UNITED STATES

for Christian Schools®

HISTORY

BJU PRESS

UNITED STATES
HIS

TORY

for Christian Schools®

Timothy Keesee
Mark Sidwell

Third Edition

Bob Jones University Press
Greenville, South Carolina 29614

This textbook was written by members of the faculty and staff of Bob Jones University. Standing for the "old-time-religion" and the absolute authority of the Bible since 1927, Bob Jones University is the world's leading Fundamentalist Christian university. The staff of the University is devoted to educating Christian men and women to be servants of Jesus Christ in all walks of life.

Providing unparalleled academic excellence, Bob Jones University prepares its students through its offering of over one hundred majors, while its fervent spiritual emphasis prepares their minds and hearts for service and devotion to the Lord Jesus Christ.

NOTE:
The fact that materials produced by other publishers are referred to in this volume does not constitute an endorsement by Bob Jones University Press of the content or theological position of materials produced by such publishers. The position of Bob Jones University Press, and the University itself, is well known. Any references and ancillary materials are listed as an aid to the student or the teacher and in an attempt to maintain the accepted academic standards of the publishing industry.

United States History for Christian Schools® Third Edition

Timothy Keesee, Ed.D.
Mark Sidwell, Ph.D.

Produced in cooperation with the Bob Jones University Division of Social Science of the College of Arts and Science, the School of Religion, and Bob Jones Academy.

Page 559:
Excerpt from "I Have a Dream" reprinted by arrangement with The Heirs to the Estate of Martin Luther King, Jr., c/o Writers House Inc, as agent for the proprietor. Copyright 1963 by Martin Luther King Jr., copyright renewed 1991 by Coretta Scott King

for Christian Schools is a registered trademark of Bob Jones University Press.

© 1991, 2001 Bob Jones University Press
Greenville, South Carolina 29614
First Edition © 1982. Third Edition © 2001

Printed in the United States of America
All rights reserved

ISBN 1-57924-605-2

15 14 13 12 11 10 9 8 7 6 5 4 3 2 1

Contents

List of Maps

Pronunciation Guide

The pronunciation key used in this text is designed to give the reader a self-evident, acceptable pronunciation for a word as he reads it from the page. For more nearly accurate pronunciations, the reader should consult a good dictionary.

Stress   Syllables with primary stress appear in LARGE CAPITAL letters. Syllables with secondary stress and one-syllable words appear in SMALL CAPITAL letters. Unstressed syllables appear in lower-case letters. Where two or more words appear together, hyphens separate the syllables within each word. For example, the pronunciation of *Marquis de Montcalm* appears as (mar-KEE deh mahnt-KAHM).

Consonant Sounds   Most consonants and consonantal combinations in the key have only their one visual sound. There are a few exceptions:

Symbol	Example	Symbol	Example
c	cat = KAT	th	thin = THIN
g	get = GET	*th*	then = *TH*EN
j	gentle = JEN tul	zh	fusion = FYOO zhun

Vowel Sounds

Symbol	Example	Symbol	Example
a	cat = KAT	ar	car = KAR
a-e	cape = KAPE	aw	all = AWL
ay	paint = PAYNT	o	bone = BOHN
e	jet = JET	oa	don't = DOANT
eh	spend = SPEHND	o-e	groan = GRONE
ee	fiend = FEEND	oh	own = OHN
i	swim = SWIM	u	some = SUM
ih	pity = PIH tee	uh	abet = uh BET
eye	icy = EYE see	oo	crew = CROO
i-e	might = MITE	*oo*	push = *POOSH*
ye	Levi = LEE vye	ou	loud = LOUD
ah	cot = KAHT	oy	toil = TOYL

innesota

LAKE SUPERIOR

Maine

Augusta •

Montpelier •

Concord • ——— New Hampshire

——— Vermont

St. Paul •

Wisconsin

LAKE MICHIGAN

LAKE HURON

LAKE ONTARIO

Albany •

Boston •

Providence •

——— Massachusetts

——— Rhode Island

Madison •

Michigan
Lansing •

LAKE ERIE

New York

Hartford •

——— Connecticut

Iowa

Des Moines •

Illinois

Springfield •

Indiana

Indianapolis •

Ohio
Columbus •

Pennsylvania

Harrisburg •

Trenton •

——— New Jersey

——— Delaware

Dover •

Annapolis •
Washington, D.C. ☆

eka •

Missouri
Jefferson City •

Central Plains

River

Charleston •

Ohio

Frankfort •

West
Virginia

Richmond •

——— Maryland

Virginia

Kentucky

Appalachian Mountains

Raleigh •

Nashville •

Tennessee

North Carolina

Piedmont

South
Carolina
Columbia •

Atlantic Coastal Plain

ATLANTIC

Arkansas

Little Rock •

Mississippi River

Atlanta •

Georgia

OCEAN

Montgomery •

Alabama

Jackson •

Mississippi

Gulf Coastal Plain

Baton Rouge •

Tallahassee •

Louisiana

Florida

GULF OF MEXICO

FEET

12,000

9,000

5,000

2,000

1,000
0

United States
of America

0   100   200   300   400   500

scale in miles

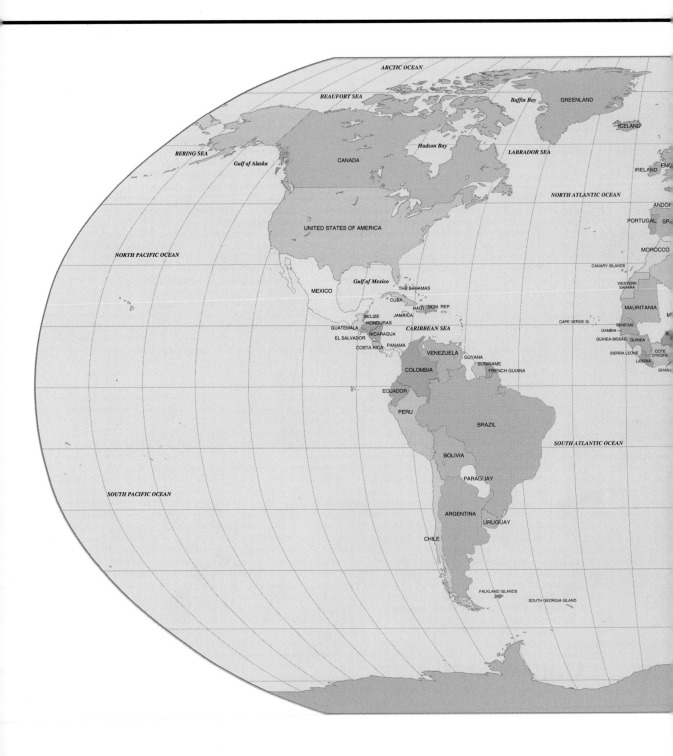

United States of America

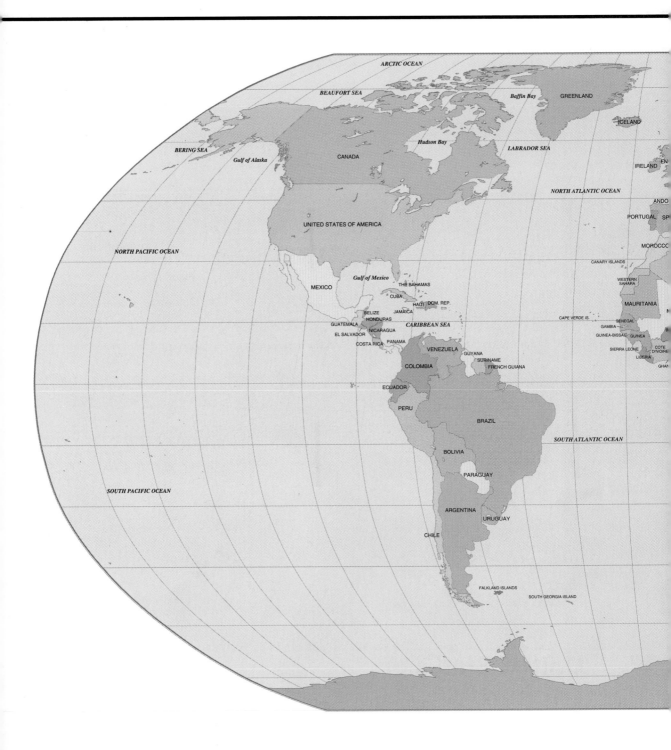

UNIT I

1492
Columbus
lands in the
New World

1517
Luther posts
his 95 Theses

1588
Defeat of
Spanish Armada

1620
Pilgrims
come to the
New World

1664
England
conquers
New Netherland

c.1720—c.1760
The Great
Awakening

1488
Dias rounds
the Cape of
Good Hope

1498
Da Gama sails
to India by way
of Africa

1522-1523
Magellan sails
around the
world

1607
Founding of
Jamestown

1630-1640
Great Migration
of Puritans to
Massachusetts
Bay

1689-1697
King William's
War

1692
Salem Witch
Trials

1702-1713
Queen Anne's
War

1743-1748
King George's
War

English ships arriving at the Roanoke Colony on the Outer Banks

Iron shackles clanked in the musty prison cell as huddled forms awakened. The eastern sun brightened the cell. One prisoner, gathering quill and parchments from beneath his pillow, continued his writing. In happier times he had been known as Rustichello of Pisa, a writer of romances and chivalric legends who had enjoyed modest acclaim. Now in 1296 the furies of war had cast him into prison with a living legend named **Marco Polo.**

Though a prisoner-of-war like himself, Polo could tell the most fantastic stories. His adventures in China had spanned nearly twenty years, during which time he had been a favorite of Kublai the grand Khan of the Mongols.

Polo described mysterious Asia, a world of shimmering silks, fragrant spices, and unlimited gold. In the land of Cipangu (seh PANG goo; an island kingdom that would someday be called Japan), Polo had heard that gold was so common that it was used for pavement.

In that prison cell, Rustichello penned the words of one of history's greatest travelers, later published under an imposing title, *Description of the World*. Polo's travel-log became the definitive work on the Orient for the next three centuries. Its vivid scenes enticed men to see the Orient for themselves, bringing them to shores even less known than the lands of the Great Khan.

Discovery and Rediscovery

Sugar and Spice

Polo's account fired the imagination of Europe's merchants and adventurers. But China's overland route was costly and dangerous. Muslim merchants, who controlled the eastern silk and spice trade,

Landing of Columbus, *United States Capitol Art Collection*

choked the highways, prompting Western Europeans to bypass the Muslim monopoly by finding a waterway to China.

The seafaring Portuguese led the way in 1488 when **Bartolomeu Dias** sailed southward along the coast of Africa and rounded its southern cape, which he optimistically called Good Hope. A decade later **Vasco da Gama** followed through on Dias's discovery by sailing to India. Da Gama returned to Portugal with a cargo of spices worth sixty times the cost of the expedition.

Such fantastic profits signaled the end of the Muslim monopoly and the beginning of the European scramble for the spice trade. Ships laden with cinnamon, gold, ivory, and sugar would revolutionize Europe's economy, politics, and world view.

As Portugal, Spain's neighbor, was turning the Indian Ocean into a private lake, Spaniards looked in another direction for trade with the Orient. Like most educated Europeans of the fifteenth century, the Italian-born **Christopher Columbus** believed the world was round. Basing his calculations, or, as it turned out, his miscalculations, on the circumference estimates of the second-century Greek mathematician Ptolemy, Columbus reasoned that the shortest route to the East was west. Columbus and Ptolemy, though correct about the earth's shape, were incorrect about its size. Columbus figured that by sailing three thousand miles west, he could reach Cipangu and its fabled riches. (Japan was in fact eight thousand miles *farther* west.)

When the king of Portugal refused to underwrite a westward voyage, Columbus turned to the Spanish for help. After receiving the reluctant support of Queen Isabella, Columbus set out in early August 1492 with three ships and a fill-in-the-blank letter of greeting from the Spanish crown to the king of Cipangu. The letter was to be personalized after Columbus learned the name of the distant potentate.

On the evening of October 11 Columbus wrote in his ship's log, "At ten at night the Admiral being in the stern castle, saw light . . . like a small wax candle. . . . The Admiral was certain they were near the land." By 2:00 A.M. the light proved to be land, and though Columbus did not realize it, he had stumbled, not onto an island of Cipangu, but onto a sliver of sand in the Bahamas. That day Columbus went ashore and named the island San Salvador (Holy Saviour) in gratitude for the merciful ocean passage his expedition had been given. Curious brown natives gathered about the strange band of pale visitors and offered gifts of parrots and raw cotton. Columbus, certain that he was on an island of the Indies in the Orient, called these people *los indios*–Indians. There would in fact be many more misunderstandings between the two races in the centuries to follow.

For an explorer looking for new lands, Columbus could not have been in a better location, since there are literally thousands of islands in the Caribbean archipelago. But for an explorer looking for Asian riches, Columbus could not have been in a more frustrating position. He would make three more voyages to the region in a vain search for China and Japan and would go to his grave believing he had reached the outskirts of Asia.

Other men, however, came to realize what Columbus did not, that there was a *new world* across the ocean. One of these men was **Amerigo Vespucci,** who made at least two voyages to the Caribbean and South America. It is one of history's interesting ironies that in 1507 a little-known German mapmaker named Martin Waldseemüller was so bold as to name this unnamed world, not after its discoverer, but *America* after Amerigo, who sailed in the wake of the great captain Columbus.

England was not idle during the race for the Orient. In 1497 the Italian Giovanni Caboto (known to the English for whom he sailed as **John Cabot**) reached Newfoundland in his search for a passage to China. The following year Cabot again sailed west for the East, but he never returned. His fate remains a mystery; yet his initial discovery changed the course of history, for it provided the basis for England's claim to and colonization of North America.

Two continents were now added to the world map. Yet the Americas seemed more of an obstacle to sail around than a land to settle. Explorers set about finding a way to bypass it, believing riches lay just beyond the new world horizon. **Ferdinand Magellan** determined that he could reach the Spice Islands of the East by sailing south around the Americas. In what would be the greatest sea voyage of all time, Magellan set out from Spain in 1519 with five ships, the largest of which was smaller than a modern tugboat. After threading his way down the coast of Brazil and Argentina, Magellan found a passage in the wild waters of Tierra del Fuego where two oceans converge.

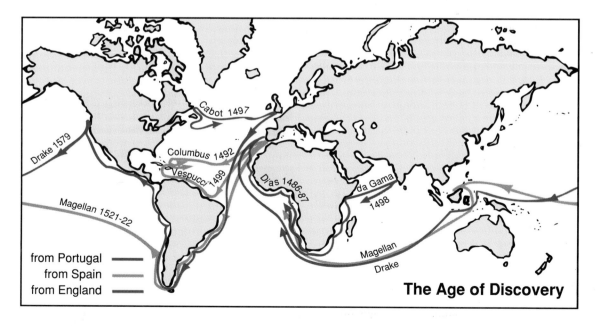

Cabot 1497

Drake 1579

Columbus 1492

Vespucci 1499

Dias 1486-87

da Gama 1498

Magellan 1521-22

Magellan
Drake

from Portugal ——
from Spain ——
from England ——

The Age of Discovery

The three ships that reached the Pacific sailed through waters never traversed by Europeans. A few years earlier, the Spanish explorer Balboa had first seen this blue expanse from a hillside in Panama, but Magellan's little fleet was now plunging through its waves. However, Asia did not lie just beyond the Americas, and as Magellan continued to pursue an ever-receding horizon, provisions ran low.

For a hundred days the crew languished on the torrid sea. The stench of foul water and death hung heavy about the ships. Gnawing hunger drove the scurvy-wracked sailors to eat leather from the ships' rigging, and rats became a prized dish. Though the ships eventually reached Guam, where the survivors were reprovisioned, it had become painfully clear that a western route to the Orient was impractical.

The ships sailed on to the Philippines, where Magellan was killed by poison arrows in a tribal squabble. Though he never lived to see it, one of his ships, the *Victoria,* reached the Spice Islands and, laden with cloves, continued the voyage westward for home. Three years after Magellan's fleet left Spain, the *Victoria* reached Seville with only eighteen of the original crew of three hundred on board. Their daring feat shook the Old World—they had sailed around the world!

Nearly five centuries later, the first circumnavigational voyage remains an incomparable achievement. Magellan had revealed the girth of the globe; yet for the time its vastness set limits on western trade routes. Increasingly the focus would be upon the Americas, a new world that offered new promise.

Here I Stand

While Magellan's little fleet was quietly making its global trek, Europe's attention was riveted by a stubborn German monk named **Martin Luther.** For a millennium Roman Catholicism had dominated the religious life of Europe. As the Roman church allowed church tradition and papal decree to supersede Scripture, spiritual darkness descended over the continent.

During this long age the pope, or bishop of Rome, amassed far-reaching political and ecclesi-

Martin Luther Discovering Justification by Faith, *by Edward Matthew Ward, Bob Jones University Collection of Sacred Art*

astical authority. Centuries before Luther challenged papal authority, the office had already degenerated into one of power politics where spiritual arrogance and ignorance, and even open immorality characterized many of its occupants. It was said of Pope Leo X, for example, that he "would have been an excellent pope if only he were also religious." With this lack of spiritual leadership and the Roman Catholic Church's emphasis on works for salvation, it is little wonder that the common people lived under spiritual bondage. Against this backdrop burst the **Protestant Reformation,** a movement that rediscovered biblical truth and shattered the religious monopoly of Rome.

The Reformation was in many ways more revolution than reformation. A number of forces—social, political, and technological—converged to strike at the roots of the existing order, shaking Europe's house to its very foundation. The social force of the Renaissance, beginning in the fourteenth century, challenged Rome's educational and cultural monopoly with a broader world view. The political force of nationalism defined and divided Europe's map. To the growing ranks of powerful kings, Rome was becoming more distant and the pope less relevant. The technological achievement of movable-type printing provided the means for the rapid dissemination of Reformation ideas and, above all, the mass distribution of the Bible in the vernacular (native languages) of Europe. As a result, men and women could for the first time hear and read the Word of God in their own tongue.

These political, social, and technological changes provided a nurturing atmosphere for the success of the Reformation, but underlying all these factors was the force of spiritual hunger born of centuries of neglect and abuse from Rome. Martin Luther's preaching rang with the simplicity of the gospel–"the just shall live by faith"–and stood in stark contrast to Rome's burdensome path.

Martin Luther was born in Eisleben, Germany, in 1483. His quest for spiritual satisfaction led him to become an Augustinian monk. Luther was brilliant, austere, and lost. Unsurpassed in his diligence, he once remarked, "If ever a monk got to heaven by his monkery, I was that monk."

While studying Paul's epistles as a professor of theology at Wittenberg, Luther's desire for spiritual peace was met when the truth of Romans 1:17 dawned over his soul. "For therein is the righteousness of God revealed . . . the just shall live by faith." Luther saw for the first time that salvation was all of God, and "not by works of righteousness which we have done" (Titus 3:5). Friar Martin's

Martin Luther's Spiritual Struggle

In the following account Luther describes the struggle he endured before finding the truth about saving faith, an event that transformed his life and changed the course of history.

Although I lived as a monk without reproach, I felt that I was a sinner before God with an extremely disturbed conscience. I could not believe that he was placated by my satisfaction. I did not love, yes, I hated the righteous God who punishes sinners, and secretly, if not blasphemously, certainly murmuring greatly, I was angry with God, and said, "As if, indeed, it is not enough, that miserable sinners, eternally lost through original sin, are crushed by every kind of calamity by the lace of decalogue, without having God add pain to pain by the gospel and also by the gospel threatening us with his righteousness and wrath!" Thus I raged with a fierce and troubled conscience. Nevertheless, I beat importunately upon Paul at that place, most ardently desiring to know what St. Paul wanted.

At last, by the mercy of God, meditating day and night, I gave heed to the context of the words, namely, "In it the righteousness of God is revealed, as it is written, 'He who through faith is righteous shall live' " [Rom. 1:17]. There I began to understand that the righteousness of God is that by which the righteous lives by a gift of God, namely by faith. And this is the meaning: the righteousness of God is revealed by the gospel, namely, the passive righteousness with which merciful God justifies us by faith, as it is written, "He who through faith is righteous shall live." Here I felt that I was altogether born again and had entered paradise itself through open gates. There a totally other face of the entire Scripture showed itself to me. Thereupon I ran through the Scriptures from memory. I also found in other terms an analogy, as, the work of God, that is, what God does in us, the power of God, with which he makes us strong, the wisdom of God, with which he makes us wise, the strength of God, the salvation of God, the glory of God.

And I extolled my sweetest word with a love as great as the hatred with which I had before hated the words "righteousness of God." Thus that place in Paul was for me truly the gate to paradise.

life was transformed; the Scripture was now the authority that directly led him to challenge Roman Catholic doctrines.

After being excommunicated from the church for opposing papal dogma, Luther was summoned to Worms in 1521 to appear before the Emperor Charles V and his assembly, or *diet*. There, when asked to recant or suffer the fate of a heretic, Luther gave a reply that was the moral equivalent of an earthquake:

> Since then Your Majesty and your lordships desire a simple reply, I will answer without horns and without teeth. Unless I am convicted by Scripture and plain reason–I do not accept the authority of popes and councils, for they have contradicted each other–my conscience is captive to the Word of God. I cannot and I will not recant anything, for to go against conscience is neither right nor safe. Here I stand, I cannot do otherwise. God help me, Amen.

Luther's prolific pen, combined with the new printing technology, flooded the continent with Reformation ideas. By 1523, only two years after he stood before the Imperial Diet at Worms, a million copies of Luther's religious and political treatises were circulating throughout Germany.

Martin Luther was the pioneer, but other reformers quickly rose up: Ulrich Zwingli in the Swiss canton of Zurich, John Calvin in Geneva and France, John Knox in Scotland, William Tyndale and Thomas Cranmer in England, and Menno Simons in the Netherlands. The geographic diversity of the Reformation mirrored its theological diversity.

The Reformers were unified in their belief in the absolute authority of Scripture and the **priesthood of all believers** (that believers can pray to God directly and interpret the Scripture without the need for an intermediary priest). However, agreement on these Biblical fundamentals ensured that there would be disagreement among the Protestant groups. If Christians could now interpret the Bible for themselves, they would not all reach the same conclusions on all the issues. Diversity, a condition

far preferable to the spiritual tyranny exercised by Rome, is the natural result of the freedom of conscience embodied in Luther's simple declaration, "Here I stand, I cannot do otherwise."

The Reformation's rapid spread drew theological as well as actual battle lines across Europe. Catholic armies were fielded to crush the Protestants into submission, engulfing the continent with intermittent war from the 1520s until the middle of the 1600s. The modern student might well ask, why did Catholics and Protestants kill each other for over a century? Why not live and let live?

Religious war in Europe must be understood in the light of the existing order. First of all, the state

This woodcut from Foxe's Book of Martyrs *illustrates persecution that many Protestants faced in defense of their faith.*

and the church were vitally connected. This relationship had existed for centuries, and now, whether Protestant or Catholic, the state exercised its responsibility to protect and promote the religion of its domain. Second, religious toleration was at first nearly nonexistent. The idea that two or more religions could exist in the same country at the same time was considered neither possible nor proper to the sixteenth-century mind. This explains the conflict between Catholics and Protestants. But it also explains the intolerance among some Protestants, such as when certain Lutheran rulers persecuted the Anabaptists. Finally, the religious wars were fueled by the political ambitions of the kings of Europe, who saw the highly motivated armies under religion's banner as tools to advance their political goals. Nowhere is this more evident than in the 1640s when French Catholics fought Spanish Catholics to aid German Lutherans and Dutch Calvinists.

To many Protestants in war-ravaged Europe, the New World was a Promised Land across a wide Jordan. America offered a refuge from persecution. Thousands of Martin Luther's spiritual descendants preferred the wilderness hardships of the New World to the religious tyranny of the Old. Of course, many colonists did not cross the Atlantic for religious reasons–they were in search of gold, not God. However, those believers that did come brought their convictions with them, and their influence would leave a lasting mark on America.

Section Review

1. Who was responsible for stirring European interest in China prior to the age of discovery? How did he do so?
2. How did Columbus's plan for reaching Asia differ from da Gama's?
3. What technological innovation helped pave the way for the Protestant Reformation?
4. On what two beliefs were all the Reformers united?
5. How did Europe's religious wars influence immigration to the New World?

In the Wilderness

The Spanish Century

Throughout the sixteenth century, Spain dominated the exploration and exploitation of the New World. From their Caribbean settlements on Hispaniola (begun by Christopher Columbus and his brother Bartholomew), Puerto Rico, and Cuba, the Spanish launched their conquests of the mainland. There in Mexico, and Central and South America, the conquistadores discovered advanced civilizations, vast cities, and incredible treasure. Within a quarter century the Spanish vanquished the Indian population, amassing an empire that was virtually unrivaled both in terms of size and wealth.

Hernando Cortés was the first great *conquistador,* a combination explorer and soldier of fortune–with the emphasis on fortune. In 1519 Cortés and his small fleet reached Mexico with strict orders from the governor of Cuba to explore the mainland coast and proceed no further. The great Aztec king **Montezuma,** hearing of the Spanish arrival, sent emissaries offering gifts that he hoped would be picked up like door prizes by these uninvited guests on their way home. However, the enticing gleam of turquoise masks, intricate gold figurines, and massive disks of hammered gold made Cortés decide he would rather try his hand at conquest than run errands for the governor of Cuba.

In order to reduce the potential for mutiny against his unsanctioned mission, and knowing he would be hanged for insubordination if he were ever forced to return to Cuba, he ordered his ships run aground. Proceeding inland to the Aztec capital with about four hundred soldiers, Cortés picked up support along the way from subjugated Indian tribes who welcomed the Spaniards as deliverers from the Aztecs. These tribes despised the Aztecs for exacting heavy tribute from them and especially for taking the best of their young warriors to offer as human sacrifices in their bloody rituals. In a daring feat of conquest, Cortés marched to the Aztec capital of Tenochtitlán (tay NAHCH tee TLAHN; present-day Mexico City) where he captured Montezuma and eventually crushed the Aztec resistance.

Despite the advanced nature of a number of the Indian tribes in central and South America, they were no match for the military superiority of the Europeans. Cortés's experiences in Mexico were indicative of the clash of cultures that would lead to European dominance in that hemisphere. At the Battle of Tlaxcala (tlah SKAHL uh) on his way to meet Montezuma, Cortés's army of four hundred was outnumbered an estimated one hundred to one; yet they were able to fight to a draw. The Tlaxcalans, equipped with spears and obsidian-bladed clubs, faced soldiers armed with muskets and artillery. Some of the Spanish soldiers were mounted on an animal never seen by these Indians before–horses.

Far more devastating to the native populations than firearms were the white man's diseases, to which the Indians had little immunity. Smallpox, measles, typhus, and other contagions devastated their numbers. The Indian population dropped from an estimated fifty million at the beginning of the sixteenth century to only four million in the seventeenth century. In the islands of the West Indies, the destruction of whole Indian populations by disease created a labor shortage for the Spanish that would be forcefully remedied with the arrival of more newcomers–African slaves.

Spain did not confine its New World interests to Mexico and South America. A number of conquistadores explored the vast hinterland of North America (southeastern, southwestern, and Gulf Coast regions) hoping to repeat Cortés's get-rich-quick conquest. **Francisco de Coronado,** for example, commanded an expedition that left Mexico in 1540 to explore what would later be the southwestern United States. Greedily believing the Indians' tall tales about the Seven Cities of Cibola, a fabulous land of gold and jewels, Coronado's search led him through Arizona, New Mexico, eastward through Texas, and on to Kansas. That any of Coronado's expedition survived the four-thousand-mile trek in the extreme temperatures of the Southwest is a tribute to their courage and Coronado's leadership. His expedition did not find gold, but one of its parties did discover and explore the Grand Canyon.

Spaniards also made a number of attempts to settle the southeastern United States, the region they called La Florida ("the flowered [land]"). **Ponce de León** was the first to explore the Florida peninsula in 1513. In 1539 **Hernando De Soto,** a veteran of the Spanish conquest of the Inca Indians in Peru, landed at Tampa Bay where he began a meandering trek through La Florida. De Soto's journey took him as far north as Charlotte, North Carolina; then, traveling through the Deep South, he eventually discovered the Mississippi River.

In the decades to follow, Spanish settlements and outposts were built along the coast of Florida, Georgia, South Carolina, Virginia's Chesapeake Bay, and as far west as Tennessee's Great Smoky Mountains. However, disease, hunger, and hostile Indians prevented Spain from becoming firmly established in North America.

Through their efforts at exploration and settlement, the Spanish claimed much of what is now the United States. Spanish rule was not beneficial to the new land, though; the Spanish preferred *exploiting* the land to *developing* it. The New World to Spain was little more than a treasure chest to be looted, not a resource to be cultivated. Also the government that Spain brought to the New World was harsh and tyrannical. The Catholic religion that the Spanish brought with them reinforced rather than reduced these authoritarian tendencies.

By the late sixteenth century it had become clear, though, that it was easier for Spain to claim territory than to keep it. The shiploads of bullion that Spain was siphoning out of the New World heightened French, English, and Dutch envy of Spain and their interest in America. In addition, the Spanish King **Philip II** (ruled 1556-1598), an ardent Catholic, was bent on crushing the Protestant menace in western Europe–and he was not altogether unsuccessful. Subsidized by Mexican gold and Peruvian silver, Philip's army was the largest, best-equipped in Europe, and thousands of Protestants were killed in its bloody wake. Bitterness over Catholic Spain's military threat made Spanish New World outposts a tempting target for Protestant sea captains such as the French Jean Ribault and England's **Francis Drake.**

Drake and his cousin Sir John Hawkins were the most famous pair in a daring class of mariners under Queen **Elizabeth I** who proudly called themselves **Sea Dogs.** Both Hawkins and Drake led attacks on Spanish shipping in the Caribbean and Central America. In 1577 Drake, commanding the *Golden Hind*, followed the course around South America that Magellan had first steered a half century earlier. Drake looted Spanish outposts on the Pacific and failing to find a northern sea route back to the Atlantic, sailed from California westward to England. His ship laden with Spanish treasure, the circumnavigator reached Plymouth Harbor in 1580. Queen Elizabeth herself came aboard the *Golden Hind* to knight the legendary Drake.

There was much more to Drake's daring raids than simply fame and fortune–he sailed with blood in his eye against the Catholic threat. Drake's father, a tenant farmer, was a fervent Protestant lay preacher who had a great influence in shaping his son's character and convictions. When Drake was a boy, he and his family were forced to flee their home during a Catholic uprising. In order to escape, the family lived in the rotting hulk of a ship on the bank of the Thames. Ironically, the boy whom the Catholics forced to live in dire poverty in the hulk of a ship would one day take a ship and greatly enrich himself at the expense of Catholic Spain.

In addition to being a strong Protestant, Francis Drake was an ardent English patriot. In 1493, for

The defeat of the Spanish Armada was a turning point in English–and American–history.

purposes of exploration and settlement, Pope Alexander VI had divided the world in half, giving rights to the east to Portugal and the west to Spain. Protestant England scorned the pope's arrogant presumption that the world was his to divide, for the English would be shut out of the New World. Sailing for the honor of England, Drake was determined to challenge Spain's monopoly in America. After his circumnavigation of the globe, Drake's concerns about Spain, however, would be much closer to home. In 1586 Philip II began amassing a huge fleet to conquer Protestant England. In the balance lay not only the fate of the island kingdom but also the determination of who would colonize most of North America–Catholic Spain or Protestant England.

The following year, Drake led thirty ships into Spain's Cadíz harbor, where Philip's Armada lay anchored being readied for their assault. The Sea Dogs destroyed thousands of tons of supplies, delaying the invasion by a year.

In 1588 the **Spanish Armada** entered the English Channel with 130 ships and 30,000 men. Drake used fireships to break up the Spanish formation and sent a number of galleons to the bottom. The Spanish admiral's attempt to outrun the English guns by sailing around Ireland ended when a fierce storm, which the relieved English later called the "Protestant Wind," destroyed much of Spain's fleet. Philip's dream of conquering Protestant England now lay amid the floating wreckage off the craggy Irish coast.

The defeat of the Spanish Armada was both dramatic in its scope and decisive in its results. It secured the future for Protestants in England. Clearly, God was providentially preserving His witness in that country. In addition, it spelled the end of the Spanish century and the beginning of English dominance on the seas and eventually in North America.

The English Foothold

In 1584 an English clergyman named Richard Hakluyt the Younger, collaborating with Sir **Walter Raleigh,** compiled for Queen Elizabeth a list of arguments favoring the colonization of North

Swashbuckler Sir Walter Raleigh and his son Wat, 1602, National Portrait Gallery, London

America. Entitled *A Discourse of Western Planting,* the document presented a number of advantages to settling the New World, including expanding Protestantism, boosting trade and national influence, reducing unemployment, and establishing military outposts to thwart Spanish dominance.

Evidently the queen liked what she read, for the following year she gave Raleigh permission to plant a colony in the land Raleigh called *Virginia* in honor of the virgin queen. Though Raleigh himself never came to North America, he sponsored an expedition of colonists to settle on **Roanoke Island,** located in the sound of North Carolina's Outer Banks. The colony under the command of Sir Richard Grenville, however, was short-lived. After wintering on the island, the colonists encountered rough treatment from neighboring Indians as well as threats of a Spanish attack. As a result, the English abandoned the lonely outpost in the summer of 1586.

The determined Raleigh financed a second group to Roanoke Island in 1587 under the command of John White, a veteran of the first expedition. White's group numbered 117, and for the first time included women and children, among them White's daughter Elenor and her husband Ananias Dare. Elenor gave birth to a daughter shortly after arriving to the New World–the first English child born in America–and appropriately named her Virginia.

Unfortunately, the colonists arrived too late in the summer to plant crops. With the prospect of a lean winter, they urged White to return to England for supplies. After he reached England, however, the war with Spain delayed his return until 1590. Mysteriously, when Governor White returned the little town of "Raleigh" was empty. The fate of the "Lost Colony" has never been determined, but it is likely the colonists were captured and killed by Indians. When Queen Elizabeth died in 1603, no trace of her colonizing efforts remained in the hostile wilderness that bore her name.

Raleigh's was the last individual effort by an Englishman to establish a colony. Later attempts were made by companies of individuals who shared the expenses of founding a colony, with the understanding that profits would also be proportionately shared. **Joint-stock companies,** whose investors shared profits without sharing liabilities, provided a means whereby enterprises could obtain large monetary resources and still remain free from the government control that accompanied government-sponsored projects. These companies provided a vehicle through which individuals could work together to establish new institutions in a new land.

On April 10, 1606, King James I granted two companies, the **London Company** and the **Plymouth Company,** a charter for colonizing "Virginia," a coastal region of two million square miles stretching from the Carolinas to Maine. The London Company was to colonize the land between the northern latitudes of thirty-four and forty-one degrees; the Plymouth Company, between the latitudes of thirty-eight and forty-five degrees. If either started settlements in the overlapping territory, the settlements were to be at least one hundred miles apart. The Royal Council, consisting of thirteen men appointed by the king, was to govern the companies and determine colonial policies.

Both companies, optimistic about potential riches, hurried to establish colonies. The Plymouth Company deposited forty-four men on the rocky coast of Maine in the summer of 1607, at a settlement they called St. George. After only one bitter winter, those who survived returned to England. The Plymouth Company made no further attempts at colonization and was dismantled in 1609.

The London Company (later renamed the Virginia Company) sent 104 men to America in December 1606. After a rough ocean passage, they reached the Chesapeake Bay in May 1607, where they found a wide inlet which they cautiously entered and went ashore. The Englishmen named both the river and their little fort after their monarch. **Jamestown** became the first permanent English settlement in the New World.

The first years were bitter ones for the colony. Malaria, typhoid fever, and dysentery took a devastating toll. By the end of the first winter, half the colonists had been shoveled into the hostile land.

Indians of the Powhatan Confederacy also complicated the settlers' existence. At first, relations between the two peoples were friendly enough, but as the colonists began to clear more land, the Indian chief Wahunsonacock, or, as the Virginians called him, **Powhatan,** (POW uh TAN) ordered war parties against the colony. Not until 1614, with the marriage of his daughter **Pocahontas** (POH kuh HAHN tus) to the Englishman John Rolfe, did a shaky peace come to the area.

Typhoid was not the only fever to wreak havoc among the colonial ranks; gold fever consumed much of the settlers' time and resources. As a result, planting and hunting were neglected–even scorned by some. This threatened the colony with starvation. Captain **John Smith** enforced the kind of discipline necessary, however, for the survival of Jamestown. Smith improved relations with Powhatan's men, who taught the settlers how to grow maize and melons, and he enforced the Biblical principle of II Thessalonians 3:10 upon the community: "If any would not work, neither should he eat."

In 1609 the Virginia Company issued a new charter appointing a resident governor, Lord De La Warr (Delaware), to direct the colony. Detained in England by personal business, Delaware sent Thomas Gates to Jamestown as his deputy, along with five hundred "reinforcements." Gates's ship was wrecked in the Bahamas, but the other ships reached Virginia. The four hundred new arrivals, without their governor, were unruly and became a severe drain on the food supply. John Smith did the best he could to whip the recruits into line, but a gunpowder explosion severely injured him and forced his return to England in October 1609. The winter of 1609-1610 was possibly the severest trial ever faced in Virginia. It was known as the "starving time," because death became a way of life. Roughly ninety per cent of the colony died during that terrible winter.

In May 1610 Thomas Gates finally arrived to find only a handful of gaunt survivors. Shocked by what he saw, Gates put the pitiful remnant on ships and set out for England–which would have meant the end of Jamestown. Just as the ships reached the mouth of the James River, three relief ships under command of Lord Delaware met them. The Englishmen returned to their desolate fort and rebuilt

The Swashbuckling Career of Captain John Smith

Captain John Smith is justly famous for his role in helping establish the Virginia colony, but his adventures there were only a part of his sensational exploits. As a teen-ager Smith fled the dull life of a farm laborer in England to seek adventure as a soldier of fortune. He fought for the Dutch in their war for independence against Spain and afterwards traveled around Europe looking for another war and an army in need of an experienced hand.

In 1600 he joined the Austrian and Hungarian forces fighting the Turks in Hungary, where he eventually rose to the rank of captain. In one glorious but gory incident, Smith took on three Turks in separate one-on-one combats and killed and beheaded all three. He was later captured by the Turks and sold into slavery. Sent to work in the fields of what is now southern Russia, Smith killed his Turkish master with a club used for threshing. After hiding the body, Smith donned his dead master's clothes, took his horse, and escaped into Russia. From there he was able to make his way back to Europe, eventually ending up in England in time to join the Jamestown expedition.

As one of the leaders of the Jamestown colony, Smith had a number of close brushes with the Indians. On one occasion, he and fifteen men on a trading trip were surrounded in an Indian village by over seven hundred Indians. Quickly Smith seized the chief of the Indians by the hair and clapped a pistol to the chief's chest. Fearing for their leader's safety, the Indians disarmed and traded peacefully with the Englishmen. The most famous encounter between Smith and the Indians (one which some historians still question) involved the Indian princess Pocahontas. As Smith related the story, the Indians captured him while he was exploring. The Indian chief Powhatan had ordered his braves to club Smith to death when the chief's daughter, Pocahontas (only about thirteen years old), dashed out, cradled Smith's head in her arms, and begged that his life be spared. A somewhat indulgent father, Powhatan agreed and Smith was saved.

Smith's adventures did not end when he left Virginia. French pirates captured him, and Smith spent several months sailing with them as they preyed on ships in the Atlantic. For the most part, however, Captain Smith spent his last years living in England, writing of his exploits, dispensing advice on colonizing to whoever would listen–and wishing he could return at least once more to the New World for more adventure.

Captain
John Smith

Jamestown. Although many more hardships await-ed the settlement, the starving time was the tough-est one, and they had grimly endured it. Their re-turn was the beginning of a new era for the English in America. They were there to stay.

Nova Britannia

Promoters attempting to attract settlers to Vir-ginia advertised the land beyond the sea as *Nova Britannia,* a new Britain. In many ways the ema-ciated survivors of the early Jamestown years could have charged that their zealous recruiters were guilty of false advertising. And yet there was much that *was* British about the settlements that multi-plied along the eastern seaboard in the seventeenth century. America's British heritage was central to the development of the colonies and the nation that would emerge.

The British colonies were quite different from the Spanish and French settlements in the New World. Spanish America was a rigidly structured plantation society controlled directly and com-pletely by the crown, run for its profit and the bene-fit of the Catholic church. Relatively few Spaniards came to the New World to live and fewer families migrated.

Similarly, the sparse French settlements in Can-ada or *New France* were largely dependent on the mother country for their success. The French king determined colonial policies and exercised complete control over his colonial subjects. In addition, the economic realities of New France did not encourage growth and independence. The long Canadian winters reduced most farming to a subsistence level, which meant that little in the way of a cash crop could be developed as an export. And though the French fur trade was profitable, it was more suited for the frontiersman than the farmer and merchant, key participants in a mature, productive settlement.

As we shall see in the next chapter, the English came in greater numbers than their rivals to the south and north, and by the 1620s they were coming as families. With them came their English heritage. Their books were printed in London, their houses were built along English lines, and their schools patterned after Oxford and Cambridge. In addition, they brought their political institutions. It is significant that in Elizabeth's original charter authorizing an American settlement, colonists and their succeeding generations were granted the full rights of English citizenship, in the words of the charter, "as if they were borne and personally residaunte within our sed Realme of England."

English patterns of self-government became an early, integral part of colonial life. In 1619 the Virginia colony at Jamestown established the House of Burgesses, an assembly modeled after the English Parliament. As other colonies developed, so did their political institutions. Living in relative isolation from the mother country, generations of colonists gained practical experience in self-government under a local political system that for them held more relevance than His Majesty's Government on the other side of the ocean.

Section Review

1. What European nation first dominated the exploration of the New World?
2. What great Indian empire formerly ruled Mexico? What Spaniard is responsible for conquering it?
3. Who were the Sea Dogs? Who were the two most famous Sea Dogs?
4. Who financed the first two English attempts to settle North America? Where were these settlements located?
5. List at least three difficulties that confronted the English settlement in Jamestown during its early years.

Chapter Review

Terms
Marco Polo
Bartolomeu Dias
Vasco da Gama
Christopher Columbus
discovery of the New World (1492)
Amerigo Vespucci
John Cabot
Ferdinand Magellan
Martin Luther
Protestant Reformation
priesthood of all believers
Hernando Cortés
conquistador
Montezuma
Francisco de Coronado
Ponce de León
Hernando de Soto
Philip II
Francis Drake
Elizabeth I
Sea Dogs
Spanish Armada (1588)
Walter Raleigh
Roanoke Island
"Lost Colony"
joint-stock companies
London Company
Plymouth Company
founding of Jamestown (1607)
Powhatan
Pocahontas
John Smith
"starving time"
New France

Content Questions
1. Name the country for which each of the following explorers sailed and note his greatest accomplishment as an explorer.
    a. Vasco da Gama
    b. Christopher Columbus
    c. John Cabot
    d. Ferdinand Magellan
    e. Ponce de León
    f. Hernando de Soto
2. List three reasons for the lack of religious tolerance in Europe during the Reformation, even among Protestants.
3. Give at least two reasons for the Sea Dogs' raids on Spanish shipping.
4. To what two companies did King James of England give charters to settle the New World? Which was more successful?
5. List at least three ways in which English settlements in the New World differed from those of the French and the Spanish.

Application Questions
1. In what ways did the teachings of Martin Luther contribute to the growth of freedom?
2. How do you think the defeat of the Spanish Armada (1588) influenced the future development of North America?

CHAPTER 2

Thirteen Colonies

"Being thus arrived in a good harbor, and brought safe to land, they fell upon their knees and blessed the God of Heaven. . . ."

William Bradford, 1650, *recalling the Pilgrim's arrival in the New World*

Discovery of the Hudson River, *United States House of Representatives Collection*

As the survivors viewed the ravages of Jamestown's starving time in the spring of 1610, it would have been impossible for them to see much of a future for England in the New World. Unlike the Spaniards to the south, busy loading their treasure fleets with gold, silver, and jewels, these Virginians had little to show for their time in the colony except their gaunt frames and a knack for digging graves.

The English, however, continued to come. Between 1607 and 1640, eighty thousand men and women came to the American wilderness. They came for many reasons. Lured by dreams of quick riches, many fortune seekers came to America. The gold and silver never materialized, however; so the settlers turned to the land for its resources. Tobacco, rice, lumber, pine tar, indigo, and furs became valuable exports, enriching both England and the colonies.

There were three types or categories of colonial administration, depending on the commercial relationship of the colony to the mother country. They were charter, proprietary, and royal. Although each type initially received a charter (a legal grant for existence), a **charter colony** was specifically one governed by a trade company (such as the Virginia Company) that received its authorization from the king. Charter colonies usually enjoyed the most independence in their government. Under the **proprietary** arrangement, the king appointed a proprietor or proprietors (ultimately responsible to the king) to govern a colony. **Royal colonies** were controlled directly by the crown, which meant that the king and his councilors appointed the governor directly. By the seventeenth century a number of charter and proprietary colonies had become royal colonies as the king assumed increasing control over colonial affairs.

Abundant land also drew many colonists to America. The charter colonies in Virginia and Massachusetts began under a communal arrangement whereby individuals were to work and share alike for the good of the colony. The absence of private ownership of property robbed the colonists of incentive and productivity. The communal system was a complete failure, and the companies soon reorganized to provide for land ownership. Beginning in 1614 Jamestown colonists were each given three acres of land–an inauspicious beginning for what was to become the most extensive real estate boom in history, the parceling off of a continent. With a seemingly endless supply of land rolling to the west, the Virginia Company offered **headrights** of fifty-acre tracts to those who paid for their passage or who fulfilled an **indenture** (work contract) for a specified period, usually between four and seven years. Nearly half of the arrivals to the colonies outside of New England came as indentured servants. A man who was willing to work, no mat-

THE AMERICAN COLONIES

COLONY	SETTLED	TYPE
Virginia	Jamestown, 1607	Charter; became royal colony, 1624
Plymouth	Plymouth, 1620	Charter; absorbed by Massachusetts, 1691
Massachusetts	Salem, 1628 Boston, 1630	Charter; became royal colony, 1686
Rhode Island	Providence, 1636	Charter
Connecticut	Hartford, Wethersfield, and Windsor, 1635-1636	Charter
New Hampshire	Odiorne's Point, 1623	Proprietary (John Mason); absorbed by Massachusetts, 1641; made separate royal colony, 1686
New York	Settled as New Netherland by Dutch, Fort Orange (Albany), 1624; conquered by English, 1664	Proprietary (Duke of York); became royal colony.
New Jersey	A part of New Netherland early settlement by Swedes	Proprietary (John, Lord Berkeley and Sir George Catteret); became royal colony, 1702
Maryland	St. Marys, 1633	Proprietary (George Calvert, Lord Baltimore; transferred to his son, Cecilius Calvert)
Pennsylvania	Philadelphia, 1682	Proprietary (William Penn)
Delaware	Settled as New Sweden by Swedes, Fort Christina (Wilmington), 1638; annexed by New Netherland, 1655; conquered by English, 1664	Proprietary (the Duke of York transferred it to William Penn, 1682); separated from Pennsylvania, 1704
North Carolina	Settlers from Virginia moved near Albemarle Sound, 1654	Proprietary (eight English nobles received grant, 1663); separated to form two colonies, 1712; both became royal colonies, 1729
South Carolina	Charles Town (Charleston), 1670	Proprietary (eight English nobles received grant, 1663); separated to form two colonies, 1712; both became royal colonies, 1729
Georgia	Savannah, 1733	Proprietary (James Oglethorpe) became royal colony, 1751

ter how poor when he arrived, after fulfilling his obligation received land, tools, seed, and, above all, opportunity.

Religious freedom was also a powerful force in attracting settlers. As we observed in the first chapter, Catholic troops on the march to crush Protestantism and the religious intolerance experienced by a number of groups sent many to America. Those believers who came for refuge and freedom were devoted to the Scriptures. That devotion would have a major impact on the development and direction of American society.

Tiny seaboard settlements grew into towns, and with new arrivals and the lure of land, the settlements multiplied. The colonies that comprised British North America had powerful political and cultural forces that united them, such as their language and their common heritage in English law. They were not, however, made in the same mold. The colonies numbered *thirteen,* an odd, diverse assortment, each having its own unique story of settlement.

New England

Massachusetts

In 1614 Captain John Smith, commissioned by the Virginia Company to explore the coast far to the north of Jamestown, found a region rich with furs and fish. Smith's account of this land he called *New England* spurred the revival and reorganization of the defunct Plymouth Company into the Council for New England.

The Pilgrims—The first settlers to New England did not go out under the sponsorship of the Council of New England, however. In November 1620 the *Mayflower,* swept off its course to Virginia by a fierce storm, anchored off Cape Cod, Massachusetts. On board were a number of Christians, known as **Pilgrims,** who had left their houses and lands and crossed an ocean in order to worship God freely. The price they were paying in terms of hardship and sacrifice was as extraordinary as their faith.

In order to study the settling of Massachusetts by the Pilgrims and a decade later by the Puritans,

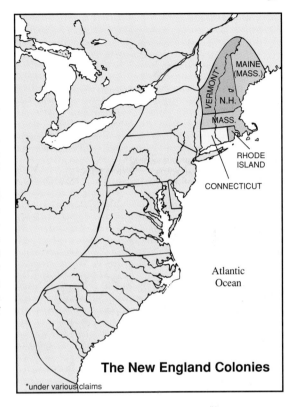

The New England Colonies

*under various claims

it is necessary to understand the religious situation in England at that time. England was Protestant, but its official break with Roman Catholicism resulted largely from political rather than spiritual concerns. This is not to say that the Reformation failed to have a spiritual impact on England. For example, William Tyndale, before he was strangled and burned at the stake by Catholics, translated the Scriptures into English. The psalmist wrote that "the entrance of thy word giveth light" (119:130), and so it was in England. Thousands of copies of Tyndale's translation were distributed, and as the gospel was preached throughout the country, many came to trust Christ as their Saviour.

However, vestiges of Roman Catholicism remained in the rituals of the Anglican church, or Church of England, and in the conduct of its clergy. Two groups, the Separatists and the Puritans, emerged in opposition to these problems. The

Embarkation of the Pilgrims, *United States Capitol Art Collection*

Puritans were a group of Anglicans who wanted to *purify* the state church from within by pushing for reforms that would rid England of Romanist influences and bring greater spiritual vitality to the nation.

The Pilgrims who settled in Massachusetts, though agreeing with many of the spiritual goals of the Puritans, were **Separatists,** or Independents. They believed that each local congregation should be independent of all other churches, free to worship and serve God without interference. As a result of the Separatists' refusal to recognize the authority of the state church, they were harassed and many were jailed.

In 1607 one congregation of Separatists from Scrooby, England, migrated to Holland because the religious tolerance there permitted them to preach and practice their faith unmolested. After they had spent a decade in Holland, though, a problem began to surface as serious as the English persecution. The Separatists' children were picking up the Dutch language and habits, and these threatened the spiritual growth of the congregation and the cultural heritage of the community. With their future in Holland becoming as bleak as it had been in England, the Pilgrims obtained a land grant from the Virginia Company to settle in the New World. Under the terms of the agreement, the Separatists were to labor seven years for the company shareholders in exchange for the land deed and, most important for these believers, the right to worship freely.

In July 1620 **William Bradford,** leading a group of thirty-five Pilgrims, sailed from Holland in the *Speedwell*. They joined the *Mayflower* in England and together set out for America. The *Speedwell* however, proved unseaworthy, forcing the expedition back to Plymouth, England, and its passengers aboard the *Mayflower*. In September the *Mayflower* set out alone with 101 passengers on board. Fewer than half of the passengers were Separatists; the others were referred to as ''strangers,'' among them Miles Standish, a soldier-adventurer.

The ocean passage was stormy, and the little *Mayflower* was blown far north of the Virginia colony to Cape Cod, Massachusetts. From there, a second attempt to reach Virginia was also beaten back by a tempest. By now it was November, and the scant provisions that remained were fit only for the vermin that infested them. The decision was made to settle in Massachusetts. A scouting party went ashore and chose a site that Captain John Smith had named ''Plymouth'' during his New England trek six years earlier.

Because they were outside the jurisdiction of the Virginia Company, the leaders drew up a contract of government to guide them until they could reorganize under the Council for New England. The agreement, known as the **Mayflower Compact,** bound the settlers into a ''civill body politick'' by which they agreed to submit to the laws and duly elected leadership of the colony. This document of self-government was the first of its kind in America.

William Bradford's history of the colony, *Of Plimmoth Plantation,* completed around 1650, records the spirit, courage, and faith of these stalwart Christian families:

> Being thus arrived in a good harbor, and brought safe to land, they fell upon their knees and blessed the God of Heaven who had brought them over the vast and furious ocean, and delivered them from all the perils therefore, again to set their feet on the firm and stable earth, their proper element.

As the Pilgrims stood in the winter's chill at the edge of a hostile wilderness, Bradford recorded their plight as well as their quiet confidence in God.

> This poor people's present condition . . . no friends to welcome them, nor inns to entertain or refresh their weatherbeaten bodies, no houses . . . to repair to. . . . Whichever way they turned their eyes (save upward to the heavens) they could have little solace. . . . For summer being done, all things stand upon them . . . and the whole country, full of woods and thickets, represented a wild and savage hue. If they looked behind them, there was the mighty ocean. . . . What could now sustain them but the Spirit of God and His grace?

The first months at Plymouth were devastating ones. Half of the little band died before spring, including their governor, John Carver. Following that first winter, however, the colony began to prosper. Friendly Indians helped the colony raise native crops of maize (corn), pumpkins, squash, and tomatoes, and under the wise and godly leadership of their new governor, William Bradford, Plymouth gained a firm foothold.

Plymouth Colony grew steadily, though after 1630 it was surpassed by the Puritans' Boston settlement in size and influence. In 1691 Plymouth merged with the rest of Massachusetts, which by then had become a royal colony. The Plymouth Colony, however, had an influence that extended far beyond the bounds of seventeenth-century Massachusetts; as the great Bradford put it, ''As one

Signing the Mayflower Compact, *painting located in the House wing of the U.S. Capitol*

small candle may light a thousand, so the light here kindled hath shone to many, yea in some sort to our whole nation.'' The enduring legacy of our Pilgrim Fathers lies in their godly testimony, their pioneering spirit, and the way in which they defined the meaning of America–as a refuge, a land of liberty for the worship of God and the preaching of His Word.

The Puritans–In 1630 an impressive fleet of seventeen ships with a thousand Puritans on board arrived at Massachusetts Bay. Their arrival opened a new chapter in the colonization of North America. In what has been called the **Great Migration,** fifty thousand settlers sailed from England to various colonies in America and the West Indies during the 1630s. Unlike the earliest settlements that dotted the coast, the Bay Colony expedition was large, well organized, and well financed. With the flood of new arrivals, a number of towns just north of Cape Cod quickly sprang up: Salem, Dorchester, Charlestown, and Boston, the Bay's seat of government.

The driving force behind the Puritan colony was its governor, **John Winthrop.** Cambridge-educated and a leading officer and financier in the Massachusetts Bay Company, Winthrop dreamed of establishing a ''wilderness Zion'' in Massachusetts, a Puritan commonwealth where the Scriptures would direct the affairs of both church and state.

The Pilgrims and Thanksgiving Day

Faith in God sustained the members of the Plymouth Colony through their tribulations. When God delivered them from such trials, they were quick to follow Paul's command to give ''thanks always for all things unto God and the Father in the name of our Lord Jesus Christ'' (Eph. 5:20). After the bitter winter of 1620-1621, the harvest of 1621 was a welcome relief to the colonists. In gratitude to God for His mercy, Governor William Bradford proclaimed a time of thanksgiving in the colony, celebrated in October 1621. For three days, the colony celebrated reverently but joyfully. They feasted on the bounty that God had provided for them–vegetables such as cabbages, carrots, turnips, onions, and beets and wild game (perhaps including turkeys, but this is not certain). Some ninety friendly Indians joined the Pilgrims, providing fresh venison as their contribution to the feast.

A day of special thanksgiving to God by His people was by no means unusual. The Israelites' Feast of Pentecost and Feast of Tabernacles, for example, were both celebrations of thanksgiving for the blessings of harvest. Moses wrote, ''And thou shalt rejoice in thy feast . . . because the Lord thy God shall bless thee in all thine increase, and in all the works of thine hands'' (Deut. 16:14-15). Christians throughout history have set aside special days of prayer, thanksgiving, and feasting to commemorate the blessings of God. However, the Plymouth feast–popularly regarded as ''the first Thanksgiving'' in America despite earlier such celebrations in Virginia–has become a part of the nation's heritage, an almost legendary event as famous as Washington's crossing the Delaware.

Though the annual celebration of Thanksgiving Day in America owes its inspiration to the Pilgrims, the official holiday is much more recent. President George Washington proclaimed the first day of national thanksgiving on November 26, 1789. Thanksgiving became a regular, annual holiday in 1863 when President Abraham Lincoln made the last Thursday in November Thanksgiving Day. This remained the standard date until 1939 when President Franklin Roosevelt moved it back one week to lengthen the Christmas shopping season. Finally in 1941 Congress officially set the fourth Thursday in November as the nation's Thanksgiving Day.

Founding governor of Massachusetts, John Winthrop, envisioned his colony as a spiritual commonwealth.

Winthrop's vision for Massachusetts was set forth in a sermon he preached aboard the *Arbella* before disembarking. In his message "A Modell of Christian Charity," the governor underscored the purpose of the colony: it was to be a Christian community in the most thorough sense of both those words. Every member of this community–pastor and parishioner alike–would contribute to the success of the whole. It was God's purpose that "they might be all knit more nearly together in the bond of brotherly affection." Winthrop further declared that the colony represented an extraordinary opportunity and responsibility: "We shall be as a city upon a hill, the eyes of all people are upon us; so that if we shall deal falsely with our God in this work we have undertaken and so cause him to withdraw his present help from us, we shall be made a story and a by-word through the world."

At the heart of this goal of establishing a community of believers was the Puritans' belief in the covenant. God had a covenant or agreement with His people in regard to their salvation, and they in turn covenanted with one another to pursue common goals–in this case to build a "Holy Commonwealth."

The Puritans set out to apply Biblical principles to every aspect of their society, including their government and educational systems. Harvard College was established near Boston in 1636 to train young men for the ministry. In explaining the purpose behind America's first college, one writer in 1643 also provided an interesting commentary on Puritan values in the New World.

> After God had carried us safe to New England, and wee had builded our houses, provided necessaries for our livli-hood, rear'd convenient places for Gods worship, and setled the Civill Government: One of the next things we longed for, and looked after was to advance Learning and perpetuate it to Posterity; dreading to leave an illiterate Ministry to the Churches, when our present Ministers shall lie in the Dust.

Unfortunately the Puritan fathers' sense of spiritual mission did not transfer to their later generations. Fish, fur, and timber enriched the industrious colonies but impoverished its churches. Ironically, Winthrop's "holy commonwealth" became a commercial success and a spiritual failure. However, God was not without His witnesses in Massachusetts, and as we shall see in Chapter 4, great revival would eventually sweep the land, awakening thousands to life in Christ.

If the Bay Colony was, in Winthrop's words, "a city upon a hill," then it was a city that resembled those of Lincolnshire or Yorkshire an ocean away. In a number of cases Puritan officials in England immigrated with their family and friends *en masse* to Massachusetts. These officials received town land grants from the Massachusetts Bay Company, which included authority to lay out the town and make property allotments. As a result the settling of Massachusetts was more organized than that of other colonies–a fact that also meant it was more tightly controlled. Property was generally distributed in relation to social position rather than through a system of headrights. Fewer indentured servants therefore immigrated to New England because of the less attractive terms.

Settlers, though, continued to come to the Puritan commonwealth. As many as twenty thousand arrived in Massachusetts in the 1630s, and Boston burgeoned into the largest city on the continent. These colonists did not all stay in Massachusetts, however. Two factors–expansion and dissension–caused Massachusetts to spawn other colonies throughout New England.

Connecticut

Not everyone wanted to live in Boston. The boundless expanse of forest laced with rivers drew land-hungry settlers further into its hold. As early as 1633, Puritans and Plymouth Pilgrims migrated into the Connecticut River Valley and established a string of settlements.

One of the most significant migrations took place in 1636, when the Puritan minister **Thomas Hooker** moved three congregations under his leadership into the Connecticut River Valley, setting up communities at Hartford, Wethersfield, and Windsor. Since those three settlements, known collectively as the River Colony or River Towns, lay outside the jurisdiction of the Massachusetts Bay Company, each developed its own simple system of local government.

Eventually these settlements joined themselves politically under the provisions of the **Fundamental Orders of Connecticut** (1639). This document, which has been called the first written constitution in America, established a framework for representative self-government in Connecticut. Though Massachusetts had a well-organized system of self-government provided through its Bay Company charter, Connecticut developed a more democratic order by not requiring church membership as a prerequisite for voting. Eventually all the Connecticut settlements, including the Puritan settlement of New Haven, were united under a royal charter obtained by John Winthrop, Jr., in 1662. This charter preserved many of the self-governing practices that had been a feature of Connecticut since its founding.

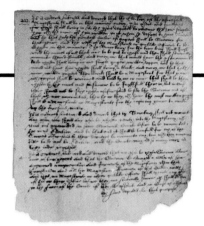

A page from the Fundamental Orders of Connecticut

The motivation behind the early political organizing among the River Towns was the need for security against the Indian threat, particularly that of the uncooperative Pequots (PEE kwots). Like the English, the Pequot Indians were newcomers to the region. Unlike the other Indians of the area, however, the Pequots did not passively accept the expansion of Massachusetts. In 1636 nine settlers in Connecticut were brutally murdered, possibly by Pequots. Colonial forces mustered out of Massachusetts and Connecticut marched on a large Pequot village on Connecticut's Mystic River. There the English demonstrated to their Indian rivals that they could beat them at brutality. The colonials reduced the village to ashes and indiscriminately killed four hundred men, women, and children. Those Pequots who escaped the fire and sword were captured and sold into slavery. The brief but decisive Pequot War, an unsavory solution to the Indian problem, permitted colonial expansion to proceed unhindered in the region for a generation.

Rhode Island and New Hampshire

The natural expansion that resulted from a massive influx of settlers was not the only cause behind the formation of new colonies coming out of Massachusetts. Dissension against the Puritan leadership in the Bay Colony contributed to the formation of Rhode Island and New Hampshire.

In 1631 **Roger Williams** arrived in Massachusetts and soon gained a reputation as a troublemaker for his ''strange'' ideas. Williams declared it a ''national sinne'' for England to take Indian land without just compensation; he denounced his fellow Puritans for not severing all ties with the Anglican church; and he advocated complete separation of church and state. This last idea flew in the face of the Puritan ideal of a "holy commonwealth." As a result, in 1635 the General Court banished Williams. After wintering with the Narragansett Indians, Williams and some of his followers established a settlement they called Providence in the coastal region known as Rhode Island.

Williams's theology often seemed to be in a state of flux. His concept of a "pure" church became so narrow that he abandoned the institutional church. As one historian has wryly observed, "Williams's belief that a true church must have no truck with the unregenerate led him eventually to the absurdity that no true church was possible, unless perhaps consisting of his wife and himself–and he may have had doubts about her."

Nonetheless Williams's ideas underscored the principle of religious liberty, a concept central to Christianity in America. In addition, Rhode Island instituted complete separation of church and state, prohibiting the government from establishing or supporting one religious group and protecting the churches from state interference. While this idea exemplified a later constitutional principle, it also attracted a variety of religious groups and malcontents. Williams lived to an advanced age, and despite his controversial views, his leadership and personality made him a likable figure both to the colonists and the Indians he befriended.

In addition to Roger Williams, Massachusetts "provided" Rhode Island with another leading dissident, **Anne Hutchinson.** Hutchinson was forty-five and the mother of fifteen children when she and her family followed their Puritan pastor, John Cotton, to Massachusetts in 1634. Her strong personality and articulateness attracted men and women of the congregation to gather at her home on Mondays to discuss Rev. Cotton's Sunday sermon.

Eventually Hutchinson went far beyond simply discussing the sermon to expounding heresy. She began to teach that outward obedience to the Scriptures was unnecessary to demonstrate an inward relationship to God (a position called **Antinomianism**). Furthermore, she taught that God had given her a direct revelation that superseded the Bible.

When the leaders of the community became aware of these teachings, they followed the Scriptural procedure and attempted to counsel her. She was completely unresponsive, however; so the court finally voted to banish her. Despite the sentence, she was not expelled until months later, in March 1638. Only a few of her supporters went with her to Portsmouth (PORTS muth), Rhode Island, where the group established a small settlement. Hutchinson soon grew restless and moved to New York, but the settlement at Portsmouth continued to grow. She continued to preach her radical beliefs in New York until she was killed in her home by Indians in 1643.

The Antinomian controversy also contributed to the first significant settlement in New Hampshire. The earliest attempt at colonization there was short-lived. David Thomson established the first settlement in New Hampshire at Little Harbor on the Piscataqua River in 1623. He named the area after the community of Hampshire, where he had lived in England. The colony consisted of only five men–not exactly a significant presence–and eventually dwindled to nothing.

The first significant settlement was not made until 1638, when John Wheelwright, along with thirty-five others, settled at Exeter. Wheelwright was an Antinomian and the brother-in-law of Anne Hutchinson; he left the Bay Colony during the Hutchinson controversy. Exeter soon became a thriving settlement. New Hampshire did not become a separate colony, though, until 1679, when the king of England made it a province under royal charter. Before that time it was under the jurisdiction of Massachusetts.

Section Review

1. Name and define the three categories of colonial government.
2. Name two factors that drew English colonists to America.
3. What is the difference between Puritans and Separatists?
4. Why did the English Separatists leave the Netherlands?
5. What two factors caused Massachusetts to spawn more colonies?

Middle Colonies

No other segment of the colonies reflected the cultural diversity of British North America quite like the **Middle Colonies.** English, Dutch, Germans, French, Finns, Scots, and Swedes all found a niche in the stretch of land from Long Island to the Delaware Bay.

The Middle Colonies

New York and New Jersey

New York began as a Dutch settlement, though it might have been England's to begin with had the English government been willing to pay the salary of **Henry Hudson.** Hudson, an Englishman, had sailed twice for his country under the auspices of the Muscovy Company in an attempt to find an arctic route to China. Frustrated by his ice-bound voyages to Greenland and Norway in 1607 and 1608, the Muscovy Company put the ambitious Hudson on a long leash. The Dutch, willing to take a chance on Captain Hudson, hired him to search again for a northern route to eastern riches. After a troublesome voyage with a quarrelsome crew off the frigid and unyielding Norwegian coast, Hudson sailed westward to America in hopes of finding a channel through which to reach China. After skirting the coast from Virginia northward, he found a wide inlet below Long Island and sailed his ship, the *Half Moon,* up the river that now bears his name. Hudson reached as far as present-day Albany, where the narrowing river convinced him that he was not nearing the Pacific. His voyage, however, provided Holland with a claim to the region.

The Dutch immediately established a flourishing fur trade and called the area **"New Netherland."** Later the Dutch West India Company received a charter from the Netherlands and in 1624 transported thirty families to New Netherland, where they settled along the Hudson River and Manhattan Island at a settlement called New Amsterdam. The Dutch governor, **Peter Minuit,** (MIN yoo wit) purchased Manhattan from the Indians by that name for $24 worth of cloth and trinkets. The Manhattans, like other Indians, had no understanding of the white man's concept of land ownership. The Indian concept of land did not include fences or property deeds. Land was a common resource that nourished all men. The Manhattans therefore must have been not only puzzled but also a little amused that they were being paid for something that they did not "own." Their descendants, however, would have little opportunity to renegotiate this most celebrated real-estate deal, since the Dutch killed most of the Manhattans during an Indian war in the 1640s.

The Dutch of New Netherland established a unique system of settlement that became known as the **patroon** (puh TROON) **system.** A patroon was a person who transported and settled fifty families in exchange for a large tract of land in the New World. The families thus transported then had to live on the patroon's land and under his control almost like feudal serfs on their lord's manor. The system gained the support of many investors but ultimately failed nonetheless because land was too easy to obtain in America, and tenants did not want to limit their freedom unnecessarily.

England was by no means content to have the Dutch as neighbors in the New World. However, from 1640 to 1660, civil war and political upheaval in England prevented her from dealing with the Dutch. When Charles II finally took the English throne in 1660, he granted New Netherland to his brother James, duke of York, who proceeded to conquer it in 1664.

When the English men-of-war massed off New Amsterdam, the peg-legged Dutch governor, **Peter Stuyvesant,** (STYE vih sent) sounded the call to arms, but no one answered. The settlers, a number of whom were Englishmen who had moved out of Massachusetts and Connecticut, simply did not view the English as a threat, and loyalty to the inept Dutch leadership did not run deep. A flustered Stuyvestant surrendered, and the English took the region by bloodless conquest.

The new owners quickly put their stamp on things. New Netherland became New York, and New Amsterdam became New York City. Dutch influence remained, however, in prominent family names such as Roosevelt and Van Buren and in place names such as Catskill, Peekskill, Spuyten Duyvil, and Wall Street, where the Dutch had built a wall as part of their Indian defenses.

New Jersey was first settled by Swedes and Dutch but came into English hands as part of the 1664 conquest of New Netherland. New Jersey was originally two colonies, East and West Jersey, during much of its colonial history. Several factors contributed to this division; one was the influence of settlements near what is now Philadelphia to the west and of New York City to the east. Most of the settlers near New York City were Dutch, whereas most near Philadelphia were Swedes. James II divided the region politically in 1664, when he gave the government of each area to different friends.

Strife developed when settlers who already lived in the Jerseys refused to pay rent to the new owners. The owner of West Jersey became disheartened and sold it to several Quakers. After 1676 both Jerseys were owned by Quakers, who included William Penn of Pennsylvania. Penn wrote a constitution called *Law, Concessions, and Agreements,* which provided for a self-governing assembly, full land rights, officially recorded deeds, religious freedom, and public trials by jury. This constitution contained many of the principles of civil and religious liberty that all thirteen colonies would eventually share.

In 1689 East and West Jersey united under common ownership, but they were not unified in spirit. The Jerseys continued to go their separate ways until 1702, when they were united as a royal colony by an act of the king.

Pennsylvania and Delaware

More than any other colony, Pennsylvania was the product of one man's vision and labor. **William Penn** always seemed to march to the beat of his own drum. Strong convictions, iron will, and fierce independence characterized the founder of Pennsylvania. Penn was expelled from Oxford for his Puritan beliefs and later joined what was a minority group even among dissenters, the Society of Friends or Quakers. (See Chapter 4.) He was imprisoned for a time in the Tower of London for writing an antitrinitarian tract, and after his release he continued to write and preach, emphasizing primarily the cause of religious liberty. Penn's involvement in colonial affairs began when he served as one of the proprietors of West Jersey. In 1681, in payment for a debt owed to Penn's late father, the cash-poor King Charles II granted the Quaker leader sole proprietorship over a vast tract north of Maryland. The king appropriately named the forested area *Pennsylvania* (meaning Penn's Woods) in honor of William Penn's father, a naval hero. This grant would be the beginning of Penn's ''Holy Experiment'' in America.

William Penn practiced what he preached in Pennsylvania. His Frames of Government provided religious toleration and political liberty for the colony. Penn's Quaker convictions concerning equality were reflected in his respectful treatment of the Indians, which provided a generally unheeded example for the other colonies.

The open political and religious environment and fertile land, as well as Penn's shrewd advertising in England and Germany, attracted thousands to

William Penn

the colony, and Philadelphia–the "city of brotherly love"–rapidly became an important commercial center.

Delaware was added to Penn's vast holdings by the king and did not become a separate colony until 1701. The little colony on the west bank of Delaware Bay had a checkered history of ownership. The area was first settled by Swedes near present-day Wilmington and named New Sweden. The Dutch later conquered the Swedes; the English conquered the Dutch; the stubborn Dutch reconquered, only to be finally ousted by the English. Delaware was granted to William Penn's proprietorship, but the settlers resisted being ruled by Quakers in Philadelphia. The colony was eventually granted the right to form a separate legislature but remained under the leadership of the Pennsylvania governor until 1776. One important contribution that came out of Delaware from the Swedes was the log cabin, a fixture in American society for the next two centuries.

Section Review

1. What nationality originally settled New York? What names did they give the colony and its capital?
2. Why did the patroon system fail?
3. In which three of the Middle Colonies were the Quakers influential in government?
4. Which colony besides New York was founded by a nation other than England?

Southern Colonies

Virginia

As we have seen in Chapter 1, the Virginia Colony got off to a shaky start but eventually stabilized. Four events occurred in 1619 that made that year pivotal to the future of Virginia. First, martial law imposed by earlier governors was lifted. These strict regulations had been necessary to the survival of the fledgling colony, but now Virginia's growing pains were less severe. In addition the need for more settlers encouraged the Virginia Company to put a happier face on a situation that had often proved grim.

The lifting of martial law and the granting of full rights to the colonists led to the formation of a representative assembly, the **House of Burgesses.** This advisory and legislative body was the first self-governing assembly in the New World. The new governor, Sir George Yeardley, organized the

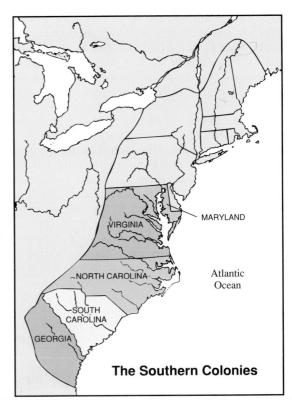

MARYLAND

VIRGINIA

NORTH CAROLINA

SOUTH CAROLINA

GEORGIA

Atlantic Ocean

The Southern Colonies

Pocahontas, *National Portrait Gallery, Smithsonian Institution. Pocahontas, daughter of the powerful Indian chief Powhatan, took the name Rebecca after her acceptance of Christianity in 1614. That same year she married the English planter John Rolfe. Their marriage produced improved relations between settlers and the Indians as well as a son in 1615. In 1616 Rolfe and his bride sailed for England where Pocahontas received a celebrity's welcome. In the spring of 1617 as she prepared for her return voyage to Virginia, Pocahontas died at Gravesend, England, where she was buried at St. George's Church.*

group of elected burgesses and held their first session in late July at the church in Jamestown. Later the assembly would build an impressive meeting place in the new colonial capital at Williamsburg.

A month after the assemblymen undertook the business of governing the colony, the arrival of a Dutch ship at Jamestown marked the third important event of the year, although no one there could have foreseen its significance. John Rolfe simply recorded in his journal that "about the last of August twenty [Negroes]" arrived. The first African slaves in British North America were treated like indentured servants, working for a period and then receiving their freedom. Gradually, though, racial distinctions were made between indentured servants, and blacks were placed in permanent

bondage. Slave labor was used throughout the colonies from New England to Georgia but was particularly widespread in the agrarian South. That day in 1619, when twenty Africans were deposited by force on the banks of the James River, was the quiet beginning of tremendous social division and moral tension for succeeding generations of Americans.

Another ship's arrival in 1619 held more immediate significance for the Virginia colonists. Ninety eligible women arrived, available to be purchased as wives for the cost of their passage. In Virginia currency for this bachelor colony, this amounted to 125 pounds of tobacco, which was an attractive price, and sales were brisk. The establishment of families in Virginia brought a more settled aspect and steadier growth to the colony.

One source of difficulty for the Virginians was Indian relations. As we have seen, the initial tension between the Indians and the English eased with the marriage of Powhatan's daughter Pocahontas to John Rolfe, famous for his introduction of tobacco as Virginia's chief cash crop. The Indian princess converted to Christianity and even made

---

"Precious Stink"

"Precious stink"–thus an early Virginian described pungent and profitable tobacco, America's first cash crop. The Spanish discovered the New World plant when they encountered Caribbean natives smoking *tabacos*–rolled leaves which were lit and inserted in both nostrils.

The Virginia settlers were the first to compete with the Spanish tobacco trade when in 1614 John Rolfe sent a shipload of tobacco to England, where it received mixed reviews. Tobacco had reached England as early as Raleigh's first colonizing effort, but Rolfe's crop was a milder variety owing to his introduction of a sweeter strain of West Indies tobacco.

Many believed that tobacco actually had medicinal qualities. A popular couplet of the time went "Divine Tobacco! which gives Ease / To all our Pains and Miseries." Actually today we know that it is the source of a great deal of pain and misery. King James I objected to the colonial crop as a "noxious weed." Yet despite its harmful effects, the "Joviall weed" remained popular. Just five years after Rolfe's first shipment, Virginia exported forty thousand pounds of tobacco, and by the late 1620s that figure had rocketed to 1.5 million pounds.

Tobacco became so crucial to the Virginia economy that the price of goods was measured not in "shillings" or "dollars" but in pounds of tobacco. For good reason, King Charles I declared that "Virginia was founded upon Smoak."

---

a celebrated tour of England, which ended tragically with her death on the eve of her return voyage to Virginia.

Not long afterward Powhatan also died, and his brother Opechancanough took control of the Indian Confederation, striking at the colonists with ferocity. On Good Friday morning, March 22, 1622, Indian warriors went on an indiscriminate rampage of murder. When the bloody massacre was over, 347 colonists had been killed. The battered Virginians gathered their forces and exacted heavy revenge. Later, another Indian massacre of whites resulted in a treaty that restricted the English to the Tidewater area of Virginia. The English soon violated this treaty, and an atmosphere of animosity continued between the two races. As a result of the Indian uprising and bickering among the Virginia Company's leadership, Charles I had the company dismantled, and Virginia became a royal colony in 1624.

Maryland

The first group of settlers arrived in Maryland in 1634, led by their proprietor **Cecilius Calvert, Lord Baltimore,** and established a settlement called St. Mary's off the north bank of the Potomac River. Charles I appropriately named the province Maryland, in honor of his Catholic wife, Queen Henrietta Maria.

There were two motives for planting a colony in Maryland: to provide a refuge for English Catholics and to make the colony a commercial success. In order to give liberty to the Catholics and still attract Protestant settlers, the colony's leaders established religious toleration through the **Toleration Act of 1649,** which provided that no one professing a belief in Christ should be troubled in the free exercise of his religion. Since Protestant settlers outnumbered the Catholic leaders from the very beginning, the act was indeed wise; by 1776 Protestants heavily outnumbered Catholics in Maryland.

The Carolinas

When Charles I dissolved the Virginia Company in 1624, he divided Virginia's vast claim, which stretched from the upper Chesapeake Bay to Spanish Florida. The region to the north of the James River settlements he named for his wife

A Brief DESCRIPTION
OF
The Province
OF
CAROLINA
On the COASTS of FLOREDA.
AND
More perticularly of a *New-Plantation*
begun by the *ENGLISH* at *Cape-Feare*,
on that River now by them called *Charles-River*,
the 29th of *May*. 1664.

Wherein is set forth
The *Healthfulness* of the *Air*; the *Fertility* of
the *Earth*, and *Waters*; and the great *Pleasure* and
Profit will accrue to those that shall go thither to enjoy
the same.

Also,
Directions and advice to such as shall go thither whether
on their own accompts, or to serve under another.

Together with
A most accurate MAP of the whole *PROVINCE*.

London, Printed for *Robert Horne* in the first Court of *Gresham-
Colledge* neer *Bishopsgate street*. 1666.

Advertisement attracting settlers to the Carolina Colony

tlement emerged: the area to the north, called Albemarle, and to the south, at a harbor settlement named Charles Town.

Northern Carolina had fewer settlers, and its scattered farms depended largely on tobacco for income. Originally the area was thought to be good for producing silk and wine. This promotion, however, proved better at attracting settlers than at sustaining them in the rough coastal plain of Albemarle.

Skulls and Crossbones

Blackbeard was the scourge of the Carolina coast for a number of years until 1718, when he was run through with a sword during a fierce fight off the Outer Banks of North Carolina. Tales of buried treasure stashed by Blackbeard still flavor many local legends along the Atlantic seaboard.

In his Generall History of the Robberies and Murders of the Most Notorious Pyrates, *(1724), Captain Charles Johnson described the fearsome pirate, Blackbeard:*

Captain Thatch, [Edward Teach] assumed the Cognomen of *Black-beard,* from that large quantity of Hair, which like a frightful Meteor, covered his whole Face, and frightn'd *America,* more than any Comet that has appear'd there a long Time.

This Beard was black, which he suffered to grow of an extravagant Length; as to Breadth, it came up to his Eyes; he was accustomed to twist it with Ribbons, in small Tails, after the Manner of our Ramellies Wigs, and turn them about his Ears: In Time of Action, he wore a Sling over his Shoulders, with three brace of Pistols, hanging in Holsters like Bandoliers; he wore a Fur-Cap, and stuck a lighted Match on each side, under it, which appearing on each side his Face, his Eyes naturally looking Fierce and Wild, made him altogether such a Figure, that Imagination cannot form an Idea of a Fury, from Hell, to look more frightful.

Maria, as we have previously noted. And being a man unfamiliar with modesty, Charles named the region to the south of the Virginia colony *Carolina* (from the Latin *Carolus* or Charles). In similar fashion to the Maryland colony, the king granted Carolina as a proprietorship to a friend. The king's favorite, Sir Robert Heath, however, did nothing to colonize the area beyond paper plans.

For several decades Carolina remained a backwater stretch for drifters and desperadoes, and among the inlets of its meandering coast were found favorite haunts for pirates. This situation began to change in 1663, when the king granted eight proprietors a new charter to develop and govern the region. From the beginning, two areas of set-

The southern Carolina settlement received more attention from the proprietors, particularly **Sir Anthony Ashley-Cooper,** the earl of Shaftesbury. Many of the original colonists in Charles Town had been small farmers in Barbados who could no longer compete with the large sugar plantations there. Initially the Charlestonians made a living by trading buckskins and Indian slaves. The slaves, acquired from Indian middlemen along the Savannah River, were generally sold in New England and the Caribbean. A more steady source of income came with the introduction of rice cultivation in the 1690s.

The geographic and economic division of Carolina was formalized in 1719, when South Carolina became a royal colony. Proprietors continued to rule North Carolina until 1729, when she too joined her sister as a royal colony.

Georgia

In terms of both chronology and geography, Georgia was at the end of the line. Settlement of the southernmost colony of British North America did not get underway until 1732, the year George Washington was born.

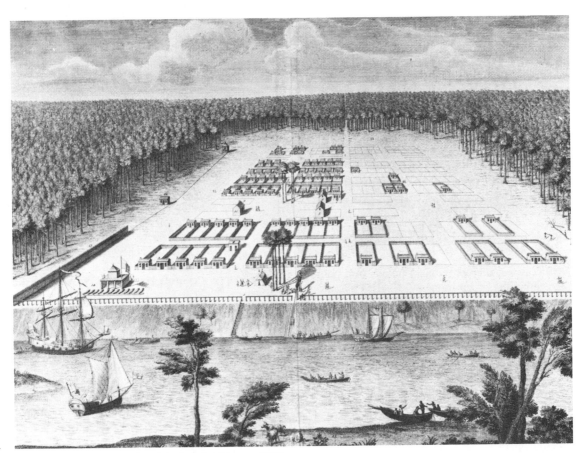

A view of Savannah on the edge of the Georgia wilderness, 1734

From the beginning the British had two purposes for Georgia: to establish a military buffer zone against Spanish Florida, and to provide a colony where debtors and vagrants, who often languished in English jails, could become productive. Emptying prison cells in England by sending their occupants to America was nothing new, but it was usually viewed as only another form of punishment, not a reprieve. In fact, Captain John Smith observed that when prisoners guilty of capital offenses were offered a choice between execution or banishment to the New World, "some did chuse to be hanged ere they would go thither, and were."

Georgia, however, was an exception. A reform-minded general named **James Oglethorpe** determined to build a colony that would provide rehabilitation through opportunity and hard work. Each settler was given fifty acres of land, and Governor Oglethorpe provided tools and seeds for the first year. Total land holdings were restricted to five hundred acres so that the small farmer was not gobbled up by land barons.

The first Georgians established Savannah in 1733, and a variety of settlers quickly followed the initial migration. Scots, Germans, Austrians, and even Portuguese Jews arrived, and Governor Oglethorpe's colony quickly distinguished itself by rapid growth and commercial success.

The Emerging American

America's thirteen colonies reflected their British heritage as well as their own upbringing. The vast Atlantic isolated the colonies from England, and the vast wilderness isolated them from one another. Isolation encouraged individualism and independence. Every colony founded in America was the result of private, even individual, effort. Smith, Bradford, Winthrop, Williams, Calvert, Penn, and Oglethorpe each had his own dream of what America was to be, and they crafted their colonies accordingly. Of course, individualism can become contagious, as the Puritan fathers learned to their chagrin on Monday mornings at Mrs. Hutchinson's.

There was also a stubborn streak of independence that ran through the colonies. This trait is underscored by a consistent pattern of settlement. After building houses for shelter and worship, the colonists organized their own government. Even where the crown refused to recognize the colonial legislature, as in the case of Virginia in the 1620s, the legislature continued to meet and make laws.

Life in the colonies could be hard, and it could even be short, but there was a newness about it, a sense of hope and opportunity that attracted thousands to America's shores to build their city in the wilderness.

The society they forged, now obscured by time, often seems to the modern reader to be as stiff and colorless as the steel engravings of the period. Yet in the days when America was ruled by a distant king, daily life had its own fascinating story to tell.

Section Review

1. What four events made 1619 a pivotal year in Virginia's history?
2. What was the religious motive in planting the Maryland colony?
3. What were the main crops of northern and southern Carolina respectively?
4. What were the two purposes the British had in founding Georgia?

Chapter Review

Terms

charter colonies
proprietary colonies
royal colonies
"headrights"
indenture
New England
Pilgrims
Puritans
Separatists
William Bradford
Mayflower Compact
Great Migration
John Winthrop
covenant
Harvard College
Thomas Hooker
Fundamental Orders of Connecticut
Roger Williams
Anne Hutchinson
Antinomianism
Middle Colonies
Henry Hudson
New Netherland
Peter Minuit
patroon system
Peter Stuyvesant
William Penn
Southern Colonies
House of Burgesses
Cecilius Calvert, Lord Baltimore
Toleration Act of 1649
Sir Anthony Ashley-Cooper
James Oglethorpe

Content Questions

1. Name the colony that each of the following men was primarily instrumental in founding.
   a. Peter Minuit
   b. Thomas Hooker
   c. James Oglethorpe
   d. Roger Williams
   e. Sir Anthony Ashley-Cooper, the Earl of Shaftesbury
   f. William Penn
   g. John Winthrop
   h. Cecilius Calvert, Lord Baltimore
2. What two colonies formed from Massachusetts as a result of dissension?
3. In what way was the Mayflower Compact, the Fundamental Orders of Connecticut, and William Penn's Frames of Government each an important step in the development of American government?
4. Which three colonies expressly permitted freedom of religion from their founding?
5. Which section of the thirteen colonies was the most diverse culturally?
6. List which Southern Colonies were originally charter colonies and which were proprietary.
7. What were the first two major settlements of northern and southern Carolina respectively?
8. Name two ways in which non-English cultures were introduced to America.

Application Questions

1. Do you think that John Winthrop's desire to make Massachusetts "a city set on a hill" was a wise goal? Why or why not?
2. Do you agree with Roger Williams's criticisms of the Massachusetts colony? Why or why not?
3. How would American history have differed if Sweden and the Netherlands had not lost their colonies in North America?

PERSPECTIVES EASTERN INDIANS

Sault Ste. Marie, *by Paul Kane, Royal Ontario Museum, Toronto, Canada*

In the far north, near the Arctic Circle, the massive continents of Asia and America each taper into slender fingers of land which rest just short of touching. It was probably here, some time after the Flood, that the ancestors of the American Indians entered the Western Hemisphere. They may have crossed the narrow Bering Sea in small boats, or they may have crossed on a bridge of ice. It is even possible that the two continents were joined at one time and that these ancient pioneers simply walked over on dry land.

However they came, these Asian immigrants slowly spread southward from Alaska. Eventually, descendants of the original pioneers had settled both continents down to the southernmost tip of South America. When Christopher Columbus came to the New World, he found it teeming with human life.

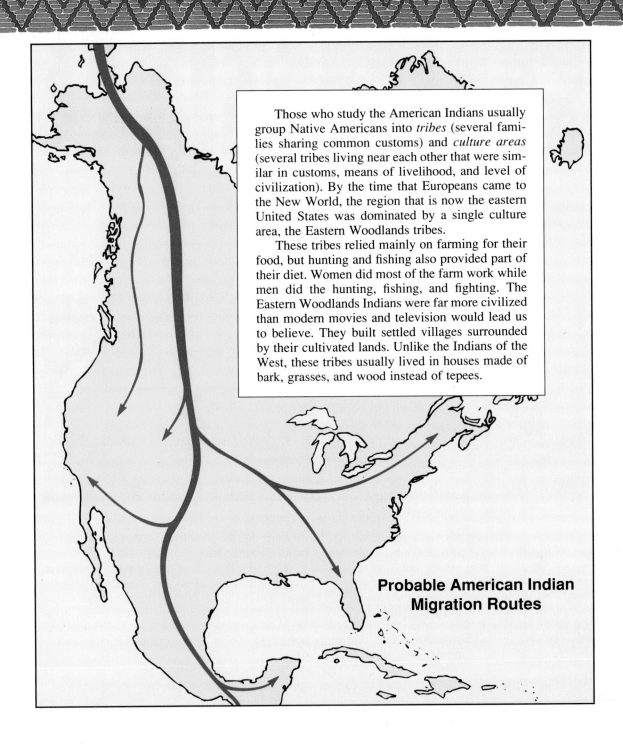

Those who study the American Indians usually group Native Americans into *tribes* (several families sharing common customs) and *culture areas* (several tribes living near each other that were similar in customs, means of livelihood, and level of civilization). By the time that Europeans came to the New World, the region that is now the eastern United States was dominated by a single culture area, the Eastern Woodlands tribes.

These tribes relied mainly on farming for their food, but hunting and fishing also provided part of their diet. Women did most of the farm work while men did the hunting, fishing, and fighting. The Eastern Woodlands Indians were far more civilized than modern movies and television would lead us to believe. They built settled villages surrounded by their cultivated lands. Unlike the Indians of the West, these tribes usually lived in houses made of bark, grasses, and wood instead of tepees.

Probable American Indian Migration Routes

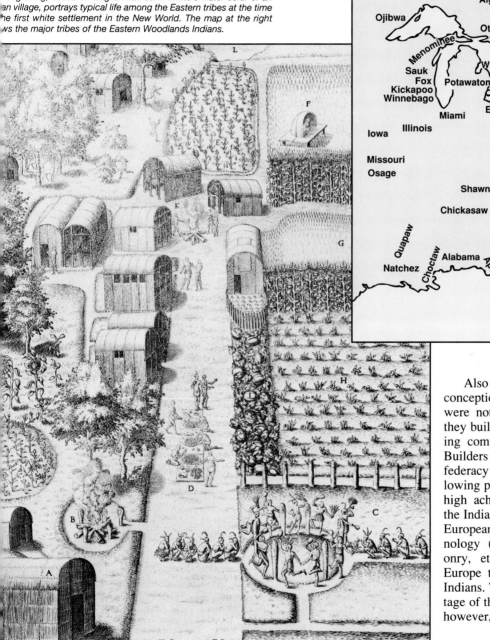

engraving, based on Englishman John White's water color of an ... an village, portrays typical life among the Eastern tribes at the time ... the first white settlement in the New World. The map at the right ... ws the major tribes of the Eastern Woodlands Indians.

Map labels: Algonquin, Ojibwa, Menominee, Ottawa, Huron, Penobscot, Abanaki, Pennacook, Sauk, Fox, Kickapoo, Winnebago, Wyandot, Iroquois, Potawatomi, Erie, Mohican, Delaware, Susquehanna, Narraganset, Mohegan, Pequot, Montauk, Miami, Iowa, Illinois, Missouri, Osage, Powhatan, Cherokee, Tuscarora, Shawnee, Catawba, Chickasaw, Creek, Quapaw, Choctaw, Alabama, Yamasee, Natchez, Apalachee, Timucua, Seminole

Also contrary to popular conception, American Indians were not backward savages; they built societies of surprising complexity. The Mound Builders and the Iroquois Confederacy discussed in the following pages demonstrate the high achievements of which the Indians were capable. The European advantage in technology (ironworking, weaponry, etc.) ultimately gave Europe the victory over the Indians. The culture and heritage of the American Indians, however, live on.

The Serpent Mound in southern Ohio is a splendid example of an effigy mound.

MOUND BUILDERS

Some fifty miles east of Cincinnati, Ohio, lies a most unnatural landform. From the ground it looks like a low, curved wall of earth stretching in a meandering course through the countryside. A bird's eye view, however, is vastly different; the seemingly purposeless curves prove to be the image of a coiled, undulating snake over a thousand feet long. This "Serpent Mound" is but one of hundreds of mounds in the United States that represent the work of one of North America's earliest Indian civilizations, the Mound Builders.

Two major groups of Mound Builders lived in North America. The first group mostly constructed *burial mounds,* piles of earth that served as grave sites. Along the Ohio River Valley, mainly in what is now southern Ohio, the mound-building Adena and Hopewell Indian cultures flourished from a century before the birth of Christ up until about A.D. 500. The Adena and Hopewell buried their dead with an elaborateness matched only by the Pharaohs of ancient Egypt.

These Mound Builders built log crypts and in them placed bodies along with various "grave goods"–elaborately decorated garments, freshwater pearls, stone-carved figurines and pipes, pottery and tools, and copper and mica effigies. The tomb was then covered with earth, not by machinery, of course, but by hand. (Archaeologists have even found baskets where presumably tired workers simply tossed in the whole load of dirt rather than take time to dump it out.) Often the Indians buried several bodies in the same mound, eventually creating an artificial hill. Archaeologists have found as many as thirty mounds within a hundred-acre area.

After the collapse of the burial mound cultures, the *temple mound* builders dominated the Mississippi River Valley from A.D. 700 to 1600. Unlike the Adena and Hopewell, these Indians constructed large mounds to use as the sites of temples rather than burial places. The largest of these temple mounds is the Cahokia Mound, also called Monks Mound, in Illinois across the Mississippi River from St. Louis. This huge mound–equal in volume to one of the pyramids of Egypt–was once the center of a thriving Indian city of perhaps thirty thousand inhabitants.

Both burial and temple mound cultures built other kinds of mounds. The Adena Serpent Mound is an example of an *effigy mound*, a mound in the shape of some animal or object. The Serpent Mound contains no bodies or artifacts and probably held some religious significance for the Adena. The Mound Builders also built a few mounds as fortifications, such as the Hopewells' "Fort Ancient" just northeast of Cincinnati.

The last of the Mound Builders were dying out when De Soto visited the Mississippi River Valley in the 1540s, and the Adena and Hopewell had disappeared entirely by that time. Today mounds such as the Cahokia Mound and those smaller mounds throughout the Midwest serve as visible reminders of North America's first important Indian civilization.

Each dot on the map below represents an Indian mound, displaying the heavy concentration of the culture of the Mound Builders along the Ohio River Valley and the Mississippi River Valley.

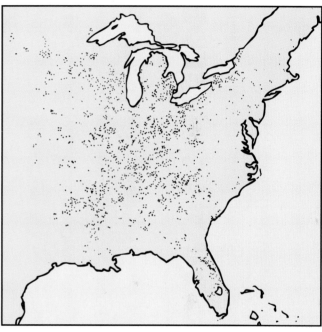

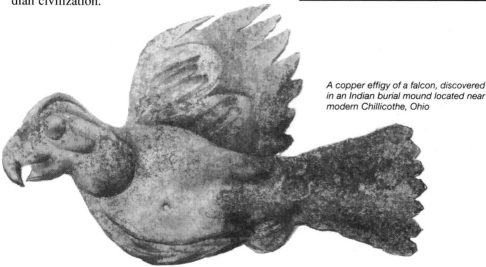

A copper effigy of a falcon, discovered in an Indian burial mound located near modern Chillicothe, Ohio

IROQUOIS CONFEDERACY

J. Grasset St. Sauveur inv. direx.   J. Laroque Sculp.

An Iroquois warrior brandishes a round-headed warclub.

"It would be a very strange thing," wrote Benjamin Franklin to a friend in 1751, "if Six Nations of Ignorant Savages should be capable of forming a Scheme for such an Union . . . and yet a like Union should be impracticable for ten or a dozen English colonies." The "Six Nations of Ignorant Savages" to which Franklin rather condescendingly referred were the tribes that made up the most advanced Indian civilization in North America, the Iroquois Confederacy of upper New York. As Franklin implied and some historians suggest, this unusual union of tribes may even have provided a pattern for the United States.

The date of the founding of the Iroquois League seems to have been between 1400 and 1450. According to Iroquois tradition an Indian named Deganwidah persuaded several Iroquois tribes to draw together under the Great Law of Peace. Deganwidah called this peace "the tree of the Great Peace," likening it to a great white pine tree whose branches sheltered the Iroquois. A total of six tribes eventually banded together: the Seneca, Cayuga, Onondaga, Oneida, Mohawk, and Tuscarora. Because all these tribes spoke the Iroquoian language, their league became known as the Iroquois Confederacy.

The alliance established a rough federal type of government which left tribes to themselves in local matters but joined them in "international" matters such as war on other tribes. A council of fifty sachems (chiefs) served as the "legislature" with each tribe allotted a specified number of seats. Each tribe had only one vote, however, and most decisions had to be unanimous. Much of the organization of the confederacy demonstrated different aspects of the unique culture of the Iroquois. They gave more voice in government to women than most Indians, for example. The sachems were always male, but they were chosen by the female head of a clan or tribe.

The Iroquois' names for their league also derived from their way of life. The "Great White Pine Tree," for example, probably reflected the many times an Iroquois had found shelter and protection beneath the spreading branches of a pine. The Iroquois also called their confederacy "the longhouse," deriving from their basic social unit. The Iroquois longhouse was a structure that outwardly resembled a modern army barracks. Covered with bark, these long, narrow houses were up to four hundred feet in length. Inside in a number of "apartments" lived several related families. A woman, usually the oldest among the families, ruled over the longhouse.

Too much can be made of Iroquois government and civilization. It was not a democratic republic by any means. Also the Iroquois could be some of the most savage of the American Indians when attacked. They executed captured enemies by slow torture, and they were known to eat parts of slain enemy warriors, believing they could absorb some of the fallen foe's bravery and valor. The confederacy nevertheless made the Iroquois one of the most powerful Indian tribes in eastern North America. In colonial days, the British, the French, and other Indian tribes could not operate without taking into account the wishes of the mighty Iroquois.

An Iroquois longhouse

Colonel Guy Johnson and Karonghyontye (Captain David Hill), *by Benjamin West, National Gallery of Art, Washington. The British relied heavily on their Iroquois allies, particularly in the American Revolution. Probably the most important of the pro-British Iroquois was Chief Joseph Brant, a Mohawk. He saw action in several battles and rose to the rank of captain in the British army.*

CORN

"When Columbus discovered the native corn of the Western Hemisphere in 1492," one writer noted, "he assuredly did not appraise his find for what it was–a potential treasure of infinitely more value than the gold of the Indies he was seeking." Indeed, of all Indian products and contributions, none has matched in worldwide importance the simple ear of corn.

Corn, or maize, as the Indians called it (scientific name *Zea mays*), probably originated in Central America and was carried from tribe to tribe until Indians on both continents cultivated it. Wild corn, much smaller and with fewer kernels than modern corn, no longer exists. Its domestic descendant, however, is–along with potatoes, rice, and wheat–one of the four most important food-

One of the earliest European drawings of corn

stuffs in the world. We often do not realize its importance because corn shows up on our dinner table mostly in the form of beef, chicken, and eggs–the result of using corn as a livestock feed.

Nearly all American Indians depended on corn as a food source. Indian methods of planting, which early settlers adopted, often differed from those of the modern farmer. The Indians first killed the trees in an area they wanted to cultivate by *girdling* them, cutting away a strip of bark around the tree. Then they burned the trees and other ground cover. (The ashes helped fertilize the soil.) Stumps and other debris remained; the Indians simply poked holes in the ground around the debris with a stick and planted their corn. Sometimes they planted beans in the hills with the corn. Not only did the cornstalk provide support for the bean vine, but also the beans fixed nitrogen in the soil and enriched it. Some Indians placed a fish with the seed to help fertilize the ground.

Corn was essential to the Indians, so much so that some tribes held elaborate dances and festivals to plead with their gods for a good crop. More practically, some tribes stationed an Indian in a shelter in the middle of the field to act as a living scarecrow to protect the harvest from pests. The men usually helped clear the ground, but the women did most of the tending and harvesting of the crop.

"Indian corn" was much like the field corn that farmers grow today. After it was harvested, much of this corn was ground into meal to be used in bread, stews, soups, and mush. Indians also grew sweet corn, the soft, pulpy corn which we are used to seeing on our plates. The Indians even raised popcorn and used it not only as a food but also in decorations such as necklaces.

Today cross-breeding and hybridization have resulted in ears of corn much larger and fuller than the Indian kinds. It is still basically the same plant, however. To hungry people all over the world Indian maize has truly proved to be more valuable than gold.

The Copley Family, *by John Singleton Copley, National Gallery of Art, Washington*

History with its flickering lamp stumbles along the trail of the past, trying to reconstruct its scenes, to revive its echoes, and kindle with pale gleams the passion of former days.

Winston Churchill here describes the difficult but rewarding task of both the writer and reader of history. This chapter reconstructs the colorful scenes of daily life in colonial America. The colo-nial era, like any period past or present, is far more than the sum of its great leaders. The farmer and merchant; the butcher, the baker, and the candlestick-maker all played a role in colonial so-ciety. A look inside their homes, meeting their wives and children, joining them for a meal, and quietly looking over their shoulder during times of leisure will tell us much about them. And whether we observe these things from a delicate Chippendale settee imported from London or an oak bench as rough as the frontiersman who carved it, we should catch a glimpse of a varied and vibrant time that has been called "the morning of America."

The Rhythms of Life

Patchwork Population

It would not have been unusual while walking the streets of the British colonial cities of New York, Philadelphia, or Charleston to hear the chatter of German, Dutch, or French mingling with the English. Although English colonists comprised a clear majority, there was a remarkable degree of ethnic diversity in the colonies, particularly after 1700.

The two largest groups of non-English settlers were **Scotch-Irish** and Germans. The Scotch-Irish were actually Presbyterian Scots from the Protestant colony of Ulster in Northern Ireland. Economic, hard times and religious intolerance sent as many as a quarter-million Ulstermen to the colonies. Many arrived in Philadelphia, but most did not stay. Hungry for land, they migrated west and southwest, funneling down the Shenandoah Valley into the Virginia and Carolina backcountry. Their avenue through the wilderness was an old Iroquois Indian trail dubbed the **"Great Philadelphia Wagon Road."** The trail, as significant as any of its better-known successors such as the National Road or the Santa Fe Trail, was the chief access to backcountry settlements from Virginia to Georgia. Tens of thou-

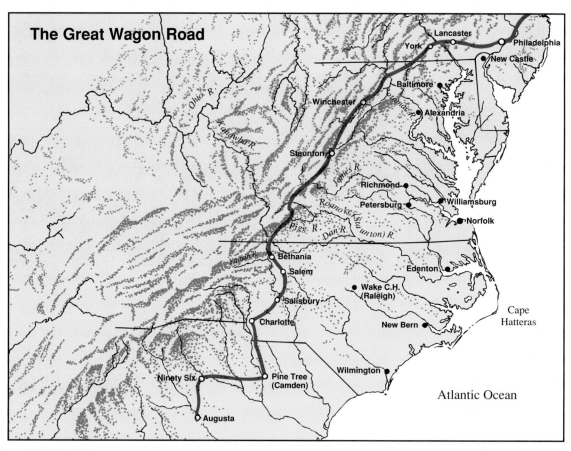

The Great Wagon Road

sands of settlers traveled the rutted pass by foot or jostled down the rugged road in wagons built by skilled Germans from Pennsylvania's Conestoga Valley. A string of inns along the seven-hundred-mile road grew into backcountry towns such as Frederick and Hagerstown, Maryland; Winchester, Staunton, and Fincastle, Virginia; Salisbury and Charlotte, North Carolina; Camden, South Carolina; and Augusta, Georgia.

The Scotch-Irish as well as the Germans generally occupied the vanguard of Appalachian expansion in the early eighteenth century. Some of them in their acquisition of wilderness land had little time or money for the ''niceties'' of land deeds and bills of sale. As squatters they often presented their own version of a land title with lead shot.

Most of the Germans were Protestants from the Rhineland Palatinate (a region in southwestern Germany) who, tiring of the incessant raids by French Catholic armies under Louis XIV (ruled 1653-1715), came to America. Thousands of Germans arrived in Pennsylvania, attracted by the religious freedom of Penn's Quaker commonwealth and the rich farm country not unlike their Rhine valley before the pillaging French arrived.

A number of German immigrants remained in Pennsylvania where they became known, as a result of a corruption of *Deutsch* (''German''), as **Pennsylvania Dutch.** Others, however, followed the Scotch-Irish into the Shenandoah or migrated from the Chesapeake settlements of Virginia into the piedmont.

The rapid growth of German settlements bothered their English neighbors. To some observers the Scotch-Irish may have had strange views on religion, but at least they spoke the same language. Germans though were, well, German. Philadelphian Benjamin Franklin lamented, ''Why should the Palatine Boors be suffered to swarm into our Settlements? . . . Why should Pennsylvania, founded by the English, become a Colony of *Aliens,* who will shortly be so numerous as to Germanize us instead of Anglifying them, and will never adopt our Language or Customs?''

Despite Franklin's fears the German and most other European immigrants quickly adapted to English ways while maintaining their own Old World traditions. For the Rhinelander, German may have been the language with which he talked to his family and to God, but English was the language of the marketplace.

The blending of non-English cultures into the social landscape was an important influence in the development of America. A pluralistic society developed in which ethnic and religious diversity existed together. However, commercial, political, and—as we shall see in the next chapter—religious bonds forged unity with diversity.

Marrying and Burying

Not only was the colonial population varied, it was also growing. In 1700 the population stood at roughly 250,000, and it increased tenfold during the next three-quarters of the century to 2.5 million at the outset of the Revolution. Immigration was of course a contributing factor here, but equally important was the high birth rate, which was twice that of Europe. Proof of this prolific birth rate was demonstrated in the 1790 census which found that over half of all Americans were under sixteen years of age.

A key reason for this increase was that colonial women married at a considerably younger age, usually around twenty. By contrast their European counterparts married in their late twenties, if they married at all. Earlier marriages were prompted by the reversed sex ratio between the Old World and the New. In England, for example, women outnumbered men, which is a typical population feature. In the colonies, particularly in the late seventeenth-century South, men outnumbered women two or three to one. As a result, few women remained single, and earlier marriages meant more childbearing years.

Earlier marriages and large families were also favored because they provided an important labor source for the home. Fully ninety per cent of the colonists depended on farming for their livelihood, and children provided helping hands and strong backs to put food on the table and in the market. Consequently, families with six to eight children were common and even a dozen or more was not uncommon.

Unfortunately for our founding mothers, childbearing could prove fatal. Midwives of the day served to the best of their ability, but obstetrics was an unknown science. Infections and difficult deliveries sent many women to an early grave, and their babies usually followed them. This 1724 epitaph of a Massachusetts wife tells an all too familiar story of the day:

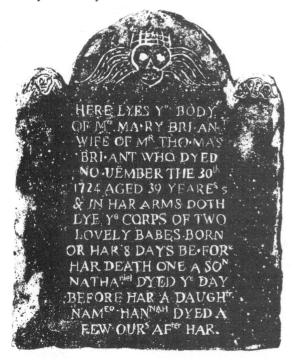

HERE LYES Y° BODY
OF M.RY BRI.AN
WIFE OF M. THO.MAS
BRI.ANT WHO DYED
NO.UEMBER THE 30th
1724 AGED 39 YEARE s
& IN HAR ARMS DOTH
LYE Y° CORPS OF TWO
LOVELY BABES BORN
OR HAR 8 DAYS BE.FOR
HAR DEATH ONE A SON
NATHA.niel DYED Y° DAY
BEFORE HAR A DAUGH.tr
NAM.ED HAN.NAH DYED A
FEW OUR.S AF.ter HAR.

As serious as the infant death rate was in the colonies, it was dramatically lower than that experienced in Europe during the same period. The mortality rate there was grim, twenty-five per cent at birth and another twenty-five per cent before the age of fifteen. Half the children in eighteenth-century Europe never reached adulthood. By contrast records from late seventeenth-century Massachusetts reveal that nine out of ten children survived infancy. The scattered settlements of the New World and its productive and plentiful land inhib-

ited the disease and famine that were prevalent in Europe's crowded conditions.

This fact offers an important clue as to why epidemics were more prevalent in eighteenth-century America than in the previous century. As cities grew, the crowded urban centers spawned contagious diseases. The problems of the Old World resurfaced in the New. Roads that emanated from the cities carried both settlers and germs to the frontier. Farmers bringing goods to the coastal market could pick up not only exotic stories from the sailors they met there but exotic diseases as well. Soldiers sent from crowded quarters in the cities to put down Indian uprisings in the wilderness sometimes killed more settlers with their contagions than the red man could with his weapons.

Epidemics of smallpox and infectious dysentery reduced the population in New England by as much as ten per cent during major outbreaks. The diph-

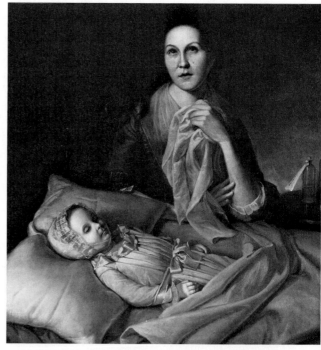

Rachel Weeping, by Charles Willson Peale, Philadelphia Museum of Art. As the model for this poignant portrait, Peale used his wife weeping over their infant daughter, who had died of smallpox.

Fighting Smallpox

One of the first men in America to urge the use of inoculations to combat deadly smallpox was Rev. Cotton Mather, a godly Puritan pastor in Boston. Mather, a member of the British Royal Society, read that exposing a person to a mild strain of smallpox would enable him to resist the full effects of the disease. However, early inoculation attempts were risky, even fatal, and opposition to Mather's new ideas was intense even from leading physicians of the day. Finally the Reverend Mr. Mather was put to the ultimate test when his son Samuel came down with the dreaded disease. In the following excerpts from his 1721 diary, Mather recorded the opposition to his pioneering efforts and his own personal struggle over the fate of his son.

[May] 26. The grievous Calamity of the *Small-Pox* has now entered the Town. The Practice of conveying and suffering the *Smallpox* by *Inoculation*, has never been used in *America*, nor indeed in our Nation, But how many Lives might be saved by it, if it were practiced? . . .

[June] 13. What shall I do? what shall I do, with regard unto *Sammy?* He comes home, when the Small-pox begins to spread in the Neighbourhood; and he is lothe to return unto *Cambridge*. I must earnestly look up to Heaven for Direction. . . .

[July] 16. At this Time, I enjoy an unspeakable Consolation. I have instructed our Physicians in the new Method used by the *Africans* and *Asiaticks*, to prevent and abate the Dangers of the *Small-Pox*, and infallibly to save the Lives of those that have it wisely managed upon them. The Destroyer, being enraged at the Proposal of any Thing, that may rescue the Lives of our poor People from him, has taken a strange Possession of the People on this Occasion. They rave, they rail, they blaspheme; they talk not only like Ideots but also like *Franticks*. And not only the Physician who began the Experiment, but I also am an Object of Fury. . . .

[August] 1. Full of Distress about *Sammy;* He begs to have his Life saved, by receiving the *Small-Pox*, in the way of *Inoculation*, whereof our Neighbourhood has had no less than ten remarkable Experiments; and if he should after all die by receiving it in the common Way, how can I answer it? On the other Side, our People, who have Satan remarkably filling their Hearts and their Tongues, will go on with infinite Prejudices against me and my Ministry, if I suffer this Operation upon the Child. . . .

15. My dear *Sammy*, is now under the Operation of receiving the *Small-Pox* in the way of Transplantation. The Success of the Experiment among my Neighbours, as well as abroad in the World . . . [has] made me think, that I could not answer it unto God, if I neglected it. . . .

25. Friday. It is very critical Time with me, a Time of unspeakable Trouble and Anguish. My dear *Sammy*, has this Week had a dangerous and threatening Fever come upon him, which is beyond what the *Inoculation* for the *Small-Pox* has hitherto brought upon my Subjects of it. In this Distress, I have cried unto the Lord; and He has answered with a Measure of Restraint upon the Fever. The Eruption proceeds, and he proves pretty full, and has not the best sort, and some Degree of his Fever holds him. His Condition is very hazardous. . . .

[September] 5. *Sammy* recovering Strength, I must now earnestly putt him on considering, what he shall render to the Lord! Use exquisite Methods that he may come Gold out of the Fire. . . .

[November] 19. Certainly it becomes me and concerns me, to do something very considerable, in a way of Gratitude unto GOD my SAVIOUR, for the astonishing Deliverance, which He did the last Week bestow upon me, and upon what belong'd unto me.

When the epidemic was over Mather was vindicated. Though the vaccine had proved fatal for three per cent of those receiving it, fifteen per cent of those not inoculated had died.

A drawing of Philadelphia in 1702 shows a bustling city where only wilderness had existed less than a hundred years before.

theria epidemic of 1735-37 began in New Hampshire and spread southward into the middle colonies, leaving thousands dead in its wake. Children were particularly susceptible to the virus; nearly all the victims were under twenty years of age. One interesting commentary on the commonness of the tragedy of childhood mortality is that among the toys that have survived the colonial period, some homemade dolls came with their own coffin.

Despite these problems, the colonies generally flourished. The abundance of land invited expansion, and young men reaching adulthood usually married and moved on. The majority of families were isolated, independent, and largely self-sufficient. The husband, his wife, and their children shared the hardships and the rewards of carving a home out of the wilderness. We shall take a closer look at these homes, the labor that sustained them, and the leisure that lightened the daily struggles of colonial life.

Section Review

1. What were the two largest groups of non-English settlers in the colonies?
2. Who were the ''Pennsylvania Dutch''? Why did they settle in Pennsylvania?
3. Why did so many colonists prefer large families?
4. Why were epidemics more prevalent in eighteenth-century America than in the previous century?

At Home

Housing

Styles of colonial houses changed with time, region, and the cultural heritage of their occupants. With the earliest houses, however, survival was more important than style. In order to weather their first wilderness winter, Plymouth settlers dug out caves and lined the walls with bark, or copied their Indian neighbors by constructing wigwams.

As a colony took on a more settled aspect, its residents built houses patterned after the styles they had known in England. Isolated by an ocean from the old country, the colonists were out of touch with the architectural ''fashions'' of seventeenth-century England. As a result, what we now consider **''colonial style''** or **''Williamsburg style''** architecture–steep gabled roofs, tall brick chimneys, brick arches over doors and windows, and interiors with exposed beam ceilings–was really the then century-old English Tudor-style construction.

The material for house exteriors depended to a large degree upon location. With rising prosperity, brick came into more common use, particularly in the tidewater regions where rich clay deposits were found. Further inland the forest yielded a less expensive but weathertight exterior of split cedar or oak clapboard. In regions where the spring thaw produced a crop of new rocks in the field, farmers often turned stumbling stones into building blocks by using field stones to produce efficient and durable cottages.

The image of the southern plantation as a sprawling, white mansion accented with magnolias and stately, wide verandas is largely mythical. Since a plantation was a large farm, the planter's house could best be described as a large farmhouse. Of course there were elaborate exceptions, particularly in the early nineteenth century, but most southern planters lived in a simple log or clapboard house. As their family and income grew, they added more rooms and elaborated on the structure–for example, replacing the translucent oiled paper windows with glass. Another popular addition to colonial plantation houses was the *piazza*, or roofed porch, a feature borrowed from the West Indies providing some protection from the hot southern sun.

In the backcountry, shelter reflected the roughness of the land and its people. One observer recorded that during the first year or two, the Scotch-Irish lived in "open Logg Cabbins," an open-face three-sided log structure with a roof–crude and cold. After getting established they generally built a cabin of notched logs, filling the chinks with moss and clay. German settlers generally squared up their logs and located the chimney in the middle of the cabin to centralize the heat source. The result was a tighter, tidier house.

Diet

The old adage "you are what you eat" would certainly hold true in the colonial period, at least in terms of social standing. The Old Colony Club at a 1769 meeting in Plymouth Massachusetts had a nine-course dinner on its menu as follows: baked Indian whortleberry pudding; steaming succotash (a soup containing fowl, pork, and corned beef); a dish of clams on the half shell; a dish of oysters and codfish; roasted venison; a dish of duck; a dish of cod and eels; and if there was any room left for dessert, steaming, spicy apple pies; and finished off with succulent cranberry tarts and cheese.

Such dinners were of course for the wealthy and well-bred. Down on the farm things were different. The standard fare for most families, particularly on the frontier, was salt pork, corn meal, Indian beans, and greens in the summer. The more settled farms often had an apple or peach orchard–a source of both food and drink. Hard cider and brandy were common beverages in the colonies; rum was more prevalent on the coast where ports provided inlets for the West Indies liquor. Drunkenness was unfortunately common, and its destructive force was felt throughout society. As we shall see later, the transforming power of the gospel proved to be a force for drying up the stills and delivering men and women from the bondage of drink.

In terms of colonial cuisine, there was a great deal of trading going on. The first Europeans to America discovered a new world of food. Corn, a variety of beans such as snaps and limas, cacao (chocolate), tomatoes, squash, pumpkins, peppers, and peanuts were all native American contributions to the colonial diet. The "Irish" potato, now a North American staple, made an interesting transatlantic trek. Spanish conquistadors first shipped white potatoes back home from Peru along with coffers of Incan gold. The unpretentious little potato would prove to be the more valuable in the centuries to follow. Cultivated in Spain, Switzerland, and later the British Isles, potatoes made their way back across the Atlantic with the Scotch-Irish in the 1700s, who introduced the plant to North America for the first time.

Europeans introduced other foods to America as well, such as bananas, melons, rice, wheat, oats, and a favorite American beverage *after* the Boston Tea Party, coffee. An array of "farm" animals were also transplanted to America: cows, pigs, sheep, and chickens.

In what has been rightly called a "green revolution," transplanted Indian crops of corn and sweet potatoes sustained burgeoning populations across the Eurasian land mass from Beijing to Belfast. From its discovery America was a breadbasket to the world and clearly God's providential hand was at work in this, providing the blessing of food to an ever-growing world that has increased tenfold during the past three centuries. The psalmist rejoiced that the Lord "giveth food to all flesh: for his mercy endureth forever" (136:25).

Education

Whether children learned the "3 Rs" at home or attended a village school, the purpose behind the education was to provide basic skills and the ability to read the Bible. This emphasis reflected the Protestant character of America. As one historian has put it, "It was the Protestant Reformation, and the Protestant insistence that every man have free access to the Word, without priestly interference, that finally broke the Church's monopoly on literacy." Just how complete was the church's medieval monopoly on reading and writing is underscored by the fact that during the five hundred years from the sixth to the eleventh century only three English kings could sign their own names.

The Reformation not only created a spiritual revolution but triggered an educational one as well, since an obvious prerequisite for the ability to read the Scripture is the ability to read. In England, "Puritan zeal" for the Word of God and widespread spiritual hunger produced a boom in education in the early 1600s. This fact is particularly important in understanding the educational climate in Puritan New England.

It has been estimated that there was a greater percentage of college graduates in Massachusetts during the 1630s than there is today. Despite the privations of the wilderness, these founders were determined that their children would not be deprived of an education. The home was the first schoolhouse in America.

A child's first "book" was ominously shaped like a paddle. The hornbook was a paddle-shaped board faced with a card containing the alphabet and the Lord's Prayer and covered with a thin sheet of horn for durability. A child usually "graduated" from the hornbook to a primer for more thorough reading training. The *New England Primer* was by far *the* standard text throughout the colonial period. It provided basic grammar and vocabulary accented with moral lessons, as well as a short catechism.

Not all colonial parents were capable of or interested in teaching their children at home. In New England in particular, the concentrated pattern of village settlements that we noted in the previous chapter contributed to the development of the village school. Such schools open to boys and girls were often called dame schools since they were generally taught by a widow or a village spinster.

Outside New England, two factors–geography and the lack of a Puritan presence with its enthusiasm for the printed page–limited the scope of colonial literacy. In the Middle Colonies and the South, farms were more scattered and families more isolated, a fact that would remain true well into the national period. As late as 1860 Virginia had 14 residents per square mile whereas Massachusetts had 127.

The majority living in the rugged outback did not have the luxury of a village school since most of them lived *days* from the nearest outpost. If parents were illiterate then their children would likely be as well. Many parents, however, made extraordinary efforts and sacrifices to have their children taught even if only through infrequent contact with literate travelers, indentured servants, or missionaries. Devereaux Jarratt, born in poverty in colonial Virginia, recorded that the highest ambition of his parents "was to teach their children to read, write, and understand the fundamental rules of arithmetic." Jarratt, like others, after learning the rudiments of reading would walk miles to borrow even a single book.

Though education in the backcountry was often hit-or-miss, those who could afford it hired private tutors for their children. A number of towns with greater resources made efforts at establishing schools. Charleston, South Carolina, for example, sponsored two *Free Schools* for the education of the poor. Charleston also led the way in 1698 by establishing the first public library in America.

In Adam's Fall
We finned all.

Thy Life to mend,
God's Book attend.

The Cat doth play,
And after flay.

A Dog will bite
A Thief at Night.

The New England Primer, *the standard reading text in New England, attempted to inculcate the truths of Scripture in students as it taught the basics of reading.*

Section Review
1. What were two of the materials used in the construction of colonial houses?
2. List at least four of the native American foods that Europeans found in the New World.
3. Why was the literacy rate higher in New England than in the other regions?

At Work

Louis Timothy, Rice Farmer, Edisto Island, South Carolina, 1718

Louis Timothy felt justly proud as the carpenters put the finishing touches on the clapboards which covered his log house. His wife wanted them white-washed, but that could wait until next year. Besides the cost, it would take time away from his work in the rice fields. For the young planter the new face on an old house was a fitting sign of the success that had marked his path in recent years.

Though successful, however, they had not been easy years. Louis arrived at the Charles Town wharves as a lad with his family, among a shipload of refugees. His father, the elder Louis Timothée, was a French Huguenot who had taken his family to the Carolina colony when life in France became too dangerous for Protestants. After arriving in Charles Town, the Timothée family had made their way down the coast and found a niche of cheap land on the Edisto River.

Their three-hundred-acre tract was not a pretty prospect when they arrived. Before them lay a tangle of swamp and sand covered with scrubby pines and imposing cypress trees. The elder Timothée felled the best pines and young Louis set about squaring them up with an adze. That first year their house was no more than a two-room cabin with a roof of palmetto palms and a floor of native sand. Aside from a table, benches, and straw bedding, the house was bare of furnishings. During the first year, food, not shelter, was the priority. A man would die of starvation before he died from exposure. Subsistence crops of corn and vegetables were the first things planted to feed a hungry family. The daylight hours were spent wrestling a farm out of the wilderness.

The coastal flats had rich, productive soil, but the land had to be cleared by cutting trees and burning and digging out stumps. It was exhausting work, the merciless sun beating down on the laborers, while mosquitoes and stinging sand flies usually joined them in the field–sometimes giving them killing fevers.

Louis's younger brother died during their second spring on the land, the family's first, but not its last, victim of malaria. The elder Timothée died of the fever in 1710 and was buried between his son and his wife beneath a moss-draped cypress. Charlotte Timothée had died in childbearing six years earlier.

Louis Timothy now stood surveying the land his father had conquered. He liked innovation. He had Anglicized his name and had moved from the subsistence farming of his youth to the cultivation of rice. The cash crop was not only suited to his land but also to the needs of his growing family and his own rising expectations.

Preparing the land for growing rice had been an exhausting, back-breaking task. To undertake this work, Mr. Timothy had purchased three slaves in Charles Town, and they joined him and his eldest son in the field, along with the two slaves that he had inherited from his father. The first task had been to turn the stream that meandered through the land into an irrigation canal complete with a sluice to provide the controlled flooding needed to grow rice. The land itself had to be leveled and divided by a grid of ditches for flooding and draining. All of this labor had been done with hoes, shovels, and muscles.

In the spring the tiny rice seeds had been planted in the fresh, dark soil, then flooded for a few days as the life in the seeds took hold beneath the warm cover of water. Through the summer the green shoots ripened to golden grain. By September the rice was ready for harvest. With sickles flashing, Timothy, his son, and their slaves slowly moved through the field cutting the rice. Sometimes the black men would sing harvest songs in strange tongues of Ibo and Mandingo, the languages of their native Africa in the happier years before they fell into the hands of an enemy African chieftain, then Dutch and British middlemen, and finally, Master Timothy.

This year's harvest would amount to forty bushels to the acre. The cutting was only the beginning, however. Four of the slaves would work until Christmas on the monotonous routine of flailing and husking the kernels. Timothy would oversee their work, as well as the cutting of timber and irrigation repairs. In late winter he would gather his finished grain on flatboats for the Charles Town market. With money in his pocket, Louis Timothy would return with cloth, shoes, nails, tools, and a bucket of paint for his patient wife.

Debora Riedhauser, House Servant, Germantown, Pennsylvania, 1747

As the coals glowed and fired the crackling wood, Debora could see her breath in the frosty November air. The sun was not yet up over the Pennsylvania countryside when she began to prepare breakfast. The house was quiet–though it would not be for long when the children awoke! For Debora it was her favorite time of her busy day, especially this morning since it was her sixteenth birthday.

Her mistress had remembered and promised her a pennysheet on her next trip to the market. After learning the hornbook Debora had only dreamed of owning a book. The pennysheet was no book, but being a page with pictures and words of wisdom from *Poor Richard's Almanack* by that witty Mr. Franklin of neighboring Philadelphia, it would still be quite a treasure.

Debora's master, Josiah Hastings, had said nothing about her birthday. She figured he was probably thinking about her birthday in two years when her indenture would end. Well, Debora was thinking about that day too, with mixed emotions. This had been her home for three years since she arrived in Philadelphia from her native Bavaria. Debora was an orphan; her mother's death was only a vague memory, and her father had been killed fighting the Austrians during one of the frequent wars that swept the German countryside. Her uncle, not wanting any more mouths to feed, had sent Debora and her two brothers to America. Their passages were paid in Philadelphia in return for five years of service. The purchasers, however, were indifferent to keeping the family together. One brother lived twenty-five miles away from Debora's Germantown home, and being a full day's journey apart, they seldom saw each other except at Christmas. Her other brother had left with his redemptioner down the Great Wagon Road and had not been heard from since.

Master Hastings had taken on young Debora as a house servant during his wife's long and uncertain recovery from complications with pregnancy. The baby had died and Mrs. Hastings had been left far too weak to care for her four other children.

Stirring noises upstairs shook Debora out of her thoughts. Fortunately yesterday's coals were glowing brightly this morning, and the fire started quickly. One day last week the embers had grown cold and no amount of coaxing could bring fire from them. Debora had to go borrow a "chunk of fire" from the neighbor's hearth to get a fire started– breakfast was late and Master Hastings was cross.

Debora adjusted the Dutch oven–a three-legged covered pot–and dropped a cut of possum fat into it. Over the sizzling grease she poured a batter of cornmeal and sour milk to make flat johnnycakes.

The table was set with seven wooden plates, seven wooden noggins, and seven wooden spoons. Pewter was only for the rich, and Debora had never even seen a China plate or a silver spoon.

The noon meal would be hearty but simple: dried apples, cold mush, and hot cider. Supper would fill the house with smells of cabbage, cheese, sausage, and maybe a stiff brew made from roasted chestnuts to warm them before the night chill set in.

Between meal preparations Debora would milk the cow, churn its milk for butter, and help her mistress weave linsey-woolsey (a mixture of linen and wool) for shirt cloth. In the meantime there was old cloth that needed repairing–the sleeve of a toddler's coat, and the seat of her master's pants. Yet as little feet scampered down the stairs to breakfast, all of these things, like her life, lay ahead of her. For on her sixteenth birthday, this German orphan thought not so much about what the past had given her as what the future offered her in this new land.

Jeremy Shrimpton, Wigmaker, Boston, Massachusetts, 1735

The list of accounts in the large ledger brought a smile to Master Shrimpton's lips–business had been good. His decision to move his business from his native London to the colonies five years earlier had paid off handsomely. Wigmakers were as much

The Cheney Family, *American 18th Century, 1795, National Gallery of Art, Washington*

in demand in America as they were in England and on the continent. Ever since French royalty started wearing wigs beginning with Louis XIII a century earlier, the powdered hairpieces had remained the fashion rage for men of station. The twenty-three-year-old Louis had donned one because of his thinning hair–his ancestor Charles the Bald was called that for good reason.

Now, however, even men with thick locks were being fitted for wigs. For many it was as essential to their business attire as a coat-and-tie would be at a later day. In the eighteenth-century professional world a wigless man might easily be taken for a witless man among the stiff upper crust of business

barons. Well, such attitudes were good for business too, Shrimpton mused, and the rising merchant class in Boston was as fashion conscious as any he had fitted in London or Liverpool.

Looking up from his shop window desk, Shrimpton could see the gleaming masts of sloops and schooners anchored in Boston Harbor. Their owners were his best customers; so he always enjoyed seeing a busy harbor. A sharp rap on the door however interrupted his deskwork. Shrimpton opened the door to a rumpled farmer, probably in town selling produce. The wigmaker eyed his visitor coolly; in his thoughts he sniffed, "A backwoods bumpkin, he certainly has no use for a wig!"

In *his* thoughts, the gristly farmer sniffed back, "Now here's a fancy little fellow, a real dandy."

In their own way, both men were too professional to give words to such thoughts–the visit was strictly business. "Do you buy hair?" the farmer began. "My wife's going to sell hers."

Shrimpton nodded and followed him to a wagon where a tense little woman sat. The wigmaker ran his bony fingers through her hair and held it up with an experienced hand, "Three shillings," he said to the farmer. With a nod the locks were snipped. After Shrimpton had applied his craft to these long locks, the hair would adorn the head of a merchant or minister, who unlike the farmer's wife, had more money than hair.

Jeremy Shrimpton made a variety of wig styles to suit the tastes and incomes of his clients. Common folks who wanted budget fashions could purchase a simple curled wig called a *Sunday Buckle*.

The wealthy had a variety to choose from, such as the *Campaign Wig* for traveling, the *Bagwig* in which the long back tresses were held in a dainty silk pouch, and the *Cadogan,* a foppish array of bows and curls. All of these hair pieces were large, flowing extravagances–their owners were not called bigwigs for nothing.

Wigmaking was a careful, customized process. First, a client would arrive at Shrimpton's shop for head measurements and style selection. Next, purchased hair was cleaned, combed, rolled, and baked in rye dough. This tempered and strengthened the hair. After this a pattern was drawn up based on the head measurements, and a foundation net known as a caul constructed into which the strands of hair were woven. The caul was lined with silk and edged with a silk ribbon that buckled or tied in the back for a snug fit.

Up to this point, Shrimpton's two apprentices did most of the work. The next two steps of finishing and dressing, however, required the master's touch. In the finishing stage curls were shaped and precision parts added. Finally the wig was "dressed" with powder and perfume. The powder was added for coloring of which there were a variety of shades from white or blonde to chestnut or black.

Despite the time and talent invested in making a wig, it seems that a wigmaker's work was never done. Not only were there new orders to fill, but the old wigs required care as well. On Saturdays, Shrimpton sent his two apprentices out to make house calls to rescue drooping curls and to refragrance smelly wigs in time for Sunday worship.

Jeremy Shrimpton would continue to do a brisk trade. For another generation, wigs would remain essential to the well-dressed man. By the end of the century, though, neither the king's army nor his fashions dominated America, and wigs became a curious relic of Mr. Shrimpton's day.

Section Review

1. Which of the three fictional characters in this section–Louis Timothy, Debora Riedhauser, or Jeremy Shrimpton–had the easiest time surviving in colonial America?
2. Which of the three characters has the brightest, most promising future?

At Play

There are several misconceptions about colonial leisure that must be dispelled before we can gain a proper understanding of it. First of all, it existed. Naturally in the early years of settlement along the coast the priority was survival; virtually the only contact between these pioneers, in a setting other than work, was on Sundays at church. When life became more settled, more leisure time was possible. This pattern was repeated over and over as the frontier moved farther and farther west. This explains some of the differences between leisure activities in the cities and backcountry settlements during the later colonial period.

Second, Americans *did* enjoy life during the colonial period. Modern views of the colonists, particularly the Puritans, as sour, dour sticklers with dark clothes and darker looks, is at best a bad caricature. Puritans had colorful wardrobes, listened to good secular music and enjoyed good literature and wholesome games. The word *pleasure* was definitely in the Puritan's vocabulary. What was also in his vocabulary was *consistency*. A godly believer did not leave off his relationship to Christ during his leisure moments; rather he honored Christ in them. In a manner of speaking he did not lay aside his robes of righteousness when he put on his play clothes. God was to be honored in all things, not just in the pew and pulpit.

As mentioned earlier, there were some definite differences between leisure activities in the urban areas and those in the backcountry. City folks were, of course, closer together and therefore had more opportunity to socialize and organize clubs and activities. Their country cousins, by contrast, were scattered and isolated by swollen rivers and miles of dense forest. Even at the risk of being dull, survival on the frontier often meant all work and no play. Yet the backwoodsmen, being innovators by necessity, found a way to combine the two.

Barn raisings, corn huskings, and quiltings gave opportunities for frontier families to gather and socialize while sharing the work load. At such events news, or probably more accurately, gossip was exchanged and children had one of their scarce opportunities to meet and play with other children.

The Domino Girl, *American 18th Century, 1790, National Gallery of Art, Washington*

The gatherings often culminated in a bonfire where there was music, dancing, and many a tall tale spun.

Even worship services became social occasions in the backcountry. One Anglican missionary to the Carolinas, the Reverend Charles Woodmason complained in his journal, "No making of them sit still during Service–but they will be in and not–forward and backward the whole time (women especially) as Bees to and fro to their hives."

These infrequent social gatherings in the isolated outback stood in sharp contrast to the other end of the geographic and economic scale. In the eastern cities of Charleston, Williamsburg, Philadelphia, New York, and Boston, wealthy planters and merchants kept a full social calendar through a myriad of clubs, balls, and parties. In Charleston, where wealthy planters escaped their swampy lands from May to December, a 1773 diary reveals a number of clubs for the movers and shakers to join, including the Smoking Club, Laughing Club, Beef-Steak Club, Monday-Night Club, Friday-Night Club, and the Fort Jolly Volunteers.

Poor Richard's Almanack

One of the most popular reading pastimes of the late colonial period was the almanac, and none surpassed Benjamin Franklin's ***Poor Richard's Almanack,*** which he published from 1733 to 1758. In addition to the usual astronomical and weather predictions, *Poor Richard's* was peppered with wit and morals that emphasized thrift, honesty, and diligence. Not all of the sayings were Franklin's, as he readily admitted, but even to those drawn from past sages he gave his own homespun touch, to the delight of his colonial readers. After two and a half centuries Franklin's sayings still flavor our conversation. Here are a few examples of *Poor Richard's* wit and wisdom:

Fish and Visitors stink after three days.

Well done is better than well said.

Tart Words make no Friends; a spoonful of honey will catch more flies than a Gallon of Vinegar.

Sloth (like Rust) consumes faster than Labour wears: the used Key is always bright.

Little Strokes Fell great Oaks.

Different Sects, like different clocks, may be all near the matter, 'tho they don't quite agree.

If your head is wax, don't walk in the Sun.

Tim was so learned, that he could name a Horse in nine Languages. So ignorant, that he bought a Cow to ride on.

An old Man in a House is a good Sign.

Beware of little Expenses: a small Leak will sink a great Ship.

Pay what you owe, and you'll know what is your own.

At 20 years of age the will reigns; at 30 the wit; at 40 the judgment.

Three may keep a secret, if two of them are dead.

Lost time is never found again.

Success had ruin'd many a Man.

Haste makes Waste.

Early to bed and early to rise makes a man healthy, wealthy, and wise.

He that falls in love with himself will have no rivals.

Keep your eyes wide open before marriage, half shut afterwards.

Forewarn'd, forearm'd.

Many a Man thinks he is buying Pleasure, when he is really selling himself a Slave to it.

Creditors have better memories than debtors.

Glass, China, and Reputation are easily crack'd, and never well mended.

A full Belly makes a dull Brain.

If Jack's in love, he's no Judge of Jill's Beauty.

Plow deep while sluggards sleep.

Not everyone in the city, however, was rich and famous enough for such exclusive merrymaking. Other city dwellers enjoyed bowling games on the village green, picnics, or trips to the tavern where the news could be heard either through the usual story swapping or from a patron reading a newspaper aloud. Such newspapers, primarily a feature of colonial life beginning in the second quarter of the eighteenth century, featured colonial happenings, advertisements, obituaries, and humor, as well as the latest from London (news that was usually several months old).

Colonial newspapers were published in all the major cities such as Boston's *New England Courant,* Philadelphia's *American Weekly Mercury* and the *Pennsylvania Gazette* (published by Benjamin

Franklin), and Charleston's *South Carolina Gazette*. Such papers filtered to outback communities by horse and rider, providing a much-needed break in the isolation of wilderness living.

Among the toys and games of colonial children are a number that are familiar today: marbles, hoops, dolls, puzzles, hopscotch, shuffleboard, shuttlecock, ''I sent a letter to my love,'' and whoop-and-hide (hide-and-seek). Most toys were homemade, simple, and highly prized since a child generally had very few of them. A girl, for example, usually had one doll during her childhood, often carved from a stick or made from a corncob. Swimming and fishing were popular in the summer and iceskating and sleigh rides in the winter where possible. Children of the more affluent could even take trips to the beach for swimming, or if they lacked the necessary skill, could wear a ''cork jacket'' which, as one 1769 New York advertisement noted, had ''saved many from drowning.''

In the growing, varied leisure time of the period there is an underlying fact–the colonies were maturing and prospering. The ''starving times'' now seemed to be but a distant footnote as each generation built upon the foundation of their fathers. As future president John Adams explained to his wife:

> I must study politics and war, that my sons may have liberty to study mathematics and philosophy, geography, natural history and naval architecture, navigation, commerce, and agriculture, in order to give their children a right to study painting, poetry, music, architecture, statuary, tapestry, and porcelain.

There was, in fact, a lot of politics and war for Adams to study in the late colonial period. The colonies *were* maturing; Britain's grip on her offspring was loosening; and there was in America a gathering sense of independence.

Section Review

1. What is the typical modern view of the Puritans? Why is this view inaccurate?
2. What are some examples of social gatherings on the frontier?

Chapter Review

Terms

Scotch-Irish
Great Philadelphia Wagon Road
Pennsylvania Dutch
''colonial style'' architecture
hornbook
New England Primer
dame schools
Poor Richard's Almanack

Content Questions

1. How did the Great Philadelphia Wagon Road aid in developing the American frontier?
2. Why was the birth rate higher in America than in Europe in the 1700s?
3. Name at least three deadly diseases that American colonists faced.
4. Why was education so important to the Puritans?

5. Where was the first public library in America established?
6. How did the Puritans reflect a Christian view of leisure?

Application Questions

1. Considering the danger of smallpox inoculation, would you have undergone such treatment if you had lived in colonial days?
2. Choose a saying from *Poor Richard's Almanack* (p. 60), and write a brief paragraph telling why it would or would not be sound advice for a Christian to follow.
3. Review the quotation from John Adams on this page and the story of Louis Timothy on pp. 55-56. What common principle can be drawn from them?

Pilgrims Going to Church, *by George Henry Boughton*

The tall, lean minister stood behind the wooden pulpit and faced his audience. He began his sermon, reading it in careful, measured tones. As he read, his words astounded his listeners. "There is nothing that keeps wicked men at any one moment out of Hell," he declared, "but the mere pleasure of God." He continued,

> O sinner, consider the fearful danger you are in! It is a great furnace of wrath, a wide and bottomless pit that you are held over in the hand of that God Whose wrath is provoked and incensed as much against you as against the damned in Hell. You hang by a slender thread, with the flames of divine wrath flashing about it and ready every moment to singe it and burn it asunder; and you have . . . nothing to lay hold of to save yourself–nothing that you have done, nothing that you can do to induce God to spare you one moment.

As the minister preached, some in the congregation cried out in fear, struck with overwhelming conviction. Others grew solemn. As the fear of divine judgment began to grip the audience, the preacher exhorted his listeners, "Therefore, let everyone that is out of Christ now awake and flee from the wrath to come."

The year was 1741, the speaker was Jonathan Edwards, and the sermon was "Sinners in the Hands of an Angry God." Next to the Pilgrims' first Thanksgiving, Edwards's preaching of this sermon is one of the most famous events in colonial American church history. The sermon was a climax to religious development in colonial America. Behind "Sinners in the Hands of an Angry God" lay over a century of diverse, complex, and intriguing religious history.

Denominational Beginnings in America

As Chapter 1 stressed, the Reformation resulted in the creation of numerous Protestant denominations and groups. The New World became the home of many of these groups–as well as Catholics and Jews. North America took on a distinctive character as a new field into which established groups could expand, as a laboratory for religious "experiments," and as a haven for persecuted sects.

English Background

The heritage of the American colonies was predominantly English. Understanding the religious history of England, therefore, helps us understand the religious history of the colonies. During the 1500s England swung back and forth like a pendulum from Catholicism to Protestantism. King Henry VIII (ruled 1509-1547) broke from the Roman Catholic church but only because he wanted to divorce his wife, and he remained doctrinally a Catholic. Under Henry's son, Edward VI (ruled 1547-1553), the Protestant leaders pushed for a thorough reform that offended a large portion of the English people by insisting on drastic and immediate changes. Edward's successor, the Roman Catholic Queen Mary (ruled 1553-1558), attempted to return England to Catholicism by means which included burning some three hundred Protestants at the stake.

After all of this turmoil, Queen Elizabeth (ruled 1558-1603) determined to put an end to religious controversy. Elizabeth wanted a Protestant church; so the creed of the Church of England was thoroughly Protestant. At the same time, Elizabeth hoped to win over the reluctant by preserving the outward trappings of the old church–its bishops, elaborate garments for priests, and so on.

Differing reactions to this **"Elizabethan settlement"** drastically affected the history of England and America. Three important groups within the Church of England and one without arose during Elizabeth's reign and shortly thereafter. The **Puritans,** as mentioned in Chapter 2, were staunch Protestants; they agreed wholeheartedly with the Anglican creed. They thought that the old ceremonies and practices, however, were too much like those of the Roman Catholic church. The Anglican church, they said, must be "purified" of such corruptions.

Low church Anglicans agreed doctrinally with the Puritans but saw no problem with the church's ceremonies and structure. Such matters were unimportant, the low church party held, as long as the church was doctrinally sound. **High church Anglicanism** held that the church's traditional practices, notably its rule by bishops, were divinely ordained. Doctrinally, the high church Anglicans differed among themselves, but they were generally more liberal in their beliefs and less opposed to Catholicism than the Puritan and low church parties.

Finally, the **Separatists** believed that the whole Church of England was corrupt and that true Christians must separate from it. Separatist groups included the Pilgrims who landed at Plymouth Rock and later the Baptists and the Quakers.

Puritanism in America

Although Virginia was the site of America's earliest settlement, New England was in some respects more influential. The Puritan views of the settlers in Massachusetts Bay and the surrounding regions affected every other colony to some extent and later shaped the religious character of the United States. In short, New England Puritanism was the most influential religious movement in colonial history.

Puritan Beliefs—Like other Protestants, the Puritans believed the basic doctrines of the Reformation: the authority of the Bible alone, justification by faith alone, and so on. As we observed in Chapter 2, the heart of Puritan theology in particular is the **idea of the covenant.** Puritans believed that God deals with mankind through a series of covenants, or agreements. For example, the Puritans held that in salvation, the believer enters into a "covenant of grace" with God. God saves an individual and in return the believer fulfills his "covenant obligations"–obeying God's law.

The covenant idea affected every aspect of Puritan society. Like Israel in the Old Testament, the Puritans believed that as a community they had made a social covenant with God to establish a model society, ruled by God's laws. The settlers hoped not only to establish a society in accordance with God's standards but also to demonstrate to England how such a godly society should operate.

The covenant idea also affected the personal lives of individual Puritans. Because each Christian is in a covenant with God, he has certain responsibilities to fulfill. Of course, the Puritans did not believe salvation resulted from good works but that good works were the natural result of salvation. Puritans agreed with Romans 12:1 that Christian dedication was simply the "reasonable service" of one who had received the "mercies of God."

Another distinguishing feature of New England Puritanism was its church polity. *Polity* refers to the system of government in a church. In **episcopal polity,** such as that in the Church of England, an authority such as a monarch appoints bishops, and the bishops in turn appoint lower officials down to the individual churches. In **presbyterian polity,** such as that in the Church of Scotland, members of the congregation elect their ruling elders. Elders from several congregations then elect officials for the next level of authority, these officials elect the next higher level, and so on.

New England Puritans chose neither of these polities. They preferred **congregational polity.** Each congregation elected its own officers, and each church remained independent of other churches. Other groups, notably the Baptists, also adopted congregational polity. Eventually most of the Puritans in America came to be called simply **Congregationalists.**

Puritan Decline—Like the children of Israel after the deaths of Joshua and the elders who outlived him (Judges 2:7-10), the Puritans declined in religious fervor after the original settlers had died. Later generations built a prosperous colony and usually remained outwardly moral, but they lacked the fervent piety of their forefathers. Materialism—the love of possessions and wealth—replaced a love for God. This decline created a serious problem in the Congregationalist churches.

In Congregationalist churches, a person joined the church upon his profession of his salvation through faith in Christ. The children of converted church members, however, were baptized as infants. These children were then considered members of the church but could not become full members and take the Lord's Supper until they "owned the covenant," declared their personal faith in Christ as Saviour. As the years passed, fewer and fewer members of the later generations owned the covenant. Most of the New Englanders did not want to leave the church, however, because privileges of citizenship, such as the right to vote in

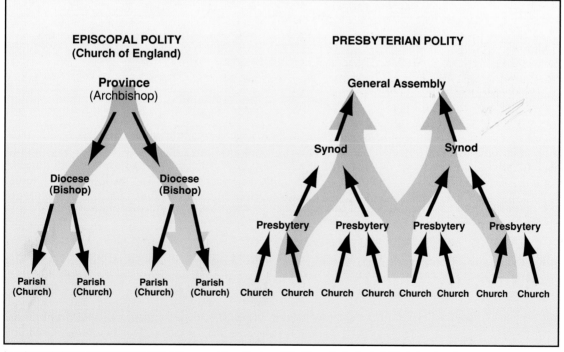

In episcopal church polity authority flows downward from the top of the hierarchy to the individual churches; in presbyterian polity authority flows upward, much like the representative form of government later adopted by the United States.

Trial of George Jacobs of Salem for Witchcraft *(Courtesy Peabody Essex Museum, Salem, Mass.)*

colonial elections, were open only to church members. Because of the Congregationalist system, the churches of New England were slowly filling up with unconverted members.

The presence of these unconverted church members led to another problem: Could the children of these unsaved members be baptized? Eventually, the ministers of New England devised what became known as the **Half-Way Covenant.** Church members who had not owned the covenant, but whose lives were outwardly moral, could present their children for baptism. The covenant also allowed unconverted members to enjoy the full privileges of citizenship. Still, neither the parents nor the children could become full members and take the Lord's Supper until they professed a personal faith in Christ. Despite its purpose of keeping people in the church and under sound preaching, the Half-Way Covenant served only to increase the number of unregenerate church members. It was a serious compromise of the principles of the original Puritans.

The year 1692 marked the low point in Puritan history. Having forsaken much of the faith of their fathers, the Massachusetts colony sank into fanaticism and hysteria. The **Salem witch trials** resulted from the claims of several young girls in Salem Village, Massachusetts, that they were being afflicted by witches. The authorities took the charges seriously and began to try those who were accused. Before the hysteria was over, at least twenty people were dead, and the reputation of Massachusetts had been permanently damaged. The spiritually chilling influences of the Half-Way Covenant and the reaction after the hysteria of the witch trials left New England spiritually depressed until the Great Awakening in the 1700s.

The Truth About the Salem Witch Trials

In 1692 in Salem Village, Massachusetts, a group of young girls began having hysterical fits. The girls claimed that witches were afflicting them and began to name certain people in the village as witches. Based virtually on the testimony of these girls alone, authorities began to arrest and then to try several astonished Salem citizens. Nineteen people were hanged; one man was pressed to death with heavy weights; an unknown number died in prison.

Ironically, only those who maintained their innocence were executed; those who confessed escaped the hangman's noose. Realizing this fact, some confessed in order to save themselves. Others could not do so in good conscience. Mary Easty said to her judges, "I know not the least thing of witchcraft, therefore I cannot, I dare not belie my own soul. I beg your honors not to deny this my humble petition from a poor dying Innocent person." She was hanged anyway.

Several facts are ignored in the blast of accusations hurled at the Puritans. The ministers of Massachusetts, rather than being persecuting fanatics, actually counseled caution and restraint to the more zealous civil authorities. It was the opposition of some of the clergy, in fact, that helped end the witch trials. Boston pastor Cotton Mather, who is often falsely accused of urging authorities on, said, "It were better that ten suspected witches should escape than that one innocent person should be condemned."

Often forgotten too is the fact that some in Massachusetts actually were practicing witchcraft–although it is difficult to tell whether this practice was mere superstition or real demonic activity. Even if this activity were only superstition, nearly everyone at that time–not just the Puritans–*believed* that it was genuine witchcraft and that it must be relentlessly punished. In the century before the Salem witch trials, for example, over three thousand accused witches were burned in the Swiss canton of Vaud alone. Salem, by comparison, was restrained.

Critics of the Puritans also ignore the repentance of Salem. Within five years the citizens of Massachusetts held a day of prayer and fasting to implore God's pardon for their actions. One of the judges in the trials, Samuel Sewall, was overcome with guilt when his son read Matthew 12:7 during the family's devotions–"But if ye had known what this meaneth, I will have mercy, and not sacrifice, ye would not have condemned the guiltless." Sewall, in remorse, went to church, confessed his guilt to the congregation, and asked for forgiveness. Anne Putnam, one of the hysterical girls, likewise stood before the congregation in Salem Village and humbly apologized for being "an instrument for the accusing of several persons of a grievous crime, whereby their lives were taken away from them, whom now I have just grounds and good reason to believe they were innocent persons."

What exactly happened in Salem Village? No one today can be quite sure. We do know certainly, however, that innocent people died because of fear and hysteria. We know too that the reputation of Massachusetts Puritans has been blemished. Regrettably, the worthy contributions of early American Puritanism have been obscured by the wild fanaticism of a few and by an eager willingness of later generations to believe only the worst.

Anglicanism in America

Anglicanism came to the colonies in 1607 with the settlers at Jamestown, and it became–after Puritanism–the most widespread religious force in seventeenth-century America.

Beginnings–Some have mistakenly viewed Virginia as a secular, materialistic colony in contrast to the more spiritually minded Massachusetts. In reality, some of the early settlers were just as devout as the Puritans. With the original settlers, for example, came Anglican minister Robert Hunt to serve as chaplain. One of Hunt's first acts on arriving in the New World was to hold services to give thanks to God for a safe arrival. He preached weekly to the settlers, holding his services under an awning made from an old sail. Hunt visited and served the many sick in the early days of the colony. As a result of his strenuous labors, Hunt died within two years of his arrival. Captain John Smith wrote of Hunt, "He was an honest, religious, and courageous Divine; he preferred the service of God to every thought of ease at home."

The early Virginians were usually low church Anglicans, agreeing doctrinally with the Puritans but having no objection to Anglican forms of worship. They were, therefore, less interested in establishing a new "holy commonwealth" like the Puritans than in re-creating England in America. Like the Puritans, however, the Anglicans of Virginia declined spiritually. This decline was slowed but not stopped by the ministries of James Blair and Thomas Bray.

Blair and Bray–Realizing that Anglicans in America needed guidance, church leaders in England sent **James Blair** to Virginia in 1685 and **Thomas Bray** to Maryland in 1700. Blair was most notable for attempting to secure better qualified ministers for that colony by helping to found William and Mary College in 1693 and by serving as its first president. Bray was even more important to Anglican history, although he spent only about six months in America. After his brief stay in Maryland, Bray returned to England to promote missionary efforts for the colonies. Two outstanding organizations resulted from his efforts. The Society for the Promotion of Christian Knowledge (SPCK) provided Christian literature for missionary work and helped establish some forty libraries in the colonies. The Society for the Propagation of the Gospel in Foreign Parts (SPG) focused more directly on securing ministers for the colonies. Later Bray helped found an organization aimed at evangelizing blacks in America.

Expansion–Due to the efforts of men such as Blair and Bray, the Anglican church grew throughout the colonies. By the time of the Revolution, Anglican churches existed in every colony, and Anglicanism had become the established (government-supported) church in Virginia, Maryland, the Carolinas, Georgia, and parts of New York and New Jersey.

Expansion did not always bring spiritual growth, however. Anglican churches constantly suffered from a shortage of pastors, and those they had were not always academically or spiritually qualified. (One glaring example was an Anglican minister in Georgia who abandoned his congregation to marry an already married Indian princess and who later urged an attack on the white settlers.) Growth also brought spiritual coldness as more high church Anglican influences entered the colonies. When the Great Awakening swept the colonies in the 1700s, the Anglican church was the least affected of the Protestant denominations.

Section Review

1. From what did Puritans want to "purify" the Church of England?
2. What are the three major kinds of church polity?
3. What is the "heart" of Puritan theology?
4. What were the provisions of the Half-Way Covenant?
5. How did James Blair and Thomas Bray help establish Anglicanism in America?

English Separatist Denominations in America

Puritans (at least initially) and Anglicans were part of the state church in England. Several groups grew in America, however, that were officially separate from the Church of England. As previously discussed in Chapter 2, the Pilgrims of Plymouth were the first of these groups in America. More important ultimately were the Baptists, the Quakers, and the Presbyterians.

Baptists—When **Roger Williams** fled from Massachusetts and founded Rhode Island, he sought to create a purer church than those in the rest of New England. In 1639 Williams and another Christian baptized each other. Williams then baptized ten others in his tiny congregation. This act marked the founding of what is generally considered the first Baptist church in America. Roger Williams remained in the church only a few months before he left to seek an even purer church. The church, however, continued without him.

The **Baptists** grew slowly at first, and they suffered persecution from colonial authorities, particularly in Massachusetts and Virginia. Nonetheless, they succeeded in establishing churches throughout the colonies and had their largest numbers in religiously tolerant Pennsylvania.

As their name suggests, Baptists emphasize the doctrine of baptism. Like the Congregationalists, the Baptists practice congregational polity and believe that only the regenerate should be church members. Unlike the Congregationalists, Baptists baptize only professing believers and then only by immersing them completely in water.

Quakers—The **Quakers,** or the Society of Friends, originated with the Englishman **George Fox.** Fox claimed to believe in guidance by the "Inner Light," an illumination from God found in every man. Exactly what Friends mean by the "inner light" is variously interpreted. Some Quakers hold that it is simply the indwelling Holy Spirit; others hold that it is some kind of "spark of divinity" and that man is saved through obeying its leading rather than through the atonement of Christ. Most—although not all—early Quakers opposed participating in war, taking oaths, or holding political

office. The name *Quaker* originated in a trial in which Fox warned authorities to "tremble at the word of the Lord."

The Quakers practiced an extremely plain method of worship. Believers sat in silence–often in a circle–and waited for the inner light to move one member to give a word of testimony or exhortation. The early Quakers did not have regular ministers or practice the church ordinances (baptism and the Lord's Supper).

Quakers did not receive a warm welcome in the colonies. The Puritans in New England quickly arrested and deported any Quaker who entered their colonies. Between 1659 and 1661, authorities in Massachusetts actually hanged four Quakers for returning to the colony after repeated warnings.

Many of the Friends lived in Rhode Island, but the center of colonial Quakerism was Pennsylvania, where William Penn established his colony as a "holy experiment" in religious liberty. Many Quakers who did not believe in the prohibition against holding office became influential political leaders in that colony.

Three distinguishing tendencies eventually emerged among the Friends. Some mystics emphasized the inner light to the point that they rejected the Bible and claimed direct communication from God. Others became moralists, emphasizing the performance of good works alone as the essence of being a Quaker. Still others held to the Biblical views of atonement only through Christ and the authority of the Bible. Many of those in the last group broke with Quaker tradition and established churches with ordained pastors and regular preaching. The moralist party came to dominate most Quaker groups, and segments of the denomination became more social than religious in emphasis, but Biblically orthodox Quaker groups continue to exist today.

Presbyterians—The **Presbyterians** were the last major English Separatist group to come to America. Doctrinally the Presbyterians were much like the Congregationalists, except that they practiced presbyterian polity. (See pp. 64-65.) The father of American Presbyterianism is **Francis Makemie** (mah KIM ee). Born in Northern Ireland, Makemie was converted at the age of fourteen and was later

Francis Makemie

ordained in the Presbyterian church of Northern Ireland. In 1683 he came to the New World to preach the gospel and start churches. Makemie preached with success throughout the colonies. He not only established numerous churches but also helped found the first presbytery (association of Presbyterian churches) in America.

Makemie also struck a blow for religious freedom for Presbyterians and other non-Anglican groups. In two separate court cases in Virginia and New York, Makemie persuaded colonial courts to recognize that the English Parliament's Act of Toleration (1689) applied equally to the colonies. These cases guaranteed freedom of worship for Makemie and others like him.

Continental Denominations in America

Although English groups dominated the religious scene in the colonies, other groups from the continent of Europe contributed to America's religious heritage. These denominations are a part of the cultural diversity that characterizes America's history.

Reformed Groups—Reformed churches, similar in doctrine and practice to the Presbyterians, emerged in several nations in Europe during the Reformation. The **Dutch Reformed** came to the New World with the settling of New Amsterdam, but not in great numbers. The Netherlands was the most religiously tolerant nation in Europe, and few had religious reasons to migrate to America. The Dutch who came to the New World were often more interested in wealth than in piety.

The French Reformed, also called **Huguenots,** settled throughout the colonies, especially after the French king Louis XIV took away their freedom of worship in 1685. The French Reformed were rarely concentrated in any one colony, however, and had a limited effect on religious life in general. Many eventually became Presbyterians.

The **German Reformed** church, from southern Germany, was probably the most important of these Reformed bodies in colonial history. Unlike the French Reformed, the Germans concentrated in one colony, Pennsylvania, and preserved their identity.

Lutherans—The **Lutherans,** followers of the teachings of the great German reformer Martin Luther, came to America in trickles rather than floods. The Swedish Lutherans of New Sweden (Delaware) were among the first, and many Dutch Lutherans settled in New Amsterdam. Most American Lutherans, however, originated in Germany. Like many of the small groups, the Lutherans flocked to Pennsylvania because of its religious freedom and abundant land.

Also like many of the small denominations, the Lutherans suffered from disorganization. The man responsible for molding the denomination was **Henry Muhlenberg,** the father of American Lutheranism. Born in Germany, Muhlenberg came to America in 1742 at the request of officials in Germany. Slogging through the muddy roads and deep snows of colonial America's frontier, Muhlenberg preached and prayed throughout the Middle and Southern colonies. Eventually Muhlenberg was able to bring about closer cooperation among the German, Swedish, and Dutch Lutherans. In doing so he laid the foundation for building the Lutheran denomination in America.

Anabaptist Groups—The Anabaptists arose during the Reformation in protest of what they considered the incomplete reforms of other Protestants. Anabaptists refused to have anything to do with the state; they refused to serve in the military, vote, or hold office. They also stressed the importance of a holy, simple life. The **Mennonites,** followers of the Dutch teacher Menno Simons, were the most important Anabaptist group numerically. The **Amish** are a more conservative branch of the Mennonites who practice a stricter church discipline.

Persecuted by governments in Europe, many of the Mennonites and Amish fled to the New World and established farms and towns in Pennsylvania. There, by thrift and hard work, these settlers built prosperous farms that their descendants farm even today. Both groups attempted to preserve their old ways of life by rejecting modern changes and having little contact with outsiders. Some modern Mennonites and Amish still use only a horse and buggy for transportation and follow farming practices that date back to the 1700s.

Pietist Groups—In Germany in the late 1600s, an important religious movement arose known as **Pietism.** Reacting to spiritually cold churches in Europe, the Pietists, like the Puritans, emphasized the importance of conversion and the necessity of a holy life. Unlike the Puritans, however, Pietists tended to downplay doctrine. Pietism touched several denominations in Europe and America. Lutheran Henry Muhlenberg, for example, was a Pietist in much of his belief and practice.

The most important Pietist group in America was the **Moravians,** persecuted followers of the teachings of preacher John Huss of Bohemia, who was burned at the stake in 1415 for rejecting Roman Catholic teachings. In 1722 a remnant of these believers found shelter on the estate of the Pietistic Lutheran nobleman Nicholas von Zinzendorf in Germany. Count von Zinzendorf was so impressed with the fervent piety of the group that he joined them and became their leader.

Evangelism was a primary concern of the Moravians. They conducted mission work among the slaves in the Caribbean and among the Indians in America. (See p. 76.) John Wesley credited his conversion in part to contact with Moravians while he was in Georgia. The Moravians built thriving communities: Nazareth, Pennsylvania; Bethlehem, Pennsylvania; and Salem (now Winston-Salem), North Carolina, to name a few. The denomination's influence diminished as the population of the nation grew while Moravian membership did not. However, as one historian noted, we still see their influence in customs such as the Easter sunrise service and even more through the work of John Wesley and others whom they influenced.

Roman Catholicism in America

Most Protestants in the colonies feared Roman Catholicism. Some of this feeling was simple prejudice, but much of it resulted from opposition to the unbiblical teachings of the Roman Catholic church and from the repression of Protestantism in Catholic countries. Also Roman Catholic Spain and France threatened the existence of the colonies, and these powers were not above using Catholic priests and missionaries to achieve their political goals.

The center of colonial Catholicism was Maryland, the colony established as a haven for Catholics. Even there, Catholics were still a minority. Some Catholics lived in Pennsylvania, and a few settled in New York, but virtually none were found elsewhere in the colonies. In the early 1700s the British government took away the limited toleration that Catholics had enjoyed. The government's act placed Roman Catholics in a difficult position until the Revolution, and their numbers remained small in America until the massive Irish immigration of the 1840s.

Section Review

1. What are the three most important English Separatist groups to be established in the colonies?
2. Who was most responsible for the founding of American Presbyterianism? of American Lutheranism?
3. How is Pietism like Puritanism in its view of Christian living? How is it unlike Puritanism in its view of doctrine?
4. Where was the center of colonial Catholicism?

Balcony (Gallery)

Bell Tower

Sounding Board

Box Pews

Pulpit

The WEST PARISH Meetinghouse

West Barnstable, Massachusetts

built in 1717

Colonial Worship

Generalizations about Christian worship in the colonial era are somewhat difficult. Some groups such as the Anglicans practiced a more formal worship than the others, whereas others such as the Quakers were much more informal. The following section provides a broad description of how colonial Christians worshiped.

Buildings

Settlers built church buildings near the center of town to indicate the central importance of religion to the community. Many early churches resembled barns in structure. (In fact, some of the earliest churches *were* barns.) The building also served as a hall for public meetings when not in use for services. Patrick Henry, for example, gave his famous "Liberty or Death" speech to an assembly of colonial delegates gathered in St. John's Church in Richmond, Virginia.

The interiors of the earliest churches were likewise plain. The first pews were simple benches with no padding or backs. Later, churches constructed pews paid for by gifts from members of the congregation, and these pews were then reserved for those who had paid for them. Sometimes members reserved pews by paying an annual rental fee. There was in all this an unwritten but understood pecking order. The higher one's social standing, the nearer to the front of the church one sat. The pews were elaborate box pews, closed on three sides in order to reduce drafts and having a door that opened into the aisle. Families could lock their pews so that no one else could use them, regardless of whether the family was present. This practice sometimes resulted in the embarrassing situation in which some people had to stand during services while locked pews sat empty.

Pulpits also grew more elaborate as the colonies grew more settled. The early roughhewn boxes gave way to graceful pulpits. One popular style was the "wine glass" pulpit, so called because the rounded pulpit sat atop a narrow stem. Above the later pulpits was a sounding board, a wooden structure designed to bounce sound waves out so that the minister could be clearly heard.

Many colonial churches contained a balcony. Often these balconies were three-sectioned, running along the back and both sides of the auditorium. Churches often reserved the balcony for certain groups such as servants, slaves, and free blacks. It was not uncommon for slaves to be required to enter by climbing a set of stairs or a ladder outside the church leading directly to the balcony.

Services

A drum or, later, a bell summoned the colonists to worship. Churches usually held two services on Sunday, one in the morning and one in the afternoon. There was no Sunday school–it was not developed until the late 1700s–but children often attended catechism class between the two services. A **catechism** is a summary of a denomination's doctrine framed in a question-and-answer form. Children were "catechized" as they gave the carefully memorized answers to the questions. For example, the Presbyterian Westminster Shorter Catechism begins as follows:

Question: What is the chief end of man?

Answer: Man's chief end is to glorify God, and to enjoy Him forever.

The first part of the services contained a long prayer by the pastor ("bills of request" were laid on the pulpit ahead of time for the pastor's notice) and the reading of the Scripture. Puritans in particular did not simply read the Bible; they commented on it and explained its meaning as they read. Singing was of course an essential part of the service. At first, most colonists sang adapted versions of the psalms. One of the most famous of these was based on Psalm 100:

Make yee a joyfull sounding noyse
　　unto Jehovah all the earth:
Serve yee Jehovah with gladnes:
　　before his presence come with mirth.

The tune to this psalm, which came to be known as "Old Hundredth," is best known today as the tune to the Doxology ("Praise God from Whom All Blessings Flow").

In 1640 the Puritans published a book of hymns called the *Bay Psalm Book,* the first book published in America. Not all congregations possessed copies of hymnals for each member, however. Often a precentor (song leader) would need to "line out" a hymn for the congregation. He would call out or sing a line of the hymn, the congregation would repeat it, and they continued alternating this way until the hymn was done.

The early churches, particularly those of the Puritans, contained no instruments. Some Christians, citing passages such as Amos 5:23, believed that the Bible forbade instruments in church. Others simply could not afford to import instruments from England. By the end of the colonial period, however, organs had come into widespread use, especially in the older churches in the East.

The sermon was the centerpiece of the church service. Most Puritan and Separatist sermons lasted at least an hour. Anglican sermons varied; normally, the closer an Anglican minister was to Puritanism in his theology, the longer his sermon. An hourglass sat by the pulpit, but it did not necessarily deter the preacher. When the sand ran out, he would simply flip it over and continue speaking.

Ministers constructed their sermons carefully. They made detailed outlines with elaborate subpoints so that listeners could easily take notes and carry them home for further study. Sleeping or talking during the sermon was frowned upon. In the early Puritan churches, in fact, ushers walked around during the sermon looking for sleepy saints. They carried a long pole with a feather at one end for tickling the women as a warning and a knob at the other end for striking the men.

The preacher might memorize his sermon for delivery, preach with only a few notes, or write the message out completely and read it to the congregation. Reading a sermon did not necessarily lessen its impact. Jonathan Edwards may have read "Sinners in the Hands of an Angry God" to his listeners, but the sermon stirred the congregation with great conviction. In general, the colonial denominations taught their own denominational distinctives, but all united in preaching the Bible as the authoritative Word of God.

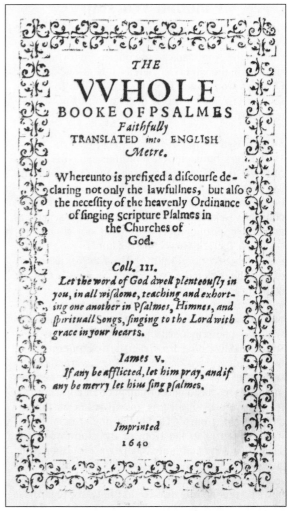

The title page to the Bay Psalm Book, the hymnal of the Puritans and the first book published in America

Section Review

1. What is a catechism?
2. What was the first book published in America?
3. Why did many colonial churches lack musical instruments?

Indian Missions

Converting native Americans to the gospel was a goal of the colonists from the very beginning. The charter for Virginia stated that the settlers aimed at "propagating [the] Christian religion to such people, as yet live in darkness and miserable ignorance of the true knowledge and worship of God." The charter of Massachusetts likewise obligated the colonists to "wynn and incite the Natives of the Country to the knowledge and obedience of the onlie true God and Savior of Mankinde, and the Christian fayth." Some historians consider these statements a cover-up to hide the ruthless exploitation of the Indians by Europeans. The evidence, however, demonstrates otherwise: many colonists were genuine in their concern. It was their success rather than their sincerity that is open to question.

Isolated Efforts

Throughout the colonial era many devout Christians attempted to reach the Indians with the gospel. Sometimes personal contact resulted in the conversion of an individual, such as Pocahontas. Ministers often preached to the Indians in addition to their other duties. Roger Williams, for example, was one of the first white men in New England to preach to the Indians. Jonathan Edwards worked with an Indian mission during one of his pastorates. John and Charles Wesley came to Georgia in 1736 to evangelize the Indians. (The Wesleys were not themselves converted at the time, however, and the work was a dismal failure).

One of the more successful early efforts was that of Swedish Lutheran John Campanius, who worked among the Delaware Indians. Among his tools for this task was his translation of Luther's catechism into the Delaware language, one of the first Christian works translated into an Indian tongue. The most extensive colonial works on the whole were those done by the Congregationalists and the Moravians.

Congregationalist Efforts

While pastoring in New England, **John Eliot** became concerned about the Algonquin Indians. With the help of an Indian who knew English, Eliot learned their language and began to preach to them.

He translated various devotional works and finally the entire Bible into the Algonquin tongue. (The Algonquin Bible was the first Bible printed in America.) His success was remarkable; some four thousand were said to be converted under Eliot's ministry. These converts, called "praying Indians," formed communities appropriately called "praying villages," with Indians often serving as pastors.

This glorious ministry came to an end, however, during a war between the English settlers and the Indians in 1675-1676. The praying Indians sided with the English, a fact that earned them the hatred of the other Indians. Nevertheless, the whites distrusted them and disbanded some of their villages. Panicky Massachusetts authorities placed many Christian Indians on an island in Boston Harbor. There, exposed to the elements, many sickened and died. Despite these setbacks, Eliot managed to establish the Society for the Propagation of the Gospel in New England, the main Congregationalist agency for conducting Indian mission work.

Other Congregationalists did not match Eliot's success, but several conducted noteworthy ministries. In the same year that Eliot started his work, Thomas Mayhew, Jr., began a work that lasted a century among the Indians on Martha's Vineyard in Massachusetts. **David Brainerd,** a close friend of Jonathan Edwards and his family, conducted a brief work among the Indians before his death from tuberculosis at the age of twenty-nine. Although Brainerd was not numerically successful, his *Journal,* published after his death, inspired many other young men to enter mission work. Eleazar Wheelock founded a school in 1754 for training Indians as missionaries to their own people. Wheelock definitely showed foresight with this idea; he realized that any race or culture is most effectively reached with the gospel by someone else from that race or culture. Eventually the school was opened to whites as well and became Dartmouth College.

Moravian Efforts

The chief shortcoming of some other Congregationalist efforts was the tendency to think that Indians must be "civilized" before they could be converted. It is true that some Indian customs could

Puritan John Eliot carried the gospel to the Indians not only by preaching (as shown at the left) but also by translating and publishing the Scripture into the native Indian tongue. Pictured at the right is a page from the Psalms from Eliot's Algonquin Bible.

not be reconciled with Christian morality, but some believed that Indians needed European standards in dress and housing as much as they needed the gospel. They often mistook "civilization" for salvation. More successful in reaching the Indians on their own terms were the Moravian missions.

While the Congregationalists performed most of their Indian mission work in New England, the Moravians conducted most of their work in the Middle and Southern colonies. The most successful Moravian mission was one near Bethlehem, Pennsylvania, called Gnadenhütten ("sheltered by grace") under the direction of **David Zeisberger** (ZICE berg ur). Like the Congregationalists, however, the Moravians saw their efforts undone by

war. During the French and Indian War, pro-French Indians attacked Gnadenhütten, killed ten missionaries, and burned the settlement. Not trusted by the English colonists either, the Moravian Indians were forced to wander through Pennsylvania, New York, and Ohio like the children of Israel seeking the Promised Land. The Indians never found rest, however. A remnant of some ninety Moravian Indians from Gnadenhütten was massacred by American soldiers during the closing days of the War for Independence.

Despite the sad end of so many Indian missions and the prejudices of some of the missionaries, colonial Indian missions were not a failure. Thousands of Indians who had never heard the gospel were converted as a result of these efforts.

Section Review

1. Who was the Swedish Lutheran who ministered among the Delaware Indians?
2. List at least two means that John Eliot used to evangelize the Algonquin Indians.
3. What was the name of the most successful Moravian Indian mission? What does this name mean?

The Great Awakening

Religious revivals have been a recurring feature in American history. The first of these revivals, the one by which all others are judged, was the **Great Awakening.** The Awakening was not simply a revival, however; it was a powerful social, political, and religious force that permanently altered the face of American history. Some historians limit the Awakening to the years 1740-1742, the years of greatest fervor and activity. Closer study, however, reveals that the whole Great Awakening and its effects cover nearly forty years, from the 1720s to the early 1760s.

Background

Religious life in the North American colonies had begun to wither by the early 1700s. Although some groups such as the Presbyterians were entering a period of growth (mostly due to immigration), most of them were in a spiritual lull. Secular historians in search of "causes" of the Great Awakening recognize the desire for security created by economic and political uncertainty as a reason for the revival. These factors may indeed have contributed to the revival, but ultimately it was simply, in the words of Jonathan Edwards, "a surprising work of God."

The colonies needed a spiritual awakening. In New England the Half-Way Covenant was slowly filling the Congregationalist churches with unconverted members. Some areas, such as the frontier regions of the Carolinas, had almost no religious life of any kind. Even those who attended church did so because of family traditions more than the genuine piety that had motivated their forefathers. There was no guarantee that even ministers were converted.

Voices Crying in the Wilderness

Early Stirrings—In 1720 Dutch Reformed pastor **Theodore Frelinghuysen** (FREE ling HYE zun) came to New Jersey. Influenced by Pietism, Frelinghuysen preached to his people of practical Christian living. He emphasized personal conversion and the holiness of life that an awareness of God's holiness brings. Frelinghuysen's faithful preaching was rewarded in the 1720s by a series of revivals in his churches. The Great Awakening had begun.

A neighbor of Frelinghuysen in New Jersey, Presbyterian **Gilbert Tennent,** was another early light in the Awakening. Encouraged by Frelinghuysen, Tennent began to preach of the need for conversion and holy living. Like the Dutch Reformed pastor, Tennent saw fruit for his labor in converted souls and rededicated saints. Tennent was soon in demand in other churches. He and other preachers carried the revival throughout the colonies.

Ironically, the revival that multiplied Presbyterian membership also divided that denomination. The **"New Lights"** supported the revival wholeheartedly, whereas the **"Old Lights"** condemned the emotional displays that accompanied the Awakening. Other Old Lights complained of preachers such as Tennent who entered an area to preach without the permission of the local Presbyterian pastor. The New Lights charged the Old Lights with obstructing the work of God and accused many of the Old Light pastors of being unconverted (a charge that was sometimes true). From 1745 to 1758, the two factions divided and formed separate organizations. When the two sides reunited in 1758, the New Lights had tripled in size, whereas the Old Lights had barely held their own.

Jonathan Edwards—The greatest theologian of the Great Awakening—and perhaps of American history—was **Jonathan Edwards.** A brilliant man (he entered Yale before he was thirteen), Edwards nonetheless lived with a constant sense of the presence of God. He did not simply practice an outward piety; he was consumed with love for God. As pastor of a Congregationalist church in Northampton, Massachusetts, Edwards sought to instill in his people the same passionate devotion that he felt in his own heart.

In 1734 Edwards began preaching a series of sermons on justification by faith. The sermons sparked a series of awakenings in the church which, Edwards admitted, surprised even him. Edwards soon became the leader of the Awakening in New England and its staunchest and ablest defender in print. He wrote glowingly of the revival's results.

Jonathan Edwards, the outstanding theologian of the Great Awakening

Even in the solemn "Sinners in the Hands of an Angry God" Edwards said,

> You have now an extraordinary opportunity, a day wherein Christ has thrown the door of mercy wide open, and stands calling, crying with a loud voice to poor sinners, a day wherein many are flocking to Him, and pressing into the kingdom of God; many are daily coming from the east, west, north, and south; many . . . are now in a happy state with their hearts filled with love to Him who has loved them, and washed them from their sins in His own blood, and rejoicing in hope of the glory of God.

George Whitefield—If Edwards was the outstanding theologian of the Great Awakening, then **George Whitefield** (WHIT feeld) was its outstanding evangelist. Born in England, Whitefield became a friend of the Wesleys while studying at Oxford.

Like them, he was later converted and became a powerful preacher. Finding the doors of England's churches often closed to him by narrow-minded ministers, Whitefield began to preach outdoors wherever he could gather a crowd to hear him.

After seeing remarkable results from his preaching in Britain, the twenty-four-year-old Whitefield came to America for the first time in 1738. Over the next thirty years, he made seven preaching tours of the colonies. He preached in Savannah, Charleston, Philadelphia, New York, Boston, and hundreds of villages and crossroads, carrying the revival throughout the colonies. In his greatest tour, that of 1740, Whitefield preached to thousands daily, and many of those thousands were converted. Whitefield's tours also united the revivalists throughout the colonies, and he became a close friend of both Jonathan Edwards and Gilbert Tennent.

Whitefield was a gifted preacher. He had a powerful, melodious, persuasive voice. Philadelphia printer Benjamin Franklin, who published some of Whitefield's sermons in America, testified to the power of that voice. Once, after a disagreement with the evangelist over his plans for an orphanage in Georgia, Franklin attended one of Whitefield's meetings. Because of this difference of opinion, Franklin determined not to give any money toward the project. Franklin later wrote,

> I had in my Pocket a Handful of Copper Money, three or four silver Dollars, and five Pistoles in Gold. As he [Whitefield] proceeded I began to soften, and concluded to give the Coppers. Another Stroke of his Oratory made me asham'd of that, and determin'd me to give the Silver; and he finsh'd so admirably, that I empty'd my Pocket wholly into the Collector's Dish, Gold and all.

On another occasion, Franklin made an experiment during one of Whitefield's outdoor sermons. Franklin walked away from the minister as he preached and measured how far he could hear Whitefield's voice. By his reckoning, Franklin figured that Whitefield could reach a crowd of thirty thousand—and this without any modern electronic amplification equipment.

The Log College

Presbyterian Gilbert Tennent graduated from an unusual college. He had no comfortable dormitory room with a private bath. The walls of his school were not covered with ivy–unless some happened to cling to the rough logs of which the building was constructed. Nor did Tennent receive instruction from a wide array of learned professors; he had only one teacher–his father, William Tennent, Sr.

Born in Northern Ireland and a graduate of the University of Edinburgh, the self-styled professor was a well-educated Presbyterian pastor who knew Greek, Hebrew, and Latin. When he came to Pennsylvania around 1718, the elder Tennent wanted a school to prepare his four sons for the ministry. Otherwise, they would have to go to New England or even back to Britain for their education.

Tennent built a large log building near his home to house his school. He began with thirteen students–his sons along with nine others who wished to study for the ministry. Enemies derisively called the school "the Log College," but there was nothing crude about the quality of the education provided there. The students worked diligently at their studies under Tennent's direction and gained practical experience by serving in his church.

The heritage of the Log College was a rich one. Gilbert Tennent, his brothers, and the other graduates of the school became Spirit-empowered agents of the Great Awakening, leading hundreds–perhaps thousands–of souls to Christ. Ironically, the often-despised Log College became an educational center as well. Over fifty colleges claim their descent from the ministry of the Log College and its graduates. Among these schools was the College of New Jersey (now Princeton University), which was chartered the year that William Tennent died (1746). The humble cabin college was indeed, as George Whitefield called it, a profoundly influential "school of the prophets."

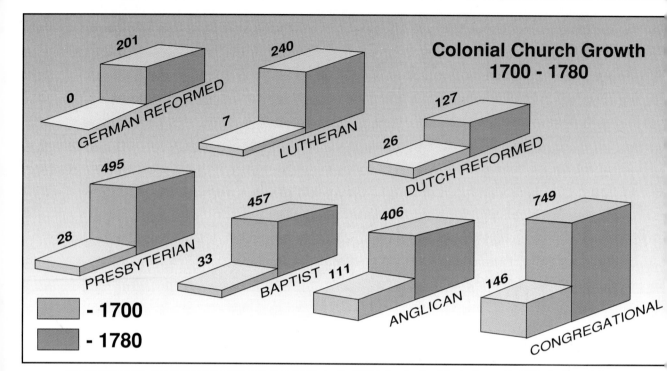

Colonial Church Growth 1700 - 1780

GERMAN REFORMED 0 / 201

LUTHERAN 7 / 240

DUTCH REFORMED 26 / 127

PRESBYTERIAN 28 / 495

BAPTIST 33 / 457

ANGLICAN 111 / 406

CONGREGATIONAL 146 / 749

- 1700
- 1780

The chart shows the number of congregations each denomination had in 1700, before the Great Awakening, and in 1780, after the revival.

The Awakening in the South—The South was the last section to experience the Awakening, but the revival's impact was no less profound. **Samuel Davies** carried the revival to the Presbyterians in Virginia. Second only to George Whitefield in pulpit oratory, Davies preached faithfully for some twelve years and also persuaded authorities to permit more religious liberty for non-Anglicans in the colony. He also promoted education by helping to found the school that eventually became Washington and Lee University and by serving as president of the College of New Jersey (Princeton).

Virginia was also the scene of the labors of Baptist Daniel Marshall. Marshall and his brother-in-law **Shubal Stearns** were New Englanders who were converted under the preaching of Whitefield in 1745. Like a number of Whitefield's converts, they became Baptists—a tendency among Whitefield's converts which caused the Anglican Whitefield to lament, "My chickens have turned to ducks."

While Marshall labored in Virginia and Georgia, Stearns enjoyed even greater success in Sandy Creek, North Carolina (south of modern Greensboro). Stearns was a small man with a penetrating stare and a powerful voice, and his bold, direct preaching brought conviction to the hearts of the rough frontiersmen. Marshall eventually joined Stearns in North Carolina, and together they oversaw the real establishing of the Baptists in the South.

Results of the Awakening—The Great Awakening affected social and political life as well as religious. First, the effect on America's churches was dramatic. Church growth was the most visible result. Both the number of churches and church membership rose markedly, with the Presbyterians and the Baptists experiencing the greatest growth. The Presbyterians, for instance, grew from under thirty churches in 1700 to almost five hundred in 1780; during the same period the Baptists grew from about thirty to over four hundred and fifty churches.

Second, the number of religious colleges increased too. Princeton, Brown, Rutgers, and Dartmouth all grew out of the revival as training centers for the ministry. Even Yale benefited from the Awakening. However, revival fires did little to thaw cold Harvard College, which had grown increasingly liberal.

Third, the Awakening transformed the spiritual life of the churches as well. The Half-Way Covenant began to vanish; increasingly, churches in America required personal regeneration for membership. The revival also promoted unity among the churches. Different congregations and even different denominations overlooked their minor doctrinal differences in the interest of evangelism. George Whitefield illustrated this tendency in an outdoor sermon in Philadelphia. Raising his eyes to heaven, Whitefield cried,

> Father Abraham, whom have you in heaven?
> Any Episcopalians? No! Any Presbyterians?

Revival Wildfire

Even in the midst of a great harvest for God there may be laborers scattering rather than gathering, destroying more than building up. When opponents wanted to attack the Great Awakening, they did not have to search far for ammunition; the ministry of James Davenport provided plenty. Davenport, pastor of a Congregationalist church on Long Island, burst onto the public scene in 1740 as an evangelist. Within a few months Davenport was almost as famous as George Whitefield–but for different reasons.

All of the Awakening's preachers stressed the need for conversion, but Davenport was quick to announce specifically who needed it. He did not make these pronouncements, as one would expect, on the basis of observable outward conduct. Davenport relied on his own snap judgments and emotions, which he claimed were direct illuminations from God. Whenever a minister opposed some aspect of Davenport's work, the evangelist denounced him, often accusing the critic of being unsaved.

Even Davenport's services were extreme. Singing, praying, and preaching were all part of the revival services, but only Davenport attempted to do all three at once. When Davenport came into the pulpit, he supposedly waited for God to tell him what to preach when he got there. Davenport admitted that he had no idea what he was going to say, and when he spoke, the fact was obvious.

Davenport received the most attention for a meeting held in New London, Connecticut. There, he tried to persuade his hearers to burn their "vanities"–wigs, plush clothing, jewelry, and so on. Gathering a crowd on a wharf, Davenport built a bonfire of what he called "unsafe" books, including works of godly Puritan authors. As the blaze crackled, Davenport declared that the smoke reminded him of the tortures that these authors must now be suffering in hell.

Officials would not put up with this firebrand for long. In trials in both Massachusetts and Connecticut, Davenport was declared mentally incompetent, and the latter colony deported him. Prorevival preachers began to fear that Davenport's excesses would bring the whole revival into disfavor.

In 1744 Davenport himself made a sudden about-face. He published a letter in which he said that he had been led by "a misguided zeal." He apologized for providing "a sad means of many persons questioning the work of God, concluding and appearing against it; and of the hardening of multitudes in their sins." The repentant Davenport spent the last thirteen years of his life working quietly as a pastor and rebuilding the reputation of a ministry he had done so much to discredit.

No! Any Independents or Methodists? No, no, no! Whom have you there? We don't know those names here. All who are here are Christians. . . . Oh, is this the case? Then God help us to forget party names and to become Christians and in deed and truth.

On the other hand, the Great Awakening also brought division to America's churches. Only the Presbyterians and the Dutch Reformed suffered formal splits between those who favored the revival and those who opposed it, but nearly every denomination saw some division within. Not all of these "antirevivalists" were necessarily against revivals; they were simply offended at the fanatical extremes of men such as James Davenport. (See p. 81.) Many of the opponents, though, were theologically opposed to the revival. They disliked the emphasis on personal experience, the attacks on unconverted pastors, and the general upsetting of "good church order." The Anglican church remained the denomination most generally opposed to the Awakening, despite the fact that many individual Anglicans supported the revival.

The Great Awakening also had political effects on the colonies. It was the first truly national movement in American history. The revival cut across sectional lines and touched every colony and nearly every class of people. The Great Awakening was not southern or northern, Presbyterian or Congregationalist, upper class or lower class; it was *American.*

The Awakening was also a breakthrough for personal liberty. By reaffirming the equality of men before God, the revival stressed the equality of all men. Also, as we have seen, the work of revivalists such as Samuel Davies resulted in greater freedom of worship for the colonists. In addition, a democratic influence swept into the churches; power moved away from traditional elites of class and education within the congregations, and all laymen began to share equally in the rule of the church. Likewise by holding large meetings–often opposed by ecclesiastical authorities–Whitefield, Tennent, and others set a precedent for the constitutional rights of free speech and the freedom of assembly.

In short, many movements unleashed in the Great Awakening saw their full development in the American Revolution. Modern historian Alan Heimert correctly noted, "What was awakened in 1740 was the spirit of American democracy."

Section Review

1. What are the names of the two factions into which the Presbyterians split during the Great Awakening? Which group grew more during the revival?
2. What was the most famous sermon preached by Jonathan Edwards?
3. Who was the important theologian of the Great Awakening? the most important evangelist?
4. Give the names and denominations of the three most important revival leaders in the South.

Chapter Review

Terms

"Elizabethan Settlement"
Puritans
low church Anglicans
high church Anglicans
Separatists
idea of the covenant
episcopal polity
presbyterian polity
congregational polity
Congregationalists
Half-Way Covenant
Salem witch trials
James Blair
Thomas Bray
Roger Williams
Baptists
Quakers
George Fox
Presbyterians
Francis Makemie
Dutch Reformed
Huguenots

German Reformed
Lutherans
Henry Muhlenberg
Mennonites
Amish
Pietism
Moravians
catechism
Bay Psalm Book
John Eliot
David Brainerd
David Zeisberger
Great Awakening
Theodore Frelinghuysen
Gilbert Tennent
"New Lights"
"Old Lights"
Jonathan Edwards
George Whitefield
Samuel Davies
Shubal Stearns

Content Questions

1. What is the difference between low church and high church Anglicans? between Puritans and low church Anglicans?
2. Why was the Half-Way Covenant dangerous to the Congregationalist churches in New England?
3. List at least three distinctive beliefs of the Quakers.
4. Describe the order of a typical service in a colonial church.
5. In what ways were the mission work of John Eliot and David Zeisberger similar?
6. List five results of the Great Awakening.

Application Questions

1. Had you lived in Queen Elizabeth's day, would you have been a Puritan, a low church Anglican, a high church Anglican, or a Separatist? Why?
2. Why, do you think, was Pennsylvania the most religiously diverse colony?
3. What was Eleazar Wheelock's reason for founding his school for training Indians in mission work? How can this principle be applied to modern missions?

UNIT II

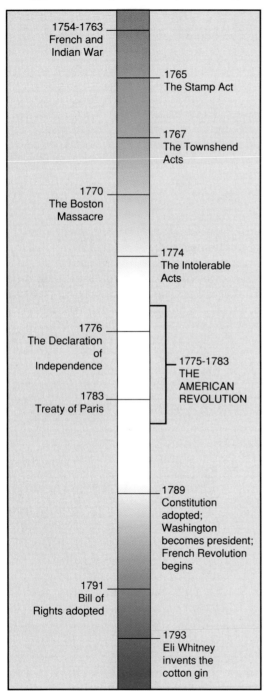

1754-1763
French and
Indian War

1765
The Stamp Act

1767
The Townshend
Acts

1770
The Boston
Massacre

1774
The Intolerable
Acts

1776
The Declaration
of
Independence

1775-1783
THE
AMERICAN
REVOLUTION

1783
Treaty of Paris

1789
Constitution
adopted;
Washington
becomes president;
French Revolution
begins

1791
Bill of
Rights adopted

1793
Eli Whitney
invents the
cotton gin

Second, the number of religious colleges increased too. Princeton, Brown, Rutgers, and Dartmouth all grew out of the revival as training centers for the ministry. Even Yale benefited from the Awakening. However, revival fires did little to thaw cold Harvard College, which had grown increasingly liberal.

Third, the Awakening transformed the spiritual life of the churches as well. The Half-Way Covenant began to vanish; increasingly, churches in America required personal regeneration for membership. The revival also promoted unity among the churches. Different congregations and even different denominations overlooked their minor doctrinal differences in the interest of evangelism. George Whitefield illustrated this tendency in an outdoor sermon in Philadelphia. Raising his eyes to heaven, Whitefield cried,

> Father Abraham, whom have you in heaven?
> Any Episcopalians? No! Any Presbyterians?

Revival Wildfire

Even in the midst of a great harvest for God there may be laborers scattering rather than gathering, destroying more than building up. When opponents wanted to attack the Great Awakening, they did not have to search far for ammunition; the ministry of James Davenport provided plenty. Davenport, pastor of a Congregationalist church on Long Island, burst onto the public scene in 1740 as an evangelist. Within a few months Davenport was almost as famous as George Whitefield–but for different reasons.

All of the Awakening's preachers stressed the need for conversion, but Davenport was quick to announce specifically who needed it. He did not make these pronouncements, as one would expect, on the basis of observable outward conduct. Davenport relied on his own snap judgments and emotions, which he claimed were direct illuminations from God. Whenever a minister opposed some aspect of Davenport's work, the evangelist denounced him, often accusing the critic of being unsaved.

Even Davenport's services were extreme. Singing, praying, and preaching were all part of the revival services, but only Davenport attempted to do all three at once. When Davenport came into the pulpit, he supposedly waited for God to tell him what to preach when he got there. Davenport admitted that he had no idea what he was going to say, and when he spoke, the fact was obvious.

Davenport received the most attention for a meeting held in New London, Connecticut. There, he tried to persuade his hearers to burn their "vanities"–wigs, plush clothing, jewelry, and so on. Gathering a crowd on a wharf, Davenport built a bonfire of what he called "unsafe" books, including works of godly Puritan authors. As the blaze crackled, Davenport declared that the smoke reminded him of the tortures that these authors must now be suffering in hell.

Officials would not put up with this firebrand for long. In trials in both Massachusetts and Connecticut, Davenport was declared mentally incompetent, and the latter colony deported him. Prorevival preachers began to fear that Davenport's excesses would bring the whole revival into disfavor.

In 1744 Davenport himself made a sudden about-face. He published a letter in which he said that he had been led by "a misguided zeal." He apologized for providing "a sad means of many persons questioning the work of God, concluding and appearing against it; and of the hardening of multitudes in their sins." The repentant Davenport spent the last thirteen years of his life working quietly as a pastor and rebuilding the reputation of a ministry he had done so much to discredit.

No! Any Independents or Methodists? No, no, no! Whom have you there? We don't know those names here. All who are here are Christians. . . . Oh, is this the case? Then God help us to forget party names and to become Christians and in deed and truth.

On the other hand, the Great Awakening also brought division to America's churches. Only the Presbyterians and the Dutch Reformed suffered formal splits between those who favored the revival and those who opposed it, but nearly every denomination saw some division within. Not all of these "antirevivalists" were necessarily against revivals; they were simply offended at the fanatical extremes of men such as James Davenport. (See p. 81.) Many of the opponents, though, were theologically opposed to the revival. They disliked the emphasis on personal experience, the attacks on unconverted pastors, and the general upsetting of "good church order." The Anglican church remained the denomination most generally opposed to the Awakening, despite the fact that many individual Anglicans supported the revival.

The Great Awakening also had political effects on the colonies. It was the first truly national movement in American history. The revival cut across sectional lines and touched every colony and nearly every class of people. The Great Awakening was not southern or northern, Presbyterian or Congregationalist, upper class or lower class; it was *American*.

The Awakening was also a breakthrough for personal liberty. By reaffirming the equality of men before God, the revival stressed the equality of all men. Also, as we have seen, the work of revivalists such as Samuel Davies resulted in greater freedom of worship for the colonists. In addition, a democratic influence swept into the churches; power moved away from traditional elites of class and education within the congregations, and all laymen began to share equally in the rule of the church. Likewise by holding large meetings–often opposed by ecclesiastical authorities–Whitefield, Tennent, and others set a precedent for the constitutional rights of free speech and the freedom of assembly.

In short, many movements unleashed in the Great Awakening saw their full development in the American Revolution. Modern historian Alan Heimert correctly noted, "What was awakened in 1740 was the spirit of American democracy."

Section Review

1. What are the names of the two factions into which the Presbyterians split during the Great Awakening? Which group grew more during the revival?
2. What was the most famous sermon preached by Jonathan Edwards?
3. Who was the important theologian of the Great Awakening? the most important evangelist?
4. Give the names and denominations of the three most important revival leaders in the South.

CHAPTER 5

The Rising Storm (1689-1770)

"My lads, they will not fire."

Samuel Gray, March 5, 1770, *last words
before being killed by the first British
volley during the Boston Massacre*

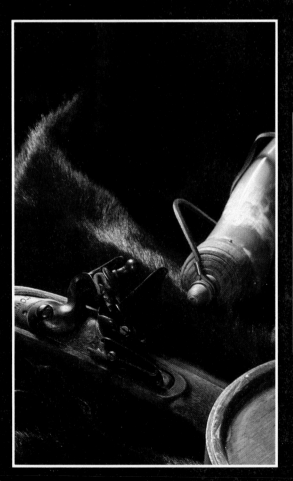

The Death of General Wolfe, *by Benjamin West, National Gallery of Canada, Ottawa. Transfer from the Canadian War Memorials, 1921 (Gift of the 2nd Duke of Westminster, Eaton Hall, Cheshire, 1918). Photograph ©1992.*

From the 1680s to the 1760s intermittent war raged on the American frontier as two colonial empires–the English and the French–fought each other from the sandy beaches of Pensacola to the snowy plains of Quebec.

At the beginning, the English had been able to safely ignore their French neighbors in the New World. Settlement of New France in Canada had amounted to little more than a scattered string of outposts along the St. Lawrence River until the arrival of Louis XIV to the throne in 1661. Louis, along with his chief adviser Jean Colbert, realized the untapped potential of the American heartland and determined to build an empire that would outflank his English adversaries.

French claims to this vast region stemmed from two important expeditions. The first was launched from Green Bay in 1673 when a trapper named **Louis Joliet** and a Jesuit priest named **Jacques Marquette** canoed down the Wisconsin River in search of the "Great River" that Indians had described. The Frenchmen reached the Mississippi and journeyed as far south as the turbulent convergence of the Missouri River. There they met Indians carrying English-made muskets, to whom the Mississippi's destination was no mystery. The red men explained to the French that the "Great River" emptied into the Sea of Florida (the Gulf of Mexico). Fearful of falling captive to the Spanish and eager to tell of their discovery of an inland water route from Canada to the Caribbean, the friar and the fur trader paddled home.

For nearly ten years Joliet and Marquette's discovery remained unexploited. Finally in 1682, Robert Cavelier, sieur de **La Salle,** set out to explore the length of the Mississippi. At the mouth of the river, the intrepid La Salle named the vast region *Louisiana* in honor of his sovereign Louis

XIV, and made a comprehensive claim of "all the nations, peoples, provinces, cities, towns, villages, mines, minerals, fisheries, streams, and rivers," as possessions of France.

The French learned, though, that it was easier to claim than to colonize. New France was never heavily populated with Frenchmen. In 1666, for example, only 3,400 French settlers lived in Canada. Though the colony grew to 80,000 by 1750, it always remained only a fraction of the populace of British America.

Several factors made the French a serious threat to the thirteen colonies. First, the French had strong Indian alliances which greatly expanded their military capabilities. Given the history of savage massacres throughout the colonies, the prospect of well-armed Indian warriors was even more fearful than facing French troops. One weak link in the French and Indian alliances was their inability to win over the powerful Iroquois. The French were aligned with the Algonquins with whom the Iroquois had a standing blood-feud. As a result, the Iroquois became allies of the British-American forces during the colonial wars.

A second factor that worked to the advantage of the French was the nature of the frontier. The American colonists had a vaguely defined western boundary of isolated farms and villages that invited attack. In the dense wilderness, finding the enemy was difficult, and effectively defending the scattered settlements was impossible.

The French threat was compounded by the failure of the American colonies to present a united front. For the most part petty jealousies and near-sightedness made the colonies divided targets for French attacks.

As bloody as the colonial wars were, the French thorn in America's side would be a key factor in changing the times and the attitudes between Britain and her colonies. Ironically, by the late 1770s American troops would be shouldering French muskets and wearing uniforms made in Paris. George Washington, who first made a name for himself by fighting the French, would one day depend on the French navy to checkmate Cornwallis and his redcoat army at Yorktown.

Frontier Feuds

As the French began to expand their claim in Canada, the Great Lakes, and the Mississippi River Basin, and as the English moved farther west, friction was inevitable. These colonial tensions were heightened by the explosive relations between their parent countries that often spilled over into America. Between 1689 and 1763 four wars erupted in Europe between England and France that were also played out in the New World under "Americanized" names: King William's War, Queen Anne's War, King George's War, and the culminating conflict–the French and Indian War.

King William's War (1689-1697)

In one of Louis XIV's many wars of expansion, the French armies crossed the Rhine and invaded the strongly Protestant German Palatinate. What Louis expected to be a quick foray turned into a nine-year war against an alliance headed by England. In Europe the war became known as the War of the League of Augsburg but the Americans dubbed their frontier version of it after their newly crowned king, William III.

Because of the need for men and materiel in his all-out war in Europe, Louis spared little for Canada. What French Canadians lacked in troops and finances, however, they compensated for in leadership. **Comte de Frontenac** (FRAHN tuh nak), a resourceful and competent leader, came to North America and, with the aid of French settlers and Indians, inflicted considerable damage and fear upon the English settlements. The English colonies had the advantage of numbers, but they did not cooperate with one another well enough to raise funds for military supplies; an intercolonial conference held in New York in 1690 failed from lack of unity. In Europe a peace treaty was finally signed in 1697 but all was neither forgiven nor forgotten; the mutual hatred between France and Britain only deepened. Meanwhile, the French continued to build forts along the Mississippi and St. Lawrence rivers.

Queen Anne's War (1702-1713)

Peace in Europe and America was short-lived. Louis XIV attempted to extend his control over

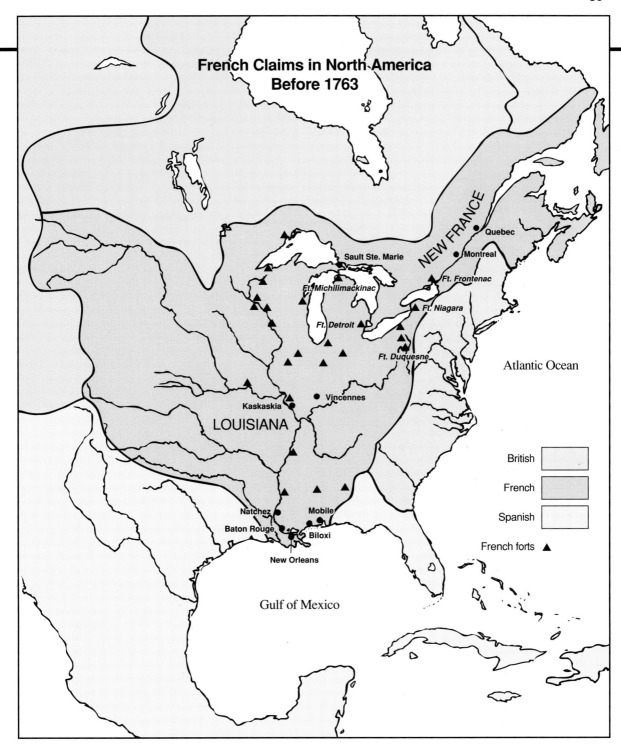

French Claims in North America Before 1763

NEW FRANCE

LOUISIANA

Atlantic Ocean

Gulf of Mexico

Quebec
Montreal
Ft. Frontenac
Sault Ste. Marie
Ft. Michilimackinac
Ft. Niagara
Ft. Detroit
Ft. Duquesne
Vincennes
Kaskaskia
Natchez
Mobile
Baton Rouge
Biloxi
New Orleans

British
French
Spanish
French forts ▲

A Redeemed Captive

The colonial wars often turned quiet backwoods settlements into the front lines of battle–catching settlers in its savage crossfire. During Queen Anne's War one man, Rev. John Williams, faced such a crisis with courage and faithfulness, leaving an enduring testimony to the sustaining grace of God.

Early on the morning of February 29, 1704, a war party of French soldiers and Indian warriors attacked the frontier town of Deerfield, Massachusetts. Pastor Williams and his family were still in bed when, with a flurry of axe blows, the enemy began to break open the doors and windows of the home. Williams seized his pistol and aimed it at the nearest Indian, but the gun misfired. Quickly the Indians captured Williams and his family. They killed two children and a slave and then marched their captives through the winter ice back to Canada.

The French and Indians had killed thirty-eight settlers and captured over a hundred citizens of Deerfield. The number of captives dwindled as the group slogged through the frigid wilderness. Anyone who could not keep up was killed. Williams's wife, who had given birth to a child only a few weeks before, was one of the victims. When her strength failed, an Indian ended her life with a blow from a tomahawk. Williams suffered from the forced march as well. He recorded how each night he had to wring the blood from his socks.

When the Indians chose a Sunday to rest on the long march, they allowed Williams to preach to his flock. He spoke from Lamentations 1:18, "The Lord is righteous; for I have rebelled against his commandment: hear, I pray you, all people, and behold my sorrow: my virgins and my young men are gone into captivity."

In Montreal the French governor took Williams and several others from the Indians. In many ways, the situation for the captives improved. The French proved surprisingly kind and sympathetic, caring for the captives' ills and giving them food and shelter. They faced a different and subtler kind of persecution, however. The Jesuit priests were determined to convert the captives to Catholicism by any means possible.

Williams noted how the Indians, for all their cruelty, had allowed the captives to keep their Bible and hymnbooks but that the priests had quickly taken them away. The Catholics worked diligently to convert Williams. They tried arguing, pleading, and even blackmail and bribery. Some captives suffered beatings for refusing to convert, but the priests seemed to realize that such treatment would not move the Massachusetts pastor. Because Williams's surviving children were separated from him, the priests told Williams that if he would convert he could have them back. In addition, they said, the governor would give him a generous pension. Williams refused. "I told them my children were dearer to me than all the world," he wrote, "but I would not deny Christ and his truths for the having of them with me; I would still put my trust in God who could perform all things for me."

Finally, in 1706, the British redeemed fifty-seven Deerfield captives and returned them to Boston. Williams and all but one of his surviving children were among them. (One daughter had become a Catholic and joined an Indian tribe; she refused to return despite her father's pleas.) Williams returned to the pastorate, and all of his sons eventually followed him into the ministry. Williams's widely read account of the ordeal, *The Redeemed Captive Returning to Zion,* first appeared in 1707. Despite his sadness for those left behind, Williams wrote, "We have reason to bless God who has wrought deliverance for so many."

Spain and her vast empire by supporting his grandson as Spanish king. The war was known in Europe, therefore, as the War of the Spanish Succession; American colonists named it after the reigning monarch of England, Queen Anne. The French king's dynastic and diplomatic expansionism was met with a military rebuff that raged for over a decade.

In America the war consisted mainly of sporadic but bloody fights on the frontier and coasts. The French and their Indian allies for example attacked Wells, Maine, in 1703, and massacred thirty-nine settlers, and in Deerfield, Massachusetts, thirty-eight were murdered by pro-French Indians. In both cases the victims were mostly women and children.

Such treachery and the potential for territorial gains in Canada finally caught the attention of Britain's Queen Anne. In 1708 five regiments and a fleet were sent to help the beleaguered colonies. In 1710 Port Royal, Nova Scotia, fell to the British forces. Despite this success, a combined attempt by English troops and colonists to take Quebec was a disastrous failure. Because of poor weather and poorer leadership, a navy of about 12,000 men failed even to reach Quebec.

The **Treaty of Utrecht** ended the fighting on both sides of the Atlantic in 1713. England gained title to eastern Canada while France retained control of the St. Lawrence and Great Lakes regions. England gained territory in the West Indies and even picked up strategic Gibraltar in the deal. Increasingly the focus of European politics would include overseas holdings, and a distant fight: a forgotten corner of the world could trigger war among the European nations on a global scale. Utrecht provided a shaky peace for a generation, but the feud between England and France was far from over.

King George's War (1743-1748)

British access to the lucrative West Indies trade as a result of Utrecht caused tensions with the Spanish that flared into a naval war known as The War of Jenkins' Ear. This curious conflict was soon merged into a general European fight known as the War of Austrian Succession, which in America was

King George II

fought out under the name of Great Britain's King George II.

The Americans made an impressive record for themselves in 1745 when four thousand New Englanders besieged and conquered French Louisbourg, considered at the time to be the most formidable fortress in North America. A truce was declared in Europe in 1748 with the Peace of Aix-la-Chapelle. The peace, however, was a mere comma in the conflict between Britain and France. Both sides seething over inconclusive and costly wars would stage an all-out rematch beginning in 1754 that would settle old problems in America and create new ones.

Section Review

1. What two expeditions provided the basis for French claims to the New World?
2. What three factors increased the danger of the French threat to the thirteen colonies?
3. What were the American names for the four wars fought by Britain and France between 1689 and 1763?

The French and Indian War

Although King William's War, Queen Anne's War, and King George's War are all sometimes referred to as "French and Indian wars," the title of *the* **French and Indian War** is reserved for the decisive conflict fought from 1754 to 1763. In contrast to these earlier, primarily European conflicts, the French and Indian War began in the New World and spread to Europe, where it broke out "officially" in 1756 and became known as the Seven Years' War (1756-1763).

The Seven Years' War eventually saw Britain and Prussia allied against Austria, Russia, France, Spain, and several other nations. With fighting on three continents among several nations (not to mention the participation of both Asian and American Indians), the war was perhaps the first "world war." This sweeping conflict began with a small incident in the backwoods of western Pennsylvania involving a twenty-two-year-old Virginia colonel named **George Washington.**

Outbreak

The Spark—In the spring of 1754, Lieutenant-Colonel George Washington led his men toward the Forks of the Ohio River (the site of modern Pittsburgh). Governor Dinwiddie of Virginia had ordered Washington to clear the territory of the French who—the English said—had illegally entered the area. On the way Washington and his troops surprised a small group of French soldiers. In the ensuing skirmish, ten Frenchmen were killed and the rest captured—despite the fact that Britain and France were officially at peace.

A much larger force of French soldiers and Indian warriors, however, was waiting at the Forks of the Ohio at the newly constructed **Fort Duquesne** (DOO KANE). Realizing that he was outnumbered, Washington retreated and hastily threw up defenses, aptly named Fort Necessity. The structure showed Washington's inexperience. Located in a low area, the fort allowed the French to fire directly into it from nearby heights. Washington was soon forced to surrender, but the French were surprisingly gracious. They allowed the Virginians to march home after Washington naively signed a note of surrender which put the blame for the whole affair on the Brit-

ish. The government repudiated Washington's note, and Britain and France went to war.

The Two Sides—In the early stages of the war, the French had an important advantage in that they understood the Indians and Indian warfare better than the British—particularly the British army—did. The French borrowed methods of forest fighting from the Indians and practiced **guerrilla warfare** on the British, sudden surprise attacks by small groups from hidden positions. The British originally tried to fight in the open, ordered style of Europe. The French also enjoyed a friendlier relationship with their Indian allies than the British had with their Iroquois allies.

In the long run, however, the British enjoyed significant advantages. British colonists outnumbered French colonists by more than twenty to one. British colonists also had a subtle but significant advantage in that they had invested something material in the New World. They had roots in America—land, businesses, and families. Many of the French, by contrast, were isolated traders and trappers who took products such as furs out of, but put little into, the New World. Above all, the British navy could control the waterways and thereby cut off French reinforcements and supplies.

The chief British disadvantage was the lack of unity in the colonies. The **Albany Congress** attempted to establish political unity when it met at Albany, New York, in June 1754, about the time that the war broke out. Delegates from most of the

Ben Franklin's 1754 appeal for cooperation among the colonies is the earliest political cartoon in American history.

colonies north of Virginia attended the meeting. On the second day, **Benjamin Franklin** proposed his "Albany Plan" for centralized colonial rule, including a president chosen by the king and a congress chosen by the separate colonies. Representatives were to be apportioned according to the amount that each colony contributed to the central treasury. The plan was finally rejected, however, because the colonists feared that it would establish a government that was too strongly centralized. Many colonists feared centralized political control even more than they feared France.

Early in the war, in 1755, the British eliminated another potential disadvantage. The presence of some six thousand **Acadians,** French Catholics living in British-held Nova Scotia, worried the British. Fearful of rebellion, the government uprooted the Acadians and forcibly moved them to English colonies further south. A few Acadians managed to escape and return to Nova Scotia. Many fled to French-held Louisiana where their descendants became known as "Cajuns." Like many civilians in the midst of war, the Acadians suffered as a result of the fears of the opposing sides.

British Setbacks

Braddock's Defeat—The early years of the war were disastrous ones for the British in North America. The government sent General **Edward Braddock** and a thousand seasoned British troops to capture Fort Duquesne. Braddock was joined by colonial forces and by Colonel Washington, who was eager to atone for his defeat at Fort Necessity. To move his men and supplies, Braddock painstakingly cut a road through the wooded wilderness to within a few miles of the French fort. Washington tried vainly to warn Braddock that the French and Indians would not fight in the open, organized fashion that the general knew in Europe.

On July 9, 1755, the French and Indians attacked. They hid in the trees and thick brush as they poured a deadly fire into the British ranks. The redcoated British regulars stood in close, ordered lines and braved the hail of bullets for three hours. "We would fight," some said, "if we could see anybody to fight with." Braddock, who was riding bravely about the field overseeing the battle, was

shot through the lungs. Eventually, the officers led by Colonel Washington organized a retreat. Over half of the British force was killed or wounded. Braddock died during the retreat after muttering, "Who would have thought it?"

Montcalm—The French assigned command of their American forces to the **Marquis de Montcalm** (mar-KEE deh mahnt-KAHM). Montcalm, a talented soldier and commander, engineered a series of stinging defeats on the British from 1756 to 1758. He destroyed two major British outposts, Fort Oswego on Lake Ontario and Fort William Henry on Lake George (both in what is now upstate New York). Montcalm also drove back a British attempt to capture the French Fort Ticonderoga. In addition, pro-French Indians raided the frontier, terrorizing the British colonists. So far the British had met the French threat mostly with bungling.

British Successes

Pitt's Plan—The situation brightened for the British in 1757 when **William Pitt** became prime minister of Great Britain. "I am sure that I can save this country, and that nobody else can," Pitt declared. Although humility was not one of his strong points, he proved as good as his word. Pitt quickly adopted a plan to win the war. He decided to let his ally, Prussia, bear the brunt of the fighting in Europe. Meanwhile Britain would use its superb navy to isolate the French forces in America and India. Pitt also discarded old, incompetent commanders and replaced them with young, energetic soldiers who would lead the army to victory. Pitt saw that British victory overseas could win an empire for Britain.

Turnaround—Among these new, energetic commanders was General **James Wolfe.** With his thin body, receding chin, and upturned nose, Wolfe did not look like an inspiring commander. His military talents, however, were tremendous. In 1758 an army under his command captured Louisbourg on the Atlantic coast, still considered the most powerful fortress in North America. With this victory Britain controlled the mouth of the St. Lawrence River. The government then entrusted Wolfe with the key campaign of the war, the attack on the French Canadian capital, Quebec.

Before the Quebec campaign, the British decided to capture Fort Duquesne and secure the Forks of the Ohio. Learning from Braddock's mistakes, a larger, well-equipped force moved methodically from Philadelphia. Seeing such an overwhelming force approaching them, the French blew up their ammunition, burned their fort, and retreated. The victors renamed the site "Pittsburgh" in honor of their prime minister. Now only Quebec remained as the main center of French strength.

"The Paths of Glory"–The Quebec campaign of 1759 matched the two greatest commanders of the war, Montcalm and Wolfe. Montcalm knew that Quebec, high on a cliff above the St. Lawrence River, was a natural fortress; if the French could simply hold out against the enemy, the bitter Canadian winter would force the British to retreat. A determined Wolfe, however, devised a plan to capture the city. For several days in early September British warships sailed up and down the St. Lawrence River, confusing the French about where they would land. Then, in the early morning of September 13, a British force rowed to a point upstream from Quebec. As they glided across the dark waters,

Wolfe relieved the tension by reciting to his officers Thomas Gray's "Elegy Written in a Country Churchyard." One line of that poem must have sounded ominous in their ears–"The paths of glory lead but to the grave."

The soldiers landed, and soon the Plains of Abraham next to Quebec swarmed with British redcoats. Deciding that he had to hit the British before they could organize, Montcalm launched his forces at the enemy. In the brief but decisive **Battle of the Plains of Abraham,** the British routed the French. Wolfe did not live to savor the victory, however: both he and Montcalm were mortally wounded. Quebec fell, and the following year Montreal followed. The war in North America was over.

Results of the War

The Treaty of Paris–The fighting in North America ended in 1760, but the war continued in Europe until 1763. The **Treaty of Paris** (1763) dramatically changed the face of North America by removing French influence as a major force in the continent. Eastern Canada and all territory east of the Mississippi River went to Britain. Spain tem-

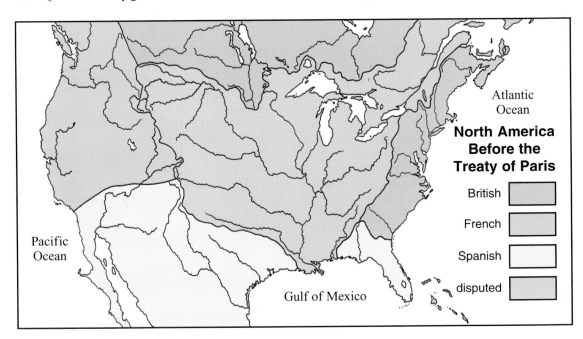

Atlantic
Ocean

**North America
Before the
Treaty of Paris**

British

French

Spanish

disputed

Pacific
Ocean

Gulf of Mexico

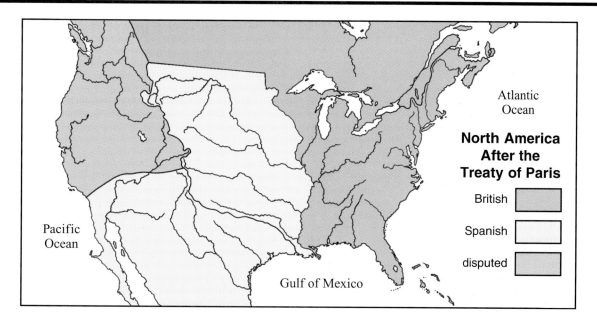

North America After the Treaty of Paris

British
Spanish
disputed

Atlantic Ocean

Pacific Ocean

Gulf of Mexico

porarily lost Florida but in return received all of France's Louisiana Territory west of the Mississippi. (See the maps on pp. 94-95.)

For the victorious British, the cost of both the war and the administration of the new possessions was high. The war alone left a debt of £140,000,000. In addition, Parliament wanted to station ten thousand troops in the colonies to protect against the Indians at a cost of £350,000 a year. Not surprisingly, the government thought the colonies should share this expense. In addition, when King **George III** came to the throne in 1760, the British government announced its intention of keeping a closer eye on the financial and political affairs of the colonies.

The colonies, after almost a century and a half of semi-independence, resented this new attitude. Furthermore, some Americans suspected that the redcoats were intended more to enforce government policies than to guard against Indian attack. Skillful statesmen such as William Pitt might have been able to calm the colonies, but Pitt had resigned in 1761. The twenty-two-year-old king and his circle of policymakers scarcely understood the growing troubles in America and were therefore incapable of resolving them.

One positive result of the French and Indian War affected the future history of the continent of North America. The nation of France in the 1700s was unbendingly and exclusively Roman Catholic. Great Britain, particularly in the colonies, was more tolerantly Protestant. A French victory could well have led to the persecution of North American Protestants. The British victory in the war paved the way for future American religious freedoms in which all faiths–including Roman Catholicism– would share.

Aftermath: Pontiac's War–One last tremor remained from the French and Indian War. The French army stopped fighting and went home. The Indians, however, could not go anywhere and had to take care of themselves. As early as 1762 a brilliant Ottawa Indian chief named **Pontiac** formed a confederacy of Indian tribes. Enraged by the Treaty of Paris, Pontiac and his forces waged a devastating war against British soldiers and settlers from 1763 to 1766. Eight of Britain's twelve frontier forts fell to the Indians, and hundreds of people–both soldiers and civilians–were slain. Pontiac proved unable to hold his confederacy together, and he eventually made peace with the British. His success, however,

King George III

raised serious questions in the minds of the colonists. What was the use of this costly British army, they asked, if it could not offer even basic protection? The French and Indian War had settled matters between the British and the French, but it had also created a host of new problems between Britain and its colonies.

Section Review

1. What event sparked the French and Indian War?
2. What was the chief British disadvantage in the French and Indian War?
3. Why was Braddock defeated so decisively at Fort Duquesne?
4. What was William Pitt's three-part plan to win the French and Indian War?
5. Who were the two greatest military commanders of the French and Indian War?

The Growing Rift

A Sense of *Nation*

For a century and a half, forces were at work creating a new man in the New World–an *American*. These forces viewed in isolation could easily be overlooked, but their cumulative effect would begin to create a *national* consciousness in the 1760s and 1770s.

Geography was an important factor in breaking the ties with the Old World. Isolated by an ocean that could be bridged only by sail, the colonists were forced out of necessity to fend for themselves. Self-reliance, ingenuity, and independence were forged during the years of settlement. When problems arose in the colonies, the mother country was more like a distant cousin. Threats from Indians, pirates, French, and Spanish were mostly dealt with by the colonists themselves. Not until King George's War in the 1740s did Britain take an active role in the defense of the colonies.

In addition, the way in which the land was settled shaped American attitudes. Private ownership of property was an attractive incentive for settlers from Europe. A man who owned property had a stake in society, and on his land he was the master of all he surveyed. This power gave him greater independence and broader horizons than he or his father had ever known in the old country. One immigrant put it this way:

A European, when he first arrives, seems limited in his intentions, as well as in his views; but he very suddenly alters his scale; . . . he no sooner breathes our air than he forms schemes, and embarks in designs he never would have thought of in his own country.

Another factor that influenced American attitudes toward Britain was the diversity of the colonists. Not everyone was British. While English language and institutions prevailed, many had a non-English heritage. Germans, French, Dutch, Swedes, Finns, and Scots by the thousands comprised a significant portion of the population of British North America. When tensions with Britain arose, loyalty to the crown was hardly uniform. Some non-English Americans took an active part in supporting the independence of their adopted homeland. For example, the son of Apollos Rivoire, a French Huguenot, became a leader in the resistance movement in Boston. Apollos himself made many sacrifices for his new country, not the least of which was his name. As he noted ''merely on account that the bumpkins pronounce it easier,'' he changed his name to Paul Revere. His son, Paul, Jr., became the famous midnight rider and a hero of the American Revolution.

Another crucial force in the development of American nationalism was the strength of colonial self-government. Colonial governments consisted of a governor, his councilors, and an elected assembly. With few exceptions colonial governors were not a strong political force since for the most part they owed their jobs to the king but their salary to the colonial assembly.

By the beginning of the eighteenth century the elected houses such as the House of Burgesses in Virginia, the House of Representatives in Massachusetts, or the House of Delegates in Maryland were clearly the most powerful force in the governing of their respective colonies. These assemblies held the all-important **power of the purse,** which meant that salaries for royal officials, military appropriations, and taxes had to pass the scrutiny of elected officeholders. In addition, the assemblies had the power to initiate their own legislation. They were not mere rubber stamps for edicts from the royal governor.

The colonies were not unaware of their political clout. Nurtured by geographic remoteness and official neglect from Britain, generations of colonists gained experience in representative government, and the assemblies were jealous of their power. Attempts to curb the self-governing power of the colonial legislatures was angrily viewed as a threat to their cherished rights and liberties.

Following the French and Indian War, the many forces that shaped America's growing sense of *nation* would be magnified by a sense of confidence and optimism. American troops had helped oust the French, clearing the way for western expansion. The Americans had also stood shoulder to shoulder with British regular troops and had come away

unimpressed. The British failure at frontier fighting, Braddock's humiliating defeat, and the grating presence of troops during peacetime built up resentment. Americans came to view the redcoats less as defenders and more as invaders. The battle lines were quietly being drawn.

Taxes and Tensions

Following the French and Indian War, the relationship between Britain and the colonies changed dramatically. Although British troops had helped to eliminate the threat of French domination, the successful conclusion of the war lessened colonial dependence on Great Britain. Increasing attitudes of independence and even hostility to Britain simply reflected the heritage of self-government in the colonies.

At the same time, however, attitudes in Britain were changing toward their colonial offspring. Britain had just bested France in a global war on land and sea, collecting an empire that would have made the Caesars envious. The triumph was a heady experience, and many in Britain decided that in keeping with the Queen Mother's advice to George III to ''be a king,'' it was time to ''be an empire''–time to gain greater control over the direction and profitability of the Thirteen Colonies. In one parliamentary act after another during the 1760s and 1770s, a policy of *coercion* instead of *cooperation* would prove to be a costly mistake for Britain.

The Proclamation Line (1763) –In October 1763 Parliament established the **Proclamation Line,** which forbade the colonists to settle beyond the Appalachian Mountains. The British government viewed the Proclamation Line as a way to diminish conflicts with the Indians, such as Pontiac's War. American colonists, however, denounced it as an arbitrary interference with their local governments, since it denied westward expansion into lands already granted by the colonial charters.

Despite the protest, expansion continued by those who had little concern for the finer points of a law laid down halfway around the world. The towns of Pittsburgh and Wheeling had their start during the decade after the line was drawn. In the western land claims of Virginia and North Carolina

To protest the Stamp Act, the Pennsylvania Journal *printed a skull and crossbones in its banner.*

(areas that include parts of West Virginia, Kentucky, and Tennessee), the defeat of a Shawnee Confederation under Chief Cornstalk and the trail-blazing efforts of the intrepid Daniel Boone beckoned land-hungry settlers and speculators across the Appalachians.

The Sugar Act (1764) — In 1764, following the lead of **George Grenville,** the king's chief minister, Parliament passed the **Sugar Act.** This act placed a tariff, or tax, on certain goods imported into the colonies, such as sugar, molasses, and coffee. The stated purpose of the Sugar Act was to raise revenue ''for defraying the expenses of defending, protecting, and securing'' the colonies. Such external tariffs (taxes on goods imported by Americans) had been levied before, but Parliament had seldom enforced them. This time, however, the British government made it clear that it intended to collect the duties. The colonists protested that since Parliament could now enforce such taxation with the standing army, the colonists and their legislatures were virtually powerless.

The Stamp Act (1765) — Grenville set about finding other ways to balance the imperial books. In February, 1765 he proposed to Parliament a stamp tax, a revenue stamp required for newspapers, diplomas, and a variety of legal and commercial documents. This **Stamp Act** levied the first **internal** tax,

or tax on goods produced and consumed entirely within the colonies, ever imposed on the colonies. The issue for Americans was not the amount of the tax but the fact that they were being taxed without their consent and that the traditional power of the colonial legislatures was being bypassed.

In Parliament the little stamp seemed innocent enough; only a handful opposed it, among them Col. Isaac Barré, a veteran of Wolfe's Quebec campaign and a man who understood America. The warrior stood in the House of Commons and, turning his scarred face to the eager tax collectors, declared that growing British contempt for the rights of the colonists had ''caused the blood of these sons of liberty to recoil within them.'' In America, word of Barré's speech was enthusiastically received, and a growing body of opposition to British rule snatched Barré's phrase and proudly called themselves the **Sons of Liberty.**

The Quartering Act (1765) — Just two days after passing the Stamp Act, on March 22, 1765, Parliament passed the **Quartering Act,** which officially subjected the colonies to a standing army in times of peace and further required that the colonists help supply provisions for them. Even Prime Minister Grenville admitted that the quartering clause was ''by far the most likely to create difficulties and uneasiness . . . especially as the quartering of soldiers upon the people against their will is declared by the Petition of Right to be contrary to law.'' The almost simultaneous passage of the Stamp Act and the Quartering Act caused the colonists to conclude that they were being oppressed by an unlawful military occupation so that illegal taxation could be enforced.

Colonial Opposition—These parliamentary decisions, particularly the Stamp Act, sparked a firestorm of protest in America. First, on May 29, 1765, **Patrick Henry** presented resolutions to the Virginia House of Burgesses that declared that Virginians possessed all the rights and privileges of Englishmen and to grant the right of taxation to *any* body beside the Virginia Assembly was an act of tyranny. In Henry's words the Stamp Act was ''A Manifest Tendency to Destroy AMERICAN FREEDOM.'' In a blunt warning to King George III about the consequences of such tyranny, Henry told the Assembly, ''Caesar had his Brutus, Charles the First his Cromwell, and George III . . . ''

''Treason! You have spoken Treason!'' interrupted the House Chairman in midsentence.

Henry always finished what he started—''may profit by their example! If this be treason, make the most of it.''

In October 1765, in the first successful example of colonial unity, delegates from nine colonies met in New York for a **Stamp Act Congress** which formally denounced the Stamp Act and the usurpation of colonial rights that it represented. Elsewhere, matters became violent. In Boston, the Sons of Liberty headed by **Samuel Adams** hanged an effigy of Andrew Oliver, the royal Stamp Distributor for Massachusetts Bay. More radical, raucous elements of the opposition ransacked Oliver's home, smashing windows and furniture. Although Samuel Adams distanced himself from the vandalism, he was pleased with the protest in general. Oliver resigned; Sons of Liberty organizations in other colonies took up the cause; and in March 1766 Parliament repealed the hated Stamp Act.

Townshend Acts (1767)—The uneasy calm in the wake of the Stamp Act repeal was soon shattered by a new revenue scheme in Parliament. In 1767 Charles Townshend, the head of the British

Treasury, proposed a series of taxes and enforcement measures that had far-reaching political consequences. The **Townshend Acts** proposed direct taxes on glass, paint, paper, and tea. Furthermore, the acts strengthened the writs of assistance, general search warrants used and often abused by customs officials in their search for taxable goods. In addition, it was proposed that the revenue raised from these taxes should go for paying the salaries of royal officials, including the governor. This was in direct conflict with the traditional ''power of the purse'' that many colonial assemblies had maintained for nearly a century.

An optimistic Charles Townshend told Parliament that the colonies should submit to this unprecedented power-grab because they were ''planted with so much tenderness, governed with so much affection, and established with so much care and

Virginian Patrick Henry, shown here in an engraving based on a famous portrait by Thomas Sully, was one of the earliest and most eloquent advocates of resistance to the increasing tyranny of Great Britain.

Patrick Henry, "Voice of the Revolution"

Among the voices raised in defense of American liberty, none was so eloquent as that of Patrick Henry. His voice was a powerful, melodious instrument that charmed and stirred its hearers. After one speech a listener said that the audience was "taken captive; and so delighted with their captivity, that they followed implicitly, whithersoever he led them; that, at his bidding their tears flowed from pity, and their cheeks flushed from indignation."

Although speaking abilities are, in part, inherited, Patrick Henry must have learned some of his oratorical skills from the matchless speakers he heard as a young man. Some historians think that young Patrick may have heard George Whitefield, the great English evangelist who helped carry the Great Awakening throughout the colonies. We know for certain that Henry heard Samuel Davies, the Presbyterian leader of the Awakening in Virginia. Indeed, Patrick Henry later called Davies the greatest orator he had ever heard.

The effect of Davies, other ministers, and the Bible itself was profound on Henry. The Virginia statesman's speeches were filled with the rhythms and cadences of Scripture, not to mention numerous allusions to the Bible. Few speeches show this tendency more clearly than Henry's most famous speech, that given in St. John's Episcopal Church in Richmond in 1775. Henry's fiery declaration "Gentlemen may cry peace, peace–but there is no peace" quotes the prophet Jeremiah, "They have healed also the hurt of the daughter of my people slightly, saying, Peace, peace; when there is no peace" (Jer. 6:14; see also 8:11). Likewise Henry's rhetorical question posed in the same speech a few moments later–"Why stand we here idle?"–alludes to Jesus' words in the parable of the laborers in the vineyard (Matt. 20:6).

Henry's early years, however, did not seem to promise future greatness. Although born into a comfortably well off Virginia family, Patrick showed little sign of possessing unusual talent. In fact, his first ventures into making a living proved to be dismal failures. He twice went bankrupt attempting to operate a store. (Some claim he preferred engaging his customers in intricate debates to selling them goods.) An effort at farming proved so troublesome that Henry seemed almost relieved when his farmhouse burned and he had to seek other employment. Almost in desperation Henry turned to law. Even then his study was so hurried that another lawyer signed his license only after Henry solemnly promised to pursue further study as he practiced.

Henry proved far more diligent at law than at his earlier pursuits, and his natural speaking ability was a tremendous advantage in arguing cases before a jury. Henry first leaped to fame, and displayed his love of American liberty, in arguing against the Two-Penny Act in 1762. This law of the Virginia legislature had fixed the Anglican clergy's annual salary of sixteen thousand pounds of tobacco at a cash value of two pence per pound. Though the salary was comfortable and guaranteed, it was set below the market value. As a result the king annulled the Two-

attention." However, the crusty Col. Barré retorted, "We did not plant the colonies. Most of them fled from oppression. They met with great difficulty and hardship, but as they fled from tyranny here they could not dread danger there. They flourished not by our care but by our neglect. They have increased while we did not attend to them. They shrink under our hand."

In America the general reaction to the Townshend Acts was expressed by **John Dickinson** in his *Letters from a Farmer in Pennsylvania to the Inhabitants of the British Colonies:* "If Great Brit-

Penny Act, and some of the parsons, looking for more than daily bread out of life, sued for their "back pay."

The twenty-seven-year-old Virginia lawyer argued that a contract existed between the king and his people. When the king acted selfishly by striking down a law beneficial to all the people, he broke his contract and the people were no longer obliged to obey him. Henry charged that a king was a tyrant if he arbitrarily trampled the will of his subjects. Shouts of "treason, treason!" filled the courtroom (an accusation that Henry would hear often over the next few years), but the jury agreed with the fiery orator.

After the Two-Penny Act case, Henry's career climbed dramatically. He became a prosperous, much sought-after attorney. He was elected to Virginia's House of Burgesses and later served in both the First and Second Continental Congresses and three terms as governor of Virginia. The greatest moment of his career came in 1775, when Virginia received word that Britain was attempting to force Massachusetts to bend to its will. Standing in St. John's Church before an assembly of the greatest leaders of Virginia, Henry raised his eloquent voice in a ringing call for the defense of liberty. As he swept to his climax, Patrick Henry, like an American Joshua, stated for his countrymen the life-and-death choice before them:

Is life so dear, or peace so sweet as to be purchased at the price of chains and slavery? Forbid it, Almighty God! I know not what course others may take, but as for me, give me liberty, or give me death!

ain can order us to pay what taxes she pleases before we take [imported goods] away, or when we land them here, we are abject slaves as France or Poland can show." Dickinson urged his fellow colonists not to give up "a single iota" of their rights and liberties.

Dickinson's argument was not an economic one; it did not center on how much the taxes would cost the colonists. His emphasis, like Patrick Henry's, was about the ideas of freedom and the rights of self-government.

Opposition to the Townshend Acts grew. **Boycotts,** or refusals to buy British goods, were organized throughout the colonies. And in Boston, the hotbed of the Patriot movement, a riot broke out in 1768 when overbearing customs officials seized the *Liberty,* one of John Hancock's merchant vessels. In the fall, British troops and artillery arrived to police Boston and to quash the growing resistance.

The British Parliament through the Sugar Act, Stamp Act, and the various Townshend measures was moving not simply to raise money–the various taxes raised more resentment than revenue–they were efforts to centralize authority in London. This centralization effort came at a time of growing nationalism in the colonies. Clearly, with Britain and America headed in different directions at the same time, they were certain to butt heads along the way.

John Dickinson, *by James Barton Longacre, National Portrait Gallery, Smithsonian Institution*

First Blood

Lord North, the latest arrival in George III's search for a competent prime minister, told Parliament, "America must fear you–before she can love you. I hope we shall never think of [repealing the Townshend Acts] till we see America prostrate at our feet." Although most of the Townshend Acts were repealed in 1770, North's words "America prostrate at our feet" had a prophetic ring to them in ways the prime minister did not expect. In the late winter of 1770 Americans would indeed be lying at the feet of the British–cut down, not with taxes, but with lead shot in the bloody **Boston Massacre.**

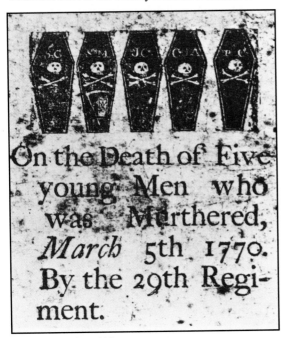

Sons of Liberty broadside

With the arrival of a thousand British troops in Boston in 1768, the atmosphere in Boston had grown from tense to explosive. The sight of an occupation force and its fleet of warships eyeing a city at peace irritated Bostonians and fueled Sam Adams's Patriot network. The spark that ignited the powder keg came in late February 1770.

On a Friday afternoon, February 23, Ebenezer Richardson, a known informant for British customs officials, took it upon himself to pull down a boycott sign placed near his home by the Sons of Liberty. A small crowd gathered and began hurling stones and exchanging insults with him. An angry Richardson retreated to his house, vowing revenge. When a rock smashed through his window, hitting his wife, Richardson took his musket and fired into the crowd, killing eleven-year-old Christopher Snider.

Over the weekend a blizzard struck Boston, and on Monday a huge funeral procession of Patriots made their way through the snowdrifts to bury the boy. Despite the February cold, tempers were hot.

By the end of the week a few minor confrontations between dockworkers and redcoats brought everything to a simmer. The soldiers vowed to settle the score on Monday. That evening, March 5, a band of Patriots gathered in the square outside the British barracks to demand the departure of the unwelcome "lobsterbacks." The angry but unarmed crowd hurled sticks and snowballs at seven soldiers under the command of Captain Thomas Preston. One of the privates, Hugh Montgomery, struck by a stick, slipped on the ice. While getting up he fired his musket into the mob; whether in anger or by accident cannot be determined. With his shot, however, the other redcoats opened fire without orders into the face of the crowd.

As the chill wind swept the smoke away, five men lay dying in the square. The bloodstained snow became a vivid reminder that sometimes the path ahead to independence would demand everything.

Section Review

1. What is "the power of the purse"?
2. Why did Parliament establish the Proclamation Line of 1763? Why did the colonists oppose it?
3. Name three of the acts of Parliament after the French and Indian War that created tension between Great Britain and its colonies.
4. What city was the site of a "massacre" in 1770?

Chapter Review

Terms

Louis Joliet
Jacques Marquette
La Salle
Louisiana
King William's War
Comte de Frontenac
Queen Anne's War
Treaty of Utrecht
King George's War
French and Indian War (1754-1763)
George Washington
Fort Duquesne
guerrilla warfare
Albany Congress
Benjamin Franklin
Acadians
Edward Braddock
Marquis de Montcalm
William Pitt
James Wolfe
Battle of the Plains of Abraham
Treaty of Paris (1763)
George III
Pontiac
power of the purse
Proclamation Line
George Grenville
Sugar Act
Stamp Act
internal tax
Sons of Liberty
Quartering Act
Patrick Henry
Stamp Act Congress
Samuel Adams
Townshend Acts
John Dickinson
boycotts
Boston Massacre

Content Questions

1. List three differences between the nature of the French and the British colonies in North America.
2. Give one advantage that the French had over the British in the French and Indian War and one advantage that the British had over the French.
3. List three ways in which the British army proved a disappointment and even an offense to the British colonists in North America.
4. What were four important factors in breaking ties between Britain and its colonies?
5. Name the parliamentary act that each phrase describes.
    a. First internal tax ever imposed on the colonies.
    b. Stated purpose was to raise revenue "for defraying the expenses of defending, protecting, and securing" the colonies.
    c. Levied direct taxes on glass, paint, paper, and tea.
    d. Levied an import tax on molasses and coffee.
    e. Required the colonies to supply provisions for the British army.
6. Why did the almost simultaneous passage of the Stamp Act and the Quartering Act make the colonists suspicious?

Application Questions

1. Review the story of John Williams of Deerfield, Massachusetts, on p. 90. Which do you think would be worse, the physical abuse he received from the Indians or the psychological abuse he received from the Jesuits? Why?
2. Do you think that the British treatment of the Acadians during the French and Indian War was fair? Why or why not?
3. Why do you think that owning property makes men more willing to fight for their country and gives them a sense of independence?

CHAPTER 6

Independence (1770-1783)

"We fight, get beat, rise, and fight again."

General Nathanael Greene,1781

The Death of General Warren at the Battle of Bunker's Hill, 17 June 1776, *John Trumbull, Yale University Art Gallery, Trumbull Collection*

"The Revolution was effected before the war commenced," John Adams, Founding Father and future president, reflected years afterwards. "The Revolution was in the minds and hearts of the people. . . . This radical change in the principles, opinions, sentiments, and affections of the people was the real American Revolution."

This "Revolution in the heart" was in many ways an evolution that began on the shores of Virginia and Massachusetts over a century before. Escalating events, however, gradually moved the revolution from the heart to the arms. The question for many Americans became not whether they would submit to taxes but whether they would submit to tyranny.

One interview with an old veteran minuteman, Levi Preston, conducted over a half-century after he fought the British, cuts to the crucial issue behind the war. The interviewer asked Preston to describe the British oppressions that led to independence. The ancient warrior replied, "What were they? Oppressions? I didn't feel them."

"What, were you not oppressed by the Stamp Act?" the reporter probed.

"I never saw one of those stamps; I am certain I never paid a penny for one of them."

"Well, what then about the tea-tax?"

"Tea-tax! I never drank a drop of the stuff; the boys threw it all overboard."

"Then I suppose you had been reading Harrington or Sidney and Locke about the eternal principles of liberty."

"Never heard of 'em." the old man answered with a shrug. "We read only the Bible, the Catechism, Watts' Psalms and Hymns, and the Almanack.''

The puzzled questioner demanded, ''Well, then, what was the matter? and what did you mean in going to the fight?''

''Young man, what we meant in going for those redcoats was this: we always had governed ourselves, and we always meant to. They didn't mean we should.''

The Eve of War

The Boston Massacre shocked the colonies into relative silence. The calm, however, turned out to be merely the eye of a storm. In June 1772 an armed British customs ship, the *Gaspee,* ran aground near Providence, Rhode Island. The ship's captain, who had earned a reputation for indiscriminate harassment around Narragansett Bay, was not welcome ashore. On the night of June 9 the *Gaspee* was boarded by locals, its crew captured and removed, and the ship burned.

This attack on one of His Majesty's ships prompted the British to establish a court of inquiry to investigate and make arrests. This arrangement was a usurpation of the power of the colonial courts. At the same time the Massachusetts governor, Thomas Hutchinson, announced that his salary would now come from the crown, not the colony. No longer would the legislature be able to keep the governor or other royal officials reined in with the purse strings. More and more the colonists came to believe that their rights were being stripped away.

Americans were encouraged in this belief by another development in 1772. In November the Boston Town Meeting authorized the formation of a **Committee of Correspondence.** Under the guidance of Samuel Adams the committee provided information to other areas of the colony on British threats to liberty.

The Boston Committee also encouraged, with considerable success, the formation of a network of Committees of Correspondence–within three months eighty new committees had sprung up in Massachusetts alone. In March 1773 the Virginia legislature voted to establish a permanent Committee of Correspondence, and other colonies quickly followed Virginia's example. These committees provided far more than information; they provided a model of intercolonial cooperation that would be an important step to a united political and military response to British encroachments. Parliament soon gave these committees ample material to write about.

The Boston Tea Party

The Tea Act–The East India Company had been one of the most profitable business enterprises in Britain, but the company had fallen on hard times, and the proof lay in warehouses along the Thames stuffed with seventeen million pounds of tea. The company, verging on bankruptcy, turned to its powerful friends for a bailout. At the urging of the prime minister, Lord North, Parliament passed the **Tea Act of 1773,** which granted the East India Company a monopoly on the shipment and sale of English tea in America. The Tea Act set only a very modest tax on tea in America, and the British tea was still cheaper to buy than the smuggled Dutch tea. However, far from being thankful for the lower tea prices, the colonies were in a rage. If Parliament could grant a monopoly on tea, then what next? In port cities from Boston to Charleston, opposition to the tea shipments was intense. In New York and Philadelphia, for example, tea agents resigned, and sea captains returned their cargoes home to England out of fear for their lives and property. Tea, like the hated stamp nearly a decade earlier, became a symbol of tyranny. Coffee replaced the British beverage on Patriot tables.

"Boston Harbor a Teapot Tonight"–When the tea arrived in Boston Harbor on November 28, 1773, aboard the *Dartmouth,* Patriots made every effort to have it returned to England; but Governor Hutchinson refused to allow the *Dartmouth*'s return. The confrontation was at a stalemate: the Patriots were determined that the tea would not be unloaded in Boston; Hutchinson was determined that it would be. Since British customs law required that the tea be auctioned and the tax paid within twenty days of the cargo's arrival, time seemed to be on the governor's side.

The twenty days expired at midnight on December 16, 1773. On that evening thousands gath-

The king's tax collectors often felt the brunt of the colonists' anger over British policies.

ered for the Boston Town Meeting in the Old South Church, not far from the waterfront. Patriot leaders made one last attempt to contact Governor Hutchinson. Shortly afterwards, to shouts of "Boston Harbor a teapot tonight," a group of perhaps one hundred and fifty men and boys, crudely disguised as Mohawk Indians, boarded the *Dartmouth* and two other newly arrived tea ships.

In less than three hours 342 large cases of tea, valued at over £10,000, were dumped into the harbor. In order to make the purpose of their protest clear, the raiders took great care to avoid damaging anything except the tea. Even a broken padlock was anonymously replaced the next day. Only one man was caught stealing tea, and he was promptly kicked off the ship. When the ships had been emptied of tea, the participants cleaned them and released their crews. They then lined up at attention on deck, emptied any loose tea from their boots, swept it into the harbor, and marched away singing,

> *Rally, Mohawks! Bring out your axes,*
> *And tell King George, we'll pay no taxes.*

Even pro-British colonists, or Tories, caustically admitted that the tea party "had been conducted as correctly as a crime could be." Across the Atlantic, however, the incident was not regarded as a mere tempest in a teapot. A law had been disregarded and property destroyed. King George III instructed Lord North that it was time for strong-arm measures against the willful colonies. "The colonists must either submit or triumph," the king declared. On this at least the Patriots and the king were in agreement.

The Intolerable Acts

The Boston Tea Party spurred the British government to action against Massachusetts. Beginning in March 1774 Parliament passed a series of four acts, known collectively as the **Coercive Acts,** intended to punish and subjugate the troublesome colony.

The first of the Coercive Acts, the Boston Port Act, closed the harbor effective June 1, 1774, until the value of the destroyed tea was reimbursed. Second, in May 1774 the Massachusetts Government Act annulled the Massachusetts colonial charter. That same month the Act for the Impartial Administration of Justice provided that British officials accused of committing crimes be tried not in Massachusetts but in another colony or in England. In June a new Quartering Act made private homes available for the quartering of British soldiers. With the arrival of a military governor, General **Thomas Gage,** to replace Thomas Hutchinson, it was clear to Bostonians that their city was under an army of occupation.

If colonial submission was the purpose behind the Coercive Acts, then clearly they were a failure. In America these measures, called the **"Intolerable Acts"** by Patriots who did not intend to be coerced, hardened opposition and created an unprecedented sense of solidarity among the colonies.

In addition, in June Parliament passed the **Quebec Act,** which was directed at British Canada, not the thirteen colonies. The timing, however, could not have been worse. The Quebec Act was designed for the particular needs of French Canadians who had lived under British occupation since Quebec became a British possession in 1763. The Quebec Act set up a rigid political system, made Roman Catholicism the official religion of Quebec, and extended the territorial boundaries of Quebec southward to the Ohio River. This specter of Catholicism rising in the west under the sanction of Parliament enraged many American Protestants who had fled Catholic oppression in Europe. They also feared that the act might set a precedent for Parliament to establish Anglicanism as the state religion throughout the colonies. The Quebec Act encouraged many believers to join the growing chorus of dissent out of fear of centralized religious authority.

First Continental Congress (1774)

Sympathy for beleaguered Boston spread throughout the colonies. In the House of Burgesses in Williamsburg, a thirty-one-year-old Virginian named Thomas Jefferson called for a day of fasting and prayer as a show of support for Boston Patriots. The royal governor, upon hearing of the resolution, dissolved the House. Unperturbed, the legislators simply reconvened in the Apollo Room of the nearby Raleigh Tavern, where they adopted a resolution calling for the meeting of a **Continental Congress.** Other calls for such a gathering came from Pennsylvania, New York, Rhode Island, South Carolina, and Massachusetts. The Massachusetts House of Representatives called for the Colonial Committees of Correspondence to meet in Philadelphia in September.

On September 5 representatives from all the colonies except Georgia gathered in Philadelphia's Carpenter's Hall. Far from being a gathering of rabid radicals, these delegates were elected by their colonial assemblies or by provincial congresses and included some of the most distinguished men in America, such as George Washington and Patrick Henry of Virginia, John Dickinson of Pennsylvania, and John and Sam Adams of Massachusetts.

The changing times required new thinking, and the delegates showed themselves equal to the task. The geographic and historic features that divided the eastern seaboard into thirteen colonies had to give way to united thinking. Patrick Henry declared, "The distinctions between Virginians, Pennsylva-

Militia vs. Regulars

To fully understand American military history, one needs to distinguish between two kinds of troops: *militia* and *regulars*. **Militia** are "citizen soldiers," part-time fighters who leave their farms and factories to fight in emergencies. The famous "minutemen" of the Revolution (citizens supposedly ready to fight on a minute's notice) are an example of American militia. Although militia units might serve for months or even years at a time, they remain nonprofessionals, serving only as long as the emergency lasts.

Regulars are professional full-time soldiers who make the military their career. The British army in the War for Independence consisted entirely of regulars, although some Loyalist militia units fought alongside them. The "Continentals" were America's regulars in the Revolution, the veteran core of Washington's army. Although militia often performed valiantly in battle, most generals–including Washington–preferred to use regulars. These seasoned veterans often proved more dependable in battle.

nians, and New Yorkers and New Englanders are no more. I am not a Virginian but an *American*."

Even in some of life's most divisive matters, there was a spirit of cooperation among the delegates that portended good things. When one member proposed that the sessions open with prayer, the idea was at first opposed on the grounds that Congregationalists, Presbyterians, Quakers, Anglicans, and Anabaptists, all represented among the delegates, could not possibly worship together. Sam Adams, who as a young man had sat under the preaching of George Whitefield, favored the prayer proposal, declaring that his faith did not prevent him from hearing anyone pray as long as the man was pious and a patriot. The other delegates conceded the point, and the next day an aged Anglican pastor Jacob Duché arrived. During the night word reached the city that General Gage's troops had opened fire on civilians in Boston. With this report fresh in his ears, the old saint read from Psalm 35: ''Plead my cause, O Lord, with them that strive with me: fight against them that fight against me. Take hold of shield and buckler, and stand up for mine help.'' Then he prayed powerfully for ten minutes for the people of Boston. When he had finished, the assembly was visibly moved and many wept openly.

Although the report of Boston casualties proved to be false–Gage had confiscated a stock of Patriot gunpowder, but there were no deaths–the Continental delegates proceeded to do serious business. In their **Declaration of American Rights** they stated that the colonies must be autonomous, or self-governing, in nearly every respect. And while maintaining their allegiance to the king, his actions, they asserted, had to be consistent with American rights. As self-governing states, the colonies had the right to raise militias to defend themselves.

After seven weeks of work on their declaration, the delegates agreed to reconvene the Congress in May 1775. None of them could foresee that by then the course of events would take a decidedly bloody turn.

"The Shot Heard Round the World"

When the Continental congressmen returned to their homes, they set about putting their words into action. Massachusetts led the way by establishing a popularly elected Provincial Congress in October 1774. This assembly, in addition to the usual legislative functions, prepared Massachusetts for the inevitable conflict that loomed over Boston. Patriot militias were organized, drilled, and supplied (often at the expense of British arsenals), and special units of minutemen were authorized by the Massachusetts Assembly to form a quick first line of defense should the redcoats invade the countryside.

Throughout the colonies the Patriots mustered their forces militarily and politically. At a gathering of the Virginia Convention in St. John's Church in Richmond in late March 1775, the issue of organizing volunteer militias was discussed. **Patrick Henry** rose to address his fellow legislators with powerful words that would soon be confirmed in Massachusetts with blood:

> Gentlemen may cry peace, peace–but there is no peace. The war is actually begun! The next gale that sweeps the north will bring to our ears the clash of resounding arms. Our brethren are already in the field!

In April 1775 General Gage decided to act against the growing militia strength in the Massachusetts countryside. Based on spy reports, Gage learned that a large stock of Patriot munitions was stored in Concord, a town sixteen miles west of Boston. In what he hoped would be a quiet show of force, he ordered 700 of his best troops to seize the stockpile.

On the night of April 18, 1775, about 700 grenadiers and light infantry stealthily gathered their arms and gear, rowed across the bay to Cambridge, and reassembled for the march to Concord by way of Lexington.

Having been forewarned by midnight riders Paul Revere and a twenty-three-year-old shoemaker named Billy Dawes, the Lexington minutemen were waiting on the village green when the redcoats arrived on the morning of April 19. Just as the sun was breaking through the chill morning mist, Major John Pitcairn, commanding the British advance, spotted the thin line of Patriot militia. Pitcairn ordered his troops to hold their fire and advance as he galloped forward, shouting to the Americans to disarm and disband. For their part the minutemen had been ordered by their commander, Captain John Parker, not to open fire either, only to take a stand in a show of defiance to the king's troops. Having accomplished this, the militia began to disperse. At this point a shot rang out–who pulled the trigger has never been determined–but the British regulars then unleashed two volleys on the scattered band of soldier-farmers, killing eight. Most of them were shot in the back. Pitcairn, angered that his men disobeyed orders, tongue-lashed his troops back into formation. Only one of his men had been slightly wounded in the skirmish, and the long scarlet line continued to wend its way to Concord.

Revolution

Addressing the United Nations in 1988, Soviet Premier Mikhail Gorbachev declared, "Two great revolutions, the French Revolution of 1789 and the Russian Revolution of 1917, exerted a powerful impact on the very nature of history." Gorbachev correctly considered the French and Russian revolutions together, for they had similar causes and consequences. Yet like most Communist leaders, accustomed to censoring history for their own purposes, Gorbachev conveniently ignored the *first* modern revolution–the American Revolution. These revolutions are separated by far more than time and place. The French and Russian revolutions were about power; the American Revolution was about freedom.

In both the French and Russian revolutions a narrow, ruthless minority, the Jacobins in France and the Bolsheviks in Russia, seized the reins of power in the name of the people. These fierce little factions overthrew the existing institutions of God and government and replaced them with atheistic dictatorships. Of course all of this was done with the bludgeoned consent of the people. Anyone who did not like the new order could make his views known before a guillotine or firing squad.

With these two revolutions in mind it is easy to see why many Americans, particularly Christians, do not feel comfortable calling *their* War for Independence a "revolution" and thereby associating it with this sort of thuggery. The War for Independence *was* a revolution that brought profound political and social changes in America, but a revolution fundamentally different from the French and Russian versions. Alexander Hamilton, observing the Paris bloodletting in the 1790s, noted: "There is no real resemblance between what was the cause of America and what was the cause of France. The difference is no less great than that between liberty and licentiousness."

Of course there was violence in America. Wars *are* violent. But a distinction must be made between violence in war and violence in peace. American colonials threw off the shackles of a distant British monarch by force of arms; yet they did not destroy their local government or close their churches. In many ways the Patriots were simply *preserving* the freedoms and rights of self-government that had been nurtured and enjoyed in America for over a century. Popularly elected assemblies continued to govern in the states, as they had for years, and many Christians who feared the religious tyranny that comes with political tyranny felt compelled to join the Continental line.

Despite a shaky start, four years after peace was proclaimed, the Constitution–the consummation of the American Revolution–was written. This remarkable charter is now entering its third century of governance. France went through three constitutions from 1789 through 1794.

To maintain their iron-fisted grip on power, revolutionary leaders in France and Russia resorted to executions rather than elections. Forty thousand Frenchmen were beheaded during their revolution, most of them peasants. And the millions of Russians killed by Lenin and Stalin in their consolidation of power exceeded the combined death tolls of both world wars. Little wonder that the Russian revolutionaries had to bind their subjects with barbed wire and draw an iron curtain across the West, lest they see the results of the *American* Revolution and feel cheated.

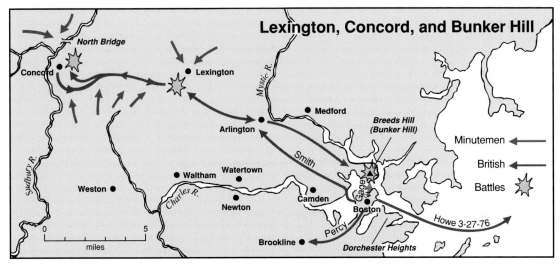

The British march to Concord, Massachusetts, on April 19, 1775, unwittingly triggered the "shot heard round the world" and marked a turning point in the path to war. As this map indicates, the British lines drew nagging and costly fire from the minutemen who had been alerted by the midnight riders and by the sound of skirmishing on Lexington Green.

Alert to the British advance, hundreds of minutemen converged on the outskirts of Concord. The British entered the town uncontested in search of munitions. At gun point they exacted enough information to locate the stockpiles, which they proceeded to burn. The Patriots, seeing smoke rising from the village, were convinced that the redcoats were torching their homes. As a result, a number of Americans advanced on the British at the North Bridge that led into Concord. Shots were exchanged with deadly effect, and the British were pushed back. Years later, poet Ralph Waldo Emerson wrote of that skirmish at Concord bridge:

> By the rude bridge that arched the flood,
>   Their flag to April's breeze unfurled,
> Here once the embattled farmers stood,
>   And fired the shot heard round the world.

For the king's men the march back to Boston was a nightmare as Patriots fired on the retreating columns from the cover of stone walls, trees, and barns. Although most of the minutemen had never had formal military training, they were used to hunting ducks, and they found the lobsterbacks to be an even easier target.

Much Patriot blood was spilled in the **Battles of Lexington and Concord,** but the Americans had clearly won the day. Forty-nine Americans had been killed and thirty-nine more wounded. But the British regulars had been hurt badly by *farmers.* Not only were 73 redcoats killed and 174 wounded, but Patriot forces now had them bottled up in Boston. The war was on.

Section Review

1. Why were the colonists offended by the decision to have the crown rather than the colony pay Governor Hutchinson's salary?
2. Why did the colonists oppose the Tea Act of 1773 even though it provided tea at lower prices?
3. Name and briefly describe each of the four Coercive Acts. What did the colonists call these acts?
4. Why did the British army send a force to Concord?

Declaring Independence

Divided Loyalties

The war that was on but undeclared left the colonies deeply divided. Many answered the call to arms as **Patriots,** fighting for the cause of independence. Others, however, were **Loyalists,** or **Tories** after the king's party in Parliament, because they continued to support the crown. The division cut across regions and social classes. It tore communities and even families apart, pitting father against son and brother against brother. In some areas the War for Independence was more like a civil war, with battles fought entirely between American Patriots and American Loyalists.

It is impossible to know how many Americans supported the king during the Revolution, although they were numerous. At least one hundred thousand Loyalists left America by the end of the war. Although it is clear that there were many more Patriots than Tories, a sizable number of Americans refused to commit themselves to either side, waiting instead for the outcome of the war to determine their loyalty.

Sympathy for the Patriot cause was not confined to America. When the war finally came, Englishmen were also divided over waging war against their colonial cousins. Such attitudes contributed to the need for hiring thousands of German mercenaries, or **Hessians,** to fill out the ranks of the British forces in America. In addition, some of the most eloquent voices in the British Parliament were raised in opposition to the king's hard-line policies against the thirteen colonies. William Pitt, Edmund Burke, and Charles James Fox repeatedly warned their colleagues and king of the hazards of ignoring American rights. Their published speeches also fired the Sons of Liberty with words such as Pitt delivered in 1777.

> If I were an American, as I am an Englishman, while a foreign troop was landed in my country, I never would lay down my arms,–never–never–never! You cannot conquer America.

Second Continental Congress

When the delegates gathered in Philadelphia on May 10, 1775, for the second session of the Continental Congress, they found themselves in an awkward situation. War in the Massachusetts countryside had erupted three weeks earlier, and thousands of New England militia had the British army pinned down in Boston. In addition, on the day of the opening session, the British **Fort Ticonderoga** in New York fell to Patriot forces from Vermont known as the ''Green Mountain Boys'' under the command of **Ethan Allen.**

The original purpose of the Continental Congress was not to make laws and supply armies but to debate and deliver cooperative resolutions concerning British colonial policies. Now, however, necessity thrust upon the shoulders of the assembly the mantle of governance. The weight of responsibilities was at first overwhelming, as John Adams wrote: ''Such a vast Multitude of objects, civil, political, commercial and military, press and crowd upon us so fast, that we know not what to do first.''

General Washington–The first priority, however, was dealing with the military situation around Boston. The delegates appointed one of their own as commander in chief. **George Washington** had arrived in Philadelphia in uniform to offer his services in command of Virginia's militia forces. Now he was being asked to take charge of a *continental* army–a ragtag collection of farmers and shopkeepers facing the best-trained, best-equipped army in the world.

Washington was a natural choice for commander in chief, and as it turned out, his appointment was one of the best decisions of the Second Continental Congress. As a Southerner, the forty-three-year-old Virginian would help link the Patriot cause in New England with the rest of the country. As commander of the Virginia forces during the French and Indian War, Washington had emerged from the conflict as a local hero, though with a war record not unmixed with failure. His greatest strength, however, was not his résumé, but his commanding presence, coolness under fire, and keen ability to lead and inspire–all essential to the seemingly impossible task to which the Continental Congress had unanimously elected him.

The Siege of Boston–As Washington traveled from Philadelphia to Cambridge to take charge of

George Washington in his French and Indian War uniform, about the time of his appointment as commander in chief of the Continental forces. Painting by Charles Willson Peale, Washington and Lee University Collection.

of artillery had come entirely from books he had read at his Boston bookstore. Nonetheless Knox was a man who got things done, even colossal things. He and his men, using oxen, sleds, and rafts, transported fifty-nine pieces of heavy artillery on a wintry, mountainous, three-hundred-mile trek.

When Knox's cannons arrived in late January 1776, Washington put them to good use. On the evening of March 4, Dorchester Heights, overlooking Boston and its harbor, was quietly fortified and the artillery wheeled into place. When the British awoke on March 5, they found themselves in an indefensible position and soon were forced to evacuate Boston. For Colonel Knox that day had a double significance. On March 5, 1770, he had stood at the front of the crowd on a snowy Boston Square when a volley of British bullets claimed its first martyrs. Now six years later the redcoats found themselves on the muzzle-end of Henry's heavy guns.

Common Sense

Even after sending Washington off to Boston to take command of the army they had inherited, delegates of the Second Continental Congress still held out hope that reconciliation could be made with Great Britain without sacrificing American rights. On July 5, 1775, the delegates drew up the **Olive Branch Petition,** which pledged loyalty to the king and requested his intervention in curbing Parliament's abusive exercise of power. The next day the Continental Congress issued a "Declaration of the Causes for Taking up Arms," in which they pointed out that British actions had left the American people with only two choices, "unconditional submission to the tyranny of irritated ministers or resistance by force." They had chosen to fight. Yet they underscored that their purpose was to gain recognition of American rights, not to pursue any "ambitious designs of separating from Great Britain and establishing independent states."

the army, word came of a major battle near **Bunker Hill** on the Charlestown peninsula north of Boston. Patriot forces on June 16, 1775, hastily built fortifications on Bunker Hill. The British commander Thomas Gage, with contempt for the soldier-farmers opposing him, ordered a frontal assault on the entrenched Patriots the next day. When the charge failed, he ordered a second assault; when that one failed, he ordered a third. The Patriots, having used all their ammunition on the redcoat ranks, were then forced to retreat. The British had won a costly victory, suffering over a thousand casualties among the two thousand soldiers sent up the slope of Breed's Hill, where most of the fighting took place. The Continental forces, by contrast, had 115 killed and 300 wounded or captured. When Washington arrived to take command of the army, the siege of Boston had returned to an uneasy standoff.

General Washington decided to break the deadlock. In December he ordered Colonel **Henry Knox** to go to Fort Ticonderoga and retrieve the captured British cannon there. Knox, portly and good natured, seemed an unlikely choice to be Washington's ordnance chief, since his knowledge

The statements were conciliatory but unbowed. The British response? George III refused even to read the Olive Branch Petition. Instead he issued a Proclamation of Rebellion and instructed his Boston army to treat the Americans as "open and avowed enemies." Parliament sent 25,000 more troops to suppress the American cause, authorized the hiring of thousands of Hessian mercenaries to help, and ordered the confiscation of all American shipping. For the Patriots the last ties of allegiance to the crown were strained and snapping.

Public opinion was solidified against the king and for American independence in part by the publication in January 1776 of a pamphlet called *Common Sense.* Its author, **Thomas Paine,** was an Englishman who had lived in America little more than a year; yet he put Patriot thinking into words that fired their will. He described monarchy as a foolish form of government whose path through history was strewn with human wreckage. Paine concluded that "the blood of the slain, the weeping voice of nature cries, 'TIS TIME TO PART.'"

Sales of *Common Sense* quickly reached a half million copies. George Washington wrote in April 1776, "I find that *Common Sense* is working a powerful change in the minds of many men."

"Free and Independent States"

During the spring and summer of 1776, one colony after another changed its constitution to a republican form of government. On June 7, 1776, Richard Henry Lee of Virginia presented a resolution to the Second Continental Congress calling for complete independence from Britain: "These United Colonies are, and of right ought to be, free and independent States."

Such a final and potentially fatal resolution required serious consideration, and debate dragged on through June. In the meantime a committee of five, which included **John Adams,** Benjamin Franklin, Roger Sherman, Robert Livingstone, and **Thomas Jefferson,** was appointed to draw up a declaration in support of Lee's resolution. Most of the work on the draft, however, was shouldered by the brilliant and eloquent Jefferson.

On July 2 the Congress approved the independence resolution. Two days later, **July 4, 1776,** the final draft of the **Declaration of Independence** was ready. It not only listed the grievances that Americans had against the king but also stated universal principles that would shape the character and direction of the emerging nation.

> We hold these truths to be self-evident, that all men are created equal; that they are endowed by their Creator with certain inalienable Rights; that among these are Life, Liberty, and the pursuit of Happiness. That to secure these rights, Governments are instituted among Men, deriving their just powers from the consent of the governed.

Fifty-six delegates from thirteen colonies inscribed their names on Jefferson's document. Their signing was an act of heroism unsurpassed on the battlefield. Each man knew that if the cause failed, he was signing his death warrant. They could be

> These are the times that try men's souls. The summer soldier and the sunshine patriot will, in this crisis, shrink from the service of his country; but he that stands it *now,* deserves the love and thanks of man and woman. Tyranny, like hell, is not easily conquered; yet we have this consolation with us, that the harder the conflict, the more glorious the triumph. What we obtain too cheap, we esteem too lightly; 'tis dearness only that gives everything its value. Heaven knows how to put a proper price upon its goods; and it would be strange indeed, if so celestial an article as *Freedom* should not be highly rated. . . . Panics, in some cases, have their uses; . . . their peculiar advantage is, that they are the touchstone of sincerity and hypocrisy, and bring things and men to light, which might otherwise have lain forever undiscovered.
>
> Thomas Paine
> *The American Crisis* (1776)

Signing of the Declaration of Independence, *by John Trumbull*

found hanging from their liberty tree. Yet they were courageous men who found the cause worth the risk. They sealed their commitment with ink and were no less willing to seal it with their blood. Jefferson, of course, put it best: ''We mutually pledge to each other our lives, our fortunes, and our sacred honor.''

Section Review

1. What was a Hessian?
2. Why did the Continental Congress choose George Washington as commander in chief?
3. Who helped break the deadlock at Boston by bringing in artillery? From where did he bring the artillery?
4. Who was largely responsible for the original draft of the Declaration of Independence?

Early Campaigns

Disaster in New York

When the British army sailed from Boston to Canada, Washington's temporary relief was mixed with apprehension. Where would the British go next? When the British turned their fleet toward New York City, Washington quickly marched his army to that city and began its defense.

New York was not really defensible, however. The Americans had virtually no navy, and the city was flanked by the East and Hudson rivers and was entered by a large harbor. The British fleet could land troops at any one of numerous points on the river and march against the American forces. Although it would have been militarily wise to abandon the city, it would also have been politically disastrous. Washington and Congress both knew that the Americans could not simply give up one of their most important cities without a fight. The American people, still divided about the war, would see such an act as a sign of weakness and cowardice. Washington, therefore, prepared for the worst when in July of 1776 General **William Howe,** General Gage's replacement, landed his forces on Staten Island.

From the summer of 1776 to late fall, the British gave the Americans a painful lesson in warfare. On Long Island, Manhattan Island, and the mainland, the British won a series of apparently effortless victories. The inexperience of Washington as a commanding general, the greenness of the American troops, and the superiority of the British navy all combined to spell defeat for the Americans. During one typical skirmish, Washington watched in disgust as some of his infantry broke and ran from the British without firing a shot. The general hurled his hat to the ground in frustration and cried, ''Are these the men with whom I am to defend America?''

A few bright spots relieved the gloom for the Continental army. After a disastrous defeat in the Battle of Long Island (August 27, 1776), for example, Washington conducted a brilliant night retreat across the East River. While brilliant retreats would not win the war, they at least saved the army to fight another day. By November, however, New York was in British hands, and the Continental army was in New Jersey.

Trenton and Princeton

Trenton—The onset of winter in late 1776 found the Continental army in a slough of despond. It had been driven smartly from New York, and the enlistments of many of the troops would expire at the end of the year. Most were not willing to re-enlist in a

"I Have Not Yet Begun To Fight!"

The American navy in the War for Independence was pitifully small, particularly in comparison to the mighty British fleet. Most American victories on the sea consisted of capturing unarmed British merchant ships for booty. At least one triumph at sea, however, was glorious enough, as one historian wrote, ''to set a tradition of victory'' for the United States Navy.

Scottish-born Captain John Paul Jones was the ablest commander in the American fleet, and he needed all of his talent on September 23, 1779. Jones was commanding the *Bonhomme Richard* (named in honor of Benjamin Franklin and his ''Poor Richard'') off the coast of Great Britain when he encountered two British warships, the *Serapis* and the *Countess of Scarborough.* The *Serapis* alone outgunned the *Bonhomme Richard,* and the presence of the second ship only increased the odds. Nonetheless, Jones joined battle.

The three-and-a-half hour fight started poorly for the Americans when two of their largest cannons exploded, killing several men. Jones tried to overcome the *Serapis*'s advantage in cannon by coming close to board her. The British crew held off the Americans, however, and their guns tore gaping holes in the side of the American ship. At one point an officer of the *Bonhomme Richard,* thinking Jones was dead, called out to the British, offering to surrender. When the British captain asked, ''Do you ask for quarter?'' Jones rose up and cried, ''I have not yet begun to fight!''

Although his ship was slowly sinking, with sheer grit Jones continued to pound at the British. Finally, the captain of the *Serapis*—his mainmast fallen–surrendered; the smaller *Countess of Scarborough* fled. Jones and his crew boarded the British warship and watched the shattered *Bonhomme Richard* sink beneath the waves. The Americans took their prize to the Netherlands, and Jones visited Paris, where the French greeted him with an uproarious celebration. John Paul Jones had given America its first great victory at sea.

Washington Crossing the Delaware, *by Emanuel Gottlieb Leutze, The Metropolitan Museum of Art, Gift of John Stewart Kennedy, 1897. (97.34). Photograph © 1992. Emanuel Leutze's famous–if romanticized–painting of Washington crossing the Delaware prior to his surprise attack on Trenton.*

losing cause. Faced with this daunting situation, Washington decided on a move as dangerous as it was daring. He would attack.

Washington's forces lay on the Pennsylvania side of the Delaware River. In **Trenton,** on the New Jersey side, lay a force of Hessians. On Christmas night of 1776, Washington led his troops across the river in the teeth of a howling storm. Snow and freezing rain pelted them as they marched through the midnight darkness. At least two men froze to death during the march.

The abominable weather did give the Americans some advantages, however. The storm hid the movements of the Americans from the Hessian forces. Furthermore, the Germans were comfortably sleeping off their Christmas merry-making. They never expected that anyone would dare to attack in such weather. When Washington attacked Trenton, he caught the astonished Hessians completely off guard. After a brief and confused resistance, they surrendered. Nearly a thousand Hessians were killed or captured. Washington did not lose a single man.

Princeton – Flushed with unaccustomed success, Washington followed the brilliant stroke at Trenton with an equally daring move. When a British force under General Cornwallis camped against him at Trenton, Washington responded with a ruse. During the night a few American soldiers stoked the campfires and made an abundance of noise while the rest of the army silently slipped away. The Americans marched toward Cornwallis's thinly defended supply base at **Princeton.**

The attack on Princeton on January 3, 1777, did not begin well. The Americans, although more numerous, were disorganized. As the small but disciplined British force advanced, Washington and his officers rode into the confused American lines to restore order. General Washington himself rode in front of his lines and directed the attack. To the horror of his aides, Washington stayed between the two enemy lines and ordered the Americans to fire.

One aide covered his face with his hat, fully expecting to see his commander lying dead on the ground. When the smoke cleared, however, Washington was completely unharmed, and the shattered British forces ran.

Trenton and Princeton were minor affairs militarily, more raids than battles. Their effect on American morale, however, was dramatic. After the disasters of New York, any victory would have been welcome. Such overwhelming victories only made the triumph sweeter. There was a visible result as well. Many of those soldiers whose enlistments had expired rejoined the army. The Americans at least had an army and hope with which to fight on.

Fight for Philadelphia

British Plans—The British launched a plan in 1777 that had the potential to win the war. A British force in Canada under General **John Burgoyne** would move south down Lake Champlain and through the wilderness of upstate New York, while General Howe was to send a force north from New York City up the Hudson River to Albany. With this move, the British would cut New England off from the rest of the colonies. Fortunately for the Americans, Howe did not cooperate with the plan. Instead he moved against the American capital, Philadelphia. Howe's action proved embarrassing to the United States initially, but in the long run it resulted in a glorious American victory.

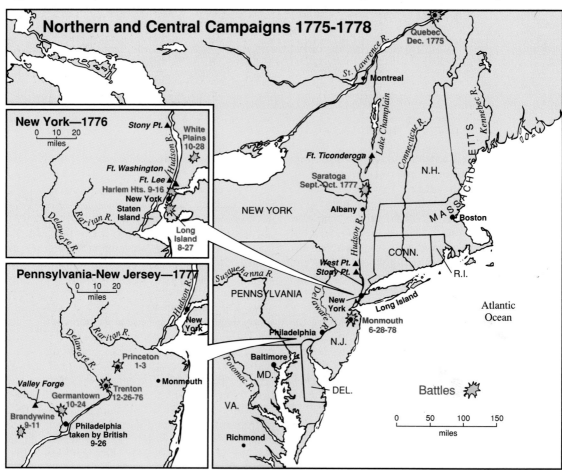

Northern and Central Campaigns 1775-1778

New York—1776

Pennsylvania-New Jersey—1777

Brandywine and Germantown—Instead of marching across New Jersey to Philadelphia, the British used their fleet to sail up the Chesapeake Bay and land in Maryland, some fifty miles from Philadelphia, the American capital. As Howe marched from Maryland through northern Delaware and into Pennsylvania, Washington placed the Continental army behind Brandywine Creek, south of Philadelphia, to await the enemy. In the **Battle of Brandywine** (September 11, 1777), Howe outmaneuvered Washington. He sent a force under General Cornwallis northward to cross the Brandywine at an unprotected ford. Then the British swept down behind the Continentals, forcing them to retreat. Washington had to fall back to reorganize, and the British entered Philadelphia unopposed on September 26. On October 4 Washington made an attempt to recapture the city by attacking the British forces stationed at Germantown, north of Philadelphia. The attack failed, and the American capital remained in enemy hands.

The Turning Point—Saratoga

While Howe was preparing his blow against Philadelphia, General Burgoyne was marching down Lake Champlain in impressive order. He easily seized Fort Ticonderoga and sent its American defenders reeling. At this point, however, the British plan began to break down. The orders to Howe from the British government were unclear, and Howe's decision to attack Philadelphia meant that only a token force would even attempt to move up the Hudson River. Another British force moving east from Lake Ontario to help Burgoyne was driven off by an American force led by **Benedict Arnold.**

Following these indirect setbacks came several defeats inflicted directly on Burgoyne's forces. A troop of Hessians sent to Bennington, Vermont, to capture American supplies was ambushed and nearly destroyed by the Americans. Then in two separate battles south of Saratoga, New York (September 19 and October 7, 1777), the Americans dealt heavy blows to the British. The American commander, General **Horatio Gates,** received much of the glory for these victories, but the real credit belonged to Gates's subordinates who led the fighting, Colonel **Daniel Morgan** and General Benedict Arnold.

Benedict Arnold

After the second battle the British attempted to withdraw to Ticonderoga, but bad weather slowed their retreat. The Americans, who were more experienced woodsmen, overtook and surrounded them near Saratoga. On October 17 Burgoyne surrendered to Gates.

The **Saratoga campaign** was the turning point of the war. Not only had an entire British invasion force of over six thousand men been killed or captured, but also France—impressed by the victory—recognized the United States as a nation and joined the war against Britain. The United States now had a powerful ally in its struggle for independence.

A Winter of Discontent and Hope

Valley Forge—Word of the French alliance did not reach America until spring of 1778. Meanwhile Washington and his army went through perhaps the darkest period of the war. With the British in control of Philadelphia, the American army made its headquarters for the winter of 1777-1778 some twenty-five miles away at **Valley Forge.** The army had to build its camp from scratch. A "city" of wooden barracks and huts soon sprouted in Valley Forge, but its "citizens" were hungry and ill clothed. Few men had whole uniforms, and even fewer had shoes. Washington grimly observed that "you might have tracked the army from White Marsh to Valley Forge by the blood of their feet."

Washington could do little to relieve the suffering of his men. For one thing the general had only the worthless paper currency of the Continental Congress to buy supplies. Farmers and merchants found it far more profitable to sell their goods to the British in Philadelphia, who paid in gold and silver. Despite the hardships, Washington's men bore up surprisingly well. Some even joked about their ragged condition. A group of officers, for example, held a party to which no one was admitted who had a whole pair of pants.

Drill and Discipline–In February of 1778 a colorful figure rode into the American camp. Lieutenant General Frederick William Augustus Henry Ferdinand **Baron von Steuben** (STOO bun) came to Valley Forge in a splendid German uniform to serve as a drillmaster for the Continental army. (Actually, Steuben was a bit of a fraud. He was not a baron, and he had never held a rank higher than major in the Prussian army.) Steuben knew no English, but he knew how to train men and how to instill pride and discipline. By memorizing a few English phrases, the German was able to drill the American forces. He taught them to march properly and showed them how to move and wheel in battle. Building on the experience that the Patriots had gained in past battles, Steuben transformed the disorganized rabble that had fled from New York into a reasonably efficient fighting force. When spring brought news of the French alliance, Washington looked at his newly drilled men and thought that perhaps the time had come to strike a major blow to the British.

Monmouth–Climax in the East

The French alliance created panic in Great Britain, and the government replaced the slow-moving Howe with General Henry Clinton. Be-

The Spirit of '76 *by Archibald Willard remains a popular patriotic painting of the Revolution, although it was painted nearly one hundred years afterward. The original painting hangs in the Selectmen's Meeting Room, Marblehead, Massachusetts.*

cause the British had decided to focus their attention on the Southern Colonies (where there was a heavier concentration of Loyalists), Clinton prepared to withdraw from Philadelphia to New York. The British move, Washington thought, would be the opportunity he had been waiting for. When the British left Philadelphia on June 18, Washington and his officers decided on a cautious plan. A segment of the American army would strike the rear of the British army on the march. If the attack went well, the rest of the Continental army could move up and join the battle. If not, the Americans could at least make things hot for the British before withdrawing without risking the whole army.

Unfortunately, Washington entrusted the initial attack to Charles Lee, his second in command. Although the most experienced officer in the American army, Lee had little confidence in the quality of the American soldiers. He was completely unimpressed with Steuben's work and claimed that the British soldiers were far superior. Furthermore,

The American Judas

In a secluded spot on the site of the Battle of Saratoga stands an odd memorial. Its inscription honors "the 'most brilliant soldier' of the Continental Army" for "winning for his countrymen the Decisive Battle of the American Revolution." The sculptor dared not mention the hero's name. He was Benedict Arnold, who was, next to Judas Iscariot, probably the most infamous traitor in history.

Arnold's war record was one of the finest in the Continental army. As joint-commander with Ethan Allen, he had captured British-held Fort Ticonderoga in New York in one of the earliest American triumphs of the war. In an otherwise ill-fated attack on Canada in 1775, Arnold conducted a brilliant march across the winter wilderness of Maine, and he was wounded while bravely supervising a night attack on Quebec during a howling winter storm. At Saratoga Arnold had broken his leg in leading a charge that shattered the British lines and turned the tide of battle.

Arnold was discontent, however. Some of his unhappiness was justified. He was often passed over for promotion by a Continental Congress that was more interested in rewarding an officer's political connections than his bravery in battle. George Washington recognized Arnold's obvious abilities and gave him command of Philadelphia after the British retreated. In that city, though, politicians and jealous fellow officers criticized him and sought to undermine his authority.

Like Simon the Sorcerer, Arnold was soon "in the gall of bitterness" (Acts 8:23). Arnold seems to have felt some genuine patriotic fervor, but he also felt an inordinate love of power, wealth, and glory. Dealing with an ungrateful Congress dampened his patriotism, and with opportunities for glory and wealth fading as he stayed in the Continental army, Arnold began to look for ways to fill his purse and feed his ego. In 1779 he secretly offered his services to the British.

George Washington still valued Arnold, and in 1780 the commander in chief thought to honor Arnold by giving him command of a section of the Continental army. Arnold astounded Washington by asking instead to be given command of West Point, an important fort on the Hudson River (now the site of the United States Military Academy). Washington was puzzled that this bold and dashing officer should request such an inactive post. Arnold pleaded that the pain from his wound at Saratoga required an undemanding command. In reality, Arnold was suffering more from wounded pride and had plotted with the British to turn the fort over to them for £20,000. Unaware of his officer's treachery, Washington granted Arnold's wish.

Arnold's plans went disastrously wrong. Arnold's contact, British major John André, was captured with incriminating papers by the Americans after a secret meeting with Arnold. Arnold fled to the British in New York; the unfortunate André was hanged as a spy.

Arnold traded his country for reward and a red coat. He spent the remainder of the war leading bloody but otherwise unimportant raids in Virginia and Connecticut. After the war he returned to Britain with Cornwallis. Although financially comfortable thanks to his treason (he received not only a reward but also a pension), Arnold was shunned by society. He died unhappy in London in 1801, no longer known as the hero of Ticonderoga and Saratoga. Rather, as Washington said, "General Arnold . . . has sullied his former glory by the blackest treason."

he actually opposed the attack and took command only because he feared someone else might receive the glory.

On June 28 the Americans attacked the British rear guard at Monmouth (MAHN muth) Court House in New Jersey. After a good start the American attack faltered, and Lee hurriedly ordered a retreat. As Washington rode to the front lines, he was astonished to run into his own men fleeing from the battle. Washington found Lee and asked angrily, ''What is all this confusion for, and retreat?'' Lee offered excuses, but Washington brushed them aside and attempted to undo the damage and save his army.

The British, seeing the American confusion, counterattacked sharply. Washington's men hurriedly fell into line to meet the attack. The temperature on the field was oppressively hot–over 100°. In fact, more men may have died from the heat than from bullets. The wife of a member of an American artillery crew, Mary Hays, became a minor legend during the battle. She carried pitchers of water to the troops (earning her the nickname ''Molly Pitcher''), and when her husband was wounded she took his place and helped fire the cannon.

The **Battle of Monmouth** vindicated Steuben's work. Despite the early disorder, the Americans quickly and professionally took their places in the battle lines and repulsed the British attacks. Clinton broke off the battle and continued his move to New York. Although the battle was a draw, it showed how far Washington's army had come since the disasters in New York. As the British marched on to New York, some must have been thinking that it was a good idea to move their campaign south and away from the increasingly dangerous army of General Washington.

The War in the West

While George Washington was trying to build an army that could stand up to the British regulars, a different kind of warfare was taking place on the frontier along the Ohio River. Here the fighting resembled the guerrilla tactics of the French and Indian War. Massacres, scalpings, and ambushes replaced the comparatively ''civilized'' battles in the East between the Continental regulars and the

George Rogers Clark, *by James Barton Longacre, National Portrait Gallery, Smithsonian Institution*

redcoats. A handful of British soldiers uneasily allied with fierce Indian tribes engaged in a brutal life-and-death struggle with hardy but scattered American frontiersmen. One great American leader arose out of the war in the West–**George Rogers Clark.**

Clark, a native Virginian, had come to the Ohio River Valley in 1772. As a resident of Kentucky, Clark recognized the threat that the frontier faced from the British and Indians. In 1778 the twenty-five-year-old Clark won Virginia's approval to lead an attack on British trading posts north of the Ohio River in the region then known as the Northwest. With a tiny force of some 175 men, Clark sailed down the Ohio River to what is now Illinois. From there Clark marched his men overland to the Mississippi River town of Kaskaskia (kus KAS kee uh). The town, populated mostly by French settlers who did not care for the British anyway, happily surrendered. Several other trading posts quickly fell, including the most important–**Vincennes** on the Wabash River in what is now Indiana.

The British commander at Detroit, Lt. Col. Henry Hamilton–known among American settlers as ''Hair-Buyer'' Hamilton for the grisly scalp trade he encouraged among his Indian allies–reacted swiftly. In December his force of regulars, Loyalists, and Indians recaptured Vincennes. Then Hamilton settled in to wait out the winter. When spring came, he thought, he would finish off the Americans farther west on the Mississippi at Kaskaskia.

Clark, however, had no intention of waiting to be attacked. Early in February of 1779 he marched a small force some 150 miles from Kaskaskia to Vincennes. The weather was wet and cold. Much of the Illinois plains were flooded, and Clark's men constantly waded through waist-deep waters. Clark alternately urged, exhorted, and encouraged his men to keep them going. When those methods began to fail, he threatened to shoot them. By February 23 they were in sight of Vincennes, the last of their food having been eaten two days before.

To deceive the British about the size of his force, Clark waited until nightfall to approach the town. He ordered his men to carry a number of banners as they marched a zig-zag route to the town. When they entered the city, Clark sent his men scurrying back and forth down side streets as though they were a huge force. Hamilton thought Clark had five hundred men; the townspeople thought he had a thousand; Clark knew he had fewer than 150. Awed by Clark's imaginary army, the worried Hamilton surrendered.

Clark's victories in the Northwest were not as significant as the battles in the East in terms of

Clark and his men attack Ft. Sackville, the British post at Vincennes.

numbers, but they had great strategic importance. Clark's expedition reduced Indian attacks, and his presence helped the United States lay claim to the territory north of the Ohio River. Much of the credit for securing Kentucky and the Northwest goes to the courage of George Rogers Clark.

Section Review

1. What militarily indefensible city did the Continental army try to defend for reasons of politics and morale?
2. Why were the victories at Trenton and Princeton so important to the American cause?
3. Why was the Saratoga campaign the turning point of the war?
4. Who was the drillmaster of the Continental army? What battle demonstrated the success of his work?
5. Why were George Rogers Clark's victories in the Northwest strategically important?

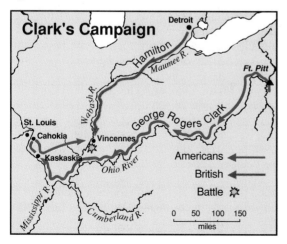

Clark's Campaign

Detroit
Hamilton
Maumee R.
Ft. Pitt
Wabash R.
St. Louis
Cahokia
Vincennes
Kaskaskia
George Rogers Clark
Ohio River
Mississippi R.
Cumberland R.

Americans
British
Battle ✷

0   50   100   150
miles

War in the South

In the early years of the war, the Southern states poured men and materiel into the military and political ranks of the Patriot cause. As a theater of war, though, the British largely ignored the region in favor of fighting Washington's Continentals and isolating New England. As early as 1776, there had been an attempt to quell the rebellion in the South, beginning with a naval attack on Charleston, South Carolina. The British fleet, however, had been sent home roughly handled. No further attempts were made until 1778, in the wake of the British defeat at Saratoga.

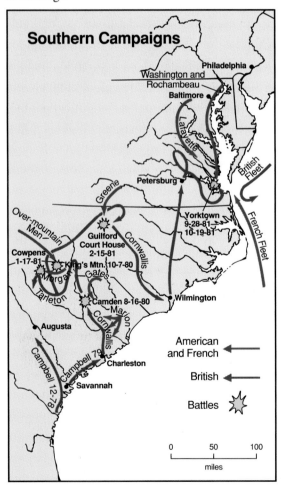

On orders from London, Sir Henry Clinton sent a British transport fleet loaded with regulars, Hessians, and Loyalists for the invasion of Georgia and the drive through the southland. Clinton hoped that the presence of His Majesty's troops would awaken Loyalist sentiment in the backcountry, soften opposition, and sever the South from the rest of the country. His plan worked so well at first that he failed to see its flaws. The southern campaign would be Britain's last.

The British Advance

Charleston—By early 1779 all of Georgia, including its chief city and port, Savannah, had fallen into British hands. Georgia became a staging area for the more important assault on **Charleston.** If the British could conquer Charleston, they would not only capture one of the most populous and important cities in America, but they would also gain access to the Carolina heartland through the navigable rivers that the city defended.

In late March 1780 Clinton's forces laid siege to Charleston. Most of the Continental forces in the South, an army of about five thousand, occupied the city. Unfortunately the American commander, General Benjamin Lincoln, gave up the advantage of mobility and heeded the pleadings of Charlestonians to hold the city at all cost. As it turned out, the cost was Lincoln's entire army. With the Americans outnumbered better than two to one and their supply lines cut by the British cavalry under the ruthless Lieutenant Colonel Banastre Tarleton, the outcome was predictable. On May 12, 1780, Lincoln surrendered his entire force to the British. It was America's worst defeat of the war.

Camden—With the fall of Charleston, the Carolinas lay invitingly open to the British. Before departing with a large force for New York, Clinton gave command of the Carolina conquest to General **Charles Cornwallis.** Soon scarlet columns of British troops were filing through the South Carolina low country.

News of the British advance sent an American expedition of about three thousand Continentals and militia to meet them. The Patriot force was under the command of General Horatio Gates, the hero of Saratoga but a man whose reputation ex-

Colonel Banastre Tarleton, *by Sir Joshua Reynolds,*
© The National Gallery, London

ceeded his abilities. When the two armies stumbled onto each other at **Camden,** South Carolina, in August 1780, the Americans were outnumbered and outgeneraled. In the heat of battle the American militia broke and ran–and leading the retreat was General Gates. The American right flank, made up of troops from Maryland and Delaware, bravely held, led by a giant German named Baron de Kalb. With only six hundred soldiers they held for over an hour against the full fury of Cornwallis's army. De Kalb was wounded eleven times before collapsing along with the Continental line. After dou-

ble disasters at Charleston and Camden the Patriot cause looked grim.

Swamp Surprises – One small band of South Carolinians that kept the war alive in the British-occupied low country of South Carolina was "distinguished by small black leather caps and the wretchedness of their attire; their number did not exceed twenty men and boys, some white, some black, and all mounted, but most of them miserably equipped." The leader of this motley assortment of guerrillas was the elusive "Swamp Fox," **Francis Marion.**

Marion and his men would slip out of the swamps and sand flats to attack British outposts and supply lines. Such small guerrilla bands, of course, could not beat a British army in open battle. Their strategic importance lay in keeping the pressure on. Marion's successful hit-and-run operations pinned down British troops, keeping them from joining the main British force, and forced Cornwallis to keep looking over his shoulder. Tarleton himself gave begrudging respect to the "Swamp Fox" when he declared that "the devil himself could not catch" Marion.

Kings Mountain – A surprising turn of events occurred in October 1780 that gave Patriots cause for encouragement. Cornwallis sent Major Patrick Ferguson to lead an all-Tory detachment of over a thousand into the western foothills of South Carolina. Ferguson warned the "over-mountain men" in the backcountry settlements of the western Carolinas and in what is now Tennessee that unless they pledged their loyalty to George III, he would lay waste to their fields, burn their homes, and hang their leaders. Unfortunately for Ferguson, these grizzled frontiersmen did not respond well to threats. Led by Isaac Shelby and "Nolichucky Jack" Sevier, a buckskinned force of nine hundred men mounted and rode to meet the blustering Briton.

The Patriot force caught Ferguson and his Tories on the wooded slopes of **Kings Mountain,** a peak that straddles the two Carolinas. There the "over-mountain men" killed Ferguson and destroyed eighty per cent of his forces. The victory at Kings Mountain strengthened Patriot resolve—something they would need much of in the final fateful year of 1781.

Greene Turns the Tide

Cowpens—In the waning days of 1780, while the American army was in winter quarters at Charlotte, North Carolina, Congress appointed a replacement for Horatio Gates. On Washington's advice they sent the "Fighting Quaker" from Rhode Island, General **Nathanael Greene.** The brilliant Greene took a small, threadbare, penniless, demoralized army and by courage, resourcefulness, and tactical genius made it into the scourge of Cornwallis's army.

Greene's first move was to divide in order to conquer. He divided his outnumbered army and sent a detachment south under General Daniel Morgan, whom he called out of retirement. The crusty Morgan, his body wracked with arthritis, rode off with six hundred Continentals, hoping that Cornwallis would also divide his force and take up pursuit.

The British commander sent out Tarleton and his Tory legion to catch the Continentals. Tarleton was particularly hated by the Americans for his reputation of killing his prisoners after they had surrendered. The daring Tarleton, however, would more than meet his match in the creaky old Dan Morgan. On some rolling meadows known as the Cowpens, which in more peaceful times offered pasturage for cattle, the two armies clashed on January 17, 1781. Morgan displayed his exceptional military skill by executing the most nearly perfect victory of the war. The Americans feigned a retreat and then dramatically halted and repelled the reckless British pursuit. In less than an hour it was all over. The British suffered 930 casualties, the Americans only 70. The **Battle of Cowpens** was the first major step toward eventual British defeat.

Race to the Dan—After unsettling losses at Kings Mountain and Cowpens, Cornwallis determined to crush Greene, the only serious and thus far most stubborn obstacle to a conclusive conquest of the Carolinas. Cornwallis decided to march through North Carolina to the fords of the Dan River, which snaked across its boundary with Virginia. The Dan would be Greene's best hope of escape from Cornwallis's superior force. Greene sensed Cornwallis's intentions, and in the bitter February of 1781 the two armies raced to the Dan. If the Continentals won, the Dan would cut off the British pursuit. If they lost, the Americans would rein up in the face of British bayonets. After a difficult two-week march in which British and American soldiers alike fell dead in their tracks from exhaustion and starvation, Greene's army ferried across the muddy, swollen river at the site of present day Danville, Virginia, and took all the boats with them. Greene had not only slipped out of Cornwallis's trap but had drawn the British far from their supply bases in South Carolina.

In mid-March the American army recrossed the Dan and advanced south to a little crossroads in

Nathanael Greene *by Charles Willson Peale, Independence National Historical Park*

Lafayette, the Republican Aristocrat

Numerous European officers served with distinction in the Continental army. Baron von Steuben, the German drillmaster; Baron de Kalb, another German who was the hero of the Battle of Camden; and Count Casimir Pulaski, veteran of a valiant but vain Polish war for independence, were among the Europeans who won glory and honor in the American cause. The most famous of these international heroes, perhaps, was the French Marquis de Lafayette (1757-1834).

Born of wealthy aristocracy in France, Lafayette seemed like an unlikely candidate for honor in a republican revolution. Lafayette's father, a soldier, died in battle when his son was only two. Young Lafayette read widely, especially military books, and he too became an officer in the French army. When he was eighteen, Lafayette attended a dinner where the American War for Independence was discussed. For some reason, the American cause fired his imagination. When an American representative came to France in 1776 seeking officers for the Continental army, Lafayette enthusiastically volunteered. Because he was enormously wealthy, Lafayette declined to take a salary. He said that he would serve only for his expenses.

When General Washington learned that he was receiving a nineteen-year-old major general in his command, he was cool to the idea. On meeting the young officer, however, Washington's doubts melted. Lafayette was gracious, humble, and eager both to learn and to serve. A strong affection grew between the American commander and the young French nobleman. For Washington, Lafayette became the son he had never had. For Lafayette, Washington became the father he had never known.

Lafayette served bravely with the Continental army. On his education as a soldier, he wrote, "I read, I study, I examine, I listen, I think, and out of all that I try to form an idea into which I put as much common sense as I can." Despite his studious nature, Lafayette was no armchair soldier; he was always in the thick of the fighting. He was wounded at the Battle of Brandywine, and a small force under his command constantly harassed Cornwallis and the British in Virginia. At Yorktown, he led an attack on a major British fortification. When he returned to France after the war, Lafayette left behind him a large group of veterans who had been impressed with the young man's unflagging cheerfulness and unquestioned courage.

Back in France, Lafayette became a leader for liberal reform in his own country. He dreamed of making his native land a model of republican virtue just like his adopted nation. When the French Revolution broke out in 1789, the marquis took the lead in drawing up and adopting a new constitution for France. At one point Lafayette was probably the most popular leader in France. The revolution turned ugly, however, and bloody violence erupted. When Lafayette tried to moderate the conflict, radicals denounced him as a traitor to the revolution. In dismay and disgust, Lafayette left France for Belgium and tried to claim American citizenship. Instead he was arrested by the Austrians and imprisoned for five years.

After his release from prison, Lafayette returned to France. He continued to fight for his republican ideals, but his battlefield was now the French legislature. He made one last visit to America in 1824. To his astonished delight, he was met by hordes of enthusiastic admirers and graying veterans. Hailed as a hero, Lafayette found that his efforts on behalf of the American republic were cherished and honored by a grateful people.

North Carolina called **Guilford Court House.** To lure Cornwallis's army out to the battlefield of his choosing, Greene dispatched ''Light-Horse Harry'' Lee and his dragoons to strike hard and feign retreat. On March 15, Lee and his green-jacketed cavaliers shattered Tarleton's Legion and turned back to Guilford Court House with Cornwallis in hot pursuit. The two armies clashed in a fierce fight in which the British won an empty victory. Cornwallis gained possession of the field, but he lost one-fourth of his men and Greene was still at large.

The battered British army marched to Wilmington, North Carolina, for fresh supplies and a fresh look at what to do next. Cornwallis decided to march north to the Virginia coast. There he would have a sea route to Clinton's New York forces, and he could wreak havoc on Virginia by destroying Patriot supplies and hanging their leaders. On August 1, 1781, Cornwallis set up his headquarters at a sleepy little tobacco port on Virginia's York River. Little did he realize that **Yorktown** would be his Waterloo.

Surrender of Lord Cornwallis, *United States Capitol Art Collection*

Victory at Yorktown

Cornwallis Cornered—During the late summer of 1781, Cornwallis amassed a large force of 7,200 troops. The **Marquis de Lafayette,** commanding the outnumbered Continental forces in Virginia, viewed the build-up with alarm. Although he shouldered the burdens of leadership well, the young Lafayette confided in a letter at the time, "When one is twenty-three, has an army to command and Lord Cornwallis to oppose, the time that is left is none too long for sleep."

Soon Lafayette would not be the only one losing sleep. At the end of August the French fleet under Admiral de Grasse sailed up the Chesapeake Bay, landed 3,000 French troops to join Lafayette, and then turned to defeat the British fleet. Suddenly Cornwallis found himself in trouble. Not only was he cut off by sea, but with the arrival of Washington's Continentals along with a large force of French regulars, he was also outnumbered and surrounded.

Washington had been leaking false reports that he intended to attack Clinton in New York, all the while screening his march to Yorktown. Admiral De Grasse's victory in the Bay had been an unexpected bonus for Washington, who now caught the hapless Cornwallis in a trap.

"The World Turned Upside Down"—After desperate attempts to break the siege, Cornwallis yielded to the inevitable, asking for terms of surrender on October 17, 1781. Two days later, amid the dappled color of the Virginia autumn, 7,000 redcoats marched between two half-mile lines of American and French troops to lay down their arms. The British band accompanying their troops, at a loss to find any dignity in the moment, struck up a rollicking nursery tune:

> *If ponies rode men,*
> *and grass ate the cow*
> *If cats should be chased*
> *into holes by the mouse . . .*

Cornwallis, who had no stomach for such a bitter occasion, called in sick. A subordinate carried the general's sword to Washington, who understood the insult of Cornwallis's absence and directed that the sword be given to *his* subordinate, General Benjamin Lincoln.

While the sword passed hands, the band blared on with their lilting, childish tune with words that captured the irony of the moment.

> *. . . If summer were spring*
> *And the other way round;*
> *Then all the world would be upside down.*

The Treaty of Paris, 1783—George III was as shaken by Yorktown as Cornwallis. The king at first raged that the war should be pressed further; then sinking into depression, he offered to abdicate. Finally, the king gave in to pressure from Parliament and the people to accept the war as over. Peace commissioners were appointed to meet the American negotiators—Benjamin Franklin, John Jay, and John Adams—in Paris.

Although the French alliance and the presence of Clinton's forces in New York at first complicated the settlement, the **Treaty of Paris** was finally signed on September 3, 1783. It acknowledged that the colonies were indeed independent. The United States was awarded all the land east of the Mississippi River with the exception of Florida, which returned to Spanish control.

Yorktown was not an end, however, as much as a beginning. A costly war paid in Patriot blood had secured independence; now the task of nation building lay before them. In many ways the challenges of peace would be greater than the challenges of war. Yet the generation of Americans who rallied on Lexington Green, weathered Valley Forge, and stormed the defenses at Yorktown would prove that they could not only win their liberty but also *preserve* it.

Section Review

1. What was the United States' worst defeat of the war?
2. Who was the leader of a band of Patriot guerrillas in South Carolina? What was his nickname?
3. Why was it so important for General Greene to reach the Dan River before the British?
4. What admiral helped trap Cornwallis at Yorktown? What nationality was he?

Chapter Review

Terms

Gaspee incident
Committee of Correspondence
Boston Tea Party
Tea Act of 1773
Coercive Acts
Thomas Gage
Intolerable Acts
Quebec Act
militia
regulars
First Continental Congress
Declaration of American Rights
Patrick Henry
Battles of Lexington and Concord (April 19, 1775)
Patriots
Loyalists
Tories
Hessians
Second Continental Congress
Fort Ticonderoga
Ethan Allen
George Washington
Bunker Hill
Henry Knox
Olive Branch Petition
Common Sense
Thomas Paine
John Adams

Thomas Jefferson
Declaration of Independence (July 4, 1776)
William Howe
Trenton
Princeton
John Burgoyne
Battle of Brandywine
Horatio Gates
Daniel Morgan
Benedict Arnold
Saratoga campaign
Valley Forge
Baron von Steuben
Battle of Monmouth
George Rogers Clark
Vincennes
siege of Charleston
Charles Cornwallis
Camden
Francis Marion
King's Mountain
Nathanael Greene
Battle of Cowpens
''Race to the Dan''
Guilford Court House
Marquis de Lafayette
surrender of Cornwallis at Yorktown (October 19, 1781)
Treaty of Paris (September 3, 1783)

Content Questions

1. What did committees of correspondence provide to the colonies?
2. Why did the colonies fear the Quebec Act?
3. What two battles marked the real beginning of the War for Independence?
4. Why were the battles of Bunker Hill and Guilford Court House empty victories for the British?
5. Place the following acts of the Continental Congress in chronological order: Declaration of Independence; Olive Branch Petition; Declaration of American Rights; appointment of George Washington as commander in chief.
6. In what way did Howe's decision to attack Philadelphia eventually work to the advantage of the Americans?
7. Identify the battle or campaign described by each of the following statements.
    a. The turning point of the war
    b. The worst American defeat of the war
    c. Horatio Gates's great defeat
    d. "The World Turned Upside Down"
    e. Won by the "over-mountain men"
    f. Surprise raid the day after Christmas
    g. American defeat allowed the British to enter Philadelphia unopposed
    h. Molly Pitcher
    i. "The most nearly perfect victory of the war"

8. Who led the initial American attack at the Battle of Monmouth?
9. The three main theaters of the Revolution were the East, the South, and the West. Which of these was characterized almost entirely by guerrilla warfare? Which of these was least characterized by guerrilla warfare?
10. In which of the theaters mentioned in Question 9 did Clinton think he could most easily end the war?

Application Questions

1. How would you answer someone who said that the American Revolution was little different than the French or Russian revolutions?
2. Why does guerrilla warfare create more destruction and hatred than warfare between regular armies?
3. Do you think the Loyalists were right in their stand on the Revolution? Why or why not?
4. Some historians have claimed that Britain lost the war because of the incompetence of its military commanders rather than because of any accomplishments by the Americans. Do you agree or disagree with this assertion? Why?

CHAPTER 7

The Critical Period (1781-1789)

"This Country must be united. If persuasion does not unite it, the sword will."

Gouverneur Morris, 1787

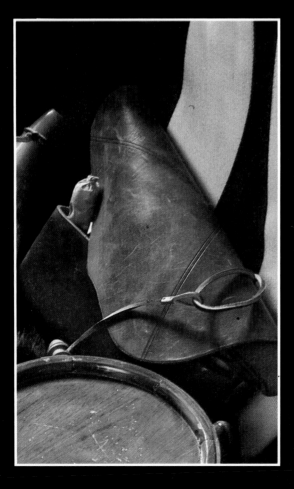

Scene of the Signers of the Constitution of the United States, *by Howard Chandler Christy*

The 1780s was the most critical decade in our nation's history. From redcoats to ratification, those years were accented with conflict and change. At the beginning of the decade, for example, British troops patrolled the streets of New York City in the name of their king, George III. By decade's end, American citizens paraded through the same streets to celebrate the inauguration of another George, President George Washington.

Americans, in fact, changed governments twice during the 1780s. Not only did they finally throw off British rule through success on the battlefield, but they also scrapped their muddling national Confederation because of its failure to govern.

Despite these difficulties there was a happy result. Forged by the experiences of that remarkable decade, the Constitution was written—America's single greatest contribution to political thought and practice. Though coming eight years after Yorktown, the Constitution really capped the independence movement, providing a stable, national government through which the states would be united

in more than just name. The new charter gave substance to the spirit of '76.

Government by Confederation

On June 7, 1776–the same day that Richard Henry Lee of Virginia moved that "these United Colonies are, and of right ought to be, free and Independent states"–the Second Continental Congress voted to draw up a charter for joining the colonies into a **confederation,** a close alliance of states. Congress entrusted the task to a committee headed by John Dickinson of Pennsylvania, and in a little more than a month, Dickinson's committee presented its work. After more than a year of debate and revision, Congress adopted these **Articles of Confederation.** By 1781 all thirteen states had approved the Articles, and they went into effect.

League of States

Dickinson originally proposed establishing a strong central government. However, the states–jealous of their power–watered down his plan. The

Articles of Confederation did little more than grant legitimacy to the loosely constructed Continental Congress and provide the minimum of authority needed to conduct the war. Although the states pledged themselves to ''Perpetual Union,'' they committed themselves only to ''a firm league of friendship with each other.'' The Articles said plainly, ''Each state retains its sovereignty, freedom, and independence.'' In effect, the central government was only as strong as the states let it be, and that was not very strong.

The legislature was the only component of the Confederation government. The Congress of the Confederation was **unicameral** (having only one house), and each state legislature could elect two to seven representatives to attend. Each state had only one vote, however, regardless of how many representatives it sent. Important legislation–such as declaring war, approving treaties, and coining money–had to be approved by nine states. Amending the Articles, like their ratification, required the unanimous consent of all thirteen states.

The chief executive was chosen by the legislature and was completely under its power. This president of Congress was virtually powerless, and three officials (the superintendent of finance and

George Washington, Our Seventeenth President?

Every first grader knows that George Washington was the first president of the United States. Before Washington took office in 1789, however, the United States had sixteen ''presidents''–the presidents of the Continental and Confederation congresses. Of course, these men did not have the prestige and power of modern presidents; they were elected annually by the Congress to serve as chairman of the sessions of Congress. Nor did the office have the high reputation of the modern presidency. During his term as president in 1785-1786, for example, John Hancock never bothered to show up for a single session. Another man, who was in poor health, asked a friend's advice when he was offered the position. The friend replied that he should take it because it was ''the Easiest in the Union for an invalid.''

The list at the right gives the names of these presidents and the dates of their election. Some of them (such as John Hancock, John Jay, and Richard Henry Lee) are justly famous in their own right. Others are almost unknown, sometimes deservedly so. None of them, however, gained any lasting fame through the office, with the possible exception of John Hancock who, as president of

Congress in 1776, was the first person to sign the Declaration of Independence.

Peyton Randolph (5 Sept. 1774)
Henry Middleton (22 Oct. 1774)
Peyton Randolph (10 May 1775)
John Hancock (24 May 1775)
Henry Laurens (1 Nov. 1777)
John Jay (10 Dec. 1778)
Samuel Huntington (28 Sept. 1779)
Thomas McKean (10 July 1781)
John Hanson (5 Nov. 1781)
Elias Boudinot (4 Nov. 1782)
Thomas Mifflin (3 Nov. 1783)
Richard Henry Lee (30 Nov. 1784)
John Hancock (23 Nov. 1785)
Nathaniel Gorham (6 June 1786)
Arthur St. Clair (2 Feb. 1787)
Cyrus Griffin (22 Jan. 1788)

Neither the office nor at times the men who filled it were held in high esteem. After she had dined with President Cyrus Griffin and several other members of the Congress of the Confederation, John Adams's daughter wrote to her mother, ''Had you been present you would have trembled for your country, to have seen, heard and observed the men who are its rulers.''

Benjamin West, American Commissioners of the Treaty of Paris. *Courtesy, The Henry Francis du Pont Winterthur Museum. The British commissioners refused to pose for the painting, leaving West's work half finished.*

the secretaries of war and foreign affairs) handled most administrative duties. A national judiciary did not exist.

The Articles simply formalized the status quo– thirteen separate states, separate historically, politi- cally, and economically. Therefore the Articles re- served to the states every ''power, jurisdiction, and right'' which was not ''expressly delegated'' to Congress. Among the most important powers re- served to the states was the power to tax. Unable to levy taxes, Congress was forced to ask the states for money, requests which the states could–and did– ignore if they wished. The central government was reduced to scraping funds together through loans from other nations (which the government usually

could not repay), the sale of public lands on the fron- tier, and the profits from the government-owned post office (a paltry $10,000-$15,000 a year). In its years of existence, the Confederation government barely made enough to cover its expenses.

Successes of the Confederation

Despite its glaring weaknesses and ultimate failure, the Confederation notched a few successes. Chief among these were the Treaty of Paris and the settlement of the western lands dispute.

The Treaty of Paris–The **Treaty of Paris** (see p. 129) was the greatest triumph in foreign affairs by the Confederation. By forcing England to rec- ognize American independence, the treaty built enormous prestige for the young nation. At the same time, the enforcing of the treaty revealed several weaknesses of the Confederation and squandered much of that prestige which the United States had so carefully built up.

By the provisions of the treaty, the United States was to restore the seized property of Loyalists and to allow British subjects access to American courts in order to recover debts owed them. The American government, however, had no means of

enforcing these provisions; it could only ask the states to comply. When the states refused, Britain used this breach of the treaty as an excuse to keep its forts in the Great Lakes region and thus protect the profitable British fur trade. When Ambassador John Adams complained to the British about their violation of the treaty, the British calmly pointed to the United States' failure to honor its obligations. When Adams tried to argue that the states would not allow the central government to do so, the Brit-

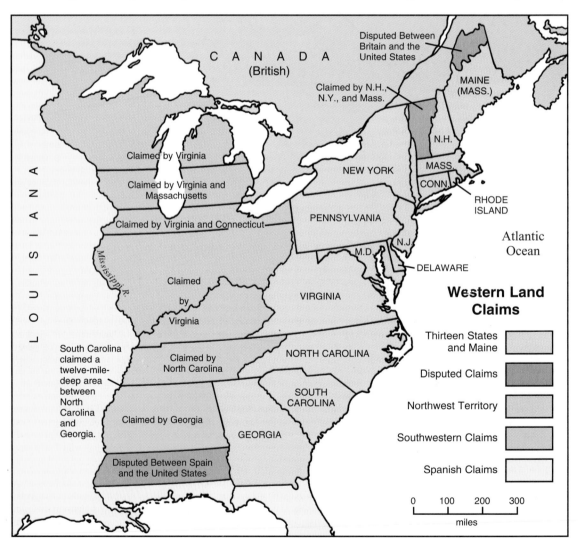

Western Land Claims

Thirteen States and Maine

Disputed Claims

Northwest Territory

Southwestern Claims

Spanish Claims

0   100   200   300

miles

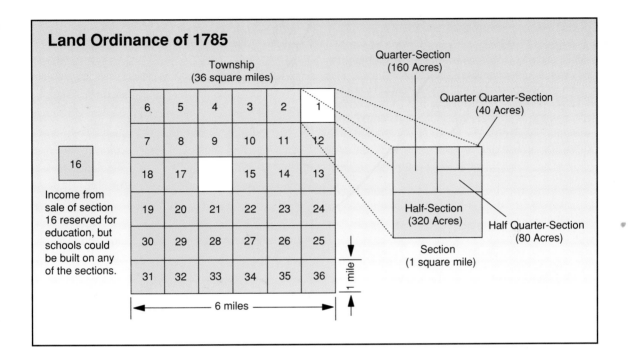

Land Ordinance of 1785

Township
(36 square miles)

6	5	4	3	2	1
7	8	9	10	11	12
18	17		15	14	13
19	20	21	22	23	24
30	29	28	27	26	25
31	32	33	34	35	36

16

Income from sale of section 16 reserved for education, but schools could be built on any of the sections.

6 miles

1 mile

Quarter-Section
(160 Acres)

Quarter Quarter-Section
(40 Acres)

Half-Section
(320 Acres)

Half Quarter-Section
(80 Acres)

Section
(1 square mile)

ish replied pointedly, Was the United States one nation or thirteen? The taunt was soon taken up by other governments that dealt with the young nation.

Western Lands—Approval of the Articles of Confederation had been delayed until 1781 because Maryland refused to ratify them until the matter of the western lands had been settled. The Treaty of Paris left the United States in control of all territory east of the Mississippi River and north of Florida and Louisiana. Several states, notably Virginia and New York, claimed parts of this huge tract of land. Several other states, including Maryland, had no such claims and feared the power of the other states if they succeeded in claiming this land. Maryland, therefore, would not ratify the Articles unless the other states abandoned their claims and turned these lands over to the federal government. When Virginia and New York agreed to yield their claims to the federal government, the others eventually followed suit, and Maryland ratified the Articles. All lands north of the Ohio River that passed into the hands of the national government became known as the **Northwest Territory.**

The question of how to develop and govern the Northwest Territory was settled by a series of ordinances. The first and most far-sighted was the **Ordinance of 1784,** written by Thomas Jefferson. He proposed creating ten new states out of the territory, each of which would be completely equal to the other states in the Union. He also proposed banning slavery in the region and giving the land to settlers instead of selling it.

Unfortunately the ordinance was so far-sighted that it never went into effect. Too many states feared the creation of ten competing states, and some opposed the ban on slavery. The **Land Ordinance of 1785** was far more cautious and avoided thorny political questions. Instead it concentrated on the settlement of the territory. The ordinance divided the new lands into orderly townships for sale and development. Each township contained thirty-six sections, or lots, of one square mile (640 acres). Each lot was to be sold for a dollar an acre ($640), contrary to Jefferson's hopes for free lands for settlers. The proceeds from the sale of lot sixteen in each township were to go toward building and maintaining schools in the area.

More sweeping was the **Northwest Ordinance of 1787.** Whereas the ordinance of 1785 concerned settlement, the ordinance of 1787 concerned government. The Northwest Territory was to be divided into at least three states but no more than five. Each would-be state went through three stages. In the first stage, the region remained almost completely under the direct control of the federal government. When a region had at least five thousand free inhabitants, it entered the second stage and became a territory. Then the people could elect a legislature and send a representative to Congress. However, the governor–still appointed by the national government– could veto any act passed by the territorial legislature, and the representative to Congress could not vote. In the third stage, once a territory had sixty thousand free inhabitants, it could draw up a state constitution and be admitted to the Union on an equal basis with the other states.

Other provisions are worthy of note. Building on the educational provisions in the Land Ordinance of 1785, the Northwest Ordinance of 1787 explicitly emphasized the importance of education: "Religion, morality, and knowledge, being necessary to good government and the happiness of mankind, schools and the means of education shall forever be encouraged." Most important, the ordinance followed Jefferson's original suggestion and prohibited slavery in the new territories. Also most states that entered the Union afterwards followed the political process set down by the Northwest Ordinance.

The Northwest ordinances were the greatest success of the Confederation government. They allowed orderly settlement of the territory, and the land sales they permitted provided income for the government. Years later Daniel Webster said that he doubted "whether one single law of any lawgiver, ancient or modern, has produced effects of more distinct, marked, and lasting character than the ordinance of '87."

Failures of the Confederation

Financial Weakness–The financial situation of the new nation was dire, as one would expect

Metropotamia, U.S.A.

When Thomas Jefferson drew up his 1784 ordinance for the Northwest Territory, he could not resist including his own plans for carving the region into ten states whose names and boundaries he had already chosen. The map below shows the division of the territory as Jefferson envisaged it, along with the boundaries of the states that were actually created.

The other thirteen states eventually rejected Jefferson's plan. They feared sharing their power with ten new competitors. Finally, only five states (Ohio, Indiana, Michigan, Illinois, and Wisconsin) along with a portion of Minnesota were carved out of the territory. We should be relieved, perhaps, or some of us might be living in Detroit, Metropotamia; Green Bay, Michigania; Saginaw, Cherronesus; Evansville, Polypotamia; or Chicago, Assenisipia. It is obvious that Jefferson was better at governing states than at naming them.

Thomas Jefferson's Plan

after a six-year war was fought on its soil. The weakness of the Articles did not help, however. The national government, of course, was almost always broke and in debt, but the individual states were not much better off. **Hard money** (silver and gold) was scarce in the United States. Paper money, the obvious answer to a lack of hard currency, presented its own difficulties. The national government printed so much money, **"Continental dollars,"** that its value plummeted and merchants would not accept it. In a short period of time the expression "not worth a Continental" came to mean that which was worthless.

Compounding the problem was the fact that each state could print its own currency. State currency was often just as worthless as the Continental notes. Smart merchants required payment in hard currency or they bartered (traded goods instead of money for other goods). One Massachusetts newspaper editor announced that he would take payment for subscriptions in salt pork.

A final financial blow was dealt the Congress of the Confederation by the states. On two occasions Congress proposed amendments to the Articles permitting it to levy small tariffs for income. In both instances failure to attain the required unanimous vote for amendments killed the measure. The second failure in particular spurred the efforts of those who desired the revision of the Articles or even a new constitution. Nothing of lasting value, it seemed, could ever be accomplished under the Articles of Confederation.

Foreign Weakness—As mentioned earlier, the separate interests of the states often hampered the national government's conduct of foreign affairs. In negotiating the Treaty of Paris and in later treaty discussions, European powers such as Britain, Spain, and France learned that they could play on jealousies between the states to undercut the United States' bargaining position. Financial and military weaknesses only worsened matters. When the United States ran afoul of the Barbary pirates in northern Africa, the nation could not even pay the demanded bribes, let alone build and arm a naval squadron to protect American shipping.

Domestic Weakness—Internal weakness resulted in part from economic confusion. The existence of fourteen different currencies (one each for the national government and the thirteen states), varying tariffs, and a postwar depression weakened

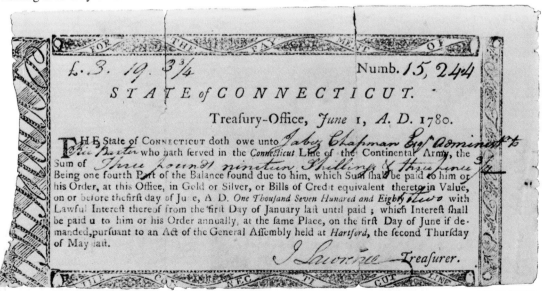

A Continental paynote for Connecticut regulars. The issuance of unbacked, inflationary paper created numerous problems for the infant nation.

This 1787 woodcut shows Daniel Shays and his lieutenant Job Shattuck. National Portrait Gallery, Smithsonian Institution.

the financial fabric that could have served to bind the nation. The most serious threat, however, was the national government's inability to keep the peace within its own borders.

In 1783 the **Newburgh Conspiracy** threatened America's young government. Frustrated by Congress's inability to pay salaries and pensions, and backed by businessmen who feared the economic chaos that they saw looming before them, a group of officers in General Washington's headquarters in Newburgh, New York, decided to take action. At the least, they intended to use the army to force Congress and the states to grant them their back pay. Some conspirators wanted more; they wanted to establish a new government under a king or a dictator. Washington was their first choice as the leader; but if he refused, they would find someone else.

Washington coldly rejected every offer to become a military ruler. When he learned that the officers planned a mass meeting in Newburgh to discuss their grievances, Washington came as an uninvited guest. He spoke kindly to the men, sympathizing with their needs but urging them not to destroy the nation they had fought for. At the conclusion of the speech, Washington started to reassure the men by reading a favorable letter from a congressman. Before reading it, he paused and with deliberation took out his glasses and put them on. "Gentlemen, you will permit me to put on my spectacles," the general said, "for I have not only grown gray but almost blind in the service of my country."

When Washington finished, tears filled the eyes of many of the men for reasons unrelated to the contents of the letter. Before them stood the patriot who had weathered the snows of Valley Forge and faced the bullets of Cornwallis, the man whose strength of character and leadership had been the greatest weapon in the American arsenal. The conspiracy collapsed, but one must wonder how a less scrupulous commander would have reacted to having a whole nation offered to him.

An even more serious problem arose in Massachusetts in 1786. Instead of simply conspiring against the government, as the ringleaders at Newburgh had done, a large body of men actually took arms against the government. Daniel Shays, a veteran of the Revolution, led an insurrection of farmers against the courts in the western part of the state. The farmers had purchased land at inflated prices; in the depression that followed, they could not meet their obligations. When many were jailed, others retaliated by using force to close the courts. The insurrection climaxed with a vain attempt to seize weapons from an arsenal. Shortly thereafter, the militia crushed the uprising.

Shays' Rebellion was quelled only a few weeks before the delegates of the Constitutional Convention met at Philadelphia in 1787. The delegates, shaken by the violence, undoubtedly considered it a warning. Americans had preserved their liberty from destruction by the British; after the war, they were faced with the task of preserving it from destruction by themselves. The Articles of Confederation looked increasingly inadequate for that task.

Section Review

1. What was the greatest accomplishment in foreign affairs by the Confederation government?
2. What were the two most controversial provisions of the Land Ordinance of 1784?
3. According to the provisions of the Northwest Ordinance of 1787, what were the three steps a region went through in order to become a state?
4. What were the two serious domestic threats to the government's authority under the Articles of Confederation?

A New Charter

The failures and weakness of the Confederation government caused thoughtful men to consider what could be done. Trade discussions gave them an opportunity to voice their ideas. Representatives from Virginia and Maryland met in 1785 at Alexandria, Virginia, and at George Washington's home at Mount Vernon to discuss trade disputes involving the Potomac River. The Mount Vernon meeting was so profitable that the legislatures of Maryland and Virginia called for another trade convention in Annapolis, Maryland, which would include all thirteen states. The **Annapolis Convention** was not well attended; only five states bothered to send representatives. Alexander Hamilton, a delegate from New York, however, wrote a resolution for the convention calling for another convention to remedy the weaknesses of the Confederation government. Faced with growing discontent and fear of anarchy, the Confederation Congress, what Washington described as a "half-starved limping government," reluctantly seconded the idea of a convention in Philadelphia for May of 1787.

The Constitutional Convention

Heavy clouds rolled off the Delaware River and opened up as the delegates arrived for the opening session on May 25. The cool rain offered welcome relief from the already unbearably warm weather that had settled over the city. Old-timers would agree that it was the hottest summer in memory, and the arriving representatives, particularly those from New England in their heavy frock coats, were easily convinced.

Drenched and mud-spattered, the delegates met at the Pennsylvania State House, where eleven years earlier the Declaration of Independence had been signed, an event which lends the old State House its present name of Independence Hall. Despite the wet weather, the delegates' spirits were undampened. They were eager to get down to work and enthusiastic about the prospects of what could be accomplished. Virginian **James Madison,** whose ideas provided much of the framework for the Constitution, justifiably earning him the title "Father of the Constitution," declared with a little indulgence that

Charles Willson Peale's watercolor on ivory miniature portrays the young James Madison, whose political thought and skills earned him the title "the father of the Constitution."

their work would "settle forever the fate of republican government."

Thomas Jefferson, overseas at the time as Minister to France, called the men who arrived for the Philadelphia Convention "an assembly of demigods"; they were indeed a remarkable gathering of talent. Numbered among the fifty-five delegates were the best political thinkers and finest lawyers in America, well read and well educated. Their talents, however, were not simply the product of book learning. They were practical men of experience, many of them as skilled with the sword as they were with the pen. Half of them had fought in the Revolution. Thirty-nine had served in the Continental or Confederation congresses, which gave them a broad range of practical political experience from which to draw. Past, present, and future governors and two United States presidents were counted among them.

The Constitutional Convention was more than a gathering of talent, however; it was also a collection of regional and individual interests. In this

regard, the "demi-gods" tended to shed their halos. Twelve independent states (Rhode Island refused even to participate) were represented. These states, apart from war-time emergencies, had never been very neighborly. Diverse delegate interests, compounded by the hot Philadelphia summer, caused heated debates and threatened the survival of the convention. That these men represented their states' interests could hardly be considered a vice since they were in fact elected as *state representatives* to the convention. Happily, though, many of them had a larger, national vision of their work and were able to hammer out compromises that kept the convention, the Constitution, and the country on track.

The first order of business was to elect a convention president to chair the proceedings. George Washington, whose very presence gave credibility to the meeting, was unanimously elected by his fellow delegates. It is interesting that in the same room in which they were meeting, a tightly packed dozen years before, Washington had been elected commander in chief of the Continental army. He likely found his war experiences beneficial in overseeing the squabbles that quickly broke out at the convention.

Crucial Compromises

The most important question that the convention faced initially was why they were meeting. Were they there to revise the Articles in an attempt to breathe some life into the Confederation corpse, or were they to allow it to die and then start over? The delegates answered the question on May 30. Acting on a resolution by a delegate named Gouverneur Morris, they agreed overwhelmingly that "a national government ought to be established consisting of a supreme Legislative, Executive and Judiciary."

Having quickly answered this basic question, the delegates soon saw their harmony fractured over the details of how such a government should be formed. The disputes grew largely out of regional interests and would require compromises on three major issues: representation, slavery, and trade.

Representation—How the states were to be represented was surely the most difficult question that the delegates had to grapple with. The battle lines were drawn between the large states (such as Virginia, Pennsylvania, and New York) and the smaller states (New Jersey, Delaware, and Maryland).

James Madison had given a great deal of thought to the composition and structure of the new Congress. His thorough study of political thought, both ancient and modern, and his careful planning resulted in a proposal known as the **Virginia Plan,** which became the basis for much of the Constitution.

Madison's Virginia Plan, which was introduced to the convention by fellow Virginian Edmund Randolph, advocated a **bicameral,** or two-house, Congress, with the number of representatives based on state population. Members of the lower house, or House of Representatives, would be elected by direct popular vote. This lower house in turn would elect members of the upper house, or Senate, from nominees submitted by state legislatures.

In contrast to the powerless, penniless Confederation Congress, the legislature under the Virginia Plan was given greatly expanded powers. For example, the new Congress would be able to enforce its laws on the states and would also be empowered to elect both the chief executive and the national judiciary. These two branches, the executive and the judicial, could join together to veto congressional acts, although their veto could be overridden by a vote in both houses of Congress.

Since representation under the Virginia Plan was based on state population, it naturally favored the larger states. The smaller states were quick to react to this proposal, setting forth a scheme of their own known as the **New Jersey Plan.** This small-state plan, presented by William Paterson of New Jersey, advocated a unicameral Congress, similar to the Confederation Congress, with each state having only one vote regardless of its population or size of its delegation. Paterson's proposal was merely a throwback to the Articles presented by delegates suddenly nervous about where the Convention was leading them. John Dickinson, representing Delaware, chided the big-state advocates, "You see the consequences of pushing things too far."

The Convention deadlocked over the issue of representation. Dickinson conceded that "some of the members from the small States wish for two branches in the General Legislature and are friends to a good National Government." But he added, "We would sooner submit to a foreign power than submit to be deprived of an equality of suffrage in both branches of the Legislature, and thereby be thrown under the domination of the large states." While the small states feared domination by the large states, the large states feared the diminishing of their power through lack of representation, arguing that basic democratic principles favored proportional representation. In short, the New Jersey Plan advocated a one-state, one-vote principle while the Virginia Plan advocated a one-man, one-vote principle.

The haggling went on for weeks as hot weather and hotter debates threatened the survival of the convention. The windows were raised at times in hopes of drawing a breeze, but they usually drew only unwelcome flies and fumes–sewer construction was underway in the streets outside the State House. Irritated delegates adjusted their sweaty collars but not their positions. Some threatened to go home.

Roger Sherman of Connecticut offered the embroiled assembly a solution to their dead-end debating. Sherman, a believer with an unwavering testimony for Christ, whom John Adams referred to as "that old Puritan, honest as an angel," put together a compromise that narrowly salvaged both the convention and the Constitution. The **Great Compromise,** or **Connecticut Compromise,** proposed that representation in the lower house be based on state population, whereas representation in the Senate be equal for all states regardless of size. "A motley measure," Alexander Hamilton sniffed; but Sherman's proposal was a classic example of political compromise: both sides gave and both sides got, and the convention continued.

Slavery–The next divisive issue that confronted the delegates of the Constitutional Convention was whether slaves should be counted in determining representation for slave-holding states. Delegates from those states, of course, said yes;

A compromise eventually eliminated slave importation.

whereas those from states that did not have slaves said no. Though slavery was predominantly in the agrarian South, it was not confined to that region. (Pennsylvania, for example, had several thousand slaves at the time.)

Many of the delegates were opposed to the institution of slavery itself, but the convention was not meeting to settle the moral issue of slavery; they were meeting to draw up a plan for a national government in which slavery was a thorny political question. Oliver Ellsworth of Connecticut reminded his fellow delegates that "the morality or wisdom of slavery are considerations belonging to the States themselves. . . . The States are the best judges of their particular interest." George Mason of Virginia countered, "Every master of slaves is born a petty tyrant. They bring the judgment of heaven on a Country." It would, however, be left to the children and grandchildren of the constitutional framers to resolve the slave question. For now, a numerical compromise known as the **Three-Fifths Compromise** was reached. Under this settlement, slaves would count as three-fifths of a person for purposes of representation in the House of Representatives, but slave states would also have to pay taxes on them at the same rate.

Trade—Part of the motivation behind calling the Philadelphia Convention was the failure of the Confederation to resolve interstate trade disputes and direct international trade. Although most delegates agreed that Congress needed to have a role in commerce, regional interests kept them at odds over the extent of that role. The South in particular was concerned that the new Congress would ban the slave trade and raise revenue through export duties that would hurt its economy, which was de-

pendent on the export of raw goods such as rice, cotton, timber, and tobacco.

A compromise, however, settled the issue. By the terms of the agreement, Congress was given power over foreign and interstate commerce. However, the legislature was forbidden to impose any export taxes on the states or to halt the slave trade for twenty years.

Constitutional Principles

Despite disputes over details, the constitutional framers agreed on certain basic principles that they incorporated into their charter. These principles have given the Constitution and the government it outlined remarkable durability.

Many of the constitutional principles grew out of the founders' clear-eyed view of human nature. They recognized that men, both the governed and the governors, are inherently sinful. As John Adams pointed out, "Whoever would found a state, and make proper laws for the government of it, must presume that all men are bad by nature."

This is not to say that the Constitution is a "Christian" document any more than its framers were all Christians. Some were godly men, some were God-fearing men, and some were neither. But what is quite clear is that the Constitution was written in a society in which Biblical principles were pervasive, and the document can be best understood only in that light. These principles are not spelled out in the fine print, but they plainly contribute to the fabric of the charter.

The key principles of our Constitution center on the issue of power–how to divide, balance, limit, and allot governmental power in view of man's corrupting tendencies. James Madison underscored this point when he wrote,

What is government itself, but the greatest of all reflections on human nature. *If men were angels, no government would be necessary. If angels were to govern men, neither external nor internal controls on government would be necessary. In framing a government which is to be administered by men over men, the great difficulty lies in this: you must first enable the government to control the governed; and in the next place oblige it to control itself.*

Striking a balance between liberty and order was the great challenge and triumph of the Constitutional Convention.

Limited Government—The underlying theme of the Constitution is **limited government.** The nation had only recently shaken off British tyranny through a long and bloody war; so the Philadelphia delegates fully understood the consequences of unlimited government—the very definition of tyranny.

The principle of limited government is expressed by the fact that ours is a *written* constitution, the first and oldest in continuous use. Unlike the unwritten British constitution, an open-ended accumulation of laws and traditions continuously subject to Parliament, a written charter more clearly defined the limits of governmental power and therefore the scope of individual liberty. In addition the principles of separation of powers and checks and balances also contribute to the limitations on state power.

Separation of Powers—In order to prevent any group or individual from gaining too much power, the national government was designed with the **separation of powers** in mind, the division of the government into three separate branches: the legislative branch, dealt with in Article I of the Constitution; the executive branch, outlined in Article II; and the judicial branch, explained in Article III. In broad terms, under our Constitution, Congress makes the laws, the president executes and enforces the laws, and the courts interpret the laws.

Though these branches are separate, they are not independent. In many areas their responsibilities intersect, and a certain amount of cooperation is necessary to make the national government work effectively.

Checks and Balances—Although separation of powers is often thought to be synonymous with **checks and balances,** there is an important difference. If power were only divided, then one branch could expand its powers within its rightful sphere and come to dominate the other branches.

The principle of checks and balances thwarts such an accumulation of power by establishing a balance of power among the three branches. For example, Congress passes a bill to become law, but the president may reject or veto the bill if he opposes it. However, his veto may in turn be overridden by a two-thirds vote in both houses of Congress. For its part, the Supreme Court may nullify acts of both Congress and the president if a majority of justices interprets a law as unconstitutional.

Federalism—**Federalism** is the division of power between national and state levels of government. The federal system was a unique contribution and was a product of American historical and political realities.

Thirteen separate, sovereign states with differing political and social backgrounds had emerged from the colonial and revolutionary periods. These fiercely independent states had no intention of giving up their political power. The delegates, though representing their regional interests, also recognized the need for the strength and order of national unity. The federal system struck a crucial balance between state and national demands. In addition, federalism provides needed flexibility in a large country of varying regions by giving citizens a greater voice in their affairs at the state and local level.

Popular Sovereignty—**Popular sovereignty,** the idea that the ultimate source of governmental power is vested in the people, is a constitutional principle evident in several areas. The **Preamble,** which introduced the charter with a full and flourishing sentence, reads:

> *We the people* of the United States, in order to form a more perfect union, establish justice, ensure domestic tranquillity, provide for the common defense, promote the general welfare, and secure the blessings of liberty to ourselves and our posterity, do ordain and establish this Constitution for the United States of America.

Despite the dramatic "We the people," the Constitution was actually formed by the agreement of states, not individuals, its approval being subject to state conventions, not a national referendum.

The principle of popular sovereignty is best expressed in the Constitution through its representation and amendment provisions. Representation allows the people to have a voice in their republican government through their elected officials. The constitutional framers, fearing the fickleness of public opinion, sought to limit the directness of the people's voice on the national level by providing direct election only for the House of Representatives.

The president and senators, by contrast, were elected indirectly by the people. Senators, for example, were initially elected by their respective state legislatures rather than by a straight vote from their constituents. Likewise, the president is elected through the indirect means of the **electoral college.** Under this constitutional provision (Article II, Section 1), each state has a number of electors equal to the state's representation in Congress. In general, all the electoral votes from a state go to the presidential candidate who receives the majority of popular votes from that state.

Constitutional **amendments,** changes in or additions to the Constitution, are also an expression of the people's sovereignty because those amendments that survive the difficult ratification process often reflect widespread popular support and are superior to the laws of Congress, the actions of the president, and the judgment of the courts. Chief Justice Marshall stated this point powerfully: "The people made the Constitution and the people can unmake it. It is the creature of their own will, and lives only by their will."

"We the people" is an enduring declaration not only of the people's power to rule themselves but also of the people's responsibility for that rule. Self-government is no easy task. It does not occur by accident, nor is it a self-propelled machine. The members of each generation must grapple with *their* government—use its principles and cherish its freedoms in order to make it work for their day and the next.

Section Review

1. How did the Constitutional Convention reach a compromise on the issue of representation?
2. What compromise allowed the convention to settle the problem of slavery in relation to taxation and representation?
3. Between what two qualities did the Constitutional Convention seek a balance?
4. What are the five principles of government contained in the American Constitution?

The Struggle for Ratification

On September 17, 1787, after a summer-long session of Constitution-making, Washington offered the final draft of the new charter to the convention to sign and forward to the Confederation Congress and from them to the states for their consent.

Eighty-one-year-old Benjamin Franklin, his frail body bowed with pain from gout and kidney stones, gave a written address to a colleague to read in hopes of swaying undecided delegates to sign. Franklin acknowledged, "I confess that there are several parts of this constitution which I do not at present approve, but I am not sure I shall never approve them: For having lived long, I have experienced many instances of being obliged by better information or fuller consideration, to change opinions even on important subjects. . . . Thus I consent, Sir, to this Constitution because I expect no better, and because I am not sure, that it is not the best." Edmund Randolph, George Mason, and Elbridge Gerry of Massachusetts objected to the expanded powers of the national government and the absence of a Bill of Rights. Mason adamantly declared that he "would sooner chop off his right hand than put it to the Constitution" because of its failure to guarantee civil liberties. Such objections foreshadowed a difficult ratification fight ahead in which the approval of at least nine states was required by Article VII of the Constitution.

After the signing and a celebration supper, the delegates parted company. Their work would now be scrutinized by the nation, and the greatest hurdles lay before them. The Constitution-makers had put forth a remarkable effort, but privately some of them worried about ratification because the stakes were so high. Washington wrote, "This or a dissolution of the Union awaits our choice." Yet he concluded, "The event is in the hand of God."

War of Words

Two days after the delegates went home, the text of the Constitution was first published in the Philadelphia daily, the *Pennsylvania Packet.* For the first time Americans learned what had been devised behind the closed doors of the Pennsylvania State House, and not everyone was pleased. The battle lines were drawn between those favoring the Constitution, who took the name **Federalists,** and their opposition, whom the Federalists dubbed the **Anti-Federalists.**

Just one week after the text was published, a New York newspaper denounced the Constitution in an article penned under the pseudonym **"Cato."** Cato was in fact the governor of the state, George Clinton. He was soon joined by "Sidney" and "Brutus" in a series of Anti-Federalist articles.

Alexander Hamilton, the lone New York delegate who had supported and signed the Constitution, returned home to find the political winds blowing against the new ship of state. He responded to the Anti-Federalist articles with some of his own under the pen name **"Publius."** Hamilton also enlisted the help of James Madison and John Jay in this war of words. Together the trio wrote eighty-five essays that were well reasoned and widely read throughout the country.

The essays were compiled and published in two volumes in May 1788 under the title ***The Federalist.***

This work, also known as *The Federalist Papers,* answered Anti-Federalist objections by carefully explaining and forcefully defending constitutional provisions of power and predicting dangers and dismemberment for the nation if the Constitution were rejected.

The Federalist was to ratification what *Common Sense* had been to the Revolution. It was a persuasive force, particularly in those states where ratification lay in the balance. But *The Federalist* is much more than a yellowed best seller; it is a comprehensive commentary on republican government. Jefferson praised it as "the best commentary on the principles of government which has ever been written." Clinton Rossiter perhaps best explained the universality of *The Federalist* when he wrote that the essays are

> now valued not merely as a clever defense of a particular charter, but as an exposition of certain timeless truths about constitutional government. . . . The message of *The Federalist* reads: no happiness without liberty, no liberty without self-government, no self-government

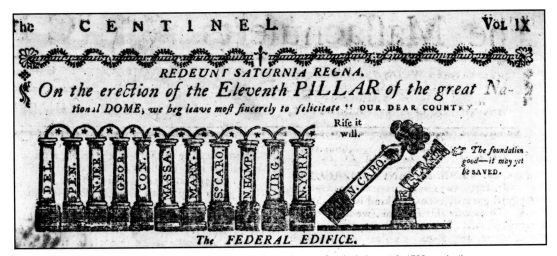

The CENTINEL. Vol. IX

REDEUNT SATURNIA REGNA.

On the erection of the Eleventh PILLAR of the great National DOME, we beg leave most sincerely to felicitate " OUR DEAR COUNTRY."

Rise it will.

The foundation good—it may yet be SAVED.

The FEDERAL EDIFICE.

This allegorical cartoon from the pro-Federalist newspaper Massachusetts Centinel, August 2, 1788, *marks the addition of New York to the ratifying states and holds out hope for the reluctant Tarheels and the recalcitrant Rhode Islanders.*

	Chronology of the Constitutional Convention, 1787
May 14-24	Preliminary meetings
May 25-28	Organization
May 29	Proposal of Randolph (Virginia) Plan and Pinckney Plan
June 15	The Paterson (New Jersey) Plan; revolt of the "small state" delegations
June 15-30	Two weeks of debate over the two plans
June 30	The Compromise Committee is appointed
July 5	Report of the Compromise Committee proposing popular representation in the lower house, equal representation in the upper, and origin of all money bills in the lower house
July 16	Compromise adopted
August 15-23	Debate on the powers of Congress (Article I, Sections 8 and 9)
August 24-25	Debate on the powers of the president
August 29	The "three-fifths" clause; the slave trade; and the commerce clause
September 12	Report of the Committee of Style
September 17	Signing of the Constitution and adjournment

	Chronology of the Ratification of the Constitution
Delaware	Thirty members ratified unanimously, December 7, 1787
Pennsylvania	Ratified by a vote of 46 to 23, December 18, 1787
New Jersey	Thirty-nine delegates ratified unanimously, December 18, 1787
Georgia	Twenty-six delegates ratified unanimously, January 2, 1788
Connecticut	Ratified by a vote of 128 to 40, January 9, 1788
Massachusetts	Ratified by a vote of 186 to 168, February 16, 1788
Maryland	Ratified by a vote of 63 to 11, April 26, 1788
South Carolina	Ratified by a vote of 149 to 73, May 23, 1788
New Hampshire	Ratified by a vote of 57 to 47, June 21, 1788
Virginia	Ratified by a vote of 89 to 79, June 25, 1788
New York	Ratified by a vote of 30 to 27, July 26, 1788
North Carolina	Rejected, 193 to 75, August 4, 1788; finally ratified, November 21, 1789
Rhode Island	Ratified by a vote of 34 to 22, May 29, 1790

without constitutionalism, no constitutionalism without morality–and none of these great goods without stability and order.

Thirteen Battles

Delaware led the states by giving the Constitution its unanimous consent on December 7, 1787. Within a month four more states–Pennsylvania, New Jersey, Georgia, and Connecticut–easily ratified the Constitution with lopsided victories. The toughest battles, however, lay ahead in Massachusetts, Virginia, and New York, where the Anti-Federalists were better organized and had leaders of considerable stature numbered among their ranks.

Massachusetts approved in a close vote in February 1788 after the Federalists gained the support of John Hancock and Samuel Adams. Three more states–Maryland, South Carolina, and New Hampshire–joined the six ratifying states to make the nine necessary for the Constitution to become law. The letter of the law, however, was not enough. Practically speaking, any hopes for a national union

had to include both Virginia, the largest state, and New York. If New York failed to ratify, then New England would be cut off geographically from the rest of the country. If Virginia refused to join, then the South would be severed.

The Anti-Federalists of Virginia were led by the fiery orator Patrick Henry and nonsigning Constitutional Convention delegates George Mason and Governor Edmund Randolph. The objections of this Anti-Federalist trio represented legitimate concerns: fear of consolidated political power in an overarching national government and the absence of guarantees of personal liberty in a Bill of Rights. It must be pointed out that the Federalists were not opposed to personal liberty; rather most viewed a Bill of Rights as unnecessary or even too restrictive by limiting rights to a written list. The Federalists also feared that the attempt to compose a Bill of Rights prior to ratification would derail the Constitution and with it the necessary precondition for such freedoms–national order. After James Madison promised to introduce amendments for a Bill

Precedent Washington

"Some achieve greatness, and some have greatness thrust upon them," Shakespeare wrote. The same could be said about Washington and the presidency, although in his case both would be true. He had the office thrust upon him, but he also made the office in his own image.

Other men have had the presidency thrust upon them, and aside from that fact we would likely never have heard of such White House occupants as Millard Fillmore or Chester Arthur. Washington, however, made the mold that he and his successors filled. Washington wanted the office to be dignified but not ostentatious, strong but not oppressive. In all this he was simply reflecting his own character, not filling a job description. He was also extremely conscious that his every public action would later be interpreted as a precedent. He, therefore, walked circumspectly.

There was, however, a man behind the marble image. He felt aches and pains. Shortly after the fifty-seven-year-old Washington was sworn in as president, he was diagnosed as having a cancerous tumor on his thigh. While recovering from crude but successful surgery, the nearly toothless president was fitted with a new set of dentures made from hippopotamus tusk and pink sealing wax. He fretted as any normal person would over the myriad problems of the new government. The reins of power that Washington was given encompassed an enormous debt, a seven-hundred-man army, no navy, and the constant challenges of new nationhood. Of course, he had weathered Valley Forge and bested the best in battle; so he and adversity were old friends.

George Washington was not a perfect man, but he provides an enduring example of how a man's character—what he is—shapes what he does. And in Washington's case his integrity shaped the dimensions of the presidency and the direction of the nation.

George Washington, *Landsdowne portrait, United States Capitol Collection*

of Rights in the first session of Congress, the Virginia Federalists won a narrow victory for ratification, 89 to 79.

Madison's concession was the tie breaker in Virginia and a catalyst for the final great state battle raging in New York. There Governor Clinton and his Anti-Federalists forces commanded a decisive majority against backers of the Constitution, led by Alexander Hamilton. News of the Anti-Federalist collapse in Virginia struck a fatal blow to Clinton's edge. By a slim margin of 30 to 27, New York ratified. North Carolina and the little state that Federalists scorned as "Rogue Island" held out for some time, but no one else seemed to care too much. Elections for the new Congress were set and the opening session was scheduled for March 4, 1789, at the temporary national capital, New York City.

Old Ben Franklin wrote with satisfaction, "Our Constitution is in actual operation, everything appears to promise that it will last, but," he added, sounding somewhat like Poor Richard, "in this world nothing is certain but death and taxes."

A Rising Sun

The office of chief executive was one of the most significant and least controversial departures from the old Confederation government. The explanation for such smooth passage among the deliberative framers of the Constitution occupied the president's chair at the Convention. George Washington, "first in war, first in peace, and first in the hearts of his countrymen," was the natural choice for the nation's highest office.

On February 4, 1789, Washington was unanimously elected president by the electoral college. His old Massachusetts ally, John Adams, was elected as the first vice president. Washington's triumphal journey from Mount Vernon to New York City for his inauguration was a swirl of speeches, suppers, and small-town serenades. The road to New York was lined with fathers and mothers hoisting up their puzzled children for a glimpse of the great man; and hands, thousands of hands, out-

stretched to touch the hero. The modest Washington was taken aback by his welcoming and privately admitted that he felt more like "a culprit who is going to his place of execution."

Washington also felt the weight of responsibility growing as he approached his inauguration. He observed, "The preservation of the sacred fire of liberty and the destiny of the republican model of government are justly considered as *deeply,* perhaps as *finally,* staked on the experiment entrusted to the hands of the American people."

On April 30, 1789, from the balcony of New York's Federal Hall on Wall Street, the great Virginian placed his hand on the Bible and promised to preserve, protect, and defend the Constitution, adding, "So help me God." With that, President Washington kissed the Bible as the city erupted with bells and booming cannons.

Washington's inauguration marked both an end and a beginning. It was the conclusion of the long struggle for liberty and self-government begun in the 1770s, and it was a *national* beginning. Benjamin Franklin summed up this sense of beginning in 1787. While the delegates were signing the Constitution, Madison recorded that

> Dr. Franklin, looking towards the president's chair, at the back of which a rising sun happened to be painted, observed to a few members near him, that painters had found it difficult to distinguish in their art a rising from a setting sun. I have, said he, often and often during the course of the session looked at that behind the president without being able to tell whether it was rising or setting: But now at length I have the happiness to know that it is a rising not a setting sun.

Section Review

1. Why did Edmund Randolph, George Mason, and Elbridge Gerry oppose the Constitution?
2. Who were "Cato" and "Publius"?
3. How did James Madison win approval for the Constitution in Virginia?

Chapter Review

Terms

confederation
Articles of Confederation
unicameral
Treaty of Paris
Northwest Territory
Ordinance of 1784
Land Ordinance of 1785
Northwest Ordinance of 1787
hard money
Continental dollars
Newburgh Conspiracy
Shays' Rebellion
Annapolis Convention
Constitutional Convention (1787)
James Madison
Virginia Plan
bicameral
New Jersey Plan
Roger Sherman
Great Compromise (Connecticut Compromise)
Three-Fifths Compromise
limited government
separation of powers
checks and balances
federalism
popular sovereignty
Preamble
electoral college
amendments
Federalists
Anti-Federalists
"Cato"
"Publius"
The Federalist
ratification of the Constitution (1788)

Content Questions

1. What were at least four of the weaknesses of the Confederation government?
2. Name at least two means that the Confederation government used in order to raise funds.
3. Which two provisions of Jefferson's Ordinance of 1784 were eventually enacted? Which two provisions were not adopted?
4. List the three major issues on which the Constitutional Convention had to compromise.
5. What basic Biblical principle concerning human nature did the framers of the Constitution recognize in writing that document?
6. How are constitutional amendments an expression of the people's sovereignty?
7. What two major states did most supporters of the Constitution believe would need to ratify the document in order for the new government to succeed, even though the necessary minimum of nine states had already ratified?

Application Questions

1. How do you think the failure of the Articles might have contributed to the Constitution's success?
2. What do you think would have happened had Washington assented to the wishes of the Newburgh conspirators?
3. Which of the five major constitutional principles do you think is most important? Why?
4. If there had been no Connecticut Compromise, which would have been better for the United States: the Virginia Plan or the New Jersey Plan? Why?

CHAPTER 8

The Federalist Years (1789-1801)

"We are not to expect to be translated from despotism to liberty in a featherbed."

Thomas Jefferson *in a letter to Lafayette*, 1790

Boston Harbor From Constitution Wharf, *by Robert Salmon, U.S. Naval Academy Museum*

Franklin's rising sun, after a rosy but brief dawn, shone across a rugged political landscape. Throughout the 1790s the fledgling republic weathered one storm after another; some blew in from Europe, others from the backcountry, and some from the halls of power.

These difficulties, not unlike those the country endured in the previous decade, had a completely different result, however. Rather than weakening the national government, they strengthened it. The Constitution proved to be a practical and powerful instrument. Despite the growing pains, the Federalist years were formative ones in which personal liberties were defended, national supremacy demonstrated, and political parties developed. The nationalist character of Federalism, so evident throughout

the decade, would not grow unchecked, however. Forces for decentralization and limited government would blunt the nationalist thrust, sparking controversy and conflict.

Launching the New Government

Getting Started

The first order of business in 1789 was to organize the new government in accordance with the new Constitution.

Cabinet—With congressional approval, President **George Washington** organized three departments in the executive branch–State, Treasury, and War–and appointed their secretaries, or chiefs.

George Washington's leadership was a crucial factor in the success of the new republic. Portrait by Gilbert Stuart, unknown source.

Thomas Jefferson, recently returned from a five-year stint as Minister to France, headed the Department of State. Washington's wartime aide, the brilliant, ambitious, and thoroughly capable **Alexander Hamilton,** became Secretary of the Treasury; and the three-hundred-pound Henry Knox of Revolutionary War fame rounded out the first cabinet as head of the War Department. In addition, Washington appointed fellow Virginian and former governor Edmund Randolph as Attorney General to provide legal counsel for his administration.

Although the term *cabinet* was not in the Constitution nor even in Washington's vocabulary in the sense of an advisory body, these department heads regularly met with the president to discuss policy decisions. Eventually this group of advisors would take on the collective name ''cabinet'' and play a key role in the first and future administrations.

Courts—The constitutional blueprint provided directly only for a Supreme Court but permitted Congress to establish lower federal courts. As a result, Congress passed the **Judiciary Act of 1789,** which organized thirteen district courts, one for each of the states, established three Circuit Courts to handle appeals, and set the number of Supreme Court justices at six. John Jay was appointed to fill the Court's chief justice position.

Despite constitutional provisions and a working system of federal courts, the Supreme Court actually mustered little power or respect during its first few years. In fact, adding insult to injury, when the national government moved to its permanent capital of Washington in 1800, planners forgot to provide a place for the third branch of government. The president had his executive mansion, Congress met in the Capitol, and the Supreme Court justices also met in the Capitol building–in the basement.

One significant section of the Judiciary Act of 1789 would have a powerful ramification in the future. It provided that state court decisions could be appealed to the federal court level if constitutional questions were involved. This little provision clearly declared the supremacy of the federal courts over the states and easily passed the predominantly nationalist Congress. Many of the Anti-Federalists leaders had become disgruntled after ratification losses and had not run for Congress. As a result, there was no significant bloc of states' rights advocates in the First Congress to thwart such nationalist legislation.

Congress—The First Congress accomplished more than any of its successors. During this remark-

Alexander Hamilton, *by John Trumbull, National Portrait Gallery, Smithsonian Institution*

able two-year session from 1789 to 1791, the Bill of Rights was drafted, the executive and judicial branches were organized, and a number of crucial measures were passed to put the country on a sound financial footing. These achievements seem all the more outstanding considering that the First Congress was breaking new ground. **James Madison,** a leader in the House of Representatives, observed, ''We are in a wilderness without a single footstep to guide. Our successors will have an easier task.''

In addition to the landmark legislation passed during the original session, the congressmen also grappled with an issue that still has a familiar ring to it: How to resolve a huge national debt problem without raising taxes. They also frittered away time over issues of pomp and protocol in search of a republican balance between respectability and regality. On what to call the president, for example, John Adams favored ''His Highness, the President of the United States and Protector of Rights of the same.'' Fortunately this breathtaking title was shelved in favor of a simple ''Mr. President.''

The First Congress also approved a salary for themselves, a whopping six dollars a day, which raised immediate howls from constituents over congressional self-indulgence. Yet considering what they were able to accomplish so quickly, particularly in drafting what would become the first ten amendments to the Constitution, their salary was a bargain.

Bill of Rights

In the summer of 1789, James Madison honored his pledge to his Anti-Federalist adversaries when he introduced amendments to the Constitution to protect individual rights. What emerged in 1791, after gaining the approval of three-fourths of the states, was the first ten amendments–the **Bill of Rights.**

The first and most fundamental of these amendments protects the freedoms of conscience and expression, specifically freedoms of religion, speech, press, assembly, and petition. The second, third, and fourth amendments protect the security rights of the individual by guaranteeing the right to bear arms, prohibiting the forced quartering of troops in private homes during peacetime, and restricting un-

reasonable searches and seizures. The fifth, sixth, seventh, and eighth amendments guarantee fair judicial procedures for the accused. The ninth and tenth amendments place further restrictions on the extent of national power by limiting its scope to constitutional bounds and by guaranteeing that freedoms not specified in the Bill of Rights nor restricted by the states belong to the people. In the words of the Tenth Amendment:

> The powers not delegated to the United States by the Constitution, nor prohibited by it to the states, are reserved to the states respectively, or to the people.

The Bill of Rights was specifically intended to restrict the power of the *national* government. For example, the First Amendment clearly states that ''*Congress* shall make no law respecting an establishment of religion''; yet in Massachusetts taxes were levied to support state churches as late as 1833. Not until the twentieth century did the Supreme Court place most of the Bill of Rights restrictions on the states, in an effort to expand national authority.

Hamilton's Plans

War debts and nearly a decade of neglect had left the country's finances in shambles. One of the greatest challenges of the 1790s was to put America's economic house in order before the walls came tumbling down. Fortunately the first Secretary of the Treasury was a man whose ideas, imagination, and energy were equal to the challenge.

Alexander Hamilton's early life gave little indication of his destiny to be, as one historian put it, ''the greatest administrative genius in America, and one of the greatest administrators of all time.'' Born out of wedlock on the Caribbean island of Nevis, Hamilton was abandoned by his father and orphaned at thirteen when his mother died. Never one to let difficulties keep him down, he managed with the help of some friends to gain admission to King's College in New York (now Columbia University) when he was seventeen. He later became Washington's chief of staff during the war and distinguished himself by his cool bravery at Yorktown.

Hamilton, having grown up in the West Indies, had none of the regional attachments that characterized many of the Founding Fathers. He viewed himself as an American first and last, not as a New Yorker or a Northerner. While his background fueled his nationalist zeal, it also made it difficult for him to appreciate the sectional sympathies that were such a delicate and sometimes volatile aspect of American politics.

Hamilton was a key figure in setting the course of the young republic. He had been instrumental in calling the Constitutional Convention in 1787, and his appointment as Secretary of the Treasury at the age of thirty-two placed him in a powerful policy-making role. In four influential reports issued to Congress in 1790 and 1791, Hamilton outlined plans for the lawmakers to resolve the nation's debt problem, establishing a national bank and national mint, and encouraging manufacturing and economic expansion. With the exception of his pro-business *Report on Manufactures,* which was too advanced for the agrarian America of that day, Hamilton's proposals were all shaped into law.

Report on Public Credit—Perhaps the most important of Hamilton's proposals was his first, the *Report on Public Credit,* which held that for the sake of national pride and future credit, government debt, both national and state, had to be paid. His ambitious plan consisted of two major aspects: **funding** and **assumption.**

Debt funding proposed that the federal government give bonds paying six per cent interest to those to whom the Continental Congress owed money for goods or military services provided during the war. The bonds were to be recognized as currency, a procedure called "monetizing the debt"–turning it into money. Despite the enormity of the debt for that day, over $77 million, Hamilton's funding plan cleared Congress rather easily.

Assumption–taking over all state debts by the national government–had a rougher passage through Congress. Most of the Southern states had faithfully paid off their debts, while the New England states were delinquent, a factor which made assumption inherently unfair as well as a brewing sectional issue. Virginian James Madison, a leader in the House of Representatives, broke with his old friend Hamilton by taking a firm stand against the assumption plan. The legislative stalemate was broken only by a major compromise that still leaves its mark on the map. The site for a permanent national capital, known as Federal City, had not been determined. Through a mediation meeting arranged by Jefferson, Hamilton promised to get sufficient Northern votes to locate Federal City in the South, on the banks of the Potomac River, in return for Southern votes on assumption. The deal was struck, and Washington himself chose the site of the capital that would one day bear his name. The new capital was set to be occupied in ten years; in the meantime Philadelphia would serve as the temporary capital during the transition.

National Bank—Having dealt with the problem of past debts, Hamilton looked to the future in his second report. He proposed the formation of a national bank, which he saw as the centerpiece of a sound, strong economy. A national bank would issue a uniform currency, and its branches throughout the country would provide a source for business loans, a spur to economic expansion.

The bill for a national bank with a twenty-year charter cleared Congress, but by the time it reached the president's desk for him to sign it into law, Madison in the House of Representatives and Jefferson in the cabinet were challenging the constitutionality of a national bank.

This was the opening round of what would be a continuing controversy over constitutional interpretation. The constitutional framers produced a brief document that provided a sturdy framework but left many areas open to interpretation. A detailed, lengthy Constitution would have quickly grown outdated because its writers in 1787 could not possibly anticipate the kinds of problems the nation would face in 1887, much less in 1987 and beyond. They wisely chose to draft a firm but flexible charter. *How much* flexibility was the thorny question. Those who advocated more flexibility on a given issue were called **loose constructionists;** those who held to a closer reading of the constitutional text were known as **strict constructionists.**

Congress had no specific authority to charter a national bank. Jefferson argued that "to take a single step beyond the boundaries thus specially

First Bank of the United States, Philadelphia

drawn around the power of Congress is to take possession of a boundless field of power.'' President Washington, concerned over the questions of constitutionality raised by Jefferson and Madison, asked Hamilton to present his side of the debate.

Hamilton was surprised by this apparent Achilles' heel in his bank bill exposed by Jefferson and Madison. After several days of thought and writing, Hamilton presented the chief executive with what has become the standard justification for expanded constitutional interpretation. Hamilton wrote,

> If the *end* be clearly comprehended within any of the specified powers, collecting taxes and regulating the currency, and if the measure have an obvious relation to that *end,* and is not forbidden by any particular provision of the Constitution, it may safely be deemed to come within the compass of the national authority.

It is interesting that the heart of Hamilton's constitutional interpretation, that specified ends justify unspecified means, was drawn from one of the *Federalist Papers* written three years earlier by his opponent James Madison.

Washington was persuaded by Hamilton's convincing nationalist argument and signed the bill into law, creating the first **National Bank** as well as the first serious rift in his own administration.

Section Review

1. What three executive departments did Washington organize after taking office? Whom did he appoint to head each department?
2. Why was Massachusetts able to continue supporting an established church years after the passage of the First Amendment?
3. Name and describe the two major points of Hamilton's *Report on Public Credit.*
4. What two benefits did Alexander Hamilton believe a national bank would bring to the United States?
5. What is the difference between a ''strict constructionist'' and a ''loose constructionist''?

Emerging Political Parties

Political parties or factions were not unknown to the Founding Fathers, but they were unwelcome. Political parties in Europe smacked of intrigue, conspiracy, and hostile division, and the founders feared that parties in America would rip the Union apart. They hoped rather that in free elections the best men, like cream, would rise to the top. This is why in presidential elections, before the growth of parties necessitated an amendment (the Twelfth Amendment), the candidate receiving the most electoral votes would be president, the second-place finisher vice president; the founders assumed leaders would act in the public not the party interest. While the idea was noble, it was also unrealistic.

America had always been a land of diverse interests: Southerner and Northerner, farmer and merchant, coastal planter and backwater bumpkin. And in a society where the freedoms of speech, assembly, and petition enjoyed constitutional protection, parties were inevitable. In addition the party spirit was already evident in the ratification battles in which the Constitution itself drove a wedge between Federalists and Anti-Federalists.

During the 1790s, two groups emerged in opposition to each other: the **Federalists,** who claimed to be the true keepers of the constitutional flame, and the **Republicans,** or **Democratic-Republicans,** who glowingly viewed themselves as the last line of defense between Federalist "tyranny" and American liberty. During this fluid stage of party development, the labels varied considerably. Federalists might be called "Hamiltonians" or something less flattering, such as "Monarchists," if the Republicans were doing the labeling. Democratic-Republicans were called "Jeffersonians" or even "Madisonians," but they generally referred to themselves as Republicans, although they were no relation to the modern party of that name.

For his part, Washington deplored political parties. He embodied the nonpartisan attitude to public office that had been the founders' ideal. His dismay, therefore, was profound when he discovered that the political fault line which would shake up the government was in his own cabinet.

Cabinet Conflicts

While James Madison was leading the opposition in Congress to Hamilton's treasury program, Thomas Jefferson was leading the opposition within the executive branch. Madison was clearly the founder of the anti-Hamilton party that called themselves Republicans, but Hamilton's clashes with Jefferson within the administration tended to place the focus on Jefferson as the leader of the opposition.

It has been said that the only thing that Hamilton and Jefferson had in common was their hatred for each other. Although this overstates the issue, the two men's backgrounds and personalities almost destined them to clash. Hamilton had risen from poverty to power by his energy and intelligence. Jefferson was a Virginia planter living on an inherited estate. Hamilton was emotionally reserved, while Jefferson tended to wear his feelings on his sleeve, particularly in letters to Washington. Jefferson viewed Hamilton as an evil genius bent on perverting the republic into a monarchy. Hamilton viewed Jefferson as a meddler, a sower of dissent who would destroy national unity. Hamilton had intense focus; Jefferson had diverse interests. Jefferson was a man of letters; Hamilton was a man of ledgers. One historian has observed that "Hamilton feared anarchy and loved order, Jefferson feared tyranny and loved liberty."

The personality clash between Hamilton and Jefferson, however, tends to overshadow the larger issues involved in the development of a two-party system in America. Jefferson's Republican party and Hamilton's Federalist party had two essentially different views of America that reflected regional and economic differences that were as old as the country. The Republican party was the friend of the farmer, and in preindustrial America this meant it had a lot of friends. The Jeffersonians distrusted centralized government and feared urban growth. Cities, they believed, were centers of vice and depositories of filthy lucre that would stain the national character. Accordingly, the key to America's future was its two great resources: its land and its people–connected by a plow.

Federalists believed that America's future was in commerce and industry, and their experiences during the Confederation period had taught them that economic growth could occur only under a strong national government. This does not mean that Federalists were motivated by financial gain. They believed, though, that power placed in the hands of a propertied, moneyed class would provide the country with a stable, conservative government.

The "spirit of party" growing within the government alarmed President Washington. He had hoped to retire to his beloved Mount Vernon. But with the election of 1792 looming, he was urged on all sides to run again. Everyone in the cabinet and the Congress and, above all, across the nation knew that no one could hold the fledgling nation together like Washington. Jefferson reminded him that "North and South will hang together if they have you to hang on."

Reluctantly the old general accepted the call, for the sake of the nation, and was unanimously re-elected. For Washington the second term would be a difficult one, both personally and politically, but for the nation, his continuing leadership was crucial. Ill winds blowing from Europe were stirring a tempest in this country, and America would need a steady hand at the helm.

Foreign Feuds

The **French Revolution** broke out in 1789, just months after America inaugurated its new constitutional government. Most Americans welcomed the news from their old ally. The French, they believed, were following the path to independence that America had pioneered. By 1792, however, it was clear that there was a decided fork in the revolutionary road. The seemingly insatiable bloodthirst of the topsy-turvy French government, which led to the beheading of King Louis XVI and the Reign of Terror, cooled much of the pro-French fever in America.

When France declared war on Britain in 1793, America met its first foreign policy crisis. According to the 1778 Treaty of Alliance, America was obligated to come to the aid of France during wartime. Should the United States honor the treaty and take up the French cause against their old nemesis, Britain? It was quickly argued that the French treaty had been made with a government and king that had been destroyed by the revolutionary regime. The United States was therefore under no obligation to go to war for France. This was hardly the end of the issue, however.

Many Republicans favored a pro-French trade policy, while Federalists were decidedly pro-British. Besides being America's chief trading partner, Britain controlled Canada to the north and a number of forts to the west, and her superior navy ruled the Atlantic. Federalists believed it better to accommodate Great Britain than the Parisian head hunters. President Washington said no to both Republicans and Federalists and issued a **Proclamation of Neutrality** in April 1793. He declared that the United States would "pursue a conduct friendly and impartial toward the belligerent powers." Challenges to American neutrality, however, would quickly rise at home and abroad.

Citizen Genêt—The already difficult neutrality policy was further complicated by the arrival of the French ambassador, Edmond Charles Genêt, who in current French fashion had rejected titles of nobility and referred to himself as **Citizen Genêt.** The flashy Frenchman, instead of honoring protocol by arriving at Philadelphia to present his credentials to the government, landed in Charleston, South Carolina. He made a grand tour through the country, stirring up pro-French sentiment in hopes of overturning American neutrality. Like a Parisian pied piper, Genêt gathered enthusiastic followers wherever he went, not the least of which was an enraptured Thomas Jefferson.

Genêt, however, overrated his charm with Washington. The president gave the ambassador a courteous but cold reception, reminding him that the United States was neutral and intended to stay that way. This was not what Genêt wanted to hear. Secretly Genêt attempted to raise an army to fight Britain's ally Spain in Florida, and he authorized privateers to raid British shipping. His plottings and personal attacks on Washington, published in Republican newspapers, eventually became an embarrassment even to Jefferson.

Daniel Boone, Backwoodsman of Kentucky

In 1792 Kentucky became the fifteenth state in the Union. The admission of the Bluegrass State was the crowning result of the pioneering efforts of many men and women. Among the heroes of Kentucky was America's best-known frontiersman, **Daniel Boone.**

Born and bred on the edge of the wilderness, Boone explored restlessly for the sheer delight of experiencing the rugged beauty of the land. He studied Indian ways of hunting and tracking until few men, white or Indian, could match him as a hunter. Part of the secret of his success as a hunter was his keen marksmanship. He called his rifle "Ticklicker" because, Boone boasted, it could "lick a tick" off a bear's nose at one hundred yards.

Boone began exploring Kentucky in the 1760s, supposedly to scout land for settlement. Actually he went more for the excitement of hunting and exploring in the wild country. Boone pioneered a trail through the Cumberland Gap, called the Wilderness Road, and it became the main route of early settlers to Kentucky, including Boone's family. He also helped establish some of the first settlements in Kentucky, one of which, Boonesborough, was named in his honor.

The Cherokee called Kentucky "the dark and bloody ground," and few areas of the United States saw such fierce and prolonged confrontation between whites and Indians. Boone experienced that conflict firsthand. His oldest son, James, was captured and tortured to death by Indians during one of Boone's first expeditions to Kentucky. Boone's second son, Israel, was killed before his father's eyes in an Indian ambush at the Battle of Blue Licks (1782). Indians killed and beheaded Boone's brother, Ned, while Boone was only a hundred yards away hunting a bear. Boone himself had close brushes with death. Once he was locked in a life-and-death struggle with an Indian, which ended when they fell into a stream.

Boone held the Indian's head under the water until he drowned, giving the stream the gruesome but appropriate name "Drowning Creek." When asked about the dangers of the frontier, Boone simply replied, "Fear's the spice that makes it interesting to go ahead."

Always restless, in 1799 Boone moved from Kentucky to Missouri, joking that someone had moved within seventy miles of him and he needed more elbow room. Actually Boone wanted to escape the debts and lawsuits piling up in Kentucky as a result of the state's irregular settlement. In Missouri Boone spent his time hunting, fishing, and trapping, although sometimes his rheumatism was so bad that his wife had to carry his rifle for him. He continued exploring, once traveling as far as the Yellowstone region of modern Wyoming while in his eighties. He died in his son's home, a legend in his own time. Even the British poet Lord Byron immortalized the frontiersman in his poem *Don Juan:*

Of the great names which in our faces stare
Is Daniel Boone, backwoodsman of Kentucky.

Daniel Boone

When a more radical faction took over the French government, their new ambassador arrived with an arrest warrant for Genêt. His return to France would almost certainly mean his execution by guillotine. The magnanimous Washington granted the troublemaker political asylum on the condition (which for Genêt was probably cruel and unusual) that he keep quiet. Grateful for his neck, Genêt settled in New York, married, and took up farming.

The Genêt episode left the country deeply divided, however. At the same time, British attacks on American shipping further complicated Washington's efforts to keep the country out of a European war.

Jay's Treaty—During 1793 the British began attacking American ships trading in the French West Indies. Not only were cargoes seized to deprive the French of them, but the British also practiced impressment, that is, seizing American sailors and forcing them into service. British violations of American neutrality particularly enraged Republicans, who were itching for a fight with England.

In 1794 Washington dispatched Chief Justice John Jay to London to settle American and British differences, including Britain's dusty promises to remove all troops from the Northwest Territory and to settle prewar debts. After difficult negotiations Jay returned with a treaty that appeared to gain little more from Britain than an agreement to keep her promise made in the Treaty of Paris (1783) to evacuate redcoats from American territory and an offer to pay compensation for the previous year of raiding carried on by the British navy against American shipping.

Given the United States' weak bargaining position (particularly because of the nation's lack of a navy) the **Jay Treaty** was the best that could be hoped for. By the narrowest of margins the treaty cleared the Senate in 1795. Republicans, though, felt the treaty was a betrayal, and Jay grimly observed that he could travel through the country at night by the light of his burning effigies. Despite the howls against the "Federalist" treaty, Jay's negotiations achieved one outstanding result—averting war with Britain.

Chief Justice John Jay, who also served as negotiator of a controversial trade treaty with Britain

Whiskey Rebellion

Discontent over Hamilton's economic policies had been simmering in the backcountry for some time. Hamilton had proposed raising revenue to pay the government's debt by taxing the production of liquor. Many backcountry farmers, who made their living raising corn and selling it in liquid form, hated the tax and refused to pay it. All along the frontier the "Whiskey Boys" were grumbling and looking for ways to avoid the tax and the tax collector. In western Pennsylvania discontent turned into violence against the government.

President Washington's response was decisive. He called up 13,000 troops to crush the **Whiskey Rebellion** and initially took command of them personally. When the huge army reached the western counties, the rebellion collapsed. The few that were captured and convicted were pardoned by the president. Washington had made his point: the national government possessed the strength and the will to enforce the law. If citizens did not like a law, they could change it through the ballot box and the courts, not through violence. In Washington's words, Americans had to "distinguish between oppression and the necessary exercise of lawful authority."

Although the rebellion ended, discontent over the tax did not. Whiskey stills were tucked away out of the sight of the pursuing "revenuers," who forced the farmers to ply their illegal trade at night, giving the word "moonshine" new meaning.

Washington's Farewell

In 1796, after two terms, Washington announced his plans to retire. He left a remarkable legacy. The Union he presided over was larger now, by the admission of Vermont (1791), Kentucky (1792), and Tennessee (1796), than when he first entered the office. Under Washington's presidency the country grew not only in size but in strength as well. Credit and commerce were stabilized, and the Constitution proved to be a practical charter.

In **Washington's Farewell Address,** however, he was not looking at the past, but to the future. Issued on the ninth anniversary of the signing of the Constitution, September 17, 1796, Washington's address urged Americans to lay aside partisan divisions and encouraged the nation to cultivate commercial ties with Europe but avoid political ones. The president warned:

> Europe has a set of primary interests which to us have none or a very remote relation; Hence she must be engaged in frequent controversies, the causes of which are essentially foreign to our concerns. . . . Our detached and distant situation invites and enables us to pursue a different course. . . . It is our true policy to steer clear of permanent alliances with any portion of the foreign world . . . [but] we may safely trust to temporary alliances for extraordinary emergencies.

Washington's influential Farewell Address outlined America's basic foreign policy until World War II.

Section Review

1. Who were the two most important leaders of the Republicans during Washington's administration?
2. Why was Washington's Proclamation of Neutrality in 1793 not popular with either the Federalists or the Republicans?
3. What was the most important result of Jay's Treaty?

Declining Federalist Influence

The election of 1796 marked the first real contest in presidential politics. During the first two elections no one had the stature even to compete with Washington. With the old general's retirement, however, and the heated partisan debate between Federalists and Republicans, the stage was set for a close race. The 1796 election demonstrated two features in the political maturing of the American republic that were remarkable then and are still so today: a peaceful transfer of power and political parties competing without resorting to violence. More immediately, the close election demonstrated that the Federalist grip on power was loosening in the face of the growing Republican challenge.

The Election of 1796

The Federalists passed over their most vocal leader, Alexander Hamilton, because of the many political enemies that he had accumulated over the years. Instead they gave the presidential nomination to Washington's two-term vice president, **John Adams** of Massachusetts. To balance the ticket geographically, the Federalists gave the vice-presidential slot to Thomas Pinckney of South Carolina. Republicans nominated Thomas Jefferson with Aaron Burr of New York as his running mate.

Hamilton, for personal and political reasons, opposed Adams for the presidency, and secretly worked to keep him as vice president. Hamilton quietly suggested to the South Carolina electors that they withhold their votes from Adams so that their state's favorite son, Pinckney, would win the presidency. When Massachusetts electors heard of the political intrigue, they refused to vote for Pinckney. Hamilton's behind-the-scenes attempt to engineer the election backfired completely.

As a result of Pinckney's loss of support, Republican Thomas Jefferson came in second to become vice president and nearly took the big prize, falling just three electoral votes short of John Adams's tally. A mixed administration of political adversaries was certainly not what the constitutional framers had had in mind less than ten years before.

The new president, John Adams, was a man whose distinguished career stretched back to the

John Adams, *by John Trumbull, National Portrait Gallery, Smithsonian Institution*

earliest days of the independence movement, when Boston was a hotbed for the Revolution. Adams was educated at Harvard, unlike his predecessor, Washington, who had less formal education than any other president in our nation's history. Despite his credentials as a lawyer, diplomat, and statesman, Adams often felt his achievements were underrated. In 1790, for example, he complained in a letter to a friend, ''The history of our Revolution will be one continued lie from one end to the other. The essence of the whole will be that Dr. Franklin's electrical rod smote the earth and out sprang George Washington.''

Yet Adams was a man of courage and conviction. Few presidents have made decisions with less concern for their own political future than he did. Such courage would prove crucial for the nation throughout Adams's troubled term.

Quasi War

During Adams's presidency the United States walked an international tightrope. To favor either France or Britain was to risk war with the other. To continue to ignore the insults of both nations toward American commerce was to irritate Americans and to risk the nation's economic future.

French hostility toward the United States following the Jay Treaty was more intense than even the British raids of 1793. By 1797 the French had seized cargo on three hundred American ships and severed diplomatic ties with the United States. This **"Quasi War,"** a conflict resembling war in nearly every particular except a formal declaration, occupied much of Adams's time in office.

XYZ Affair – In 1797 French belligerence led Adams to send diplomats to negotiate with the revolutionary government in France, at that time a five-man Directory. The French foreign minister was the wily Charles Maurice Talleyrand, who hinted through three of his agents that he would negotiate with the Americans–for a price–say, $250,000 for each of the Directors and a $12 million loan to the French government. The American representatives–John Marshall, C. C. Pinckney, and Elbridge Gerry–replied "No, no, not a sixpence."

Americans of all political persuasions were incensed by France's action. When Congress later demanded to see the correspondence regarding the affair, Adams complied but substituted the letters X, Y, and Z for the names of the French agents. The episode soon became known as the **XYZ Affair.**

Retaliation – French arrogance in the XYZ Affair raised the cry in America, "Millions for defence, but not one cent for tribute." In 1798, as war fever raged, Congress authorized a larger army to prepare to stop a French invasion that seemed imminent. In addition, a Department of the Navy was formed that same year and a strong shipbuilding effort funded. Within two years the United States Navy had over thirty ships in its fleet.

Many of these ships were quickly tested in battle during the undeclared naval war against the French. The Federalists and a growing number of Republicans, however, wanted an all-out war effort against the French. Instead President Adams put the interests of his country ahead of his party, a decision that probably cost him his re-election. Adams wanted to protect national honor and preserve freedom of the seas, but at the same time he believed that war would destroy the hard-fought

A crude political cartoon scathingly satirizes clashes between factions in Congress during the late 1790s.

gains the young republic had made. When the French hinted at the possibility of peace negotiations, Adams seized the opportunity.

Adams sent a peace commission to France in late 1799, even though many Federalists opposed the idea and though he knew that it would further erode his support. Napoleon Bonaparte had assumed the leadership of France and was playing the role of peacemaker at the time. Under Napoleon's favorable terms, France promised to leave American ships alone and to suspend the old Treaty of Alliance in exchange for an American promise not to seek compensation for shipping damages during their quiet little Quasi War.

Alien and Sedition Acts

Quieting the Critics—The anti-French sentiment that swept the country in the late 1790s provided the Federalists with an important political opportunity, since Jefferson and his Republicans had been identified with the French cause from the beginning. In a series of four acts, known as the **Alien and Sedition Acts,** the Federalist-controlled Congress sought to silence their political opponents. Three of the acts placed restrictions on immigrants–particularly the French and Irish, ethnic groups that were predominantly Republican. The Alien Acts gave the president greatly expanded powers to expel or imprison such undesirables. The Sedition Act not only outlined penalties for antigovernment activities such as riots, but it also went so far as to make it illegal to speak or write anything ''false, scandalous and malicious . . . against the government of the United States, or the President of the United States, with intent to defame . . . or to bring them or either of them, into contempt or disrepute.'' Stiff penalties of fines and imprisonment awaited anyone convicted of such ''treasonous'' speech.

Only ten men were convicted under the Sedition Act, but it was clear that the opposition Republican party was getting the brunt of the law. Matthew Lyon, for example, an outspoken Vermont congressman, was fined $1,000 and spent four months in jail for accusing President Adams of having an "unbounded thirst for ridiculous pomp, foolish adulation, and selfish avarice."

The Sedition Act was clearly unconstitutional—that is, as clear to us today as it was to Republicans then. At the time, however, when anti-French hysteria and the fear of anarchy gripped the government, it was genuinely viewed as a means to preserve order. Many Republican newspaper editors unwittingly encouraged the act's passage by printing articles that were bitter, false, and inflammatory toward the Federalists.

Kentucky and Virginia Resolutions—In November 1798 Jefferson responded to the Alien and Sedition Acts by writing the **Kentucky Resolutions;** in December Madison further responded by writing the **Virginia Resolutions.** Both lists of resolutions opposed the Alien and Sedition Acts as a violation of the First Amendment, and both expressed the rights of the states to judge the constitutionality of a law. The resolutions held that under the Constitution the national government existed by consent of the states and, by extension, that the dissent of the states could nullify government acts that the states considered unconstitutional. The documents even suggested that the states had a right to secede when the federal government acted unconstitutionally. Neither Jefferson nor Madison wanted secession; both had worked too hard to establish the federal government. What they wanted was the repeal of the Alien and Sedition Acts. However, their nullification theory would gain importance a generation later.

The limited political persecution resulting from the Alien and Sedition Acts was short-lived. Jefferson urged his supporters to make their views known through the ballot box, not violence. The upcoming election of 1800 would give Republicans the opportunity to determine the future of the Alien and Sedition Acts as well as Federalist control of the government.

The Election of 1800

In the summer of 1800, John Adams moved to the new national capital, called Washington City in honor of the late president. His stay in the executive mansion, however, would be brief. Adams's efforts to make peace with France divided his own party, and the Alien and Sedition Acts had galvanized opposition to him. The election of 1800 was one of the bitterest ever.

The Candidates—The presidential and vice-presidential candidates for both parties were very nearly repeats of the 1796 election. The Republicans chose Jefferson and Burr again, and the Federalists picked Adams and Pinckney, only this Pinckney was Charles Cotesworth, brother of Thomas.

Ridiculous accusations flew between the rival camps. Jefferson described the Federalist administration as a "reign of witches," while Federalists warned the public that if Jefferson were elected they could expect "dwellings in flames, hoary hairs bathed in blood, . . . children writhing on the pike and halberd."

Too Many Chiefs—The results of the election would have been comical if they had not been so serious. The Federalist electors arranged to have one of their electors not vote for Pinckney in order to distinguish between their presidential and vice-presidential candidates; Adams received 65 electoral votes and his running mate Pinckney, 64 votes. The Republicans could have learned something from their Federalist foes. The Republican electors each cast their votes for both Jefferson and Burr, giving them a tie at 73 votes apiece. As a result, the election was thrown into the House of Representatives for the Federalist-controlled Congress to decide between the lesser of two Republican evils. After a lengthy deadlock Jefferson, considered slightly less repugnant than Burr by the reluctant kingmakers, was elected president on the thirty-fifth ballot. (The Republicans quickly lent support to an amendment to the Constitution, the Twelfth, to avoid such a situation in the future.)

The "Midnight Appointments"—The Federalists lost control of both the executive and the legislative branches in 1800. The only branch left to them was the judicial. After the election but before

Jefferson's inauguration, Adams took steps to strengthen Federalist control of the judiciary. In February 1801 he appointed the Federalist John Marshall as chief justice of the Supreme Court. Marshall, who would serve as chief justice for thirty-four years, delivering some of the court's most important decisions, was perhaps the most enduring legacy of the Adams administration. Also, before newly elected Republican congressmen replaced the Federalists, Congress passed the **Judiciary Act of 1801,** which increased the number of federal judges. Adams, of course, filled these appointments with Federalists. He was accused of staying up until midnight the night before Jefferson's inauguration on March 4, 1801, signing commissions for the new judges. The appointments were thus called the **"midnight appointments."** Jefferson remarked begrudgingly that the wily Federalists had "retired into the judiciary as a stronghold."

A Time to Heal

When Jefferson took the oath of office, John Adams did not stay to watch what he believed was the beginning of national ruin. After thirty years of public service, the old patriot was turned out of office and returned to his home in Quincy, Massachusetts, to retire and to brood. Contrary to Federalist predictions the Great Tribulation did not begin with Jefferson's inauguration. Two terms later, Jefferson also retired to Monticello, nestled in Virginia's Blue Ridge. After a few years the two ex-presidents started corresponding and became ex-enemies. The lengthy letters of these presidential pen pals reveal more than witty commentaries on national politics; they reveal true friendship, the healing of old wounds. Even in death, the two men who at one time could not even stand each other's presence were knit together. On the fiftieth anniversary of the Declaration of Independence, a document that first brought Adams and Jefferson together in 1776, both men lay on their deathbeds. Adams's last words were about his old enemy and new friend; he whispered "Jefferson lives." Ironically, his friend had died at Monticello a few hours earlier.

The friendship between John Adams and Thomas Jefferson illustrates much about the 1790s. The formative Federalist decade established national supremacy and enduring precedents, but it also produced deep political divisions. In time these wounds would heal. After some maturing, the political parties brought healthy competition, not open conflict, to America. The fiery trials of the 1790s tempered the young nation, fitting it for a growing role at the dawn of a new century.

Section Review

1. Name the president and vice president, along with their political parties, who were elected in 1796.
2. What is the origin of the phrase "Millions for defence, but not one cent for tribute"?
3. Why was Adams's decision to pursue peace with France a politically brave act?
4. What political theory did the Virginia and Kentucky resolutions advocate?
5. How did the Judiciary Act of 1801 allow the Federalists to continue their influence in government after the election of Jefferson in 1800?

Chapter Review

Terms

George Washington
Thomas Jefferson
Alexander Hamilton
cabinet
Judiciary Act of 1789
James Madison
Bill of Rights
funding
assumption
loose constructionist
strict constructionist
National Bank
Federalists
Republicans (Democratic-Republicans)
French Revolution
Proclamation of Neutrality
Citizen Genêt
Jay Treaty
Whiskey Rebellion
Washington's Farewell Address
Daniel Boone
John Adams
Quasi War
XYZ Affair
Alien and Sedition Acts
Kentucky Resolutions
Virginia Resolutions
Judiciary Act of 1801
"midnight appointments"

Content Questions

1. What was the most significant section of the Judiciary Act of 1789? Why?
2. Match the following phrases with the amendments to the Constitution that they describe.
   a. Fair judicial procedures for the accused
   b. Extent of the national government's power restricted to the bounds of the Constitution and powers reserved to the states and the people
   c. Security rights of the individual
   d. Freedoms of conscience and expression
   (1) Amendment 1
   (2) Amendments 2-4
   (3) Amendments 5-8
   (4) Amendments 9-10
3. What did Hamilton offer the South in order to win Southern support for assumption of state debts by the federal government?
4. How did the Federalist and the Republican parties differ concerning constitutional interpretation?
5. With what two nations did Washington have the most difficulty during his administration?
6. How did the elections of 1796 and 1800 reveal flaws in the presidential election system devised by the Constitution?
7. Why was the French-American conflict of the 1790s called a "Quasi War"?
8. What acts gave the president the power to expel or imprison immigrants? What acts prohibited "treasonous" speech?

Application Questions

1. Which view of constitutional interpretation do you think is better, loose or strict constructionism?
2. Compare and contrast the course and results of Shays' Rebellion (p. 141) and the Whiskey Rebellion.
3. How was the presence of political opponents Alexander Hamilton and Thomas Jefferson in Washington's cabinet both good and bad for the young nation?

UNIT III

	c. 1800—c. 1825 Second Great Awakening
1801 Thomas Jefferson inaugurated	
	1803 Louisiana Purchase
1811 Battle of Tippecanoe	
	1812-1815 War of 1812
1817 Construction of Erie Canal begins	
	1820 Missouri Compromise
1823 Monroe Doctrine proclaimed	
	1828 "Tariff of Abominations"; Andrew Jackson elected president
1836 Texan independence	
	1844 Samuel F.B. Morse demonstrates telegraph to government
1845 Annexation of Texas	
1846 Oregon controversy settled	
	1846-1848 Mexican War
1857-1859 Prayer Meeting Revival	

CHAPTER 9

The Jeffersonian Era (1801-1825)

"Our country! In her intercourse with foreign nations may
she always be in the right; but *our country, right or wrong.*"

Commodore Stephen Decatur *in a toast given in*
Norfolk, Virginia, April 1816

The U.S.S. Constitution *("Old Ironsides") relentlessly hammers the H.M.S.* Guerriere, *during the War of 1812. Courtesy U.S. Naval Academy Museum.*

In the first year of the nineteenth century, Washington, D.C., was as raw and unfinished as the nation of which it was the capital. The country's leaders trudged down muddy pathways (imaginatively referred to as streets) from the ramshackle, overcrowded boarding houses in which they lived to the half-completed buildings in which they worked. On March 4, 1801, **Thomas Jefferson** left his boarding house, strolled over to the unfinished Capitol, and took the oath of office as the third president of the United States. Afterwards he delivered his inaugural address in a whispery, indistinct voice, much of which was lost on his audience. The simple ceremony would not have impressed the cultured rulers of Europe, a fact which undoubtedly impressed Jefferson.

The tall and lanky president, his red hair now peppered with gray, was certainly not a pretentious man. He soon offended the English ambassador by greeting him while wearing a pair of carpet slippers. On another occasion the president astounded Washington society by taking his nephew shopping around the city to buy back-to-school items. Jefferson may not have been pretentious, but he was

certainly remarkable. By 1801 his accomplishments included writing the Declaration of Independence and serving as ambassador to France, governor of Virginia, secretary of state, and vice president–not to mention developing numerous inventions and architectural designs in his spare time. "Science is my passion," Jefferson once said, "politics my duty." So wide-ranging were Jefferson's abilities in politics, art, and science that in 1962 President John F. Kennedy told a gathering of Nobel prize winners, "I think this is the most extraordinary collection of talent, of human knowledge, that has ever been gathered together at the White House, with the possible exception of when Thomas Jefferson dined alone."

The administrations of Jefferson and his hand-picked successors, James Madison and James Monroe, were the era of **Jeffersonian Republicanism.** The period bears Jefferson's stamp and embodies his philosophy at work. Through events ranging from a magnificent land purchase which doubled the size of the United States to the burning of the nation's capital by a foreign power, Jeffersonian principles endured in both prosperity and adversity.

President Thomas Jefferson

By the end of the period, Jefferson's party and his philosophy stood virtually unopposed on the political landscape of America.

"The Revolution of 1800"

Jefferson called his election "the revolution of 1800," suggesting that his victory marked a transformation as dramatic as that of 1776. Although time would demonstrate that the change was not as great as Jefferson imagined, it proved to be a discernible shift from the Federalist era.

Nature of Jeffersonian Republicanism

Republican ideas may be best understood in contrast to the ideas of the Federalists. The Federalists were the party of finance, the great defenders of the merchant class. Jefferson's Republican party, on the other hand, concerned itself with the interests of the farmers. Jefferson believed that liberty in the United States would be preserved only as long as the country remained predominantly a nation of independent, self-sufficient farmers. The Federalists preferred a strong central government to protect and further national interests. The Republicans operated on the principle that the less

government there is, the better. Jefferson had vigorously demonstrated his adherence to the idea of states' rights against the claims of the national government in the Virginia and Kentucky resolutions (see p. 165).

Despite their defense of states' rights and the farmer, the Jeffersonian Republicans were not truly a party of the "common man." Like the Federalists, the Republicans believed in rule by an elite class. The Federalists wanted rule by an elite of birth, those who came from the "best," almost aristocratic, families. The Republicans preferred the creation of an elite of talent; in each generation the most brilliant and most capable men would rise from the masses (probably through education) and take the reins of government. It is not too much to say that most Republicans took as their ideal a man much like Jefferson himself–intelligent, cultured, and accomplished.

Jefferson was right perhaps in seeing his election as a change, but it was no revolution. There was no wholesale repudiation of the Federalist method of governing, only an alteration of those practices Republicans found offensive. With the benefit of hindsight, we can see that Jeffersonian Republicanism was not so much a revolution as a middle step in the transition from the elitism of the Federalists to the more truly "common man" politics of Andrew Jackson which arose in the 1820s.

The U.S. Capitol as it appeared in the time of Thomas Jefferson

Thomas Jefferson's Religious Views

When word of Jefferson's election reached New England in 1800 some Christians began hiding their Bibles for fear that government agents would seize them. As odd as it may sound to us today, Jefferson was widely regarded as an atheist and enemy of religion. Part of that perception arose from the fact that Jefferson opposed established (tax-supported) churches, such as the Anglican church in Virginia, and had promoted legislation to disestablish such churches. It was certainly true, however, that Thomas Jefferson was no orthodox Christian.

Jefferson professed an admiration for the teachings of Jesus, calling them "a system of morals" which is "the most perfect and sublime that has ever been taught by man." Jefferson denied, however, most of the Scriptural teaching concerning Christ. Of the virgin birth, for example, he wrote to John Adams, "The day will come when the account of the birth of Christ as accepted in the Trinitarian churches will be classed with the fable of Minerva springing from the brain of Jupiter." Jefferson also believed that much of the New Testament, such as the writings of the Apostle Paul, were corruptions of Jesus' teaching.

While president, Jefferson began to compile his own version of the "true" teachings of Jesus. Using scissors, paste, and two English and two Greek New Testaments, Jefferson literally pieced together an account of Jesus' life and teaching, an account shorn of every miracle and every reference to Christ as God. The resulting work–variously called "The Philosophy of Jesus of Nazareth," "The Morals of Jesus," or "Jefferson's Bible"–limited itself almost entirely to the moral teachings of Jesus. Jefferson read from his edition nearly every night and called it "a document in proof that *I* am *a real Christian,* that is to say a disciple of the doctrines of Jesus."

Thomas Jefferson was an outstanding political thinker and statesman, but his religious views demonstrate that not all great Americans were necessarily Christians. American believers can appreciate Jefferson's rich contribution to the development of their nation, but they must beware of his view of Christ as a good teacher but not the incarnate Son of God. As the Apostle John said, "Who is a liar but he that denieth that Jesus is the Christ? He is antichrist, that denieth the Father and the Son" (I John 2:22).

Making Changes

Jefferson undeniably made changes when he took office. The Republicans quickly repealed the offensive Judiciary Act of 1801 and allowed the Alien and Sedition Acts to lapse. To guard against a repetition of the deadlocked election of 1800 (see p. 165), Congress and the states adopted the **Twelfth Amendment,** which enabled electors to cast separate ballots for president and vice president. The extremely formal receptions that Washington and Adams had held with political leaders gave way to Jefferson's informal discussions with congressional leaders around his dinner table. Eager to reduce the size of the national government, Jefferson ordered his secretary of the treasury, Albert Gallatin, to draw up a plan for both reducing taxes and eliminating the national debt.

Jefferson knew when to leave well enough alone, however. He made no attempt, for example, to destroy the National Bank. In fact, after the bank's charter expired, a Republican Congress under Jefferson's successor, James Madison, created another bank in 1816. Apparently, holding the reins of government themselves convinced the Republicans that the power of the federal government was not all bad.

John Marshall and the Supreme Court

One institution remained a bastion of Federalism and its nationalistic policies–the Supreme Court. The leader of that court, and its first great chief justice, was **John Marshall.** A Virginia Federalist and cousin of Jefferson, Marshall was appointed and took office in the waning days of the Adams administration. The Supreme Court was not as honored then as it is today. The first chief justice, John Jay, resigned the office in order to become governor of New York, an office which Jay considered more prestigious. Marshall received the nomination only after two others had turned Adams down. (Perhaps these refusals caused Adams to nominate Marshall without asking him first.) After Marshall's thirty-four years on the bench, however, no one would doubt the power and prestige of the Court.

Marshall was a Federalist in the mold of George Washington. He envisioned a tremendous future for the young nation as long as the central government held the power to develop the potential of the new land. In a series of landmark decisions, the Marshall Court upheld the authority of the national government and increased the scope of the Court's authority.

Marbury v. Madison–The first major case before the Marshall court involved the infamous Judiciary Act of 1801. William Marbury had received one of Adams's "midnight appointments." However, Jefferson's secretary of state, James Madison, refused to deliver Marbury's commission, meaning that Marbury could not take office. Marbury asked the Supreme Court to issue an order forcing Madison to deliver the commission. Marshall knew that he had no means of forcing Madison to obey, and some Republicans eagerly awaited the opportunity to flout the authority of the Federalist judge.

Marshall cleverly handed down a ruling that preserved the authority of the Court without giving the Republicans an opportunity to defy the Court. Although Marbury was right in his complaint, Marshall said, the power to issue such orders was not one of the powers delegated to the Court by the Constitution. The law that permitted such orders, then, was unconstitutional and therefore invalid.

John Marshall, *by James Reid Lambdin, National Portrait Gallery, Smithsonian Institution*

Thus, in **Marbury v. Madison** the Supreme Court established the principle of **judicial review,** the right of the Court to declare a law unconstitutional. As Marshall wrote in handing down the decision, "A legislative act contrary to the Constitution is not law. . . . It is emphatically the province and duty of the judicial department to say what the law is."

Gibbons v. Ogden–Another important ruling, handed down in 1824, protected the federal government's **delegated powers,** those powers specifically given to the national government by the Constitution. This case involved Congress's right to regulate interstate commerce. New York had attempted to grant a monopoly on the use of its waterways to one steamship company, a monopoly which also limited the federal government's use of those waterways. In *Gibbons* v. *Ogden* the Court ruled that the delegated powers given to the national government by the Constitution could not be limited by state boundaries. Where the Constitution entrusted Congress with a power, the states had no right to interfere with that power.

McCulloch *v.* **Maryland**—Perhaps the most far-reaching decision of the Marshall court was *McCulloch* v. *Maryland* (1819). The state of Maryland, opposed to the idea of a national bank, attempted to tax the Baltimore branch of the Bank of the United States out of existence. Claiming that "the power to tax involves the power to destroy," the Court overruled the state's action. The Constitution is the supreme law of the land, Marshall said, referring to Article VI of the Constitution. Therefore, the states had no authority to interfere with the ability of Congress to enact legislation that is "necessary and proper" to carry out its delegated powers (Article I, Section 8, Clause 18). (These "necessary and proper" powers needed to carry out the delegated powers are called **implied powers.**) In this decision, Marshall placed the Court squarely on the side of the loose constructionists and national supremacy. The Supreme Court may have been a Federalist island in a sea of Republicanism, but John Marshall made sure that it was an island that the Jeffersonians could not ignore.

Section Review

1. How did the Federalists and the Republicans disagree concerning the power of the central government?
2. What is judicial review? What Supreme Court decision established judicial review?
3. List the three important court cases that the Marshall Court ruled on and the important long-range principle established by each one.

Jefferson's Triumphs Abroad

Despite his overriding concern with domestic affairs, Thomas Jefferson achieved his two greatest successes in the field of foreign affairs. Through his clash with the Barbary pirates and even more through the Louisiana Purchase, Jefferson dramatically increased the international prestige of the young nation.

To the Shores of Tripoli

As part of his plan to cut federal expenses, Jefferson wanted to reduce the size of the navy. Several petty Muslim kingdoms in North Africa, where piracy and kidnaping were the chief sources of national income, however, forced the president to reconsider his budget cuts. The ships of these **Barbary states** raided Mediterranean shipping and occasionally ventured out into the Atlantic. These pirates captured unarmed merchant ships, enslaved the crews, and demanded ransom from the owners. Most nations found it cheaper and easier to pay ransom to the Barbary states than to send in their warships.

The United States was among those who paid tribute money, until Jefferson took office. Offended at this practice, Jefferson sent a squadron of warships to Tripoli to frighten the most important Barbary state with a show of force. In a brief war the squadron bombarded Tripoli harbor, and a group of eight U.S. Marines fought alongside an army of Muslim rebels who captured the Tripolitan city of Derna. There Lieutenant Presley O'Bannon became the first soldier to plant the American flag on foreign soil. The exploits of O'Bannon and his companions fired the pride of the young nation. O'Bannon's act later inspired a phrase in the Marine Corps' hymn—"to the shores of Tripoli."

The Louisiana Purchase

"A Noble Bargain"—In 1800 France and Spain secretly signed a treaty returning the Louisiana Territory to France. Word of this deal leaked out and caused panic in Washington. New Orleans was vital to American interests; the western states shipped millions of tons of American goods down the Mississippi River to New Orleans, whence they were shipped out to other markets. Dealing with

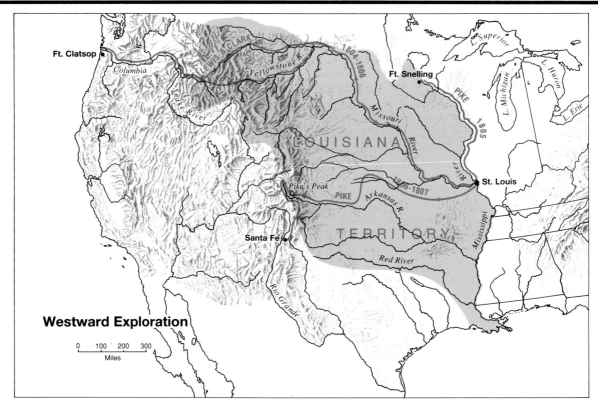

Westward Exploration

0   100   200   300
Miles

the relatively weak Spanish had often been trouble-some. Dealing with the French under the powerful **Napoleon Bonaparte** could be potentially disas-trous for the Americans.

Jefferson instructed James Monroe and Robert Livingstone, the ambassador to France, to go to Napoleon and offer him up to $10 million for New Orleans. Napoleon's foreign minister astounded the Americans with a counteroffer: *all* of the Louisiana Territory–a region larger than the whole United States–for $15 million. The American representa-tives hurriedly sent word to Jefferson and urged him to accept. The offer bothered Jefferson. It was certainly a splendid opportunity, but the Constitu-tion gave the government no authority to purchase land in this way. Jefferson briefly toyed with the idea of adopting a constitutional amendment to per-mit the purchase, but his ministers in France warned him to hurry before Napoleon changed his mind. Casting his constitutional scruples aside, Jefferson

submitted the treaty to the Senate. A majority quickly approved, and with the **Louisiana Pur-chase** the United States more than doubled its size in one stroke.

Why did Napoleon so eagerly sell such a huge tract of land for less than three cents an acre? Al-though Napoleon was currently at peace, he was preparing again for war with Great Britain. When war broke out, Napoleon would be pressed to de-fend Louisiana thousands of miles away across the Atlantic. Being land-rich and cash-poor, it made more sense to sell the territory to the United States; Napoleon would have more funds for his expected war with Britain, and he would build up favor with the United States–not a bad bargain in exchange for a territory that he probably could not keep anyway.

An important question remained: Exactly what were the boundaries of Louisiana? The French for-eign minister replied evasively to Livingstone that they were the same as those France had received from Spain. Livingstone persisted. What were *those* boundaries then? The minister declined to answer but said simply, "You have made a noble bargain for yourselves, and I suppose you will make the most of it."

Exploring the New Lands — To help answer the questions of what the territory was and what it contained, Jefferson had Congress authorize army officers **Meriwether Lewis,** the president's private secretary, and **William Clark,** brother of George Rogers Clark, to head an expedition to explore the Louisiana Territory.

On May 14, 1804, their group of about fifty men left St. Louis. The party traveled up the Missouri River through the Dakotas and Montana, crossed the Rocky Mountains, and by December 1805 had paddled canoes down the Columbia River to the Pacific. The explorers saw wonders of the American West previously undreamed of by white men. Raging, swirling rivers tumbled through the land, threatening to swallow any boat foolish enough to challenge them. Strange animals stalked them, such as the fierce grizzly bear and the cougar. In the mountains shrieking winds shot pellets of ice and snow like bullets at the explorers.

In addition to the dangers were breathtaking beauties. Some of the streams may have been fierce, but they were also sparklingly clear and

Sacajawea

Accompanying the intrepid explorers Lewis and Clark through the Pacific Northwest was a remarkable young woman in her late teens who was no stranger to the hardships of the wild west. The woman was a Shoshone (shu SHOW nee) Indian named Sacajawea (SAC uh juh WEE uh), wife of a French fur trader. The expedition met the woman and her husband while at an Indian village near modern-day Bismarck, North Dakota. Sacajawea had been kidnaped from the Shoshones as a young girl, and she regarded the American expedition as an opportunity to see her people again. Lewis and Clark knew that they would need horses from the Shoshones in order to cross the Rocky Mountains. Therefore, the two sides quickly struck a deal, and Sacajawea and her husband joined the group.

Sacajawea was already several months pregnant when she joined the expedition, and in February 1805 she gave birth to a son. The child quickly won the affection of the members of the party, particularly Clark. Rather than being a burden, the woman and her infant often proved to be a blessing when meeting suspicious Indians. "A woman with a party of men is a token of peace," observed Clark.

When the expedition met the Shoshones, Sacajawea proved to be more helpful than even she had imagined. As she began to interpret, she suddenly stopped, began weeping, and ran over to the Shoshone chief. He was, it turned out, her brother. Her presence, to say the least, smoothed the way for Lewis and Clark among the Shoshones.

Contrary to popular belief, Sacajawea did not act as a guide for the party, although she did help point out some important landmarks in Shoshone country (the Snake River area of modern Idaho). On one occasion when a boat was nearly swamped in a river, she calmly held her child with one arm while she used the other to snatch papers and supplies from the water.

When the expedition returned to civilization, Sacajawea and her family stayed behind. Clark later wrote to her husband, "Your woman who accompanied you that long dangerous and fatigueing rout to the Pacific Ocian and back diserved a greater reward for her attention and services on that rout than we had in our power to give her." Clark repaid at least part of that debt after Sacajawea's death in 1812 by paying for the education of her son in St. Louis. That act was his memorial to a brave and daring woman.

fresh. The Rocky Mountains may have held dangers, but their craggy outline and dizzying heights must have amazed those who were used to the lower, rounded peaks of the Appalachians. The explorers returned by way of the Yellowstone River and saw much of the awe-inspiring scenery now contained in Yellowstone National Park. The climax of the trip must have been when the explorers stood on the shores of the Pacific and gazed at an ocean that dwarfed even the mighty Atlantic. The adventures finally came to an end when the party reached St. Louis again in September 1806. Few explorations in history can rival the Lewis and Clark expedition for extensive travel, spectacular sights, and fruitful discoveries.

Zebulon Pike, another army officer, directed two important expeditions about the same time as Lewis and Clark's trip. The first (1805-1806) went northward to the upper reaches of the Mississippi River. The second trip, in 1806 and 1807, crossed the Great Plains to the Colorado Rockies, where Pike discovered (but did not actually climb) the mountain named for him, Pikes Peak. The expedition then turned southward into Spanish-held Mexico. As a result of these and other explorations, Americans learned increasingly more about their continent and could realistically begin to envision a nation stretching "from sea to shining sea."

Section Review

1. What were Jefferson's two great triumphs in foreign affairs?
2. Why did Napoleon sell the Louisiana Territory to the United States?
3. Who were the three great explorers of the American West during Jefferson's administration?

Aaron Burr: The Schemer Snared

Thomas Jefferson had many problems as president, but none greater than his own vice president, **Aaron Burr.** Burr's enemy Alexander Hamilton accurately stated that the driving force in Burr's life was his "inordinate ambition." For Aaron Burr, principles were merely weaknesses in other men of which he could take advantage.

If a godly heritage were any guarantee of success, then Burr was doubly blessed. He was the grandson of Jonathan Edwards, and his father was a Presbyterian pastor and president of Princeton. Unfortunately, Burr never personally embraced Christianity. He was orphaned at the age of two, a fact that embit-

tered him and blunted the impact of his godly family. Later, after briefly studying for the ministry, Burr turned to the more lucrative study of law.

After serving in the army during the Revolutionary War, Burr entered New York politics and became one of the most influential men in the state. So important was Burr that the Republicans added him to the ticket as Jefferson's running mate in 1800 to pull New York's electoral votes into the Republican column. In the deadlocked election of 1800, Burr publicly denied that he had any interest in becoming president. Privately, rumors floated about that Burr was secretly intriguing to displace Jefferson when the House of Representatives voted. The rumors were never proved, but Jefferson believed them and came to distrust his vice president.

An outcast in Jefferson's administration, Burr began looking for a new outlet for his talents. In 1804 he ran for governor of New York. Again rumors flew about. Some suspected that Burr's campaign was part of a plot to separate New York and New England from the Union. The question became pointless, however, when Burr lost—due at least in part to the opposition of Alexander Hamilton. Angered by Hamilton's interference, Burr challenged him to a duel. In the early hours of July 11, 1804, the two met at Weehawken, New Jersey. Burr's aim was sure and Hamilton fell, mortally wounded.

If Burr had problems before, he was in deeper trouble now. Jefferson had already dropped him from the ticket for the 1804 election, and now the vice president found himself wanted for murder in New York and New Jersey. Desperation, perhaps, drove Burr to his most daring scheme. He wrote a number of secret letters and began a series of meetings with politicians, military officers, and other influential men. With their help, Burr began stockpiling boats, supplies, and weapons on an island in the Ohio River between Virginia and Ohio.

To this day no one is quite sure what Burr had in mind. Some think he intended to install himself as ruler of Mexico. Others claim that he planned to lead the western states and territories out of the Union and form his own empire. At any rate, it all came to naught when one of the conspirators decided to save himself by revealing the plot. Jefferson arrested Burr without hesitation and had him tried for treason, but he was acquitted when Chief Justice John Marshall ruled that there were not two witnesses to the act of treason, as the Constitution required.

The scandal dealt the final blow to Burr's career. His last years were spent practicing law in New York in near obscurity. Burr's failure proved to be the embodiment of a Scriptural principle: "Whoso diggeth a pit shall fall therein: and he that rolleth a stone, it will return upon him" (Prov. 26:27).

Indians and the Northwest Territory

The Treaty of Paris after the Revolution gave the Great Lakes region to the United States, but no one asked the Indians who lived there what they thought of the matter. If settlers were to move into the Ohio River Valley and north to the Great Lakes, the Indians would have to be dealt with somehow. Unfortunately, the means of dealing with them were usually violent.

Fallen Timbers and the Opening of Ohio

As early as George Washington's administration, settlers and Indians had been locked in a bloody struggle for Ohio. Treaties existed in abundance, but the Americans did not always honor them and the Indians did not always understand them. For example, the idea of private property belonging to a single person was strange to a people who shared all lands among the members of the tribe. "Sell a country!" Indian chief Tecumseh

The signing of the Treaty of Fort Greenville, which opened Ohio to white settlement

once said. "Why not sell the air, the clouds and the great sea, as well?" An old Indian once complained to William Henry Harrison that the French had been friendlier to the Indians than the Americans. He said,

> They [the French] never took from us our lands; indeed, they were common between us. They planted where they pleased, and they cut wood where they pleased, and so did we. But now, if a poor Indian attempts to take a little bark from a tree to cover him from rain, up comes a white man and threatens to shoot him, claiming the tree as his own.

When the Indians realized that the Americans intended to keep the lands forever–and keep the Indians *off*–they went on the warpath.

Whites, on the other hand, considered the Indians' way of living wasteful. Using the land, as the Indians did, only to raise a few crops and to hunt did not begin to tap the potential resources of the country. Many white settlers used their desire to "improve" the land as an excuse to take it from the Indians. They considered themselves better stewards of the nation's resources. These differing philosophies of whites and Indians only increased the opportunity for conflict.

In 1790 and 1791 the Indians inflicted two stinging and humiliating defeats on the American army. Faced with an increasingly dangerous situation, President Washington appointed Revolutionary War hero **"Mad Anthony" Wayne** to crush the Indians. In a careful, meticulously planned campaign, Wayne and his force marched from Fort Washington on the Ohio River (modern Cincinnati) to a site near modern Toledo. In the **Battle of Fallen Timbers,** so called because most of the fighting occurred in a maze of tangled trees knocked down by a storm, Wayne's forces routed the Indians. In the resulting **Treaty of Fort Greenville,** the Indians surrendered all rights to the southern half of Ohio.

After Fallen Timbers, settlers began to pour into the Ohio region of the Northwest Territory. A series of land acts passed in 1796, 1800, and 1804 reduced the size of a minimum purchase to 160 acres and lowered the price from $2.00 to $1.64 an acre. In addition, these acts allowed the settler to purchase on credit with a down payment of $80. As a result, ordinary farmers and not just land speculators could buy land in the Ohio Valley. By 1799 Ohio's population had grown so much that Congress sliced it off the Northwest Territory and made it a separate territory. In 1803 Ohio was admitted to the Union as the first state from the Northwest Territory.

Harrison vs. Tecumseh

Looking over the names of the men who fought at Fallen Timbers is much like looking at a "Who's Who" of American history. Meriwether Lewis, William Clark, and Zebulon Pike, for example, all served loyally in Wayne's force. The two most important veterans of Fallen Timbers, as far as the Northwest Territory was concerned, were two young men on opposite sides–a nineteen-year-old officer named **William Henry Harrison** and an Indian scout named **Tecumseh.**

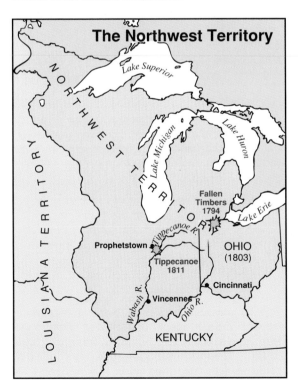

The Northwest Territory

William Henry Harrison–Harrison was the son of Benjamin Harrison, governor of Virginia and signer of the Declaration of Independence. Lured by the promise of glory and adventure, Harrison joined the army in which he served as an aide to Wayne in the Fallen Timbers campaign. In 1798 Harrison left the army and entered politics. In 1800 he was appointed governor of the Indiana Territory (modern Indiana, Illinois, Michigan, and Wisconsin), and he served in that office until 1812.

Harrison was much fairer in his dealings with the Indians than the average frontier settler–whose philosophy can be summed up with the callous statement "The only good Indian is a dead Indian." Harrison followed Jefferson in believing that Indians should receive the full help and protection of the government. It genuinely distressed Harrison, for example, that he could never find a white jury which would convict a white man for killing an Indian. Harrison also approved of Jefferson's plan to encourage the Indians to give up hunting and take up farming. In that way, the Indians would lead a more settled life, and they would not need large tracts of undeveloped forests in which to hunt. As well intentioned as Jefferson, Harrison, and men like them may have been, they nonetheless insisted that the Indians give up their traditional way of life and open their lands to white settlement.

Tecumseh–Harrison's chief adversary was Tecumseh, one of the greatest Indian leaders in the history of North America. Born around 1768 near modern Springfield, Ohio, Tecumseh led the last great Indian challenge to the United States in the Northwest Territory. As part of the Shawnee tribe, he was raised as a warrior, and since his father and two brothers were killed in battle against the whites, he retaliated with a vengeance.

Tecumseh realized that, individually, the Indian tribes could never stand against the United States. Therefore, he proposed joining all the Indian tribes into a single confederation with himself as head. When Harrison protested Tecumseh's actions, the Indian replied calmly that he was simply following the example of the United States in joining his people into one nation. Although resented by chiefs who feared him as a threat to their power, Tecum-

Shawnee chief Tecumseh (left) and
General William Henry Harrison
(right) personified the clash between
Indian and white in the Northwest
Territory. William Henry Harrison, by
Rembrandt Peale, National Portrait
Gallery, Smithsonian Institution.

seh began building his confederation by sheer force
of personality. His persuasive speeches wooed Indians to his cause. His fearlessness and code of honor
won respect even among white men. (Unlike some
Indians, Tecumseh never tortured prisoners or attacked women and children.)

Contributing to Tecumseh's success was a religious movement led by his brother, a man known
as **the Prophet.** Maimed (he had lost an eye in an
accident with a bow and arrow), somewhat cowardly, and a virtual alcoholic, Tecumseh's brother
suddenly claimed in 1805 to have received a revelation from the "Master of Life." After this experience, he quit drinking and began to preach to
the tribes. Indians must reject the white man's
ways, the Prophet said, especially his whiskey. All
Indians must learn to treat each other fairly and to
draw together against the whites, who were the offspring of an evil god.

When the Prophet began to win converts among
the tribes of the Northwest, Harrison unwittingly
played into his hands. The governor sent a message
to the Indians, urging them to reject this so-called
prophet. He said,

> Demand of him some proofs at least of his
> being the messenger of the Deity. . . . If
> he is really a prophet, ask of him to cause
> the sun to stand still–the moon to alter its
> course–or the dead to rise from their graves.
> If he does these things, you may then be-
> lieve that he has been sent by God.

The message backfired. Somehow (perhaps
through British agents in Canada), the Prophet
learned of a total eclipse of the sun that was to occur
in 1806. The Prophet announced to every Indian he
could reach that he would indeed make the sun stand
still. The Indians were awed when the Prophet an-

nounced, "Behold! darkness has shrouded the sun," and the sun apparently did vanish. Multitudes flocked to Tecumseh and his brother. As their headquarters, the brothers built a village called Prophetstown in the Indiana Territory at the juncture of the Wabash and Tippecanoe rivers–only about a hundred and twenty miles from Harrison's territorial capital in Vincennes.

Tippecanoe–As his warrior army grew, Tecumseh announced that no more Indian lands would be opened to the white man without the consent of *all* the tribes. Harrison knew full well this demand would mean that no more land sales would be made. The governor met Tecumseh personally in 1810, but they could reach no agreement. When Harrison suggested sending Tecumseh's demands to the president, the Indian leader replied that the president "is so far off he will not be injured by the war; he may sit still in his town and drink his wine, whilst you and I will have to fight it out."

Thinking that a clash seemed inevitable, Harrison decided to act quickly. In 1811 when Tecumseh was away in the South trying to rally the tribes there to his cause, Harrison took a force of some eight hundred men up the Wabash and camped near Prophetstown on the Tippecanoe River. In his brother's absence, the Prophet ordered a night attack on the American camp, promising to charm the white man's weapons so that they would not harm the warriors. In the **Battle of Tippecanoe,** Harrison's forces drove off the Indians but took heavy losses. The Indians abandoned Prophetstown, and Harrison destroyed it. When Tecumseh returned, he found that he must begin all over again. This time, however, he had an ally. The United States and Great Britain were about to go to war.

Section Review

1. What battle opened the Ohio Territory to white settlement?
2. Who were the single most important white and Indian leaders, respectively, in the Northwest Territory?
3. How did Harrison's plea to the Indians to test the Prophet backfire?

The War of 1812

In 1808 Thomas Jefferson refused to run for a third term, but he persuaded the Republicans to nominate his secretary of state, **James Madison,** as his successor. Madison crushed Federalist Charles Cotesworth Pinckney in the election, and in 1809 he took office as the nation's fourth president. A keen political philosopher (he was, after all, "the father of the Constitution") and experienced politician, Madison was nevertheless not a great president. He was too passive and tended to allow Congress to dominate him. Also he was distracted for most of his two terms as the United States rushed headlong into war with Great Britain.

Background to the War

Worsening Relations–In 1803 Great Britain and Napoleonic France went to war again. The British navy was too powerful for Napoleon to invade Great Britain, and Napoleon's army was too strong for Britain to defeat France in battle on land. As a result each side tried to starve the other by destroying its trade. Unfortunately, the neutral United States was caught between the two. Both Britain and France seized American ships which they thought were bound for enemy ports, but Britain–with its powerful navy–seized more than the French. In addition Britain claimed the right of **impressment,** the right to stop American ships, forcibly remove British deserters, and put them back into service. The discipline in the Royal Navy was harsh and cruel and the living conditions squalid; so it was no wonder that British seamen (many of whom had been forced into the navy in the first place) fled to American ships. As if stopping and searching American ships were not enough, British officers–in desperate need of sailors–sometimes "mistakenly" took Americans as well. Although both Britain and France oppressed American shipping, the greater number of British provocations made Britain seem more villainous to the United States.

Tension began to mount during Jefferson's second term. British and French trade restrictions merely harassed the Americans, but an incident of violence–the *Chesapeake* affair–nearly brought war in 1807. The British warship *Leopard,* suspecting that British deserters were aboard the

U.S.S. *Chesapeake,* stopped the American ship and demanded the right to search the vessel. When the *Chesapeake*'s captain refused, the British opened fire and killed or wounded over twenty men. The *Chesapeake* surrendered, the British took four ''deserters'' (three of whom were actually Americans), and Americans were outraged.

Jefferson did not want war, however. Instead he persuaded Congress to adopt the **Embargo Act** which banned all American trade with the rest of the world. In keeping needed American goods from Europe, Jefferson hoped to force Britain and France to lift their restrictions. The embargo failed miserably. France did not need American goods as much as Jefferson thought. Britain needed the goods more, but it could not risk helping Napoleon by lifting its restrictions. Those most hurt by the embargo were Americans. Shipping dropped dramatically, and economic recession threw merchants, sailors, shipbuilders, and many others out of work. Foods rotted on docks as owners could find no market for them. New England suffered the most, but all of the states felt the pinch.

Just before Jefferson left office, the government admitted its failure. Congress replaced the embargo with the **Non-Intercourse Act.** This act restored some international trade (though not with Britain or France), but more importantly it offered to restore trade with either nation if either would lift its trade restrictions. Non-intercourse was no more successful than the embargo, and in 1810 Congress tried a new approach with what was known as **Macon's Bill Number Two.** This bill made the European belligerents a frank offer. It abolished the non-intercourse policy and restored all trade. The act then stated that if either country would repeal its antitrade regulations, the United States would restore trade with that side in the war and refuse to trade with the other. England and France themselves would determine which side gained the trade.

Napoleon jumped at the chance. He seemingly repealed his restrictions in 1810, and the United States resumed non-intercourse with Britain. The British correctly doubted Napoleon's honesty and rejected the offer. Despite Napoleon's continued interference with American shipping, the United States shut its eyes, took Napoleon at his word, and tried to force the British to comply. Both England and France viewed the American action as virtually bringing the United States into the war on France's side. At any rate, the action hastened America's entering into a real war against Britain.

The War Hawks—The congressional elections of 1810 nudged America closer to war. In the West and the South a number of intensely nationalistic, prowar representatives joined the House. These **''War Hawks,''** led by **Henry Clay** of Kentucky and **John C. Calhoun** of South Carolina, pushed for war with Britain. The War Hawks feared that British trade restrictions would harm western trade down the Mississippi River. They also believed that the British were supporting, and perhaps equipping, the Indians under Tecumseh in the Northwest. Some War Hawks were frankly expansionists who wanted to seize Canada. Above all, the group saw British acts such as impressment as insults to American honor. In short order the War Hawks elected Clay Speaker of the House and began pressuring Madison toward war.

Declaration, Division, and Disarray—Madison did not need to be pressured too much. On June 1, 1812, the president sent a war message to Congress. He gave the legislators five reasons for declaring war on Britain: (1) impressment of American sailors, (2) violations of American territorial waters, (3) plunderings of American goods, (4) refusal to revoke trade restrictions, and (5) incitement of the Indians to violence.

Debate over the declaration of war was bitter. In general Federalists, New Englanders, and easterners opposed the war. They depended on the sea for their livelihood and could see no advantage in making matters worse. If anything, they preferred a war against France. Those in the South and West, such as the War Hawks, favored the war. The Middle States were divided, but the prowar faction managed to build a majority in both houses. The House voted 79-49 for war and the Senate 19-13. Ironically, only days before the declaration, Great Britain had revoked its trade restrictions. If there had been some quick means of communicating the news, there might never have been a war at all.

Fighting a war is a difficult endeavor even in the best of circumstances. The United States entered the War of 1812 divided and unprepared. The New England states in particular resented the war and resisted giving money or men to the war effort. They called it "Mr. Madison's War," as though the whole affair had nothing to do with them. The War Hawks were eager to fight but were reluctant to pay the costs. After declaring war, they voted down an attempt to enlarge the navy. With only sixteen seagoing warships, America entered a war against the world's greatest naval power.

The United States Army was not ready either. Jefferson and the Republicans feared a large standing army as a threat to liberty. In 1812 the army numbered a mere seven thousand men, and it would take time to raise and train new recruits. The nation had thousands of state militiamen, but these often proved undependable in real fighting. As one historian noted of the militia, "Many of the troops had obviously come to see a show, not to fight a war." Most of the army's commanders were aged veterans of the War for Independence. Only the fact that Britain was tied down by the war with Napoleon gave the Americans an initial advantage.

Course of the War

Disasters in Canada—Henry Clay had bragged that "the militia of Kentucky alone" would be enough to conquer Canada. In reality, the task was far more difficult because of the land's enormous size and pro-British population. The government assigned General William Hull to attack Canada from Detroit in the west and General Stephen Van Rensselaer from New York in the east. A brilliant British general, Isaac Brock, derailed this plan. First, his British-Indian force darted into Michigan and surrounded Hull in Detroit. By hinting that his Indian allies would be uncontrollable in an attack, Brock frightened Hull into surrendering his entire force without a fight. Thus the entire Northwest was open to the British and Indians. Then Brock rushed to meet Van Rensselaer's force near Niagara Falls. In the ensuing battle, Brock was killed, but the Americans were driven back into New York. The United States' opening campaign was a fiasco.

The War at Sea—The disasters in Canada were at least partly offset by early victories at sea. In engagements with single British warships American vessels fared quite well. The U.S.S. *Constitution, United States, Hornet,* and others defeated British ships in combat. The *Constitution* was particularly effective. In battles with the British *Guerrière* and *Java,* the *Constitution* shattered the enemy with devastating broadsides. British cannonballs, however, often bounced off the solid oak sides of the *Constitution,* leading Americans to nickname it **"Old Ironsides."**

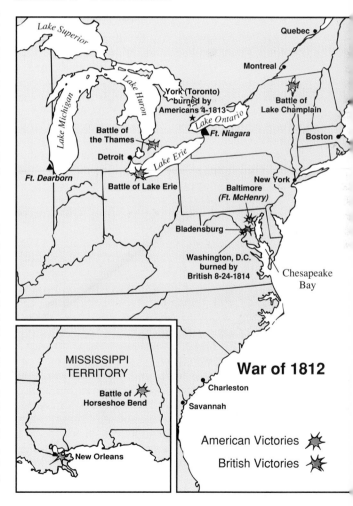

War of 1812

American Victories

British Victories

The British navy, however, outnumbered the American fleet in ships by at least fifty to one. As the British tightened their blockade along the coast, they forced American warships to stay in port or spend the rest of the war at sea preying on British shipping. The American victories soon ceased, but the early triumphs on the high seas encouraged the American public.

Recovery of the Northwest—After Hull's surrender at Detroit the government gave William Henry Harrison command of operations in the Northwest. Harrison realized that he could never secure the territory unless the United States controlled Lake Erie. American captain **Oliver Hazard Perry** rose to the challenge. By building his own ships, dragging cannon and ammunition through the wilderness to Lake Erie, and using as sailors Kentucky militiamen who had never been on anything larger than a flatboat, Perry defeated the British fleet in the **Battle of Lake Erie** (September 10, 1813). Perry sent a triumphant message to Harrison: "We have met the enemy and they are ours."

With Lake Erie secured, Harrison moved against the British army. The two armies met near the River Thames (TEMZ) some sixty miles east of Detroit on October 5, 1813. In the **Battle of the Thames,** Harrison routed the British-Indian force. Tecumseh was killed in the battle, and with him died his dream of an Indian confederation. The Northwest was never again seriously threatened by the Indians or the British.

The British Drive for Victory—Despite Harrison's victory, the American situation remained grave early in 1814. Napoleon had surrendered, allowing Britain to turn its full attention to its upstart former colonies. The British devised a threefold plan to win the war. First, an army would descend from Canada and separate New York and New England from the rest of the states. Second, an amphibious force would attack and raid major cities on the eastern coast. Third, another force would attack and capture New Orleans.

The first stage of the campaign ended in failure when a small American naval squadron defeated a larger British fleet on Lake Champlain on September 11, 1814. Without control of the lake, the British commander would not risk an invasion, and the force turned back.

"Don't Give Up the Ship"

When Perry won his great victory on Lake Erie he was flying a flag above his ship which read, "Don't Give Up the Ship." Perry's flag quoted a commander who had lost his life–and his ship–in battle only a little more than three months earlier.

On June 1, 1813, the U.S.S. *Chesapeake* (the same ship which the *Leopard* had humiliated in 1807) under Captain James Lawrence sailed out of Boston Harbor to meet the British warship *Shannon*. The two ships were relatively equal, but the crew of the British ship was more experienced and better trained. The *Shannon* manhandled the *Chesapeake* in battle. When Captain Lawrence was hit by a musket ball in the stomach, he said to his men as they carried him below, "Fight her 'till she sinks, and don't give up the ship."

The command was vain. The British boarded the *Chesapeake* and captured it, and Lawrence died before the ship reached harbor. His words lived on, however. The phrase became a motto for the U.S. Navy, and Perry's flag is now on display in Memorial Hall at the U.S. Naval Academy in Annapolis, Maryland.

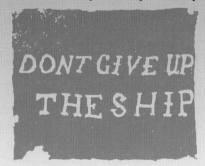

The second stage was initially more successful. A British force landed in Maryland in August and marched toward Washington. In the **Battle of Bladensburg,** the British scattered a large force of American militia and cleared a path to the American capital. President Madison and other government leaders fled in haste, and the British army marched into the city unopposed. British officers dined in the president's mansion on a meal that the Madisons had left cooking. Soldiers soon set fire to the Capitol, the president's mansion, and several other important government buildings. British admiral Sir George Cockburn (KOH burn) personally ordered the destruction of an anti-British newspaper; he told his men to particularly destroy all the type for the letter *C* so that the paper could print no more attacks on him. Only a series of severe thunderstorms prevented the entire city from burning to the ground.

The British had no intention of holding Washington, the value of which was more symbolic than strategic; so they turned their attention next to Baltimore. That city, however, was protected by a larger, more disciplined force and by the well-designed **Fort McHenry.** The British fleet tried vainly to bombard the fort into submission. After three days of fighting in which the British commanding general was killed, the British abandoned the task. The whole force left Chesapeake Bay and joined the effort to capture New Orleans.

*The War in the South—*In the South, the War of 1812 was complicated in a manner never expected by the British. As a result of Tecumseh's efforts among the southern tribes, civil war broke out among the Creek Indians in the Mississippi Territory (modern Alabama and Mississippi). The conflict between pro-American and anti-American Creeks grew sharp, and white settlers bordering Indian lands began to suffer. The government authorized Tennessee general **Andrew Jackson** to help the friendly Creeks and to defend the South against the British. Jackson was not a brilliant strategist, but he was a firm and unflinching leader. Jackson's men called him "Old Hickory" because he was as lean and tough as a hickory branch. Jackson knew how to handle his frontier army. When some of his militia tried to leave during the campaign, for example, Jackson laid his rifle across his horse's neck and promised to personally shoot the first man who tried to leave. Jackson's force won a series of victories against the Creeks, climaxing in the **Battle of Horseshoe Bend** (1814) in which he nearly annihilated the unfriendly Creeks.

Jackson had little time to savor his victory, however. He marched quickly to New Orleans late in 1814 to meet the British thrust there. At New Orleans Jackson stationed his troops and artillery behind fortifications made of earthworks and cotton bales. On January 8, 1815, the overconfident British, believing that their troops would make short work of the American rabble, marched directly on Jackson's lines. Old Hickory's massed artillery tore huge gaps in the British lines, and his frontier sharpshooters picked off those who managed to survive the cannons. The British lost two thousand men; the Americans lost thirteen.

The **Battle of New Orleans** was the most stunning victory of the War of 1812, but it was fought after the war was over. The **Treaty of Ghent** (signed December 24, 1814), climaxing four months of negotiations, had ended hostilities some two weeks earlier. Slow communications from Europe, however, kept that news from America for several weeks. Nonetheless, the battle made Jackson the greatest hero of the war.

Results of the War

The Treaty of Ghent was a peace without victory; conditions returned to much what they were in 1812. Britain and the United States simply wanted to stop fighting, and both were willing to settle their differences diplomatically later. The United States did profit from the war, however. Tecumseh's confederation was finished, and the Northwest was wide open to settlement. Also the British blockade unintentionally spurred the growth of American industry and manufacturing (discussed in Chapter 11).

The war brought changes in attitude too. For years the United States had tried vainly to distance itself from affairs in Europe. After the war the nation was secure enough to retreat from the rest

"By the Dawn's Early Light"
Just prior to the British attack on Fort McHenry, Baltimore lawyer **Francis Scott Key** and some friends sailed out to the British fleet under a flag of truce to ask for the release of a civilian doctor who had been captured by the British. The British commander graciously received the party and agreed to release the doctor, but the commander refused to allow them to leave. The fleet was preparing to attack Fort McHenry, and they had to stay aboard until the battle was over.

Key and the other Americans had front-row seats for the battle as they watched the British fleet shell the fort. As the pounding continued into the night, the anxious little group strained to see what was happening. As dawn broke, they saw the American flag flying proudly above the fort, signaling that the attack had failed. As he gazed at the flag, Key was inspired. He began to write on the back of an envelope the words to a poem that came into his head. He called it "The Defense of Fort McHenry." We know it, of course, as "The Star-Spangled Banner."

The first verse of the poem remained much as Key wrote it on the ship, although the first line originally read "O say, can you see, *through* the dawn's early light." He wrote the other, less familiar verses, after returning to the shore. After the poem was set to music, it became one of the most popular patriotic songs in America. Eventually, in 1931, Congress officially proclaimed "The Star-Spangled Banner" the national anthem of the United States.

of the world into a shell of isolationism. Not until World War I over a century later would Americans again become deeply involved in foreign affairs.

Perhaps the chief result was a sense of national pride and honor. In a toast after the war, naval commander Stephen Decatur captured this spirit when he said, "Our country! In her intercourse with foreign nations may she always be in the right; but *our country, right or wrong*." This surge of patriotism became an important influence in shaping the period after the war, the "Era of Good Feelings" under President James Monroe.

Section Review

1. By what three pieces of legislation did the United States hope to use economic pressure to avoid war with Great Britain?
2. Give at least two reasons the War Hawks offered for going to war with Britian.
3. What five reasons did President Madison give for going to war against Britain?
4. What was Britain's threefold plan for winning the War of 1812? How did each stage of the plan fare in the actual fighting?

"The Era of Good Feelings"

The "Virginia Dynasty" of presidents continued in 1816 when Secretary of State **James Monroe** was elected to succeed James Madison. Monroe, a former law student of Jefferson's, maintained the dominance of the Jeffersonian philosophy into the 1820s. Monroe's quiet, modest manner pleased and impressed even the staunchest of anti-Jeffersonians. So popular–or at least so unobjectionable–was Monroe that in the election for his second term he came within one electoral vote of becoming the only president besides Washington to be elected unanimously. The president's popularity, the glow of postwar triumph, and the collapse of all political opposition to the Republicans caused Monroe's two terms to be known as **"the Era of Good Feelings."**

Demise of the Federalists

One cause of the Era of Good Feelings was the collapse of the Federalist party. In 1812 the Federalists had halted their decline by joining antiwar Republicans against Madison. The election of 1812 was so close in the electoral college that the switch of Pennsylvania alone would have given the victory to Federalist-Republican DeWitt Clinton instead of Madison. Throughout the War of 1812 the Federalists led a loud chorus of protest against the progress and conduct of the war.

During the conflict's darkest days in 1814, representatives of the New England states–mostly Federalists–met in Hartford, Connecticut. The **Hartford Convention** opposed the war and hinted that New England might just secede from the Union if its demands were not met. Unfortunately for the Federalists, the Treaty of Ghent and the Battle of New Orleans soon followed the Hartford Convention. In the flush of victory, the convention's action looked, and perhaps was, treasonous. If the Federalist party was dying before the war, then it was clearly dead after it. Within a few years the discredited party disappeared entirely.

Mending Fences with Britain

The good feelings were not necessarily limited to the United States. The Treaty of Ghent stopped the fighting with Britain, but it did not settle the problems between the two nations. The United States and Great Britain, therefore, carried out extensive negotiations to iron out their differences. One of the first and most important of these agreements was the **Rush-Bagot** (BAG ut) **Treaty** (1817), which called for disarmament in the Great Lakes. This treaty has the distinction of being one of the few disarmament treaties in history that has succeeded. Its provisions were eventually extended along the entire U.S.-Canadian border as the nations advanced westward, and the two countries have maintained peaceful relations throughout their history. Today the Peace Arch in Blaine, Washington, on the Canadian border commemorates over a hundred and fifty years of extended peace between neighboring countries with no fortifications, barbed wire, or large armies between them. In addition, in 1818 the United States and Britain agreed to occupy the Oregon Territory on the Pacific Ocean jointly until they could decide how to divide it.

Conflict in Florida

Some members of Congress, especially the War Hawks, had hoped that the War of 1812 would result in the conquest of Florida. Although Spain exercised nominal control over the area, anarchy would be a better description of the government. Pirates, escaped slaves, and renegade Indians not only lived in Florida but also used it as a haven from which to make raids across the U.S. border. When violence broke out between the Indians and settlers in Georgia, the American government authorized Andrew Jackson to take a force into Florida and crush the Indians. In 1818, in his usual blunt and thorough manner, General Jackson punished the Indians in a swift campaign. He also arrested two British citizens who were accused of aiding the Indians. After speedy trials, Old Hickory had one hanged and the other shot. Then, for good measure, Jackson's army captured Pensacola, the capital of Spanish Florida.

Jackson's actions exceeded his orders; the government was certainly not interested in offending the British again. Jackson's campaign was enormously popular in the United States, however. Fortunately, the British were not interested in going to war over a couple of obscure Indian traders. The

Spanish were understandably angry, but Secretary of State **John Quincy Adams** decided to take a hard line with the Spanish government. Jackson was only defending American lives and property, Adams said, and the Spanish should do a better job of policing their territory. Jackson's campaign showed Spain how helpless it would be if the United States found sufficient excuse to simply take Florida. Rather than end up with nothing, the Spanish government decided to sell the region. Under the provisions of the **Adams-Onis Treaty,** the U.S. took possession of Florida in 1821 at a cost of $5 million. The United States now possessed all territory south of Canada and east of the Mississippi River, as well as its holdings in the Louisiana Territory.

The Monroe Doctrine

The impact of Napoleon's conquering armies and ideas was not limited to Europe. When Napoleon conquered Spain and Portugal, the Spanish and Portuguese possessions in Latin America leaped at the chance to be free. Led by revolutionary leaders **Simón Bolívar** and **Jose de San Martín,** most of Latin America broke from its European overlords and founded independent republics. After the fall of Napoleon, Spain began to look longingly at its former colonies, and the other powers of Europe indicated that they would be willing to help crush these ''dangerous'' revolutionary republics. One exception to this mood of reconquest was Great Britain. The British had established a profitable trade with these new nations and had no desire to see them become colonies again. So the British government asked the United States if it would like to join Britain in proclaiming that European powers should not intervene in the Americas.

President Monroe and Secretary of State Adams thought over the offer. They decided that rather than tying America to Britain, the nation should issue its own warning. In 1823 in his annual message to Congress, President Monroe declared, ''The American continents, by the free and independent condition which they have assumed and maintain, are henceforth not to be considered as subjects for future colonization by any European powers.'' Furthermore, he added, ''In the wars of the European powers in matters relating to themselves we have never taken any part, nor does it comport with our policy so to do.''

With the **Monroe Doctrine,** as Monroe's statement of policy came to be called, the United States established two principles: European nations could not intervene in the Western Hemisphere (except where they already held colonies), and the United States would not meddle in European affairs. When issued, the statement was little more than a paper pledge since the United States lacked the military might to back it up. The Monroe Doctrine, however, has become a cornerstone of American foreign policy. Since 1823 numerous presidents and statesmen have defended its principles and expanded its meaning. It affects the manner in which the United States conducts its foreign policy even today.

The Monroe Doctrine embodied one of the cherished tenets of Jeffersonianism and also solidified one result of the War of 1812–it formalized America's determination to remain isolated from Europe and its affairs. The decision to remain aloof proved to be a wise one. As Monroe's term of office and his Era of Good Feelings drew to a close, the nation confronted serious internal problems and important internal developments. The young nation had to direct all of its energies toward expanding and developing the frontier, harnessing new technologies, and grappling with the problem of slavery–all of which would test the character of America's government. The Era of Good Feelings, and of Jeffersonianism in general, ended with ominous clouds of conflict on the horizon.

Section Review

1. Why was Monroe's time in office called ''the Era of Good Feelings''?
2. Whose campaign in Florida motivated Spain to sell that territory to the United States?
3. What treaty settled a border dispute between the United States and Great Britain? What treaty enabled the U.S. to purchase Florida from Spain?
4. What are the two basic principles of the Monroe Doctrine?

Chapter Review

Terms

Thomas Jefferson
Jeffersonian Republicanism
Twelfth Amendment
John Marshall
Marbury v. *Madison*
judicial review
delegated powers
Gibbons v. *Ogden*
McCulloch v. *Maryland*
implied powers
Barbary states
Napoleon Bonaparte
Louisiana Purchase
Meriwether Lewis
William Clark
Zebulon Pike
Aaron Burr
"Mad Anthony" Wayne

Battle of Fallen Timbers
Treaty of Fort Greenville
William Henry Harrison
Tecumseh
the Prophet
Battle of Tippecanoe
the War of 1812 (1812-1815)
James Madison
impressment
Chesapeake affair
Embargo Act
Non-Intercourse Act
Macon's Bill Number Two
War Hawks
Henry Clay
John C. Calhoun
U.S.S. *Constitution* ("Old Ironsides")
Oliver Hazard Perry

Battle of Lake Erie
Battle of the Thames
Battle of Bladensburg
Fort McHenry
Francis Scott Key
Andrew Jackson
Battle of Horseshoe Bend
Battle of New Orleans
Treaty of Ghent
James Monroe
the Era of Good Feelings
Hartford Convention
Rush-Bagot Treaty
John Quincy Adams
Adams-Onis Treaty
Simón Bolívar
Jose de San Martín
Monroe Doctrine

Content Questions

1. What was the view of Thomas Jefferson and William Henry Harrison concerning American Indian policy? Why was their view unsatisfactory to the Indians?
2. How did Tecumseh hope to slow the advance of the Americans into the Northwest Territory?
3. List at least three difficulties the United States faced when it entered the War of 1812.
4. What was the chief importance of each of the following battles to the overall course of the War of 1812: Lake Erie, the Thames, and Horseshoe Bend?
5. Name at least four results of the War of 1812.
6. What policy statement confirmed America's determination to remain isolated from European affairs after the War of 1812?

Application Questions

1. Do you think that Thomas Jefferson's dream of a dominantly agricultural America was a realistic idea?
2. Does the principle of judicial review make the Supreme Court too powerful? Defend your answer.
3. Consider the statement from p. 188, "Our country! In her intercourse with foreign nations may she always be in the right; but *our country, right or wrong.*" Do you agree or disagree with this statement?
4. Does the fact that Jackson's invasion of Florida resulted in the United States' acquiring that territory excuse his exceeding his orders?

CHAPTER 10

The Age of Jackson (1820-1840)

"Just think, Mama! This sofa is a millionth part mine."

A young democrat to her parents as she romped on White House furniture during Jackson's inauguration, 1829

All Creation Going to the White House. *Robert Cruikshank's engraving of Jackson's inaugural*

It seemed to run in the family. John Adams had been swept from the White House in 1800 and now nearly thirty years later, his son John Quincy Adams was suffering the same fate at the hands of "the people." The people's hands, however, were damaging more than Adams's pride the day he left office. They were stripping wall paper from the White House walls for souvenirs, scooping out globs of melting ice cream, dripping trails of it on the carpet, smashing furniture and glass, and gripping the hand of the mansion's newest occupant, Andrew Jackson—just before he slipped out a back door to leave the house to its fate. As one unamused observer grumbled, "The reign of King Mob seemed triumphant."

While it is true that the invading army of supporters could be blamed for being a bit raucous, they should also be credited with providing a fitting start to a new American era–the age of Jacksonian democracy, the age of the common man.

Crosscurrents

Though the era is named after its hero, **Andrew Jackson,** it was actually well underway before Jackson's 1829 inauguration. Since the beginning of the century, powerful crosscurrents were roiling the political and social seas. Jackson would ride into office on its turbulent crest, but the age was shaped by forces much larger than any man. These were widespread currents of nationalism, sectionalism, and democratization that originated before Jackson's presidency and would shape America's future long after Old Hickory had gone.

Nationalism

The years immediately following the War of 1812 saw a growing spirit of nationalism throughout the country. The relief and the prospects that came with peace bolstered national pride and vision. The rapid expansion of the period gave the Star-Spangled Banner a larger constellation, including six more states in the West and deep South by 1821: Louisiana (1812), Indiana (1816), Mississippi (1817), Illinois (1818), Alabama (1819), and Missouri (1821). In addition a new breed of leaders, men such as John Quincy Adams and Daniel Webster of New England, Henry Clay of Kentucky, and John C. Calhoun of South Carolina–young, capable, and energetic–were advancing the vision of a strong, burgeoning America.

At the heart of this new nationalism was a concern for the economic strength of the nation, a union of states bound by cords of commerce. **Henry Clay,** the chief advocate of this economic nationalism in Congress, dubbed it the **American System.** Clay's system consisted of three parts: protective tariffs, internal improvements, and renewal of the National Bank.

Protective Tariff–Necessity being the mother of invention, Jefferson's Embargo Act (p. 184) and the trade disruptions brought on by the War of 1812 had the unexpected benefit of spurring the growth of American manufacturing. This was an important step toward economic independence from Europe. Since colonial days America had served both as a source of raw materials for Europe, particularly Britain, and as a market for British finished goods. American manufacturing would shake up this longstanding arrangement. The British were quick to see the threat to their own interests posed by America's infant industry, and they determined to nip it in the bud. One member of the British Parliament even urged his country to sell goods to America well below cost in order "to stifle in the cradle, those rising manufactures in the United States, which war has forced into existence, contrary to the natural course of things."

A **tariff** is a tax on imported goods, and a **protective tariff** is an unusually high tariff designed to shield a nation's manufactures from potentially fatal foreign competition. The **Tariff of 1816** was America's first such protectionist legislation. The tariff, however, was a two-edged sword. Though encouraging some economic growth, the tariff would also discourage competition, which would mean higher consumer prices. In addition, regions of the country that produced raw goods, such as the agrarian South, or that depended upon shipping for their livelihood, such as New England, would be hurt by the loss of foreign trade. In the postwar nationalist euphoria, economic independence outweighed other considerations, but eventually protective tariffs would become a sore point between the sections.

Second National Bank–The charter for the first National Bank expired in 1811, setting off an avalanche of inflationary paper money issued by a motley assortment of private banks. The financial problems created by inflation were only compounded by the war, all of which made it difficult for the national government to meet its obligations.

It is interesting that the Republicans of the 1790s were vehemently opposed to a national bank as well as to a protective tariff for industry. When in power, however, they tended to set aside their constitutional qualms in favor of such "Federalist" issues. In 1816 nationalistic Republicans approved a twenty-year charter on a second Bank of the United States, patterned after Hamilton's first central bank. Such a bank would assist economic growth by providing uniform currency, a source for loans to the public and private sectors, and a depository for government revenue.

Internal Improvements–Another key element of the American System was **internal improvements,** funding for roads, canals, and harbor developments that would bolster commerce and communications. Such improvements would help link western goods with eastern markets as well as provide better routes for trans-Appalachian settlement.

Despite the many advantages of internal improvements and their popularity in the growing West, this was the least successful aspect of the American System. President Madison and others believed they lacked constitutional authority to fund such projects. Why should Maine, they reasoned, be taxed to pave a road in Maryland? It was argued that roads and canals were the responsibility of the state or locality that they served. Younger Republicans complained that the president's narrow views were hindering economic growth. Calhoun, for example, protested to the president that the Constitution "was not a thesis for the logician to exercise his ingenuity on; . . . it ought to be construed with plain good sense."

Before the issue of internal improvements bogged down in the constitutional quagmire, one important step was approved: the building of the **National Road.** Begun during Jefferson's Administration, the graveled road extended from Baltimore to Cumberland, Maryland, but lack of funding brought construction to a halt. After considerable debate during the Madison years, additional funds were appropriated to extend the route to Wheeling, Virginia (now West Virginia). Further funding in 1825 drove the road into the heart of the new western states, reaching Zanesville, Ohio, and by 1839 ending in Vandalia, Illinois. Today motorists on Interstate 70 east of St. Louis travel basically the same route that pioneering families took in the 1830s by covered wagon, ox cart, and foot.

Sectionalism

Monroe's Era of Good Feelings turned out to be little more than that—just feelings. When hard times came to the country and tough questions were raised in Congress, the good feelings went bad and drove the sections North, South, and West further apart. Sectional strife would have a large impact on the politics of the coming Jacksonian era.

Panic of 1819—Following the War of 1812 the resumption of trade as well as the growth of domestic industry and western land sales brought economic good times to the country. Two unrelated events an ocean apart, however, quickly sent America's postwar prosperity tumbling, resulting in a depression, or *panic,* the **Panic of 1819.**

In Liverpool, England, the price of cotton fell sharply, owing to higher American prices and the introduction of cheap Asian cotton from India. The cotton collapse brought other American goods down with it. The financial failure was due in part to the high protectionist Tariff of 1816, a fact that

many, particularly in the hard-hit South, were quick to point out. The Virginia Agricultural Society told Congress in 1820 that the tariff was an unequal tax that favored a privileged class by granting them "oppressive monopolies, which are ultimately to grind both us and our children after us 'into dust and ashes.' "

The second factor contributing to the Panic of 1819 was the irresponsible action of state banks and the National Bank. The opening of western land purchases seemed to present a golden opportunity for banks to make loans to speculators and settlers. Banks, paper money, and loans all multiplied in the race for riches. When the economy soured, the Bank of the United States tried to whip the state banks into shape by tightening the money supply. As a result, many people defaulted on loans, and some lost their lands and homes. Many in the West and South felt that the Bank of the United States, which had been rife with fraud and scandal, was saving itself by oppressing the people. In these regions, a legacy of bitterness grew toward the National Bank.

Missouri Compromise—The routine admission of new states suddenly sparked a heated controversy, one that John Quincy Adams afterward described as a "title page to a great tragic volume."

When Missouri applied for statehood in 1818, its constitution permitted slavery (an understandable provision, considering that Missouri had ten thousand slaves at the time). Since there were already eleven slave states and eleven free states, the question of political balance between the South and North lay at the heart of the debate. The South, some time before, had lost control in the House of Representatives to the more populous North; balance in the Senate, therefore, remained critical to maintaining political control for the region.

In February 1819 Representative James Tallmadge of New York recommended that the act authorizing Missouri to become a state be amended in a way that would virtually prohibit slavery. The Tallmadge Amendment brought an outcry from the slave states for its interference in a state's prerogatives and for its threat to the balance of the Senate. Voting along sectional lines, House members approved the Tallmadge Amendment despite Southern objections. On a more even playing field, however, the amendment was defeated in the Senate.

The application of Maine for statehood in the summer of 1819, as well as Speaker of the House Henry Clay's skillful handling of the controversy, helped provide a compromise solution to the statehood stalemate. The **Missouri Compromise** of 1820 proposed that Maine be admitted as a free state and Missouri as a slave state, and that in the rest of the Louisiana Territory, slavery not be permitted north of 36° 30', Missouri's southern boundary. By a narrow margin the Missouri Compromise was approved, and Congress authorized Missouri to submit a constitution, the final step in the statehood process.

The Missouri controversy boded ill for the future. Political lines were drawn between the sections, and with the ever-expanding westward settlement, Missouri represented a problem that would

not soon go away. Speaking of the Missouri debate, Thomas Jefferson said, ''This momentous question, like a firebell in the night, awakened and filled me with terror. I considered it the knell of the Union.''

Democratization

Another growing force during the first quarter of the nineteenth century was the increasing openness of the political process. This democratization gave the average citizen a greater voice in his government.

Political expansion was evident in three major changes during the period. First was the extension of voting rights to all adult white males, not just property owners. New western states entering the Union, unbound by the political customs of the older states, drafted more democratic constitutions that helped open the way for universal manhood suffrage for whites and some free blacks by the

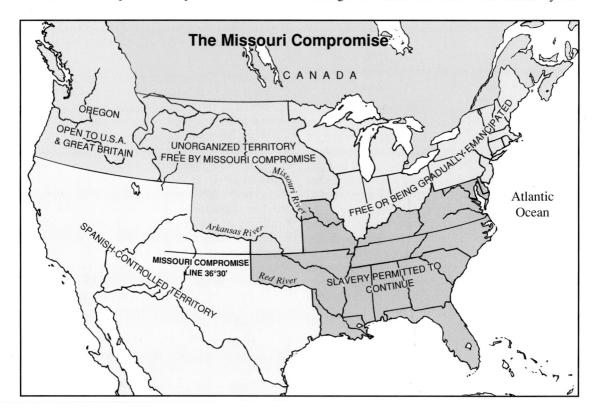

The Missouri Compromise

1830s. Second, the people gained a greater voice in presidential elections. In 1800 most electors in the electoral college were chosen by their state's legislature. After 1816, however, the majority of presidential electors were selected by popular vote, giving voters a greater influence in the choosing of their president.

These democratic changes in turn encouraged the third important change–the fracturing of the one-party system and the emergence of a strong two-party system. Since Jefferson's "Revolution of 1800" victory, the Republicans had dominated national politics. In fact, with the exception of Madison's unhappy presidency, the Federalists ceased even to be a threat in presidential contests. Without genuine competition, this single party dominance was in effect a nonpartisan system. It seemed for a time that national politics had returned to President Washington's ideal. It became popular to criticize any hint of political division. Even Andrew Jackson, who would one day be among the most partisan of presidents, urged Monroe in 1816 "to exterminate the monster called party spirit." Nonpartisan unity, however, like the "Era of Good Feelings" of which it was a part, proved to be a fragile thing.

Death of "King Caucus"–From 1796 to 1820, a congressional caucus selected the presidential and vice-presidential nominees for their party. (A **caucus** is a closed meeting of party leaders.) After Republicans became the dominant party, this meant that a handful of congressmen in effect picked the president of the United States. The "Virginia Dynasty" of Jefferson, Madison, and Monroe, serving a total of twenty-four years, was selected by the closed-door caucus method.

Despite those impressive presidential choices, the reign of "King Caucus" understandably came under fire as undemocratic. As early as 1800 one newspaper criticized "this factious meeting, this self appointed, self elected, self delegated club or caucus, or conspiracy," charging that about twenty-four men were deciding "for the people of the United States who should be president and vice president."

The 1824 election proved to be a political turning point in America. The caucus system of nomi-

John Quincy Adams

nating candidates was completely discredited, and the divisive presidential campaign that year ended the myth of a nonpartisan government.

A "Corrupt Bargain"–Four men threw their hats into the ring as candidates for president in 1824. William H. Crawford of Georgia was the choice of the dying congressional caucus, a fact that did him more harm than good. **John Quincy Adams,** son of the former president and Monroe's brilliant secretary of state, announced his candidacy. In addition two westerners joined the slate of candidates, the popular Speaker of the House, Kentuckian Henry Clay, and the "Hero of New Orleans," General Andrew Jackson of Tennessee.

The four-way race was not among competing parties, since all the candidates were at least in name Republicans, heirs of Mr. Jefferson. Rather the race was between competing personalities and regions of the country. The results were predictable–no candidate received a majority of the votes. In the electoral college tally Jackson polled 99, Adams 84, Crawford 41, and Clay 37. The popular vote,

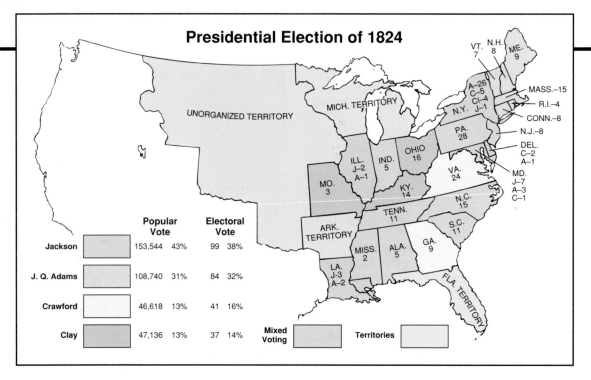

Presidential Election of 1824

	Popular Vote		Electoral Vote	
Jackson	153,544	43%	99	38%
J. Q. Adams	108,740	31%	84	32%
Crawford	46,618	13%	41	16%
Clay	47,136	13%	37	14%

which was recorded for the first time, gave Jackson 154,000, Adams 109,000, Crawford 46,000, and Clay 47,000. Since no candidate won a majority, the Twelfth Amendment required that the election be thrown into the House of Representatives. There the president would be chosen from among the top three candidates from the electoral college.

Clay, who did not make the cut, was placed in a unique position. He could not win the election, but as the powerful Speaker of the House he could decide who would. Clay preferred the nationalist policies of Adams, and he considered Jackson unqualified. Also Clay nursed his own ambitions of being the first president from the western states. It was an easy decision. He guided the voting to give Adams a victory on the first ballot.

Jackson's supporters were outraged. Old Hickory had won the most electoral and popular votes in the general election; why then was Adams president? Adams then compounded the problem by appointing Clay as secretary of state, a position that had already produced three presidents. Jackson's supporters claimed that Adams and Clay had made a **"corrupt bargain,"** an underhanded deal to give Adams the presidency in return for making Clay secretary. Although there is no proof of a prior deal, these charges stung Adams personally and impaired his administration from the start.

John Quincy Adams had had a distinguished political career, having served capably in several offices. His performance as secretary of state under James Monroe–particularly his settling of differences with Britain and his negotiation of the purchase of Florida from Spain–have caused some historians to rate him one of the greatest secretaries of state in history. He was unquestionably intellectually brilliant and morally conscientious and consistent. Nevertheless, John Quincy Adams was an ineffective president. Like his father, Adams had little patience for the backslapping ways of politics, and he never seemed to quite understand the people he was asked to lead. In his first annual address to Congress, for example, Adams urged the members to support his sometimes unpopular programs, saying they should not fold up their arms "and proclaim to the world that we are palsied by the will of our constituents." Handling voters so ineptly strengthened the pro-Jackson forces all the more.

One of the key features of Adams's administration was its strong nationalist emphasis. Expanding on Clay's American System, Adams worked for higher protective tariffs to encourage American manufacturing, internal improvements, and even proposed federal funding for higher education and the arts.

This nationalist thrust became a distinguishing mark of Adams's wing of the party, which became known as the **National Republicans.** The Jackson wing kept the old name, Democratic-Republicans, but eventually dropped the "Republican" part, keeping the name by which the party is still called, the **Democratic party.**

Rematch and Revenge—The candidates and perhaps the outcome of the 1828 election were probably determined four years earlier. It was to be an Adams-Jackson rematch. This time, however, many of the former Crawford and Clay supporters had moved into the Jackson camp, including a shrewd New York senator named **Martin Van Buren.** Van Buren's skill as a politician earned the 5' 6" native of Kinderhook, New York, the name "Little Magician." He helped organize the Democratic effort and urged Jackson to avoid mentioning divisive issues, emphasizing instead a *symbolic* campaign—Old Hickory, the friend of the common man.

Jackson and his running mate, **John C. Calhoun** of South Carolina, won by a landslide, getting 56 per cent of the popular vote and an electoral tally of 178 to 83. The election's two-party competition also boosted voter participation. For the first time a million voters cast ballots for the presidency, double the number of the 1824 election. This was just one of the signs that Jackson's victory marked a turning point in America.

Section Review

1. What were the three components of Henry Clay's American System?
2. What was America's first protectionist legislation?
3. What two factors contributed to the Panic of 1819?
4. What were the three provisions of the Missouri Compromise?
5. What two men did supporters of Andrew Jackson accuse of making a "corrupt bargain" in the presidential election of 1824?

The Jackson Years

Old Hickory

The democratic movement that won Jackson the presidency was underway before Old Hickory became its popular hero. While it could be argued that had there not been an Andrew Jackson, it would have been necessary to invent one, Jackson's remarkable life supplied more than enough material for his hero's image. By 1828 Jackson's biography read like *A Brief History of the United States.*

Jackson was born in the Carolina backcountry in 1767. His parents were Irish-Presbyterians who left Ulster just two years before their son was born. Frontier life then was crude and perilous. Andrew, Sr., died in an accident clearing his fields for spring planting. A few days later his grieving widow,

The *"people's president"*: Andrew Jackson, *by Thomas Sully, National Gallery of Art*

Betty, gave birth to a third son, giving him the name of her dead husband.

Young Andrew's early life was as rough-and-tumble as the land in which he lived. At thirteen he joined Patriot forces against the invading British, serving as a messenger. In April 1781 Andrew and his brother Robert were captured by British cavalry. When one of the officers ordered Andrew to clean his boots, Jackson refused to give the redcoat so much as a bow. The enraged officer slashed the boy on his head with a saber and hacked at his raised arm. Jackson would bear the scars of his defiance for the rest of his life.

After the war Jackson studied law in Salisbury, North Carolina, and was admitted to the bar. The young lawyer soon landed a position as a public prosecutor in the Tennessee territory. The opening West well suited the fiery, energetic Jackson. He acquired land, slaves, horses, and a taste for politics. Jackson became a state judge and in 1796 was elected to a term in Congress, where he gained some respect for his straightforward though roughshod manner.

Jackson's reputation, however, was not made in Washington; it was forged on the frontier, fighting Indians and redcoats. General Jackson drove his men hard, but he drove himself harder. His grit earned him the admiration of his ranks. "He's tough as hickory," they would say, and so he was. In 1805 he dueled with Charles Dickinson, a man who had repeatedly insulted his wife. Dickinson, a famed marksman, got off the first shot, putting a .70-caliber bullet next to Jackson's heart. Standing motionless, with a gaping chest wound, Old Hickory took aim and fired, killing Dickinson.

Opponents hurled epithets of "murderer" and "hangman" at him in 1828 (the latter name referring to his Florida campaign in 1818; see pp. 189-90), but with little effect. His code of honor was something instinctively understood in the raw country he represented.

As president, Andrew Jackson was not an innovator. His great success was as a symbol of what America had become. In broad strokes his life mirrored the life of the young republic. With Jackson in the White House, Jefferson's self-evident truths were indeed evident. America offered ordinary people extraordinary opportunity, and this is why Jackson's tumultuous inauguration was a celebration for common folks.

The People's President

Spoils of Victory—Jackson's partisan victory for "the people" ushered in a change in the filling of government jobs. The new president believed that public service should not be a lifelong career. Up to that time bureaucratic officials such as clerks, postmasters, revenue collectors, and court officers were appointed on a fairly permanent basis. Jackson held that men who stayed in public office for too long were prone to be corrupted by their power. Accordingly, after reasonable intervals, particularly with the change of administrations, rotation in office should occur.

Jackson actually took a low-key approach to replacing officeholders. During his first year in office he turned out only nine per cent of the appointed officeholders he inherited, and less than twenty per cent during his term.

The significance of Jackson's replacement of government officeholders was not so much what he did as what he started. The **spoils system,** as this patronage came to be called, would endure for half a century, taking on a highly partisan political character. While it is true that Jackson's policy did shake up an entrenched bureaucracy, it also removed some highly qualified individuals from office at times and replaced them with highly unqualified individuals. Neither did the spoils system necessarily make public servants more responsive to the public, since the bureaucrats owed their jobs to their party leaders, not to the people.

Kitchen Cabinet—Jackson's cabinet members were given their posts as political rewards for services rendered during the campaign, but they actually had little influence with the president. Jackson's real advisors were a close circle of friends critics called his **"Kitchen Cabinet."** It included newspaper editors, prominent Democrats in Congress, and his secretary of state, Martin Van Buren—all political insiders. Increasingly the president was taking on the role of party leader.

The Preacher and the President

One of the most colorful preachers of the Jackson era was Methodist Peter Cartwright. Cartwright was as much the product of the frontier as Jackson himself. He was born in Virginia and reared in Kentucky, and he preached in the frontier regions of Kentucky, Tennessee, Ohio, Indiana, and Illinois. Cartwright was a fearless preacher who said, "It was a part of my creed to love everybody, but to fear no one."

Once, during an outdoor meeting in southern Ohio, Cartwright's sermon was interrupted by a drunken mob bent on breaking up the service. Soon a riot had broken out, and the drunken leader of the rowdies swung at the preacher and missed badly. As the off-balance ringleader lurched past him, Cartwright said, "It seemed at that moment I had not power to resist temptation, and I struck a sudden blow . . . and dropped him to the earth." Soon the mob was outnumbered and overpowered, and Cartwright was able to complete his meeting.

Cartwright displayed his fearlessness even more publicly in Nashville in 1818. He had been invited to preach in a large church in town, and General Andrew Jackson, having heard of the fiery preacher, decided to attend. Cartwright had already begun his sermon when the general walked in. Not finding a vacant seat, Jackson leaned against a pillar to listen. The pastor of the church, seeing the hero of New Orleans in the congregation, worried that the blunt Cartwright might offend this distinguished visitor. Urgently, the pastor began to pull on Cartwright's coattail and whisper, "General Jackson has come in; General Jackson has come in." Cartwright roared from the pulpit, "Who is General Jackson?" He warned that if the general "don't get his soul converted," then "God will damn him" as quickly as He would any other sinner.

The next day Cartwright met Jackson on the streets of Nashville. Jackson may not have had much appreciation for religion, but he admired bravery. The general said to the fiery Methodist, "Mr. Cartwright, you are a man after my own heart," adding that "a minister of Jesus Christ ought to love everybody and fear no mortal man."

Cartwright later joined Jackson's Democratic party and served as a representative in the Illinois state legislature. In 1846 Cartwright even ran for Congress, but he lost to an up-and-coming figure in Illinois politics—a young man named Abraham Lincoln.

Almost from the outset Jackson's administration was torn by infighting, particularly the jockeying for power between Martin Van Buren and Vice President Calhoun. The Red Fox of Kinderhook increasingly curried the favor of President Jackson against Calhoun. In addition the sectional differences between the New Yorker and the South Carolinian heightened the dispute, particularly over the tariff question. Calhoun, who had been an ardent nationalist in the War of 1812, was becoming the major spokesman for the interests of the South.

Nullification Crisis—At the time of Jackson's inauguration, the tariff controversy was raging again. In 1828 Congress passed a new higher protective tariff with rates of up to fifty per cent on some imports. The more industrialized North welcomed the tariff, while the South dubbed it the **"Tariff of Abominations."**

Southern leaders recognized the constitutional right of Congress to levy modest tariffs in order to raise revenue (Article 5, Section 8, Clause 1). They declared unconstitutional, however, tariffs aimed at protecting a particular class or favoring one section of the country over another. As we have seen, the North favored a high protective tariff to curb competing foreign imports. The South, however, depended on foreign imports in exchange for its agricultural exports. Higher tariffs meant higher prices in the South and higher sales in the North. Southerners argued that this was unfair since agricultural exports of cotton and tobacco from their region, which made up two-thirds of the country's total exports, already paid for the imports. Revenue the government received from the tariffs therefore came largely from the South but was mostly spent to fund internal improvements in the North. In short, the high tariff was a discriminatory tax.

In December 1828 the South Carolina legislature denounced the tariff as unconstitutional. It further suggested, as had Jefferson and Madison in the Kentucky and Virginia resolutions, that any unconstitutional federal act could be nullified by the states. Georgia declared the tariff unconstitutional that same month. Mississippi and Virginia did the same two months later.

The issue of nullification was drawn from an antitariff pamphlet written anonymously by Vice President Calhoun. The South Carolinian proposed the doctrine of **nullification** whereby states could nullify or reject congressional acts they deemed unconstitutional. Congress then could either change the law or send it to the states in the form of a constitutional amendment to be ratified or rejected. Nullification was Calhoun's skillful attempt to find a constitutional middle ground between submission and secession.

Nullification raised both constitutional questions and tempers in Congress. In a celebrated debate in January 1830, Senator Robert Y. Hayne, a gifted orator from South Carolina, rebuked New England's opposition to secession as inconsistent since it had considered secession itself in the Hartford Convention of 1815. (See p. 189.) Hayne further denounced the Tariff of 1828 and proclaimed nullification the only hope of self-preservation for the South and the West.

Daniel Webster, a senator from Massachusetts and perhaps America's finest orator, defended New England in his response to Hayne. He insisted that the people of the United States as a whole, not as individual states, had ratified the Constitution. Webster declared, "It is the people's Constitution, the people's government, made for the people, made by the people, and answerable to the people."

John C. Calhoun, *by Charles Bird King, National Portrait Gallery, Smithsonian Institution*

Therefore, he said, a state could neither secede nor nullify an act. Webster's speech climaxed with the famous phrase, "Liberty and Union, now and forever, one and inseparable." His views, however, like others involved in the controversy, appeared to be inconsistent; in 1815 he, too, had supported the Hartford Convention's decision to secede if Congress denied its demands. Opponents charged that Webster was seeking simply what was best for his state and region. In 1815 secession had appeared to be best for New England; in 1830 enforcement of the tariff was best for New England.

Although nullification was talked about in 1828 and 1830, it was tested in 1832. In May 1832, John Quincy Adams, who had returned to Congress after his unsuccessful bid in 1828 for re-election to the presidency, proposed a revision to the Tariff of 1828. Congress passed the revised tariff, which was lower than that of 1828, but still higher than most Southerners wanted; Jackson signed it in July. The South Carolina legislature responded by calling for a special state convention that in turn declared the tariffs of both 1828 and 1832 unconstitutional and therefore null and void. The convention further threatened that South Carolina would secede if there were any attempts to collect the tariff duties.

Senator Hayne resigned his Senate seat to head the nullification forces as governor in South Carolina. John C. Calhoun resigned as vice president to take Hayne's place on the Senate floor. Calhoun's resignation climaxed months of worsening relations between the president and vice president, bad relations which had become increasingly public. At a banquet in 1830 Jackson had pointedly looked at Calhoun as he raised a toast: "Our Union; it must be preserved!" Without missing a beat, Calhoun rose and presented his own toast: "The Union: next to our liberty, most dear."

Despite Calhoun's maneuverings, only a little sympathy and no support could be found for South Carolina's action. An angry Andrew Jackson threatened to hang Calhoun and secured from Congress consideration and later passage of the **Force Bill,** which gave the president war powers against South Carolina. In his *Proclamation to the People of South Carolina,* Jackson warned,

> The laws of the United States must be executed. I have no discretionary power on the subject; my duty is emphatically pronounced in the Constitution. Those who told you that you might peaceably prevent their execution deceived you; they could not have been deceived themselves. . . . Their object is disunion. But be not deceived by names. Disunion by armed force is *treason.* Are you really ready to incur its guilt?

South Carolina declared that Jackson's constitutional views were "erroneous and dangerous," and despite their friendless position the state was prepared to "repel force by force . . . and maintain its liberty at all hazards."

Behind these bare-knuckle pronouncements was an attempt on both sides to find a bloodless solution. At this juncture Henry Clay, "the Great Compromiser," proposed a new tariff that substantially, though gradually, reduced the Tariff of 1832, making it acceptable to South Carolina. Clay's proposed tariff, known as the **Compromise Tariff of 1833,** passed on March 1. In a parting shot to the

president, though, South Carolina nullified the Force Bill.

War had been averted, but there was little to cheer about. The crisis heightened tensions between the sections, and throughout the South there was a growing uneasy sense of loss of control over the future. As one South Carolinian observed at the time of the nullification crisis, "It is useless and impracticable to disguise the fact that the South is a permanent minority, and that there is a *sectional* majority against it—a majority of different views and interests and little common sympathy."

Busting the Bank—The major campaign issue as Jackson faced re-election in 1832 was the future of the **Bank of the United States.** Jackson had little understanding of banking practices but had a westerner's distaste for banks nonetheless. The Panic of 1819 was still a vivid and bitter memory in the West and South, and the Bank was the culprit in the popular mind.

In the summer of 1832 the president of the National Bank, Nicholas Biddle, submitted the Bank's charter to Congress for a twenty-year renewal, though the existing charter did not expire until 1836. When Jackson learned that his old political rival Henry Clay had instigated the early renewal of the charter, hoping that it would help him to be elected president, Jackson growled, "The bank . . . is trying to kill me, but I will kill it."

The Bank had such strong support in Congress that Clay believed he had a winning campaign issue. The recharter bill passed Congress; as predicted, Jackson vetoed it, claiming that it was unconstitutional. The Senate was unable to gain a two-thirds majority to override Jackson's veto; thus the Bank was to expire in four years. Clay thought the stage was now set for him to win a great victory.

The election of 1832 introduced three political precedents. A **"third party,"** the **Anti-Masonic party,** arose shortly before the election, stimulated by the questionable activities of the Masonic Lodge and other secret societies. It also opposed Catholic immigration and supported federal funding for internal improvements. The party, a precedent in itself, established two other precedents. First, it issued a **platform,** a written statement describing where the party stood on various issues. More important, it held a **national convention** where state delegates gathered to nominate the party's presidential and vice-presidential candidates. The major parties quickly followed its example, and nominating conventions have since become a standard part of the American political process.

The election itself was not so interesting. Clay had miscalculated badly; support in Congress for the Bank and support in the countryside turned out to be two different things. Jackson swept to victory with his old ally Van Buren as his new vice president. His re-election having convinced him more than ever that he was the choice of the people, Old Hickory again marched off to fight the Bank. His terms were unconditional surrender. Jackson claimed that withdrawing federal funds from the Bank would lessen the negative effects of the charter's expiration in 1836. After two secretaries of the treasury refused to remove the federal deposits, Jackson appointed Roger B. Taney as secretary in September 1833. The next month Taney began removing federal deposits and placing them in state banks–Jackson's **"pet banks,"** as his enemies called them.

The Bank's defeat was not a victory for the common man over the wealthy financiers, as Jack-

Genuine as a $3 Bill

Jackson's successful war against the National Bank helped open a new era in American banking from 1836 to 1864. Although state banks and branch banks had been in operation before, the absence of both a national banking system and regulations on state and private banks spawned a colorful period of "free banking."

Hundreds of banks sprang up representing towns, canal companies, insurance agencies, railroads, and factories. These diverse, largely unregulated banks issued a motley supply of money. Bills were issued in various colors, sizes, and engravings. Denominations were also varied, such as $1, $2, $3, $4, and $5 bills. They could also be, it seems to us today, a little bizarre, such as the 6 1/4¢ bill issued in the state of Virginia or the $9 bill issued from Paterson, New Jersey. In contrast to the somber gallery of statesmen on our currency today, bank notes of the antebellum period were adorned with birds, bees, buffaloes, children, trains, steamboats, coal miners, cotton pickers, and timber cutters.

Twenty-five thousand varieties of notes were issued throughout the country during this period. In 1864, however, the National Bank Act brought about a uniform national currency and greater Treasury control which condemned most of the private banks to extinction. Three-dollar bills and the like soon became only historical curiosities and colorful collectibles.

son had claimed that it would be. Jackson's actions turned out to be a two-edged sword on which he inadvertantly impaled the economy. The loss of federal deposits in the Bank of the United States forced it to tighten credit, which in turn hurt business expansion. At the same time the federal funds deposited in state banks fueled wild speculation in western land sales, financed with mountains of worthless paper money that these banks issued in order to stay ahead of the inflation they were creating.

Jackson attempted to slow down the spiraling inflation by issuing the **Specie Circular of 1836.** It ordered the prohibition of the use of anything except gold or silver coin–"specie," or "hard money"–for the purchase of public land. In other words, no one could use paper money to buy land. Jackson intended the circular to restrict speculation, since there was not nearly so much specie available as there was paper money. What it did, however, was to increase radically the demand for specie and thus to increase the Bank's control over credit. The speculative collapse brought on a severe depression during the term of Jackson's successor, Van Buren. Unfortunately Old Hickory handled the complexities of the economy as roughly as he had the British at New Orleans and with equal effect.

The Indian "Problem"

In his first inaugural address President Jackson promised,

> It will be my sincere and constant desire to observe toward the Indian tribes within our limits a just and liberal policy, and to give that humane and considerate attention to their rights and their wants which is consistent with the habits of our Government and the feelings of our people.

The old Indian fighter, however, pursued Indian policies that were anything but "just and liberal" and that showed a remarkable lack of "humane and considerate attention to their rights and their wants."

Indian Removal—Even before Jackson took office, the United States had discussed the idea of moving all Indian tribes in the East to lands west

Sequoyah, *attributed to Henry Inman, National Portrait Gallery, Smithsonian Institution. Sequoyah displays the Cherokee alphabet that he developed.*

of the Mississippi River and east of the Rockies. Such a policy seemed only fair to the government, since it wanted the Indian lands and did not want the western lands–yet. The Indians were understandably less impressed with the fairness of the idea. When he took office, Jackson pursued the **Indian removal policy** zealously. Under his administration no less than ninety-four treaties were made with the Indians, some of them forcibly. With the treaties as legal justification, the United States began moving the Indians westward and opening Indian lands in the East to white settlement.

Indian Resistance—Not all of the Indians gave in meekly to this treatment. Some responded with violence. In 1832 a group of Sauk (SAHK) and Fox Indians under Chief Black Hawk crossed the Mississippi River back into northern Illinois to reclaim their land. A force of regular soldiers and Illinois militia moved to intercept the Indians. The resulting **Black Hawk War** was brief but bloody. As with most U.S.-Indian conflicts, the Indians suffered the most and lost the war.

More challenging was the **Seminole War** (1835-1842). The Seminoles, led by the canny Osceola (OSS ee OH luh), also resisted efforts to move

"The Trail Where They Cried"

Perhaps the saddest event in the Indian removal was the Trail of Tears, the forced march of over ten thousand Cherokee from North Carolina to Oklahoma (then known as the Indian Territory) in 1838-1839. The name of the journey comes from a Cherokee phrase describing it, *Nunna-da-ul-tsu-yi*, "the Trail where they cried." Beginning in virtual prison camps in the Carolinas, the Cherokee were herded like cattle by the U.S. Army through freezing winter weather. Without adequate food, shelter, or even blankets, many Cherokee died along the way. The sick, the aged, and the very young suffered the most.

Ironically, many of these same Indians had fought under General Andrew Jackson in the Creek campaign during the War of 1812. One chief who had fought alongside the Americans in the crucial Battle of Horseshoe Bend (1814) said bitterly, "If I had known that Jackson would drive us from our homes, I would have killed him that day at the Horse Shoe."

A handful of Cherokee escaped the army dragnet and hid in the Smoky Mountains for several years. These Indians eventually emerged from hiding and were able to legally reclaim about fifty thousand of the seven million acres of Cherokee land that had been seized. This grant was an extremely small reparation to a people who had suffered so much so unjustly.

them west. They hid in the swamp lands and marshes of Florida as American troops tried fruitlessly to track them down. Over 1,500 Americans and an unknown number of Indians died in the conflict. Most Seminoles were rounded up and sent west, but some held out in Florida until the government gave up and left them to live in peace.

The Cherokee, one of the "the Five Civilized Tribes" (along with the Chickasaw, Seminole, Choctaw, and Creek) in the southeastern United States, tried a different approach. As their name suggests, the Civilized Tribes adopted many of the features of white civilization. They built communities with roads and schools and developed prosperous farms using European methods of agriculture. A brilliant Cherokee named **Sequoyah** even developed a written Cherokee alphabet, allowing the Indians to publish newspapers and the Bible in their own language.

Believing the promises contained in their treaties with the United States that they would be left to govern themselves, the Cherokee resisted removal. In keeping with their civilized character, they did not go to war; they went to court. In 1832 Supreme Court Chief Justice John Marshall handed down a decision in favor of the Cherokee. Unfortunately, the government ignored it. Jackson is reported to have said, "John Marshall has made his decision. Now let him enforce it." The Cherokee and the other Civilized Tribes were forcibly moved west to what is today Oklahoma. The hard journey from their homes resulted in the deaths of many Cherokee and became known as the **"Trail of Tears."**

Section Review
1. What is the difference between a revenue tariff and a protective tariff?
2. What were the three political precedents of the presidential election of 1832?
3. What did President Jackson issue to slow the inflation caused by the proliferation of paper money and to restrict land expansion?
4. How did the reactions of the Seminoles and the Cherokee to Indian removal differ? What was the result for each tribe?

Party Politics

A strong indication of the democratic forces at work during the Jackson years was the growing, organized, even turbulent, political competition of the era. Within a span of just a dozen years, from 1828 to 1840, two new national parties–Jackson's Democratic party and Jackson's opposition, the Whig party–competed effectively for the presidency and control of Congress.

Jackson and Anti-Jackson

Andrew Jackson's strong leadership at the presidential helm often made as many foes as followers. By the time of his second term, though Jackson was still popular, opposition to him was growing. His fight against the Bank of the United States and federal funds for internal improvements angered many nationalists allied with Henry Clay and John

An anti-Jackson cartoon

Quincy Adams, while his willingness to lower the tariff to ease the pressure on the South angered New England business interests represented by Daniel Webster. In addition, Jackson's gruff treatment of South Carolina aroused opposition throughout the South.

These anti-Jackson forces, despite their differing regions and interests, formed a political alliance in the early 1830s that became known as the **Whig party.** The Whigs derived their name from the British party that traditionally opposed royal tyranny. Jackson's highhanded methods and the manner in which he dictated his policies to Congress and his cabinet seemed to his opposition to have the trappings of monarchy. The Whigs dubbed the so-called people's president ''King Andrew I'' and insisted that he did not have a monopoly on the common man's support.

Besides being anti-Jackson, the Whigs were also a nationalist party. They sought to breathe new life into Clay's American System. Whig emphasis on optimism and opportunity had a national appeal across the young republic and attracted a freshman class of public men such as Abraham Lincoln, Horace Greeley, and William Seward. The Whig party quickly demonstrated that they had a *national* organization as well as a nationalist platform when they competed in the presidential election in 1836.

Van's Victory—Having won 98 seats in the House of Representatives in 1834, the upstart Whigs devised an ambitious strategy for the 1836 election. Due to their fledgling status, their strategy was to run several candidates, each strong in his own region, who would carry enough states to prevent Van Buren from gaining a majority of the electoral votes. The election would then go to the House of Representatives, where the Whigs hoped to be strong enough to maneuver one of their men into office. Daniel Webster from Massachusetts ran in New England; William Henry Harrison, popular Indian fighter from Ohio, ran in the West; and Tennessee's Hugh White ran in the South.

On the Democratic side, Martin Van Buren had been Jackson's hand-picked successor almost from the start. In the case of Jackson and Van Buren, it seemed true that opposites do attract. Though both

President Martin Van Buren

were born in humble circumstances, they grew up in different worlds. Jackson became a planter and an Indian fighter, Van Buren a politician with polish. The 6' 1" Jackson, with his shock of iron-gray hair, certainly contrasted with his balding, sandy-haired vice president who was seven inches shorter. Despite their differing backgrounds, appearances, and temperaments, Old Hickory owed the Little Magician a great deal for his political skills in winning elections. With general prosperity (though short-lived) at the time of the election, Jackson's endorsement was really the deciding vote in Van Buren's favor.

Even with Jackson's help Van Buren won the popular vote by only 25,000 out of the 1.5 million votes cast. Van Buren became the last sitting vice president to be elected president until 1989, when George Bush succeeded Ronald Reagan.

Hard Times—Just weeks after Van Buren took office, the economy collapsed, pulling the country down into a deep, five-year depression known as the **Panic of 1837.** Banks and businesses failed, and unemployment grew across the nation.

The economic hard times were brought on by a number of factors. Jackson's economic policies, of course, had been a financial fiasco, but his malpractice worsened–though it did not cause–all of the problems of the ailing economy. Wild, irresponsible practices among the state banks, as well as a massive wheat crop failure and the collapse of cotton prices, brought the economy to its knees. As one historian put it, "By its shortsighted financial measures Jackson's administration had sown the wind. Van Buren was to reap the whirlwind." When it came to the economy, the Little Magician had run out of tricks. Blame for the depression would dog his administration throughout his term.

Van Buren had few solutions for the problems he had inherited, but he was determined at least to put the government's financial house in order. As a result Van Buren proposed an **independent treasury** to replace the state banks as a depository for federal funds. The treasury was to have only federal funds deposited in it, and only government employees were to manage it. Subtreasuries were planned for major cities throughout the nation. (Van Buren's proposal was often called the "subtreasury system.") This system would divorce private banks from federal funds so that the government's funds and credit could not be used to support speculation and credit expansion. The plan was proposed in 1837, but because of opposition, Congress did not pass it until 1840.

Log Cabin Campaign

The 1840 campaign was one of the most colorful in our nation's history, a remarkable fact considering the bland candidates that the two parties offered the country. The excitement came from the images and enthusiasm that the parties, particularly the Whigs, were able to generate.

The Democrats renominated President Van Buren and hoped to stretch General Jackson's popularity for yet another election. The Whigs realized that it would take more than the battered economy to turn the entrenched Democrats out of office. In 1840, Whigs reasoned, "If you can't beat them, learn from them." As a result they nominated an old Indian fighter, **William Henry Harrison,** the hero of the Battle of Tippecanoe nearly thirty years earlier. They added **John Tyler,** a states' rights Virginian and friend of Clay, as running mate to broaden the ticket's appeal. In the campaign to follow, the Whigs would outgeneral the general's party.

The Democrats thought bringing Harrison out of retirement was ludicrous. One Democratic newspaper in Baltimore mocked "that upon condition of his receiving a pension of $2,000 and a barrel of cider, General Harrison would no doubt consent to withdraw his pretensions, and spend his days in a log cabin on the banks of the Ohio." Unwittingly the Democrats gave the Whigs a winning theme.

The Whigs presented Harrison as a humble but heroic backwoodsman in contrast to the dainty, aristocratic Van Buren who lived at the White House, or the "Palace," as the Whigs referred to it. Actually Harrison was born into Virginia aristocracy; his father was the governor of the state and a signer of the Declaration of Independence. Van Buren, who was the son of a New York tavernkeeper, hardly grew up in the lap of luxury. But facts were never allowed to interfere with either party's campaign.

Torch-light parades, log cabin floats, and quantities of hard cider drew crowds for the Whigs. Throughout the country the Whigs were just as imaginative with their campaign slogans: "Tippecanoe and Tyler too!" and "Van, Van is a used up man!" Songs often accented the raucous Whig parades:

Old Tip he wears a homespun coat
He has no ruffled shirt-wirt-wirt
But Mat has the golden plate
And he's a little squirt-wirt-wirt

The Whigs rode their log cabin theme all the way to the White House, with an electoral landslide of 234 to 60. The *Democratic Review* mourned, "We have taught them to conquer us!"

Harrison's inauguration was certainly anticlimactic compared to his campaign. On that dreary, drizzling day of March 4, 1841, Old Tippecanoe stood on the east steps of the Capitol and read in the rain for nearly two hours his ponderous inaugural address to a shuffling assortment of umbrellas and slickers.

The sixty-eight-year-old general was not well as it was, and in the days after he moved into the White House he found the flood of office seekers trying to cash in on the campaign overwhelming. Besides, his wife, Anna, was back home in Ohio. She had not been well enough to join him on the difficult journey by steamboat and stage to Washington. As a result the White House was simply not in order, and the general was not one to sit around and wait for the sun to shine–literally. In the chill spring rain he journeyed to the fish market and the butchers to stock the White House cupboards. A cold that had nagged him since his inaugural speech worsened. In that speech he had pointedly declared himself to be a one-term president; ironically, he was to be a one-

PUBLIC MEETING.

A general MEETING of the friends of

HARRISON & REFORM,

In the City of Alton will be held at the Old Court Room, Riley's Building on THIS EVENING, the Ninth inst., at Seven o'clock, to make arrangements for the approaching Convention at Springfield on the Fourth of June next.
Alton, May 9, 1840.

A Harrison campaign poster presents the general as a simple farmer who lived in a log cabin. In reality, Harrison was moderately wealthy and the son of a leading Virginia family.

month president. Stricken with pneumonia on April 1, Harrison died three days later, a bare month after taking office.

The president's death stunned the nation. Harrison's larger-than-life campaign image suddenly turned mortal. The oldest president yet elected was now replaced by the youngest president yet to serve. The nation now faced its future under the leadership of Tyler, a man who it had never expected would actually govern.

"OK"

The 1840 campaign did more than change the political landscape in America and shape the style of future campaigns; it also made an enduring contribution to our language. Van Buren's supporters rallied followers for "Old Kinderhook" by organizing O.K. Clubs. The Whigs, the masters of one-upmanship during the campaign declared that *O.K.* did not stand for Old Kinderhook but rather for "Oll Korrect," a spelling the Whigs jokingly pinned on the backwoods Jackson–who was a genuinely poor speller. The Whigs then, ironically, took what began as a Democratic slogan and stamped it on their kegs of campaign cider.

The popular term *OK* has long survived the log cabin campaign to become a nearly universal expression, what H. L. Mencken called "the most successful of Americanisms." Hardly a day or hour goes by in which "OK" is not used in our conversation–a tribute to the classic, colorful contest of 1840.

Section Review
1. What three anti-Jackson forces came together to form the Whig party?
2. What was the Whig strategy in the presidential election of 1836? What was the result?
3. Name two causes of the Panic of 1837.

Chapter Review

Terms

Andrew Jackson
Henry Clay
American System
tariff
protective tariff
Tariff of 1816
internal improvements
National Road
Panic of 1819
Missouri Compromise
caucus
John Quincy Adams
"corrupt bargain"

National Republicans
Democratic party
Martin Van Buren
John C. Calhoun
spoils system
"Kitchen Cabinet"
"Tariff of Abominations"
nullification
Force Bill
Compromise Tariff of 1833
Bank of the United States
third party
Anti-Masonic party
platform

national convention
"pet banks"
Specie Circular of 1836
Indian removal policy
Black Hawk War
Seminole War
Sequoyah
Trail of Tears
Whig party
Panic of 1837
independent treasury
William Henry Harrison
John Tyler

Content Questions

1. In what three ways did the National Bank assist economic growth?
2. Why did many American leaders, such as James Madison, generally oppose federal funding of internal improvements?
3. Why did Missouri's application for statehood create controversy?
4. Why did Henry Clay favor John Quincy Adams over Andrew Jackson when the presidential election of 1824 went to the House of Representatives?
5. Why did the South oppose protective tariffs?
6. What idea did John C. Calhoun advocate as a middle ground between submission to unpopular federal legislation and outright secession from the Union?
7. Put the following events from the nullification crisis in their proper chronological order from earliest to latest.
   a. Senators Hayne and Webster debate nullification.
   b. Henry Clay proposes the Compromise Tariff of 1833.
   c. The Tariff of Abominations is passed.
   d. President Jackson proposes the Force Bill.
   e. Vice President Calhoun anonymously advocates the doctrine of nullification.

8. With what two great compromises of the 1820s and 1830s did Henry Clay demonstrate his ability as "the Great Compromiser"?
9. Why was the 1840 campaign called the "log cabin campaign"?
10. What did the *Democratic Review* mean after the election of 1840 when it said, "We have taught them to conquer us!"?

Application Questions

1. Review the toast given by Jackson and Calhoun in 1830 (p. 203). With whose statement do you agree more? Why?
2. Why is Andrew Jackson's reaction to the Supreme Court decision concerning the Cherokee Indians a dangerous one?
3. Do you think the Whig approach to the election of 1840 is a proper one? Why or why not?

CHAPTER 11

The Growth of American Society (1789-1861)

"What hath God wrought!"

First telegraph message, May 24, 1844

Flax Scutching Bee, *by Linton Park (c. 1860), National Gallery of Art*

The face of the United States changed dramatically between 1789 and 1861. Transportation improved markedly, for one thing. In 1789 George Washington traveled to his inauguration over muddy roads in a carriage; in 1861 Abraham Lincoln traveled to his on iron rails in a train. The speed of communication also increased at an incredible rate. In 1815 the United States defeated Britain at the Battle of New Orleans, unaware that the war had actually ended with the Treaty of Ghent two weeks before. With the laying of the trans-Atlantic telegraph cable in 1858, however, the time for such communications was reduced from a matter of months to a matter of minutes. The religious face of the nation changed too. From a spiritual lull after the Revolution, the country soared to new spiritual heights through two major nationwide revivals. The era from 1789 to 1861 was one of remarkable cultural growth for the United States—technologically, intellectually, and spiritually.

American Technology

Manufacturing and Industry

The history of American manufacturing and industry is, basically, the history of inventions and applications of processes. But it is also the history of the people who devised the inventions and developed the processes. American industry is more than the story of machines; it is the story of the creative men and women behind the machines.

Textiles—In 1789 Great Britain was the world's leader in manufacturing, and the British intended to keep it that way. The British government carefully guarded not only all machinery relating to Britain's textile industry but even the blueprints for the machinery. Skilled workers in the textile industry were kept by law from emigrating. This situation did not deter **Samuel Slater,** however. Although a successful apprentice in an English textile mill, Slater saw greater economic opportunities for

Old Slater Mill, Pawtucket, Rhode Island

himself in America. Slater carefully memorized the construction of the textile machines, disguised himself as a farm hand, and escaped to the United States in 1789.

In Providence, Rhode Island, Slater–working entirely from memory–constructed an English-style mill with the financial support of American investors. This mill proved to be the first of a series of mills which sprouted across New England. The region was a natural site for the textile industry, because of its numerous streams and rivers to drive the water wheels used to power the machinery. Textiles became America's first major industry.

Interchangeable Parts–Slater's contribution in textile machinery was only one of several advances in American manufacturing. Probably the most important was **Eli Whitney's** work. Although Whitney was better known in his own day for inventing the cotton gin (discussed later), his work with **interchangeable parts** was ultimately more important. In 1798 Whitney took an order to provide ten thousand rifles for the United States government. Until that time, guns, like most machinery, were handmade by a craftsman who individually made and fitted each part. Repairs required the craftsman to make each replacement part by hand. Whitney designed a gun that was made of standardized, identical, machine-manufactured parts. When a piece broke, a new one could be easily inserted. Building on Whitney's process, every industry soon began to use standardized, interchangeable parts.

Patents and Inventors–American inventors benefited from the support of the United States government, which clearly saw the importance of developing industry. The government's most important help to industry was the passage of the first national **patent** law in 1790, which allowed inventors to secure a patent for new devices and processes. While the inventors held the patent, no one else could legally copy the inventor's work, and the inventor could reap the profits from a useful invention.

Spurred by the patent law and the promise of sure profits, inventors flooded the United States with new devices. Elias Howe, for example, perfected a mechanical sewing machine. With the improvements that Howe and others made, the sewing machine permitted the quicker, cheaper manufacture of clothing and other cloth products. Samuel Colt made his mark on the firearms industry. He patented and manufactured a ''six-shooter,'' a pistol with a revolving cylinder which allowed a user to fire six times before reloading. Colt's sales started slowly, but his weapon caught on during the Mexican War when it became the standard side-arm of the United States Army.

Heavy Industry–Americans had dabbled in coal and iron production in colonial days, but most iron products had to be imported from England before the Revolution. Much of the coal used in colonial days was bituminous, or ''soft,'' coal, which smoked a great deal when burnt and did not

Samuel Colt

heat up enough to "smelt" (melt) iron ore properly so that the pure iron could be separated from waste materials. Americans soon discovered large deposits of anthracite, or "hard," coal and iron ore in western Pennsylvania. With the cleaner burning, higher heating hard coal, American manufacturers could produce both more and better iron. As roads, canals, and railroads reached into the American interior, iron products soon spread throughout the nation, and western Pennsylvania became a center of American heavy industry.

Most iron went into the growing railroad industry to provide rails and engines. Smaller amounts of iron went into producing items such as tools and cooking utensils. An efficient process of producing steel from iron developed in the 1850s in Great Britain and spread to the United States. Although steel was much stronger and more durable than iron, its production did not become important to the United States until after the Civil War.

Agriculture

The United States had been dominantly agricultural since its founding. The period from 1789 to 1861, however, saw important advances in agricultural technology. The applications of that technology led to an increasing division between the agricultural system of the South and that of the rest of the nation.

Agricultural Advances—As settlers streamed into the wilderness of the Northwest Territory and across the Mississippi River, they found an abundance of rich and fertile soil. The soil was so rich, in fact, that farmers had difficulty harvesting their bountiful crops. The untapped potential of the frontier lands presented a challenge to the young nation.

The rich soil of the Northwest and particularly the plains across the Mississippi was sticky and was covered with a tough sod. Several men experimented with iron plows that would cut through the sod and turn the soil over cleanly without sticking to such a plow. Eventually a blacksmith from Vermont named **John Deere** perfected the plow. He put an edge of steel over the iron blade of the plow, and his improved plow proved ideal for the new lands of the West. Reaping the harvest became simpler due to the work of **Cyrus McCormick.** In 1834 McCormick received a patent for a reaping machine, a horse-drawn device that allowed one man to cut and stack ten to twelve acres of grain in a single day. Spurred by easterners who mocked his invention, McCormick moved his headquarters to Chicago, where his business had made him a millionaire by 1860. A devout Christian, McCormick used his wealth to support Christian efforts such as seminaries and the work of evangelist D. L. Moody.

Through technical advances in agricultural machinery, such as those of Deere and McCormick, American farm production grew at a tremendous rate. In 1789 farmers had generally eked out only enough to feed their families. By 1861 the United States was producing nearly $2 billion worth of agricultural products each year.

The Cotton Kingdom—The situation in the South differed from that in the North and the West. Foodstuffs were important, but the South did not produce the abundant grains of the West. Tobacco was important to some areas, particularly upper Southern states such as Virginia and Kentucky. A single cash crop, however, dominated the agriculture and economy of the region—**cotton.** "Cotton is King" was the motto of many Southerners, and King Cotton placed its distinctive stamp on the culture of the South.

In 1789 cotton was a relatively unimportant

The Rubber Man

Ralph Waldo Emerson is credited with saying, "If a man can write a better book, preach a better sermon, or make a better mousetrap than his neighbor, though he builds his house in the woods the world will make a beaten path to his door." Inventor Charles Goodyear, however, had "a better mousetrap"—a superior idea—and had trouble selling it even though *he* tried to beat a path to the *world's* door.

Goodyear became convinced of—some would say obsessed with—the industrial and economic potential of rubber goods. The problem with making goods out of rubber, however, was that the material would become hard and brittle in cold weather and would melt in hot weather. Goodyear believed that if rubber were mixed with some other substance, it could become a useful product. The inventor tried blending rubber with all sorts of materials, including cream cheese. One day in 1839 Goodyear accidentally dropped an experimental rubber-sulfur mixture on a hot stove. The result was what Goodyear had been searching for: the combination of sulfur and heat created a rubber product that was waterproof and flexible at all temperatures. This new process eventually became known as "vulcanization," after Vulcan, the Roman god of fire.

Despite his years of research, Goodyear found that making his discovery was easier than marketing it. The inventor tirelessly but vainly traveled from potential investor to potential investor. He became almost fanatical in his advocacy of rubber products. A neighbor described Goodyear to an acquaintance: "If you meet a man who has on an India-rubber cap, stock, coat, vest, and shoes, with an India-rubber money purse *without a cent of money in it, that is he.*" Another neighbor recalled watching Goodyear's hungry children grub for half-grown potatoes in their garden. Even when he found investors, Goodyear's problems were not over. He was once thrown into prison in France for some of his partners' debts.

At the time of Goodyear's death in 1860, vulcanization was widely recognized and accepted. Its inventor made little money from the process, however. He had spent many years fighting numerous legal battles to protect his patents and died $200,000 dollars in debt. Years afterward, the rubber industry gave him a belated tribute when it named one of its largest companies after him, the Goodyear Tire & Rubber Company. Charles Goodyear may have been a prime example of an individual whose ideas were genuinely ahead of his time.

---

crop. Most cotton grown in the South was a short-staple variety whose seeds clung to the cotton fibers. A slave had to work a whole day to clean just one pound of cotton. Eli Whitney changed that situation in 1793. While working as a tutor on a Georgia plantation, Whitney hit upon the idea of making a machine to clean cotton. In just ten days Whitney devised the **cotton gin,** a machine containing a series of metal teeth mounted on rollers which separated the cotton from the troublesome seeds. The cotton gin cleaned cotton fifty times faster than slaves working by hand.

Whitney's invention transformed the Southern economy. With a strong demand for cotton in the textile mills of the North and Europe, farmers in the lower South rushed to plant cotton. In 1790 the United States produced two million pounds of cotton; in 1860 the nation produced over two *billion* pounds—seven-eighths of the cotton produced in the world. Cotton was by far the most important export of the United States.

The growth of the Cotton Kingdom, however, widened the gap between the South on the one hand and the North and the West on the other. Cotton growing, for one thing, revitalized slavery. In 1790 slavery appeared to be an increasingly unprofitable and dying institution. With the advent of the cotton gin, slavery again became necessary—many planters

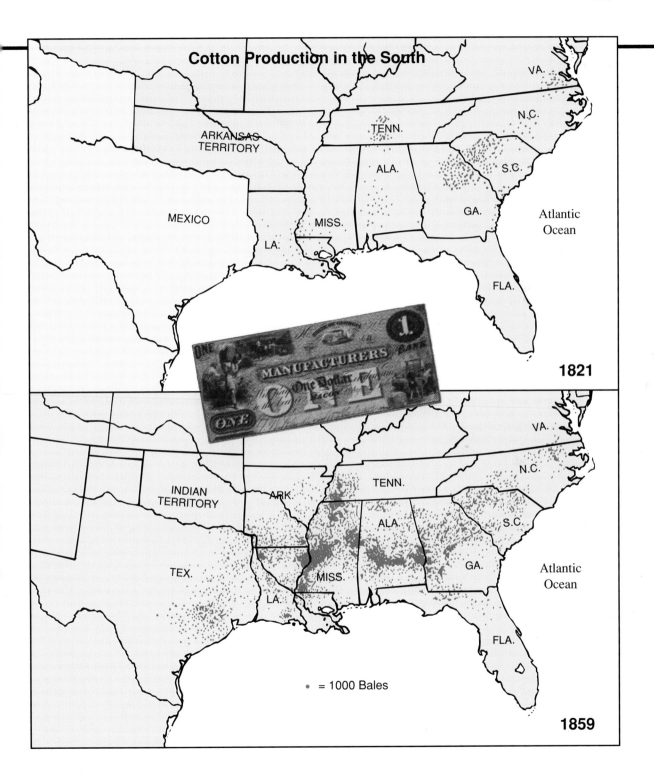

Cotton Production in the South

1821

1859

• = 1000 Bales

thought–to the region's prosperity. The value of field hands soon doubled, and the South became increasingly sensitive to Northern attacks on slavery. In addition, the overwhelming value of cotton hampered Southern industrial development. The majority of Southerners simply saw no use in developing industry and transportation networks as the North was doing. "King Cotton" by itself seemed sufficient to take care of all the region's needs.

Section Review

1. What was America's first major industry? In what region of the nation did it center?
2. Name three of this era's important inventors and their respective inventions.
3. Why was the discovery of "hard" anthracite coal in western Pennsylvania important?
4. How did the invention of the cotton gin increase the differences between the South and the rest of the nation?

Slavery

One of the most offensive features of American society between the Revolution and the Civil War was the existence of slavery. Slavery was hardly new; it is nearly as old as the human race. A regular slave trade in blacks, however, did not develop until the Middle Ages, when Muslims began to purchase slaves from black tribal leaders in Africa. In fact, an important object of African tribal warfare was to take prisoners to sell to Muslim and later to European slave traders.

When the North American colonies were founded, slavery was already common in other colonies and throughout southern Europe. Since few opposed it initially, black slavery was introduced in all of the thirteen American colonies (although not all blacks in colonial America were slaves). By 1775 the North American colonies held five hundred thousand slaves, of which two hundred thousand were in Virginia and one hundred thousand in South Carolina.

The attitude toward slavery in both America and Europe began to change in the last half of the 1700s. Often, the moral offense was an argument against slavery. Although the Bible does not specifically condemn slavery, it was difficult to reconcile the practice with the admonition to "love thy neighbour as thyself" (Matt. 22:39; see also Philem. 15-17). It was likewise difficult to reconcile slavery with the principles of American government and the belief in man's "inalienable rights," including liberty, as expressed in the Declaration of Independence.

When the Constitution was written in 1787, most of its framers, even those from the South, opposed slavery. Many, such as George Washington, eventually freed their own slaves. Several Northern states had already abolished slavery by 1789, and the Northwest Ordinance of 1787 prohibited slavery in that territory. The United States entirely prohibited the importation of slaves in 1808, the earliest date allowed by the Constitution (Article 1, Section 9). The framers of the Constitution, however, did not deal directly with slavery. Some thought it best to avoid the divisive issue in the interest of national unity. Others thought that each state should decide the issue for itself.

Yet many times moral arguments had to overcome economic and political motives for keeping slavery. In New England, for example, economic reasons helped change attitudes. As the region became more mercantile and less agricultural, slaves became a nuisance rather than an asset. It was fairly easy for the Northern states to abolish slavery. Blacks made up less than ten per cent of their population, and the economic price for abolition was negligible.

In the South, however, the situation was different. First, Eli Whitney's invention of the cotton gin in 1793 made slavery vital to the economy of the lower South. Second, the high percentage of blacks in the South (over a third of the population) caused Southerners to fear the effects of freed slaves on Southern culture and society. Though rare, the violence of slave uprisings, such as Nat Turner's Rebellion (p. 224), only reinforced these fears. Unfortunately, many Southerners convinced themselves that slavery was the only system that enabled whites and blacks to live together in harmony.

A slave family on a plantation in Beaufort, South Carolina, 1862

Physical treatment of slaves varied. Some slave holders were undeniably cruel. Examples of slaves beaten to death were not common, but neither were they unknown. Much more common was the use of flogging and other physical punishment to ensure obedience. The large majority of slave holders fed their slaves enough to sustain them in their work, housed them well enough to keep them dry, and clothed them well enough to keep them warm. For most owners, this was simply good business; slaves cost too much to mistreat. Some owners treated slaves well out of humanitarian motives. Such owners not only fed and clothed them but took them to church and taught them to read and write.

Nonetheless, physical mistreatment was only part of the offense of American slavery. Former slave Richard Allen noted, "Slavery is a bitter pill," even, Allen said, when a slave had "a good master." The slave was completely under the control of his owner. Whom the slave would marry, where (and whether) he would go to church, what would happen to his children—all of these decisions belonged entirely to the slave owner. Even some of the well-intentioned slave owners often broke up slave families as finances forced them to sell some of their slaves to make ends meet. As far as most black Americans were concerned, the slavery system sacrificed the rights and responsibilities that God granted to the family.

Nearly everyone, including slave owners themselves, had to admit that slavery raised a host of problems. For most Southerners, however, compelling political, social, and economic needs outweighed its disadvantages. Politically, the South considered slavery a matter for the states to decide; it involved larger constitutional questions concerning state sovereignty. Socially, neither the South nor the North knew what to do with freed slaves. One common but unworkable suggestion was to send them back to Africa, a solution only somewhat better than slavery for Americanized blacks. Economically, the South needed cotton to prosper and needed slavery to grow cotton. These reasons were so strong that the South would not abolish slavery until compelled to do so by military force and constitutional amendment.

The story of slavery in America is an excellent example of the far-reaching consequences of sin. The sin in this case was greed—greed on the part of African tribal leaders, on the part of slave traders, and on the part of slave owners, all of whom allowed their love for profit to outweigh their love for their fellow man. The consequences of such greed and racism extended across society and far into the future. It resulted in untold suffering—most obviously for the black race but for the white race as well. It led, at least in part, to the division of a nation and a bloody civil war to reunite it. It instilled a tension and even bitterness between the races in the United States. The Lord has never exaggerated in warning us of sin's devastating consequences—for us and for our descendants (Exod. 34:7).

Transportation and Communication

Manufacturing products and growing crops was one matter; getting those products to market was another. The United States could not tame its frontier until it built a network of transportation and communication to unite the sections of the nation. The United States rose to that challenge in dramatic fashion during the period between the Revolution and the Civil War.

River Transportation—The oldest avenues in America were rivers and streams. Indians and early settlers used canoes on the numerous waterways to penetrate the dense forests. Later settlers, needing some means of moving farm products to market, used flatboats and keelboats. These were sufficient for sailing downstream but were obviously of limited use in going up. The nation needed some kind of powered water transportation.

The answer to this problem was the steamboat. Several Americans had been trying since 1763 to develop a steam-powered ship. The idea was finally perfected by a talented, imaginative inventor from Philadelphia, **Robert Fulton.** In 1807 Fulton unveiled his steamboat, the *Clermont,* on the Hudson River. Critics called it "Fulton's Folly," but it successfully sailed upstream to Albany. The steamboat soon revolutionized river traffic. Goods and passengers could now move cheaply and easily through the interior wherever navigable rivers existed.

Roads—The rather obvious shortcoming of steamboats was that they could go only where rivers went. To link landlocked points, Americans built a system of roads across the countryside. Colonial roads, such as the Great Philadelphia Wagon Road (pp. 48-49), had provided the earliest means of reaching the frontier. Braddock's Road, built for military purposes during the French and Indian War (p. 93), became an important commercial route. Pioneer Daniel Boone blazed the Wilderness Road, which carried travelers from southern Virginia through the Cumberland Gap and into Kentucky all the way to the Ohio River. Branches of the Wilderness Road also led to Nashville, Tennessee, and into the Carolinas.

The most important early American road was the **National Road** (also known as the Cumberland Road because it originally began in Cumberland, Maryland), begun in 1811. Following roughly the same route as modern Interstate 70 and U.S. Highway 40, the National Road eventually linked Baltimore to Vandalia, Illinois. The road was a major transportation route for early settlers of the Old Northwest. It was also the first federal highway; the federal government had spent some $7 million on it by the time the road was finished in 1839.

Early roads were obviously not modern superhighways. A good road had a surface of gravel or perhaps stone. Many consisted of a series of boards laid side by side (**"plank roads"**) or logs (called **"corduroy roads"** because of their bumpy texture). Some roads were nothing more than dirt trails—or mud in wet weather. Most roads were built by private companies who paid for them by charging tolls (fees) for their use. Such roads were called **toll roads** or **turnpikes.** Maintenance of roads was almost nonexistent. By the time the National Road reached Vandalia, its eastern portions were already decaying. Nineteenth-century roads were helpful in providing transportation, but rapid economic expansion soon outstripped the road-making technology of the day.

Canals—Canals combined some of the best features of rivers and roads. Like rivers, canals permitted pioneers to use boats, a cheaper and generally faster mode of transport than wagons. A horse pulling a canal boat, for example, could pull fifty times more weight than it could pull in a wagon. Like roads but unlike rivers, one could build a canal practically wherever it was needed.

The beginning of the canal era was in 1817, when New York, under the urging of Governor **DeWitt Clinton,** began building a canal from Albany to Lake Erie. With the backbreaking labor required for the task, the idea of a 363-mile canal seemed, as Thomas Jefferson said, "little short of madness." At a cost of some $6 million, the canal was a gamble for the state. Critics called it "Clinton's Big Ditch." Yet the **Erie Canal** proved such a success that it had paid for itself in tolls in less than ten years. Furthermore, the cost of shipping goods plunged. Before the canal opened, it cost twenty cents a pound to ship goods from Buffalo

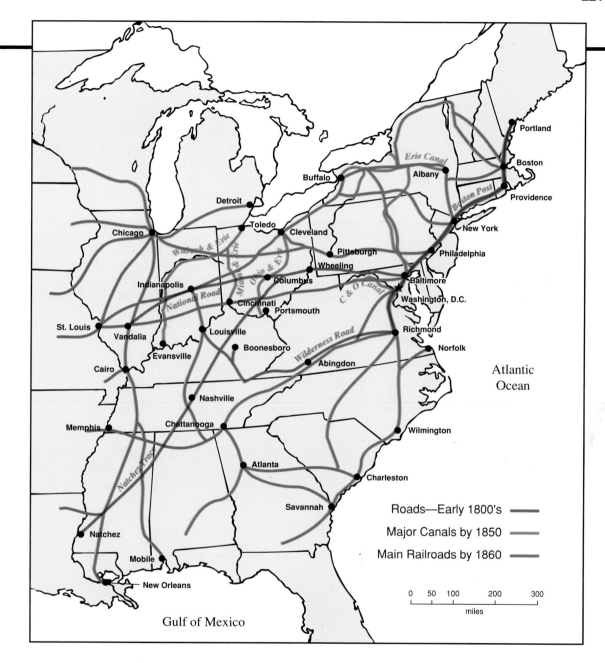

Roads—Early 1800's
Major Canals by 1850
Main Railroads by 1860

0 50 100   200   300
miles

Atlantic
Ocean

Gulf of Mexico

to New York City. After the canal opened, the price dropped to less than a penny a pound. In 1827 the governor of Georgia complained that wheat from upstate New York was selling more cheaply in Savannah than wheat from central Georgia.

The success story of the Erie Canal encouraged other efforts. The Wabash and Erie Canal in Indiana and the Miami and Erie Canal in Ohio connected Lake Erie to the Ohio River. The Illinois and Michigan Canal connected Lake Michigan to the Mississippi River by way of Chicago. By the 1830s one could travel from New York City to New Orleans completely by inland waterways.

Canals had their shortcomings, though. Most of them were in the North, for example, where winter freezes rendered them useless for months at a time. Also, they were expensive to build. By the 1840s the "canal craze" was nearly over. Canals gave way to a new and better form of transportation: the railroad.

Railroads – Nineteenth-century American transportation climaxed with the development of the railroad, which combined the flexibility of canals and roads with the dependable power of steam. The first economically successful railroad in America was the **B & O (Baltimore & Ohio) Railroad.** Originally the B & O consisted of horse-drawn carriages on metal rails. Inventor Peter Cooper believed that the line could develop a steam-driven engine, like the ones British companies were using. Working mostly with scrap metal, Cooper constructed the *Tom Thumb.* This small but powerful steam engine was well designed to handle the sharp curves and steep climbs of the B & O rail line. As a display of the engine's capabilities, Cooper agreed to run the *Tom Thumb* in a thirteen-mile race against a horse. Although the horse won narrowly because of a mechanical failure, the future of American transportation was clearly with steam power. South Carolina's Charleston to Hamburg line opened in 1833, and its 137-mile length made it the longest line in the world. Other lines, usually local in service, grew around major cities.

Several inventions smoothed the way for the growth of railroads. Iron rails replaced wooden ones covered with iron strips. A cowcatcher attached to the front of an engine reduced damage from collisions with animals. The perfection of the steam engine rendered trains faster, safer, and more powerful. Most important of all, railroads, particularly in the North and West, began using a standard gauge (width) of track of 4' 8". The resulting ability of trains from different companies to use the same tracks became vitally important during the Civil War in linking the war efforts of the Northeast and the West. Virtually the only drawback to railroads

was that they initially cost more to build than steamboats, canals, and roads.

In 1830 the United States contained a total of 32 miles of track. By 1860 over 30,000 miles of track fanned out across the country, and over 20,000 miles of that had been built since 1850. Previously unimportant cities such as Chicago and Indianapolis became major centers of rail traffic. Chicago, for example, mushroomed from a population of about 4,000 in 1840 to over 100,000 by 1860. By the time of the Civil War, railroads had become not only the nation's most important means of transportation but also a growing economic, social, and political force.

Sea Transportation—American sea trade on both the Atlantic and Pacific oceans boomed in the 1840s and 1850s due to one of the most beautiful inventions in transportation history. The **clipper ship** differed from previous seagoing vessels. With its slender, streamlined hull and its hundreds of square feet of canvas sails, the clipper was the fastest sailing ship ever built, and those of Donald McKay of Boston were the fastest of all. McKay's *Lightning,* for example, set a record by sailing 436 miles in a single day. From 1845 to 1860, the United States carried more sea trade than any other nation.

The clipper ship eventually fell victim to another technological advance, the steamship. At first steam power was impractical for oceangoing vessels. They could not carry enough coal to fuel their

Peter Cooper's Tom Thumb *in its famous race against a horse-drawn carriage*

engines for a long ocean voyage. Improvements in engine design, however, soon enabled the steamship to replace the clipper. Steam gave ships a constant source of power, one not dependent on winds and currents. Also steamships were bigger and could carry more cargo. By the time of the Civil War, the British had retaken the lead in sea trade. The reign of America's clipper ships was glorious but brief.

Communications—As fast as travel became in the period between the Revolution and the Civil War, communication became even faster. Some attempts to improve communication were colorful—if not practical. William Russell, for example, established the **pony express** in 1860. With a stable of 500 horses and a series of 190 stations stretching from Missouri to California, Russell promised to carry mail across the continent in the shortest possible time. A series of riders working in relays carried the mail from St. Joseph, Missouri, to San Francisco in ten to twelve days. The company went broke in 1861, however, a victim of the most important communications invention of the era, the telegraph.

The telegraph was the invention of **Samuel F. B. Morse,** a talented painter who studied under the famous Benjamin West in England. (See p. 228.) While he was in England, Morse's contacts with British evangelicals led to his conversion to Christ. Also while in Europe, Morse became interested in the semaphore communications system in France. The semaphore system worked by flashing signals with flags from mountaintop to mountaintop from one location to another. Morse hit upon the idea of using electricity to carry messages over wire much more quickly and over longer distances than semaphore could.

Back in the United States, Morse spent several years developing his system. A series of tests of his method impressed Congress enough to cause it to appropriate $30,000 for constructing a model telegraph system. Stringing wire on poles from Baltimore to Washington, D.C., Morse sent the first intercity telegraph message on May 24, 1844, before a host of important political leaders in the United States Capitol. Appropriately, the first mes-

Samuel F.B. Morse in his later years

sage was a Bible verse: "What hath God wrought!" (Num. 23:23). Soon telegraph lines stretched all across the United States. People living hundreds of miles apart could now communicate almost instantly. In 1858 the first successful trans-Atlantic cable was laid between North America and the British Isles. A message between the United States and Britain would have taken weeks to deliver in 1789. Now it was a matter of minutes. Perhaps no improvement better symbolizes the rapid changes produced by technology than this linking of continents.

Section Review

1. Name two methods of surfacing roads in the nineteenth century.
2. What event marked the beginning of the canal era?
3. What was America's most important method of transportation by 1861?
4. What was the first economically successful railroad in America? Who designed its first steam engine?
5. What system of carrying mail to California began in 1860? What invention put it out of business?

American Culture

Balancing the economic and technological side of American life was the cultural side. American expansion in technology was matched by an expansion in art and thought. Americans may have thought of themselves primarily as "doers" in that era, but some were also accomplished thinkers. American achievements in art, literature, and reform were just as important as the nation's technological advances.

Reform

Paralleling American efforts to improve technology were efforts to improve society. Reform movements, attempts to eliminate evils in society, blossomed and flourished in the first half of the nineteenth century. Most of these reformers were religiously inspired; some were guided by simple humanitarian ideals. All believed that glaring evils in America should–and could–be rooted out. Many freedoms and advantages that we enjoy today resulted from the efforts of nineteenth-century reformers.

Abolition–Without doubt the most controversial reform movement in the first half of the nineteenth century was **abolitionism,** the movement to eliminate slavery. Much of the impulse for abolitionism came from religious motives. A church in Oberlin, Ohio, was typical of many Northern churches when it resolved that "as Slavery is a Sin, no person shall be invited to preach or Minister to this church, or any Brother invited to commune who is a slaveholder." Quakers in particular had been leading advocates of abolition since colonial days.

The most important and most militant abolitionist leader was **William Lloyd Garrison.** Although he looked mild and benign, Garrison was fierce and zealous in his hatred of slavery. In 1831 he launched a newspaper, the *Liberator,* dedicated to attacking the moral evil of slavery. His methods could be extreme. He once denounced the Constitution as "a league with death, and a covenant with hell" because it did not condemn slavery. On another occasion he publicly burned a copy of the Constitution. In the pages of the *Liberator* Garrison reported every atrocity against slaves that he could find–including a few that were not true.

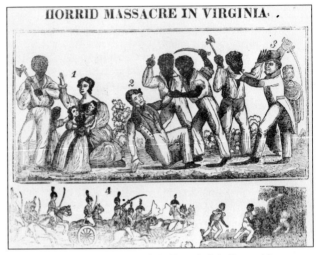

A lurid contemporary engraving of Nat Turner's Rebellion and its bloody aftermath

Garrison enraged many Southerners with his violent attacks not only on slavery but also on slave holders. He once called them the "meanest of thieves and the worst of robbers." Nor was Garrison particularly popular in the North. His uncompromising attacks on slavery offended both those who preferred gradual reform and those who cared little for any reform at all. Furthermore, some Northerners disliked Garrison's linking of his attacks on slavery with attacks on discrimination against free blacks in the North. The editor scathingly pointed out that blacks in some states in the North were denied access to public schools or opportunities to serve as apprentices. In short, he noted that blacks in the North were sometimes little better off than slaves in the South.

In the South hatred of Garrison and the other abolitionists reached new heights in 1831. In August of that year, a slave and radical preacher named **Nat Turner** led a slave rebellion in Southampton County, Virginia. Some sixty whites and perhaps a hundred blacks died in the rebellion and the bloody repression that followed. Turner, along with eighteen alleged leaders, was hanged. Southerners–probably incorrectly–blamed the revolt on abolitionist meddling. The economic need for slavery, the fear of revolts such as Turner's, and the resentment of abolitionist criticism made the South determined to protect slavery.

Undismayed by opposition, abolitionists pressed their cause zealously. Several former slaves helped by writing and speaking of their experiences. **Frederick Douglass** was one of the most brilliant, most eloquent, and most radical. His understandably strong hatred of slavery caused him to make statements such as "Slaveholders not only forfeit their right to liberty but to life itself." **Harriet Tubman** not only spoke at antislavery meetings but also made some twenty trips to the South to help lead more than three hundred blacks to freedom. Despite all these efforts, however, only a major war would succeed in eliminating slavery from the American continent.

Education—Two important trends developed in the reform of American education during this period: the growth of both public education and

Escaped slave Frederick Douglass was one of abolitionism's most powerful and persuasive speakers.

teacher education. Most schooling since colonial days was a private affair. Children often snatched a few months of training, usually during the winter when farm work eased, to learn the "three Rs" from someone in their church or community.

Despite its mixed character, private education was remarkably successful. The 1840 census, for example, revealed that seventy-eight per cent of the entire population was literate and that nine out of ten whites could read and write. Despite possibly the highest literacy rate in the world, beginning in the 1830s a movement was underfoot to make American schools better and more available. Reformers argued that the states should assume a larger role in schooling their young citizens to help ensure that the rising generation of voters make informed decisions.

One of the leading reformers in the drive for public education was **Horace Mann.** As head of the Massachusetts Board of Education, Mann brought a crusader's zeal to the task. After Mann had been at his post for eleven years, every child in the state could go to school for six months out of the year, fifty new high schools had been built, and teachers' salaries increased by half. Massachusetts became a model for public education in the rest of the country.

In addition, Mann led a growing movement to educate the educators. Previously, teaching was generally viewed as something a law student or seminary student did to earn money before entering his profession. But teaching as a profession itself became an important part of educational reform. Teacher colleges—called "normal schools" because they offered a uniform curriculum—developed, and more trained women began to join the profession.

Unfortunately for Horace Mann, his energetic reforms were motivated by faulty reasons. As a young man he had willfully rejected the orthodox Christian influence of his parents and pastor and drifted to liberal Unitarianism. Mann came to believe that people could find deliverance from ignorance and social problems through sound moral education. He believed, in the words of a friend, "If we can but turn the wonderful energy of this

Slavery and the Churches

American Christians diverged widely on the issue of slavery. Many, almost entirely in the North, called slavery a sin and slave owners sinners. A Baptist group in Maine said, "Of all the systems of iniquity that ever cursed the world, the slave system is the most abominable." Others, almost entirely in the South, defended slavery as a "positive good" for the benefit of blacks and claimed that slavery was sanctioned by the Bible. A leading South Carolina Baptist said that "the right of holding slaves is clearly established in the Holy Scriptures both by precept and example." Some, in both the North and the South, tried to straddle the issue, such as a Presbyterian who wrote, "The Presbyterian Church has stood at an equal remove from the extremes of Abolitionism and Pro-slaveryism. She has refused to pervert God's word to make it either denounce or sanction slavery."

The issue could not be avoided, as several denominations discovered to their sorrow. Two of America's largest denominations divided over slavery in the same year, 1844. First the Methodists split when a majority of the delegates in that church's General Conference voted to suspend a bishop in Georgia who owned slaves. Southern delegates left and formed their own denomination, remaining separate until 1939, nearly a hundred years later. The Baptists underwent a similar struggle. Baptists in the South decided to test abolitionist sentiment among Baptists in the North by presenting a slave owner as a candidate to the denominational mission board. After a fierce internal battle, the board rejected him. As had happened with the Methodists, the Southerners left and set up their own denomination, the Southern Baptist Convention, in 1845. Northern Baptists remained loosely organized until the founding of the Northern Baptist Convention in 1907. Unlike the Methodists, the Baptists have never reunited.

Many denominations avoided schism over the slavery issue. The Congregationalists, for example, were both antislavery and completely unified. But then, the overwhelming majority of Congregationalist churches were in the North, mainly in New England. The denominations that avoided division, such as the Episcopal church, usually did so by simply avoiding the issue as often as they could. Slavery remained a burning and inescapably divisive moral question until after the Civil War.

people into right channels, what a new heaven and earth might be realized among us."

In aiming for the head, however, Mann missed the heart. As the Apostle Paul reminded Titus, "Unto them that are defiled and unbelieving is nothing pure; but even their mind and conscience is defiled" (1:15). Only Christ can provide deliverance as He cleanses the heart and mind in salvation.

Unlike Mann, one Christian who saw the importance of the public education movement and its potential for the gospel was **William H. McGuffey.** In a series of elementary reading books, McGuffey taught generations of Americans rules for living as well as rules for grammar. By the beginning of the twentieth century, 120 million copies of his *Eclectic Readers* had been sold. McGuffey believed that Biblical values had a natural and necessary role for shaping character in the classroom, and his work was enormously successful.

Mental Illness—One of the most important reformers of the era was a quiet schoolteacher and writer, **Dorothea Dix.** As the head of a young women's school and author of children's books, she seemed an unlikely reformer. When she began teaching a Sunday school class in a prison in Massachusetts, however, Dix was appalled to find four mentally ill persons imprisoned there. They had simply been thrown into prison by officials who knew of nothing else to do with them. Secretly, she visited numerous prisons and insane asylums to get firsthand information about conditions there. Appalled by what she found, Dix wrote and lectured, attempting to inform the public about the situation. Through her efforts, legislatures in several eastern states voted to improve sanitary conditions and the treatment of inmates in asylums.

Prohibition—Alcohol was another evil that reformers attacked. The problem of drunkenness had been long recognized, but efforts to reduce drinking had enjoyed limited success. Reformers eventually replaced their call for temperance, or moderate drinking, with a call for the outright **prohibition,** or banning, of the sale and consumption of alcohol. Support for prohibition was widespread. Christians supported prohibition as a moral principle. Social reformers supported prohibition because of the suffering that drinking brought to drinkers and their families. Employers supported prohibition because drunkenness affected production. The movement scored its first major victory in 1846, when Maine voted for statewide prohibition. The prohibition movement's greatest success, however, came in the early twentieth century. (See Chapter 18.)

Women's Rights—As demonstrated by the work of Dorothea Dix, many of the leading advocates of reform in the first half of the nineteenth century were women. In the prohibition and abolition movements particularly, women were both numerous and active. Some male reformers resented this ''unladylike'' activity. An antislavery convention in London, for example, refused to seat women delegates simply because of their sex. This rejection, combined with activism in other fields, led naturally to agitation for women's rights, notably women's suffrage (the right to vote). In 1848 a number of women reformers held a convention in Seneca Falls, New York, in which they passed resolutions calling for equal rights for women, such as the right to vote. This **Seneca Falls Convention** is now commonly regarded as the birth of the modern women's rights movement. Dramatic gains in women's rights, however, did not come until the twentieth century.

Utopian Reformers—Most reformers focused on a single major problem in society, such as prison reform or alcohol, and aimed at eliminating the

Dorothea Dix was one of several influential female reformers in the pre–Civil War era.

problem throughout society. **Utopian reformers,** on the other hand, sought to establish a small, perfect community that would serve as a model for the reform of society at large. (A ''utopia'' is an ideally perfect place.) Some of these reformers operated from religious motives. The Harmony Society, also known as the Rappites after their leader, George Rapp, founded a religiously based community in Harmonie, Indiana, in 1815. The Harmony Society established a society based on the idea of mutual helpfulness and support. (They also practiced celibacy, the abstaining from all sexual relations, a belief which limited their growth and eventually caused the group to die out.)

Other utopians operated from secular, rationalistic motives. British reformer **Robert Owen,** for example, purchased Harmonie from the Rappites in 1825. Renaming it New Harmony, Owen sought to establish a perfect society based on common ownership of property. After two years of internal fighting and a loss of $200,000, Owen abandoned the New Harmony project. The utopian reformers,

Isaiah's Lips Anointed with Fire, *by Benjamin West, Bob Jones University Collection of Sacred Art*

whether religious or secular, all ultimately failed because of their faulty view of the nature of man. Man's inherent sinfulness dooms any human attempt to build a perfect society on earth.

The Arts

Americans in the early nineteenth century did not pursue the fine arts with the same enthusiasm that they did the technological arts. Samuel F. B. Morse, for example, was an accomplished painter, but he found it far easier to put bread on the table as an inventor. However, American painters, architects, musicians, and writers produced works that displayed remarkable talent. Furthermore, they produced works that copied European models less and were more distinctly American in nature. This period was the real beginning of truly *American* art.

Painting and Architecture—The period from the inauguration of George Washington to that of Andrew Jackson is usually called the era of the **"Federalist style"** in art. The Federalist approach more or less duplicated the neoclassical style of Europe. It emphasized balance, emotional restraint, and a respect for the artistic styles of ancient Greece and Rome. Federalist art borrowed heavily from European models. **Benjamin West,** America's first great painter, was really more English than American, although he often painted New World subjects. He was born in Pennsylvania, but he studied in Europe and eventually settled in England. He continued to influence American painting, though, through his teaching of leading American artists.

Several of West's students came to dominate American art. One was **Gilbert Stuart,** one of the young nation's finest portrait painters. He is best known for his different portraits of George Washington, especially his "unfinished portrait" which appears on the $1 bill. (One of Stuart's portraits of Washington appears on p. 154.) Possibly the greatest of the Federalist artists was **John Trumbull,** another student of West's. Trumbull, in fact, specialized in the realistic historical paintings that West had pioneered. Among Trumbull's works are *The Battle of Bunker's Hill* (pictured on p. 105) and *Signing of the Declaration of Independence* (p. 115).

Federalist architecture also borrowed from classical ancient civilizations. The **"Greek re-**

This 1846 view of the U.S. Capitol reveals clearly the neoclassical Federalist influence of its design.

vival,'' led by architects such as **Charles Bulfinch** and **Benjamin Latrobe,** re-created the columns and porticos of ancient Greek and Roman buildings. Bulfinch was so eager to further classical styles that he even drew architectural designs free of charge to encourage people to build in the Federalist style. Both Bulfinch and Latrobe worked at different times on the design of America's most famous Federalist style building, the United States Capitol. Ironically, Republican president and amateur architect Thomas Jefferson was a proponent of the Federalist style. Jefferson thought that Greece, the great example of ancient democracy, and Rome, the great example of ancient republicanism, provided ideal models for America's young democratic republic. Among Jefferson's designs were his home in Virginia (known as Monticello), the Virginia state capitol, and the University of Virginia rotunda.

After the rise of Jacksonian democracy, American art began to shift in emphasis. The formal portraits of the Federalist era gave way to casual portrayals of the common man in everyday life. No one surpassed the self-described ''thorough democrat'' **George Caleb Bingham** in drawing the common man. His *Stump Speaking* and *The County Election,* for example, captured the boisterous, sometimes crude, but always lively activity of American politicking. Bingham also captured the beauty and tranquility of the new land in such works as *Fur Traders Descending the Missouri* (pictured on p. 230). Carrying the love of American beauty even further was the so-called **Hudson River school** of painters. These artists specialized in landscapes, capturing the land in its serene and majestic beauty. Post-Federalist art in general left European models and sought to celebrate the glories of American life.

Literature—America's most lasting contribution in culture in this era probably came in the field of literature. Although some American writers had achieved a degree of success in the colonial period, the first great age of American literature began with the romantic movement (1820-1865). **Romanticism** rejected the balanced unemotionalism of the Federalist and neoclassical styles. Instead romanticism emphasized the emotional, the colorful, and the imaginative. Furthermore, this style placed greater stress on the love of nature and on the individual person rather than on society. (The Hudson River school of painters, for example, were romantic in their stress on portraying nature.)

The first American writer to gain fame outside America was novelist **James Fenimore Cooper.** His ''Leatherstocking Tales,'' one of which was *The Last of the Mohicans,* created an exaggeratedly romantic view of life on the American frontier. Although Cooper's works sound dated today, his novels paved the way for later writers. **Washington Irving** rose to fame with *Knickerbocker History,* a comic fictional history of Dutch New York. Through his later stories such as ''Rip Van Winkle'' and ''The Legend of Sleepy Hollow,'' Irving helped develop the greatest American contribution to world literature, the short story.

Romanticism's central belief in the goodness—or even godhood—of man and the glory of nature, expounded by **Ralph Waldo Emerson** (see p. 236) in his works *Nature* and *Self-Reliance,* drew both supporters and critics. Essayist **Henry David Thoreau,** author of *Walden,* and poet **Walt Whitman,** in his work *Leaves of Grass,* both celebrated the glory and nobility of man. Whitman expressed this belief, and his belief in the unity and brotherhood of man, in his ''Song of Myself'':

> I celebrate myself, and sing myself,
> And what I assume you shall assume,
> For every atom belonging to me as good
>   belongs to you.

Other romantics attacked the idea of man's inherent goodness. **Nathaniel Hawthorne,** for example, realized the truth of man's depravity. *The Scarlet Letter,* perhaps his finest work, attempts to deal with the problem of sin and its effects, but the novel criticizes what Hawthorne considered the narrow, hypocritical views of Puritanism. **Edgar Allan Poe** delved even deeper into the dark, tortured depths of man's soul in stories such as "The Tell-Tale Heart" and poems such as "The Raven." In the process, Poe became the master short-story writer of America before the Civil War. Sadly, neither Hawthorne nor Poe recognized that the solution to man's sin is found only through the atoning work of the Lord Jesus Christ.

Music–American music from 1789 to 1861 probably represents the character of American culture better than any of the other arts. In Europe this was the period of great classical composers such as Beethoven. America had no such musical giants. Instead, popular music dominated the United States. America's most important composer of the period was **Stephen Foster.** Foster wrote lyrical ballads such as "I Dream of Jeanie with the Light Brown Hair" (written for his wife) and spirited songs about the South such as "Camptown Races," "Oh, Susanna," and "My Old Kentucky Home" (although Foster had never even visited the South).

Another great composer of the time represented the importance of religious faith to the era. Hymn-

Fur Traders Descending the Missouri, *by George Caleb Bingham, The Metropolitan Museum of Art, Morris K. Jesup Fund, 1933. (33.61) Photograph © 1992.*

Stephen Foster, one of America's most beloved songwriters

writer **Lowell Mason** published several popular hymnbooks and composed the tunes for such hymns as ''Nearer, My God, to Thee'' and ''My Faith Looks Up to Thee.'' Mason constantly sought to introduce classical European ideals into American hymn music. He arranged his tune for Isaac Watts's ''When I Survey the Wondrous Cross,'' for example, from a medieval Gregorian chant. In addition to his work with hymns, Mason was a leading promoter of music education, particularly the teaching of music in public schools.

Newspapers and Magazines—The fine arts were not the only examples of American cultural growth. Rising literacy rates caused by educational improvements created a market for popular literature: newspapers and magazines. Improvements in technology not only allowed printers to publish a greater number of materials but also enabled them to produce them more quickly and more cheaply. In 1835 America published 1,258 newspapers; by 1860 the number had swelled to 3,343. The daily penny newspaper (in contrast to more expensive weekly ones) was an important means of making information more available and more affordable. Two papers, the *New York Sun* (founded 1833) and the *New York Tribune* (1841), represent two different approaches to journalism. The *Sun* contained sensational accounts of murders, scandals, and other lurid events in order to appeal to the baser tastes of readers. The *Tribune,* edited by Horace Greeley, supported reform efforts and attempted to educate and uplift its readers. The two approaches proved equally successful, and both the *Sun* and the *Tribune* attracted readers even outside of New York.

Magazines were another vehicle of popular culture. Containing short stories, serialized novels, poems, travel articles, engravings of the latest cuts in fashion from Paris, and reviews, magazines served almost as miniature libraries. *Harper's New Monthly* (founded 1850) and the *Atlantic Monthly* (1857) were two of the most popular and longest lived. Magazines aimed to reach either general audiences or some specific group, such as *Godey's Lady's Book,* (1830), one of the first women's magazines. Magazines served not only to meet American literary tastes but also to increase them. Significantly, *Harper's* began by reprinting British material, but it soon found a wider audience for the work of American writers.

Section Review

1. What were the two important trends in American education in the early 1800s?
2. What is the difference between temperance and prohibition?
3. How did utopian reformers differ from other reformers?
4. What was the most controversial reform movement of the first half of the nineteenth century? Who was its most important leader?
5. Which authors defended romanticism's idea that man is basically good? Which authors denied this idea?
6. How did the journalistic approach of the *New York Sun* differ from that of the *New York Tribune?*

American Religion

Religious life in America also expanded from 1789 to 1861. Some of the expansion was only numerical, not spiritual; a few of the religious movements of the era were sources of spiritual darkness instead of spiritual light. Many of the movements, however, seem to have been genuine expressions of the work of the Holy Spirit. Significantly, this period in American history began and ended with a sweeping national revival.

The Second Great Awakening

Shortly after the ratification of the Constitution, America experienced its second great revival of religion. The **Second Great Awakening** was longer and more complex in nature than the first. It touched different regions of the nation in different manners, and its effects reached even across the sea.

Background—American religion was in a sorry state after the Revolution. **Deism** was the "faith" of several American leaders. A deist believed that God created the universe, set it into operation, and then stood back to allow it to work. Deists denied the deity of Christ, the inspiration of the Bible, the reality of miracles, and any other belief that struck them as "superstitious" because they could not explain it by their own reason. Revolutionary War veteran Ethan Allen wrote one of the first American defenses of deism, a crude, anti-Christian work. Thomas Paine, author of *Common Sense,* wrote a more polished—but no more orthodox—exposition of deism, *The Age of Reason.* Other American leaders, such as Thomas Jefferson and Benjamin Franklin, at least leaned toward deism.

Besides this "intellectual religion," there was a lack of any religion at all. For many Americans, the pleasures of the day—drinking, gambling, and the like—were far more important than any kind of creed, Christian or otherwise. Looking over this situation, John Marshall remarked sadly that the church was "too far gone ever to be revived."

The situation was not all darkness and despair, however. One of the brightest spots for Christianity was the birth of American Methodism. The **Methodists** were followers of the teachings of English minister **John Wesley.** After a long and desperate struggle with a sense of guilt and sin, Wesley had been converted. He began to travel around Great Britain preaching the need for conversion to Christ and holy living. The Methodists remained technically part of the Church of England until Wesley's death, but afterwards they became a separate denomination.

Methodism in America grew slowly at first, partly because of its association with Anglicanism and partly because of Wesley's opposition to the War for Independence. Much of the credit for the denomination's growth must go to the "father of American Methodism," **Francis Asbury.** Sent from England to America in 1772, Asbury worked for years to establish Methodist congregations. He developed the most important institution of American Methodism, **circuit riding.** The United States was too vast and its population too scattered for Asbury to be able to establish a minister in every community. Asbury therefore divided the land into sections, or circuits. One minister, called a "circuit rider," traveled on horseback from settlement to settlement, ministering to Christians and preaching to the lost. Facing the challenges of an untamed wilderness, Methodist circuit riders were tough men with tender hearts. Asbury himself traveled nearly three hundred thousand miles on horseback. On the frontier in particular, Methodists became some of the most important contributors to the awakening.

Revival in the East—The Second Great Awakening began in the East. There the revivals centered in the churches and colleges, where Christian zeal had lapsed into apathy and even open sin. Yale, founded in 1701 to train ministers, was an example of how low spirituality had fallen. One minister recalled his student days at Yale in the years before the awakening:

> The College was in a most ungodly state. The college church was almost extinct. Most of the students were skeptical, and rowdies were plenty. Wine and liquors were kept in many rooms; intemperance, profanity, gambling, and licentiousness were common.

Into this situation at Yale came **Timothy Dwight,** a grandson of Jonathan Edwards. Elected

Richard Allen

Methodism proved enormously successful at reaching all classes of society with the gospel, including both free blacks and slaves. One instrument God used in reaching blacks was a former slave himself, Richard Allen. Born in Pennsylvania, Allen was converted under the preaching of a Methodist in Delaware in 1777. Shortly thereafter Allen's master allowed the young slave to purchase his freedom.

Although freed, Allen did not find life easy. He chopped wood, worked in a brickyard, and delivered salt in order to make a living. Allen also began to preach in the evenings and on Sundays. A Methodist minister

noted Allen's efforts and helped instruct and train the former slave. Allen became a circuit rider in New Jersey and Pennsylvania, although his financial situation often forced him to be a "circuit walker" instead.

Allen came to Philadelphia and enjoyed a fruitful ministry among blacks there. Allen and the blacks he reached originally attended a predominantly white Methodist church in the city. Some members resented the increased numbers of blacks in their service, however. This tension finally climaxed in a service in 1787 in which one of the church officers tried during prayer to forcibly move one of the blacks to a seat in the back of the balcony. Allen and the others walked out.

After much discussion, the group decided to build its own church. After years of labor, sacrificial giving, and strong opposition, Allen's group built the African Methodist Episcopal (AME) Church in Philadelphia. Bishop Francis Asbury dedicated the church in 1794, and he later ordained Allen. When several other black congregations expressed an interest in closer fellowship with Allen's church, they decided to form their own denomination, and Allen became their first bishop. Under the leadership of Allen and others, the denomination became one of the most effective means of reaching blacks with the gospel before the Civil War.

president of Yale in 1795, Dwight confronted the challenge of a rebellious student body. He met it by openly taking on all comers in public debates on the truths of the Christian faith. Dwight also preached a series of sermons in chapel on basic Christian theology. The fruit of Dwight's labors was a series of revivals in which at least a third of Yale's students were converted.

Revival in the other schools and churches of the East followed the pattern of Yale. Order and restraint were the key characteristics. The preaching was urgent in its message but calm in its tone. The spiritual fervor of the revivals in the East was deep—but quiet—and the results were profound.

Revival in the West—On the frontier, the awakening appeared a little later and in a different form. The chief feature of the western revivals was the **camp meeting,** a series of religious services lasting several days and often held outdoors. Usually several preachers exhorted the crowds in simple but fiery gospel sermons. The originator of the camp meeting was Presbyterian James McGready. In

The camp meeting was one of the main means of reaching the frontier with the gospel.

1800 in Logan County, Kentucky, McGready, three other Presbyterians, and a Methodist preacher held an outdoor communion service to welcome new members into the church. During this and other services that followed, hearers began to profess a deep sense of their own sinfulness and to cry out for salvation. The results in Logan County proved so remarkable that other preachers began to hold camp meetings. Probably the greatest camp meeting was held at **Cane Ridge,** Kentucky, in 1801. Estimates of the attendance at Cane Ridge range from ten thousand to twenty-five thousand. This attendance was phenomenal, especially considering that nearby Lexington, the largest city in Kentucky at that time, had a population of only eighteen hundred people.

Camp meeting revivals contrasted markedly with the revivals in the East. Noisy, boisterous energy in the West replaced the quiet order and restraint of the East. The preaching in the camp meetings was loud and lively, but the audiences were often louder and livelier. Some hearers punctuated the sermons with hearty amens. Others cried out in fear or horror as a conviction of their sinfulness came over them. Some underwent strange physical maladies such as uncontrollable shaking, jumping, and jerking. Undoubtedly, some of the excesses of the western revivals resulted from mass hysteria and the rough, uncultured character of the frontiersmen. Some historians note only these excesses, but the real importance of the camp meet-

ings lies in their lasting results: the changed lives of those who were converted.

Foreign Missions—The effects of the Second Great Awakening were not limited to the shores of the United States. The first great American missions movement resulted from the revival. Among the colleges in the East that were touched by the revival was Williams College in Massachusetts. In 1806 a group of students from the college was holding an outdoor prayer meeting when a fierce thunderstorm blew in. Taking shelter under a nearby haystack, the little group began to discuss the need to carry the gospel throughout the world. One member of that group, Samuel Mills, decided to fulfill that dream and helped establish the **American Board of Commissioners for Foreign Missions** (ABCFM), America's first foreign mission board.

The ABCFM, a Congregationalist organization, sent many missionaries throughout the world, but it was not the only American mission board. **Adoniram Judson** and Luther Rice went to India in 1812 under the ABCFM. On the way, however, Judson and Rice decided that their theological views were closer to those of the Baptists. Judson remained in Asia while Rice returned to the United States to raise support among Baptists. Judson eventually moved to Burma, where his faithful translation work and preaching made him the first great hero of the American missions movement. Rice helped start a Baptist mission organization that became a major

Evangelist Charles G. Finney

force in sending missionaries overseas. Through the efforts of men such as Mills and Rice and through the labors of missionaries such as Judson, thousands of lost souls throughout the world found salvation in Jesus Christ.

Charles Finney and the "New Measures"—By the 1820s, as the first wave of revivals began to subside, the awakening began to take a new direction with the ministry of **Charles Finney.** While practicing law in upstate New York, Finney was converted in 1821 during a revival. After informal study with a Presbyterian pastor, Finney began preaching in small towns across New York. Reports of numerous dramatic conversions increased Finney's reputation. By the 1830s he was preaching to huge crowds in New York City and was America's leading evangelist.

Humanly speaking, Finney's success lay in his personality and his methods. A tall man with piercing eyes which seemed to bore into a man's soul, Finney preached in a plain but relentlessly logical style on God's judgment on sin. He developed what others dubbed the **"New Measures,"** new and un-

usual methods for conducting revivals. He always kept an "anxious bench" in his meetings, reserved seats for sinners who sensed a conviction of sin. Finney also held "protracted meetings," services held daily for up to several weeks in one location. Finney combined elements of both eastern and western revivals. He insisted on order and restraint in his meetings, like those in the East. His aggressive sermons and extended meetings, however, had the flavor of the West about them. Whatever the source of Finney's methods, his success guaranteed that many would copy him.

Finney set the standard for American evangelists, and most evangelists today use at least some of his methods. Finney received much criticism too, some of it deserved. For one thing, Finney stressed human ability in conversion so much that some Christians thought that he made salvation more man's work than God's. Finney himself admitted in 1846, after the height of the revivals, "I have laid . . . too much stress on the natural ability of sinners to the neglect of showing them the nature of their dependence upon the grace of God." Still, through his hugely successful campaigns and later his influential position as professor and president of Oberlin College in Ohio, Charles Finney was the single most dominant figure in American religion in this era.

Results of the Awakening—Like the colonial Great Awakening, the Second Great Awakening produced dramatic results. First and most important, thousands of people were converted to Christ and joined churches. American Methodists, for example, numbered 15,000 in 1785. By 1840 their numbers had grown to 850,000, and Methodism had become the largest denomination in the United States. Second, as mentioned earlier, was the birth and growth of America's foreign missions movement. Third were moral results. Moral sins declined in the wake of the revival; for example, drunkenness on the frontier declined. Also the revival fueled the drive for moral reform. Many of the leaders in the prohibition and abolition movements were zealous converts of the revival. Fourth, new methods of evangelism resulted from the revival. The camp meetings and many of Charles Finney's

"New Measures" became standard features of American Christianity. In all, the Second Great Awakening touched and transformed the lives of a large segment of the American people.

Unorthodox Religion

Not all of the religious movements in the first half of the nineteenth century reflected Biblical teaching and standards. In fact, several influential movements denied Scriptural truth and promoted error.

Unitarianism—One of the most prestigious unorthodox religions was **Unitarianism.** Its name derives from its basic belief in the "unity" of God; that is, Unitarianism denies the Trinity and therefore the deity of Christ. Jesus, to the Unitarians, was a great religious teacher, but He was only a man and His death provides no atonement for sin. Instead, Unitarianism teaches that men should simply live moral, upright lives in order to please God.

The first Unitarian church in America began in 1785, but the denomination's real growth came after 1805, when Harvard appointed its first Unitarian professor. Within twenty years, Harvard had become a center of Unitarian teaching, and many of the old Congregationalist churches in the East lapsed from orthodoxy to Unitarianism. The denomination's influence was even greater than its numbers, in part because many of the wealthy and prominent leaders of eastern society became Unitarians. The denomination experienced little growth outside of New England, however, causing one wit to remark that Unitarian preaching was limited to "the fatherhood of God, the brotherhood of man, and the neighborhood of Boston."

Transcendentalism—Unitarianism eventually gave birth to an even more liberal, more un-Biblical philosophy: **transcendentalism.** Transcendentalism was primarily the creation of writer and lecturer Ralph Waldo Emerson. A graduate of Harvard, Emerson entered the Unitarian ministry. He found even liberal Unitarianism too confining, however, and developed his own optimistic, man-centered "faith." Transcendentalism denied the miraculous, like Unitarianism, but went even further in its teachings. Basically, the philosophy put

man in the place of God. Emerson taught that man was good and ultimately perfectible. He rejected the Christian view of God and taught instead that everything is part of God and that God dwells within every man. Emerson denied, as he put it, a faith "in Christ" in favor of a faith "like Christ's," which Emerson said was "faith in man." Transcendentalists were never numerous, but they were influential. Among those influenced by transcendentalism were author Henry David Thoreau and poet Walt Whitman.

Millerites—Unlike many of the unorthodox movements of the era, the error of the **Millerites** was not so much wrong doctrine as wrong emphasis. William Miller was a Baptist minister in New York who began to attract attention in the 1830s. Like many Christians throughout history, Miller was a premillennialist; he believed that Christ would return to the earth and establish the millennium, a perfect kingdom of peace lasting a thousand years. (The word *millennium* comes from two Latin words meaning "thousand years.") Miller differed, however, in that he set a date for Christ's return, sometime between March 21, 1843, and March 21, 1844. Thousands of people in the northeast heard Miller, and perhaps as many as one hundred thousand became followers of his teaching. The frenzied year of Miller's prediction came–and went. Mockers ridiculed Millerites, and they poured their scorn on premillennialism in general. Unproved rumors circulated of how Millerites dressed in white "ascension robes" waited on top of barns for the great event. Miller unwittingly brought reproach on the doctrine of the Second Coming by ignoring Jesus' own words about His return: "But of that day and that hour knoweth no man, no, not the angels which are in heaven, neither the Son, but the Father. Take ye heed, watch and pray: for ye know not when the time is" (Mark 13:32-33).

Cults—Several other unorthodox groups developed in this era. Many of these were cults, groups that call themselves Christian but which deviate from orthodox doctrine on one or more points. One such group was the **Shakers,** who began in England in the 1700s but enjoyed their greatest growth in America in the early 1800s. Shakers took their name

Brigham Young

from the shaking or dancing which accompanied their worship. They practiced celibacy, because they considered any sexual relations sinful, and owned property in common. Shakers believed that their founder, Mother Ann Lee, was an incarnation of God just as Jesus was. The Shakers built prosperous, well-ordered farms in New England, New York, Ohio, Indiana, and Kentucky. The group won many converts in the early 1800s, but it eventually died out because of its practice of celibacy.

Probably the most important cult to arise at this time was **Mormonism,** also known as the Church of Jesus Christ of Latter-Day Saints. Mormonism was founded by **Joseph Smith** in 1830. Smith claimed that an angel showed him some golden plates inscribed with ancient writing. With the help of the angel, Smith said, he translated the plates to form the Book of Mormon, one of the holy books of Mormonism. The Mormons teach that salvation rests primarily on good works and that one who is good enough eventually becomes a god. Mormons stirred up the most controversy by their practice of polygamy, the taking of more than one wife at the same time.

Opposition drove the Mormons from New York to Ohio to Nauvoo, Illinois. In Illinois, conflicts between Mormons and local residents led to the jailing of Smith in Nauvoo. There a lynch mob attacked the jail and killed Smith. **Brigham Young** then assumed the leadership of the group. He led the Mormons on an enormous trek west, where they founded Salt Lake City, capital of a territory that eventually became the state of Utah. The Mormons eventually abandoned the practice of polygamy officially and built a huge temple in Salt Lake City.

The Prayer Meeting Revival

Despite the growth of false religious movements such as the Mormons, the first half of the 1800s was a time of triumph for many Biblical groups. The climax of American religious life in that era came just before the Civil War. This event was the "third great awakening" of American history, the **Prayer Meeting Revival** of 1857-1859.

The revival began shortly after a serious financial crisis, the Panic of 1857. In September of that year in New York City, a lay evangelist named Jeremiah Lanphier began holding a weekly prayer meeting during the noon lunch hour. Attendance grew from six the first week, to twenty the next, to forty the next, and then more. Soon the group decided to meet daily, and the church building was full to overcrowding. Other churches, first in New York and then in other eastern cities, began to hold daily prayer meetings. Within months churches and auditoriums across America were filled with men and women who met to pray for an hour. Every day in cities throughout the United States, life stood still for an hour as shopkeepers, laborers, and others paused to pray.

There was no formal organization to the prayer meetings. Each group usually met under the leadership of some Christian, often a layman. They sang a few hymns, shared requests, and listened to short devotionals, but mostly they prayed. Afterwards pastors and other Christian workers remained to help those who sought spiritual counsel.

The results of the revival were astounding. Between a half million and a million people were converted. Encouraged by the revival, Christians raised money to found Christian schools and support foreign missionaries. Established Christian organizations received floods of new volunteers whose lives had been transformed by the awakening. For example, the Young Men's Christian Association (YMCA; established 1844 in Great Britain) was able to expand its ministry of providing wholesome recreation and fervent religious instruction for young people, primarily in the cities. The Prayer Meeting Revival also marked perhaps the first time that laymen had dominated the leadership of a revival. The overall impact of the revival was remarkable. One Presbyterian pastor, who earlier had been skeptical of the revival, wrote to a friend,

> Study I cannot, being run down by persons, many of whom I never knew, in search of counsel. . . . The openness of thousands to doctrine, reproof, etc., is undeniable. . . . You may rest assured that there is a great awakening among us.

The revival came at an opportune time. Within two years of its close, the United States would go to battle against itself in the Civil War. The blessings that God so graciously shed upon the young nation in revival would help to sustain it in the fiery furnace of war.

Section Review

1. What system did Francis Asbury develop to solve the problem of having too few ministers to cover a large area of land?
2. What were the "New Measures"?
3. How did Charles Finney combine elements of both the eastern and western revivals of the Second Great Awakening?
4. Give four results of the Second Great Awakening.
5. Name at least four of the unorthodox religious movements of the era. How did the Millerites differ from the other movements?

Chapter Review

Terms

Samuel Slater
Eli Whitney
interchangeable parts
patent
John Deere
Cyrus McCormick
cotton
cotton gin
Robert Fulton
National Road
plank roads
corduroy roads
toll roads
turnpikes
DeWitt Clinton
Erie Canal
B & O (Baltimore & Ohio) Railroad
clipper ship
pony express
Samuel F. B. Morse
abolitionism
William Lloyd Garrison
Nat Turner
Frederick Douglass
Harriet Tubman
Horace Mann
William H. McGuffey
Dorothea Dix
prohibition
Seneca Falls Convention
utopian reformers
Robert Owen
Federalist style
Benjamin West
Gilbert Stuart
John Trumbull
Greek revival
Charles Bulfinch
Benjamin Latrobe
George Caleb Bingham
Hudson River school
romanticism
James Fenimore Cooper

Washington Irving
Ralph Waldo Emerson
Henry David Thoreau
Walt Whitman
Nathaniel Hawthorne
Edgar Allan Poe
Stephen Foster
Lowell Mason
penny newspaper
Second Great Awakening
deism
Methodists
John Wesley
Francis Asbury
circuit riding
Timothy Dwight
camp meeting
Cane Ridge revival
American Board of Commissioners for Foreign
   Missions
Adoniram Judson
Charles Finney
''New Measures''
Unitarianism
transcendentalism
Millerites
Shakers
Mormonism
Joseph Smith
Brigham Young
Prayer Meeting Revival

Content Questions

1. For what two technological innovations was Eli Whitney responsible?
2. Why did western Pennsylvania become an early center of American heavy industry?
3. What three agricultural inventions drastically affected the agricultural output of the United States during this era?
4. List at least one advantage and one disadvantage for each of the following methods of transportation: steamboats/rivers, roads, canals, railroads.

5. Describe at least three characteristics each of the Federalist style and the romantic style in art and literature.
6. During the Second Great Awakening, which were more emotional, the revivals in the East or the revivals in the West? In which region did the revivals center in the schools and churches?
7. Name the religious figure described by each phrase.
   a. foreign missionary to Burma
   b. originated the camp meeting
   c. founded the African Methodist Episcopal Church
   d. sparked the Prayer Meeting Revival
   e. oversaw the Yale revivals
   f. founded Mormonism
   g. ''Father of American Methodism''
   h. taught ''faith in man'' instead of ''faith in Christ''
   i. practiced the New Measures
   j. incorrectly predicted the Second Coming
8. What were at least three arguments offered by Southerners in defense of slavery?

Application Questions

1. How would the history of America have been affected had the South developed a system of transportation and communication by 1860 as the North and West did?
2. Read the quotation from Walt Whitman on p. 229. How does this reflect the transcendental philosophy taught by Ralph Waldo Emerson?
3. Which do you think is more important: mission work as conducted by Adoniram Judson or mission-support work as conducted by Luther Rice?
4. Read Philemon 15-17 on the relationship of Paul, Philemon, and Onesimus. How does this passage undercut the religious arguments in support of slavery?

A crowd eagerly awaits news from the Mexican War in this nineteenth-century engraving.

According to a popular story, when Henry Clay was traveling through the Cumberland Gap in 1850, he stopped and began to concentrate as though he were listening intently to something. When a curious onlooker asked what he was doing, Clay replied, "I am listening to the tread of the coming millions."

Since the founding of the first settlements on the Atlantic coast, Americans had been courageously, stubbornly, almost irresistibly moving ever westward to settle the continent. As one pioneer wrote in her diary,

> When God made man,
> He seemed to think it best
> To make him in the East
> And let him travel west.

The 1840s saw that pattern continue with violent vigor as a burst of expansion resulted in the nation's stretching "from sea to shining sea." Supporting and motivating this growth was a philosophy which urged, even demanded, expansion. In 1845 New York journalist John Louis O'Sullivan both named and described this philosophy when he wrote that

> our manifest destiny [is] to overspread and to possess the whole of the continent which Providence has given us for the development of the great experiment of liberty and federated self-government entrusted to us.

The idea of **Manifest Destiny,** that America was providentially ordained to possess the North American continent, dominated American history in the 1840s. Americans asserted boldly–perhaps even arrogantly–that some "higher power" had given the whole continent to the United States. All that remained was for Americans to take it.

Across the Wide Missouri

Expansion in the 1840s was not as sudden as it might have seemed at the time. The background of that dramatic decade lay in over twenty years of dealings between the United States and Britain on the one hand and the United States and Mexico on the other. The background of Manifest Destiny in the 1840s lay in the history of the territories of Oregon and Texas and in the development of the western trails.

Oregon

Joint Occupation–As mentioned in Chapter 9, the United States and Great Britain agreed in 1818 to occupy the Oregon Territory jointly until the two nations could decide how to divide the area. At first Britain did the most toward developing the territory. Attracted by Oregon's abundance of beaver and other animals, British fur traders and trappers flocked to the region, but they were a wandering breed, and few of them settled down to build houses and to farm. In 1840 the number of whites living in Oregon, aside from those involved in the fur trade, was only two hundred. As the 1840s proceeded, however, that situation changed rapidly.

Missions to the Northwest–One of the more positive aspects of Manifest Destiny was an increased interest in missions. In fact, the great spur to the settlement of Oregon came from American missionaries to the Indians. In 1833 an Indian convert to Christianity published an appeal for Christians to reach the Indians of the Northwest with the gospel. Many eagerly responded, the most famous of whom were two missionary couples: **Marcus Whitman** and his wife, **Narcissa,** and Henry Spalding and his wife, Eliza. The Spaldings, settling in what is today northern Idaho, enjoyed some success among the Nez Perce (NEZ PURS) Indians. They

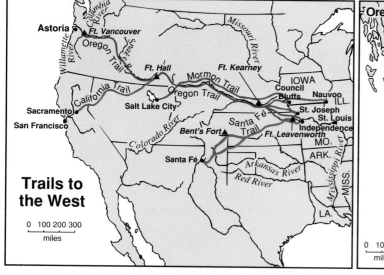

Trails to the West

0 100 200 300 miles

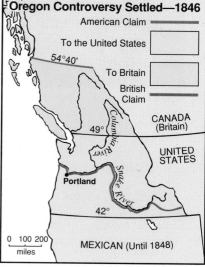

Oregon Controversy Settled—1846

American Claim

To the United States

To Britain

British Claim

CANADA (Britain)

UNITED STATES

Portland

MEXICAN (Until 1848)

0 100 200 miles

Narcissa Whitman

By her journey to and labors in Oregon, Narcissa Whitman soundly refuted the argument that the Oregon country was no place for a white woman. But then, Narcissa Whitman was not a typical woman in many ways. A lovely and well-educated woman from New York, she wrote revealingly in her letters and diary of the new land. In doing so, she presented a vivid picture of the courage and faith of a pioneer missionary.

After her conversion at the age of eleven, Narcissa Prentiss became interested in the mission field, but the American Board of Commissioners for Foreign Missions refused to consider an unmarried woman missionary. When she met physician Marcus Whitman, Narcissa eagerly shared in his dream of carrying the gospel to the Indians of the Pacific Northwest. They were married, and the board approved them as missionaries.

She began the difficult trip to Oregon with great optimism. Full of the flush of newly married love, she wrote to her sister, "Jane if you want to be happy, get a good husband as I have got and be a missionary." As she traveled, Narcissa meditated on Christ and the love for Him that had motivated her decision to go: "It is good to feel that He is all that I want, & all my righteousness, & if I had ten thousand lives I would give them all to Him."

The trip itself fascinated her. She noted her first encounter with buffalo meat: "I never saw anything like it to satisfy hunger. I have eaten three meals of it, and it relishes well." She later tired of it, however, and began to recall longingly the pork and potatoes of home. She noted with amusement the speech of westerners. "In speaking of quantity they say 'heap of man, heap of water, she is a heap sick.' If you ask, 'How does your wife do today?' they answer, 'Oh, she is smartly better, I reckon, but she is powerful weak, she has been mighty bad.' "

Like most travelers to Oregon, she had to sacrifice some of her possessions because of the unexpected rigor of the trip. Forced to leave her trunk in the wilderness, she noted in her diary: "Poor little trunk, I am sorry to leave thee. Thou must abide here alone. . . . Twenty miles below the Snake River. This shall be thy place of rest. Farewell little trunk. I thank thee for thy faithful services and that I have been cheered by thy presence so long."

Once in Oregon, the romance of mission work quickly wore off. The work of building and keeping up their mission compound/farm was heavy, and the Indians did not respond as readily as the Whitmans had hoped. Narcissa was comforted by the birth of a blond-haired daughter, but the child tragically drowned in a river at the age of two. Narcissa noted that the grave of her daughter was "in sight every time I step out the door." The unvarying, unending labor wore on Narcissa not only physically but also spiritually. She wrote that "never in my whole life have I been led to see so distinctly the hidden iniquity and secret evils of my heart. Of all persons I see myself to be the most unfit for the place I occupy on heathen ground. I wonder I was ever permitted to come."

Through the years she stayed with the task. She wrote to her parents in April 1846: "There has been considerable evidence of the movings of the Holy Spirit. . . . For ourselves, we feel that our own souls have been greatly revived, and I hope and pray that we may never again relapse into such a state of insensibility and worldly-mindedness as we many times have found ourselves in." Then in November 1846, about a year before her murder at the hands of the Indians, she wrote home again with some optimism: "We feel that God has heard prayer, for many precious souls give evidence of having passed from death to life, some among the Indians and many more among our own countrymen. . . . It would be well for the Home Missionary Society . . . to look this way, for this country is destined to exert an influence that will be felt the world over."

were able to establish both a church for the Nez Perce and a school for their children. Eliza hand-painted visual aids, such as charts, to present the gospel pictorially to the Indians. In addition the Spaldings attempted to help the Indians learn better methods of agriculture. Spalding said, ''We point them with one hand to the Lamb of God, with the other to the hoe as the means of saving their famishing bodies.''

The Whitmans had less apparent success as missionaries but had greater impact on the settlement of Oregon. The Whitmans, soon joined by other missionaries, built a mission compound near the site of modern Walla Walla, Washington, and tried to reach the fiercely independent Cayuse (kye YOOS) Indians. Although the mission featured a thriving farm, the area proved less fertile for the gospel. The suspicious Cayuse distrusted the settlers. The missionaries did not help matters by suggesting that the Indians could better please God by abandoning hunting and fishing and taking up farming like the whites. Instead the Whitmans proved more successful at recruiting settlers than reaching Indians. They sent back not only calls for more workers but also exciting descriptions of the rich unsettled lands. Whitman even served as a scout for some parties of settlers from the East.

The increasing stream of white settlers angered the Cayuse and caused them to suspect that the white man was more interested in taking Indian land than in saving Indian souls. Whitman wrote optimistically in a letter in 1844, ''The Indians are anxious about the consequence of settlers among them, but I hope there will be no acts of violence on either hand.'' Whitman's hopes proved vain, especially when a measles epidemic, apparently carried into Oregon by settlers, wiped out nearly half of the tribe despite Whitman's efforts to treat the ill. Finally in 1847 a party of Cayuse ambushed the mission compound, murdering Marcus, Narcissa, and twelve others.

Growing Numbers—The missionaries had unwittingly opened the door for a flood of immigrants. A thousand settlers came to Oregon in 1841; within two years the number had tripled and continued to grow. Extravagant stories of the region's

beauty and wealth filtered back to the East, such as the tall tale that ''the pigs are running about . . . already cooked, with knives and forks sticking in them so that you can cut off a slice whenever you are hungry.'' The truth about Oregon was enough to lure most settlers: abundant land, fertile soil, and a mild climate. By the mid-1840s, southern Oregon was far more American than British, and the joint occupation agreement of 1818 no longer seemed to be satisfactory to many Americans.

Texas

American Settlement—As part of Spain's vast North American empire, Texas remained almost unsettled until the 1820s. In 1822 **Stephen Austin,** with the permission of Spanish authorities, led the first of many land-hungry American settlers into Texas. Soon after arriving, Austin received the disturbing news that the Mexicans had overthrown the Spanish and gained their independence. Austin quickly secured approval for his venture by pledging allegiance to the new government of Mexico. Under the firm and diligent leadership of Austin, the transplanted Americans prospered, and others soon streamed in to take advantage of the riches of the new land. Cotton growing and cattle raising in particular became major businesses in Texas. By 1835 Americans in the area numbered between twenty and twenty-five thousand—far more than the Mexican population.

''Remember the Alamo!''—The influx of Americans also increased the tension between Texas and the central government of Mexico. A series of revolutions in Mexico City brought to power a government that was determined to reduce the independent ways of the province of Texas. In 1835 the Texans took arms, at first to defend the Mexican constitution of 1824, which guaranteed them a degree of autonomy within Mexico. When the Mexican dictator General **Antonio López de Santa Anna** approached Texas with some 5,000 troops, however, the Texans changed their demands to a call for outright independence from Mexico.

Santa Anna planned to drive through the heart of Texas, execute the leaders of the revolt, and expel the American pioneers. His first stop on the drive was San Antonio, which was defended by a Catholic mission turned fortress called the **Alamo.** The commander of the Texan forces, **Sam Houston,** ordered the tiny force holding the Alamo to destroy the fort and fall back. However, the commanders at the Alamo, Jim Bowie and William Travis, decided to hold the post and block the Mexican advance. In February 1836 Santa Anna marched into San Antonio and laid siege to the Alamo. The Mexicans flew a blood red flag, meaning that no mercy would be shown to the defenders. The 183 defenders, who included Bowie, Travis, and the legendary Tennessee frontiersman Davy Crockett, held out for thirteen days, and they exacted somewhere between 600 and 1,500 casualties on the Mexicans. In the end, though, the Mexicans stormed the fort and killed all the defenders.

Sam Houston did not panic. Despite the pleas of his men to attack the Mexicans and avenge the slaughter, Houston slowly fell back, forcing the Mexicans to stretch their supply lines. Santa Anna split his army into three forces to speed the crushing of the revolt. Seizing his opportunity, Houston

attacked part of Santa Anna's divided army near the San Jacinto (hah SEEN toh) River on April 21, 1836. In the brief but bloody **Battle of San Jacinto,** 800 enraged Texans–many shouting "Remember the Alamo!"–routed 1,200 Mexicans. The Texans captured Santa Anna himself and forced the dictator to sign a treaty recognizing Texan independence.

The Republic of Texas–Although the Mexican government quickly repudiated the treaty, Texas was in fact free from Mexico. Most Texans would have preferred to join the United States. President Andrew Jackson, however, realized that accepting Texas into the Union might spark a war with Mexico. Also antislavery forces in the United States opposed Texan annexation because Texas would almost certainly enter as a slave state. All that Jackson would do was to recognize the independence of Texas. Reluctantly, the **Republic of Texas** began a ten-year history of independence.

The Alamo (shown above in a nineteenth-century drawing as it appeared during the time of the Texan War for Independence) became a symbol to Texans as revered as Valley Forge had been to Americans of an earlier generation. The success of the Texan quest for independence from Mexico, however, owed less to the Alamo than to the inspired generalship of Sam Houston (pictured at the right).

Sam Houston, American Giant

He was an American swashbuckler. A 6' 6" giant, Sam Houston was a soldier, statesman, and adventurer whose life was even larger than his legend.

As a boy in Tennessee, Houston hated farm work and took every opportunity to go into the forests hunting and exploring. While in his late teens, he ran off and lived with the Cherokee Indians for three years. The tribe adopted him and gave him the name "the Raven," a title of honor. When only twenty-three, Houston served as a lieutenant under Andrew Jackson at the Battle of Horseshoe Bend (1814), where he was badly wounded by an arrow in the thigh and two bullets in the shoulder while leading a daring charge.

Houston's unflinching bravery in battle won him not only glory but also the friendship of Jackson. When Old Hickory began his rise to national power, Houston followed. The younger man was elected to Congress and in 1827 became governor of Tennessee. Then, suddenly, his career came crashing down. Houston married the daughter of a prominent Tennessee family, but within three months she had left him. Neither Houston nor his bride would ever give the reason for their sudden split. The angry and embittered Houston, however, resigned as governor and–like other Tennesseans such as Davy Crockett–went to Texas.

In Texas Sam Houston was not a pleasant man to be around. He became a brawling, moody loner who tried to drown his troubles in alcohol. The Indians gave him a new and more appropriate name, "Big Drunk." Houston might have sunk into obscurity in the backwaters of Texas were it not for the Texan War for Independence, which gave him new purpose and drive. His natural leadership and military talents won him the command of the Texan forces. Only his strong personality was able to keep in line this ragged assortment of strong-minded settlers and roughnecks. After his great victory at San Jacinto, Houston was the most popular man in Texas.

Sam Houston put his life back together. He served two terms as the president of the Republic of Texas, and after statehood he served the state as both U.S. senator and governor. He also married again in 1840 to twenty-one-year-old Margaret Lea, a devout Baptist. Friends privately predicted that the marriage would not last six months. Instead, Houston proved a devoted family man as he and Margaret raised eight children. His former acquaintances were even more astounded when he later professed his faith in Christ for salvation and was baptized at the age of sixty-one in a Texas creek.

The final crisis of Houston's career came in 1860 when he was governor. Texas strongly favored joining the other Southern states in

Trails West

One important aspect of Manifest Destiny was simply *getting* to the West. Traveling to the new lands of the West in the 1800s was obviously not a matter of hopping in a car and driving down an interstate. The goal of the pioneers was the far West, and the means of getting there were the overland trails. *Trail* is an accurate term, for these routes were certainly not roads. At best, they consisted of the ruts left by preceding wagons. Packing all their belongings into sturdy, ox-drawn wagons, settlers journeyed west seeking a new and better life. Often, as trails climbed into the steep passes through the Rocky Mountains, pioneers had to lighten their loads. Oak chests, chairs, trunks, even grandfather clocks littered the wayside, victims of the craggy heights of the Rockies. The discards could have furnished many houses–if one had only had the means of carrying them.

Traveling the trails was dangerous. Indian attack, of course, was always a possibility. More mundane, but nearly as deadly, were broken axles or the death of an exhausted ox, events which would strand families in the wilderness to die.

seceding from the United States. As loyal to the Union as he was to Texas, Houston tried to argue his fellow citizens out of secession. He said, "You may, after the sacrifice of countless millions of treasure and hundreds of thousands of lives, as a bare possibility, win Southern independence . . . but I doubt it." His pleas were in vain.

When the new Confederate government ordered all officials to take an oath of allegiance to the Confederacy, Houston refused. He resigned from office and retired from public life. He died in 1863, his last words being "Texas . . . Texas . . . Margaret. . . ."

Weather was also a factor. Storms and floods could slow the advance of a wagon train, and woe to the pioneer who did not reach his destination before winter set in. Probably the most horrible example of the dangers of the trails was the fate of the Donner Party. Heading to California in 1846, a group under the leadership of George Donner was trapped for months in the Sierra Nevada range by the winter snows. Only forty of the eighty-seven members of

the party survived, and they did so by resorting to cannibalism.

Three main trails reached westward. The **Oregon Trail** was obviously the most important. Not only did the trail lead to Oregon, but also branches (called "cutoffs") reached into California. The **Santa Fe Trail** was also important, but it was more of a commercial route than a means of pioneer transportation. During the era of Spanish domination, American merchants began a thriving trade between Santa Fe in New Mexico and Independence, Missouri. Even after Mexican independence, the trade flourished. Fear of growing American activity in Texas eventually caused the Mexican government to close the trail, but memories of earlier profits caused many Americans to covet New Mexico. The **Mormon Trail,** as its name indicates, was blazed by the Mormons when they fled from Nauvoo, Illinois, to Salt Lake City in 1846-1847. (See p. 237.) More Mormons followed the trail, and eventually non-Mormons found it a convenient route to California. The constant stream of pioneers along the trails began to fill the West. It also began to increase tension between the United States and both Great Britain and Mexico.

Section Review

1. Who first spurred American settlement of Oregon?
2. Name two characteristics of Oregon that attracted settlers to that region.
3. Why did Andrew Jackson refuse to annex Texas?
4. Name three dangers of traveling on the western trails in the first half of the nineteenth century.
5. Using both the text and the map on p. 242, name which of the three western trails (Oregon Trail, Santa Fe Trail, or Mormon Trail) is described by each of the following phrases:
   a. Involved trade with the Spanish
   b. Had "cutoffs" that went into California
   c. The southernmost trail
   d. Blazed primarily by a religious sect

Politics and Protocol

While Americans boldly settled in the West, politics in the East moved more prudently. Jackson's refusal to annex Texas, for example, displayed a caution that was alien to those who had defended the Alamo. Political developments in Washington, D.C., in the 1840s, however, profoundly affected affairs in far-off Oregon, California, and Texas. Manifest Destiny increasingly became an article of faith to American politicians.

And Tyler Too

"His Accidency"—The sudden death of President Harrison in 1841 created confusion in the Whig ranks. Party leaders had chosen Vice President **John Tyler** to win votes in the South, not to run the country. Since Harrison was the first president to die in office, some questioned Tyler's position. Was he simply "Acting President," or did he have the full powers of the presidency? At any rate, most Whig leaders in Congress and the cabinet assumed that Tyler should submit to their guidance and instruction. **Henry Clay,** the real head of the party, said, "Tyler dares not resist me. I will drive him before me."

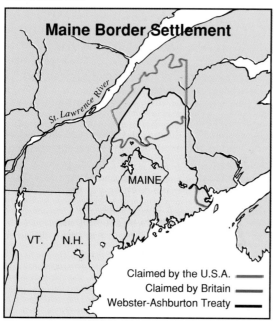

Maine Border Settlement

St. Lawrence River

MAINE

VT. N.H.

Claimed by the U.S.A. ━━━
Claimed by Britain ━━━
Webster-Ashburton Treaty ━━━

Tyler, however, refused to be driven. He left no doubt that he was president in the full sense of the term. Rather than follow the bidding of Clay, Tyler shocked the Whigs by his policies. Really more of an anti-Jackson Democrat than a true Whig at heart, Tyler vetoed Clay's measures for higher tariffs, a new national bank, and internal improvements. The Whigs responded by voting Tyler out of the party, and the entire cabinet–except Secretary of State **Daniel Webster**–resigned in the fall of 1841. Embittered Whigs began to refer to Tyler as "his Accidency."

Webster-Ashburton Treaty—One of the reasons that Webster remained in the cabinet was his ongoing negotiations with Great Britain over the American-Canadian border. The northern border of Maine was the main point of controversy. Because of ambiguities in the Treaty of Paris (1783), Britain and the United States argued over some twelve thousand square miles of territory. The conflict heightened in 1840 when lumberjacks from Maine and Canada clashed over timber claims in the disputed region. Webster and the British representative, Lord Ashburton, sought to settle the issue. After much discussion, the pair hammered out the **Webster-Ashburton Treaty** (1842). Under the treaty, the United States received seven-twelfths of the disputed area, and the British received the rest. The diplomats also clarified the border between Minnesota and Canada so that the United States received clear title to land that later was found to contain valuable deposits of iron ore.

"Who Is James K. Polk?"

Campaign of 1844—As another presidential election approached in 1844, Clay emerged as the leading Whig candidate over the discredited Tyler. The president would have liked to run for reelection on the Democratic ticket, but the Democrats were not about to trust a man who had been a Whig only four years before. The leading Democratic candidate was in fact former president Martin Van Buren. Tyler tried to rally support for himself by making the annexation of Texas (which he favored) a major issue in the campaign; Clay and Van Buren tried to eliminate this issue by publishing letters stating their opposition to annexation.

President James K. Polk

A Dark Horse−Clay easily won the Whig nomination, but the Democrats surprisingly rejected Van Buren. Pushed by expansionists, the party turned to a **"dark horse,"** a nominee who had not been a serious candidate before the nominating convention and about whom little was usually known by the general public. In this case, the dark horse was **James K. Polk** of Tennessee. During the campaign, Whigs derisively asked, "Who is James K. Polk?" But Polk was not a political unknown. He had served for fourteen years in the House of Representatives, including four years as Speaker of the House. He was also a former governor of Tennessee whose close association with Andrew Jackson earned him the nickname "Young Hickory." Even more important, as far as Democratic expansionists were concerned, Polk was more than willing to run on a platform which called for "the reoccupation of Oregon and the reannexation of Texas."

As fervor for annexation began to grow, Clay began to hedge his position. He declared that he was not necessarily opposed to annexing Texas if such an act would not result in war with Mexico.

Opponents of slavery objected to Clay's shift, and many supported James Birney, the candidate of the tiny antislavery **Liberty party.** Polk won the election by a narrow margin of 38,000 out of 2.7 million votes cast and by a count of 170 to 105 in the electoral college. Birney drew only 62,000 votes, but he may have cost Clay the election. Polk carried New York by only 5,000 votes, and Birney polled 15,000 in that state. Had Clay not lost the antislavery vote, he might have become president.

Texas Annexed−After the election, but before Polk took office, President Tyler took the election results as a mandate to push for the **annexation of Texas.** Tyler realized that he could not raise the needed two-thirds majority in the Senate to ratify a treaty of annexation. Therefore he proposed to annex the region through a **joint resolution** of Congress, an act which required only a simple majority in both houses. The resolution passed, and Tyler signed it two days before leaving office. Thus Texas became the twenty-eighth state in the Union.

Polk's Administration

A Disciplined Executive−Polk was perhaps the hardest working, most self-disciplined president in our history. He approached each task before him with an almost grim determination. Eighteen-hour workdays were common for him, and he rarely took vacations. Polk paid for this unceasing labor, however. His health declined during his term, and he died within four months of leaving office.

One historian noted that Polk "knew how to get things done, which is the first necessity of government, and he knew what he wanted done, which is the second." Polk is unusual among American politicians in that he faithfully kept his campaign promises. He pledged, for example, to serve only one term as president, and he never relented. A cabinet member recalled that on his inauguration day, Polk outlined four goals for his administration. He wanted to (1) lower the tariff, (2) restore the independent treasury system of Van Buren (see p. 209), (3) settle the Oregon Question, and (4) acquire California from Mexico. With his Democratic majority in Congress, Polk achieved his first two goals rather easily. The last two, however, involved entering the confused and sometimes dangerous world of international diplomacy.

The Oregon Question—The Oregon country stretched from 42° latitude in the south to 54° 40' latitude in the north. Fired by the fervor of the 1844 presidential campaign, some expansionists began clamoring for the United States to take the whole region. Polk entered delicate negotiations with Britain while zealous members of his party were proclaiming slogans such as "Fifty-four-forty or fight!" and "All of Oregon or none!" The British, on the other hand, had long maintained that the proper boundary should be the Columbia River, a border which would have made most of the modern state of Washington part of Canada.

Polk offered to extend the U.S.-Canadian border along the 49th parallel (49° latitude), the line that formed the border from Minnesota to the Rockies. Since the fur trade had declined along the Columbia River, the British now had less interest in that region and were more open to compromise. In 1846 the two nations signed a treaty that settled the Oregon Question. The 49th parallel became the international boundary to the Pacific, but Britain retained all of Vancouver Island, and its fur traders kept the right to travel on the Columbia. Polk did not please die-hard expansionists with this compromise, but he made what most Americans considered a fair settlement.

Section Review

1. Why was Tyler unpopular with the Whig party?
2. Who received most of the disputed territory in Maine under the provisions of the Webster-Ashburton Treaty?
3. Why did Tyler annex Texas through a joint resolution of Congress rather than a treaty in the Senate?
4. What were James Polk's four goals for his administration?
5. Where did extreme American expansionists want to draw the Oregon boundary? Where did Britain originally contend it should be drawn? What became the actual boundary?

War with Mexico

Polk's fourth goal, acquiring California, involved diplomatic dealings with Mexico. Affairs with that nation, however, were neither so smooth nor so amicably settled as they had been with Britain. In fact, the American desire for California coupled with difficulties over Texas plunged the United States into war with its neighbor to the south. The **Mexican War** (1846-1848) was the climax and the most violent phase of Manifest Destiny.

An American force enters Saltillo, Mexico, in one of the earliest photographs of American soldiers taken in time of war.

Background of the War

Causes—The causes of the Mexican War were complex. First, and most obvious, was Mexican resentment over the annexation of Texas. Mexico had never recognized Texan independence and therefore refused to accept the American action. Second was the longing of many expansionists in the United States for California and New Mexico. Some coveted the rich, fertile lands of California and its fine harbors, while others fondly recalled the profitable trade that had existed along the Santa Fe Trail. In addition, Mexico's shaky control over these far-off regions caused some expansionists to urge that the United States seize them before some other power, such as Britain, beat them to it. Third was a history of hostility between the two nations. Americans often looked down on the Mexicans as somehow crude and inferior. Many angrily recalled the slaughter at the Alamo. Mexicans, on the other hand, resented the arrogance of the United States and feared its expansion at their expense. Mexico's unstable political situation did not help relations. The constant series of Mexican revolutions allowed little time for the two nations to work out their differences.

A fourth cause was, ironically, the failure of an attempt at a peaceful settlement. In 1845 Polk sent an envoy to negotiate with Mexico. Polk was prepared to pay $5 million to settle the disputes about Texas and up to $30 million to purchase California and New Mexico. Mexicans considered the offer an insult to their national honor, and the Mexican government could not even discuss the offer for fear of starting another revolution among the angry populace. The result of the offer was to drive another wedge between the nations. Polk's envoy, furious at the treatment he had received, wrote back to his chief, "Depend on it, we can never get along with them until we have given them a good drubbing."

A fifth cause–the real spark of the conflict–was a dispute over the Texas-Mexico boundary. The Mexicans claimed that the southern border of Texas was the Nueces (noo AY sis) River; the United States claimed that it was the Rio Grande, some miles to the south. After Texas officially entered the Union, Polk sent a force under General Zachary Taylor into the disputed area between the two rivers. The Mexicans demanded they leave immediately and posted an army on the southern bank of the Rio Grande. On April 25, 1846, Mexican troops attacked a detachment of American cavalry across the river. Polk, saying "The cup of forbearance had been exhausted," called on Congress to declare war, which it did on May 13, 1846. The conflict had begun.

Problems at Home–Although the attack in Texas enabled Polk to persuade Congress to declare war, the administration was hampered by division at home. A sizable minority of Americans considered the conflict an unjust war of conquest.

Some thought the war a brazen attempt to create more slave states. New England poet James Lowell Russell wrote scathingly:

> They just want this Californy
>> So's to lug new slave-states in
> To abuse ye, an' to scorn ye,
>> An' to plunder ye like sin.

Even Southern spokesman John C. Calhoun warned, "Mexico is to us the forbidden fruit; the penalty of eating it would be to subject our institutions to political death." Young Whig congressman Abraham Lincoln of Illinois called for the administration to announce the exact spot of the Mexican attack so that Congress could decide whether the war was truly defensive or had been provoked. Nor did matters improve after the war dragged on. Less than a year after voting to declare war, the House narrowly passed a resolution stating that the conflict had been "unnecessarily and unconstitutionally begun by the President of the United States." Some opponents simply referred to it as "Mr. Polk's War."

The United States was not ready for the war either. The regular army was tiny, about 7,000 men. Volunteers flocked in to fight, but, though brave, they often proved unruly and undisciplined. The two leading generals, Winfield Scott and Zachary Taylor, were Whigs whose every success created jealousy in the Democratic ranks. Furthermore, neither Polk nor the army had any real master strategy for winning the war. Typical of the president's ignorance of the situation was his suggestion that Taylor's army "live off the land" in northern Mexico, land that was mostly desert scrub. The credit for the American victory ultimately rested on the nation's clear-cut naval superiority, the valor of its troops in battle, and the fact that Mexico's lack of preparedness matched that of the United States.

Campaigns of the War

The course of the Mexican War divides neatly into four campaigns: (1) Taylor's campaign in northern Mexico, (2) the New Mexico campaign, (3) the California campaign, and (4) Scott's campaign in central Mexico, which climaxed in the capture of Mexico City.

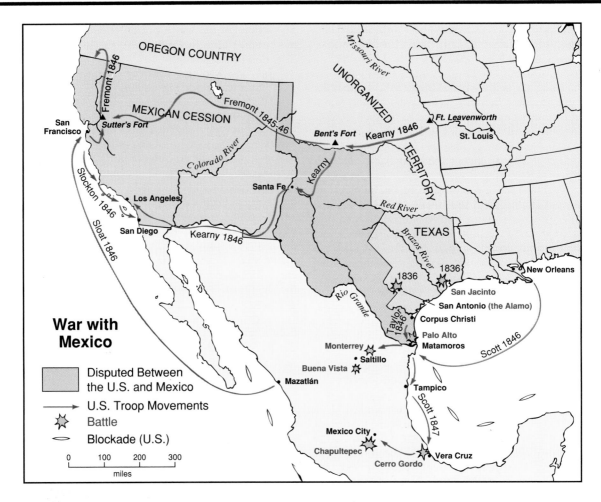

War with Mexico

Disputed Between the U.S. and Mexico

→ U.S. Troop Movements

✦ Battle

◯ Blockade (U.S.)

0   100   200   300
miles

*Taylor in Northern Mexico—*Zachary Taylor, the commander of the troops on the Rio Grande, was a veteran of the War of 1812 and several Indian wars. Nicknamed "Old Rough and Ready" by his men, Taylor dressed sloppily and lacked the superior air that many generals carefully cultivated. New recruits often failed to recognize their slouchily dressed, rumpled-looking commander on first meeting. For example, one new lieutenant, seeing Taylor sitting behind his tent cleaning his sword, unwittingly asked him if he would take a dollar to clean the lieutenant's sword too. "Sure thing," replied the general cheerfully.

Taylor's undeniable bravery and his simple, friendly manner won him the unflinching devotion of his men. But he was not a particularly good strategist, and his battles with the Indians had given him little experience in fighting a regular army. In addition, his easygoing manner did not create the most organized or disciplined of camps.

Somehow Taylor overcame his shortcomings as a commander. He began the campaign with two sharp victories which drove the Mexicans from the Rio Grande. Then gathering his force of 6,600 men, Taylor marched to Monterrey, the main city of northern Mexico, and confronted a well-entrenched force of 7,000 Mexicans. For three days (September 21-23, 1846), the Americans assaulted the fortifications of Monterrey. After the forts fell, fierce street fighting ensued as the Americans battled house by house toward the city's central plaza. Realizing his hopeless situation, the Mexican commander finally surrendered.

Taylor had won a great victory, but several factors worked to undermine his position. Defeat at Monterrey was not enough to force the Mexican government in far-off Mexico City to make peace. In the meantime, so many Whigs were speaking of running "Old Rough and Ready" for president that the Democratic administration resolved to give him no more opportunities for glory. A planned thrust on Mexico City was instead entrusted to Winfield Scott, Taylor's superior. Scott soon took the best of Taylor's men and left him with a smaller force of 4,500 volunteers. To top it all off, after Scott had removed the troops, Taylor suddenly found

American cavalry charges the Mexican lines in one of the battles of the northern Mexico campaign.

himself facing a new army of 15,000 Mexicans under the leadership of the scourge of the Alamo, Santa Anna.

Santa Anna's presence on the field was the result of a diplomatic blunder by Polk. Living in exile in Cuba when the war broke out, Santa Anna convinced the Americans that if they allowed him back into Mexico, he would arrange a peace settlement. On returning to Mexico, however, he seized power again and vowed to drive the Americans from Mexican soil. After intercepting some correspondence that revealed American plans, Santa Anna marched north to crush Taylor. In the **Battle of Buena Vista** (February 22-23, 1847), Taylor's outnumbered army held out in a desperate defensive battle that brought the Americans as close as they came to defeat during the entire war. Finally, the exhausted Mexicans broke off the fighting and began a demoralizing retreat to Mexico City to meet the next American thrust.

New Mexico Campaign—"Campaign" is almost too glorious a term for the capture of New Mexico; it was more a desert march than anything else. Polk appointed General **Stephen Kearny** to lead a force of 1,500 men, mostly cavalry, down the Santa Fe Trail to capture New Mexico. Kearny's army left Fort Leavenworth on June 5 and captured Santa Fe on August 18 after almost no resistance. Leaving most of his troops to occupy the newly conquered province, Kearny took part of his men west to aid in the conquest of California.

*California Campaign—*California proved to be much more difficult to capture than New Mexico. Although a number of Americans had settled in the province, the Spanish-speaking population outnumbered them ten to one. Furthermore, the Spanish Californians were suspicious, and for good reason. In 1842 an American naval commander, hearing a rumor that Mexico and the United States had gone to war, sailed into Monterey Bay in central California and captured it. When the rumor proved unfounded, the red-faced Americans quickly apologized, but the action left the Californians understandably wary of American intentions.

Captain **John C. Frémont,** an explorer known as "the Pathfinder of the West," struck the next blow in California. Before the war broke out, Frémont had led a group of sixty men into California. To this day no one knows exactly what they were doing there. Supposedly in the area to explore, Frémont's party was too numerous and too well armed to be a simple exploration team. Since Polk was trying to purchase California from Mexico, however, he was not likely to have sent Frémont there to stir up trouble. At any rate, Frémont found the Spanish-speaking population divided into two hostile camps and the American settlers afraid of both. When the settlers revolted from Mexico and established the **"Bear Flag Republic"** (because their flag featured a bear) on July 4, 1846, Frémont supported them–despite the fact that as far as he knew Mexico and the United States were still at peace.

Shortly thereafter the American fleet arrived at California's Monterey Bay with the news that war had broken out. Relieved, Frémont joined forces with the naval commander, and they quickly subdued all of California. Initially, most Californians greeted the Americans enthusiastically. The contempt and harsh treatment which some American soldiers displayed toward the Spanish Californians, however, quickly soured relations. A revolt broke out, and the Spanish insurgents recaptured Los Angeles. At this point, Kearny arrived from New Mexico with his men. With an unusual army consisting of Frémont's explorers, armed settlers, marines from the American fleet, and Kearny's cavalry, the Americans recaptured Los Angeles and ended the revolt. The victors treated the defeated foe generously this time, and by January of 1847, California was once again quiet and firmly under American control.

Scott in Central Mexico—Taylor's victories in northern Mexico and the conquest of New Mexico and California meant little if Mexico would not make peace. Finally, Polk approved an attack on Mexico City in an attempt to end the war. The administration assigned this task to General **Winfield Scott,** probably their most capable commander. Called "Old Fuss and Feathers" because of his love for military pomp and discipline, Scott lacked the warmth of Taylor and was not as popular with the rank-and-file soldiers. He had a better grasp of strat-

Mexico: Boot Camp for the Civil War

The Mexican War was the first conflict in which graduates of West Point, the United States Military Academy, played a major role. It also proved to be a training ground for many of those graduates in preparation for more arduous service on the battlefields of the Civil War.

Many young officers first gained distinction in Mexico. Captain Robert E. Lee, an engineer on General Scott's staff in central Mexico, played an important role in the movements of the American army. While scouting the field at Cerro Gordo, Lee found a potential route for the Americans that would allow them to slip behind the Mexican position. As he scouted the route, Lee suddenly heard the voices of Mexican soldiers. Lee scrambled behind a log to hide. He lay com-

pletely still while a party of Mexican soldiers gathered and talked, some of them even sitting on the log behind which Lee was hiding. Insects added torment to the suspense as they crawled over the motionless American and bit him. After several hours, the Mexicans left, and Lee hurried back to Scott's headquarters.

With the captain's information, the American army outflanked Santa Anna and won a smashing victory. Lee's unflinching personal discipline and his self-sacrificing character were even more evident years later when he led the Confederate army.

Many other famous names won their first glory in Mexico. Lieutenant Ulysses "Sam" Grant also served under Scott in central Mexico. Grant was honored in particular for his actions during the final assault on Mexico City. He and a gun crew performed the remarkable feat of disassembling a cannon, pulling it into the belfry of a church, reassembling it, and then using it to shell the Mexican position. Sixteen years later in the siege of Vicksburg, Grant displayed that same kind of ingenuity on a much larger scale.

Another lieutenant, Thomas J. Jackson, also won praise for his bravery with an artillery unit in the attack on Mexico City. Assigned to fire on an entrenched fortress, Jackson could not persuade his crew to come out into the open and man the gun in the face of fierce enemy fire. As bullets and shells whizzed about him, Jackson walked about in the open calling, "There is no danger. See! I am not hit." Only a sergeant would join Jackson, and together they fired the gun until the fortress fell. It was this same kind of brave determination that won Jackson the nickname "Stonewall" fourteen years later at the First Battle of Manassas.

Not all of the great generals of the Civil War won glory in Mexico. Lieutenant William Sherman, much to his disgust, began the war as a recruiting officer in Pittsburgh. Finally, Sherman was assigned to the forces in California. The seven-month sea journey around South America, however, landed him on the west coast after the fighting was over. "We'll have . . . no fighting," Sherman lamented. "That's too bad after coming so far." In a few years, the Civil War provided Lee, Grant, Jackson, Sherman, and thousands of others more than enough opportunity to display their fighting prowess.

egy, however, and his Mexican campaign was one of the most brilliant in American military history.

Scott planned to follow the route that the Spanish *conquistador* Cortés had followed over three hundred years before. Scott's army landed south of the Mexican port of **Vera Cruz** early in March of 1847, and he captured the city in less than three weeks. Santa Anna, recovered from his setback at Buena Vista, blocked the American path. By quick movement and shrewd maneuvering, Scott drove the Mexicans back toward their capital. At least three times Scott outwitted the enemy by sending his troops over ground that Santa Anna thought impassable for an army. In August and September, Americans and Mexicans engaged in a series of bloody battles outside of Mexico City. As the Americans edged nearer, Santa Anna realized the hopelessness of his cause. With his army defeated and the populace of the capital calling for his head, Santa Anna abandoned the city. Scott led the victorious Americans into Mexico City on September 14, 1847.

Results of the War

The loss of Mexico City was a final blow to Santa Anna's government. He resigned in disgrace, and a new government began negotiating with the United States. The result was the **Treaty of Guadalupe Hidalgo** (gwah-duh-LOO-pay ee-DAHL-go) in 1848. Mexico recognized American claims to Texas to the Rio Grande and ceded New Mexico and California to the U.S. The United States in turn paid Mexico $15 million and assumed all debts that Mexico owed American citizens. The cost of the war was high in more than dollars. About 1,700 Americans died in combat, and over 11,000 perished from disease. The war also provided a training ground for an even larger conflict scarcely a dozen years later; over two hundred officers who served in the Mexican War became generals in either the Union or Confederate armies in the Civil War.

In 1853, almost as a footnote to the war, the United States paid Mexico $10 million for a chunk of territory bordering on the southwestern United

General Winfield Scott, America's greatest commander of the Mexican War

States. Known as the **Gadsden Purchase,** the land was needed for the path of a transcontinental railroad. Ironically, the Mexican president who negotiated the purchase–Santa Anna once again–was overthrown the following year in reaction to the sale. The Gadsden Purchase filled out the continental United States to its present boundaries. It was in many ways the climax of Manifest Destiny. The United States now stretched from the Atlantic to the Pacific.

Section Review

1. List at least three causes of the Mexican War.
2. What were the four main campaigns of the Mexican War?
3. How did Santa Anna return to power in Mexico during the Mexican War?
4. What were three results of the Mexican War?

Chapter Review

Terms
Manifest Destiny
Marcus Whitman
Narcissa Whitman
Stephen Austin
Antonio López de Santa Anna
Alamo
Sam Houston
Battle of San Jacinto
Republic of Texas
Oregon Trail
Santa Fe Trail
Mormon Trail
John Tyler
Henry Clay
Daniel Webster
Webster-Ashburton Treaty
"dark horse"
James K. Polk
Liberty party
annexation of Texas
joint resolution
Mexican War (1846-1848)
Zachary Taylor
Battle of Buena Vista
Stephen Kearny
John C. Frémont
Bear Flag Republic
Winfield Scott
Vera Cruz
Treaty of Guadalupe Hidalgo
Gadsden Purchase

Content Questions
1. What business attracted British citizens to Oregon?
2. Why did Secretary of State Daniel Webster decide not to resign with the rest of Tyler's cabinet in 1841?

3. Give the dates for the following steps in American expansion and then place them in their proper chronological order.
   a. Treaty of Guadalupe Hidalgo
   b. Annexation of Texas
   c. Maine boundary settlement
   d. Gadsden Purchase
   e. Oregon boundary settlement
4. How did the Santa Fe Trail differ in purpose from the Oregon and Mormon trails?
5. Which commander was more popular with his men, Winfield Scott or Zachary Taylor? Which was the better strategic commander?
6. Why did the Polk administration entrust the Mexico City campaign to Winfield Scott instead of Zachary Taylor?
7. Name the campaign of the Mexican War (northern Mexico, New Mexico, California, or central Mexico) described by each of the following phrases.
   a. a difficult march with no hard fighting
   b. commanded by Zachary Taylor
   c. commanded by Winfield Scott
   d. led in part by the "Pathfinder of the West"
   e. Battle of Buena Vista
   f. Bear Flag Republic
   g. siege of Vera Cruz
   h. Stephen Kearny's *first* campaign

Application Questions
1. How would you evaluate the missionary work of the Whitmans? What lessons can we learn from their experience?
2. How did Henry Clay's stand on Texas possibly cost him the election of 1844?
3. In his later years, Ulysses S. Grant called the Mexican War "one of the most unjust ever waged by a stronger against a weaker nation." Do you agree with this statement? Why or why not?

UNIT IV

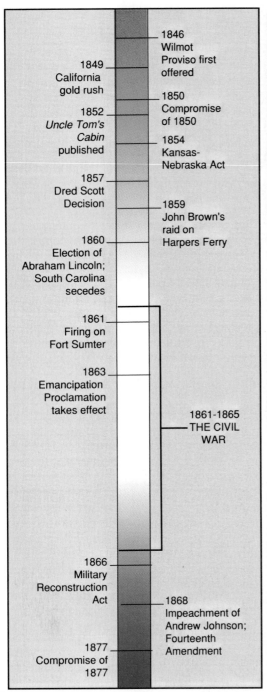

1849
California
gold rush

1852
*Uncle Tom's
Cabin*
published

1857
Dred Scott
Decision

1860
Election of
Abraham Lincoln;
South Carolina
secedes

1861
Firing on
Fort Sumter

1863
Emancipation
Proclamation
takes effect

1866
Military
Reconstruction
Act

1877
Compromise of
1877

1846
Wilmot
Proviso first
offered

1850
Compromise
of 1850

1854
Kansas-
Nebraska Act

1859
John Brown's
raid on
Harpers Ferry

1861-1865
THE CIVIL
WAR

1868
Impeachment of
Andrew Johnson;
Fourteenth
Amendment

CHAPTER 13

A House Dividing (1848-1861)

"And so we fool on into the black cloud ahead of us."

> Mary Boykin Chestnut, *diary entry from Charleston,*
> *South Carolina,* April 11, 1861, *the day before the*
> *firing on Fort Sumter*

Members of the Kansas Free State Battery, partisans of "Bleeding Kansas"

The 1850s was perhaps America's most decisive decade since nationhood, the 1860s its most divisive. Yet the one preceded the other in more than a chronological sense. Far from the coming war's being an "irrepressible conflict" as William Seward declared, there were opportunities in the 1850s for peace and compromise, though like sand in an hourglass they diminished with time. Americans of that day have rightly been called "the blundering generation" as extremists in the North and South, with their ravenous rhetoric, tore at the cords of union, while most people were content to watch them. One by one the lines of communication were severed until Americans were talking past each other, then shouting past each other, then shooting *at* each other. The seeds of discord that had been in the soil since the founding of the republic were warmed in the 1850s by hateful rhetoric and watered with blood. They would soon yield a grim harvest.

Controversy

New Territories, Old Questions

As a result of the Mexican War, the United States made the largest single acquisition of territory in its history, larger even than the Louisiana Purchase. With these new lands came a revival of old problems that had plagued the nation since its founding. This time, however, the problems would not go away. They would continue to fester throughout the 1850s and finally plunge the nation into war. Events seemed to vindicate the gloomy prediction that Ralph Waldo Emerson had made during the Mexican War: "The United States will conquer Mexico, but it will be as the man who swallows arsenic which brings him down in turn. Mexico will poison us.''

Wilmot Proviso—In 1846 President Polk sent an appropriations bill to Congress for funds to pursue negotiations with Mexico even while the fighting was going on. A Democratic representative from Pennsylvania, David Wilmot, attached an amendment to the bill. In what became known as the **Wilmot Proviso,** the freshman congressman proposed that the United States prohibit slavery in any territory acquired from Mexico. The South was outraged, and Southern voting strength in the Senate kept the proviso from becoming law. Nevertheless, Wilmot's amendment became a rallying point for antislavery forces. Over the next few years antislavery congressmen repeatedly offered the Wilmot Proviso to Congress. Several times the act passed the House only to be rejected by the Senate.

Calhoun Resolutions—Reacting to the threat of the Wilmot Proviso, many Southerners rallied to the position of Southern spokesman John C. Calhoun. In his **Calhoun Resolutions,** offered to the Senate in 1847, Calhoun set down the Southern view of the status of slavery in the territories. Territories are the common possession of the states and not the federal government, Calhoun argued. Therefore slave owners have the same constitutional protection of their property (i.e., slaves) in the territories as they had in their home states. Neither Congress nor territorial legislatures, Calhoun said, had the right to limit slavery. Only when a territory became a state could it prohibit slavery. When confronted with the fact that Congress had previously prohibited slavery in the territories under, for example, the Missouri Compromise, Calhoun claimed that such measures were extra-constitutional acts that the South had permitted in order to preserve the Union.

Popular Sovereignty—Between the extremes of Wilmot and Calhoun arose a compromise position, **popular sovereignty.** According to this idea, the residents of a territory should decide on the status of slavery. If citizens wanted slavery, they could have it. If they did not want it, they could prohibit it. The doctrine of popular sovereignty was strongest among the Democrats. Lewis Cass of Michigan

President Zachary Taylor

and later Stephen Douglas of Illinois became its leading proponents.

Election of 1848

When the presidential election of 1848 rolled around, the Democrats and the Whigs sought to skirt the thorny questions raised by Wilmot and Calhoun. The Democrats nominated Lewis Cass, champion of the compromise view of popular sovereignty. The Whigs decided to avoid the question altogether. They nominated **Zachary Taylor,** hero of the Mexican War. Although Taylor owned slaves on his plantation in Mississippi, his political views were little known, and, in fact, Taylor had never even voted in a presidential election before. Copying their successful formula of 1840, the Whigs nominated a general, avoided adopting a platform, and stressed the military achievements of their candidate.

The positions of Cass and Taylor were not likely to please the antislavery forces. Nor did they please **free-soilers,** those who favored leaving slavery alone in the South where it already existed but opposed its extension into the territories. These antislavery and free-soil groups joined forces to form a third party, the **Free Soil party.** Under the slogan ''Free Soil, Free Speech, Free Labor, and Free Men,'' the new party warmly supported the Wilmot Proviso and nominated former president Martin Van Buren as its candidate. With Van Buren drawing off dissatisfied Democrats in the North (particularly in New York), Taylor won a narrow victory over Cass. The new president, however, faced a difficult situation. A dramatic discovery in California was about to spark a renewal of the sectional controversy.

California

Gold Rush—Swiss immigrant John Sutter arrived in California in 1839 while the region was still under Mexican control. Winning a grant of 50,000 acres of land from the Mexican government, Sutter began building a large, self-sufficient ranch at the junction of the Sacramento and American rivers (the site of the modern city of Sacramento). The transfer of California from Mexico to the United States in 1846 did not affect Sutter—at first. He continued his construction, planning to build a sawmill to provide lumber for his extensive ranch. In 1848, during the building of the mill, one of Sutter's foremen found some glittering stones below the mill's water wheel. The stones, he soon discovered, were gold. The foreman took the gold to Sutter, who decided to try to keep the matter quiet.

News such as that, however, could not be kept quiet. Word spread first throughout California and then back to the eastern United States and overseas. ''Gold fever'' seized thousands of otherwise sensible men and sent them to California where wealth was seemingly theirs for the taking. The **California gold rush** was on. Because the first wave of gold hunters came in 1849, they all became known as **forty-niners.** Most forty-niners followed the overland route to California, like the pioneers who had followed the Oregon Trail. A number, particularly on the east coast, went by sea. Some sailed to Central America, crossed the narrow bridge of land by canoe and mule, and tried to find a ship on the Pacific side going to California. More took the all-water route, the long and dangerous journey around the southern tip of South America. In all, some 80,000 men came to California in 1849, and over 400,000 came in the ten years from 1848 to 1858.

The lure of wealth drew men irresistibly to California. Whole crews deserted when their ships landed on the west coast, leaving the hulks to rot in the harbors. (Some captains learned to take the precaution of putting their crew in chains before landing in San Francisco.) Even soldiers stationed in California began to desert to the gold fields. Lieutenant William Sherman complained bitterly, ''None remain behind but we poor devils of officers who are restrained by honor.''

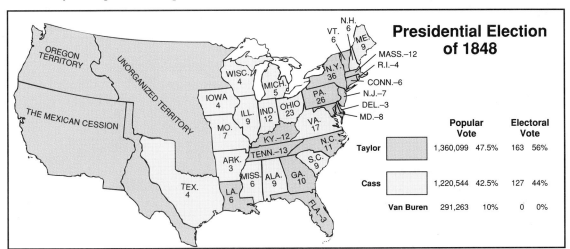

Presidential Election of 1848

	Popular Vote		Electoral Vote	
Taylor	1,360,099	47.5%	163	56%
Cass	1,220,544	42.5%	127	44%
Van Buren	291,263	10%	0	0%

Seeking gold was a gamble; there were only a few winners and many losers. Many gambled their savings, their occupation, and even their lives, believing that they would win. Some of those who hoped to strike it rich died in shipwrecks or on the trails without ever reaching California. Those who successfully staked claims found that standing in water all day and wielding a pick and shovel was hard, discouraging work. The few who found rich ore, however–if they were not murdered or swindled out of their claims–became enviably wealthy and inspired stories that encouraged others to come.

Whether or not a prospector found gold, he seldom left California. The trip home was too long and the beauty of the region too appealing. Ironically, one man who did not share in the wealth was John Sutter. He lost his land to greedy gold hunters and died in Pennsylvania in 1873, never having profited from the gold rush he had started.

Statehood Question–The rush of people into California resulted in governmental chaos. The military rule installed after the Mexican War proved insufficient to govern the large number of sometimes unruly forty-niners. Out of necessity, California organized a government. Encouraged by President Taylor, California decided to skip the territorial stage, write a constitution, and apply directly for statehood. Because the Californians adopted a free-state constitution, Southerners opposed the move. The admission of California would upset the balance between slave and free states in the Senate, for one thing. Also, Southerners had a tactical reason for resisting statehood. Even according to the Calhoun Resolutions, California had the right to determine the status of slavery within its boundaries once it became a state. Some Southern leaders would not consent, however, until Congress clarified what would be done with the other lands

Ships rot in the harbor of San Francisco where crews have abandoned them to hunt for gold in California.

Clay addresses the Senate in the historic debate over the Compromise of 1850.

taken from Mexico, the Utah and New Mexico territories. The fact that President Taylor was also encouraging New Mexico to apply for direct admission as a free state did not reassure Southerners. An old and bitterly divisive controversy was heating up once more.

The Great Debate

The West was driving a new wedge between the North and the South. The resulting crisis was played out on the Senate floor in what was perhaps the most extraordinary debate in congressional history. Three aging giants–Clay, Calhoun, and Webster–climbed into the political ring for the last time. The trio had begun their congressional careers in the days of Madison when they and the nation were young; now the old warriors were searching for a peaceful solution to calm the Republic's troubled waters.

Compromise of 1850–Henry Clay again taking the lead, as he had in the Missouri Compromise

and nullification crisis, offered the sections a compromise package. As a concession to the North, he proposed that (1) California be admitted as a free state and (2) the slave trade–but not slavery–be abolished in the District of Columbia. To the pro-slavery forces he offered (3) a federally enforced fugitive slave act, which would put the government solidly behind the return of runaway slaves, and (4) the protection of slavery in the District of Columbia. In addition, Clay offered the two sides a joint concession, proposing that (5) the new territories of New Mexico and Utah be organized without reference to or restrictions on slavery.

Clay's proposals, collectively known as the **Compromise of 1850** underwent intense debate from all sides. President Taylor opposed the Compromise for making any concessions that might extend slavery into the territories. He thought debate on the Compromise would succeed only in deepening sectional division and delaying the admission of new territories. Despite the apparent

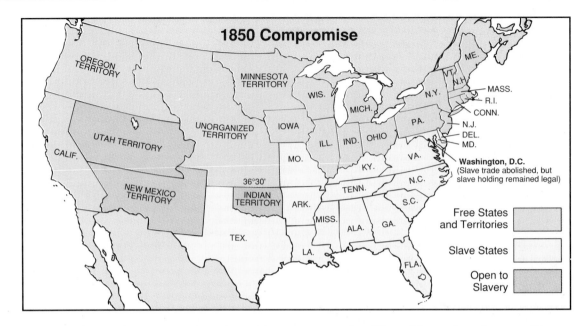

1850 Compromise

OREGON TERRITORY

MINNESOTA TERRITORY

WIS.

MICH.

N.Y.

ME.

VT. N.H.

MASS.

R.I.

CONN.

UTAH TERRITORY

UNORGANIZED TERRITORY

IOWA

ILL. IND. OHIO

PA.

N.J.

DEL.

MD.

CALIF.

MO.

KY.

VA.

Washington, D.C.
(Slave trade abolished, but
slave holding remained legal)

NEW MEXICO TERRITORY

36°30'

INDIAN TERRITORY

ARK.

TENN.

N.C.

S.C.

MISS.

ALA.

GA.

TEX.

LA.

FLA.

Free States
and Territories

Slave States

Open to
Slavery

efficiency of Taylor's direct assault on the problem, the old general quickly learned that he could not run the Senate or the country as he had his army.

The aging Calhoun came to the Senate on March 4 to present the South's position. Gaunt and wracked with pain–he would be dead within three weeks–Calhoun was too weak to speak but gave his written remarks to a fellow senator to read. Calhoun declared that the compromise did not go far enough in protecting Southern rights. Constitutional guarantees needed to be extended so that neither section could dominate the other.

Three days later the eloquent Daniel Webster rose to speak. His "Seventh of March" speech was the most crucial and courageous of his distinguished career. Webster declared, "I wish to speak today, not as a Massachusetts man, not as a Northern man, but as an American. . . . I speak today for the preservation of the Union. 'Hear me for my cause.' "

Webster went on to point out that the bounds of slavery were already set by the Northwest Ordinance and the Missouri Compromise, as well as by geography. The arid conditions of the new territories could not support a slave economy anyway. Therefore, the Wilmot Proviso was needless and

provocative. "I would not take pains to reaffirm an ordinance of nature nor to re-enact the will of God," Webster asserted.

The silver-tongued senator then turned his arguments in favor of union and compromise against the extremists in both sections. Webster blasted the "infernal fanatics and abolitionists" in the North for their agitations and chided the hot-headed secessionists in the South: "Secession! Peaceable Secession! Sir, your eyes and mine are never destined to see that miracle." If either extreme prevailed, Webster believed, the future was a "cavern of darkness." A far brighter future for the nation lay in "liberty and union."

Abolitionists heaped every abusive adjective available upon Webster for his conciliatory speech. Despite such criticism, Webster's support of the Compromise was a critical factor in sparing the country war and disunion. Another factor in the passage of the Compromise was the sudden removal of one of its most influential critics. On July 4, Zachary Taylor strolled to the unfinished Washington Monument for some Independence Day speechmaking. It was a blistering day, and when the president returned to the White House, hot and

Daniel Webster

the South and North over the Whigs' candidate, General Winfield Scott. The Free Soilers, the party of Wilmot, polled only 156,000 votes out of over three million cast.

Ironically, the peace that the Compromise produced was soon shaken by the Compromise itself. One of its provisions, a concession to the South, was a new, tougher **Fugitive Slave Law.** The return of runaway slaves to bondage became a powerful emotional tool of the abolitionists in gradually turning public opinion. A number of abolitionists, such as Ralph Waldo Emerson, urged citizens to break the law on "the earliest occasion," and some states practiced a Northern version of nullification by passing "Personal Liberty" laws in defiance of the federal statute. Even some Northerners who were

hungry, he ate some cherries and cucumbers and washed them down with quantities of milk and ice water. The President quickly grew sick and died five days later, a victim of food poisoning. Had he lived, the forceful pro-Union Southerner could possibly have effected a completely different outcome between the sections. Taylor's death removed all such possibilities to the realm of speculation, however. The new president, Millard Fillmore, solidly backed Clay's proposals, and by September they had cleared Congress and were signed into law.

Sectional Strains—The Compromise of 1850 brought a shaky sense of relief. Tensions eased for a time even within the political parties. In 1852 the controversies over slavery expansion that had torn the Democrats apart in 1848 were laid aside. The Democrat's platform and their nominee, **Franklin Pierce** of New Hampshire, were solidly behind the Compromise. Evidently most of the voters were, too. Pierce won a lopsided electoral victory in both

CAUTION!!

COLORED PEOPLE

OF BOSTON, ONE & ALL,

You are hereby respectfully CAUTIONED and advised, to avoid conversing with the

Watchmen and Police Officers of Boston,

For since the recent ORDER OF THE MAYOR & ALDERMEN, they are empowered to act as

KIDNAPPERS

AND

Slave Catchers,

And they have already been actually employed in KIDNAPPING, CATCHING, AND KEEPING SLAVES. Therefore, if you value your LIBERTY, and the *Welfare of the Fugitives* among you, *Shun* them in every possible manner, as so many *HOUNDS* on the track of the most unfortunate of your race.

Keep a Sharp Look Out for KIDNAPPERS, and have TOP EYE open.

APRIL 24, 1851.

Although incidents of escaped slaves being returned were rare, abolitionists used the Fugitive Slave Law to stir public opinion.

The Underground Railroad

One divisive North-South issue from the 1830s to the Civil War was the existence of the **Underground Railroad,** the escape route for fugitive slaves through the Northern states (particularly Illinois, Indiana, Ohio, and Pennsylvania). The origin of this curious name is uncertain. Some legends credit the name to a slave owner who lost track of a fugitive slave he was pursuing. According to the story, the frustrated owner grumbled that Northerners must have an "underground railroad" to spirit off slaves. In theory, and in keeping with the railroad idea, the system consisted of a series of *safe houses* (also called *stations* or *depots*), each overseen by a *conductor*. Fugitives, called *passengers,* traveled secretly from house to house until they were safe either in the far north of the United States or in Canada.

In actuality, the Railroad was not as well organized as later tales might indicate. The Railroad did not exist at all in the South, the most dangerous portion of the trip for a fugitive slave. Escaping slaves had to use their own ingenuity to reach the North. One married slave couple escaped through disguise. The light-skinned wife, who could "pass" for white, dressed herself as an ailing, elderly white planter, and her husband posed as the "planter's" devoted slave. In this guise, the couple easily traveled north. Another slave, in Virginia, escaped in a more direct manner. He had a carpenter to build him a large wooden crate, and then he mailed himself to Philadelphia and freedom.

Once slaves reached the North, they found more help, although some slaves escaped without ever being aware of the existence of the Underground Railroad. When they found "conductors," slaves received food, shelter, and further directions on the route to safety. (Despite the legends, few fugitives hid in secret rooms or scurried through secret tunnels.) The best known of these conductors were white abolitionists. Levi Coffin of Newport (now Fountain City), Indiana, and later Cincinnati, Ohio, was a Quaker who openly aided fugitive slaves. His work was so extensive that some called him the "president" of the Underground Railroad. Most of the conductors, however, were free blacks and escaped slaves–brave men and women whose names are mostly unknown today.

How many slaves escaped via the Underground Railroad? Exact figures are almost impossible to come by. They certainly numbered in the thousands, but how many thousands is unknown. At any rate, in contrast to the millions of blacks who remained slaves, the number is tiny. The Underground Railroad had great symbolic value, however. For the South, it symbolized Northern refusal to keep faith and to honor the fugitive slave laws. For the North, it was a protest against the injustice of slavery. For slaves, the Underground Railroad simply meant freedom.

not abolitionists opposed the law. They feared that the lack of safeguards in the act could result in free blacks being kidnaped and sent into slavery.

Despite all the clamor less than two hundred runaway slaves were actually returned during the first six years after enactment of the Fugitive Slave Law. The abolitionist press was active, however, churning out biting reproach and bitter stereotypes of life in the South, many of which have been perpetuated for over a century. The most successful abolitionist literature, however, was not William Lloyd Garrison's radical *Liberator* but was a piece of fiction by Harriet Beecher Stowe entitled *Uncle Tom's Cabin,* published in 1852. The book sold three hundred thousand copies the first year and was perhaps the most influential piece of propaganda since Thomas Paine's *Common Sense*. Interestingly, Stowe never identified herself with the leading abolitionists, whom she considered fanatics. Yet, her *Uncle Tom's Cabin,* with its sentimental images of slaves and searing portrayal of the degradation of slavery, surpassed the abolitionists in capturing popular support.

By the 1850s the abolitionist message was changing from an attack on slavery to an attack on the South as an evil empire built on the backs of black slaves. Despite the fact that only five per cent of the population owned slaves, the abolitionist attacks had a decisive effect on the Southern mind in general. In 1827 antislavery societies in the South actually outnumbered those in the North. Southerners, however, grew defensive over repeated attacks. Extremists began to promote slavery as a positive good, trying to put the best face possible on an ugly situation. The most radical Southerners were the **"Fire-Eaters,"** extremists who advocated the South's leaving the Union as the only way to preserve the Southern way of life.

Lines of communication began to break down. Institutions that bound the regions together, such as religious denominations and political parties, fell apart along sectional lines. After 1850 the common ground of compromise would be increasingly difficult to find.

Section Review

1. What view of the status of slavery in the territories was expressed in the Wilmot Proviso? the Calhoun Resolutions? popular sovereignty?
2. What two sea routes did forty-niners take to California?
3. What were the five provisions of the Compromise of 1850?
4. Why did some Northerners who were not abolitionists oppose the Fugitive Slave Law?
5. What was the single most important piece of abolitionist propaganda? Who was its author?

Senator Stephen A. Douglas

Conflict

Kansas-Nebraska Act

Despite the growing sectional conflicts and its own weaknesses, the Compromise of 1850 might have kept the peace for several years. The overwhelming support for the pro-Compromise Democrats in 1852 would certainly seem to indicate that most Americans wanted an end to these bitter and divisive struggles. The wounds of sectional conflict were unwittingly reopened in 1854, however, by the actions of the major Democratic leader of the 1850s, Senator **Stephen A. Douglas** of Illinois.

Douglas, like many farseeing Americans of his time, envisioned the construction of a transcontinental railroad to link the East with the far West. The United States had bought the Gadsden Purchase from Mexico (p. 256), for example, as part of a potential southern route for a transcontinental line. Douglas, like any good politician, wanted his home state to benefit from the railroad by building it through Illinois. A transcontinental route from that state, however, would have to go through the unorganized portion of the Louisiana Purchase which lay west of Missouri. The region would need an organized government to allow construction and maintenance of the line. Many Southerners opposed territorial organization, though, because of the still-unanswered questions about the expansion of slavery.

Douglas sought to win Southern support for his railroad by a clever piece of legislation. In the **Kansas-Nebraska Act** (1854), the Illinois senator proposed organizing two territories from the region, the Kansas Territory west of Missouri and the Nebraska Territory west of Iowa. To settle the slavery issue, Douglas returned to the idea of popular sovereignty; each territory would decide on the status of slavery for itself. To make popular sovereignty work and to please Southern congressmen, the act repealed the provision of the Missouri Compromise that banned slavery north of 36° 30' latitude.

Southerners, of course, welcomed this opportunity to expand slavery into an area that had been previously closed to it. Northern resistance, on the other hand, was strong. Due to the large Democratic majority in Congress and the support of nearly all the South, the Kansas-Nebraska Act passed. Afterwards, however, a storm of protest broke out across the North and West as people objected to both the expansion of slavery and the scrapping of the Missouri Compromise. Douglas bore much of the fury himself, but his party did not escape. Over two-thirds of the Northern incumbent Democrats in Congress lost their seats in the next election. Only seven of forty-four Northern Democrats in the House who voted for the act were re-elected. More important, the Kansas-Nebraska Act resulted in two events which eventually destroyed Democratic dominance of American politics: the rise of the Republican party and a virtual civil war in Kansas.

Rise of the Republicans

Collapse of the Whigs—The Whigs had never been a party of strong ideas. The party had existed primarily as a coalition of various opponents to Democratic policies. The two times the party had won a presidential election, for example (1840 and 1848), it had done so in part by refusing to adopt a platform. The poor showing in the presidential election of 1852 weakened the Whigs; the Kansas-Nebraska Act destroyed it. Southern Whigs almost unanimously supported the act; Northern Whigs almost unanimously opposed it. No political party could survive such a traumatic split. Within a few years, the Whigs had disappeared completely, and their demise left a gaping hole in America's two-party system.

The Know-Nothings—For a time it appeared that the Whigs might be replaced by the American party, better known as the **Know-Nothings.** This curious nickname arose from the secret societies, such as the Order of the Star-Spangled Banner, that had given birth to the movement. When members were asked about the nature of their secret order, they were taught to reply that they knew nothing about it. The phrase also aptly describes the party's ideology, for it was rooted in ignorance and fear. The Know-Nothings arose in reaction to increasing immigration from Europe in the 1840s and 1850s. The potato famine in Ireland and wars in Germany sent hundreds of thousands of Europeans fleeing to America for refuge. Many Americans feared that these immigrants would take jobs from native-born Americans. The fact that many of these immigrants were Catholic also caused uneasiness. Catholicism had been closely linked with tyranny and repression in Europe, and American Protestants feared for the democratic institutions of the United States.

In 1854 the Know-Nothings capitalized on both fears of immigrants and resentment to the Kansas-Nebraska Act to score big gains in Congress and state legislatures. Although the Know-Nothings were strongest in the North, they displayed surprising strength in slave states such as Kentucky and Texas. The movement turned out to be a passing fad, however. Simple negativism was not a strong base on which to build a party, and the Northern and Southern wings of the Know-Nothings turned out to have almost as little in common as Northern and Southern Whigs. After the 1856 presidential elec-

THE GREAT REPUBLICAN REFORM PARTY,
Calling on their Candidate.

This contemporary cartoon portrayed the new Republican party as an odd assortment of interest groups.

tion, most Southern Know-Nothings eventually joined the Democrats. A number of Northern Know-Nothings joined a new party, the Republicans.

The Republicans—The real successor to the Whigs was the **Republican party.** Although many cities compete for the title "birthplace of the Republican party," the honor seems to go to Ripon, Wisconsin. On February 28, 1854, a rally of anti-Nebraska forces in that town called for others of like mind to join under the label of Thomas Jefferson's old party, "Republican." Soon the Republican movement spread across the North, and the party was able to offer candidates in the 1854 election.

The Republicans began as a generally "anti-slavery party," but even that description covers a wide range of beliefs. Abolitionists naturally gravitated to the Republicans. Free-soilers, those who opposed simply the growth of slavery, also joined. The party was not necessarily problack, however. In fact, some free-soilers were more interested in preserving the territories for white settlers than in helping blacks. Nor was the appeal of the Republicans built entirely on the slavery issue. The Republicans appropriated many of the probusiness,

nationalistic ideas of the Whigs, such as a protective tariff and government support of railroads, roads, and other internal improvements. Many Know-Nothings joined as well, if for no other reason than the fact that the Democrats seemed to be the party of the immigrants. Republicans appealed to the small farmer by promising the distribution of inexpensive land to settlers in the western territories. Despite this range of interests, though, the Republicans remained strictly a sectional party. The Republicans were nonexistent in the South.

Election of 1856—The election of 1856 revealed both the strengths and weaknesses of the Republicans and marked the decline of the Know-Nothings. Borrowing from the Whigs' bag of tricks, the Republicans bypassed their most prominent political leaders, such as New York senator William Seward, in favor of a colorful hero. The party nominated explorer-soldier **John C. Frémont,** "Pathfinder of the West" and hero of the Mexican War. The Republicans also borrowed from the Free Soil slogan of 1848 as they said that they were for "Free speech, free press, free soil, free men, Frémont and victory." The American party (Know-Nothings) nominated former president Millard Fillmore, but his devotion to the anti-immigrant, anti-Catholic principles of the party

President James Buchanan

was at best lukewarm. (Fillmore's daughter had, in fact, been educated by nuns.)

The Democrats ignored their colorless incumbent, Pierce, and nominated a lackluster if accomplished legislator and diplomat, **James Buchanan.** As a native Pennsylvanian who was generally sympathetic to the South, Buchanan was the ideal candidate to unite all factions of the party. Also, he had been minister to Great Britain since 1853 and was therefore, unlike prominent Democrats such as Stephen Douglas, not associated with the controversial Kansas-Nebraska Act. Running on a platform defending popular sovereignty, Buchanan offered himself as the safe, sensible alternative to the "extremists," Frémont and Fillmore. Frémont ran well in the North and West, carrying eleven states and winning 114 electoral votes. Fillmore ran surprisingly well in the South but carried only Maryland with its 8 electoral votes. However, Buchanan, as the head of the only party with a truly nationwide following, carried the entire South and enough Northern states to win 174 electoral votes and the election. Again the voters had chosen the moderate, middle course. Signs of trouble were evident, though. Buchanan had won only a plurality, not a majority of the votes, and several Southern leaders had threatened secession during the campaign if Frémont won.

"Bleeding Kansas"

One issue that the Republicans had used to good effect in 1856 was the increasingly ugly situation that had developed in Kansas. Douglas's system of popular sovereignty meant that the settlers in the Kansas Territory would decide the fate of slavery there. Because of this fact, hordes of proslavery and antislavery advocates streamed into the territory in an attempt to win the region for their position. Bloody fighting broke out between the two factions, and the dissension-torn territory became known as **"Bleeding Kansas."**

Lawrence—The situation in Kansas steadily worsened. Proslavery "border ruffians" from Missouri and antislavery "free-staters" clashed in open violence. In May of 1856, three events within the span of five days (May 21-25) brought the Kansas conflict to national attention. On May 21 an army of border ruffians sacked the town of Lawrence, Kansas, a center of free-state strength. Because the citizens chose not to resist the attackers, only one man died, a proslavery "ruffian" who was killed when a collapsing building fell on him. The ruffians freely burned, looted, and destroyed, however, and the **sack of Lawrence** outraged free-staters.

Brooks-Sumner Episode—Two days later, in Washington, D.C., Representative Preston Brooks of South Carolina approached Senator Charles Sumner of Massachusetts in the Senate chamber. A few days earlier, Sumner, who had a reputation for angry ranting, had given a heated speech denouncing "the crime against Kansas." In the process, Sumner had heaped vile and abusive scorn on South Carolina senator Andrew Butler, who was not present to defend himself. Brooks, a relative of Butler's, confronted Sumner. The harsh language the Massachusetts senator had used was inexcusable, but Brooks's response was hardly justified. As Sumner sat at his desk, Brooks began to hit him repeatedly with a cane. Brooks continued to beat him mercilessly until the cane snapped and Sumner was bloody and badly injured. To the North, Brooks's action confirmed the prejudice that Southern leaders were violent brutes. The Southern reaction did not help matters. Brooks's district overwhelmingly reelected him to the House, and admirers from all over the South sent him new canes. Brooks wrote proudly, "The fragments of the stick are begged for as sacred relics."

Pottawatomie Massacre—The news of this **Brooks-Sumner episode** enraged one Northerner to a murderous fury. **John Brown** was a fanatical abolitionist from Connecticut who had come to Kansas to help win the territory for the antislavery forces. A failure in every business venture he attempted, Brown proved frighteningly successful as a terrorist. The sack of Lawrence infuriated Brown not only because the border ruffians had attacked the town but also because the free-staters had not fought back. When, on top of that, he received news of Brooks's beating of Sumner, Brown, in the words of his son, "went crazy–*crazy*." Gathering his followers about him on the night of May 24-25, this grim, self-styled "avenging angel" attacked

A Northern cartoon reflects the outrage that Northerners felt over Representative Preston Brooks's beating of Senator Charles Sumner in the Senate chamber.

several proslavery families along Pottawatomie (PAHT uh WAHT uh mee) Creek. In the grisly **Pottawatomie Massacre,** Brown's men butchered five proslavery settlers with razor-sharp swords.

The first reaction was almost universal horror among both pro- and antislavery groups. As news of the massacre traveled east, however, antislavery forces changed the story to suit their views. Northern newspapers claimed that the killings had been in self-defense, or that Indians had done it, or even that Brown had not been anywhere near the site of the killings. A congressional investigating committee, thanks to an antislavery majority, suppressed testimony condemning Brown. The "avenging angel" soon found himself free to pursue other plans, and in a few years he would burst onto the national scene with even greater impact.

The Dred Scott Decision

On March 6, 1857, only two days after James Buchanan took office, the Supreme Court handed down a decision that further agitated the conflict over slavery. The case ***Dred Scott* v. *Sandford*** revealed that even the Supreme Court could not pro-

vide a solution to the problems that so vexed the nation.

Dred Scott was the slave of an army surgeon named John Emerson from Missouri. During the 1830s Emerson had taken Scott to the free state of Illinois and the unorganized free territory of the Louisiana Purchase. Scott later returned to Missouri, a slave state, with his master. After Emerson's death in 1843, Scott sought to gain his freedom on the grounds that he had become free by entering free territory and could not be re-enslaved. The case eventually found its way to the Supreme Court.

With its pro-Southern majority, the Supreme Court under Chief Justice **Roger Taney** (TAH nee) welcomed the opportunity to settle the slavery question. In a splintered decision (most justices issued separate opinions), the majority ruled that as a slave Dred Scott was not a citizen and therefore had no right to sue. Some justices carried the matter further, with Taney's views being the most extreme. According to the chief justice, the Constitution did not recognize slaves *or* free blacks as citizens. Blacks, in Taney's words, "had no rights which the white man was bound to respect." Taney

The Mormon War

In 1857 Robert Tyler, son of former President John Tyler, wrote a letter to President Buchanan suggesting how to divert the nation's attention from the sectional controversy: "I believe that we can supercede the Negro-Mania with the almost universal excitement of an Anti-Mormon Crusade." The nation, Tyler assured the president, would "rally to you with an earnest enthusiasm" if he declared war on the Mormons. Buchanan eagerly seized on the idea. The Mormons were almost universally disliked. Most Americans objected to their practice of polygamy (marriage to more than one wife at a time). The Republican platform of 1860, for example, condemned slavery and polygamy as "twin relics of barbarism." Others suspected the Mormons of treason. They pointed with alarm to the militant groups that the Mormons had organized and armed.

When the government organized the Utah Territory in 1850, President Fillmore tried to keep the peace by appointing Mormon leader Brigham Young as territorial governor. Buchanan, in an effort to break the political power of the Mormons, removed Young in 1857 and replaced him with a non-Mormon. To support the new governor, the president sent him west in the company of 2,500 soldiers. The Mormons reacted with fury. "Woe, woe to those who came here to unlawfully meddle with me and this people," Young cried.

The worst atrocity in the Mormon War took place in southern Utah in September of 1857–without the knowledge of Young and the other major Mormon leaders. Just as tension was mounting between the Mormons and the federal government, a party of 137 California-bound settlers entered Utah. Foolishly, some members of the group insulted both Mormons and Indians as they traveled. A few men even bragged that they had killed Mormons when the sect had been located back in the East. Brigham Young, with enough problems on his hands, sent word to Mormon elders in the south to ignore the group and let them pass through. His letter arrived two days too late.

On September 6, 1857, the pioneers made camp at Mountain Meadows, Utah. There they were surrounded by two hundred hostile Indians. The next day, a group of Mormons approached the now terrified camp. If the settlers would surrender their weapons and give their supplies to the Indians, the Mormons said, their lives would be spared. As the settlers filed out of their circle of wagons, however, the Mormons and Indians fell on the pioneers. They butchered 120 men, women, and children. The Mormons saved only 17 children, whom they thought too young to be able to tell anyone what had happened. So thorough was the slaughter that details of the "Mountain Meadows Massacre" remained hazy for years. Only after twenty years was the Mormon elder chiefly responsible for the killings finally arrested, tried, and executed.

In northern Utah, some Mormons urged violent resistance to the oncoming troops, but Young knew better than to confront the army in open battle. Instead he announced that he would burn Salt Lake City and other Mormon settlements to the ground and take his people to Mexico or Canada if the troops entered Mormon territory. Buchanan had not expected such resistance, and the campaign did not prove as popular among the American people as he had hoped. Therefore, Buchanan and Young compromised. The new governor could take office, and the U.S. Army could enter the territory. The army, however, would not camp in Salt Lake City. Peace settled uneasily over the territory, and the troops remained until the outbreak of the Civil War.

Dred Scott

then went on to examine the Missouri Compromise, which he ruled unconstitutional on the grounds that it had unfairly deprived slave holders of their property in territories north of 36° 30'.

Of course, Taney's decision that Congress could not forbid slavery in the territories was hailed in the South and castigated in the North. It made slavery theoretically legal in all territories until it should be voted out when the territory became a state. Such a decision could not come close to settling the sectional conflict. Proslavery forces claimed that the case forever closed the issue. Antislavery forces argued ingeniously if inaccurately that as soon as the court ruled on Scott's citizenship, the case was decided and all the rest was merely the opinion of the justices and therefore nonbinding. The two sides remained unreconciled. If anything, the animosity had grown worse.

Lincoln-Douglas Debates

One man caught in the crossfire over the Dred Scott decision was Stephen A. Douglas. Although Douglas personally did not care whether a territory adopted or prohibited slavery, he stoutly maintained under the doctrine of popular sovereignty that the citizens of a territory had the right to decide for themselves. In light of the Dred Scott case, Douglas had to find a way to reconcile popular sovereignty with the Supreme Court's ruling. In what became known as the **Freeport Doctrine** (after one of the cities in which he enunciated the idea), Douglas argued that a territory could still prohibit slavery by refusing to adopt laws establishing and protecting it.

Douglas's Freeport Doctrine, as one would expect, drew the wrath of the proslavery forces. Douglas's political career was further threatened when he broke with President Buchanan over Kansas. Proslavery forces in that territory had, through fraud, elected a convention to draw up a state constitution that established slavery—despite the fact that the majority of settlers were free-staters. Buchanan, eager to please the South and to bring Kansas into the Union as a Democratic state, pushed Congress to accept the slavery constitution and admit Kansas. Douglas led a courageous group of Democrats who resisted the administration's attempts to thwart the will of the majority in Kansas. Under pressure from the Republicans and the Douglas Democrats, Congress put the constitution to a vote in the territory, and the Kansans rejected it overwhelmingly. As Douglas prepared to run for re-election in 1858, he faced opposition from his own Democratic president. In addition, the Republican party had grown markedly stronger in Illinois and was offering a strong challenger to Douglas, Illinois lawyer **Abraham Lincoln.**

Abraham Lincoln—The story of Abraham Lincoln's life sounds like one of the classic ''rags to riches'' tales. He was born into the family of a poor farmer living near Hodgenville, Kentucky, in 1809. The family then moved to southern Indiana when Abraham was only seven. In both places, the Lincoln family experienced the grinding poverty that oppressed many settlers on the frontier. Young Lincoln spent his youth performing the backbreaking labor of a pioneer farmer—clearing and cultivating the land, splitting rails for fences, and generally trying to help keep his family from starving.

Lincoln's standard of living improved when the family moved to Illinois in 1830. There Lincoln was able to find work as a store clerk, postmaster, and surveyor. He had always had a hunger for education but had been able to attend school only infrequently; his total formal education probably totaled only about a year. Lacking formal schooling, Lincoln became an avid reader, eagerly consuming the works of Shakespeare, the poems of Robert Burns, and the Bible. He also began to study law on his own, and in 1836 he was licensed to practice.

Lincoln also developed a taste for politics. He joined the Whig party, headed by his idol, Kentuckian Henry Clay, and became an influential leader in the Illinois party. He served four terms in the Illinois state legislature and one term as a member of the House of Representatives. By 1850, however, Lincoln thought that his political career had gone about as far as it could go, and he left politics to devote himself to his profitable law practice in Springfield, Illinois.

Abraham Lincoln's character was a mixture of genuine kindness, personal ambition, and unflinching determination. His reputation for honesty earned him the nickname "Honest Abe." Even political opponent Stephen Douglas said that Lincoln "is as honest as he is shrewd." His thoughtfulness and generosity, not to mention his sense of humor and talent for telling amusing stories, charmed those who met him. The driving force behind his political thinking was that slavery was wrong. He often quoted the Declaration of Independence's famous phrase "All men are created equal." As Lincoln said after his election to the presidency, "I have never had a feeling, politically, that did not spring from the sentiments embodied in the Declaration of Independence." Primary among those sentiments, he said, was the "promise that in due time the weights would be lifted from the shoulders of all men, and that all should have an equal chance."

Yet Lincoln was a realist. He knew that slavery could not be easily eliminated, and he believed that the federal government had no right to interfere with slavery in the states where it already existed. Lincoln satisfied himself with the free-soil doctrine that slavery should not be allowed to expand any farther than it already had. The territories must be kept free. Perhaps then, Lincoln thought, slavery would die out.

The Kansas-Nebraska Act brought Lincoln out of his political retirement. "I was losing interest in politics," Lincoln wrote in 1859, "when the repeal of the Missouri Compromise aroused me again." Lincoln denounced the act because it offered the possibility of slavery's expansion into the territories. His eloquence and homey manner pleased listeners and attracted the attention of the anti-Nebraska forces. Conservative by nature, Lincoln tried to work at first through the dying Whig party. Eventually, however, he realized that the Republicans offered him a better political future. By 1858 he was the leading Republican in Illinois and the natural choice to oppose incumbent Stephen Douglas for the U.S. Senate.

The Debates—Lincoln launched the campaign by giving one of his most famous speeches. Quoting Mark 3:25, Lincoln said,

> "A house divided against itself cannot stand."
> I believe this government cannot endure, permanently half slave and half free. I do not expect the Union to be dissolved–I do not expect the house to fall–but I do expect it will cease to be divided. It will become all one thing or all the other.

Douglas immediately charged Lincoln with promoting conflict and dissension. After all, Douglas argued, the nation had existed as half slave and half free since its founding. Why should it not continue to do so? Lincoln responded by challenging Douglas to a series of debates. Douglas accepted, and the **Lincoln-Douglas debates** became a platform not only for the Illinois election but also the national debate on slavery.

Lincoln and Douglas met seven times at different sites in Illinois. Douglas continued to promote popular sovereignty as the answer to the slavery question. He also played on the racist prejudices of his listeners by accusing Lincoln of preaching the absolute equality of the races. "I do not believe that the Almighty ever intended the negro to be the equal of the white man," said Douglas. "He belongs to an inferior race, and must always occupy an inferior position."

Put on the defensive, Lincoln–reflecting the prejudices of the day–backed off from the issue of

Abraham Lincoln was beardless for most of his life, as shown by the photograph at the left taken shortly before his election as president. After his election, Lincoln grew a beard at the suggestion of an eleven-year-old girl who wrote that "if you will let your whiskers grow . . . you would look a great deal better for your face is so thin."

equality. "I am not, nor ever have been in favor of bringing about in any way the social and political equality of the white and black races," he told one audience. Lincoln refused to deny that slavery was immoral, however, and restated his conviction that its expansion must be prohibited. In another town, Lincoln declared,

> Notwithstanding all this, there is no reason in the world why the Negro is not entitled to all the natural rights enumerated in the Declaration of Independence–the right to life, liberty, and the pursuit of happiness. . . . [I]n the right to eat the bread, without the leave of anybody else, which his own hand earns, he is *my equal and the equal of Judge Douglas, and the equal of every living man.*

The heart of the controversy, Lincoln said, was not black equality but the immorality and expansion of slavery. "The real issue in this controversy . . . is the sentiment on the part of one class that looks upon the institution of slavery as a wrong, and of another class that does not look upon it as a

wrong." Douglas, with his indifference to slavery, was in the second group. Lincoln was part of the first group, believing that slavery should "be treated as a wrong, and one of the methods of treating it as a wrong is to make provision that it shall grow no larger."

Douglas won a close election and returned to the Senate. Lincoln lost, but he had gained a national audience for his views. Two years later, Lincoln would win a greater prize.

Section Review

1. Why did Stephen Douglas propose the Kansas-Nebraska Act?
2. What three events during the period May 21-25, 1856, focused national attention on Kansas?
3. What did the Dred Scott decision do to the Missouri Compromise?
4. Why did Stephen Douglas break with President James Buchanan?
5. How did Abraham Lincoln and Stephen Douglas differ concerning the expansion of slavery?

Crisis

John Brown's Raid

"Old Man" Brown had more work to do. After his grisly Pottawatomie murders, Brown kept a low profile in the rough Kansas backcountry, then later turned up in the plush parlors of Boston's elite. That a man of Brown's sordid credentials could gather such audiences says as much about the temper of the times as the charisma of the man.

Between 1857 and 1859 Brown raised money and an army for his grand, harebrained scheme to incite a general slave revolt in the South and establish a state for the freed slaves in the Allegheny Mountains between Maryland and Virginia. If the far-fetched plan of mass murder and mayhem seemed to confirm Brown's madness, he was not alone. A group of supporters known as the **Secret Six,** which included some of the most prominent clergymen and abolitionists in the Northeast, backed the bizarre plan. In addition dozens of others were aware of Brown's intentions, including prominent Republican leader Senator William Seward. Brown's ties with such well-placed supporters, revealed after the plot unraveled, would have a significant impact in further poisoning sectional relations.

Raid on Harpers Ferry—In the fall of 1859, Brown and several followers moved secretly to a farmhouse near **Harpers Ferry,** Virginia (now West Virginia), to wait for promised supplies to arrive from supporters in New England. In October Brown was ready to attack the federal arsenal at Harpers Ferry, strategically located at the junction of the Shenandoah and Potomac rivers. Brown expected to conquer the arsenal from which he would supply a spontaneous slave revolt with weapons. He apparently believed that enough slaves and abolitionists would join him to make the liberation possible.

During the night of October 16, 1859, Brown and his army of twenty-one raiders captured the arsenal and cut the telegraph lines. By the next morning, alarmed citizens and militia from Harpers Ferry and nearby towns had surrounded the arsenal. As the day wore on, several on both sides were mortally wounded, including two of Brown's sons. Ironically, the first person that Brown's raiders killed was a free black working as a baggage man on a train.

Word of the raid spread quickly. Colonel Robert E. Lee of the 2nd United States Cavalry was at home on leave when he received orders to take command of federal troops in the area and recapture the arsenal. Without taking time to put on his uniform, Lee in civilian clothes saddled up and headed for Harpers Ferry. On the morning of October 18, Lee ordered a detachment of marines under the command of Lieutenant James Ewell Brown (Jeb) Stuart to take Brown's stronghold. After a brief fight Brown and his remaining raiders were captured and imprisoned.

Aftermath—After being convicted of murder and treason, Brown spent the month of November

The notorious John Brown of Pottawatomie fame

in prison awaiting his execution. Southerners were of course eager for the man who had such ruthless designs against them to receive his just reward. But a number of Republicans, embarrassed by Brown's ties to their party, were also anxious that he be soon silenced. As for the old man himself, he eagerly awaited his execution date. The self-styled martyr saw it as a date with destiny when he would gain greater glory in death than he had achieved in life. In a letter to his wife, Brown wrote, "I have been *whiped* as the saying *is,* but am sure I can recover all the lost capital occasioned by that disaster, by only hanging a few moments by the neck; & I feel quite determined to make the utmost possible out of a defeat."

On December 2, 1859, John Brown's body swung from a gallows in Charlestown, Virginia, but this was no routine execution. It was the inauguration of a period of mourning in the North that shocked the South by its excess. Buildings were draped with black bunting, church bells rang their dirges, and poets and pulpiteers poured out their most eloquent words on Brown, so recently convicted for murder and treason. Abolitionists found his death a useful symbol, and writers such as Emerson, Thoreau, and Louisa May Alcott, in words frankly blasphemous, compared Brown to Christ. Ironically, Thoreau also called Brown "an angel of light," apparently unaware that this was a Scriptural name for Satan (II Cor. 11:14). In that context, most Southerners would have heartily agreed with Thoreau.

The majority of Northerners, however, did not support slave revolts or Brown's methods. Lincoln noted that although Brown "agreed with us in thinking slavery wrong, that cannot excuse violence, bloodshed and treason." Others went even further in denouncing Brown's actions as "among the gravest of crimes." These voices of moderation, however, were not being heard in the South above the abolitionists' clamor and the siege mentality that had developed there. Understandably, unionist sympathies in the South evaporated, and fear of both secret plots and slave revolts multiplied after Harpers Ferry. Across Dixie, Brown's ties with Republican leaders meant guilt by association.

If the Republicans came to power, they believed, the South was not safe. Such dark thoughts boded ill for the future as the nation stumbled into the new and fateful year of 1860.

Election of 1860

The election of 1860 was surely the most critical contest in American politics. Perhaps, with the nation at fever-pitch following the Harpers Ferry plot, it was not a good time to be choosing a new president. But the Constitution and the calendar required it. The outcome of the campaign would shatter the last truly *national* institution tying the sections together–the Democratic party–and serve as a catalyst for the dissolution of the Union.

Democratic Division–The Democratic party held its convention in Charleston, South Carolina, in April 1860. Going into the convention, Stephen Douglas was generally the preferred nominee over the hapless incumbent Buchanan. The struggle over the party platform, however, created a serious rift.

Douglas supporters wanted simply to rerun the 1856 platform, which called for congressional noninterference with the slave question in the territories. A number of representatives from the Deep South states called for federal protection of slavery in the territories. Buchanan's supporters, in an effort to deny Douglas the nomination, advocated this impossible plank in the platform. When the Northern delegates rejected the Southern plank, delegates from the Gulf states, Arkansas, Tennessee, and Delaware bolted the convention.

Eventually the sectional factions reconvened separately in Baltimore. Northern Democrats nominated Douglas, while Southern Democrats nominated Buchanan's vice president, **John C. Breckinridge** of Kentucky. In addition, between these two wings emerged a coalition of conservative Southerners and Northerners calling themselves the **Constitutional Union party.** Also meeting in Baltimore, they nominated **John Bell** of Tennessee for the presidency. The Constitutional Union platform was probably the most concise in American history: "The Constitution of the Country, the Union of the States and the Enforcement of the Laws."

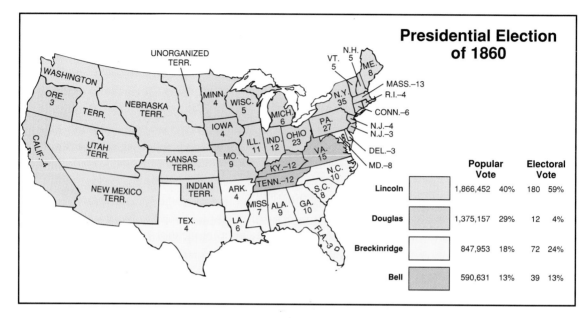

Presidential Election of 1860

		Popular Vote		Electoral Vote	
Lincoln		1,866,452	40%	180	59%
Douglas		1,375,157	29%	12	4%
Breckinridge		847,953	18%	72	24%
Bell		590,631	13%	39	13%

Bell's party, representing much of the sentiment in the Upper South and border states, offered a pro-Union alternative to those who believed that a Republican victory would bring disunion.

Despite the attempts by all of the Democratic factions to keep the Union intact in their own way, the three-part division in their ranks virtually assured Republican success.

Lincoln's Victory—Republicans met in Chicago for their convention. Although William Seward appeared to have the lead for the nomination, Abraham Lincoln quickly passed him in the balloting to win the top spot on the ticket. The Republican platform reflected the coalition character of the party. The party opposed the expansion of slavery into the territories, supported a protective tariff for Northern business interests, and endorsed a transcontinental railroad and opening western lands to appeal to farmers and immigrants. The Republicans also tried to calm Southern fears by pledging not to interfere with slavery where it already existed.

The presidential campaign was really two sectional races: Lincoln and Douglas competing in the North, Bell and Breckinridge in the South and border states. With the Democrats hopelessly divided,

Lincoln won by a plurality with just under 40 per cent of the popular vote. Since his sectional strength was confined to the more populous North, however, he gained a strong majority in the electoral college.

Secession—The election results triggered disunion. Leaders in the Deep South had promised that if Lincoln won, they would not submit themselves to what they considered a hostile, strictly Northern party. They would **secede,** or leave the Union.

Talk of secession had occurred at various times for various reasons in both the North and the South since the earliest years of the Republic. South Carolina, however, actually led the way on December 20, 1860, by unanimously approving an **Ordinance of Secession.** It was South Carolina's Declaration of Independence. By February 1, 1861, Georgia and all of the Gulf states from Florida to Texas had joined South Carolina in seceding. On February 7 in Montgomery, Alabama, the seven Southern states drew up a constitutional league to form the Confederate States of America. **Jefferson Davis,** a former Senator from Mississippi and Secretary of War under Franklin Pierce, was elected its first President.

Attempts at Compromise—As the nation unraveled, men frantically searched for a compromise to avert war. Unfortunately there were no Clays, Websters, or Calhouns to be found. Lesser men were in charge now. Buchanan sat in the White House fretting, frustrated, and indecisive. President-elect Lincoln only repeated his campaign promise not to interfere with slavery in the states where it already existed, and he refused to commit himself to any course of action until he took office and held the reins of power himself.

As precious time slipped away in the weeks following the election, Senator **John J. Crittenden** of Kentucky proposed a series of amendments that would have extended the Missouri Compromise line of 36° 30' for the western territories and would guarantee the protection of slavery where it already existed. Crittenden, who had succeeded Henry Clay upon that statesman's retirement from the Senate, was no "Great Compromiser"; yet he made a noble effort to save the Union and preserve the peace. When his compromise ultimately failed in the Republican-controlled Congress, he lost more than a political initiative. His was the last, best hope of avoiding war. Its failure would cost Crittenden dearly—one of his sons would become a general in the Union army, the other a general in the Confederate army.

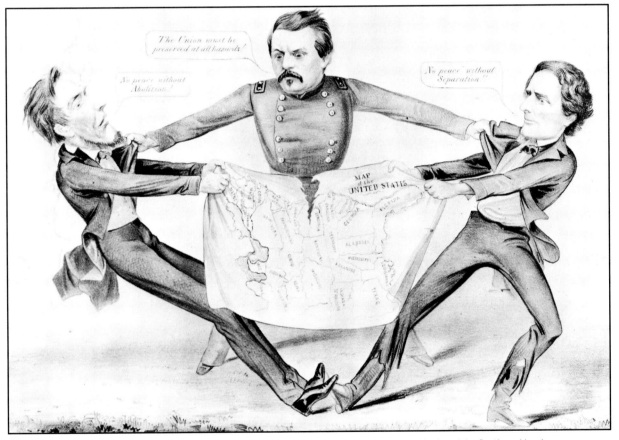

"The True Issue." This cartoon places the blame for disunion on the political leadership in both the North and the South—as Lincoln and Davis pull the nation apart at the center.

First Fire

Only a spark was needed to bring the country to war. Fear in the South of Northern aggression and frustration and anger in the North over the Southern secession put neither side in the mood for reconciliation. The spark came over the issue of federal forts in the South, particularly **Fort Sumter,** strategically centered in the mouth of Charleston Harbor.

In March the Confederacy sent three peace commissioners to Washington to resolve the problem of federal forts. Both Lincoln and Secretary of State Seward refused to meet the commissioners personally, since to do so would be, in effect, to recognize the Confederate government. Seward, however, sent word that Fort Sumter would be evacuated and on April 7 confirmed his promise in writing–although it is unclear whether Lincoln knew of Seward's actions. On April 9, when the commissioners learned that a squadron of ships had been sent to take supplies to the garrison at Sumter, they could only conclude that they had been deceived. Although Lincoln notified the governor of South Carolina of his intentions, Confederate leaders interpreted his actions as a declaration of war and advised capturing the fort if necessary.

President Jefferson Davis wrote, ''The order for the sending of the fleet was a declaration of war. The responsibility is on their shoulders, not on ours. A deadly weapon has been aimed at our heart. Only a fool would wait until the first shot has been fired.'' Lincoln, on the other hand, believed that he would virtually be recognizing the legitimacy of secession if he did not defend federal property in the South. As he said in his inaugural address, ''The power confided to me will be used to hold, occupy, and possess the property, and places belonging to the government.''

When Lincoln's heavily armed naval expedition neared Charleston, on April 12, 1861, Confederate General Pierre G. T. Beauregard opened fire on Fort Sumter, which was commanded by Major Robert Anderson. Ironically, when Beauregard was a cadet at West Point, his artillery instructor was the same Robert Anderson. Now Beauregard had a chance to show his old teacher just how well he had learned his lessons. After a two-day bombardment Anderson surrendered the garrison; Union troops were permitted to leave for New York on steamships.

Miraculously, no one on either side had been killed in the two-day fight. The war, however, was on. The Lincoln-Seward maneuvering produced the desired result. In a letter to a friend, Lincoln wrote, ''The plan [reinforcing Major Anderson] succeeded. They attacked Sumter–it fell, and thus did more service than it otherwise could.'' One distinguished historian has summed up the Sumter situation this way: ''Lincoln, having decided that there was no other way than war for the salvation of his administration, his party, and the Union, maneuvered the Confederates into firing the first shot in order that they, rather than he, should take the blame of beginning bloodshed.''

The day after the surrender, Lincoln called up 75,000 troops to suppress the secessionist states. Extremists in the North and South welcomed the war as an opportunity to teach the other section a lesson. Their enthusiasm was not shared, however, in the upper South where many had hoped that reconciliation would be made. However, when Lincoln called up his army to invade the South, Virginia, Arkansas, Tennessee, and North Carolina also seceded, refusing to fight their sister states.

The time for debate and compromise had slipped through the fingers of leaders fumbling with the future. Differences would now be settled by the force of clashing arms rather than the force of constitutional arguments. The spring of '61 was the beginning of desolations for the nation. Four bloody, bitter springtimes would pass before Americans had exhausted themselves in killing each other.

Section Review

1. Why did John Brown raid the federal arsenal at Harpers Ferry?
2. Name the four presidential candidates and their parties in the election of 1860.
3. Which was the first Southern state to secede from the Union? When?
4. What event marked the beginning of the Civil War?

Chapter Review

Terms

Wilmot Proviso
Calhoun Resolutions
popular sovereignty
Zachary Taylor
free-soilers
Free Soil party
California gold rush
forty-niners
Compromise of 1850
Franklin Pierce
Fugitive Slave Law
Uncle Tom's Cabin
Fire-Eaters
Underground Railroad
Stephen A. Douglas
Kansas-Nebraska Act
Know-Nothings
Republican party
John C. Frémont
James Buchanan
"Bleeding Kansas"
sack of Lawrence
Brooks-Sumner episode
John Brown
Pottawatomie Massacre
Dred Scott v. *Sandford*
Roger Taney
Freeport Doctrine
Abraham Lincoln
Lincoln-Douglas debates
Secret Six
Harpers Ferry
John C. Breckinridge
Constitutional Union party
John Bell
secede
Ordinance of Secession
Jefferson Davis
John J. Crittenden
Fort Sumter

Content Questions

1. For what two reasons did Southerners resist the admission of California to the Union?
2. What did Daniel Webster mean in his "Seventh of March" speech when he said, "I would not take pains to reaffirm an ordinance of nature nor to re-enact the will of God"?
3. Why did both abolitionist and nonabolitionist Northerners generally oppose the Fugitive Slave Law included in the Compromise of 1850?
4. What is the difference between an abolitionist and a free-soiler?
5. Why did Southerners generally welcome the Kansas-Nebraska Act?
6. What was Abraham Lincoln's basic belief concerning the morality of slavery? How did he modify this belief in practice?
7. How did most Northerners react to Brown's raid on Harpers Ferry? How did most abolitionists react?
8. What event caused the lower South to secede? What event caused the upper South to secede?

Application Questions

1. Do you think that the free-soilers were right in believing that Americans should tolerate slavery in areas where it already existed? Why or why not?
2. If you had lived in the North at the time of John Brown's raid, how would you have reacted? Why?
3. Why did the Compromise of 1850 succeed in avoiding war, whereas Senator Crittenden's compromise failed to do so?

CHAPTER 14

War Between the States (1861-1865)

"Duty is ours; consequences are God's."

Thomas J. "Stonewall" Jackson, 1863

Over 600,000 young men who saw the beginning of the Civil War in 1861 would not live to see its conclusion four years later.

Dogwood blossoms and yellow jasmine danced in the warm spring breeze. Across the country, the boys of '61 gathered on village greens, their knapsacks laden with goodies, their cheeks with kisses, their heads with laurels. Most had seen little or none of the world beyond their horizons, and now they were eager to go teach the Yankees or Rebels–depending upon where those horizons happened to lie–a thing or two.

Shiny brass, scarlet sashes, golden trim, and glistening muzzles all drew the admiration of wives and sweethearts and the envy of little boys with stick guns marching through the milling crowd.

The spring of '61 with its pageantry and patriotism gave little hint of the reality ahead. Four years later these village scenes were, like a tintype, drained of the color and clamor of that first spring. Veterans, pale and disfigured, hobbled past their old parade ground. Black-draped widows shuffled about the square. The little boys so anxious to trade their sticks for swords never made it to the battlefront; many of their fathers never made it back home.

In the fight both sides demonstrated remarkable courage. The Southern soldier heroically fought in the face of insurmountable odds; the Northern soldier tenaciously pursued victory in the face of devastating casualties. The war produced more than courage, however; the bitterness of civil war in which countrymen killed each other had far-reaching consequences. The war that swept the land changed forever the face of its people and its politics. Issues that should have been settled with ballots were settled with bullets. As one historian has starkly observed, when the war was over, ''Slavery was dead, secession was dead, and six hundred thousand men were dead.''

War of Brothers

Causes

Mr. Lincoln's War, Jeff Davis's War, War of the Rebellion, War for Southern Independence, War of Northern Aggression, War Between the States, the Civil War, the Needless War. People neither then nor now can even agree on what to call the war, much less what caused it. A number of complex, competing forces, however, converged and clashed to produce the bloodiest chapter in American history.

Union vs. Independence—The central issue that sparked the Civil War concerned the nature of the Union. Could states that voluntarily joined the Union by ratifying the Constitution voluntarily *leave* the Union? This was hardly a novel question in 1860; it had been hotly debated since the earliest years of the Republic. Historically, secession was not tied to a particular section but rather to particular circumstances. As early as 1798 Jefferson and Madison proposed secession as a political tool to curb excessive federal power. During the War of 1812 opposition to the war in general and Jeffersonians in particular created a strong undercurrent of secessionist sentiment among disgruntled Federalists in New England. After 1830 the growing sense of frustration over the South's minority role in Congress simply renewed what was in fact an open constitutional question at the time: Do the states have the right to secede?

The fact that the secession question was the central cause of the war was underscored by the warmakers themselves. The war resolution approved in the House of Representatives on July 22, 1861, by a vote of 121 to 2 stated plainly that

> in this national emergency, Congress, will recollect only its duty to the whole country; that this war is not waged on their part in any spirit of oppression, or for any purpose of conquest or subjugation, or . . . of overthrowing or interfering with the rights or established institutions of those States, but to defend and maintain the *supremacy* of the Constitution, and to preserve the Union with all the dignity, equality, and rights of the several States unimpaired; and that as soon as these objects are accomplished the war ought to cease.

For their part Southern leaders asserted the constitutional right of secession based on state sovereignty. According to the **states' rights** view, each state was largely an independent entity joined in a compact of union but a union in which they maintained their identity and were not subservient to a centralized national authority.

In his address to the Confederate Congress, in response to Lincoln's call for troops, Jefferson Davis presented a careful constitutional defense of states' rights. Davis said that in both the Articles of Confederation and the Tenth Amendment to the Constitution, states had preserved their rights to independence and sovereignty. In addition, Davis asserted that, while secession was constitutional, Lincoln's declaration of war without congressional approval was unconstitutional. In the view of the secessionist states, the Confederacy was made in the same mold as the Confederation: Sovereign states in league to throw off the shackles of an oppressive, centralized authority. In the South the war was a Second American Revolution.

Thus the war opened with the constitutional questions and countercharges that had been haggled over for decades. The North argued that the Union must be preserved above all else; the South argued that the rights and liberties of the states must be preserved, even at the expense of the Union. Now the questions would be settled on the battlefield. Whoever won the coming war would get to stamp their interpretation on the Constitution.

Slavery—Slavery was another issue over which the sections parted company. While the institution of slavery was not the primary cause of the war, it was a highly charged, emotionally divisive issue among certain influential groups in the North and South.

In the North abolitionists had made gradual gains in public opinion, at least in opposition to the expansion of slavery. Of course, racial prejudice in the North and fear of the impact of emancipation on the job market made many Northerners indifferent to the plight of blacks in bondage. Nonetheless, the moral high ground of moderate abolitionists–those not associated with the radicalism of Garrison or the terrorism of John Brown–was difficult to ignore. There was an obvious contradiction between "the proposition that all men are created equal" and the institution of slavery.

In the South opinion on slavery was as varied as its people. The overwhelming majority of Southerners did not own slaves. Of the minority who did, most had but a few field hands or a house servant. Large plantations with large numbers of slaves were concentrated in the tobacco and cotton belts of the South and comprised only a fraction of Southern households; yet it was an influential fraction. These wealthy planters with their tremendous investments in their labor force felt threatened by abolitionist talk. Southern leaders reacted angrily to what they viewed as Northern interference in their lives. Some even went to lengths to defend slavery as a positive good. These radicals coupled with Northern radicals dominated public debate and poisoned it at the same time.

Patriotism—The emotionally charged issues of secession and slavery, union and abolition were not shared by everyone. There is often a tendency to characterize each section with uniform sympathies and motives. Nothing could be further from the truth. There were, for example, proslavery men fighting for the Union just as there were antislavery, antisecession men fighting against it.

Robert E. Lee, perhaps, best illustrates the dilemma that many Southerners faced at the outset of war. Lee was the heir of a great American heritage. He was the son of Revolutionary War hero

"Light-Horse Harry" Lee, and his wife was the step-granddaughter of George Washington. Lee had already given thirty years of distinguished service to his country as an officer in the army. In April 1861 Lincoln made him a seemingly irresistible offer–field command of the Union armies. Lee opposed secession and abhorred slavery; yet when Virginia seceded, he refused the offer of command and resigned, declaring, "Save in defence of my native state, I never desire again to draw my sword." In a letter to his sister, Lee explained his difficult decision: "With all my devotion to the Union, and the feeling of loyalty and duty of an American citizen, I have not been able to . . . raise my hand against my relatives, my children, my home."

There is an important difference between causing a war and going to war. Most soldiers were indifferent to or even ignorant of the motives they are often charged with for taking up arms against their countrymen. They answered the call to arms out of a sense of duty, whether as Southern patriots or Northern patriots. Many would have instinctively understood Lee's words, words which characterized his life. "There is a true glory and a true honor, the glory of duty done, the honor of integrity of principle."

Though such men fought the war, they did not cause it. The Civil War resulted from a leadership failure that permitted extremists to take the terms of debate to their own ends. Historian James Randall has summed up the issue this way:

> Let one take all the factors–the Sumter maneuver, the election of Lincoln, abolitionism, slavery in Kansas, cultural and economic differences–and it will be seen that only by a kind of false display could any of these issues, or all of them together, be said to have caused the war if one omits the elements of emotional unreason and overbold leadership. If one word or phrase were selected to account for the war, that word would not be slavery, or state-rights, or diverse civilizations. It would have to be such a word as fanaticism (on both sides), or misunderstanding, or perhaps politics.

CHRONOLOGY

	1861 Apr.-June	July-Sept.	Oct.-Dec.	1862 Jan.-Mar.	Apr.-June	July-Sept.	Oct.-Dec.	1863 Jan.-Mar.
EASTERN FRONT	Firing on Ft. Sumter (April 12-13)	First Battle of Manassas (July 21)		Peninsular Campaign / *Monitor* vs. *Merrimac* (C.S.S. *Virginia*) (March 8-9)	Jackson's Valley Campaign	Second Battle of Manassas (Aug. 29-30) / Battle of Antietam (Sept. 17)	Battle of Fredericksburg (Dec. 13)	
WESTERN FRONT				Battle of Mill Springs (Jan. 19) / Capture of Forts Henry and Donelson (Feb. 6, 16)	Capture of Island No. 10 (April 8) / Battle of Shiloh (April 6-7) / Capture of New Orleans (April 25)		Battle of Perryville (Oct. 8) / Battle of Stones River (Dec. 31—Jan. 2)	
HOME FRONT	Lincoln calls for troops (April 14) / Upper south secedes		Trent Affair			Emancipation Proclamation Issued (Sept. 22)		Emancipation Proclamation takes effect (Jan. 1)

Some battles during the Civil War were given different names by the Union and Confederate leadership. Below is a chart of such battles. Those names in **bold type** are the names used in this book.

Union Name	**Confederate Name**
First Bull Run	**First Manassas**
Logan's Cross Roads	**Mill Springs**
Pittsburgh Landing	**Shiloh**
Fair Oaks	Seven Pines
Second Bull Run	**Second Manassas**
Antietam	Sharpsburg
Chaplin Hills	**Perryville**
Stones River	Murfreesboro

Apr.-June	July-Sept.	Oct.-Dec.	**1864** Jan.-Mar.	Apr.-June	July-Sept.	Oct.-Dec.	**1865** Jan.-Mar.	Apr.-June
Battle of Chancellorsville (May 1-4)	Battle of Gettysburg (July 1-3)			Wilderness Campaign Battle of Cold Harbor (June 1-3)	**Siege of Petersburg**			Richmond Falls (April 3) Lee surrenders at Appomattox (April 9)
	Fall of Vicksburg (July 4) Battle of Chickamauga (Sept. 19-20)	Battles of Chattanooga (Nov. 24-25)		Battle of Kennesaw Mountain (June 27)	Battle of Atlanta (July 20-22)	"March to the Sea" Battle of Nashville (Dec. 15-16) Fall of Savannah (Dec. 20)		
West Virginia admitted to Union (June 20) New York draft riot (July 13-16)	Bread riots in Richmond (April 2)	Gettysburg Address (Nov. 19)				Re-election of Lincoln (Nov. 8) Nevada admitted to the Union (Oct. 31)		Assassination of Lincoln (April 14)

Comparisons

Behind the massing armies of the North and South were numbers of sectional differences that would prove to be critical factors over the course of the war.

Resources—In terms of the basic resources of population, food production, and industrial output, the North had the advantage in every area. The eighteen Northern states had a population of 18.5 million, twice that of the eleven Confederate states with nine million people, of which 3.5 million were slaves.

Napoleon once remarked that an army "marches on its stomach." In this regard the Northern army marched farther. The agriculture of the South in terms of volume was geared toward the cash crops of cotton and tobacco, which would do little to sustain hungry troops. Production of the major grains of wheat, corn, and oats was dominated by the North's midwestern breadbasket. There was a closer balance between the regions, however, in the number of livestock.

In addition, the North had twice the railroad mileage of the South and the capacity to produce more. Sharp differences existed between the sections over manufacturing ability. The North had five times the number of factories and ten times the number of industrial workers. In retrospect it is difficult to see how the determined South fought on for four years in the face of such odds.

Commanding Leads—One area in which the South surpassed the North, particularly in the early years of the war, was in superior military leadership. Because of a strong military tradition, a number of Southerners attended military academies in the South as well as West Point, the national military academy. As a result, many of the Confederate officers were better trained than their Union counterparts at the outset of the war. This command difference was particularly pronounced in the eastern campaigns, where Robert E. Lee, "Stonewall" Jackson, and J.E.B. Stuart displayed a brilliance and resourcefulness that often mystified their opponents. Lee faced a half dozen different Union commanders over the course of the war, forcing most of them into less strenuous employment.

Strategy—The two sides also differed in their strategy for winning the war. The North would have to go on the offensive by invading the South and defeating the Southern armies in the field. In addition, General Winfield Scott, commander of the Union army at the beginning of the war, proposed a blockade of Southern ports to compound the Confederacy's supply problem. Scott's plan also included the capture of the Mississippi River to split the Confederacy and hamper its ability to move men and supplies from east to west.

Unlike his more enthusiastic subordinates, Scott—himself a Virginian—believed a quick military victory over the South was unlikely. Rather, his plan involved slowly cutting off the Confederacy's ability to make war. The Northern press, reflecting the popular view that the war would last only a few weeks, derisively called Scott's scheme the **Anaconda Plan,** after a large South American snake which slowly crushes its prey within its coils. Scott's ideas, though, would eventually prove both realistic and successful.

The Confederate strategy was largely defensive, to outlast the enemy's will to fight. In general, the Southern soldier took up arms for clearer, more compelling reasons than his Northern adversary. The Confederate was fighting to protect home and family from an invading force, which over the long term provided a more driving motivation in the face of death and deprivation than the Northern soldier's effort to preserve the abstract concept of union.

Section Review

1. What was the main issue that sparked the Civil War?
2. Why did some Southerners consider the Civil War to be a Second American Revolution?
3. Which side in the war had the advantage in basic resources (population, food production, and industrial capacity)?
4. Why was Winfield Scott's plan to win the war called the "Anaconda Plan"?

War in the East

The contest in the East, fought largely in Virginia, centered on the North's attempt to rout the Confederate army and capture the new capital at Richmond, Virginia. The Confederate government's move from Montgomery, Alabama, to Richmond linked the success of the Confederacy to the fortunes of the state that would contribute the most to the cause. "On to Richmond" was the battle cry that characterized much of the Union strategy. However, Richmond had capable and courageous defenders who would force the Union army into a long and costly campaign.

In the spring of 1861, in both the North and South, most people believed that a quick, decisive duel held somewhere between Washington, D.C., and Richmond, Virginia, would end the war. Lincoln's initial call for troops in April was for enlistment of three months. These summer soldiers, like their Southern counterparts, were eager for fame and fighting. They would soon get a chance to prove themselves at a little Virginia crossroads called Manassas Junction.

First Manassas (July 1861)

With the Northern press clamoring for something to write about and the three-month enlistments nearing an end for about 80,000 troops, Lincoln felt the pressure to go on the offensive. General Irvin McDowell, field commander of the Union forces, was ordered south to take Richmond. On July 18 McDowell's troops encountered the Confederate troops under General Beauregard, the Southern commander, near Manassas Junction, a railroad intersection about twenty-five miles southwest of Washington.

In Washington, news of the massing armies was the talk of the town. Hundreds of spectators from senators to socialites turned out in their finery with picnic baskets in hand for the gala event: the beginning and–they believed–the end of the war. Typical of this curious crowd was Illinois Congressman John Logan, who, after arriving for the front-line festivities, decided to join the troops. He went into battle wearing a top hat and tuxedo.

The Confederates chose to take a stand at a little stream near Manassas called Bull Run. On Sunday morning July 21, McDowell launched his attack. At first the raw Federal troops did well, pushing the equally raw Confederates back. However, the timely arrival of troops under South Carolinian Barnard Bee and Virginians under **Thomas J. Jackson** stemmed the tide. Standing against heavy fire and repeated assaults, Bee galloped among his troops urging them to hold the line. Pointing to Jackson's brigade, he shouted, "There stands Jackson like a stonewall! Rally behind the Virginians!" The name stuck, and Jackson was ever after known as "Stonewall." As for Bee, his inspiring words were among his last. Riding at the front of his troops under murderous fire, he was struck down, an early casualty in a long train of war dead.

The Confederate line held and by mid-afternoon McDowell's troops were being pushed back. The retreat turned into a complete rout as green Union troops and panicky picnickers headed back to

War in the East 1861-1863

PENNSYLVANIA

Antietam
Sept. 1862

Gettysburg
July 1863

Philadelphia

MARYLAND

Harpers Ferry

Baltimore

Jackson's Valley Campaign

2nd Manassas
Aug. 1862

Manassas

Washington, D.C.

1st Manassas
(Bull Run)
July 1861

DEL.

Chesapeake Bay

Chancellorsville
May 1863

Jackson to the Peninsula

Fredericksburg
Dec. 1862

Richmond

The Seven Days
June 1862

VIRGINIA

Petersburg

Monitor vs. Merrimac (Virginia)
March 1862

• Danville

0   50
miles

Union Movements
Confederate Movements

Battles

Washington in earnest. The victorious Confederates, however, were too disorganized to follow up their win.

Following the Confederate victory at the **First Battle of Manassas,** the South was relieved and confident, the North demoralized. The next day Lincoln replaced McDowell with General **George B. McClellan** and rumors flew through Washington of a Confederate attack. The most significant result, however, was that both sides realized that the war would not be over quickly. Many of the congressmen, veterans of the Sunday afternoon picnic near Bull Run, voted for a half million more troops for three-*year* enlistments. The season for summer soldiers had passed.

Peninsular Campaign (March–July 1862)

In the months following Manassas, McClellan took the shattered remnants of McDowell's army and the flood of raw recruits and organized and drilled them into an impressive force, called the **Army of the Potomac.** That, however, was about all McClellan did with his army–organize and drill them. By the spring of 1862 Lincoln ordered McClellan south to Richmond. The general, however, offered a better plan. He would move his troops up the peninsula between the James and York rivers and attack Richmond from the east; he could then send a separate force sweeping from the north and crush the capital in the grip of the two armies.

The Monitor *and the* Merrimac *(March 1862)*–McClellan's plan to use the James River as a supply line was nearly upset before the campaign began. The Confederates unveiled a new weapon, an **ironclad** (an iron-plated warship). This ugly but dangerous monster was built on the damaged hull of an abandoned Union warship, the U.S.S. *Merrimack.* Southerners renamed it the C.S.S. *Virginia,* but it has traditionally been known as the **Merrimac** (the final *k* usually being omitted). This vessel with its heavy iron armor, ten guns, and iron ram attached to its bow, sailed out against the Union blockade fleet at Hampton Roads, Virginia, on March 8, 1862. The *Merrimac,* virtually invulnerable to Union cannon, easily sank two large Northern warships. Word quickly spread throughout the

panic-stricken North about the South's new weapon. Abraham Lincoln watched out the window of the White House, expecting to see the *Merrimac* steaming up the Potomac River.

When the *Merrimac* returned to Hampton Roads the next day, it faced a strange opponent. Described as "a cheese box on a raft" and "a tin can on a shingle," this was the U.S.S. **Monitor,** the Union's newest ironclad, just arrived from New York. The *Monitor* was an unusual craft. Instead of the usual fixed guns on each side of the ship, the Union vessel had only two guns mounted in a revolving turret that could fire in any direction. The *Monitor* and the *Merrimac* battled for over four hours without either seriously damaging the other. As the tide began to go out, however, the *Merrimac* was forced to retreat to avoid running aground. Although the battle was a draw, the *Monitor* had saved the Union fleet at Hampton Roads. More important, the clash was the first between iron warships, and it spelled the end of the age of wooden ships.

Diversion in the Valley (March–June 1862)– Considering the numerical advantages of the Union forces, McClellan's plan to capture Richmond might have worked had it not been for Stonewall Jackson and one of the most brilliant campaigns of the war. During the **Valley Campaign** (March 23 to June 9, 1862) Jackson, with a scant fighting force of less than 15,000 Confederates, ranged up and down Virginia's Shenandoah Valley, defeating two separate armies and effectively pinning down 50,000 Federal troops before slipping out of the valley for Richmond to help stop McClellan. Returning from his incredible campaign, "Old Jack" declared, "God has been our shield."

On to Richmond!–Beginning in April 1862, McClellan, with 100,000 troops, pushed up the neck of land toward Richmond. The outnumbered **Army of Northern Virginia** under General **Joseph E. Johnston** delayed the Union advance, grudgingly giving ground to the overly cautious McClellan. Eventually, however, the Union forces came within sight of the spires of Richmond.

On the last day of May, Johnston struck McClellan hard at Fair Oaks on the outskirts of Richmond. The two-day fight left heavy casualties on both sides, including the Confederate commander. Johnston, severely wounded, would be out of action for months. With the enemy at the gates, Jefferson Davis turned to his military adviser, **Robert E. Lee,** to command the army. Lee, always a man of action, sized up the situation and seized the initiative, launching what would be known as the **Seven Days' Battles.** From June 25 to July 1, at obscure little creeks and crossroads such as Gaine's Mill, Savage's Station, White Oak Swamp, and Malvern Hill, the Confederates pushed McClellan's grand army back to the James River with both sides taking heavy losses. Having been outgeneraled by Lee, McClellan was ordered to abandon the peninsula and return to Washington, D.C., where he

General Robert E. Lee, photograph by Mathew Brady

would join General John Pope for a new drive on Richmond. Lee, however, had no intention of waiting to be attacked.

Second Manassas (August 1862)

It was clear to Lee that when McClellan's army linked up with Pope's army, they would have an overwhelming advantage in manpower and firepower. He had to break this equation by removing Pope's menacing force. Lee's strategy was as daring as it was successful. He sent his cavalry commander, **J.E.B. Stuart,** to raid Pope from the rear. Stuart swooped down on Pope's headquarters and, while the general was away, Stuart took the Federal payroll, battle plans, and for good measure Pope's dress coat.

While Stuart was creating havoc at Pope's back door, Lee sent the elusive Jackson around Pope's army. Stonewall's men marched sixty-two miles in forty-eight hours, capturing Federal supplies at Manassas Junction and attacking Pope's lines on the evening of August 28. Just as Pope was preparing to attack Jackson's thin lines the next day, the rest of Lee's army came crashing down on the Federal flank. On the second day of the battle, brave Federal assaults were cut down by Southern defenders with devastating effect. With a piercing "Rebel yell" the Confederates counterattacked, appearing to one retreating Federal "like demons emerging from the earth." As a result of this **Second Battle of Manassas,** Pope's army was sent reeling back to Washington. Remarkably, after only two months, Lee had cleared practically all of Virginia of Federal forces.

Antietam (September 1862)

After his victory at Manassas, Lee decided to take the war into enemy territory to relieve the pressure on the Confederate capital. In September he crossed the Potomac into Maryland, hoping to disrupt transportation and communication systems to Washington and gain foreign assistance for the Confederacy. He did not plan to occupy Washington but only to panic the government into terms of peace.

On September 13, Private B. W. Mitchell of the 27th Indiana Volunteers was setting up camp when he found three cigars wrapped in papers that turned out to be Lee's orders to one of his generals, orders

Alexander Gardner's photograph of Confederate dead by the fence at the cornfield in the aftermath of bloody Antietam

that revealed Lee's battle plan. When an exuberant McClellan received the lost orders, he waved them boasting, "Here is a paper with which, if I cannot whip Bobby Lee, I will be willing to go home."

Thanks to J.E.B. Stuart's scouts, Lee knew within a day that McClellan knew his positions. Quickly Lee gathered his army, a force of about 30,000, and drew up a defensive line at **Antietam** Creek near Sharpsburg, Maryland. There they awaited the onslaught of McClellan's legions, 87,000 strong.

At dawn on September 17, Union forces fell upon the Confederate line. At one point between the two armies a forty-acre corn field stood ripe and full, ready for harvest. There was in fact a grim harvest that day, as the corn field became a killing field. One survivor wrote that the terrific fire cut down the charging soldiers "like a scythe running through our line."

All along the line, the day was a furious swirl of blood and sweat and smoke as the armies held each other in a death grip. One Confederate recalled, "The sun seemed almost to go backwards, and it appeared as if night would never come." When night finally did come, 24,000 men had fallen. It was the bloodiest day in American history.

The next morning Lee drew up a line of defense, expecting another attack, but McClellan had no stomach for it. On September 18 Lee slipped his battered army back across the Potomac into Virginia. Technically, Antietam was a Union victory, because the Confederates had withdrawn. In reality, the battle was a draw. Even so, Lincoln used news of this "victory" to announce the Emancipation Proclamation (see p. 308).

Fredericksburg (December 1862)

After Antietam, Lincoln gave up on McClellan and turned command over to General Ambrose Burnside. The modest Burnside never felt himself capable of high command. At **Fredericksburg, Virginia,** it was clear that he felt that way for a good reason.

On December 13, 1862, Burnside launched repeated attacks on entrenched Confederate positions on the outskirts of the quaint colonial village of

Fredericksburg. Before the frigid day was over, 12,000 Union soldiers had fallen before the steady gray line along a slope called Marye's Heights. Before the stone wall, where the Confederates took their stand, the dying were strewn among the dead, begging for water. One South Carolina sergeant, nineteen-year-old Richard Kirkland, was overwhelmed by their pitiful cries. With hostile fire raging, Kirkland gathered canteens of water and repeatedly crawled out among the wounded Yankees to quench their thirst–a moving example of Christ's command to "Love your enemies." Kirkland's selfless heroism earned him the title "the Angel of Marye's Heights."

As a dismal December closed on 1862–the first but not the last full year of the war–Burnside, overwhelmed by his losses, broke off the assault. When Lincoln heard of the defeat, he turned command over to yet another general, "Fighting Joe" Hooker.

Chancellorsville (May 1863)

"Fighting Joe" was a popular, proven general, but he was also a braggart. "May God have mercy on General Lee," the new commander declared, "for I will have none." For three days in May 1863, Lee would give Hooker cause to regret his words.

Hooker, with a huge force of 130,000 men, returned to the Fredericksburg area to crush the Southern army. Lee, with less than half the number of troops, made up in daring what he lacked in numbers. In a bold move, Lee divided his badly outnumbered army into three parts, half of it going with Stonewall Jackson on a flank march around the end of the Union position. Jackson's men completely surprised the Federals and rolled up the Union line. Fierce fighting continued for three days in the **Battle of Chancellorsville,** but Hooker never recovered from the shock of Jackson's attack. Baffled and battered, the Union general dragged his huge army northward in retreat.

Lee's triumph, however, was marred by the fatal wounding of Stonewall Jackson. Tragically for the South, Jackson was mistakenly shot by Confederate troops while he rode at the front of his lines at dusk amid the tangled fighting on May 2. The loss to Lee and the Southern cause was inestimable. None-

theless, Lee's decisive win at Chancellorsville threw back the Union threat, paving the way for more ambitious plans.

The Confederacy's victories in the East from First Manassas to Chancellorsville were important for more than just military glory. First, these victories succeeded in completely frustrating one of the Union's chief war aims, the capture of Richmond. The only Union "victory" in the campaign was the bloody stalemate at Antietam. Even then, the battle only drove Lee back into Virginia; it did not bring the Northerners any closer to the Confederate capital. Second, the victories raised the morale of the South and lowered that of the North. Despite defeats in the West (discussed in the next section), Confederates took hope from Lee's triumphs that they might yet win the war. Northerners, on the other hand, became wearied with defeat. Because all that the South needed in order to win was for the North to give up, Northern weariness was itself a Southern victory. Third, the longer the South held out and continued to inflict defeats on the Federals, the more likely it was that a European power, such as Britain, would recognize the Confederacy and aid its cause. After Chancellorsville, Southern hopes for independence seemed close to fulfillment.

Gettysburg (July 1863)

The plight of Vicksburg (pp. 300-301) and growing shortages among his own troops convinced Lee that a victory on Northern soil was needed to help turn the tide. In late June the Confederate army marched through Maryland into Pennsylvania, being careful to follow Lee's orders not to destroy property or to molest citizens. The citizens were surprised to see that the lean soldiers who had put the Union army to flight so often were poorly clothed and equipped and that many were barefoot.

A Search for Shoes–On June 30 an advance party of Confederates neared Gettysburg, Pennsylvania, in hopes of finding shoes for their ragged troops. There they clashed with an advance unit of Federals under the command of General George Meade, who had replaced Hooker. The two armies had found each other.

Stonewall Jackson: Soldier of the Cross

One of the greatest heroes of the South was also one of its most devout Christians. General Thomas Jonathan Jackson, nicknamed "Stonewall" for his bravery at First Manassas, was converted to Christ shortly after he served in the Mexican War. After the Civil War broke out, Jackson served brilliantly in the Confederate army, but he combined fervent piety with military genius.

His courageous faith in God carried him through many dangerous battles. For example, after First Manassas an aide asked General Jackson how he managed to remain so calm as bullets and shells whistled about him. Jackson replied, "Captain, my religious belief teaches me to feel as safe in battle as in bed. God has fixed the time for my death. I do not concern myself about *that,* but to be always ready no matter when it may overtake me." He paused and then added, "Captain, that is the way all men should live, and then all would be equally brave."

Jackson unhesitatingly expressed his gratitude to God for victory. After the Second Battle of Manassas, an officer on the general's staff said, "We have won this battle by the hardest kind of fighting." Jackson disagreed: "No, No, we have won by the blessing of Almighty God." After victory in the Battle of Port Republic during the Valley Campaign, Jackson turned to General Richard Ewell and said gently, "General, he who does not see the hand of God in this is blind, Sir, blind!"

Jackson cared for the spiritual needs of his men as well. He ordered regular religious services to be held in camp, and the general himself faithfully attended. He carried saddlebags of religious tracts for his men and welcomed others who wanted to distribute religious literature among his troops. Jackson told one such distributor, "I am more anxious than I can express that my men should be not only good soldiers of their country, but also good soldiers of the Cross."

The consistency of Jackson's testimony impressed those who knew him. One evening during the Seven Days' Battles, General Ewell and General William Whiting asked Jackson if they could change their route of march for the next day. Jackson said that he would think it over. After they left, Ewell said to Whiting, "Don't you know why 'Old Jack' would not decide at once? He's going to pray over it first!" Then, realizing he had forgotten his sword, Ewell re-entered the headquarters and in fact found Jackson on his knees beside his bed praying.

On another occasion, Kyd Douglas, a member of Jackson's staff, reported how Jackson walked through his camp on the way to services. Without the general's noticing it, his men silently left their tents and filed in behind him. Stonewall Jackson's men followed him to a prayer meeting just as loyally as they followed him into battle.

On July 1 the Confederates drove the Federals back, where they entrenched on high ground south of Gettysburg. The next day Lee renewed the assault on Meade's position, hitting both flanks, but Union reinforcements held the line.

Pickett's Charge—On July 3 Lee made one final attempt to dislodge Meade's army by ordering an assault on the center of the Union position along Cemetery Ridge. Fresh troops, mostly veteran Virginians under command of General George Pickett, formed a line nearly a mile long and marched into the face of a murderous artillery barrage. Those who survived the charge took the ridge in fierce hand-to-hand combat. One Massachusetts soldier present described the high-water mark of the battle—and possibly the war—that day on Cemetery Ridge:

> Foot to foot, body to body and man to man they struggled, pushed and strived and killed. The mass of wounded and heaps of dead entangled the feet of the contestants, and, under-

After Jackson received his mortal wounds at Chancellorsville, his calm faith and composure deeply impressed those who attended him on his deathbed. He said, ''You see me severely wounded, but not depressed; not unhappy. I believe it has been done according to God's holy will, and I acquiesce entirely in it.'' When told that he was dying, Jackson took the news calmly. A little later he said, ''It is the Lord's Day. . . . My wish is fulfilled. I always wanted to die on Sunday.'' On Sunday, May 10, 1863, Stonewall Jackson said quietly, ''Let us cross over the river, and rest under the shade of the trees,'' and then he died. He left behind the testimony of a man who combined unflinching bravery with unflinching faith. As his wife said after Jackson's death, ''The fear of the Lord was the only fear he knew.''

neath the trampling mass, wounded men who could no longer stand, struggled, fought, shouted and killed–hatless, coatless, drowned in sweat, black with powder, red with blood, with fiendish yells and strange oaths, they blindly plied the work of slaughter, valor could do no more.

Surrounded on three sides with no reinforcements, Pickett's valiant men were quickly overwhelmed. The **Battle of Gettysburg** was over; the two sides had suffered 50,000 casualties between them. Two days later the remnants of Lee's army retreated to Virginia, and Meade, exhausted by his costly victory, failed to stop him. The South would never again have the strength to launch a major offensive. Yet the war was far from over.

Gettysburg Address—With the human wreckage of war strewn across the Pennsylvania countryside, seventeen acres of the hotly contested ground was set aside to bury the men who had fallen there. At the dedication of the cemetery in November 1863 Lincoln summed up in ten eloquent sentences– his **Gettysburg Address**–the common courage and sacrifice of the soldiers of the North and South:

> In a larger sense, we cannot dedicate–we cannot consecrate–we cannot hallow–this ground. The brave men, living and dead, who struggled here have consecrated it, far above our poor power to add or detract. The world will little note, nor long remember, what we say here, but it can never forget what they did here.

Section Review

1. Why did the Confederates not follow up their victory at the First Battle of Manassas?
2. How did the First Battle of Manassas affect Northern and Southern morale?
3. What is the significance of the clash between the *Monitor* and the *Merrimac?*
4. What event marred for the Confederates their victory at Chancellorsville?
5. In what three ways were the series of Confederate victories in the East from First Manassas to Chancellorsville important to the Southern cause?

War in the West

The Civil War in the West differed from the fighting in the East. There were two main campaigns in the West, for example, instead of the prolonged single contest between the Army of Northern Virginia and the Army of the Potomac in the East. In the West, the war from 1861 to 1863 divided between the Mississippi River campaign and the Kentucky-Tennessee campaign. The West also saw a lopsided number of Union victories, in contrast to the Confederate triumphs in the East. In addition, while the South's greatest generals (Lee and Jackson) fought in the East, the North's best commanders (U. S. Grant and William Sherman) rose to fame in the West. In one respect, though, the two theaters of war were identical: the fighting was hard and bloody.

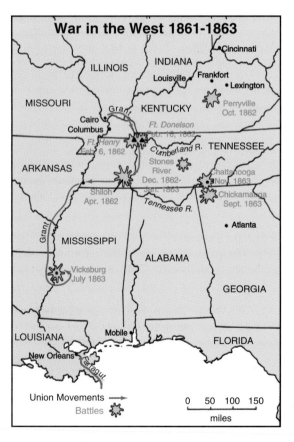

Mississippi River Campaign

One of the most important features of Winfield Scott's "Anaconda Plan" was the capture of the Mississippi River. Union control of the Mississippi would serve two purposes. First, it would split the Confederacy in two. Second, it would provide Northern farmers in the Midwest a needed outlet for their products. Control of the Mississippi was therefore crucial to both sides. The Confederacy sought to maintain its grip through major fortifications on the river, primarily those in Columbus, Kentucky; on Island No. 10 near the Kentucky-Tennessee border; in Vicksburg, Mississippi; and in New Orleans. To win the river, the Union had to break these strongholds.

A Fleet and a General—One major Union advantage was its river fleet of gunboats. These ungainly, ugly ironclad warships were nicknamed "turtles" for their appearance and slow speed. These ships were not as mighty as the *Merrimac,* but they were the most powerful force on the western rivers. Another Union advantage in the West was the presence of one of the North's finest generals, **Ulysses S. Grant.**

No one who looked at Grant thought of him as a great warrior. He was short and slight and looked rather commonplace. On first meeting Grant's staff, Secretary of War Stanton unknowingly bypassed the general, shook hands with the staff surgeon, and said, "How are you, General Grant? I knew you at sight from your pictures." Nor was Grant particularly accomplished. His record at West Point had been mediocre, and he had resigned from the army in the 1850s under threat of a court-martial for drunkenness. In civilian life Grant failed as a farmer and real-estate salesman, and, when the war broke out, he was working in his father's leather shop in Galena, Illinois. After volunteering for the army, Grant was made a brigadier general and entrusted with a command at Cairo, Illinois, the point at which the Ohio and Mississippi rivers join. General Grant soon surprised his superiors with his abilities.

Forts Henry and Donelson (February 1862)—The Union high command knew that a frontal attack on heavily fortified Columbus, Kentucky,

General Ulysses S. Grant

Donelson in Union hands, the Confederates abandoned Columbus and fell back from western Kentucky. In addition, Nashville fell to the Union, and Tennessee was open to Union advances.

Shiloh (April 1862) — Grant's popularity lasted only until his next battle. As the Union army moved south along the Tennessee River, Confederate commander General Albert Sidney Johnston decided to strike the enemy a sudden blow. Johnston was helped by the fact that Grant and his men, thinking that the Confederates were on the run, let down their guard. On the morning of April 6, 1862, Johnston's force of 40,000 soldiers attacked a Union force of about equal size near an abandoned Methodist church called "Shiloh." The astonished Federals staggered and reeled under the punishing blows of the Confederates. The screaming hail of shells and bullets was so intense that one Union soldier watched in wonder as a rabbit crawled out of the brush and snuggled next to a soldier for safety. The disorganized Union forces steadily fell back toward the Tennessee River. As darkness fell, the Union army was barely holding on to its positions.

During the night, however, Northern reinforcements arrived. The Confederates had taken heavy losses, including General Johnston, who had suffered a leg wound and bled to death before he realized how serious the wound was. At the dawn of April 7, Grant counterattacked and drove the enemy back. The **Battle of Shiloh** was technically a Union victory, but it was a costly one. Each side lost over 10,000 men killed and wounded. Angry newspapers and politicians called for Grant's dismissal. Lincoln refused, saying, "I can't spare this man. He fights." For his part, Grant learned an important lesson; he would not soon be caught napping again.

Island No. 10 and New Orleans (April 1862) — April of 1862 also brought some good news to the Union. The day after Shiloh, Island No. 10 fell to a combined force of Federal gunboats and troops under General John Pope (before his promotion to the East and his loss at Second Manassas). Then on April 25, Union naval commander **David G. Farragut** led the fleet up the Mississippi from the Gulf of Mexico and captured New Orleans, the

would be foolhardy. Therefore, Grant was ordered to take his troops and the gunboat fleet and capture two important forts behind Columbus in northern Tennessee: **Fort Henry** on the Tennessee River and **Fort Donelson** on the Cumberland River. Grant easily captured the poorly designed Fort Henry on February 6, 1862. Even as the fort surrendered, flood waters from the river were slowly submerging it.

Fort Donelson, only twelve miles to the east, was far more difficult. This fort was well designed and staffed with some 20,000 Confederate troops. The winter fighting for the fort was hard and bitter, and Grant's men outside the fort suffered terribly. Finally, on February 16, the Confederate commander sent a message asking for terms of surrender. Grant replied, "No terms except unconditional and immediate surrender can be accepted." The fort fell, and a jubilant Northern public, playing on the general's initials, honored its new hero, "Unconditional Surrender" Grant. With Henry and

South's largest city and most important seaport. One major obstacle remained for Union control of the river, the Mississippi city of Vicksburg.

***Fall of Vicksburg (July 1863)*—Vicksburg** was an important river port even before the war. Its high bluffs above the river made it a natural fortress, and the swampy lands near the city made it difficult for an enemy to approach. Jefferson Davis called Vicksburg ''the nailhead that held the South's two halves together.'' As long as the Confederates held the city, they could bring supplies and troops from their western regions. Vicksburg therefore became the key to the Mississippi campaign.

Despite the near-disaster at Shiloh, U. S. Grant was the Union's top general, and to him was en-trusted the capture of Vicksburg. In the Vicksburg campaign, Grant revealed both a talent for experimentation and a streak of daring. When his first attack on the city in December 1862 failed, Grant decided to gather his forces north of the city and to try to find a way to bypass the guns of the forts. Throughout the winter of 1862-63, Grant tried first digging a canal and then floating his gunboats and troop transports along the bayous, swamps, and streams surrounding the city. All of these attempts failed.

Finally, Grant tried a risky maneuver. First, he marched his men down the swampy western bank of the Mississippi to a point below Vicksburg. Then he floated his fleet of gunboats and transports past

Under cover of night, the Union gunboat fleet runs past the blazing guns on the heights of Vicksburg as part of U.S. Grant's plan for capturing the Mississippi River fortress.

the guns on the bluffs under cover of night. This accomplished, Grant ferried his troops across the river below the city. The Union army had outmaneuvered the Confederates, but it had also abandoned its supply line. The army had only what its soldiers carried on their backs. Calmly, Grant wrote that he wanted ''to get up what rations of hard bread, coffee and salt we can and make the country furnish the rest.''

Grant's bold strategy worked. His move mystified the Confederates and allowed his army to sweep north and surround Vicksburg by May 1863. The defenses of the city were too strong to assault; so Grant laid seige to Vicksburg to starve it into submission. Conditions inside the besieged city worsened. Horses, cats, and dogs disappeared as the starving populace sought food. Finally, on July 4, 1863–the same day that Lee began his retreat from Gettysburg–Vicksburg surrendered. With Vicksburg gone, the last Confederate garrison on the Mississippi surrendered a few days later. The Mississippi River was completely in Union hands. Abraham Lincoln declared with satisfaction, ''The Father of Waters again flows unvexed to the sea.''

Kentucky-Tennessee Campaign

While Grant was slowly pushing down the Mississippi River, an equally important but less famous campaign was going on–the struggle for control of Kentucky and Tennessee.

Situation in Kentucky–Kentucky was one of the most divided border states. When the war broke out, for example, the governor was pro-Confederate and the state legislature was pro-Union. Faced with such drastic division, the state declared that it would remain neutral. Such neutrality was impossible to maintain, considering Kentucky's location. However, Lincoln and Jefferson Davis–each eager to win the state to his side–promised to respect Kentucky's wishes. Eventually the need to protect the Mississippi River forced the Confederates to move north to occupy Columbus, Kentucky. The Union responded by happily sending in troops to ''avenge'' this violation of Kentucky's neutrality.

At first, the Confederate position looked strong in the state. The Confederates held Columbus in the west, and another force in the east guarded the Cumberland Gap, the gateway to the mountains of eastern Tennessee and western Virginia. Then in January 1862 the Confederate commander at the Cumberland Gap foolishly pushed north across the Cumberland River. On January 19 a small Union force under General **George Thomas** routed the Southerners at the Battle of Mill Springs. That defeat, coupled with Grant's capture of Forts Henry and Donelson in February, forced the Confederates from Kentucky.

Perryville (October 1862)–After the death of Albert Sidney Johnston at Shiloh, the Confederate government appointed General **Braxton Bragg** to head its armies in the West. Bragg had a distinguished military record, but he tended to anger easily and often refused to listen to suggestions. Bragg's harsh discipline caused one soldier to remark, ''Not a single soldier in the whole army ever loved or respected him.''

Bragg nonetheless came up with a good plan to revive the Confederate cause in the West–an invasion of Kentucky. Such a campaign, Bragg thought, would raise new troops from among the pro-Confederate citizens of Kentucky and might even bring the state into the Confederacy. He also hoped that the attack would force Union forces on the Mississippi River to retreat or at least halt their advance.

In August the great campaign began. A smaller force swept up through eastern Kentucky, capturing the Cumberland Gap, Lexington, and the state capital, Frankfort. Bragg followed with a larger force through the center of the state, about a hundred miles to the west. Soon the Southerners were threatening Louisville and Cincinnati, and the hard-pressed Union commander, Don Carlos Buell, moved his forces between Bragg and the Ohio River.

The campaign did not work as Bragg had hoped. Although some Kentuckians rallied to the Confederate standard, even more volunteers enlisted in the Union cause to expel the invaders. Pro-Confederate Kentuckians said they would support Bragg–if he could win a great victory. Buell and Bragg finally met in the center of the state in the confused **Battle of Perryville** (October 8, 1862). The outnumbered Southerners, not realizing that Buell's whole force was present, actually attacked and drove back the Federals. When Bragg realized the strength of the enemy force, however, he quickly ordered a retreat into Tennessee. Bragg's great invasion had failed, and Kentucky was never again seriously threatened by the Confederacy.

Stones River (December 1862–January 1863)—Buell's mixed success at Perryville resulted in his replacement by General William Rosecrans, who set up his headquarters in Nashville. The new commander then pushed his reorganized army southeast to Murfreesboro, Tennessee, where Bragg was gathering his forces to strike Nashville. In the chilling cold of a frigid December, the two armies met near Stones River, northwest of Murfreesboro. The night before the battle, the bands of the two armies serenaded each other with strains of "Yankee Doodle" and "Dixie." Then the Union band began playing "Home Sweet Home," and the Confederate band joined in. For a few moments, enemy soldiers were countrymen once again, united in thoughts of home.

The next morning the only music came from a chorus of cannon. The **Battle of Stones River** (also known as the Battle of Murfreesboro) was two days of hard fighting with a rest day on New Year's Day between (December 31, 1862 to January 2, 1863). Although Bragg's troops succeeded in pushing back the Federals at several points, the Confederates could not destroy the Union army. As Northern reinforcements poured in from Nashville, Bragg was forced to retreat again.

Chickamauga (September 1863)—Union losses at Stones River forced Rosecrans to pause and rebuild his forces. When the Federals began to move in late June, they steadily pushed back the outnumbered Confederates through Chattanooga and into northern Georgia. Rosecrans pushed his men on for what he thought would be the final blow. Bragg's army was not routed, however. Reinforced by 12,000 veteran troops from Virginia, Bragg took his stand near the banks of a creek named **Chickamauga,** Cherokee for "river of death." In two days (September 19-20), the Confederates shattered the Union forces, and Rosecrans fled the field with his battered troops.

Christ in the Camp

Christians served on both sides in the Civil War. The Christian testimonies of Southern generals Robert E. Lee and "Stonewall" Jackson are well known, and several Union officers were likewise followers of Christ. For example, Admiral Andrew Foote, commander of U. S. Grant's gunboat fleet and the hero of the capture of Fort Henry, was a devout Christian who was known to preach to his men on the deck of his ship. Lay evangelists, such as Northerner Dwight L. Moody, labored among the soldiers, preaching and witnessing and ultimately leading many of them to Christ.

The greatest recorded moving of God's Spirit during the war, however, took place in the Southern armies, particularly Lee's Army of Northern Virginia. Revivals in the Confederate ranks occurred throughout the war, but the most sweeping came during the fall and winter months between the Battle of Antietam (September 17, 1862) and the Battle of Chancellorsville (May 1-3, 1863). In that period, Confederate chaplains and civilian pastors saw a remarkable harvest of souls. Hundreds of soldiers, realizing that they might face death in battle as early as the next day's march, gathered in sober, solemn as-

Complete disaster for the Union was avoided only through the courage of General George Thomas. He calmly held his troops on the field to protect the retreating forces and then slowly withdrew. A member of Rosecrans's staff, General (later President) James Garfield, wrote that Thomas was "standing like a rock" and thereafter Thomas was known as the "Rock of Chickamauga." Despite the heroics of Thomas and his troops, the Battle of Chickamauga was a major Confederate victory and a disastrous Union defeat. Bragg trapped the Union army in Chattanooga and threatened to starve it out just as Grant had starved out Vicksburg.

semblies to listen to the preaching of God's Word. When weather permitted, the men met outdoors, where enemy sniper fire was sometimes a danger. In cold weather, they met in nearby churches or in crude log huts that they constructed just so that they might hold services.

Nearly all Southern denominations joined hands in promoting the revival. On one occasion a minister noted, "We had a Presbyterian sermon, introduced by Baptist services, under the direction of a Methodist chaplain, in an Episcopal church!" The men responded in large numbers. Some of the converts were earnest, outwardly moral men who were searching for inner peace. Others were hardened, ungodly sinners whom no one had ever expected to be converted.

Estimates of the number of converts vary. In his book *Christ in the Camp,* Virginia

chaplain J. W. Jones estimated the number of converts in Lee's army during the whole four years of the war as 15,000. Jones admitted that he took only the most certain and unquestioned numbers that he could find and said that the actual total was probably much higher. The lives of those who professed salvation generally indicated that the conversions were genuine. After the war Jones attempted to follow up on the 410 soldiers that he had personally baptized and found that only three had abandoned their professions and returned to their old sinful ways.

Revivals were not limited to Lee's forces, either. During the period between the Battles for Chattanooga (November 1863) and the beginning of Sherman's march on Atlanta (May 1864), a similar revival swept General Johnston's forces in their winter quarters in Dalton, Georgia. Another Southern historian of the revivals estimates that over 100,000 Confederate soldiers were converted during the course of the war. Chaplain Jones wrote at the close of his book: "And surely Christian men of every section and of every creed will unite in thanking God that Christ *was* in the camps of Lee's army with such wonderful power to save, and that out of that terrible war God brought such rich blessings."

Scene in Stonewall Jackson's Camp, *by Adalbert Volck, National Portrait Gallery, Smithsonian Institution*

Chattanooga—Climax in the West

Union Reorganization—Rosecrans's disastrous defeat forced the Lincoln administration to make changes. George Thomas replaced Rosecrans as commander of the forces in Chattanooga. Meanwhile, Lincoln rewarded Grant by making him chief of all Union forces in the West. Grant and part of his troops left the Mississippi region for Chattanooga. First, Grant broke the siege that Bragg had laid and got supplies into the hungry

city. Then he prepared to drive the Confederates from their strong positions south of the city on Lookout Mountain and Missionary Ridge.

Battles for Chattanooga (November 1863)— The Yankees rather easily captured Lookout Mountain on November 24 in a mist-enshrouded encounter romantically known as "the Battle Above the Clouds." The Southerners still held the more formidable position on Missionary Ridge, however. None of Grant's plans in the **Battle of Missionary Ridge** (November 25) worked as he had envisioned them. When attacks on the flanks of the Confederate line failed, Grant ordered George Thomas's

General U. S. Grant (left) surveys the damage on Lookout Mountain following the Union's victory there.

men to create a diversion by capturing enemy rifle pits at the base of Missionary Ridge. The troops captured the rifle pits and then almost spontaneously began to swarm up the ridge toward the main Confederate positions. Watching from a distance, an unpleasantly surprised General Grant asked, "Thomas, who ordered those men up the ridge?" "I don't know," replied General Thomas. "I did not." After watching for a few minutes, Grant muttered, "It's all right, if it turns out all right. If not, someone will suffer."

The Union attack, however, surprised the outnumbered Southerners almost as much as it had Grant. Missionary Ridge was soon in Northern hands, and Bragg's troops were once more retreating into Georgia. Bragg resigned, and President Jefferson Davis replaced him as commander with Joseph Johnston. President Lincoln promoted U. S. Grant and made him commander of all Union forces. Georgia was open to invasion, and the tide in the West was definitely flowing in the Union's favor.

Section Review

1. What were the two main campaigns of the Civil War in the West?
2. For what two reasons did the Union want to control the Mississippi River?
3. How did the South seek to maintain control of the Mississippi River?
4. The capture of what city was the key to the Mississippi River campaign?
5. What were the three goals of Braxton Bragg in his invasion of Kentucky in 1862?

On the Home Front

War consists of more than the dramatic clash of arms on the battlefield. In addition to the suffering of the wounded was the quieter–but nonetheless real–suffering of those at home. Behind the lines of battle lay large civilian populations and their governments, all of which tried to function as effectively as they could in the strained circumstances of war.

Life Behind the Lines

In the South–Because most of the fighting took place on Southern soil, life in the South during the war was far more difficult than life in the North. In addition, the Confederate leaders, having to build a central government almost from scratch, confronted problems that the Lincoln administration never faced. The South, for example, possessed very little gold and silver. The Confederacy therefore found itself printing paper money with little to back it up except confidence in the government. As people realized how worthless the money was and as Confederate fortunes on the battlefield declined, prices soared. By late 1864, hams were selling in Richmond for as much as $350 apiece, and by the following January, flour was $425 a barrel. By the end of 1864, Confederate money was worth one-fortieth of its face value. After the war, of course, it was worth nothing. Those who invested most heavily in the Confederate cause often lost everything they had.

Some goods were extremely scarce, and both civilians and soldiers suffered from shortages of food and clothing. Some learned to make do with what was on hand. Newspapers in Vicksburg, for example, printed their issues on wallpaper when supplies of newsprint ran out. A Memphis newspaper used shoe polish when it ran out of ink. Sometimes the shortages resulted in anger and violence. In Richmond in April 1863, hungry women started a riot over shortages of bread. Rioting mobs smashed windows, broke into stores, and stole food. The violence was halted only when Jefferson Davis personally confronted the rioters and persuaded them to disperse.

The primary cause of these shortages was the Union blockade of the Confederacy. Some daring merchant ships, called **blockade runners,** risked the wrath of the Union navy to bring supplies into Southern ports, where these goods were sold for enormous profits. Even at the beginning of the war, however, when the North had few ships to enforce the blockade, Southern trade dropped below prewar levels. One of the primary reasons for this drop was the fact that the British–with the mightiest navy in the world–chose to honor the blockade. Had Britain been determined to trade normally with the South, the North could not have stopped the British short of declaring war on them. As the war progressed, the Union built more ships and captured more Confederate seaports. As a result, the effectiveness of the blockade increased, and blockade running became too hazardous to be profitable.

*In the North–*The situation on the Northern home front was easier than in the South, but it was not without its problems. Inflation and shortages also plagued Northern families, but neither became as severe as they did in the South. In fact, after the first shock of secession, the North actually entered a period of prosperity. With most farm hands away fighting, farmers learned to rely more heavily on machinery, such as McCormick's reaper (see p. 216), to do the work. As a result, Northern farms began to produce more foodstuffs during the war than they had before. Likewise, heavy industries, such as ironworking, profited from the Union army's need for cannon, iron for ships, and other armaments. At the close of the war, an increasingly prosperous North stood in marked contrast to a devastated and war-torn South.

Government in Time of War

*Filling the Ranks–*The main challenge to both the Union and the Confederacy was putting an army in the field. At first, volunteers were more than enough to fill the ranks. As the war dragged on, however, men became less willing to serve in the army as they saw the casualty lists and realized how their families back home were suffering. Eventually, first the Confederacy and then the Union adopted **conscription,** the "drafting," or

Confederate currency

compulsory enrollment, of men into military service. The resulting draft laws were unfortunately not always fair. Anyone drafted could avoid serving by hiring a substitute or paying an exemption fee. These provisions led to mutterings in both North and South that this was ''a rich man's war and a poor man's fight.''

Resistance to the draft arose in both sections. In the South, a surprising amount of the opposition came from state government officials. Having gone to war over the issue of states' rights, many officials resisted giving the central government the power to draft recruits. The governors of Georgia and North Carolina particularly resented the draft. Because the draft law exempted justices of the peace from the draft, for example, the governor of Georgia appointed hundreds of new ''justices'' to save them from conscription. In all, North Carolina and Georgia accounted for over ninety per cent of the exemptions granted to the Confederate draft.

Although a few Southerners resisted the draft with violence, the North was the scene of most violent resistance. The most vicious example was the **New York draft riot** in July 1863. The city of New York was home to many recent immigrants, many of whom did not understand the war and few of whom wanted to fight in it. In four days of rioting, mobs attacked not only government officials but also the city's black population. One mob, for example, burned an orphanage for black children, and another seized a crippled black coach driver and hanged him from a lamppost. By the time the riots were suppressed, 119 people had died and 306 had been injured. The results of the draft were scarcely worth the cost. Only six to seven per cent of the Union ranks were filled by conscripts or their hired substitutes.

Blacks provided a valuable pool of recruits for the ranks. The South used some free blacks behind the lines in noncombatant roles such as wagon drivers and also used slaves in the construction of fortifications. At the very end of war, Robert E. Lee even suggested granting slaves their freedom in return for fighting for the Confederacy, but the idea came too late to be enacted. Most blacks fought in the Union army, where they saw themselves as fighting for the freedom of their race. Blacks provided about ten per cent of the Union army's fighting men and about a fourth of the navy's enlistees. The brave performance of these men in battle did much to dispel prejudices that blacks were inferior to whites, and they proved important to the Union cause.

Border States—Of interest to both the Union and the Confederacy were the **border states,** slave states which did not secede from the Union (Missouri, Kentucky, Maryland, and Delaware). Missouri, despite a miniature civil war among its citizens, remained in the Union. Delaware never seriously considered seceding, and Kentucky, after an initial declaration of neutrality, joined the Union cause.

Maryland was a special case. The loyalty of its citizens was evenly divided, and no one knew for certain which way the state would go. The secession of Maryland, however, would leave Washington, D.C., rather uncomfortably located within the Confederacy. To avoid this risk, Lincoln ordered the virtual military occupation of the state. The national government jailed pro-Confederacy leaders without trial and stationed troops in the secessionist ''hot spots,'' such as Baltimore. Only in the middle of 1862, after the first crisis had passed, did Lincoln order the release of the political prisoners.

Another ''border state'' owed its formation to the Civil War. When Virginia seceded from the Union, citizens in the mountainous western portion of the state refused to follow. With the help of the Union army and the federal government, western Virginia set up its own state government. Despite the fact that the Constitution clearly states that ''no new state shall be formed or erected within the jurisdiction of any other state . . . without the consent of the legislatures of the states concerned'' (Article IV, Section 3), the federal government recognized this pro-Union state, and Congress admitted it to the Union on June 20, 1863, as the state of **West Virginia.**

Lincoln and the Constitution—As the situations in Maryland and West Virginia indicate, the Civil War strained the North's strict obedience to the Constitution. In fact, Lincoln's opponents complained that the president was making himself a dictator by ignoring the Constitution. Lincoln, for example, suspended writs of habeas corpus, meaning that the government could arrest a person without charging him with a crime or bringing him to trial. Such unchecked, sweeping powers led to abuses. A minister in Union-controlled Alexandria, Virginia, for example, was arrested simply for omitting a standard prayer for the president from the service.

Lincoln defended his actions by pointing out that the Constitution allowed suspending writs of habeas corpus ''in cases of rebellion or invasion'' (Article I, Section 9). Critics correctly replied that such power belonged only to Congress, for Article I deals with the power of the legislature and not the president. As the war progressed and the government felt more secure, such arrests became less common, and the prisoners already seized were released. In March 1863, to eliminate all such questions, Congress officially gave the president the power that he had been exercising all along.

Copperheads—One reason for Lincoln's arbitrary actions was his fear of Southern sympathizers in the North. Northerners labeled such men **Copperheads,** after the poisonous snakes of that name. In the border states and the states of Illinois, Indiana, and Ohio particularly, Copperhead sentiment was strong, and paranoid Union sympathizers discerned numerous plots—real and imagined—to destroy the war effort. In reality the Copperheads were not as numerous as the administration feared, and many of them were more interested in securing peace than in directly helping the Southern cause. Their presence, however, was one more constant worry for the Lincoln administration.

Diplomatic Maneuvers

The Civil War was fought largely within the borders of the United States, but its impact was international. The main goal of Southern diplomacy was to persuade a European power—preferably Great Britain—to recognize the independence of the Confederacy, just as France had recognized the United States during the Revolutionary War. The North, obviously, sought to keep Europe out of the affair.

Southern Efforts—Southerners hoped at first that simple economics would force Britain to rec-

ognize the Confederacy. The British textile industry depended heavily on Southern cotton to supply its mills. Surely, the South thought, when the British felt the pinch of losing their source of cotton, they would come to the South's aid. Great Britain, however, was not eager to risk war with the United States over what seemed–to the British, at least–a purely internal American matter. The use of inferior cotton from India and Egypt also enabled the British to do without the South's cotton.

The South came closest to receiving British help not because of its diplomacy but because of Union bungling. In November 1861 an incident on the sea nearly brought Britain into the war on the side of the Confederacy. The Confederate government had commissioned two agents, John Slidell and James Mason, to go to Europe to negotiate for aid. They were sailing on a British mail ship, the *Trent,* when Captain Charles Wilkes of the United States Navy forced the British ship to surrender the agents.

The *Trent* **affair,** as it was called, outraged the British. Britain demanded an apology and the release of Mason and Slidell. Secretary of State Seward released the agents and managed to apologize in a way that satisfied the British but did not offend the Northern public. The Union thus narrowly avoided British intervention.

Ultimately, Britain would recognize the Confederacy only if it thought the South could actually win. This fact led many Southerners to hope that a great military victory would bring Britain to their side, much as the Battle of Saratoga had persuaded France to help the United States during the Revolution. One of the motives for Lee's Maryland campaign, for example, was to win a victory that would impress the British. The uncertain results of the Battle of Antietam, however, dashed those hopes. Despite numerous victories in the early years of the war, the South could never seem to gain the decisive victory that it needed to win the British to its cause.

Emancipation Proclamation—Fear of British intervention was one motive behind Abraham Lincoln's most important diplomatic maneuver of the war. As late as August 22, 1862, Lincoln wrote to newspaper editor Horace Greeley:

Abraham Lincoln meets with General George McClellan and his staff at Antietam following the Union victory there. Success in that battle allowed Lincoln to issue the Emancipation Proclamation.

My paramount object in this struggle is to save the Union, and is not either to save or to destroy slavery. If I could save the Union without freeing any slave I would do it; and if I could save it by freeing all the slaves, I would do it; and if I could do it by freeing some and leaving others alone, I would also do that.

Circumstances, however, forced Lincoln to attack slavery as a means of winning the war. In September 1862, after the Battle of Antietam, Lincoln issued the **Emancipation Proclamation**. As of January 1, 1863, Lincoln declared, all slaves in rebel-controlled territory would be freed. The proclamation, therefore, excluded slaves in the Union's border states and in Confederate territories already under Union control, such as New Orleans. In fact, should the Confederacy surrender by January 1, 1863 (an unlikely event), no slaves would be freed at all. It was, to use Lincoln's words, an attempt to save the Union "by freeing some and leaving others alone."

Although Lincoln opposed slavery and was happy to strike a blow against it, his motives were primarily political. Lincoln had three main purposes in issuing the proclamation. He wanted (1) to keep Britain from recognizing the South by appealing to the strong British antislavery feeling; (2) to encourage blacks to join the war effort and fight for the Union; and (3) to revive flagging spirits in the North by giving Northerners another reason for fighting the war in addition to preserving the Union.

Lincoln achieved his goals. Britain did not recognize the Confederacy, and thousands of blacks joined the Union forces. Although some Northerners initially resisted fighting "to free the slaves," by the end of the war most were describing their fight as a battle for freedom. Lincoln admitted that the Emancipation Proclamation was a war-time emergency act, like his suspending of the habeas corpus, that would expire when the war was over. (Otherwise, of course, the president had no power to make such a sweeping act without the consent of Congress, a fact his opponents repeatedly stressed.) The president knew, however, that whatever happened, those who were freed by the act were not likely to be re-enslaved. Regardless of its limitations, the Emancipation Proclamation was an important step toward the elimination of slavery.

Section Review

1. How did the fact that so many farm hands went off to fight actually help the growth of agriculture in the North?
2. What were the four border states at the beginning of the war?
3. What was the main goal of Southern diplomacy during the Civil War?
4. What event in 1861 nearly brought Great Britain into the war on the side of the Confederacy?
5. What were Lincoln's three main purposes in issuing the Emancipation Proclamation?

Road to Appomattox

War in the Wilderness

After his success in the West, Grant was given field command of Union forces in the East. Grant, however, would learn, according to General Meade, "that Lee and the Army of Northern Virginia are not the same as Bragg and the Army of Tennessee." For Grant and his army, it would be an expensive lesson indeed.

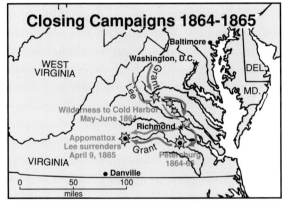

Closing Campaigns 1864-1865

Baltimore

WEST VIRGINIA

Washington, D.C.

DEL.

MD.

Wilderness to Cold Harbor May-June 1864

Richmond

Appomattox Lee surrenders April 9, 1865

Grant

Petersburg 1864-65

VIRGINIA

Danville

0   50   100
miles

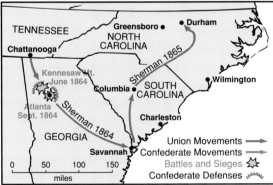

TENNESSEE

Greensboro   Durham

NORTH CAROLINA

Chattanooga

Kennesaw Mt. June 1864

Sherman 1865

Columbia

SOUTH CAROLINA

Wilmington

Atlanta Sept. 1864

Sherman 1864

Charleston

GEORGIA

Savannah

Union Movements →
Confederate Movements →
Battles and Sieges ☆
Confederate Defenses

0   50   100   150
miles

Wilderness Campaign—With a huge force of 122,000 troops, Grant marched south for Richmond. Lee, with half that number, blocked his advance near the scene of his Chancellorsville triumph a year earlier. In the dense woods and tangled underbrush, appropriately called the Wilderness, the two armies began a month-long series of battles that were among the closest, costliest, most desperate of the war.

At the battles of the Wilderness (May 5-6, 1864), Spotsylvania Court House (May 8-12), and the North Anna River (May 16-23), the Confederates dealt punishing blows to the Union forces. Yet Grant kept the pressure on. Unlike previous Union commanders, such as McClellan, Grant did not retreat after a major setback. At Spotsylvania he wrote, "I propose to fight it out along this line if it takes all summer." After successive defeats, however, Grant did break off the fighting and continued to push southward.

"Grant's Slaughter Pen"—At a dusty crossroads called Cold Harbor, east of Richmond, Grant made his costliest mistake of a campaign that was already being termed a continuous "funeral procession." The **Battle of Cold Harbor** (June 1-3) climaxed on the final day with a massive assault on entrenched Confederate positions that left 7,000 Union soldiers dead and dying before the sun was fully up. When the soldiers were ordered to renew

A burial party gathers the grisly remains of the Battle of Cold Harbor.

the suicidal assault, they simply refused. Between the two armies lay acres of bodies, what soldiers from both sides dubbed "Grant's Slaughter Pen."

Cold Harbor capped a month of devastation for the bludgeoned Union army. In four weeks of nearly continuous fighting, Grant had lost more men than Lee had in his entire army. The difference, however, was that Grant could replace his numbers; Lee could not. Every assault on the thin gray lines made them thinner yet. In addition, while the Union supply lines were choked with food and clothing, some Southern soldiers were literally starving. In late May, for example, many Confederates received a ration of only one biscuit, with perhaps a slice of bacon, every two days. Their endurance in the face of such deprivation was a remarkable testimony to their struggle for independence.

War in Georgia

When Grant was made commander of all the Union forces, he left the troops in Chattanooga under the command of his most trusted officer, General **William Tecumseh Sherman.** A tense and excitable man, Sherman had earlier been relieved of a major command in Kentucky in 1861 because of what amounted to a nervous breakdown. Grant, however, believed in Sherman's talents and helped rebuild Sherman's confidence. At Shiloh, Vicksburg, Chattanooga, and other battles, Sherman justified Grant's faith. Now on his own, Sherman sought to prove that he could lead as well as follow. His task was to destroy Joseph Johnston's Southern army and to capture Atlanta, one of the South's most important remaining railroad and manufacturing centers. Sherman approached this job with a grim determination devoid of romanticism and sentiment. "War is cruelty," he said, "and you cannot refine it."

Atlanta Campaign (May-September 1864)—In May 1864 the stern Sherman began his campaign a hundred miles from his goal. Between the Union forces and Atlanta stood a smaller but resolute force under the resourceful General Johnston. A master of defensive tactics, Johnston carefully constructed fortifications of earth, timber, and stone and waited for his adversary to make a mistake. Sherman usually knew better than to attack such strong positions.

General William Tecumseh Sherman

Instead, he used his superior numbers to slip around the flanks of the Southerners and force them to retreat or be overwhelmed. Once, however, at the Battle of Kennesaw Mountain (June 27), an impatient General Sherman ignored his instincts and launched a head-on attack against entrenched Confederate positions. The bloody results quickly forced Sherman back to his original strategy.

Johnston's slow and skillful retreats frustrated Sherman, but they also frustrated Jefferson Davis, who thought that the Southern general was risking the loss of Atlanta. When the Union armies forced Johnston back across the Chattahoochee River just north of Atlanta in July, Davis dismissed the general. He replaced him with the fiery, energetic John B. Hood. True to his reputation as a fighter, Hood attacked the more numerous Union forces in the **Battle of Atlanta** (July 20-22, 1864). The attack surprised Sherman, but the Federals recovered quickly. The valiant Southerners—with a smaller army–suffered greater casualties, more than twice the number of the Northerners. Slowed but not halted, Sherman continued to encircle the city. Faced with destruction if he stayed, Hood abandoned the city on September 2. Sherman sent a jubilant telegram to President Lincoln: "So Atlanta is ours, and fairly won."

The March to the Sea (November-December 1864)–As he sat in Atlanta, Sherman devised an idea to hasten the end of the war. He would march his force across Georgia three hundred miles to Savannah on the coast. Such a march would serve two purposes. First, Sherman's men could destroy food, animals, and other supplies that supported the Confederate army. Second, the march would show Southerners that the Confederacy was rapidly losing the ability to resist. As Sherman himself said, "If the North can march an army right through the South, it is proof positive that the North will prevail." As he prepared what became known as his **"March to the Sea,"** Sherman told his superiors in Washington, "I can make the march, and make Georgia howl!"

Before he could march, however, Sherman had to consider Hood's Confederate army, still loose in Georgia and Alabama. Sherman sent a detachment of 30,000 men under General George Thomas back to Nashville, where further reinforcements waited. Thomas was to watch Hood while Sherman made his march. When Sherman began marching toward Savannah on November 15, Hood launched a desperate invasion of Tennessee. Thomas, showing the firmness he had displayed at Chickamauga, successfully repulsed Hood's attacks. Then at the **Bat-**

Union troops huddle in the siege lines near Petersburg, Virginia. Grant's methodical squeezing of the Confederate lines was slow but certain.

Oliver O. Howard

Oliver O. Howard possessed an impressive résumé. He was a Union general in the Civil War, the head of Howard University and West Point, the director of the Freedman's Bureau in the South after the war (see p. 337), and a peace negotiator with the Indians. Yet, near the conclusion of his autobiography, Howard wrote simply, "It is a fitting close to my life story to lift up my heart in thanksgiving to my Heavenly Father for the mercies and blessings which he has unceasingly showered upon me and mine. . . . His precept—Love the Lord thy God with all thy heart and thy neighbor as thyself—expresses the aim and aspiration of my soul."

Although Howard had attended church all of his life, he had no inner peace. After graduating from West Point in 1854, he was assigned to a lonely outpost at Tampa, Florida. There, through meditating on the verse "the blood of Jesus Christ . . . cleanseth us from all sin" (I John 1:7), Howard was converted. He wrote, "The joy of that night was so great that it would be difficult to attempt in any way to describe it. The next morning everything appeared to me to be changed—the sky was brighter, the trees more beautiful, and the songs of the birds were never before so sweet to my ears."

During the Civil War, Howard fought in more major battles than nearly any other Union general. He participated in First Manassas, Fair Oaks, Second Manassas, Antietam, Fredericksburg, Chancellorsville, and Gettysburg. Then he was transferred to the West where he served under Grant at the Battle of Missionary Ridge and under Sherman in both the Atlanta campaign and the March to the Sea. At Fair Oaks, his right arm was shattered by two bullets and had to be amputated. Afterwards, General Phil Kearny, who had lost his left arm in the Mexican War, tried to comfort Howard. The wounded Howard replied, "There is one thing that we can do, general; we can buy our gloves together!"

As a commander, Howard was deeply concerned with the spiritual needs of his men. He made sure that services were held each Sunday, and the general himself filled in as speaker when a chaplain was not available. General Howard held sessions of prayer and Bible study for his officers, even on the mornings of battles. Howard went about the wounded after battles, attempting to comfort his men. After the Battle of Resaca in northern Georgia, he found a young man in the hospital, obviously dying. Gently, the commander asked if there was anything he could do. The young soldier replied, "Yes, I want

---

tle of Nashville (December 15-16, 1864), the Union forces attacked and completely shattered their foe. Hood's broken army retreated south, no longer a threat to the Northern forces.

Meanwhile, Sherman's men were marching effortlessly through Georgia. They blazed a trail of destruction fifty to sixty miles wide from Atlanta to Savannah. Anything that could be used to support the Confederate war effort—crops, livestock, valuables—was either seized for the Union forces or destroyed. With only loose control from their officers, some men became little more than vandals, wrecking, looting, and pillaging at will. Worse than the

regular troops were the "bummers," an ugly collection of renegades on the fringes of Sherman's army. Most of these bummers were Union deserters, but the group also included some newly freed blacks and even a few Confederate deserters. Under no discipline whatsoever, the bummers committed the worst atrocities of the march—robbery, rape, and murder. Sherman's inability to control his troops would leave a bitter legacy long after the war was over.

When Sherman reached Savannah in December (which he offered as "a Christmas gift" to Lincoln), the general estimated that his army had done

somebody to tell me how to find the Saviour.'' Gladly, Howard shared the gospel with the man and was able to lead him to Christ before the soldier died.

Even those who did not sympathize with Howard's religious views learned to respect him. When the mayor of Columbia, South Carolina, came to General Sherman to ask for help for his devastated city in 1865, the irreligious Sherman replied, ''Go to Howard. Howard runs the religion of this army. Go to him. . . . He will treat you better than one of your own generals.''

$100,000,000 worth of damage. The March to the Sea was a deadly blow to the materiel and morale of the Confederate war effort.

Election of 1864

Sherman's success almost came too late for Abraham Lincoln. Grant's bloody slugfest with Lee in northern Virginia and Sherman's slow advance in northern Georgia were creating weariness with the war in the North. No end to the fighting seemed to be in sight, and by the summer of 1864, Lincoln's chances for re-election looked slim. On August 23, Lincoln wrote, ''This morning, as for some days

past, it seems exceedingly probable that this Administration will not be re-elected.'' Facing Lincoln as the Democratic nominee was none other than George McClellan, former head of the Army of the Potomac. Although McClellan insisted that the Union must be preserved, most members of his party were seeking an end to the war–almost at any price.

The fall of Atlanta to Sherman in September, however, changed the situation. Suddenly, victory looked probable, even certain. War weariness melted in the warmth of military triumph. On election day, Lincoln won 55 per cent of the vote and swamped McClellan 212 to 21 in the electoral college. The election of 1864 guaranteed that the effort to preserve the Union would go on. Interestingly, Lincoln captured 78 per cent of the recorded soldiers' vote against his former general. The Union army was apparently even more united behind the president in the drive for victory.

Confederate Collapse

Siege of Petersburg (July 1864-March 1865)– After Grant's Cold Harbor disaster he continued to move southward, slipped across the James River, and laid a twenty-five-mile-long siege line against Petersburg, Virginia. Petersburg was the major railroad junction that fed into Richmond from the south. If Petersburg fell to the overwhelming Union forces, Richmond would be cut off.

For nine months from July 1864 through March 1865, the two armies eyed each other and tested each other's defenses. Battle deaths and disease took their toll on both sides, but the drain was particularly noticeable in the Confederate ranks where there were no replacements to be had. Supply problems for Lee's army were compounded by the torching of the fertile Shenandoah Valley by Union forces. In addition the situation in the Carolinas was quickly sealing the fate of the Confederates. From Savannah, Sherman marched his army north through the Carolinas, wreaking the same havoc there that he had in Georgia. Although General Joseph Johnston was doing his best to pull together an effective fighting force, he could only harass Sherman's army, not stop it. The Union forces pushed north, leaving destruction and bitterness in its wake.

Furling the Flag, *by Richard N. Brooke, The West Point Museum, United States Military Academy, West Point, New York*

Furling the Flags

When the proud and sensitive sons of Dixie came to a full realization of the truth that the Confederacy was overthrown and their leader had been compelled to surrender his once invincible army, they could no longer control their emotions, and tears ran like water down their shrunken faces. The flags which they still carried were objects of undisguised affection. These Southern banners had gone down before overwhelming numbers, and torn by shells, riddled by bullets, and laden with the powder and smoke of battle, they aroused intense emotion in the men who had so often followed them to victory. Yielding to overpowering sentiment, these high-mettled men began to tear the flags from the staffs and hide them in their bosoms, as they wet them with burning tears.

From General John B. Gordon's eyewitness account of the Confederates at Appomattox

On April 1, 1865, when the fall of Petersburg was imminent, it was clear that Lee's only hope was to slip out of the siege and link up with Johnston in North Carolina. Jefferson Davis and his cabinet abandoned Richmond for Danville in southern Virginia. The Confederate army also made a desperate attempt to reach the rail lines first at Danville and then Lynchburg. At every turn they were cut off by Grant's encircling army.

Some urged Lee to send his soldiers into scattered units to conduct guerrilla warfare. But Lee would have no part in creating a legacy of bitterness. Sadly he told his men he was "compelled to yield to overwhelming numbers and resources" and he was "determined to avoid the useless sacrifice of those whose past services have endeared them to their countrymen."

Appomattox (April 1865)—On Palm Sunday, April 9, 1865, Lee met Grant at **Appomattox Court House,** Virginia, where they agreed on the terms of surrender for the Army of Northern Virginia. Grant, recalling his impression of their meeting, later wrote that he felt "sad and depressed. I felt anything rather than rejoicing at the downfall of a foe who had fought so long and so valiantly." Grant's generous terms–basically that the Confederates would lay down their weapons and go home–gave an unbowed Lee the opportunity to surrender with honor. He appreciatively accepted Grant's offer.

When word spread of Lee's surrender, the noise of celebration and gun salutes erupted throughout the Union lines. Grant, however, quickly ordered the commotion to cease. "The war is over," the General said. "The Rebels are our countrymen again."

Bitter Harvest

Appomattox closed the bloodiest chapter in American history. More Americans died during the War Between the States than in all other wars *combined* from 1775 to 1975, from the Revolution through Vietnam. Over 650,000 men died in the four-year War of Brothers. Tens of thousands would be maimed for life.

One closing casualty occurred five days after Appomattox. On Good Friday, April 14, a crazed

Casualties

Union Armed Forces

Army

Killed in action/mortally wounded	110,100
Died of disease	224,580
Died as prisoners of war	30,192
Nonbattle deaths	24,881
Wounded in action	275,175

Navy

Killed in action/mortally wounded	1,804
Died of disease/accident	3,000
Wounded in action	2,226

Total Union Casualties: 671,958

Confederate Armed Forces

Army

Killed in action/mortally wounded	94,000
Died of disease	164,000
Died as prisoners of war	31,000
Wounded in action	194,026

Navy

No figures available.

Total Confederate Casualties: 483,026

actor named John Wilkes Booth shot President Lincoln in Ford's theater in Washington. At his last cabinet meeting on the day he was assassinated, Lincoln had extended his hand to the fallen South. According to a cabinet member, the president had warned that "there were men in Congress who . . . possessed feelings of hate and vindictiveness in which he did not sympathize and could not participate." In restoring the Confederate states to the Union, Lincoln had wanted "no persecution, no bloody work." Cut down in the hour of his triumph, Lincoln became part martyr, part myth after his death. The new leadership that Booth's bullet provided the nation, however, little understood Lincoln, the man. With Lincoln gone, the hateful and vindictive men would have their way in the South.

In Jefferson Davis's last address to his beleaguered citizens, written from his last capital at Danville in those final desperate days in April, he urged, "Let us not then despond, my countrymen, but, relying on the never failing mercies and pro-

tecting care of our God, let us meet the foe with fresh defiance, with unconquered and unconquerable hearts." Across the South, that was about all that had not been conquered. It was an impoverished land of widows and orphans where the wounds of war were nursed in bitterness until the scars became badges of pride. Ahead of the country lay a long and difficult road to national healing.

Section Review

1. Why were the casualties in the eastern campaigns of 1864-1865 harder on Lee's army than on Grant's even though Grant's losses were greater?
2. Why did Jefferson Davis replace Joseph Johnston as commander of the Confederate forces in Georgia?
3. What were Sherman's two purposes in launching the March to the Sea?
4. What military victory helped Abraham Lincoln win the election of 1864?

Chapter Review

Terms

states' rights	Battle of Antietam	Battle of Missionary Ridge
Anaconda Plan	Battle of Fredericksburg	blockade runners
Thomas J. Jackson	Battle of Chancellorsville	conscription
First Battle of Manassas	Battle of Gettysburg	New York draft riot
George B. McClellan	Pickett's Charge	border states
Peninsular Campaign	Gettysburg Address	West Virginia
Army of the Potomac	Ulysses S. Grant	Copperheads
ironclad	Fort Henry	*Trent* affair
Merrimac	Fort Donelson	Emancipation Proclamation
Monitor	Battle of Shiloh	Wilderness Campaign
Valley Campaign	David G. Farragut	Battle of Cold Harbor
Army of Northern Virginia	Vicksburg	William Tecumseh Sherman
Joseph E. Johnston	George Thomas	Battle of Atlanta
Robert E. Lee	Braxton Bragg	March to the Sea
Seven Days' Battles	Battle of Perryville	Battle of Nashville
J.E.B. Stuart	Battle of Stones River	siege of Petersburg
Second Battle of Manassas	Battle of Chickamauga	Appomattox Court House

Content Questions

1. List the Union and Confederate commanders at each of the following battles: Second Manassas, Antietam, Fredericksburg, Gettysburg. What Southern advantage at the beginning of the war does this list illustrate?
2. What was the most important result of the Battle of Fair Oaks during the Peninsular Campaign?
3. What two battles ended Lee's two attempts to carry the war into Northern territory?
4. Why was life on the home front more difficult in the South than in the North?
5. What were the two ways in which a man could exempt himself from the draft?
6. Why did many state governments in the South oppose conscription?
7. How did the Lincoln administration keep Maryland in the Union?
8. Name at least one act of the Lincoln administration that opponents considered unconstitutional.
9. Why did the South assume at first that Great Britain would come to its aid?

10. Identify the battle described by each of the following phrases.
   a. worst Union defeat in the western campaigns
   b. a technical Union "victory" which Lincoln used as the basis for issuing the Emancipation Proclamation
   c. opened Georgia to invasion from Tennessee
   d. "Grant's Slaughter Pen"
   e. Albert Sidney Johnston surprises Grant
   f. Lee pushes McClellan back from within sight of Richmond

Application Questions

1. Why did the South think it was right in the Civil War? Why did the North think it was right?
2. Consider William Sherman's statement: "War is cruelty, and you cannot refine it." Do you think this statement is true? What are the potential dangers in this attitude?
3. Review Chaplain J. W. Jones's follow-up of the 410 converts he baptized during the Civil War (pp. 302-3). What do his findings indicate concerning the genuineness of the conversions of the Confederate soldiers during the revivals?

PERSPECTIVES
Photography

The Face of America

It has been suggested that photography "imprisons time in a rectangle," and plainly the camera has done more to preserve and popularize the past than anything else since the invention of the printing press. But photography has not only captured the panorama of great events and the portraits of great men; it has also kept for us the common faces and places of life long ago. The United States, being a relatively young country among the community of nations, has enjoyed the benefit of having the camera for much of its existence.

In the late 1830s Frenchman Louis Daguerre and Englishman William Henry Talbot developed photography independently. The early photographers were part chemist, part artist, and all pioneer. The process, first described by Talbot as photogenic drawing, was a struggle with salts and silvers, glass, paper, and iron to create a light-sensitive surface upon which images could be fixed permanently. Because of the long exposure times, the first photographs were mainly still lifes or pictures of buildings. Portraits were difficult, for even when the subjects were kept in bright sunlight with their faces powdered with flour, exposure time still lasted several minutes. Improvements came rapidly in the 1840s, however, and "daguerrian artists" set up shop or roved the countryside on both sides of the Atlantic. Families of modest means, who could never afford to have portraits painted, could now own whole albums of pictures that were in

An ambrotype (c. 1860) captures
the delicate features of three children
whose names have been lost to time.

Perspectives

many ways more realistic than the best portraits. Photographers such as Mathew Brady, Alexander Gardner, and Alfred Stieglitz became renowned for their work in capturing the great American experiences of war and expansion.

Yet photography remained the work of photographers, for only professionals had equipment and experience enough for the delicate art of picture taking. By the 1880s, however, two factors had changed that: the development of faster shutter speeds made hand-held cameras possible, and the introduction of roll film by George Eastman made photography affordable. Eastman's famous Kodak camera, invented in 1888, was an instant success. The camera had now become an important tool of popular culture and an accessible means of personal expression. Photography not only recorded the face of America; it changed it as well.

An ambrotype was essentially a glass negative with a layer of black-coated glass beneath to complete the image. The fragile ambrotypes and daguerreotypes were usually packaged in ornate cases.

These carte-de-visite *photographs, or CDVs, from the 1860s show a young lady from Galena, Illinois, and a young man from Lexington, Kentucky. Unlike bulky glass images, CDVs were easy to handle and affordable.*

The original *daguerreotype* used a silver-coated copper plate to capture the image. Daguerre's process, after some improvement, used other surfaces such as glass (known as an ambrotype) and enameled iron (called a ferrotype or tintype). The ambrotype and tintype enjoyed wide popularity in the United States from the 1850s through the 1870s.

The smooth enameled metal of the tintype permitted a very sharp image that could also be hand-tinted.

This Wilmington, North Carolina, couple found the bigger format cabinet photograph well suited for capturing their large brood.

George Eastman, shown here in 1890 with an early Kodak camera, revolutionized photography.

Paper photographs first developed by the Englishman Talbot were based on the negative process and could therefore be reproduced (unlike the daguerreotype, in which each image is unique). By the 1860s small paper photographs called *carte-de-visite* (French for ''visiting card'') became the craze. People could now exchange pictures with friends and family. For families separated by great distances, photographs provided an important link. A larger style paper image known as a cabinet photograph gradually replaced the carte-de-visite, but by 1890 both styles were largely swept aside by Eastman's remarkable Kodak.

The first Kodak cameras were loaded with film by the Eastman Company. After a roll was exposed, the entire camera was mailed back so that the film could be unloaded and processed. By the time of this turn-of-the century Kodak "Brownie" camera, improvements permitted amateurs the ease of loading and unloading their own film.

The stereoscope, which provided a three-dimensional view of interesting and faraway places, made photography a form of popular home entertainment from the late nineteenth century and into the early twentieth century.

The Face of War

Cameras saw limited use in the Mexican War and Britain's Crimean War (1854-1856), but their first significant use came during the Civil War. Mathew Brady and his skilled assistants, such as Alexander Gardner and Timothy O'Sullivan, photographed not only the generals and their foot soldiers but also the battlefields strewn with the human debris of death—forever changing the way we view war. After viewing photographs of the dead at Antietam, a *New York Times* reporter wrote in the October 20, 1862, edition:

> Mr. Brady has done something to bring home to us the terrible reality and earnestness of war. If he has not brought bodies and laid them on our dooryards and along the streets, he has done something very like it.

Oliver Wendell Holmes, after seeing the photographs of the aftermath of Gettysburg, wrote,

> It was so nearly like visiting the battlefield to look over these views, that all the emotions excited by the actual sight of the stained and sordid scene, strewed with rags and wrecks, came back to us, and we buried them in the recesses of our cabinet as we would have buried the mutilated remains of the dead they too vividly represented.

Death in Devil's Den, Gettysburg, July 1863. This photograph by Alexander Gardner, supposedly of a Confederate sharpshooter, is one of the most famous images of the war. Gardner, however, just ahead of the burial party, dragged the corpse on a blanket from a nearby field where he had earlier photographed the body under the title of a Union sharpshooter.

Private James Allen Oakes, 38th Virginia Infantry, wounded in action during Pickett's Charge, died at Gettysburg July 15, 1863

Private Edwin Francis Jemison, 2nd Louisiana Regiment, killed at Malvern Hill, July 1, 1862

Corporal Nailer, 13th Pennsylvania Cavalry, with his model 1840 dragoon saber, a cumbersome weapon the horsemen often referred to as "old wristbreaker"

Michigan volunteer

The aftermath of war: Ruins of the Gallego Flour Mills, Richmond, Virginia, 1865. Photograph by Mathew Brady.

Edward Curtis's captivating portrait of a Mojave girl named Mosa. Curtis noted, ''She had the eyes of a fawn as it emerges from the forest, questioning all the strange sights, sounds, and colors of civilization.''

The Face of the Frontier

As the frontier slipped beneath the wagon wheels and steel rails of the American advance, photographers were present to capture the fleeting images. Edward Curtis for example devoted thirty years of his life to photographing the western Indians. Curtis, born on a farm near Whitewater, Wisconsin, was early on driven by the realization that the white man's advance was destroying or altering the diverse Indian cultures of the Plains and Pacific region. Curtis's two thousand published images of eighty different tribes is the most impressive and extensive visual documentation of America's vanished cultures.

Like Curtis, William Henry Jackson was a pioneer photographer of the American West. The energetic Jackson, whose life spanned ninety-nine years, captured the grand beauty of the West, from Yellowstone to Yosemite. His influential work, in fact, spurred Congress to establish national parks to preserve facets of the wilderness as a national treasure.

In this Curtis photograph, Atsina warriors of the Blackfoot alliance gather, recalling war councils of earlier years.

Photographing in high places. William Henry Jackson in Lincoln County, Wyoming, as part of a U.S. Geological and Geographical Survey of the Territories, 1872.

The Face of Change

Photographers such as Lewis Hine, who took this picture of a young girl working in a Carolina textile mill, heightened awareness of the problems of child labor.

The camera's work was not universally welcomed. Some artists and philosophers objected to the way photography replaced idealism with realism. The French poet and critic Charles Baudelaire complained, "Our squalid society rushed, Narcissus to a man, to gaze at its trivial image on a scrap of metal." Ironically, despite his bitter observations, a number of photographs of Baudelaire survive. His views and those of other critics were soon swept aside by the advance of photography which forever changed the way we see the world. By the late nineteenth century, photographers were raising the realism of the camera to the level of art and social expression. Faster shutter speeds fixed on film the quickening pace of modern life.

"Lodgers in a Crowded Bayard Street Tenement: Five cents a Spot." Jacob Riis's photographs of the slum squalor in New York's Lower East Side encouraged housing and sanitation legislation.

Empire State Building construction, 1930. As the city touched the sky the camera was present to capture the event.

CHAPTER 15

Reconstruction (1865-1877)

"May God forgive, unite and bless us all."

*Inscription on a rocking chair given by a Union
veteran to a Confederate acquaintance*

Black-draped women in mourning walk amid the ruins of Richmond, April 1865.

On March 4, 1865, Abraham Lincoln closed his Second Inaugural Address with a plea for Americans to put away past hatreds and to unite for the healing of the nation:

> With malice toward none, with charity for all, with firmness in the right as God gives us to see the right, let us strive on to finish the work we are in, to bind up the nation's wounds, to care for him who shall have borne the battle and for his widow and his orphan, to do all which may achieve and cherish a just and lasting peace among ourselves and with all nations.

A little more than a month later, John Wilkes Booth's bullet forever prevented Americans from learning whether Lincoln could have achieved these noble goals. Instead, to Lincoln's vice president, **Andrew Johnson,** fell the task of "binding up the nation's wounds."

The period from 1865 to 1877 is usually known as the era of **Reconstruction.** In its narrowest sense, *Reconstruction* refers to the national government's attempts to rebuild the South after the war. Such recovery was not easy, and Southerners understandably resented many aspects of Reconstruction rule. In a broader sense, Reconstruction refers to changes in the whole nation. The nation that went into the war in 1861 was not the same nation that emerged from Reconstruction in 1877. In particular, the nature of the federal government and its relationship to the states changed dramatically from the relationship intended by the Founding Fathers. For good or ill, Reconstruction shifted the direction of the growth of the American nation.

President Andrew Johnson

Struggle over Reconstruction

Plans for Reconstruction

The obvious question facing the national government was how to treat and administer the Southern states after the war was won. Events soon proved that there was little agreement in the North as to what policy should be followed.

Lincoln's Ten Per Cent Plan—In 1863 Lincoln formulated his **"ten per cent" plan** for restoring the South. As the Union army pushed into the South, Lincoln appointed a military governor for each controlled state. The governor was then to re-establish civilian government as soon as ten per cent of the citizens who had voted in 1860 had taken an oath of allegiance to the Union. Lincoln also intended to grant presidential pardons to many Confederate leaders. This was in many ways a fairly lenient plan.

Radicals' View—Opposing Lincoln in Congress was a group known as the **Radical Republicans.** Although only a minority within the Re-

An Old Warrior's Last Campaign

The fate of Confederate leaders after the war was an uncertain matter. At first, many Northerners—especially after the assassination of Lincoln—called for treason trials and hangings. After his capture, Jefferson Davis, who probably suffered the most of any Confederate leader, found himself shackled in chains within a cell at Fort Monroe, Virginia. He was released in 1867, however, and granted amnesty in 1868. Northern passions quickly cooled, and most former Confederate leaders quietly began to put their lives back together.

The greatest Southern soldier entered into an entirely new career. After Appomattox, Robert E. Lee wondered what he would do to support himself and his family. An answer came with an offer from a little school in Lexington, Virginia: Would Lee consider becoming president of tiny Washington College? The institution was admittedly in poor shape. It had only forty students, and its buildings were in disrepair. Its presidency was hardly the most prestigious position that the South could offer its greatest hero.

Lee, however, accepted. Rebuilding this school seemed to embody in a small way the general's desire to see the whole South rebuilt and reestablished. Lee oversaw the repair and restoration of the campus. He broadened the school's curriculum to make it more flexible in order to accommodate the changing eco-

publican party, the Radicals were highly influential. The Radical view of Reconstruction was set forth in 1864 in the **Wade-Davis Bill.** This bill required military governors for each Southern state until a majority of all adult white males, rather than just ten per cent of those who had voted in 1860, had signed an oath of allegiance. The bill also demanded several provisions for new state constitutions: the denial of suffrage (the right to vote) and political offices to all former Confederate leaders,

nomic needs of the South. He administered the school in a fair and firm manner, always displaying his characteristic gentlemanly restraint and kindness. In dealing with a student who had cut classes to go hunting, President Lee did not scold. Instead he said gently, "Yesterday was such a pretty day, and you would kill the birds that enjoy the day so much. I don't think I would do so again." Under Lee's guidance, Washington College grew from forty students to four hundred.

Lee's Christian character was plainly evident in Lexington. Every day the president faithfully took his seat for morning chapel. During the war, General Lee had encouraged

prayer meetings and preaching among his soldiers. President Lee continued to promote the faith among his students. Lee once told a local pastor, "Oh, Doctor, if I could only know that all of the young men in the college were good Christians, I should have nothing more to desire!"

Lee also manifested his Christian character by laying aside bitterness and hatred after the war. He once told a young lady, "I believe I may say, looking into my own heart, and speaking as in the presence of God, that I have never known one moment of bitterness or resentment." On hearing a faculty member speak insultingly of U. S. Grant, Lee–with a rare flash of anger–said, "Sir, if you ever again presume to speak disrespectfully of General Grant in my presence, either you or I will sever his connection with this university."

Five years of toil in behalf of the college wore down the health of the old soldier. He collapsed one evening in 1870 while preparing to say grace before a meal and died a few days later. His last words–an old marching order–were "Strike the tent." His words seemed to both wander back to the gallant war years and commence his final glorious march.

The college trustees honored the general by changing the name of the school he had rebuilt. Washington and Lee College (now a university) became a memorial to *two* of the noblest sons of Virginia.

Joseph Johnston and Robert E. Lee meet after the war.

the abolition of slavery, and the repudiation of Confederate war debts (that is, the refusal of the federal government to pay the debts the Confederate states had incurred during the war). No state was to be readmitted until it had fulfilled these requirements. Lincoln vetoed the bill.

The Wade-Davis Bill clearly showed that the Radical Republicans did not view the South's

status as Lincoln did. Lincoln held that since the South could not legally secede, it was still in the Union. His plan was to restore the rebellious members. The Radicals, on the other hand, viewed the South as a conquered enemy. The leading Radical in the House of Representatives, Pennsylvania's Thaddeus Stevens, viewed the Southern states as "conquered provinces" under the direct authority of Congress. Charles Sumner, the Senate's leading Radical, believed that the Southern states had "committed suicide" and had ceased to exist. Sumner's view, however, was too radical even for the Radicals.

The motives of the Radicals were a mixture of idealistic sentiment, bitter hatred, and crass political opportunism. Some Radicals undeniably believed that only a strict policy of Reconstruction would secure and protect the rights of blacks in the South. Others, as illustrated by Thaddeus Stevens, seemed at times to have no higher motive than simple revenge. Many Republicans thought that a heavy-handed policy would ensure Republican control of the region and, in turn, Republican control of the nation.

Johnson's Plan—After Lincoln's assassination, all eyes turned to Andrew Johnson to see what course he would take. Like Lincoln, Johnson was born in poverty and had risen through sheer hard work and dogged determination. He was illiterate until he married a schoolteacher who taught him to read and write. A Democratic senator from Tennessee when the war broke out, Johnson remained loyal to the Union, and he served as provisional governor of the state after it was captured by the Northern armies. The Republicans added Johnson to their ticket in 1864 in hopes that, as a Southerner and a Democrat, he would broaden the ticket's appeal and help promote unity when the war ended. In addition to his accomplishments, however, Johnson had a streak of stubbornness and a short temper.

Johnson's plan for Reconstruction was a modification of Lincoln's. Like the latter, it based readmission on the allegiance of ten per cent of those who had voted in 1860, but it proposed a stricter policy on qualifications for Southern leadership and on pardons for ex-Confederates than had Lincoln's plan. Further, Johnson believed—like Lincoln—that the responsibility for Reconstruction belonged to the president rather than to Congress. As a result, Reconstruction became, in part, a struggle for power between the legislative and executive branches.

President vs. Congress

Division in Washington—Because Congress was not in session when Johnson took office and would not be for several months, the new president decided to proceed with Reconstruction by himself. If he "reconstructed" the South before Congress met, Johnson believed that the congressmen would have to go along. When Congress met, however, it rejected Johnson's moves. It refused to seat members from the newly "reconstructed" states and sought to take control of the Reconstruction process.

At this point, Johnson's temper caused him to blunder. Democrats in Congress, along with some conservative and moderate Republicans, were still willing to work with the president. Johnson, however, launched into a speaking tour defending his plan. In a series of poor performances, the president alienated the Northern public. He got into shouting matches with hecklers in the crowds, and, in one tasteless display, compared his enemies to Judas Iscariot and himself to Jesus Christ! As Johnson's unpopularity grew, more Republicans drifted into the Radical camp.

Congress Acts—In the congressional elections of 1866, the Republicans gained over two-thirds of the seats in both houses of Congress, more than enough to override any vetoes Johnson might issue. The Radicals acted quickly to limit the power of the president and to seize control of the Reconstruction process. Among the bills passed over Johnson's veto were the Military Reconstruction Act (discussed later) and the **Tenure of Office Act,** which forbade the president from dismissing cabinet members without the consent of the Senate.

The Radicals intended the Tenure of Office Act to protect Secretary of War Edwin Stanton, the most important Radical in the cabinet. Johnson thought the act unconstitutional. (The Supreme Court eventually agreed with him.) Furthermore, he disliked the vain, difficult Stanton and viewed him as a Radical spy. Johnson therefore tested the act by dismissing the secretary of war. Stanton responded by literally barricading himself in his office. The president's action delighted the Radicals because it gave them an opportunity to get rid of the obstructive Johnson.

Impeachment—The Radicals began to agitate for Johnson's **impeachment,** or indictment by the House of Representatives. Impeachment would

The Senate committee for President Johnson's impeachment (left) and a facsimile of an admission ticket to the impeachment hearings (right)

then be followed by trial before the Senate. If convicted by the Senate, Johnson would be removed from office, and Benjamin Wade, president pro tempore of the Senate and a leading Radical, would become president. In February 1868 the House of Representatives presented a list of formal charges against Johnson and voted to impeach him. The main charge was Johnson's violation of the Tenure of Office Act by dismissing Stanton. The recommendation went to the Senate, where the case against Johnson was tried.

Many political leaders questioned the wisdom of removing Johnson for what was in reality no greater "crime" than disagreeing with the Radicals about the best means of Reconstruction. Such an act would reduce the president to a servant of Congress and potentially destroy the balance between the branches of government. When the final vote was tallied, the count stood at 35 to 19 to convict—exactly one vote short of the two-thirds needed to remove Johnson from office. Seven Republicans risked their political careers to follow their consciences and joined twelve Democrats in voting for acquittal. Saved from removal but still at odds with Congress, Johnson rode out the rest of his term quietly and did not again attempt to take control of the Reconstruction process.

Amending the Constitution

Although Congress passed many important pieces of legislation during the Reconstruction pe-

riod, the most far-reaching were three amendments to the Constitution. The Thirteenth Amendment (ratified 1865), the Fourteenth Amendment (1868), and the Fifteenth Amendment (1870) are often known collectively as the "Reconstruction amendments." No set of amendments, with the exception of the first ten (the Bill of Rights), have proved so influential in American life.

Thirteenth Amendment—Before the war, Senator Crittenden of Kentucky had attempted to avoid the conflict by proposing a thirteenth amendment to the Constitution that would permanently *protect* the institution of slavery. Crittenden's amendment failed to pass. Ironically, when a thirteenth amendment was actually adopted, it *prohibited* slavery. The **Thirteenth Amendment** eliminated the last traces of slavery in the border states and climaxed the work of abolition begun by the Emancipation Proclamation.

Fourteenth Amendment—The Thirteenth Amendment freed the slaves, but questions remained about the legal status of blacks. Congress therefore sought to define the rights of all citizens, including blacks, in the **Fourteenth Amendment**. The amendment contained three important provisions. First, it granted blacks full citizenship in both the United States and the states in which they lived. Second, it applied to the states the Constitution's provision that the federal government may not deprive any person "of life, liberty, or property, without due process of law." This provision virtually invalidated the Tenth Amendment, which reserved to the states all powers not directly delegated to the national government, when courts later interpreted this clause to give the federal government increased authority over the states. Third, the amendment prohibited all former Confederate leaders from holding any office unless first approved by a two-thirds majority of the House and Senate. Because of the way that it increased the power of the national government, the Fourteenth Amendment proved to be the most important and most influential of the three Reconstruction amendments.

Fifteenth Amendment—During Reconstruction, Southerners claimed that the North was being hypocritical in forcing the South to give the vote to blacks when, as late as 1868, only eleven Northern states had legalized black suffrage. Republican leaders agreed with the logic of this complaint and sought vainly to convince other Northern states to give black males the same voting rights as white males. After most of these efforts failed, Congress passed the **Fifteenth Amendment,** which stated clearly, ''The right of the citizens of the United States to vote shall not be denied or abridged by the United States or by any state on account of race, color, or previous condition of servitude.''

These three amendments—the Thirteenth (abolition of slavery), Fourteenth (guarantee of citizen rights), and Fifteenth (guarantee of voting rights)—are the most lasting heritage of the Reconstruction period. Their full impact would not be felt, however, until after the middle of the twentieth century.

Section Review

1. How did Lincoln's ten per cent plan differ from the Radicals' Wade-Davis Bill concerning the number of white males taking the oath of allegiance?
2. What is *suffrage?*
3. How did Johnson test the Tenure of Office Act? How did the Radicals respond to his action?
4. Why did seven Republican senators vote for President Johnson's acquittal at his impeachment?
5. What were the three important provisions of the Fourteenth Amendment?

Reconstruction in the South

At the end of the Civil War, the South lay devastated. Nearly 300,000 Southern men had died in the war in battle, in prison camps, or from disease. The economy of the South was in a shambles, devastated by the heavy fighting that had taken place throughout the region. One observer described Charleston, South Carolina, as the scene of ''vacant houses, of widowed women, of rotting wharves, of deserted warehouses, of weed-wild gardens, of miles of grass-grown streets, of acres of pitiful and voiceless barrenness.'' Some Northern observers touring the region said that morale was so low that Southerners would accept almost any government that the North chose to impose on them. Andrew Johnson's lenient approach, however, encouraged the South. Perhaps, thought Southerners, recovery would not be as painful as they had thought. Then, when the Radicals took control of Reconstruction from the president, the South faced harsher policies. Leniency followed by strictness only embittered the South and strengthened the region's will to resist. Reconstruction was not off to a good start.

Reconstruction Rule

Military Reconstruction Act—At the same time it passed the Tenure of Office Act, Congress passed the **Military Reconstruction Act.** This legislation more or less imposed military occupation on the South, like the army of a conquering nation occupying a defeated foe. Tennessee was exempted from this law because it had already ratified the Fourteenth Amendment and had been ''reconstructed.'' The act divided the remaining ten former states of the Confederacy into five military districts. Each district was headed by a military governor (usually a general in the Union army) appointed by the president. Congress instructed the governors to keep peace in the South, through federal troops and military courts if necessary. The act also required each state to write a new constitution providing for universal male suffrage regardless of color and to pass the Fourteenth Amendment. (Later legislation added passage of the Fifteenth Amendment to the requirements.) Only when a state fulfilled all of these requirements would it be considered ''reconstructed.'' Then the army would be removed and the state's representatives admitted to Congress.

Freedman's Bureau—One of the most important agencies in Southern Reconstruction was the **Freedman's Bureau,** founded in 1865 to provide help to the newly freed slaves. The Bureau originally concerned itself with aiding blacks in the South—distributing food and clothing and building schools for black children. When Congress took control of Reconstruction, the Bureau became a channel for Radical Reconstruction. When Congress decided that state courts in the South were not being fair to blacks, for example, it set up ''Freedman's United States Courts'' administered by the Bureau. These Bureau courts protected the rights of the freedmen, but the Bureau offended Southerners by overriding local courts.

The Bureau also sought to counteract the **Black Codes** passed by President Johnson's ''recon-structed'' states immediately after the war. These codes were attempts to regulate the conduct of the former slaves, often in an unfair manner. For example, they allowed blacks to be jailed for vagrancy (lack of self-support) much more easily than whites. The extremes of some of the codes created the most controversy. When South Carolina and Mississippi, for instance, allowed courts to hire out convicted black vagrants to plantations to work off their fines, Northerners believed that the South was actually trying to re-establish slavery. The codes likewise prohibited blacks from voting, holding office, or serving on juries. Southerners defended the codes by arguing that the uneducated former slaves could be easily manipulated and thus should not have the right to vote. Northerners replied that denial of the right to vote was hardly a long-range solution. Unless blacks were treated as full-fledged citizens, they would sink into an endless cycle of failure.

Former slaves gather in a school run by the Freedman's Bureau. Education was one of the benefits the Bureau brought to blacks in the postwar South.

Carpetbaggers and Scalawags—By denying the vote to many former Confederates, a coalition of blacks and white Radical Republicans was able to elect Radical governments in the South. The majority of white Southerners opposed the Radical Republican governments. They called Northern Radicals who moved to the South "**carpetbaggers**," after the cheap luggage made out of carpet in which most of them supposedly brought all their belongings. Southern Radicals were known as "**scalawags**." Not all of these men were as low and corrupt as the white majority claimed. Some carpetbaggers had come south from idealistic motives, such as aiding in the region's recovery. Likewise most scalawags had been pro-Union men since before the War Between the States, and their behavior was not at all inconsistent with their political beliefs. However, the corruption of many Radicals, the dishonest ways in which the Radicals kept power, and the association of Radical rule with black rights all combined to embitter most Southerners against Radical rule.

Evaluation—How good or bad were the Reconstruction governments? Many were undeniably corrupt, as men sought to use political power to enrich themselves. The Radical legislature of South Carolina, for example, voted a bonus of $1,000 to its speaker of the house after he had lost that amount betting on a horse race. Corruption, however, was not limited to the "carpetbaggers" of the South in this era. The scandals of the Grant administration and the corruption of Tammany Hall in New York (both discussed in the next section) demonstrate that corruption was fairly widespread. In fact, some of the Southern state governments after Reconstruction were just as bad as those of the Radicals.

The Radical governments in the South could also point with pride to some accomplishments. They enacted universal manhood suffrage; organized public school systems; and rebuilt roads, railroads, and other transportation systems destroyed by the war. Even at their best, however, the Radical governments still relied on the military might of the army and the **disfranchisement** (denial of the right to vote) of many Southern whites to stay in

Hiram Revels

When Congress met in January 1870, a new member drew an unusual amount of attention. He was Hiram Revels, senator from Mississippi and the first black to serve in the United States Congress.

Hiram Revels was born to free black parents in Fayetteville, North Carolina, in 1822. Because higher education was closed to blacks in North Carolina at that time, he moved to the Midwest, where he attended schools in Indiana, Ohio, and Illinois. Revels became a minister in the African Methodist Episcopal Church, the black denomination founded by Richard Allen (see p. 233). He preached and taught in the Midwest and the

power. It was basically a government imposed against the will of the majority. As one Republican said, "We cannot always control these states by the bayonet." When the bayonet was removed, the Radical governments collapsed quickly.

Southern Reactions

As different people in the South confronted the difficulties of Reconstruction, they reacted in a va-

border states and at the outbreak of the Civil War was pastoring in Baltimore.

Revels first came to Mississippi in 1864 to preach to the blacks and to help care for the needs of the freed slaves. He was elected to the state senate in 1868 on the Radical Republican ticket. Revels, as a minister, was asked to give the prayer of the opening session of the legislature. His rich voice, dignified presence, and polished manner impressed his fellow legislators. Revels seemed to them to be an ideal choice for an important symbolic role–the first black to serve in Congress. He was elected to finish the last year of an unexpired Senate term.

Serving only a year in the Senate obviously meant that Revels's importance was more symbolic than real. As a result, his legislative role was limited. He successfully persuaded the War Department to hire qualified black mechanics in the United States Navy Yard and spoke out against segregation in the schools of Washington, D.C., but none of the bills he presented to Congress passed. Revels in fact disappointed some of the Radicals by his conservatism. Although he supported the presence of the army in the South, because he believed that only the army could protect the rights of blacks in the region, Revels opposed efforts to deprive former Confederates of the vote. Having seen his own people deprived of the right to vote because of their race, Revels could not see the justice in depriving others of the vote because of their political views.

After his term of office ended, Revels returned to Mississippi. He served as president of Alcorn College, a black college in the state, and a brief term as Mississippi's secretary of state. Revels became increasingly disgusted with the corruption of Radical rule in Mississippi, however. In 1875 he surprised the nation when he resigned from the Republican party and called for an end to Reconstruction in the South. In a widely published letter to President Grant, he complained that blacks were being used as ''mere tools'' by the Republicans to keep power. ''If the state administration had adhered to Republican principles, advanced patriotic measures, appointed only honest and competent men to office, and sought to restore confidence between the races,'' he wrote, ''bloodshed would have been unknown, peace would have prevailed, Federal interference been unthought of; harmony, friendship, and mutual confidence would have taken the place of the bayonet.''

After retiring from the presidency of Alcorn due to health problems, Revels returned to the ministry. He spent his last years preaching and died in 1901 while attending a church conference in Mississippi.

riety of ways. Some lashed out in blind violence. Others dedicated themselves to regaining self-rule for the states of the region. Many avoided political questions altogether and concentrated simply on surviving.

Extremism–Denied participation in the political process, some former Confederates turned to violence to express their opinions. Groups of white vigilantes terrorized parts of the South, directing their wrath against carpetbaggers, scalawags, and particularly blacks. The most important of these extremist groups was the **Ku Klux Klan.** Dressed in white hoods and robes that supposedly made them look like ghosts, klansmen rode about at night threatening blacks to keep them from exercising their newly gained political rights. When threats did not work, the klansmen resorted to beatings and even murder. The Klan became so successful at intimidating blacks that Congress passed legislation aimed at curbing the organization. The Ku Klux Act of 1871 broke the power of the Klan. As a result of this act, the government arrested thousands of klansmen and convicted over twelve hundred. The Klan did not die out completely, however, and it rose to prominence again in the twentieth century. (See Chapter 20.)

Sharecropping—The Southern economy, devastated by the war, did not improve markedly under Radical rule. The freed slave returned to farming, the only occupation he knew, and agriculture remained the leading Southern "industry." Land was, in fact, the only Southern resource of consequence. Southern landowners, however, soon found the wage system unsatisfactory. Since there was little cash available, they had difficulty paying their workers in cash, and the workers became discontent because of low wages. Also the workers, feeling no particular loyalty to their employers, often left at crucial times, such as during planting, to look for better wages elsewhere.

Sharecropping developed as an answer to the economic deprivations of the South. There were several different arrangements under the share-cropping system. Some laborers leased the land, provided their own tools and seeds, grew what they wanted, and then paid their rent with cash or crops. Others provided only labor while the landowner provided land, tools, and other supplies. The landowner's share of the crop ranged from one-fourth to one-half the harvest, depending on how much material he supplied. Because of the need for profits, landowners usually insisted that their tenants

grow cash crops such as tobacco or cotton. These crops quickly depleted the soil of nutrients and obviously provided nothing for the sharecropper to eat. Low prices for cotton and tobacco after the war only worsened the situation for both sharecroppers and landowners.

Sharecropping was not limited to blacks. About three-fourths of the black farmers in the South and one-third of the white farmers were sharecroppers. In many cases, sharecroppers purchased groceries and supplies on credit and paid after harvest. Interest on the credit was so high that most sharecroppers remained constantly in debt. A sharecropper worked as hard as a slave and often received less for his efforts. If he owed money to the landowner or store, the sharecropper could not even leave. As years passed, the debts increased as interest grew and further debts were incurred. Thousands of Southerners—both white and black—became involved in this endless cycle of annual debt and were unable to save enough money to purchase their own land, even after many years. Sharecropping allowed many Southerners to survive, but it did not enable them to prosper.

Redemption—Most Southerners desired to take control of their states back from the Radicals. Because they wanted "Redemption" from congressional control, men who led the fight for white

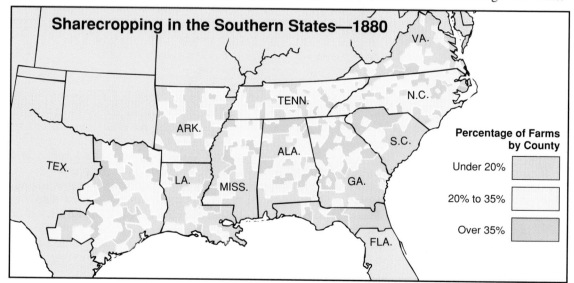

Sharecropping in the Southern States—1880

Percentage of Farms by County

Under 20%

20% to 35%

Over 35%

VA. • TENN. • N.C. • ARK. • S.C. • TEX. • ALA. • GA. • LA. • MISS. • FLA.

majority rule were called **Redeemers.** As in the case of the carpetbaggers and scalawags, wide generalizations about the Redeemers can sometimes be unfair. Some of these men undeniably hoped to strip blacks of the rights and privileges they had gained since the war. The majority of Redeemers, however, simply wanted fair play. They wished to elect their own governments and run their own affairs without outside interference. A good example of a fair-minded Redeemer was Democrat Wade Hampton, a former Confederate cavalry general who served two terms as governor of South Carolina after Reconstruction. During his first campaign for governor, Hampton said,

> The only way to bring about prosperity in this state is to bring the two races in friendly relations together. The Democratic Party in South Carolina . . . has promised that every citizen of this state is to be the equal of all; he is to have every right given to him by the Constitution of the United States and of this state. . . . And I pledge my faith, and I pledge it for those gentlemen who are on the ticket with me, that if we are elected, as far as in us lies, we will observe, protect, and defend the rights of the colored man as quickly as [of] any man in South Carolina.

To his credit, Hampton kept these promises after his election. One by one, Southern states turned to the leadership of Redeemers like Hampton and regained control of their own affairs. By 1876 federal troops remained only in Louisiana, Florida, and South Carolina.

Section Review

1. What requirements did the Military Reconstruction Act set down for the states in order for them to be "reconstructed" and restored to full status?
2. What is the difference between a "carpetbagger" and a "scalawag"?
3. What was the most notorious extremist vigilante group in the South during Reconstruction?
4. What system of farming was the South's main economic response to the devastation caused by the Civil War?

Ulysses S. Grant proved as great a failure as a president as he had proved a success as a general.

Reconstruction in the North

The North did not undergo Reconstruction as the South did. There was no widespread destruction in the North, no need to rebuild the state governments, and certainly no military occupation. The Reconstruction *era,* however, brought changes to the North just as it did to the South.

The Grant Administration

When the presidential election of 1868 rolled around, the Republicans turned to the nation's leading hero, General **Ulysses S. Grant,** as their candidate. Grant seemed to be the pillar of honesty and strength that the nation needed after the Civil War and the bitter struggle between President Johnson and Congress. Grant captured the mood of the people in his campaign slogan: "Let us have peace."

A Radical President—Grant proved to be a weak president, however, one of the poorest in history. He was a president in the Radical mold, for one thing. Grant believed that the president should be relatively passive and allow Congress to run the nation. He let Congress control the Reconstruction of the South, for example, unlike President Johnson. Another reason for Grant's failure was his lack of political experience. Grant soon learned that leading a nation was far different from leading an army. He had virtually no preparation for the office of president, and the duties of the office seemed to confuse and frustrate him. One visitor to the White House said that Grant looked like "a man with a problem before him of which he does not understand the terms." The major problem with Grant's administration was corruption. Although Grant himself was unquestionably honest, his friends, cabinet members, and other associates seemed to believe that Grant had won the presidency so that they might enrich themselves. A new word, **"Grantism,"** became a synonym for political corruption.

Scandals—Several scandals rocked the Grant administration. One of these, the **Credit Mobilier** (CRED-it moh-BEEL-yur) **Scandal,** actually began before Grant took office. The Credit Mobilier was a railroad construction company controlled by promoters and officers of the Union Pacific Railway. During the construction of the transcontinental railroad (see pp. 382-83), the company padded construction expenses and then paid the excesses to the stockholders, most of whom were Union Pacific officers. To discourage congressional investigation, the company sold stock in the Credit Mobilier to congressmen and other government officials at prices far below the market value. A congressional investigation in 1872 revealed that several prominent Republicans had received shares of the stock, including Vice President Schuyler Colfax.

Perhaps the most notorious scheme that cast shadows on Grant's political reputation was one in which James Fisk and Jay Gould, two unscrupulous financiers, tried to gain control of the gold market. They planned to buy gold on the New York Stock Exchange until the price of gold rose. Then they would sell theirs and make an enormous profit. For their plan to work, however, the federal treasury had to refrain from selling any of its gold reserves, or the price of gold would drop. Fisk and Gould

William Belknap, Grant's secretary of war and close friend, resigned from office amid charges that he had accepted bribes.

therefore convinced Grant that the nation would be racked with inflation if the secretary of the treasury sold any federal gold. They even bribed Grant's brother-in-law to use his influence to ensure the government's cooperation. Then on September 24, 1869, "Black Friday," Fisk and Gould began to bid up the price of gold. When Grant learned of the scheme, he ordered the treasury to release gold for sale, and the Fisk-Gould plan only partially succeeded. The two schemers did quite well financially, however. "Nothing is lost save honor," said Fisk happily.

Some scandals reached into Grant's inner circle of cabinet members and advisers. Secretary of War William Belknap, Grant's close personal friend, was accused of receiving $24,000 in bribes in return for granting special licenses to sell goods to the Indians. After the House began impeachment proceedings, Belknap resigned in March 1876. One of the worst scandals, revealed in 1875, was the **Whiskey Ring.** This group of whiskey distillers and distributors and federal tax collectors conspired to cheat the government out of millions of dollars in revenue from excise taxes. Because his private secretary, Orville Babcock, was among the swindlers, Grant was hesitant to demand a thorough investigation; he even testified as a character witness for his secretary. In all, Grant's was probably the most scandal-ridden administration in American history.

Tammany Hall—The most notorious political corruption in this period was not in the Radical state governments in the South or even in the Grant administration; it was in the city government of New York run by the Democratic **Tammany Hall** under the direction of **William ''Boss'' Tweed.** Tammany Hall was a political organization founded after the Revolution that soon grew in influence until it controlled most of New York's political affairs during the last half of the nineteenth century. Under the leadership of Boss Tweed, its corruption in the 1860s and 1870s reached astonishing depths.

New York City's debt increased from $36 million in 1868 to more than $136 million in 1870, largely because Tweed and other Tammany leaders diverted city funds into their own pockets. It has been estimated that fraudulent expenditures from 1865 to 1871 totaled over $75 million. In only one of his many frauds, Tweed charged New York taxpayers about $11 million to build a courthouse that actually cost about $3 million. (Thermometers for the building, for example, were listed as costing $7,500 each.) Excess funds, entered on the records as fictitious expenditures, were literally stolen by Tweed and others in Tammany Hall. Hospitals, asylums, and other institutions that never existed except on paper received large funds from the city—money which then went into the wallets of Tweed and company.

Boss Tweed and his crooked cohorts managed to stay in power by delivering large blocs of Democratic votes in each election. Needing Tammany's help to win, many Democrats in New York closed their eyes to the corruption in New York city. Tammany politicians used bribes to persuade Republicans to leave them alone.

As a result of a reform movement aimed at destroying Tammany Hall, Tweed was finally arrested in 1871, although Tammany's political influence continued well into the twentieth century. Tweed's arrest and imprisonment were encouraged by the gifted Republican cartoonist **Thomas Nast,** who attacked Tweed and Tammany Hall without mercy. Tweed feared the cartoons more than any other opposition; as Tweed himself said, his uneducated supporters could not read editorials, but they could understand Nast's drawings. Ironically, when Tweed escaped to Spain in 1876, he was identified and arrested through one of Nast's cartoons.

Liberal Republicans—The corruption of the Grant administration and the excesses of Radical Reconstruction in the South offended some elements within the Republican party. As a result, a splinter group calling itself the **''Liberal Republicans''** decided to oppose Grant's re-election in 1872. The Liberal Republicans called for an end to military occupation of the South and the purging of corruption from the national government. The Democrats, agreeing with these positions and still weakened by the Civil War, decided to join forces with the Liberal Republicans in hopes of defeating Grant.

Unfortunately, this diverse coalition of politicans had trouble finding a candidate acceptable to all factions. Eventually—almost in desperation—they chose New York newspaper editor **Horace Greeley.** Although Greeley was well known and thoroughly honest, he had long been a bitter critic of the South and aroused little excitement among Southern Democrats. (Greeley had once said, ''All Democrats may not be rascals, but all rascals are Democrats.'') Furthermore, Greeley was an eccentric, advocating such things as vegetarianism and spiritualism (communication with the dead). Presidential corruption or not, most voters did not see Greeley as an improvement over Grant. The president crushed Greeley in the election and in so doing destroyed the Liberal Republican movement. Exhausted by the campaign, Greeley died three weeks after the election.

Thomas Nast

The cartoonist who helped bring down Boss Tweed was a short, bespectacled German immigrant who looked more like a bookish professor than a fearless reformer. But Thomas Nast was a man whose firm principles and fierce sense of right gave his political cartoons in *Harper's Weekly* a sharp edge that made him the leading political cartoonist in America. A diehard Republican through and through, Nast was not exactly unbiased. Even at the height of the Grant scandals, the cartoonist stubbornly defended the president in his cartoons. Yet even Nast's opponents could not deny the power of his work. When Boss Tweed died, those who went through his belongings discovered that the political boss had saved a copy of every cartoon that Nast had drawn of him.

In addition to the Tweed drawings, Nast contributed richly to the imagery of American life. He created the symbol of the Republican party, the elephant, and helped popularize the Democratic symbol, the donkey. Nast's most popular figure, however, had nothing to do with politics. When illustrating Clement Moore's poem "A Visit from St. Nicholas" (better known today as "The Night Before Christmas"), Nast established the modern conception of Santa Claus—the round-bellied, red-cheeked, white-haired "right jolly old elf" that everyone today instantly recognizes as "Saint Nick." The illustrations on this page display some characteristic examples of Nast's work.

THE " BRAINS "

Economic Boom and Bust

One of the reasons Grant won re-election so easily was the general prosperity of the nation, particularly the North. As mentioned in the last chapter, the War Between the States had spurred the growth of both agriculture and heavy industry. After the war, business continued to boom as manufacturing quickly shifted from wartime to peacetime goods. A rifle-making plant in Hartford, Connecticut, for example, became a plant for manufacturing sewing machines. For most voters, economic good times covered many of the failures of Grant's administration.

Prosperity came to a devastating halt during Grant's second term, however. A financial collapse called the **Panic of '73** touched off a six-year depression, the worst depression that the United States had endured up to that time. One of the causes of this panic was a struggle over the nation's currency. At the outset of the Civil War, Congress had issued paper money called **"greenbacks"** (because they were printed in green ink) to help pay for the war effort. Unlike earlier currencies, the greenbacks were not backed by gold or silver but simply by the government's promise to honor them. As a result, most Americans viewed greenbacks as less valuable than "hard money" (gold and silver or notes redeemable for gold and silver).

After the war, conservative financiers wanted to get rid of the greenbacks and return to money based entirely on gold. "Easy money" advocates wanted not only to continue using greenbacks but also to print more. Debtors and those on the poorer end of the economic ladder liked the greenbacks because the more money that was in circulation, the more everybody would have. Wages would rise, and it would also be easier to pay off debts. Bankers and other conservative economists quickly pointed out that higher prices on goods and services would also result from an increase in the amount of currency in circulation.

Eventually a compromise of sorts was reached. Over $300 million in greenbacks were left in circulation, but the government pledged to begin redeeming them for their face value in gold. In this way the greenbacks became "as good as gold." Although taking steps to establish the currency on a gold standard may have been wise, doing so during a depression almost certainly was not. The government's acts actually restricted the amount of money in circulation and thereby made the depression worse. The nation's economic problems began to stir opposition and gave the Democrats a potent political weapon.

Election of 1876

Southern Reconstruction, Republican corruption, and economic hard times were the themes of the presidential election of 1876. Even if there had not been a tradition against electing a president for a third term, the Republicans were not eager to run the scandal-marred Grant again. Nearly all important Republican leaders, however, were tinged with at least a hint of scandal. Finally the Republicans chose a dark horse, **Rutherford B. Hayes.** Although Hayes had a rather colorless personality, he had served as a Union general in the Civil War, had been a three-time governor of Ohio, and–most important to the Republicans–possessed a reputation for unimpeachable honesty. The Democrats nominated **Samuel J. Tilden,** a brilliant railroad lawyer and former governor of New York. Tilden, who had gained a national reputation by breaking the "Tweed ring" and by reforming the state judiciary system, was an excellent candidate for the Democratic campaign against Republican corruption.

Waving the Bloody Shirt—Since the Democrats had the powerful issues of corruption and economic depression on which to campaign, the Republicans needed an issue to distract voters. Hayes wrote to one Republican leader, "Our strong ground is the dread of a solid South, rebel rule, etc., etc. I hope you will make these topics prominent in your speeches. It leads people away from 'hard times,' which is our deadliest foe." Republicans resorted to "waving the bloody shirt," that is, blaming the

Copyright 1876, by Currier & Ives, N.Y.

The Hayes-Wheeler ticket won one of the most hotly disputed presidential elections in American history.

Democrats for the Civil War and treating them as traitors. One Republican speaker in 1876, for example, made the following attack on the Democrats:

> Every State that seceded from the Union was a Democratic State. . . . Every man that shot down Union soldiers was a Democrat. . . . The man that assassinated Abraham Lincoln was a Democrat. . . . Soldiers, every scar you have on your heroic bodies was given you by a Democrat. Every scar, every arm that is missing, every limb that is gone, is a souvenir of a Democrat.

Obviously, reason and logic were not strong points of the Republican campaign of 1876.

A Disputed Election—When the election returns came in, it appeared that Tilden had won. The Democrats won the popular vote by a margin of 250,000, and Tilden had 184 of the 185 electoral

votes needed to win. However, three Southern states—Florida, Louisiana, and South Carolina (all states that federal troops still occupied)—sent in conflicting returns. The Republicans claimed that Hayes had won these states, and the Democrats, of course, claimed that Tilden had won them. If Tilden could capture at least one of these disputed electoral votes, he would be president. If Hayes captured all nineteen, he would be president.

Congress set up a commission of fifteen men—five each from the Supreme Court, the Senate, and the House—to determine which party should receive the disputed votes. By a vote of eight to seven along strict party lines, the commission gave all the disputed votes to the Republicans. The final tally gave Hayes 185 electoral votes to Tilden's 184.

It is difficult to decide who—if anyone—was in the right in the disputed election. Voting corruption marked the efforts of both parties. Southern Democrats, for example, made obvious efforts through threats and fraud to prevent black Republicans from voting. Likewise, the Republican majority on the special congressional election commission was more concerned with electing its candidate than in honestly determining who had won. It may be, as one historian observed, "that the Democrats stole the election first and the Republicans stole it back."

Compromise of 1877 – As one might expect, the Democrats contested the commission's decision. The party threatened to hold up the official counting of the electoral votes in Congress so that Hayes could not take office. No one knew what would happen if the Democrats carried out this threat, and a few even hinted that another civil war might result. The deadlock was broken, however, when a group of Southern Democrats secretly met with the Republicans to make a deal. This agreement, known as the **Compromise of 1877,** was essentially a trade-off. Southern Democrats would help Hayes by allowing the electoral votes to be counted. Hayes, in turn, would remove the last federal troops from the South. Both sides kept their part of the bargain. Hayes took office on schedule, and within two months he had withdrawn the last troops from the South. Reconstruction was officially over.

A Reconstructed Nation

As a result of Reconstruction, the United States was a markedly different nation than it had been before the Civil War. Three important, far-reaching events resulted from the Civil War and Reconstruction: the slaves were freed, the South became solidly Democratic, and the powers of the federal government expanded dramatically. Freeing the slaves was a great triumph, but the impact of that freedom was probably greater than anyone expected. The economy of the South–so long dependent on slavery for its prosperity–was devastated. Furthermore, the struggle over the rights of the newly freed blacks became a heated political issue that has divided and tested the nation up to the present.

The South, now bitterly opposed to the Republicans because of the Civil War and Radical Reconstruction, became known as **"the Solid South"** for

the Democratic party. With some exceptions, the region elected only Democratic governors, state legislators, and congressmen for nearly a hundred years. Not until 1972 would a Republican candidate for president again carry the South. This unusual political unity gave the region great influence in the Democratic party and enabled the region to influence the national party's policy and to make sure that the national government left the South alone to run its own affairs for at least seventy-five years.

Perhaps the most important change was the alteration of the nature of the federal government. Before the Civil War, the United States had been a Union of States, with the national government limited to a certain defined role with certain delegated powers. The Founding Fathers attempted to balance the powers of the state and national governments and allow them to hold each other in check. The South, of course, believed strongly in the rights of the states and went to war to fight for them. Most Northerners, however, believed in the principle too. Lincoln, for example, opposed secession but did not oppose the idea that many rights are reserved to the states. His insistence that he could not constitutionally interfere with slavery in states where it already existed demonstrated Lincoln's belief in the limited powers of the national government.

The Civil War altered these attitudes. The association of the idea of "states' rights" with the secessionist South caused many Northerners to suspect the whole concept. Perhaps, they thought, another civil war might result if they did not repudiate the idea. Also the abolition of slavery removed one of the main differences between the sections. Abolition at least opened the door for the sections of the nation to draw closer in culture, technology, and economy. Increasingly, Americans began to speak less of "the Union" and more of "the nation." Sentences that had previously begun "The United States *are* . . ." now began "The United States *is.* . . ."

Whatever advantages the United States may have gained from this change, there was one great disadvantage: The power of the national government increased significantly. The reduction of the idea of states' rights removed one check on the

Electoral Commission of 1877, *United States Senate Collection. The controversial decision of the electoral commission gave Republican Rutherford B. Hayes the victory over Democrat Samuel Tilden.*

central government's power. The Fourteenth Amendment, as mentioned earlier, eventually became a wedge that the central government used to enter and eventually control many state and local affairs. One historian noted that before the Civil War virtually the only agency of the national government that touched the lives of the average citizen was the Post Office. Today, the American citizen usually cannot avoid contact–even conflict–with the national bureaucracy.

The Civil War and Reconstruction transformed the "Federal Union" into the "American nation." The goals that motivated this change–preserving the Union and granting the rights of citizenship to blacks–were certainly important. Could these goals have been achieved without the resulting growth of government power, bitter sectional hatred, and longstanding racial tension? Only after this question has been answered can the wisdom of the process of Reconstruction be evaluated.

Section Review

1. List at least three major scandals of the Grant administration.
2. Who was the leader of the corrupt city government of New York during the Reconstruction era? What was his political party?
3. What were the three main campaign themes of the Democrats in 1876?
4. What did Southern Democrats promise in the Compromise of 1877? What did the Republicans promise?
5. What was the effect of the Civil War and Reconstruction on Southern voting as a whole region?

Chapter Review

Terms

Andrew Johnson
Reconstruction
ten per cent plan
Radical Republicans
Wade-Davis Bill
Tenure of Office Act
impeachment
Thirteenth Amendment
Fourteenth Amendment
Fifteenth Amendment
Military Reconstruction Act
Freedman's Bureau
Black Codes
carpetbaggers
scalawags
disfranchisement
Ku Klux Klan
sharecropping
Redeemers
Ulysses S. Grant
"Grantism"
Credit Mobilier Scandal
Whiskey Ring
Tammany Hall
William "Boss" Tweed
Thomas Nast
Liberal Republicans
Horace Greeley
Panic of '73
greenbacks
Rutherford B. Hayes
Samuel J. Tilden
Compromise of 1877
"the Solid South"

Content Questions

1. How did Lincoln and Johnson differ with the Radicals concerning the ultimate responsibility for Reconstruction?
2. How did the Fourteenth Amendment provide a way for the central government to extend its power over state and local governments?
3. Which of the "Reconstruction amendments" abolished slavery? Which guaranteed voting rights? Which guaranteed citizen rights?
4. Name at least two positive accomplishments of the Radical governments of the South. Why did Southerners nonetheless resent these governments?
5. Give at least two reasons explaining why Grant was a poor president.
6. Why did the Liberal Republicans' choice of a candidate in 1872 harm their efforts to defeat Grant?
7. What is meant by "waving the bloody shirt"?
8. Why did one historian say of the presidential election of 1876 "that the Democrats stole the election first and the Republicans stole it back"?

Application Questions

1. Why was sharecropping more popular than the wage system in the South during Reconstruction?
2. What was beneficial about Reconstruction? What aspects of Reconstruction were harmful then and since?

UNIT V

1859
Charles Darwin
publishes
*Origin of
Species*

1862
Homestead
Act passed

1867
Purchase of
Alaska

1869
First
transcontinental
railroad
completed

1870
Rockefeller
forms the
Standard Oil
Company of
Ohio

1871
Treaty of
Washington

1873
D.L. Moody
begins
evangelistic tour
of Great Britain

1876
Alexander
Graham Bell
invents the
telephone

1876-1877
The Sioux War

1881
American
Federation of
Labor formed

1883
Pendleton Act
creates Civil
Service
Commission

1890
Sherman
Anti-Trust Act
passed

1896
McKinley
defeats
Bryan

1898
Spanish-
American War

1901
U.S. Steel
formed;
Theodore
Roosevelt
becomes
president

1903
Henry Ford
founds Ford
Motor Company;
Wright brothers'
first flight

1914
Panama Canal
opens

1914-1918
WORLD WAR I

1917
U.S. enters
World War I

CHAPTER 16

The Gilded Age (1877-1896)

"Well, well, my boy, things are looking pretty bright now I tell you. Speculation—my! The whole atmosphere's full of money." *Con man Colonel Beriah Sellers discussing a business venture over a dinner of water and raw turnips in* Mark Twain's *The Gilded Age* (1873)

The Champion Single Sculls (Max Schmitt in a Single Scull), *by Thomas Eakins, The Metropolitan Museum of Art, Purchase, The Alfred N. Punnett Endowment Fund and George D. Pratt Gift, 1934. (34.92). Photograph © 1994.*

America's horizons were never the same. As the country hurried headlong toward the twentieth century, the skyscraper and smokestack replaced the steeple as the skyline's most prominent feature. Steel replaced stone; machines replaced muscle; concrete replaced cobblestones; the future replaced the past.

In his 1873 work *The Gilded Age,* Mark Twain unwittingly but fittingly named the postwar era. Industrialization put its golden stamp of prosperity on much of society. The rich got richer, and even the poor got less poor. Yet behind the glitter of America's burgeoning wealth were contrasts and divisions that would transform national life.

Industry and Invention

The Rise of Industrialism

The period after the Civil War witnessed a rapid rise in the importance of industry in the United States. From a few small iron factories and oil wells in the 1850s, American industry grew until the United States became a leader in the world's industrial community.

There were several causes of American industrial growth. First and most obvious was the growth of the nation itself. In fact, a modest postwar baby boom combined with immigration nearly tripled the population from 32 million in 1860 to 92 million in 1910. Increased population led to an increased demand for products and an increased work force to produce them. It also encouraged the movement westward and the accompanying development of farmland and mining in the resource-rich West. This development gave the nation an increased supply of raw materials with which to produce goods. Another result of the westward movement was the rapid expansion of the railroads, connecting manufacturers with new markets and binding East and West with steel rails.

Second, the innovative spirit of the times fostered new machines and methods that were crucial contributions to industrial expansion during the postwar period. Third, industry also benefited from a sympathetic government; its generally high tariff laws reduced foreign competition, and the nation's liberal immigration laws provided a vast and inexpensive work force for prospective employers.

Fourth, new sources of power sprang up during this period to supplement or supplant the water power that had driven America's early industry. Whole new energy industries in oil and electricity spurred greater manufacturing and opened new markets.

Captains of Industry

At the top of America's growing industrial empire were men whose ideas, energy, and money dominated the age. Their lives often illustrated the best and worst aspects of industrialization. These men were called the "captains of industry," and their efforts helped forge America into a prosperous and productive nation. For some of them, however, greed for gain and aggressive business practices earned them the less flattering title of **"robber barons."** Nonetheless these men did more to shape America's future than anyone who sat in the White House or Congress at the time, and their lives illustrate a number of important trends during this formative period.

Cornelius Vanderbilt, Railroad Baron—As a young man, **Cornelius Vanderbilt** borrowed one hundred dollars from his mother to start a ferry business. From this small beginning the aggressive and ambitious Vanderbilt gained control of much of New York's water-borne shipping through hard work and cutthroat competition. He duplicated his success across the Northeast and into the expanding West so that by 1860 Vanderbilt controlled much of the nation's shipping. Besides a fortune, Vanderbilt's steamboat business also gained him the inflated title of "Commodore."

The threat of wartime disruptions caused Vanderbilt to direct his business interests toward railroads. Beginning in 1862 Vanderbilt began buying out rail lines in New York. Typical of Vanderbilt's ruthless tactics was his takeover of the New York Central Railroad in 1867. Vanderbilt's rail lines provided access for that railroad's traffic. After failing to gain concessions from New York Central's stockholders, Vanderbilt shut his line down and thus cut off Central's business. When outcries arose from a strangled New York Central, Vanderbilt casually replied, "Can't I do what I want with my own?" Vanderbilt won concessions from the stockholders, and by the end of 1867 the Commodore was president of the New York Central. Vanderbilt's acquisitions gradually extended his rail lines from New York to Chicago. Others followed Vanderbilt's example of empire building, so that eventually most of the railroads in America were controlled by only a half dozen groups.

Andrew Carnegie, Steel Giant—**Andrew Carnegie** was born in Scotland, but hard times forced his poor family to immigrate to western Pennsylvania in 1848. His life in America would become a classic "rags to riches" story. Carnegie's first job after arriving in America was as a bobbin boy in a textile mill earning $1.20 a week. The following year he worked as a telegraph messenger boy. Because he was diligent, efficient, and a quick study with anything he undertook, Carnegie rapidly advanced to become superintendent of the Pitts-

Andrew Carnegie

burgh division of the Pennsylvania Railroad in 1859. He saved what he could and began to invest in several industries such as oil, iron, bridge building, and railroads.

By the early 1870s Carnegie determined to focus his diverse interests and investments on the steel industry. Through a method known as **vertical integration,** Carnegie controlled every aspect of steel production literally from the ground up, from the mine to the market. Such a conglomerate effectively dismantled most of Carnegie's competitors, most of whom dealt with only one segment of the steel industry. When financier John Pierpont Morgan bought out Carnegie Steel in 1901 the former bobbin boy's personal share was nearly $300 million.

Carnegie was not only a financial genius; he was also a philosopher of big business. In his 1889 book *The Gospel of Wealth,* Carnegie revealed the influence of evolutionist Charles Darwin on his thinking. The accumulation of wealth, Carnegie believed, simply illustrated the survival of the fittest–and Carnegie clearly considered himself among ''the fittest.'' Wealth, however, was not an end in itself. Carnegie wrote, ''The man who dies rich dies disgraced. . . . Surplus wealth is a sacred trust which its possessor is bound to administer in his lifetime for the good of the community.''

Carnegie was as good as his word. Although he disdained the word ''philanthropy'' (giving to charitable causes) because it implied a handout, Carnegie gave millions of dollars to causes that would promote self-improvement. Libraries, hospitals, universities, and concert halls were built across the country through Carnegie's generosity. Unfortunately, despite his good works, Carnegie was an avowed unbeliever who scorned the Scriptures. His *Gospel of Wealth* was a gospel of works. The man who had everything died in spiritual poverty because he had rejected Christ and the only gospel that saves.

John D. Rockefeller, Trust Maker–America's first billionaire was **John D. Rockefeller,** the founder of Standard Oil Company. As a young businessman, Rockefeller saw his future in oil. In 1859 the discovery of petroleum in western Pennsylvania set off a ''black gold'' rush, but Rockefeller shrewdly

John D. Rockefeller

calculated that there was too much risk in oil drilling. He realized that oil refining, turning petroleum into useful products, was where the safest investments and largest profits lay. In 1870 Rockefeller consolidated his refining interests to form the Standard Oil Company of Ohio.

Rockefeller was not the only one who saw the profits in oil refining. The resulting competition was, in Rockefeller's words, ''chaotic.'' By systematically, sometimes deviously, eliminating all competitors, Rockefeller controlled ninety-five per cent of the nation's oil refining industry by 1879. Unlike the vertical integration practiced by Carnegie, in which a company controlled a *part* of *all* segments of the production of a good from raw material to finished product, this consolidation of *all* of *one* entire segment of an industry was called **horizontal integration.** At this level, Rockefeller controlled every aspect of the process from barrel-making to pipelines and transportation.

In 1879 Rockefeller organized his oil refining empire into a **trust.** The trust was a legal device by which a board of trustees was empowered to make decisions and control the operations of a

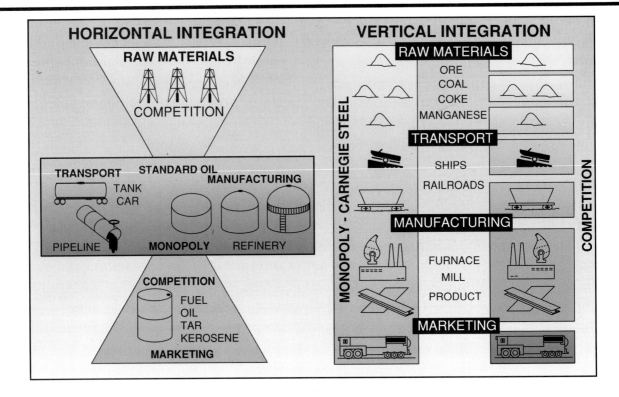

whole group of companies. As a result the Standard Oil Trust took over the operation of twenty-seven competing oil companies.

Rockefeller's mighty oil trust became the pattern for the formation of other trusts during the 1880s by businessmen who also had the means to eliminate their competition. Such monopolies drew outcries from farmers and small businessmen for the government to break up the giants and to create a fair playing field. The result was the Sherman Antitrust Act, passed in 1890 (see p. 363). The law, however, was loosely enforced and easily evaded. Most trusts such as Standard Oil simply sought refuge in more legal forms of organization without conceding any of their economic empire.

J. P. Morgan, Financier—From the last quarter of the nineteenth century until his death in 1913, **John Pierpont Morgan** was the leading investment banker in America. Whether paying a half-billion dollars to buy out Andrew Carnegie's steel empire or sitting in his three-hundred-foot yacht making decisions that rearranged whole companies like chess pieces, big J. P. Morgan came to symbolize the power and prestige at the top of America's industrial pyramid.

Morgan's business was not particularly oil, or steel, or railroads; it was money—buying and selling stocks on a grand scale in a variety of industries. Morgan shared Rockefeller's hatred of free competition and bought up a controlling interest in competing companies in order to reorganize them into streamlined corporations.

Morgan's mergers began in the railroad industry, where he reorganized a number of major lines such as the Northern Pacific, Union Pacific, B & O, and Southern railways. Morgan's biggest deal, however, was the consolidation of much of the steel industry. Through a series of mergers, culminating in the purchase of the giant Carnegie Steel, Morgan formed the first billion-dollar supercorporation,

J. P. Morgan

United States Steel Corporation in 1901.

The power of one man and his money to control so much of the economy drew the ire of the popular Irish humorist of the day, "Mr. Dooley," who remarked,

> Pierpont Morgan calls in wan iv his office boys, th' presidint iv a national bank, an' says he, "James," he says, "take some change out iv th' damper an' r-run out an' buy Europe f'r me," he says. "I intind to re-organize it an' put it on a paying basis," he says. "Call up the Czar an' th' Pope an' th' Sultan an' th' Impror Willum, an' tell thim we won't need their savices afther nex' week," he says. "Give thim a year's salary in advance."

James Buchanan Duke, New South Leader— After the war, as they had done for two centuries, Southerners returned to the soil for their livelihood. Nonetheless, many Southerners began to envision a **"New South,"** one that would match the North in economic and industrial capacity. The economic house of the New South was built on the twin pillars of the two "Ts"—tobacco and textiles. Virginia and Carolina piedmont towns, such as Dan-ville, Virginia, and Greensboro and Charlotte, North Carolina, largely spared the ravages of war, became leaders in the economic revitalization of the postwar New South. By 1900 four hundred cotton mills dotted the old Confederacy, far surpassing the textile production of New England.

Tobacco, the South's original cash crop, even gained a new lease on life during the postwar period. Bright leaf tobacco, a mild variety of the weed, was little known beyond upper North Carolina until Union soldiers tramped through in 1865. Capitalizing on the popularity of bright leaf, **James Buchanan** ("Buck") **Duke** of Durham Station, North Carolina, seized upon new marketing techniques to create a national and an international market for his tobacco products.

Buck Duke once described the tobacco industry as "half smoke and half ballyhoo," and he quickly showed himself to be a master of ballyhoo. Through the skillful use of advertising and promotion, Duke outstripped all of his competitors. In 1890 Duke formed the American Tobacco Company, which controlled ninety per cent of the nation's cigarette market. The New South's captain of industry also became a leader in developing hydroelectric power, opening the way for greater economic expansion in the South.

Innovations

Behind the rapid industrialization in America were new methods, new ideas, and new inventions that fueled expansion and created whole new markets. Thousands of inventions from the telephone to the tin can would completely change the way Americans lived.

Diet and Dress— The rising standard of living brought on by industrialization made significant changes in the American diet. Refrigerator cars brought beef and pork from the vast midwestern plains, and strawberries, tomatoes, and oranges from the South and West to the growing cities and the waiting iceboxes of middle-class homes. By 1880 the perfection of the mass-production of tin cans and new methods of cooking and sealing allowed the preservation of a wide variety of foods.

Americans enjoyed not only changes in their diet but also changes in their dress as well. The de-

H. J. Heinz

Not all the great captains of industry were "robber barons," always eager to enrich themselves at the expense of others. The unbendingly honest food-producer H. J. Heinz of Pittsburgh was one exception. The key difference was his Christian faith. A devout Methodist, he wrote in his will: "I desire to set forth, at the very beginning of this Will, as the most important item in it, a confession of my faith in Jesus Christ as my Saviour." Although Heinz pioneered much of modern billboard and newspaper advertising, he refused to allow his products to be advertised in Sunday newspapers, because he believed such advertising desecrated the Lord's day. Heinz gave liberally to Christian works, particularly Sunday school organizations, and he served as an officer in various Sunday school associations himself. When Heinz visited England, his "tourist stops" included the graves of John Bunyan, Isaac Watts, and John Wesley. He also visited a chapel that John Wesley had founded, where he sat in Wesley's chair. He later wrote, "I felt I was upon holy ground."

Heinz was a leader in producing bottled and canned foods: horseradish, ketchup, pickles, and dozens of other products. His honesty became a byword in the food industry. Other producers added fillers to their products, such as mixing ground turnips or even wood pulp with their horseradish, and sold their goods in green-tinted bottles to hide the impurities. Heinz insisted on one-hundred-per-cent pure products, and he sold them in clear bottles so that everyone could see the purity for themselves. When the government proposed regulating the quality of packaged foods, other food producers protested this "government interference," but not Heinz. Realizing that he had nothing to fear from regulation and believing that the public had a right to expect the food they bought to be pure, Heinz supported the Pure Food and Drug Act (1906) and helped secure its passage.

Other business leaders endured strikes and labor unrest. The H. J. Heinz Company never suffered a single strike during Heinz's lifetime. Heinz intended that his employees should have no reason to strike. He provided them with free medical care; recreation facilities such as gyms, swimming pools, and gardens; and educational opportunities such as libraries and free concerts and lectures. Employees of other companies labored in dark, dirty, noisy factories. Heinz's workers enjoyed clean, well-lighted, well-ventilated plants where dining halls provided food at discount prices while they were serenaded by the piano or organ.

Heinz never believed that there was any "secret" to his success other than honesty and hard work. "To do a common thing uncommonly well brings success," was one of his mottoes. Another was "Do the best you can, where you are, with what you have today." Heinz illustrates the Christian's response to the challenge of business management: "And whatsoever ye do, do it heartily, as to the Lord, and not unto men; knowing that of the Lord ye shall receive the reward of the inheritance: for ye serve the Lord Christ" (Col. 3:23-24).

velopment of the sewing machine and its widespread use during the Civil War spawned a huge retail market for mass-produced clothing. For the first time, standardized sizes and designs were applied to clothing. Most tailors and seamstresses, who at one time made clothing, now only repaired it.

Fashion and comfort became important considerations in the American wardrobe. By the turn of the century, suits of lighter weight and color were being produced for men's summer wear. The generous Victorian styles for ladies were gradually being trimmed down as well. By 1920 a woman's dress required only three yards of material to produce, compared with ten yards in the 1890s.

In addition, mass-produced clothing hastened democratization, since the availability of high quality, stylish clothing lessened class distinctions. Armed with a *Sears and Roebuck Catalog,* men and women of modest means could dress like the Rockefellers and Vanderbilts, and–given the American thirst for status–many of them did just that.

Communications–Industrialization also created a communications revolution during the Gilded Age. The growth of businesses across the nation resulted in increased correspondence and more sophisticated record keeping. The invention of the typewriter (1867) and an improved system of shorthand (1888) met these new demands of the business world.

The development of cheap paper from wood pulp and the invention of continuous action roller presses resulted in the birth of mass media. Inexpensive newspapers, magazines, and books became available for an increasingly literate, increasingly sophisticated society.

The crowning communications achievement of the time came in 1876 with the invention of the telephone by **Alexander Graham Bell.** A Scottish immigrant, Bell arrived in the United States at the age of twenty-four to teach speech to the deaf. Bell was an innovative thinker who combined his interest in sound with his propensity for experimentation. For three years, Bell struggled with the idea that he could "make iron talk." On March 10, 1876, Bell transmitted his first message over wire by calling an assistant in another room of his house: "Mr. Watson, come here, I want you." People have been answering phone calls ever since.

After the long and numerous legal battles to defend his telephone patent, as well as patents on various long-distance improvements, Bell and his associates formed American Telephone and Tele-

"Genius is one per cent inspiration and ninety-nine per cent perspiration"–Thomas Edison in his laboratory, 1888.

graph Company in 1885. By 1900 AT&T held a monopoly over the country's entire phone service.

Age of Electricity—America's most versatile and prolific inventor was **Thomas Alva Edison.** Though lacking in formal education, Edison had a knack for new ideas and a thirst for discovery. After several successful inventions beginning at age twenty-one, Edison established an "invention-factory" at Menlo Park, New Jersey, the forerunner of today's industrial research laboratories.

Edison was responsible for over a thousand inventions during his lifetime, but the most influential ones were the phonograph, the motion-picture projector, and the one that turned night into day—the incandescent light bulb. After years of experimentation in developing the light bulb and the power system that could make indoor lighting practical, on September 4, 1882, Edison flipped a switch that lit up New York's financial district. A new age was born in the eerie glow on Wall Street.

With the contributions of George Westinghouse and Hungarian immigrant Nikola Tesla in devising alternating current generators and transformers, electrical power gained long-range practicality. In 1893, for example, the Columbian Exposition in Chicago was lit by power generated at and transmitted from Niagara Falls. Men rightly marveled at the potential that electricity offered the world. As Harvard President Charles Eliot declared at the turn of the century, electricity is the "carrier of light and power; devourer of time and space; bearer of human speech over land and sea; greatest servant of men."

Section Review

1. What were the four causes of American industrial growth after the Civil War?
2. In what two businesses did Cornelius Vanderbilt make his fortune?
3. What two industries dominated the Southern economy after the Civil War?
4. What was the most important invention in communications in the late nineteenth century? Who invented it?
5. Name two of Thomas Edison's most influential inventions.

Reform and Reaction

The rapid and far-reaching changes of the last quarter of the nineteenth century did not occur in a vacuum. They touched the lives of all Americans, from rich industrialists to ragged immigrants. The changes that produced prosperity also caused problems and spawned reform movements in a number of areas.

Politics

Four issues dominated American politics from the mid-1870s to the end of the century: civil service reform, government corruption, tariff revision, and regulation of the trusts. Debate over these issues was heated up by some of the closest, most evenly matched party politics in American history.

The "Spoiled" System—During the early part of Rutherford Hayes's administration, reform of the spoils system was the pressing issue. (The spoils system was the tendency of new administrations to replace appointed officeholders from the previous administration with supporters of their own. See p. 200.) Grant's name had become an adjective for corruption in high places, and Hayes had been nominated largely because he was a reformer.

Hayes courageously attacked political "machines," groups that sought to control voters, even though his action cost him political support. He particularly attacked a notorious New York Republican political machine—similar to the Democrats' Tammany Hall—controlled by Senator **Roscoe Conkling.** This machine controlled New York's tariff-collecting agency, the Customs House, where New York politicians manipulated records and siphoned off money belonging to the federal government. Hayes, hoping to check the corrupt practices, removed the Collector of the Port, future president Chester Arthur. The removal angered Conkling and other influential Republicans.

Stalwarts vs. Half-breeds—This clash between Hayes and Conkling reflected a growing division within the Republican party. On the one hand was Conkling's faction, the "Stalwarts," who favored high tariffs, hard money, and the spoils system. Opposing them were moderate Republicans, called **"Half-breeds,"** who had earlier been dissatisifed with Grant, the Radical Republicans, and Reconstruction and who tended to favor reform. The internal struggle between Stalwarts and Half-breeds intensified over the Republican presidential nomination in 1880. When the convention deadlocked, the Republican factions eventually compromised by nominating Ohio's **James A. Garfield,** a Half-breed, for president and New York's **Chester A. Arthur,** a Stalwart, for vice president.

In the general election, Garfield faced Democratic nominee Winfield S. Hancock, who had gained fame as a Union general at Gettysburg. Garfield won the electoral vote easily, but the popular vote was extremely close; the Republican candidate won by fewer than ten thousand votes out of nine million cast.

James A. Garfield was a man of ability and character, but his efforts at reform were short-lived. On July 2, 1881, just a few months after the inauguration, a distraught office-seeker, Charles J. Guiteau (gih TOH), shot Garfield at a railway station in Washington, D.C., and cried, "I am a Stalwart, and Arthur is now president." After enduring eleven weeks of pain and crude medical care, Garfield died on September 19, and Vice President Arthur became president.

Arthur's past attachment to New York's political machines led Conkling's supporters to rejoice and caused others to feel uneasy. However, Arthur, called "the gentleman president," turned out to be a pleasant surprise. He conscientiously assumed his responsibilities as president and refused to use his high office to provide special favors for Conkling's Stalwarts. Arthur also backed civil service reform and favored lowering the tariff.

Civil Service Reform—Arthur's presidency is perhaps best known for reform of the civil service (government employee) system. George H. Pendleton, a Democrat from Ohio, introduced a bill, called the **Pendleton Act,** that recommended establishing an independent **Civil Service Commission** and eliminating much of the spoils system. Garfield's death at the hands of a disappointed office-seeker had stimulated interest in such an act, and Pendleton's proposal was enacted in January 1883.

The Pendleton Act authorized the president to appoint three civil service commissioners, who

President Chester A. Arthur

were to be responsible for seeing that offices were filled by men who scored well on examinations. The act was intended to prevent the awarding of political offices for no other reason than party loyalty. To some extent it succeeded. Although only about twelve per cent of the federal offices were filled by the commission during Arthur's term, eventually about ninety per cent would be.

The Mongrel Tariff—Arthur's presidency is also noted for attempts to revise the tariff. Because general prosperity had led to government surpluses, a commission appointed by Arthur recommended a general tariff reduction of twenty to twenty-five per cent. Congressmen who wanted to protect the trade interests of their constituents, however, added many amendments to the proposed tariff. As a result when the tariff passed in 1883, it was a mixture of inharmonious policies. Critics soon dubbed it the **"Mongrel Tariff."** This legislation completely failed to reform the tariff as had been intended. All that it succeeded in doing was to clarify party positions on the tariff issue. The Republicans, coming mainly from industrial areas, more commonly favored protective tariffs; the Democrats, representing the South and the West, favored low tariffs.

The Election of 1884—In 1884 the Republicans bypassed Arthur, who had offended some Republicans by refusing to grant party members special favors. Instead they nominated Maine's James G. Blaine, a long-time Republican leader mildewed from an earlier railroad corruption scandal. The Democrats nominated New York's former governor **Grover Cleveland,** a courageous opponent of Tammany Hall noted for his honesty. Even many Republicans, disgusted by the tainted Blaine, supported Cleveland. Stalwarts sneeringly called these party deserters "Mugwumps," from an Indian word meaning "big chief." The joke quickly circulated that these straddling Republicans had their "mugs" on one side of the fence, and their "wumps" on the other. The Mugwumps, however, took the name as a badge of honor for their stand in favor of reform.

The 1884 election was a hard-fought, spirited affair better remembered for its mudslinging than for any issues that were debated. The campaign produced such memorable political poetry as the Democratic cry "Blaine, Blaine, James G. Blaine, the continental liar from the state of Maine." The Republicans responded with a ditty of their own over the allegation that the bachelor Cleveland had fathered an illegitimate child. "Ma, Ma, where's my pa?" they would wail. "Gone to the White

President Grover Cleveland

House, ha, ha, ha." Cleveland won a narrow victory. Had Blaine won the extremely close race in New York–he lost there by only 1,149 votes out of over a million cast–he would have won the election. Cleveland's election was the first Democratic victory in twenty-eight years.

Challenging the Trusts–During Cleveland's first term, Congress passed the first comprehensive act to provide for federal regulation of commerce. Some railroad trusts had been engaged in activities that called for regulation, such as rate-fixing schemes and discriminatory rates. The railroads proved unwilling to police themselves, however, and state railroad commissions had no authority to regulate activities outside the borders of their states. Nearly all Americans favored federal regulation of the railroads under the interstate commerce clause of the Constitution.

In February 1887 Cleveland signed the **Interstate Commerce Act,** which (1) directed that railroad rates must be "reasonable and just"; (2) required that railroad companies publish all rates and make financial reports; and (3) provided for the creation of the Interstate Commerce Commission (ICC), an independent regulatory agency, to investigate alleged abuses and stop them.

The Election of 1888–The Democrats renominated the popular Cleveland in 1888. The Republicans, however, abandoned Blaine and nominated Indiana's **Benjamin Harrison,** who, though somewhat colorless, was a capable, honest man. He was also the grandson of ex-President William Henry Harrison, a fact the Republicans loudly proclaimed. Some of Cleveland's aides feared that the president's stand in favor of lowering the tariffs might offend some voters and cost him the election. Cleveland retorted, "What is the use of being elected unless you stand for something?" Cleveland won more popular votes, but Harrison won more electoral votes and, hence, the election. Once again, New York's thirty-six electoral votes determined the election's outcome. In 1884 Cleveland had barely won them from Blaine; in 1888 he barely lost them to Harrison.

Although personally honest, Harrison was a disappointingly weak president. He appointed Blaine as secretary of state, and Blaine in turn dominated both the administration and the Republican party. The Republicans sought to win favor with the voters and maintain control of the government through liberal spending, such as giving generous pensions to army veterans. The Fifty-first Congress (1889-1891) became known as "the Billion-Dollar Congress," because, for the first time in history, the annual budget exceeded a billion dollars. Weak leadership in the White House and Congress combined with free-spending policies only squandered the Treasury surplus that Cleveland had left without improving Republican popularity.

The Sherman Antitrust Act—One law during the Harrison years, however, was extremely influential. Congress greatly expanded its potential power to regulate business with the passage of the **Sherman Antitrust Act** in 1890. The public had become increasingly wary of big business's tendency to form monopolies, or "trusts"; companies such as Rockefeller's Standard Oil, after driving all competition out of business or forcing a merger, took advantage of their monopoly by raising prices to an exorbitant level. If the consumer needed the product and could get it nowhere else, he simply had to pay.

The Sherman Antitrust Act made such monopolizing illegal. It declared, "Every contract, combination in the form of trust or otherwise, or conspiracy, in restraint of trade or commerce . . . is hereby declared to be illegal." The act was difficult to enforce, however, because there were no specific definitions of "contract," "combination," or "restraint of trade." For this reason the act was relatively ineffective until the passage of tougher federal regulations in the twentieth century.

Raising the Tariff—A major goal of the Republicans in the Fifty-first Congress was to raise the tariff again. Because their majority in both houses of Congress was slim, the Republicans bolstered their strength by admitting six new predominantly Republican states: North Dakota, South Dakota, Montana, and Washington in November 1889 and Idaho and Wyoming in July 1890. The addition of Republican representatives and senators from these states strengthened the Republican majority in Congress and allowed the party to pass the **McKinley Tariff** in 1890.

The new tariff placed higher duties on manufactured and agricultural imports than had any previous tariff in history. Consequently, to a higher degree than ever before, inefficiency in American industry was protected from foreign competition. In addition, the high tariff actually lowered revenue by radically decreasing trade. This decrease in the government's income, combined with the lavish congressional spending, reduced the treasury's reserves at an alarming rate. The general public demonstrated its anger at the tariff in the congressional election of 1890. The voters reduced the Republican majority in the Senate and gave the Democrats an overwhelming 235-88 advantage in the House. Even William McKinley, whose name had graced the titan tariff, was turned out of office.

The result of the 1890 election was a prelude to the 1892 presidential rematch between Benjamin Harrison and Grover Cleveland. Ex-president Cleveland made an ex-president out of Harrison by recapturing the White House with a clear victory. In addition, Democrats regained control of both the House and the Senate. Unfortunately for the Democrats, a financial collapse shortly after Cleveland's inauguration, called the **Panic of '93,** plunged the nation into four years of the worst depression it had yet seen. The Democrats watched helplessly as banks and businesses failed and unemployment mounted to a record twenty per cent.

Section Review

1. What four issues dominated American politics from the mid-1870s to the end of the nineteenth century?
2. How did the Half-breeds and the Stalwarts compromise in choosing candidates for the Republican presidential campaign of 1880?
3. How did Republicans and Democrats differ concerning the tariff in the late nineteenth century?
4. What were the three provisions of the Interstate Commerce Act?
5. Why was the Fifty-first Congress called "the Billion-Dollar Congress"?

Labor

The demands of industrialization and the flood of immigration swelled the ranks of America's labor force. The rising standard of living that industrialization brought in its wake touched all Americans. Even unskilled immigrants living in difficult circumstances in most cases had better prospects for themselves and their children than they had in the "old country," stricken by war and poverty.

Yet there was a human cost to industrialization. Although they had been accustomed to working long hours on farms, workers found that six twelve-hour days or more could be trying when combined with other factors such as unsafe factories and wage cuts. Hard times also brought war widows and children into the factories in order to make ends meet, further burdening the problems of the labor system.

After the war, unorganized strikes were occasionally held in response to wage cuts, and the effectiveness and potential of labor organizations soon became apparent. Responding to the challenge and human cost of industrialization, organized labor became a powerful political and social force during the period.

Labor Unions—The earliest significant labor union was the **Knights of Labor,** formed in 1869 as a secret society of skilled and unskilled workers from various occupations. Though weakened by the Panic of 1873, the union emerged as an effective force under the leadership of **Terrence V. Powderly,** former mayor of Scranton, Pennsylvania.

The Knights advocated an eight-hour workday, laws prohibiting child labor, and equal pay for men and women. However, the Knights, like most early American labor unions, tended to be much more conservative than the radical and even violent unions of Europe. Powderly, in fact, personally favored boycotts and arbitration over strikes to settle wage dispute, since strikes often resulted in violence. A number of successful strikes, however, gained the Knights new clout and new members, and the group reached a peak of 700,000 members in 1886.

A more influential labor organization was formed in 1881. The **American Federation of Labor** (AFL), a splinter group from the Knights of Labor, formed craft unions for skilled laborers. Grouping skilled workers together by profession gave union members greater bargaining power with management. Under the leadership of **Samuel Gompers,** the AFL supported higher wages, shorter working hours, safer and cleaner working conditions, and elimination of child labor. The AFL's goals, however, were not entirely humanitarian. Unions in the AFL did not oppose child labor primarily out of sympathy for children, but because child labor contributed to low wage rates and made jobs for adults more scarce.

The most enduring achievement of the AFL was the acceptance of the eight-hour workday as a standard. Despite such accomplishments and the rapid growth of its membership, the image of the AFL as well as that of other unions was marred by the violence of strikes and infiltration by radical elements.

Labor Unrest—During the late 1860s and the 1870s only scattered, poorly managed strikes occurred over labor grievances. As unions grew in membership and purpose, however, strikes–and violence–became more common. Probably the most famous example of labor violence was the **Haymarket Riot** of 1886. Factory workers in Chicago, agitated by anarchists, went on strike, demanding an eight-hour workday. On May 4, 1886, police attempted to disperse a crowd of strikers listening to an anarchist speaker at Haymarket Square in Chicago. Someone threw a bomb into a group of policemen, touching off a riot. When the subsequent fighting ended, seven policemen and four civilians had been killed and many others seriously wounded. The Haymarket Square episode discredited the Knights of Labor and ended the "eight-hour" movement for the time being.

In 1892 violence erupted during a strike at the Carnegie Steel Company in Homestead, Pennsylvania, a suburb of Pittsburgh. Carnegie's assistant at the company, Henry C. Frick, proposed lowering the workers' wages because of the use of new labor-saving machinery. When the workers threatened to strike, Frick closed the plant, an action that has become known as a "lockout." Frick then hired three hundred guards to subdue picketers.

When fighting broke out on July 6, 1892, nine people were killed, and the hired guards were beaten back. Despite this temporary victory for the workers, however, the **Homestead Strike** gained nothing. After five months of striking, the workers agreed to Frick's proposal. The union was broken.

Another violent strike occurred at the Pullman Palace Car Company in Chicago. The leader of the strike was **Eugene V. Debs,** founder of the American Railway Union. The **Pullman Strike** was precipitated by five successive wage reductions, totaling twenty-five per cent, in the spring of 1894. Though these reductions were made necessary by the depression at the time, the company did not simultaneously reduce the rent on the houses it provided its employees or the cost of goods in the company stores. When the workers retaliated by striking, the Pullman Company withdrew the strikers' credit from the company stores. Facing starvation, the Pullman workers appealed to Debs's American Railway Union.

On June 26 Debs ordered union members to cut all Pullman passenger cars out of trains and leave them standing on the side tracks. The boycott of Pullman cars affected all western railroads. When boycotters were fired, the strike became general, and traffic including the mail between the West and Chicago came to a virtual standstill. Strikers and unemployed ruffians destroyed engines, cars, and equipment, causing owners to demand that federal troops be sent to break the strike. President Cleveland complied, declaring, ''If it takes every dollar in the Treasury and every soldier in the United States to deliver a postal card in Chicago–that postal card should be delivered.''

In addition, the federal courts issued an **injunction,** or court order, forbidding Debs and other strike leaders to continue further encouragement of the strike. Debs ignored the order and promoted the general strike and consequently spent six months in jail. He claimed that it was while in jail that he became an avowed socialist, though in fact his views had been socialistic for all of his adult life. (**Socialism** advocates collective or government ownership of the means of production.) After Debs's release he became the leader of the Social

Democratic party of America (later called simply the Socialist party), a position he was to hold until the 1920s. He was four times that party's candidate for president.

The violence and radicalism of the movement discredited unions for nearly a half century. Perhaps in part because of this radicalism, the government tended to side with management by providing court orders to end strikes and even providing troops to quell violence. Although organized labor made some gains for some workers, most union goals remained unrealized until the twentieth century.

Rural Revolt

The forces and politics of industrialism and innovation caused important changes in American agriculture. Improved farm machinery and methods increased production and made agricultural commodities an important export. Railroads, however, were the essential link between the farm and the market. High shipping costs siphoned off farm profits into the pocket of the railroads and left the farmers outraged. Abundant production itself became a problem, because, with such high yields of agricultural goods, prices stayed low.

The Grange–During the 1870s protesting farmers organized under the leadership of the Patrons of Husbandry, more commonly called the **Grange.** The organization had been founded by Oliver H. Kelly in 1867 to encourage social contacts and scientific methods of farming. Its growth and influence were negligible until farmers began to use it as a means of confronting railroads. The Granger movement made state regulation of railroads its chief goal, one that gained increasing support during the 1870s.

As a result of Grange influence, several midwestern states passed Granger Laws, legislation regulating railroads. In response, the railroads went to the Supreme Court in the case of *Munn* v. *Illinois* in 1877. The Court ruled against the railroads, deciding that a state through its ''police powers'' had the right to regulate a business that was public in nature, even though it was privately owned.

Lacking organizational strength, the Grange eventually disappeared but re-emerged in the 1880s

A Granger poster credits American prosperity to the farmers' labor.

as the Farmers' Alliance. Taking a lesson from industrial labor, the Farmers' Alliance united farm cooperatives across the country and looked to politics to meet agrarian demands such as railroad regulation, favorable currency policies, and anti-trust laws.

Populism—Grassroots, independent organizations sprang up throughout the Midwest and eventually merged through the politics of discontent to form the People's or **Populist party.** The Populist party seemed to prove the truth of the adage that "misery loves company." The hard times in Middle America between the Great Blizzards of 1886-1887 and the Panic of '93 attracted thousands of farmers and reformers to the party's banner. Though officially formed only in 1891, the Populists polled over a million votes with their presidential candidate, James B. Weaver, in 1892. In fact, this new third party carried four western states and showed remarkable strength in the solidly Democratic South.

The issue that dominated the Populist movement during the mid-nineties was currency policy. After the failure of the greenback efforts under Grant (see p. 345), easy money advocates began to view coinage of silver as the answer to their problems. Basically, the Populists wanted to make sil-ver in addition to gold the standard for American currency. The depression meant that money was scarce, and, for a growing number of Americans feeling the squeeze, the solution was the unlimited coinage of silver. Such purposeful inflation would make more money available to the hard-pressed working man. In the words of the 1894 best seller, *Coin's Financial School,* **free silver** would "make it possible for the debtor to pay his debts; business to start anew, and revivify all the industries of the country, which must remain paralyzed so long as silver as well as all other property is measured by a gold standard." For the farmers, more money in circulation would mean higher prices for crops.

Amid the hard times and the economic complexities of industrialism, silver became a simple solution for the down-and-out, a kind of patent medicine for all economic ills. In the Midwest free silver became the battle cry for the Populist legions. Not even the major parties were immune from their growing force. Lacking, however, the organizational, financial, and numerical strength of the major parties, the Populists decided to cast their lot with the more sympathetic Democratic party in the 1896 presidential election. The result was a colorful, crucial contest—part campaign, part crusade.

Goldbugs vs. Silverbugs

The Panic of '93 and the ensuing depression hounded Grover Cleveland throughout his second term and left the Democratic nomination in doubt in 1896. Republicans, however, had a candidate on the first ballot, Ohio's **William McKinley.** A likable though somber figure, McKinley was the friend of industrialists, a fitting candidate for the gold-standard, protariff, big-business platform of the Republicans.

When the Democrats arrived in Chicago for their convention, the place was abuzz with talk of silver and the inevitable question of who would get the nomination and stamp out the "goldbugs." The answer was a thirty-six-year-old Nebraskan named **William Jennings Bryan.**

Bryan, called "the Great Commoner" because of his genuine sympathy for the common man, was both a remarkable political figure and a fervent Christian. His silver-tongued oratory sprang from

The silver-tongued orator from the Great Plains, William Jennings Bryan on the stump in 1896

roots which ran deep into America's heartland. In Chicago his eloquent appeals for economic deliverance through silver sealed his nomination. Bryan stood before the convention and declared to a sea of rapt faces, ''I come to speak to you in defense of a cause as holy as the cause of liberty–the cause of humanity.'' The government must have a social conscience, he cried. Its voice must be the people's voice, and the people would be heard. He concluded,

> Having behind us the producing masses of this nation and the world, supported by the commercial interests, the laboring interests, and the toilers everywhere, we will answer their [the business interests'] demand for a gold standard by saying to them: You shall not press down upon the brow of labor this crown of thorns, you shall not crucify mankind upon a cross of gold.

Bryan swept the convention like a prairie fire.

The campaign to follow was the first modern campaign as well as a study in contrasts. Leading a cash-poor campaign (Republicans outspent Democrats as much as twenty to one), Bryan went on a whirlwind tour of the country. He made hundreds of whistlestops during an 18,000-mile trek and was seen and heard by an audience totaling five million. McKinley, however, stayed home. In a carefully orchestrated effort, McKinley ran a ''front porch campaign'' from his home in Canton, Ohio. Trainloads of select audiences were given all-expense-paid trips to Canton to hear McKinley read a prepared script, while hundreds of speakers fanned out across the country to promote him.

On election day Bryan polled six and a half million votes, but McKinley got over seven million. The Great Commoner, however, was not the only casualty on election day. The Populist party, in giving up its reform efforts for a single issue and in losing its identity by casting its lot with the

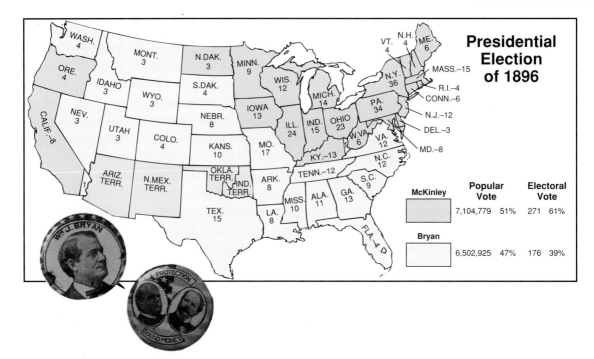

Presidential Election of 1896

	Popular Vote		Electoral Vote	
McKinley	7,104,779	51%	271	61%
Bryan	6,502,925	47%	176	39%

Democrats, had betrayed its cause for a few pieces of silver. Many of its reforms would be taken up by others but won under different labels and circumstances in later years.

The 1896 election was a turning point in American political history, the culmination of the struggle between the past and the future, between the farm and the factory–and the factory won. The rural leadership that Populism represented was growing old with the century. For good or bad, America's future lay amidst her crowded city streets.

Section Review

1. What was the most enduring achievement of the American Federation of Labor?
2. Name two major labor strikes of the late 1800s.
3. What industry did most farmers blame for their low profits?
4. What political party eventually emerged from the agricultural reform movement begun by the Grange? What economic issue dominated this party in the 1890s?

Change and Challenge

Growth of Cities

One of the reasons that the rural revolt of Populism came up short was that many farmers had moved to the city. The 1890 census revealed that for the first time, the majority of Americans were in nonagricultural occupations. The concentrations of industry with the resulting concentrations of labor made **"urbanization"** (movement of the population to the cities) the most significant social movement of the period.

During the half century from 1860 through 1910 increases in the urban population outstripped increases in the rural population by nearly two to one. The dramatic shift was reflected in the size and number of cities. In 1860 only New York and Philadelphia had populations in excess of 500,000 people. In 1910 Chicago, St. Louis, Boston, Cleveland, Baltimore, and Pittsburgh had joined the ranks of the big cities, with New York City (including Brooklyn) approaching a population of nearly five million by that time. The most phenomenal urban growth, however, was in the small cities with populations of 2,500 or greater. Such cities numbered 400 at the outset of the War Between the States; that number jumped sevenfold in fifty years to 2,200 cities.

What was the attraction of city dwelling? Jobs, for one. The boom in manufacturing and service industries provided employment for the huge influx of immigrants, as well as for down-and-out farm laborers squeezed off the land by hard times or labor-saving machinery. In addition, many found the services and attractions of city living alluring. As Horace Greeley observed, ''We cannot all live in cities, yet nearly all seem determined to do so. Hot and cold water, baker's bread, gas, the theatre and the streetcars . . . indicate the tendency of modern taste.''

To those who lived there, however, the ''gilded metropolis,'' as one wide-eyed farm boy described Kansas City, became a tinsel town. There was an ugly side to urbanization in the squalor of slums, the rise of crime and prostitution, and the dangers of disease. In fact, the infant mortality rate in the city was double that in the country. In Chicago in the 1880s, for example, only half the children born there lived past their fifth birthday.

Industrialization gradually created a substantial, growing middle class, but the path to prosperity was choked with moral as well as industrial pollutants, and the promises offered by smoke-stacked cities often proved empty.

Immigration

Aggravating the problems of the cities was a new wave of immigration. The American continent had been receiving immigrants, of course, since the English settled at Jamestown and Plymouth. After the Civil War, however, came a wave of immigrants so different from those in the past that it was called the **''New Immigration.''** As the turn of the twentieth century neared, the percentage of British and German immigrants (who had previously made up most American immigrants) began to shrink in comparison to ''new immigrants'' from Southern and Eastern European countries such as Italy, Greece, and Russia. By 1900, for the first time in American history, immigrants from Southern and

Eastern Europe outnumbered those from Northern and Western Europe. Another new element in immigration was the large number of Chinese who began to settle on the west coast, where they provided labor for the railroads.

Some of the more fortunate immigrants, particularly those from Scandinavia and Germany, were able to move directly to the Midwest and immediately find work in farming or logging. Most of the immigrants, however, had no money or job skills to enable them to move from the cities to which they first came. New York, Chicago, Philadelphia, and other large cities swelled in population. Immigrants tended to band together in the cities so that different neighborhoods often had their own distinct ethnic character–Polish, Italian, Greek, or any one of a number of others. Often illiterate and knowing little English, many of these immigrants were forced to take low-paying jobs in ''sweat shop'' factories and to live in squalid tenements.

As the ''New Immigration'' grew in proportion to the ''old,'' so did opposition to immigration. American labor leaders feared–rightly in some cases–that immigrant workers would take jobs from other Americans by agreeing to work longer

For many European immigrants, America provided new hope and opportunity.

hours for less pay. The poverty of ethnic slums created fears that immigrants would lower the nation's standard of living and breed crime and disease–although obviously no immigrant *wanted* to live under such conditions. The large number of Catholic, Jewish, and Eastern Orthodox immigrants raised religious fears among America's dominantly Protestant population. A tiny minority of radicals and revolutionaries among the immigrants caused many of them to be branded as potential enemies of American freedoms and institutions. Racial prejudice, especially in California against the Chinese, also motivated calls for limits to immigration. The simple fact that immigrants tended to form churches and sometimes schools where only their native language was spoken led many Americans to fear that the cultural unity of the nation was being undermined. As a result of these fears, Congress placed an increasing number of quotas and restrictions on immigration. By 1930 immigration from Southern and Eastern Europe had been reduced to less than a fifth of what it had been in 1910.

Despite the many cultural obstacles, the immigrants continued to come and many prospered. The children of the immigrants, able to learn the language and American customs more easily than their parents, often rose higher economically than their elders. Immigrants provided labor for construction projects and for factories; they built rich and fertile farms in the Midwest; some became prosperous shopkeepers and small businessmen. Immigrants, in short, provided much of the backbone and muscle needed to transform the United States into an industrial giant. As immigrants began to adopt American culture, fears of an ethnically fragmented society began to subside. In fact, some began to speak of the United States as the **"melting pot"** in which diverse racial and ethnic cultures would blend to form a new and unified nation.

As immigrants streamed into the United States, over a million a year passed through the immigrant reception center on Ellis Island in New York Harbor. There in the harbor they saw a gleaming torchbearer, a bronze lady–the Statue of Liberty. Inscribed in the statue's pedestal were these words of welcome:

> Give me your tired, your poor,
> Your huddled masses yearning to breathe free,
> The wretched refuse of your teeming shore.
> Send these, the homeless, tempest-tossed, to me,
> I lift my lamp beside the golden door!

New Forces

Machines alone were not changing America; new ideas, philosophies, and attitudes were also challenging old systems. Whether these new philosophies were accepted or rejected, they had and continue to have a wide influence throughout society.

Darwinism–The book *The Origin of Species* (1859) by **Charles Darwin** found a receptive audience in burgeoning, industrial America. Darwin's basic theory involved "natural selection," a process through which all present species, including man, have supposedly struggled and evolved. The survival, development, and improvement of species depend upon their ability to adapt to the changes of a sometimes cruel world. For Christians, Darwin's theory lacked scientific credibility and contradicted Biblical truth; nonetheless a number of Darwin's disciples came to apply his ideas to every area of a rapidly changing society. Darwinism to them became more than a biological staircase of mud, monkeys, and men; it became the key to the riddle of life.

The chief proponent of **Social Darwinism** (the application of the evolutionary theory to social institutions) was Englishman Herbert Spencer, whose only memorable contribution out of eight dense volumes on the new philosophy was the phrase "survival of the fittest." On this side of the Atlantic, Spencer's Social Darwinism fit well into the unfettered business climate of the Gilded Age. Andrew Carnegie's *Gospel of Wealth* applied Spencer's views to the economy. John D. Rockefeller eagerly seized the concept as an article of faith, declaring, "The growth of a large business is merely a survival of the fittest. . . . This is not an evil tendency in business. It is merely the working-out of a law of nature and a law of God." For these men and for those who longed for what they had, millionaires were the marathoners in the race of life, having outperformed and outdistanced lesser breeds.

Not all Darwinists were satisfied with Spencer's conclusions. In the late nineteenth century a movement known as **Reform Darwinism** emerged as a result of the work of a Washington bureaucrat named Lester Frank Ward. Unlike the Carnegies and the Rockefellers of the world, Ward could view the evolutionary process only from the bottom up. From that perspective, he determined that human progress was best achieved not through competition but through cooperation. Not surprisingly, Ward believed that government was best equipped to promote human progress through cooperation. As a result, government as an active agent for social change could remove the two great barriers to a better world, poverty and ignorance. Ward's ideas would have a tremendous impact on social thinking and public policy in the twentieth century.

Despite the fact that Darwinism was opposed to Biblical truth, liberal theologians and pulpiteers accommodated and incorporated the new philosophy. Evolution was used to explain not only the origin of the earth but the origin of the Scriptures as well. According to these new thinkers, the Bible was not "given by inspiration of God" (II Tim. 3:16); rather it was the result of a "process" of human aspirations.

In addition, building on a liberal tradition, the Reform Darwinists among the evolutionists believed that man was not, as the Scriptures taught, sinful; rather man was inherently good. The ailments of society could be cured through improvement of the human condition. This social gospel often grew out of a genuine concern to relieve the misery of the slums, believing that the essence of Christianity was the command "Thou shalt love thy neighbor as thyself." This love, however, was misdirected and inadequate since it embraced the body only and not the soul. Christ, our great example, fed the hungry with bread in order to teach them about the Bread of Life. Love for our neighbor is hardly complete if it gives him food and shelter but leaves his soul in darkness.

The marvels of the machine age and the miracles of science and invention seemed to offer irrefutable proof of the Darwinist view of human progress. Such millennial optimism, however, would eventually sink in the mud and blood of 1914, as global war brought man's triumphant march to a grinding halt.

Trends in Literature – A number of literary styles emerged during the late nineteenth century, reflecting the changes in society and capturing the spirit of the times. Perhaps the most popular writer of the day was Samuel Langhorne Clemens, who under the pen name **Mark Twain** produced such American classics as *The Adventures of Huckleberry Finn* and *Life on the Mississippi.* Twain's work reflected the literary school of **realism.** In contrast to the emotional, exotic character of romanticism (see p. 229), realists such as Twain drew a picture of simple, ordinary life colored with his captivating humor. In a similar vein, realist painters such as Winslow Homer and Thomas Eakins portrayed daily life from the common man's perspective, revealing both its strength and its mundane quality.

By the 1890s a new literary approach, known as **naturalism,** developed. In some ways an extreme form of realism that was shaped by Darwinism, naturalism emphasized man's helplessness and struggle with the world. **Stephen Crane,** for example, in *Maggie: A Girl of the Streets* (1893) portrayed a girl who is overwhelmed by circumstances and driven to prostitution, a tragic victim of the city. In the *Red Badge of Courage* (1895) Crane described a young soldier caught up in the whirling fates of war. **Jack London,** also writing from the naturalist perspective, portrayed the triumph of brute force over the cruel world in his *Call of the Wild* (1903), the story of a fierce dog who ran with an Alaskan wolf pack.

Another popular literary form of the time described triumph not in the tradition of Jack London's red fang but in the tradition of Benjamin Franklin's Poor Richard. Success literature emphasized the virtues of hard work, thrift, and honesty. **Horatio Alger** was the premier writer of such rags-to-riches tales. A generation of young readers grew up reading about the heroes of *Luck and Pluck, Bound to Rise,* and *Tattered Tom* who triumphed

Winslow Homer, 1836-1910, Croquet Scene, *oil on canvas, 1866, 15 7/8 x 26 1/16 in, Friends of American Art Collection, 1942.35*
© *1991 The Art Institute of Chicago, All Rights Reserved.*

over adversity, often on the new frontier of America's urban jungle.

Materialism—Jefferson's phrase "the pursuit of happiness" took on a whole new meaning during the Gilded Age. In the wake of industrialization, mass production and labor-saving machinery provided more people with more things and more time to enjoy them. America increasingly became a consumer society in which people associated with each other on the basis of what they owned. Brand names, advertising, and new mass marketing techniques took on greater importance in the economic choices of daily life. Unfortunately, **materialism**—the desire for worldly possessions and the belief that only they can bring true happiness—became the philosophy of an alarming number of Americans.

Prior to industrialization, markets were local, their stock confined to the produce of the region. With the rise of national companies and the mass market, cupboards from Savannah to Seattle held many of the same labels. Nabisco, for example, underscored the national scope of their line of crackers, the *Uneeda Biscuit,* with this 1904 ad:

> When San Francisco folks are eating Uneeda Biscuits for breakfast, New Yorkers are having them for lunch, and the people in between are just getting hungry for more. We were right when we said to the whole country, "Uneeda Biscuit."

With the increase of leisure time that mechanization provided, Americans sought a number of new outlets for recreation and amusement. Organized sports took on the broad appeal that other "consumables" had. Baseball became the *national* pastime beginning in 1869 when the Cincinnati Red Stockings, the first all-professional team, toured the country. In the decades that followed, thousands flocked to city ball parks. In 1903 the first World Series was played as crowds watched the Boston Pilgrims defeat the Pittsburgh Pirates to become the first "world champions."

Other recreational activities–such as golf, tennis, and particularly croquet–enjoyed an even broader appeal because both women and men could play. Throughout the entire period croquet was the sport of choice for upper- and middle-class people. Some enterprising croquet clubs even organized night parties with candles attached to the wickets. The popularity of mixed sports prompted illustrator Charles Dana Gibson to produce the "Gibson girl," the quintessential American woman–athletic yet without the loss of feminine charm.

Bicycles were immensely popular during the 1890s, with sales figures showing over a million pedal-pushers by 1893. Cycle clubs were so numerous that they even became a political force, lobbying with municipal and state governments for more paved roads. Courting couples in particular found bicycling appealing, inspiring turn-of-the century beaus to croon

It won't be a stylish marriage–
I can't afford a carriage–
But you'll look sweet
Upon the seat
Of a bicycle built for two.

The material prosperity not only changed social conditions but also influenced spiritual conditions. For many the goal of gain became paramount. In his "Acres of Diamonds" speech, prominent lecturer Russell Conwell declared to audiences totaling thirteen million people that it was the Christian's duty to be prosperous. The Baptist minister exhorted, "I say, get rich, get rich." Conwell forgot Christ's words in Luke 12:15 that "a man's life consisteth not in the abundance of the things which he possesseth."

Boston versus New York in a 1904 American League game at Boston's old Huntington Avenue Park, the predecessor to Fenway Park.

Jumbo!

"The only burning question between England and America is Jumbo," the American ambassador James Russell Lowell reported in March, 1882. What was this huge foreign policy crisis? A twelve-foot-high, seven-ton elephant named Jumbo. Circus owner P. T. Barnum, the indisputable master of show and sham, had purchased the elephant from the London Zoo to the outrage of all of England, from Queen Victoria to the thousands of children who had ridden on Jumbo's enormous back during weekends at Regent's Park.

Jumbo was an African bull elephant, the largest ever held in captivity. Captured as a baby in Ethiopia, the elephant changed hands from Cairo to Paris and finally to London where the "elephantine toddler" was named "Jumbo" after the African title "Mumbo Jumbo" (a West African village official charged with warding off evil spirits). By the time Jumbo approached twelve feet high, zoo officials knew they had a record-breaking ani-

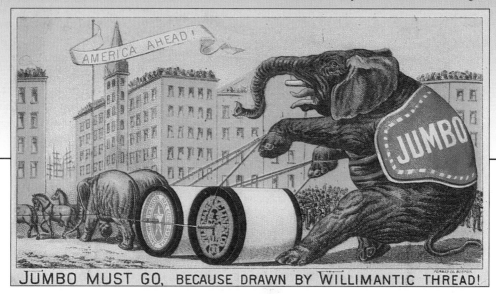

JUMBO MUST GO, BECAUSE DRAWN BY WILLIMANTIC THREAD!

A number of American advertisers found Jumbo's size a fitting complement for their extravagant claims about their products.

The transformation of the celebration of Christmas perhaps best illustrates the changes that materialism brought. In 1880, F. W. Woolworth, pinching pennies for his Five and Ten Cent Store in Lancaster, Pennsylvania, cautiously ventured to spend $25 for Christmas ornaments. Surprised when the decorations were snapped up by eager customers, Woolworth began to pour more and more into his Christmas stock to meet the demands of the market. By 1891 Woolworth was reminding the managers of his chain of stores that Christmas "is our harvest time, make it pay." Increasingly for retailers and consumers alike Christmas was "good" in proportion to its gain. Somewhere amid the growing materialism, many Americans were trading off spiritual values at bargain prices.

Meeting the Challenge

Christians did not let the challenges of urbanization, materialism, immigration, and class conflict go unanswered. Many Christians sought to deal with these problems in Scriptural ways. Some, for

mal. His huge size contributed a colossal new adjective to the language—jumbo!

After Jumbo had been with the London Zoo for nearly twenty years, officials began to fear that the gentle giant might grow erratic with advancing age. They were therefore looking for a buyer, and Barnum was only too eager to add Jumbo to his "Greatest Show on Earth." A deal was quickly struck.

While custom-made accommodations were being prepared for Jumbo's Atlantic passage, a period of near national mourning followed in England, which Barnum encouraged and manipulated wherever he could to increase the drama and the ticket sales when Jumbo finally arrived in America. Jumbo's arrival at New York on April 9, 1882, drew huge, enthusiastic crowds that only foreshadowed Jumbo's fabulous future on the circus circuit. Within two weeks Barnum had recovered the $30,000 it had cost him to acquire the elephant. His ticket take the first season with Jumbo approached $2 million.

Jumbo would probably have been little more than a big elephant, but under Barnum's skillful promotion he became "the Colossus of his kind" and the "monstrous mammal." Through the avenues of mass appeal, thousands flocked into Barnum's tents to see what no words could describe. For over forty years Barnum's shows had given the country the lovable dwarf General Tom Thumb, the Swedish nightingale Jenny Lind, and such oddities as the Bearded Lady and the Siamese Twins. Jumbo, however, capped the showman's remarkable career and captured something of America's boisterous spirit.

Sadly Jumbo's American career was cut short when in 1885 he was struck and killed by a train in Ontario, Canada. Barnum, however, did not consider it a complete loss. He had the skeleton mounted and the skin stuffed for separate display. Only Barnum could have figured out a way to make *two* Jumbos.

example, confronted the squalor of city slums by establishing rescue missions, centers located in the middle of the slums for preaching the gospel and ministering to the physical needs of city dwellers. The most widespread method of meeting these challenges with the gospel, however, was **urban evangelism,** the conducting of large, city-wide campaigns in huge auditoriums or large churches in major cities. The leader of the movement during this period was Evangelist **Dwight L. Moody.**

D. L. Moody—Dwight Lyman Moody was born in Northfield, Massachusetts, in 1837. At the age of seventeen, Moody went to seek his fortune in Boston. He worked for his uncle in a shoe store, and at his uncle's insistence, young Moody went to church regularly. There Moody sat in the class of a concerned Sunday school teacher, who eventually led the young man to Christ. Despite his salvation, Moody was in some ways still worldly-minded. He desired above all to be rich, and to that end he moved to Chicago in 1856, where he thought lay greater opportunities for wealth.

In Chicago, however, Moody was touched by the Prayer Meeting Revival (see pp. 237-38), and as a result he became more involved in Christian work than in the search for wealth. In 1859 he began a Sunday school in the slums of Chicago that grew under his leadership to over fifteen hundred students. In 1860 Moody completely abandoned his materialistic goals, quit his high-paying job with a shoe company, and devoted himself entirely to working with his Sunday school, the YMCA, and other Christian organizations. He began a church in Chicago, although he was not an ordained minister, and he became a popular speaker at conventions and churches on subjects such as Sunday school organization and promotion.

Evangelism—Moody's transformation from Sunday school lecturer to world-renowned evangelist was unexpected. In 1873 Moody began a speaking tour of Great Britain. At first it was a small affair and little noticed. As the tour continued, however, crowds swelled, and newspapers began to report the success of this "Yankee evangelist." In four

D. L. Moody, America's evangelist to the cities during the Gilded Age

months in London alone, Moody conducted 285 meetings attended by two and a half million people. Even the English nobility, including the Princess of Wales, came to hear this remarkable American.

When Moody returned to the United States in 1875, he found himself deluged with requests to hold city-wide campaigns across the United States. Moody eagerly agreed to as many of these invitations as he could because he believed that reaching the major cities with the gospel would reach the whole nation. "Water runs down hill, and the highest hills in America are the great cities," he said. "If we can stir them we shall stir the whole country." Over the next twenty years, Moody preached to millions in the United States, Canada, the British Isles, and Mexico. Reported conversions numbered in the thousands at each campaign.

Methodology—The ultimate reason for the success of the Moody campaigns was, of course, the moving of the Holy Spirit in the hearts of men. In human terms, however, some credit must go to Moody's approach and organization. Although not formally educated, Moody had a gift for communicating. He spoke plainly from the heart to the heart and filled his sermons with compelling stories, jokes, and illustrations. His theme was simple but profound: God loves sinners and wants to save them. Moody also avoided denominational ties. He wanted all true Christians of all denominations to join together in winning the lost to Christ.

Moody was tremendously well organized–like successful businessmen of his time. One minister noted, "As he stood on the platform, he looked like a businessman, he dressed like a businessman; he took the meeting in hand as a businessman would." Although Moody's services were informal, he demanded order. Each element of the massive meetings was carefully planned and meticulously organized. Although Moody rejected the materialism of big business, he insisted on businesslike efficiency in his campaigns. The all-important "business" of saving souls, Moody thought, certainly required at least as much care, planning, and forethought as the operation of some secular company.

Moody also became one of the first evangelists to use music in his campaigns as a means of attracting and winning over a crowd and of presenting "the gospel in song." He recruited baritone **Ira Sankey** to serve as his song leader and soloist. Sankey helped popularize the "gospel song," a sacred tune that is less formal than a hymn and has a more popular, easily sung melody. Sankey composed the tunes for such gospel songs as "A Shelter in the Time of Storm," "Hiding in Thee," and "Faith Is the Victory!"

Effects—Moody launched the urban evangelism movement, and scores of evangelists followed after him. Methodist **Sam Jones,** often called "the Moody of the South," was probably second only to Moody himself in popularity and success. Like Moody, Jones preached in a direct–almost blunt– and colorful manner that spoke to listeners on their own level. Led by evangelists such as Moody and

Fanny Crosby: Her Saviour First of All

The most prolific writer of gospel songs and hymns in the nineteenth century was Fanny Crosby. Blinded by the blundering of a quack doctor when she was only six months old, Fanny spent most of her life in darkness. She refused to be bitter, however, and she found an outlet for her talents in writing poetry.

Christian musician William Bradbury persuaded Fanny to write the words for hymns and gospel songs. Her songs, popularized by the Moody-Sankey campaigns, soon filled the churches of America and Great Britain. She wrote songs to call the penitent to Christ (''Pass Me Not, O Gentle Saviour,'' ''Jesus Is Calling''), songs to rouse Christians to evangelize the lost (''Rescue the Perishing''), songs of comfort and fellowship (''Blessed Assurance,'' ''All the Way My Saviour Leads Me''), and songs of praise (''To God Be the Glory,'' ''Praise Him! Praise Him! Jesus Our Blessed Redeemer!'').

Her output was so phenomenally large that music publishers asked her to write some songs under pseudonyms so that people would not think *all* the songs in their books were by her. Her inspiration might come from some passing thought or a comment overheard somewhere. She reportedly wrote ''Pass Me Not, O Gentle Saviour,'' for example, after hearing someone in a rescue mission pray, ''Saviour, do not pass me by.'' Sometimes a melody would suggest the words to Fanny. Phoebe Knapp, for example, played a tune and asked, ''What does it say to you, Fanny?'' The poetess replied, ''Blessed assurance, Jesus is mine,'' and the song was born.

Fanny Crosby's life spanned nearly a century (1820-1915). In that time she wrote hundreds of verses, not for fame or wealth but out of a sense of love and devotion to Christ in return for His matchless love for her. One of her more poignant songs, ''My Saviour First of All,'' demonstrates that despite her physical blindness, she had set her spiritual sight on the proper goal:

When my life-work is ended, and I cross the swelling tide,
When the bright and glorious morning I shall see;
I shall know my Redeemer when I reach the other side,
And His smile will be the first to welcome me.

Jones, the period from 1875 to 1915 was the golden age of urban evangelism.

Moody and Sankey also helped establish the gospel song as part of American church life. The works of songwriters such as P. P. Bliss and blind poetess Fanny Crosby became standards in most church hymnals. Bliss in particular–with songs such as ''Let the Lower Lights Be Burning,'' ''Wonderful Words of Life,'' and ''Hallelujah, What a Saviour!''–may have done even more to popularize gospel songs than Sankey did.

In Moody's campaigns alone, millions of people heard the gospel and tens of thousands professed salvation through Christ. It is difficult to measure what impact these conversions had on American society at large, but it became clear in the 1890s and 1900s that the urban revivals gave at least a push to reform efforts such as prohibition. For Moody and the urban evangelists, however, the salvation of the lost was clearly the most important result. Their motto was best summed up in the title of a gospel song–''Rescue the Perishing.'' As Moody said on one occasion, ''I look upon this world as a wrecked vessel. God has given me a lifeboat and said to me, 'Moody, save all you can.' ''

As the century drifted into twilight, the great urban revivals underscored the remarkable change America had undergone since 1800. At the beginning of the century, Methodist circuit riders and frontier camp meetings were on the leading edge of American Christianity. By Moody's day, however, congregations had moved from brush arbors to big auditoriums. The nation now bridged two oceans, and half the country had moved to the city. As the twentieth century dawned on America's streets, more change and new challenge lay ahead.

Section Review

1. List at least two advantages and two disadvantages of living in the city in the late 1800s.
2. Name at least three popular leisure-time activities in the late nineteenth century.
3. What was the ultimate reason for the success of the Moody campaigns?
4. What is a gospel song?

Chapter Review

Terms

robber barons
Cornelius Vanderbilt
Andrew Carnegie
vertical integration
John D. Rockefeller
horizontal integration
trust
John Pierpont Morgan
United States Steel Corporation
"New South"
James Buchanan Duke
Alexander Graham Bell
Thomas Alva Edison
Roscoe Conkling
"Stalwarts"
"Half-breeds"
James A. Garfield
Chester A. Arthur
Pendleton Act
Civil Service Commission

"Mongrel Tariff"
Grover Cleveland
Interstate Commerce Act
Benjamin Harrison
Sherman Antitrust Act
McKinley Tariff
Panic of '93
Knights of Labor
Terrence V. Powderly
American Federation of Labor
Samuel Gompers
Haymarket Riot
Homestead Strike
Eugene V. Debs
Pullman Strike
injunction
socialism
Grange
Populist party
free silver
William McKinley

William Jennings Bryan
urbanization
"New Immigration"
"melting pot"
The Origin of Species
Charles Darwin
Social Darwinism
Reform Darwinism
Mark Twain
realism
naturalism
Stephen Crane
Jack London
Horatio Alger
materialism
urban evangelism
Dwight L. Moody
Ira Sankey
Sam Jones

Content Questions

1. What is the difference between vertical integration and horizontal integration?
2. With which captain of industry do we associate oil refining? With which do we associate steel production? the "New South"?
3. Widespread use of what invention spurred the growth of the mass-produced clothing industry?
4. What crime in 1881 helped promote civil service reform by the passage of the Pendleton Act?
5. In which presidential election in the late 1800s did a candidate win in the electoral college but lose in the popular vote?
6. Which of the two major political parties embraced the free silver issue in 1896? Who was their candidate for president in that election?
7. Give at least three reasons that many Americans opposed the "New Immigration" of the late nineteenth and early twentieth centuries.

8. What was the most widespread method of meeting the challenges of the city with the gospel?

Application Questions

1. In what ways was the growth of American industry during the Gilded Age a benefit to the nation? In what ways was it detrimental?
2. Review the discussion of the spoils system under Andrew Jackson (p. 200) and in this chapter (p. 360). What are some advantages of the spoils system? What are some of the disadvantages? Do you think the system is good or bad on the whole?
3. Was federal regulation of the railroads, such as the Interstate Commerce Act, necessary? Why or why not?
4. Read Matthew 6:19-21, 24-34. What do these passages teach the Christian concerning his reaction to materialism?

A sod house, such as this one in Nebraska, provided shelter for many early settlers of the Great Plains.

Americans were a restless and energetic people. During the Gilded Age they not only built their cities and factories but also settled the continent, pushing the frontier to the Pacific and beyond. With the climax of Manifest Destiny in the Mexican War (1848), the United States faced a new challenge. It now faced the daunting task of developing not only the huge tracts of land won from Mexico but also large segments of the Louisiana Purchase and Oregon territory that were still relatively unsettled. This challenge was met by railroaders, cowboys, miners, and farmers–all pioneers who pushed toward the Pacific in the last great wave of westward expansion in American history.

Yet Manifest Destiny did not really end with victory over Mexico. With the continent now possessed from Atlantic to Pacific, some Americans began to look across the seas to other lands where they could plant the Stars and Stripes. Part of this ''overseas Manifest Destiny'' was simply economic, the securing of new markets for the prod-

ucts of a growing American economy. Part of this expansion, however, was the same lust for territory that had helped spark the Mexican War. Most of this expansion–to the credit of the United States– was peaceful, although before the century closed, the United States found itself involved in its first foreign war in fifty years.

Western Expansion
Rails to the West

The history of the American West rode on iron rails. The railroads crisscrossed the country, uniting the western half of the nation with the eastern half. Trains carried settlers into the West, of course, but they also carried out the products of the West to the East. Development of the region's resources was not impossible without the railroad; the California gold rush had proved that. There is no question, however, that precious metals and rich land for grazing and agriculture became even more valuable when supply sources and markets were only

Workers for the Union Pacific Railroad lay track westward across the Great Plains.

as far as the nearest rail junction. Railroads proved to be the main instrument of "civilizing" the American West.

The Transcontinental Idea – After the California gold rush created a population explosion on the Pacific coast, Americans began to dream of linking East and West. The ideal "bridge" over the intervening mountains and prairie was, of course, the railroad. The mammoth cost of a **transcontinental railroad,** however, frightened railroad investors. The federal government came up with two railroad acts which provided a system of incentives for builders. First, for each mile of track laid, the railroad company would receive land grants of alternating ten-mile-square sections of land along each side of the road. This land grant was doubled in 1864 to twenty-mile-square sections, ultimately giving the participating railroads about twenty million acres–an area nearly as large as the state of Indiana. Second, the government provided loans to the railroads: $16,000 for each mile of track laid in the plains, $32,000 per mile in the foothills, and $48,000 per mile in the mountains.

Two railroads received charters to build the first transcontinental railroad. The **Union Pacific** was to begin in Omaha, Nebraska, and build westward, and the **Central Pacific** was to begin in Sacramento, California, and build eastward. Eventually the two companies raced to see which could lay the most track–and therefore receive the most money. The Union Pacific, with mostly plains to cross, had an easier time than the Central Pacific, which had

to cross the steepest part of the Sierra Nevada. Even so, the Union Pacific still had to contend with searing heat, waterless plains, and Indian attacks. Neither company faced an easy task.

Building the Line – The Union Pacific hired mostly Irish immigrants, many of them former Union army veterans. The Central Pacific relied mainly on immigrant Chinese workers called "coolies." Both sets of workers overcame tremendous challenges and astonished their employers with the speed at which they laid track. An English visitor described the process:

> A light car, drawn by a single horse, gallops up to the front with its load of rails. Two men seize the end of a rail and start forward, the rest of the gang taking hold by twos until it is clear of the car. They come forward at a run. At the word of command the rail is dropped in its place, right side up. Less than thirty seconds to a rail for each gang, and so four rails go down to the minute!

Almost poetically, the observer went on to note that there were "three strokes to the spike, . . . ten spikes to the rail, four hundred rails to a mile, eighteen hundred miles to San Francisco." The Central Pacific set the single-day record for laying track. At 7:00 A.M. on April 28, 1869, 5,000 men set to work using five trains full of over 25,000 railroad ties, 3,500 rails, 55,000 spikes, and 14,000 bolts. By the time they had stopped at 7:00 P.M., the crews had laid ten miles of track.

The joining of a continent: workers of the Union Pacific and Central Pacific railroads celebrate the meeting of their lines at Promontory Point, Utah.

The climax came on May 10, 1869, when the two lines were joined at Promontory (PRAH mun TORE ee) Point, Utah. Officials drove in four special spikes–two gold, one silver, and one a mixture of gold, silver, and iron. On one of the gold spikes was inscribed, ''May God continue the unity of our Country as this Railroad unites the two great Oceans of the world.'' Within twenty-five years, four more transcontinental lines spanned the country: the Southern Pacific (finished 1883); the Northern Pacific (1883); the Atchison, Topeka, and Santa Fe (1885); and the Great Northern (1893). The railroads quickly became the vehicles for tremendous change in the West.

Resources of the West

Mining–One of the first spurs to the settlement of the West and the building of the transcontinental railroad was the mining of precious metals. The California gold rush in 1849 was but the first of several western scrambles to dig wealth out of the earth. One of the earliest after California was the **Pikes Peak gold rush** in 1859, which resulted in the settlement of Colorado. Thousands of pioneers seeking to ''get rich quick'' streamed into Colorado, particularly the wildly expanding ''boom town'' of Denver. On their wagons, gold hunters boldly advertised, ''Pikes Peak or Bust!'' When the gold in Colorado gave out, however, many fortune seekers rode back with a new message: ''Busted!''

Miners often found more than gold in the Rockies. Leadville, Colorado, is a splendid example of the diverse resources of the region. After a gold boom in Leadville gave out in the early 1860s, the town became a center for silver and lead mining. After the silver ran out, Leadville also became a center for mining zinc and copper. The story of Leadville and similar communities often made it seem that the mineral resources of the West were limitless.

Farther west one of the largest and richest mines was the **Comstock Lode** in Nevada. Miners there eagerly dug gold out of the ground, but they were disappointed to find that it was contaminated by some other metal and therefore sold for less. Upon closer examination, the "other metal" turned out to be silver. In fact, over half of the ore eventually mined from the Comstock Lode was silver and the rest was gold. In all, miners extracted some $400 million worth of gold and silver from the Comstock Lode between 1859 and 1900.

The mining of the Comstock Lode was typical of mining in the latter half of the nineteenth century. No longer was mining a matter of a lone grizzled prospector with his pickaxe and shovel digging for gold in the side of a mountain; mining was big business. Large companies hired dozens of miners, sank shafts hundreds–even thousands–of feet into the earth, and brought in huge drills, pumps, and other heavy machinery to extract the precious ores. Comstock was also typical in spurring the growth of mining towns. Near Comstock was Virginia City, a metropolis of 30,000 at its height, containing only four churches but a hundred saloons. Yet after the mine gave out, the population plummeted to fewer than a thousand permanent residents.

With all of his equipment loaded on a single burro, a miner sets out to seek his fortune in the mineral-rich American West.

Other mines throughout the West drew workers and investors to the region. Gold was always the chief attraction, but fortunes were to be made in other metals as well. The Anaconda Mine in Montana, for example, began as a rather poor silver mine. It was soon discovered, however, that the claim included one of the richest veins of copper in the world. Nearby deposits of zinc and lead further enriched the region. Wealth in the West, it seemed, was there for the digging.

Cattle–One romantic element of the American West, celebrated in numerous motion pictures and television programs, was the **cattle drive.** After the Civil War, ranchers in Texas found themselves with herds of cattle too large for nearby markets. In the East, however, there was a large demand for beef. The problem, though, was how to get the meat to market. The answer was simple in concept but enormously difficult in practice: Cattlemen drove the herds overland to railroad terminals to the north. Soon "cow towns" such as Kansas City, Missouri; Dodge City, Kansas; and other frontier settlements were thriving centers of the cattle trade. From these towns the cattle were shipped east by rail.

Driving the herds were **cowboys,** men now shrouded by myth but who were actually tough, hard-working ranch hands. The cattle they drove were longhorns–stubborn, ornery, independent cattle. Their meat was not the best beef, but only the tough longhorns could survive the rigors of the cattle trails. Several of these trails stretched north from Texas; the Goodnight-Loving Trail and the Chisholm Trail were perhaps the most famous. The cowboys guided the cattle across the **"open ranges"** (so called because the ranges were unfenced public lands) and allowed them to feed on the grasses of the plains. For all of the romance later attached to the drives, they were grueling work with more than their share of dangers. Stampedes, cattle "rustlers" (thieves), and Indian attacks were the more dramatic threats. A more common and constant danger was simply a lack of water. If the cattle failed to reach the next watering hole in time, the entire herd could perish and leave an owner financially ruined.

The cattle-raising industry owed at least part of its success to the development of a related industry,

The Life and Hard Times of the American Cowboy

The strenuous life on the cattle trails is best recounted by the "cowpunchers" who went through them. "Teddy Blue" Abbott, the younger son of an English nobleman who came to the United States to make his fortune, gave this account of a trail drive in 1883.

After some experience in the business, they [the cattle drivers] found that about 2,000 head on average was the best number in a herd. . . . Eleven men made the average crew with a trail herd. The two men in the lead were called point men, and then as the herd strung out there would be two men behind them on the wing, two on the flank, and two drag drivers in the rear. With the cook and horse wrangler and boss, that made eleven. The poorest men always worked with the drags [i.e., rode behind the herd], because a good hand wouldn't stand for it. I have seen them come off herd with the dust half an inch deep on their hats and thick as fur in their eyebrows and mustaches. . . . They would go to the water barrel at the end of the day and rinse their mouths and cough and spit and bring up that black stuff out of their throats. But you couldn't get it up out of your lungs. . . .

But when you add it all up, I believe the worst hardship we had on the trail was loss of sleep. There was never enough sleep. Our day wouldn't end till about nine o'clock, when we grazed the herd onto the bed ground. And after that every man in the outfit except the boss and horse wrangler and cook would have to stand two hours' night guard. Suppose my guard was twelve to two. I would stake my night horse, unroll my bed, pull off my boots, and crawl in at nine, get about three hours' sleep, and then ride two hours. Then I would come off guard and get to sleep another hour and a half, till the cook yelled, "Roll out," at half past three. So I would get maybe five hours' sleep when the weather was nice and everything smooth and pretty, with cowboys singing under the stars. If it wasn't so nice, you'd be lucky to sleep an hour. But the wagon rolled on in the morning just the same.

meat packing. The idea of meat packing had first gained popularity during the Civil War when the Union army used treated meat packed in barrels or tins to feed its soldiers. After the war, city dwellers in particular found the process convenient for purchasing and storing food. Meat-packing plants opened first in midwestern cities such as Cincinnati, Chicago, Milwaukee, and Minneapolis. At first, cattle were shipped live by train to the packing houses. The invention of the ice-cooled refrigerator railcars allowed meat packers to slaughter the beef in the West and ship it to the plants. Eventually packing houses opened in the West as well, shortening the process even further. The names of meat packers such as Philip Armour and Gustavus Swift became household words as their canned meat products stocked the shelves of American pantries.

The open-range cattle industry came to an end in the 1880s. Cattle overgrazed much of the land, ruining it for large herds. In addition, bitterly cold winters in 1886 and 1887 killed thousands of cattle and bankrupted many cattlemen. As railroads expanded in the West, long drives were no longer necessary to reach markets; the chief advantage of the longhorns–their ability to survive long and difficult drives–no longer mattered. Some cattlemen began fencing in their ranches and breeding smaller, meatier stock. Beef remained a profitable product, and related industries such as meat packing continued to thrive, but the era of the cattle drive and the longhorn ended.

Settlers and Sod-busters

The most significant factor in the demise of the open range was farming. The railroads that hauled cattle to meat-packing plants also brought back settlers who farmed the land instead of using it for grazing. To help protect their crops from ranging

Homesteaders in Nebraska cut a cattleman's wire fences in 1885 during one of the many farmer-cattleman clashes on the Great Plains.

cattle, frontier farmers fenced their properties, breaking up the open ranges and hindering trail drives. Ranchers sent cowboys to drive off the "sod-busters," as farmers were called, and "range wars" often developed between cattlemen and farmers.

These were wars that the farmers were destined to win. In the first thirty years after the Civil War, more new land was settled than in all of America's previous history. By the 1880s, farmers far outnumbered cowboys, and the open ranges began to dwindle as more and more land was fenced.

Acquiring Land—Acquiring land was the farmer's first priority. Railroads sold their land grants to settlers, but the location of the lands near the tracks (and hence to supply sources and markets) made them much more valuable than other lands. Many settlers could not afford the railroad's prices. The federal government, eager to see the West settled, passed the **Homestead Act** in 1862. This act provided 160 acres of land to any settler who would live on the land for five years and "improve" it by building and farming. The Homestead Act proved to be a tremendous success, and by 1900 nearly a million settlers had filed for homesteads under this law.

Most of the influx of homesteaders was gradual, but the **Oklahoma land rushes** were an exception. When the government decided to open large sections of the Indian Territory (Oklahoma) to white settlement, it decided to do so in two large blows. Each Oklahoma land rush–three million acres thrown open in 1889 and six million in 1893–began like a race on a set day at a set time. With the sounding of a signal, a massive flood of settlers rushed across the borders to claim the land. In the 1889 rush, over fifty thousand people entered the territory on the first day. The effects of this rush were dramatic. The town of Guthrie, for example, was founded and immediately grew to a population of six thousand, leading residents to joke, "Rome was not built in a day, but Guthrie was."

Developing the Land—The **Great Plains** is the region between the Mississippi River Valley and the Rocky Mountains, stretching north to south from Canada to southern Texas. Prior to the Civil War, Americans often called the region "the Great American Desert," not because it was really a desert but because the grassy plains were nearly tree-less and suffered from infrequent rainfall. This tree-less, semiarid region provided daunting challenges to settlers.

To make up for the lack of rain, some farmers irrigated their fields from the region's rivers. Others pumped water up from the water table below the ground by using windmills to drive the pumps. There was widespread practice of **dry farming,** the cultivation of crops with the careful conservation of water. In dry farming, farmers used ground covers–such as stubble from the previous crops or a top layer of powdery soil–to hold in precious moisture. Because plants use more water while growing than when mature, farmers also planted crops such as winter wheat, which grew to maturity before the heat of summer increased the rate of evaporation. Wheat, in fact, became the main crop of the Great Plains, making that region one of the great "breadbaskets" of the world.

The lack of trees on the plains created a major problem in the construction of buildings. Many early pioneers lived in "soddies," houses built of blocks of earth and sod. Sod houses were warm in the winter and cool in the summer, but they were hardly luxurious living. Rain, on the rare occasions when it fell, was a particular menace to sod houses. One pioneer wife said,

> Sometimes the water would drip on the stove while I was cooking, and I would have to keep tight lids on the skillets to prevent mud from falling into the food. With my dress pinned up, and rubbers on my feet, I waded around until the clouds rolled by. Life is too short to be spent under a sod roof.

If rains were heavy or prolonged, the sod house might collapse completely. At best, a soddie lasted only a few years. Usually this was long enough for a settler to import materials such as lumber by rail and build a more permanent house–or another soddie.

Fencing was likewise a problem in the treeless plains. Obviously, the split-rail fences used in the East were out of the question. Some farmers experimented with hedges, but these took time to grow. The ideal invention for fencing the plains

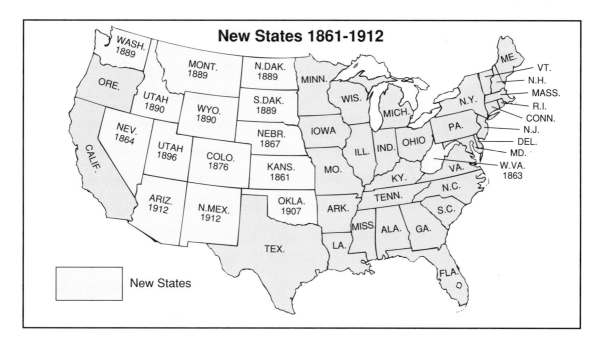

New States 1861-1912

New States

came from Joseph Glidden of Illinois. He developed **barbed wire** in the 1870s, two twisted strands of wire studded with sharp metal barbs at various intervals. Pioneers strung the wire along posts, thus fencing their property more easily and quickly than they ever could have done with rail fences. The barbs kept wary livestock away from the fence so that they would not break it down.

These innovations, combined with inventions brought from east of the Mississippi, such as the reaper and the steel plow, allowed the plains farmer to transform the grasslands into an agricultural paradise. When traveling on vacation in the West in 1893, Wellesley College teacher Katherine Lee Bates was moved by the sight of these rich and lovely lands. In a notebook she carried, she wrote a poem celebrating this divinely blessed land:

O beautiful for spacious skies,
　For amber waves of grain,
For purple mountain majesties
　Above the fruited plain!
America! America!
　God shed His grace on thee,
And crown thy good with brotherhood
　From sea to shining sea!

Section Review

1. What two incentives did the federal government give the railroads to build a transcontinental line?
2. Name the two railroad companies that were given charters to build the first transcontinental railroad and the city from which each started.
3. Name at least three metals that were profitably mined in the West.
4. Why did ranchers raise longhorn cattle for the cattle drives?
5. How did pioneers overcome the lack of trees in the Great Plains in building houses? in building fences?

Indian Affairs

One could wish that the story of the American West was one of unbroken triumph, of courageous settlers overcoming the obstacles they faced in order to build a new and better land. Unfortunately, there is a darker side to the story. As white men moved west, they clashed with the Indians, just as they had done since the days of the Jamestown colony in Virginia. This time, however, the conflict would be the final, climactic struggle between white and Indian for control of the remainder of the American continent.

Plains Indians—The Great Plains region was not uninhabited when the white settlers came. It was home to the **Plains Indians,** tribes such as the Cheyenne, Comanche, and **Sioux** (SOO). These tribes came closer to the popular conception of Indians than the eastern tribes. They lived in tepees, hunted buffalo on swift Indian ponies, and fought American cavalry with bows and arrows. Such superficial stereotypes, however, do not do justice to the surprisingly complex culture of these people.

The key to the survival of the Plains Indians was the buffalo. The men of the tribes, riding on horses descended from those left by the Spanish centuries before, were the ones who usually hunted the buffalo that wandered in herds so huge that they blackened the Great Plains with their numbers. The Indians ate a great deal of buffalo meat, either fresh, in dried strips (jerky), or dried and mixed with berries (pemmican). Buffalo hides provided clothing, blankets, tent coverings, curtains, drumheads, and other necessities. Buffalo sinews and tendons provided bowstrings and the "thread" for sewing coverings together. Some Indians made dice out of buffalo bones for gambling. Even the dung of the buffalo was dried and burned as fuel in the treeless plains. Buffalo were so important to the Indians that during the Indian Wars the U.S. government quietly encouraged slaughtering the herds in order to rob the Indians of their means of livelihood. By 1900 the huge herds of the Great Plains had become nearly extinct. Some historians believe that the destruction of the buffalo was more important in the conquest of the Plains Indians than any military campaign.

Buffalo Chase, *United States House of Representatives Collection. The buffalo were essential to the survival of the Plains Indians and their nomadic way of life.*

White settlers soon learned that the Plains Indians were skilled warriors, dashing about on their horses and firing arrows almost as fast as a man could fire a repeating rifle. The Indians were hardy, independent fighters. One on one, few whites could stand up to them. Only disunity among the tribes and the Indian tendency to fight as individuals kept them from overwhelming the undersupplied soldiers they often faced.

The Plains Indians were also fiercely proud of their heritage, and they became ferociously protective of their lands as white settlers encroached upon them. The Plains tribes did not intend to simply give their land away, and they soon learned–as other tribes had learned earlier–that the government's word was not always trustworthy. Even when government officials intended to be fair, their lack of understanding of Indian culture sometimes caused them to make fatal errors. Whites never seemed to understand, for example, that Indian chiefs were more honorary than official and that few chiefs could bind all of their people to a treaty–treaties which, incidentally, the chiefs themselves often did not understand. Misunderstanding fueled by greed resulted in bloody conflict on the Great Plains.

Indian Wars–From the 1850s until the 1870s, the U.S. Army fought a series of campaigns against the Plains Indians. The army demonstrated a remarkable ability to underestimate its opponents. For example, during the "First Sioux War" in the Wyoming-Montana region (1866-1868), Captain William Fetterman bragged that with eighty men, he could ride through the entire Sioux nation. Ironically, Fetterman had exactly eighty men with him when he met a large Sioux war party near Fort Phil Kearny, and he and his troops were slaughtered to the last man. This war may in fact have the unusual distinction of being the first war that the United States ever lost. The Sioux won every battle and forced the government to give them a treaty granting all of their demands. Unfortunately for the Indians, the government had little intention of honoring the treaty.

The Indian Wars were brutal, bloody affairs. Both sides committed atrocities and slaughtered without mercy. Whites and Indians did not merely kill each other; they tortured the living and mutilated the dead, including the women and children of both sides. Whites called the Indians "savages" with some reason, but the supposedly civilized white man proved hardly less brutal than his red counterpart.

The goal of the Indian Wars for the American government was to force the tribes onto **reservations,** special tracts of land set aside for the Indians where they could theoretically live in peace. Some whites undoubtedly thought this policy to be a means of helping and protecting the Indians. Many others, however, viewed it as an opportunity to move the Indians out of the way so that they could seize rich Indian lands. The Indians, for their part, could see no reason for abandoning their tribal lands. Even some Indians who agreed to move to the reservations rebelled when they saw how poor the lands were, for the government tended to set up reservations on arid, barren land that was useless to whites. Perhaps, given the superior numbers and technology of white culture, the result of the Indian Wars was a foregone conclusion. It took long, hard fighting, however, for the American army to emerge victorious.

The Sioux War—The climax of the Indian Wars was what is commonly known as the **Sioux War** (1876-1877; also known as "the Second Sioux War" and "the Great Sioux War" to distinguish it from the conflict of 1866-1868). The fame of this war lies partly in the fact that it was the last great Indian War and partly in the personalities involved: cavalry colonel George Armstrong Custer and Indian leaders Sitting Bull and Crazy Horse.

Ohio-born **George Armstrong Custer** was a dashing, rash, self-centered army officer. He had risen from the rank of lieutenant to major general during the Civil War as a result of his reckless daring and his constant efforts to impress his superiors. Reduced to the rank of colonel when the army shrank after the war, Custer became a renowned Indian fighter. Typical of his method was the Battle of the Washita (WASH uh TAH) River (1868) in what is today Oklahoma. Coming upon an Indian camp on the banks of the river, Custer divided his force and prepared to attack without any reconnaissance. The attack was a smashing success for the cavalry as they routed the surprised Indians. It turned out that some of the Indians had been raiding white settlements, but Custer had not

known that beforehand–nor did he care. To the impetuous Custer, the fact that they were Indians was enough.

Opposing Custer in the Sioux War were **Sitting Bull** and **Crazy Horse.** Although both men were Sioux chiefs, Sitting Bull was more the political leader of the Sioux forces. He provided moral inspiration to the Indians and led in all negotiations with the whites. Crazy Horse served more as the commander of the Sioux warriors. Under Crazy Horse's leadership, the Sioux warriors fought one of the most unified, best-organized Indian campaigns in history.

The major battle of the Sioux War took place on June 25, 1876. Custer's cavalry regiment came upon a huge Indian camp on the banks of the Little Bighorn River in what is now Montana. Unknown to Custer, Sitting Bull and Crazy Horse had noted his approach and were prepared to meet him. Custer's scouts looked at the size of the camp and warned the colonel that the Sioux had more warriors than the soldiers had bullets. Custer brushed these warnings aside. As he had done at the Washita River eight years before, Custer divided his forces to attack the Indians from two directions. One force, under Major Marcus Reno, attacked the camp head-on and was soon driven back with heavy losses. Even so, Reno's force was the fortunate one. Custer took some two hundred men and swept north of the Indian camp to launch what he thought would be a surprise attack. Instead the Indians surprised Custer by coming out to meet him in overwhelming numbers. Perhaps two thousand braves attacked the two hundred soldiers. Custer and all of his force lost their lives in the Battle of the Little Bighorn, what is popularly known as **Custer's Last Stand.**

This great Indian victory actually worked to the advantage of the U.S. Army. Thinking that the war was won, many Sioux left Sitting Bull's force. Shocked and sobered by the defeat, the government quickly sent more men and supplies west to defeat the Sioux. Within months of Custer's defeat, the army had forced the Indians to accept peace on the government's terms. Most Sioux went sadly to the reservations. Crazy Horse, after giving himself up,

Custer's Last Stand, *by Edgar S. Paxson, Buffalo Bill Historical Center, Cody, WY. Paxson's painting is generally considered one of the most historically accurate portrayals of the Battle of the Little Bighorn.*

was killed in a scuffle with soldiers as they attempted to put him in a guardhouse. Sitting Bull fled to Canada for a time. He eventually returned to live on a reservation, only to be killed by Indian police in 1890 during his arrest for allegedly inciting Indians to rebel.

Later Indian Affairs – The fate of the Sioux was typical of what happened to the tribes of the West. Some Indians still resisted the idea of living a dull, impoverished life on the barren reservations. The Apache Geronimo, for example, led a small band of Indians who for several years frustrated the army's attempts to force them onto a reservation. He and his band were finally captured. The Nez Perce Chief Joseph conducted a masterful campaign to save his tribal lands or at least lead his people to refuge in Canada (see the next page), but he was forced to surrender in 1877.

The final volleys of the Indian Wars came in 1890 near

Chief Sitting Bull of the Sioux

Wounded Knee Creek in South Dakota. There the army tried to disarm and capture a band of Sioux who were resisting removal from their lands. The chief, knowing he was outnumbered, surrendered. One brave resisted, however, and fired a wild shot at the soldiers. Fighting quickly broke out. When it was over, 25 soldiers and over 150 Indians (half of them women and children) were dead. The **Wounded Knee Massacre** was a sad and bloody epilogue to the Indian Wars.

In 1881 Helen Hunt Jackson published *A Century of Dishonor,* a work portraying the government's ruthless and sometimes dishonorable dealings with the Indians. Jackson's book, combined with the decreasing threat of the Plains Indians, inspired some belated sympathy for the Indians' plight. In 1887 Congress tried to undo some of the damage by passing the **Dawes Act.** This legislation allowed Indian lands to be parceled out to individual Indian families to use and develop as they liked. Unfortunately, this act tended to break down the

Chief Joseph, Man of War and Peace

Of those Indians who fought against the United States Army in the nineteenth century, none won more sympathy among the American public than a chief of the Nez Perce tribe, In-mut-too-yah-lat-lat (''Thunder-traveling-over-the-mountain''), better known as Chief Joseph. He conducted a military campaign and march so brilliant that newspapers and even opposing generals called him the ''Indian Napoleon.''

Joseph and his tribe lived in the Wallowa Valley in what is now Idaho. In 1877 the government tried to force the Nez Perce onto a reservation. Joseph did not want to leave his land but he hated war. He thought that the tribe must submit or risk destruction at the hands of the army. While he was trying to organize his people for the move, however, a handful of young warriors attacked and killed some white settlers who had mistreated their tribe. With little hope of peace now, Joseph prepared to flee and–if necessary–to fight.

Joseph took his people east, eventually deciding to escape to Canada, where Sitting Bull and his Sioux were already living. What followed was an epic journey. In 108 days Joseph marched over 700 Indians–most of them women, children, and old men–nearly 1,400 miles. In eight separate battles and skirmishes, the Nez Perce defeated contingents of four separate cavalry units. At the Clearwater River, for example, about a hundred braves entrenched and surrounded 600 soldiers and pinned them there for two days.

Joseph refused to fight a savage war, however. He forbade the killing of women and children and the taking of scalps from the dead. He simply wanted to get his tribe to a place where they could live in peace. Americans followed with interest the newspaper reports describing his trek through the mountains and how he seemed to be outwitting and baffling the army at every turn.

Finally, on September 30, 1877, the cavalry caught up with Joseph's band just forty miles from the Canadian border. Outnumbered and numbed by a chilling cold, the tribe could go no farther. As he surrendered, Chief Joseph spoke with an eloquence that moved the hearts of thousands who later read his words: ''It is cold and we have no blankets. The little children are freezing to death. . . . Hear me, my chiefs, I am tired; my heart is sick and sad. From where the sun now stands, I will fight no more forever.''

Joseph was eventually settled on a reservation in Washington. ''You might as well expect the rivers to run backward as that any man who was born a free man should be contented penned up and denied liberty to go where he pleases,'' he once said. Joseph died ''penned up'' on the reservation on September 21, 1904, collapsing as he sat by the fire in his tepee. A doctor on the reservation said, ''Joseph died of a broken heart.''

unity of the tribes, and many Indians sold their allotted lands to whites and were soon more impoverished than before.

In the twentieth century, the United States government has attempted to redress some of the wrongs done to the Indians. In 1924 Congress gave

GERONIMO

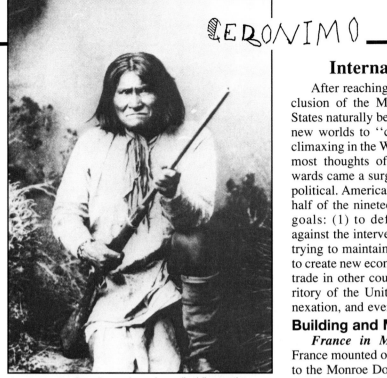

Apache warrior Geronimo, using only small raiding parties, harassed and tied down large numbers of U.S. cavalry before he finally surrendered.

Indians full citizenship. In 1934 the Indian Reorganization Act halted the allotment program of the Dawes Act, in order to preserve remaining Indian lands, and gave the reservations limited self-government. Congress has also made it easier for Indians to seek damages for past violations of treaties and other agreements. These acts, however, seem little enough in the face of the injustices done to the Indians.

Section Review

1. What animal was the key to the survival of the Plains Indians? What were at least two uses of this animal?
2. What was the goal of the American government in its campaigns against the Indians?
3. Who was the most famous cavalry officer of the Sioux War of 1876-1877? Which two chiefs were his main opponents?
4. Why did the great Indian victory at the Little Bighorn actually work to the advantage of the U.S. Army?

International Expansion

After reaching the Pacific Ocean with the conclusion of the Mexican War (1848), the United States naturally began to look across the oceans for new worlds to "conquer." The sectional conflict climaxing in the War Between the States postponed most thoughts of overseas expansion, but afterwards came a surge of growth, both economic and political. American foreign policymakers in the last half of the nineteenth century pursued three main goals: (1) to defend the Western Hemisphere against the intervention of European powers while trying to maintain good relations with Europe, (2) to create new economic opportunities for American trade in other countries, and (3) to extend the territory of the United States through purchase, annexation, and even conquest.

Building and Mending Fences

France in Mexico—During the Civil War, France mounted one of the most serious challenges to the Monroe Doctrine in American history. Taking advantage of the distractions of the war, Napoleon III (grandnephew of Napoleon Bonaparte and ruler of France) established a "puppet emperor," the Austrian nobleman **Maximilian I,** in Mexico in 1864. Napoleon III ignored American protests, particularly since the United States government was far too busy to do anything about it. After the war, however, the United States stationed 50,000 veteran troops on the Rio Grande. Secretary of State William Seward then gave Napoleon an ultimatum to withdraw French soldiers from Mexico. The French, worried by the troops and plagued by troubles in Europe, quietly withdrew. After losing the support of the French, Maximilian was executed by a Mexican firing squad in 1867. The United States had successfully met one challenge.

Treaty of Washington—After its confrontation with France, the United States sought to settle three longstanding differences with Great Britain. First, the United States sought compensation for the ravages its merchant fleet had suffered from commerce raiders during the Civil War. **Commerce raiders** were warships owned and commanded by the Confederates but built in British shipyards. The American government rightly believed that Britain was partly responsible for the damage caused by these raiders. Second, the United States and Britain had been arguing since the 1840s over who owned a group of islands between Vancouver Island and the state of Washington. Third, the United States and Canada had long disagreed over fishing rights off the coasts of North America.

The **Treaty of Washington** (1871) settled these matters by setting up international tribunals to deal with each question. One tribunal awarded the United States over $15 million in damages from Britain in payment for the destruction caused by the commerce raiders. Another tribunal awarded possession of the islands off Vancouver to the United States. A third required the United States to pay Canada over $5 million for special fishing privileges. The importance of the treaty was not simply in settling these individual questions; the treaty also paved the way for greater friendship and cooperation between the United States on the one hand and Britain and Canada on the other.

Economic Expansion

Because of improvements in transportation and technology, the United States was able by the mid-1800s to produce more goods–food, raw materials, and manufactured products–than it could use. The nation therefore sought more foreign markets in which to sell its goods.

The Arrival of the "American Barbarians"

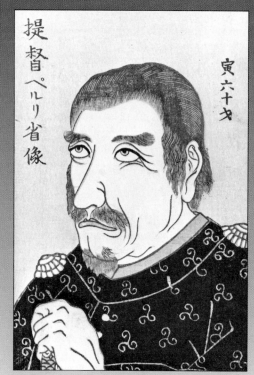

Matthew Perry, *unidentified Japanese artist, National Portrait Gallery, Smithsonian Institution*

The visit of Commodore Perry, while having an important influence on the futures of Japan and the United States, certainly did not have a favorable effect on those Japanese who were present. The insult that the Japanese felt rose as much from the ignorance that both Americans and Japanese had of each other's manners as from any actual arrogance on the part of the naval commander. Sakuma Shōzan, in a contemporary account, records the immediate effect of Perry's visit and the fate of Perry's gift to the Japanese of a portrait of U.S. president Franklin Pierce.

Last summer the American barbarians arrived in the Bay of Uraga with four warships, bearing their president's message. Their deportment and manner of expression were exceedingly arrogant, and the resulting insult to our national dignity was not small. Those who heard could not but gnash their teeth. A certain person on guard in Uraga suffered this insult in silence, and having ultimately been unable to do anything about it, after the barbarians had retired, he drew his knife and slashed to bits a portrait of their leader, which they had left as a gift. Thus he gave vent to his rage.

Perry in Japan (1854)—The California gold rush and the acquisition of Mexican territories after the Mexican War had established America as a potential Pacific power and had made increased trade with Asia a major American goal. However, Japan, one of the main powers in Asia, had isolated itself from the rest of the world for some two hundred years. Hoping to open a door for trade, the United States government commissioned Commodore **Matthew Perry** to take a small squadron of warships to Japan and to negotiate with Japan's rulers. Perry's squadron awed and offended the Japanese. Despite opposition by many in his government, the Japanese ruler agreed to make a trade agreement with the United States. This agreement, the **Treaty of Kanagawa** (1854), was a major victory for American foreign trade. It was also the first step in opening Japan to western influences and in molding that island nation into a major economic and military power.

Pan-Americanism—After the Civil War, the United States resumed its push for new markets abroad. One obvious potential market was Latin America. The nations south of the Rio Grande, although rich in raw materials and some foodstuffs, had little industry. The United States hoped to increase inter-American trade and lessen Latin American trade with Europe.

James G. Blaine, secretary of state under Garfield and Harrison, was a major promoter of closer relations with Latin America. He advocated **Pan-Americanism,** a movement favoring greater cooperation and unity among the nations of the Western Hemisphere. Blaine hoped to create economic unity by reducing trade barriers such as tariffs among the nations. Blaine and others even dreamed of creating a loose political confederation of American nations, which the United States would dominate. With some delight, then, Blaine hosted delegates from Latin American countries at the First Pan-American Congress in 1889, but the meeting was not a resounding success. These southern nations feared political and economic domination by the United States, and most could not forget past offenses such as the Mexican War. Furthermore, the secretary of state's own Republican party

A FAIR FIELD AND NO FAVOR!
UNCLE SAM: "I'M OUT FOR COMMERCE, NOT CONQUEST!"

Uncle Sam—saying, "I'm out for commerce, not conquest"—holds back the great powers of Europe in this Harper's Weekly *cartoon supporting the idea of free trade in China.*

was wary of lowering tariffs. The congress did at least provide a precedent, however, for further discussion and friendlier relations as the years passed.

An Open Door in China—Although the United States pioneered efforts to open Japan for trade, it found itself in the middle of intense competition when attempting to trade with China, the other major nation in Asia. Each European power, along with Japan, was attempting to set up "spheres of influence" in China, regions where one foreign nation could dominate Chinese trade. Some diplomats even talked of carving up China into colonies. The United States, however, was interested only in trading freely in China, not in sending in a military force to establish a colony. Therefore in 1899 Secretary of State John Hay proposed the **Open Door Policy.** Hay's policy called for all nations trading in China to refrain from interfering with one another and to allow free trade in China. Although the United States could do little to enforce such a policy, the idea fit well with what some European powers–notably Great Britain–already wanted to do in China. Because the policy suited the inclinations of the major powers, it succeeded.

Hay nearly saw his open door close as soon as it had opened, however. The Chinese understandably resented attempts by foreign powers to determine the future of their country. In 1900 an antiforeign movement, the **Boxer Rebellion,** broke out in China. (The name ''boxer'' comes from a leading organization in the rebellion, ''the Righteous and Harmonious Fists.'') Chinese rioters destroyed anything foreign they could lay their hands on. Boxers slaughtered missionaries, diplomats, foreign merchants, and Chinese converts to Christianity (which Boxers considered a ''foreign'' religion). An international military force, including troops from the United States, intervened to protect foreigners in China. Boxer power was broken.

The peace terms imposed by the victors were harsh. Secretary Hay, who opposed dividing China among the victors, persuaded the others to accept payments from the Chinese rather than insist on territorial concessions. The nations involved accepted Hay's proposal. The payments totaled $333 million; the United States was promised $25 million, but Congress reduced that amount and sent what it did collect back to China with the understanding that the money would be used to educate Chinese students in America. American efforts to help China, although not free from self-interest, created kind feelings between the two countries.

Territorial Expansion: Imperialism

As the events in China demonstrated, the nineteenth century was the great century of **imperialism,** the extension of power by one people or country over another country or region. An imperialist nation might acquire territory by purchase, annexation, or conquest. Today the word *imperialism* has a negative connotation. Critics of imperialism picture the practice as the ruthless conquest and brutal exploitation of people and nations for the enrich-

ment of the imperialist nation. It is true that the imperialist movement had its abuses; even the history of American imperialism, probably better than average among imperialist nations, has its darker side of acquisition by conquest and duplicity. It is also true, however, that imperialism brought some benefits to colonized regions: better medical treatment, development of natural resources, and improvements in education. Perhaps the greatest benefit of imperialism was the opportunity it presented for missionaries to take the gospel to people who had never heard of Jesus Christ.

Seward's Folly–The largest single American acquisition after the Civil War was the **purchase of Alaska** from Russia in 1867. When Secretary of State William Seward announced the purchase, many Americans–believing Alaska to be only an empty wasteland of snow and ice–called the sale ''Seward's Folly'' or ''Seward's Icebox.'' Still, at a cost of only $7.2 million (less than two cents an acre), Alaska looked like a bargain, and the treaty of purchase passed the Senate easily.

Within a few years, Alaska had proved its value to the United States. First gold and then oil were discovered in the region, making it a source of enormous wealth. Furthermore, the rise of communism in the twentieth century increased Alaska's value as a military base and vindicated the wisdom of those who wanted to take the region out of Russian hands. ''Seward's Folly'' turned out to be a very shrewd bargain indeed.

Pacific Expansion–Trade with Japan and China was not America's only interest in the Pacific in the last half of the nineteenth century. The United States also began building a Pacific empire. The U.S., for example, simply annexed the tiny coral island of Midway in the middle of the Pacific in 1867. In 1889 the United States joined Britain and Germany in a joint protectorate of the Samoan islands. Disagreements among the three nations, however, led to the division of the islands, the United States forming the eastern islands into the U.S. territory of American Samoa.

The most important Pacific addition to the United States was **Hawaii.** The Hawaiian Islands had been an important supply point for whalers, merchant ships, and warships since the 1700s. In the early 1800s American missionaries had come to the islands and had enjoyed remarkable success in winning many islanders to Christ. Unfortunately many Americans who followed the missionaries and, sadly, the sons of the missionaries themselves proved more interested in profits than in the souls of the Hawaiians. These American investors soon built a thriving sugar industry which dominated the economy of the islands and, indeed, helped the islands to prosper.

Until 1891 Hawaii was ruled by native kings who usually went along with the planters' wishes. In that year, however, Queen Liliuokalani (lee LEE oo oh kah LAH nee) took the throne. She attempted to reestablish native control of the island and limit the power of the planters. In 1893 the planters revolted against "Queen Lil" and asked to be annexed to the United States. President Grover Cleveland, however, refused to approve this upstart uprising and blocked annexation of the islands. Like Texas after its war for independence, Hawaii was forced to exist for several years as an independent republic. In 1898, however, when McKinley was in office and a war with Spain was making the United States nervous about the security of the Pacific, Congress voted to annex the islands.

Missions

One of the most positive elements of imperialism was a growth in Christian missions. Some historians criticize missionaries as "agents of imperialism" who secretly made colonies for their homelands under the cloak of preaching the gospel. Actually, the opposite was often true. For example, Hiram Bingham, one of the first Congregationalist missionaries to go to Hawaii in 1820, clashed with Americans and others who were bent on exploiting the Hawaiians. When Bingham helped end prostitution among the native women, for example, outraged white sailors armed with knives and clubs physically assaulted him.

Missionaries went to all corners of the globe in the nineteenth century. One nation that attracted many was China, where Methodists took an early lead in establishing American gospel outposts. The most prominent North American leaders in Chinese work in the late nineteenth and early twentieth centuries were not from the United States but from Canada: Jonathan Goforth and his wife, Rosalind. Together they faithfully preached to the Chinese despite major difficulties, such as the Boxer Rebellion in which they were nearly killed. Another hero of Chinese missions was American Lottie Moon. She bravely traveled into the dangerous interior of China to minister to the Chinese people. She did more to arouse enthusiasm among Baptists for missions than anyone else since Adoniram Judson.

One of the most important movements in foreign missions was the **Student Volunteer Movement** (SVM). This organization began in 1886 at a Bible conference in Massachusetts hosted by D. L. Moody. Spurred by an appeal to consider foreign missions, one hundred college students pledged themselves to become missionaries. Taking as its

Queen Liliuokalani in her later years

motto "The evangelization of the world in this generation," the SVM grew rapidly. It is ultimately credited with sending twenty thousand missionaries to the field.

The latter part of the nineteenth century also saw the growth of a new kind of mission board. Up to this time, most mission boards had been tied directly to a major denomination. The denomination collected money from its member churches and in turn paid salaries to the missionaries so that they could continue their work. **Faith missions,** on the other hand, are usually independent mission boards which have no guaranteed income. Even today missionaries under "faith boards" go on "deputation" to visit local churches directly and solicit support for their work. One of the first faith mission boards in America was the Christian and Missionary Alliance (CMA), founded by A. B. Simpson in 1887. The CMA grew so much that it eventually became a separate, independent denomination. Most faith missions focused on one region of the world. One example was the Central American Mission, founded in 1890 by C. I. Scofield, Congregationalist pastor in Dallas and later editor of a famous reference Bible.

Whether they served under a denominational or a faith board, American missionaries labored loyally and diligently throughout the world. Some suffered martyrdom; thirty-five CMA missionaries and their children, for example, died in the Boxer Rebellion. Because of these sacrificial labors by so many brave and daring missionaries, many souls came to find Jesus Christ as their Saviour.

Section Review

1. What was the most serious challenge to the Monroe Doctrine during this era?
2. Why did the United States claim that Britain was partly responsible for the damage caused by Confederate commerce raiders during the Civil War?
3. What event almost ended John Hay's Open Door Policy for China?
4. What was the largest single American acquisition of territory after the Civil War?
5. What is the difference between a denominational mission board and a faith mission board?

Climax of Imperialism: The Spanish-American War

The climax of American imperialism came in 1898, when the United States went to war with Spain over that nation's treatment of its colony of Cuba. Although the Cubans had intermittently revolted against the Spanish government for decades, a revolt that broke out in 1895 was unusually serious. A depression with its resulting unemployment, combined with weak, corrupt Spanish rule over the colony, provided ideal conditions for an insurrection. Bands of guerrillas destroyed sugar mills, plantations, and anything else valued by those loyal to Spain. In order to stop this wanton destruction, Spanish troops arrested rebels and put them in barbed-wire concentration camps, where many died of starvation or disease. As American newspapers reported the brutal Spanish suppression of the rebels, American sympathy for the Cubans began to grow.

Causes—Sympathy alone, however, was not enough to push the United States into war. Three other factors fanned American hatred of Spain and hastened the war: (1) yellow journalism, (2) the de Lôme letter, and (3) the sinking of the U.S.S. *Maine.* **"Yellow journalism"** is sensationalized news reporting aimed more at attracting readers than at reporting the truth. Two of the leading "yellow journals" were William Randolph Hearst's *New York Journal* and Joseph Pulitzer's *New York World.* Each paper attempted to outdo the other in reporting sensational stories that would boost sales. Hearst, for example, paid a famous illustrator, Frederic Remington, to go to Cuba to draw sketches of the revolt. When Remington arrived in Cuba and reported back that conditions were not bad enough to warrant U.S. intervention, Hearst reportedly replied, "You furnish the pictures and I'll furnish the war."

American public opinion, inflamed by the yellow journalism of Hearst and Pulitzer, began to favor war with Spain to establish Cuba's independence. In spite of journalistic propaganda, however, President McKinley intended to avoid hostilities. The situation was actually improving, and the Spanish government was willing to meet McKinley's demands for better treatment of the Cubans when two incidents gave the prowar party new reason to demand military action.

First, on February 9, 1898, the *New York Journal* published a stolen letter written by the Spanish ambassador in Washington, Enrique Dupuy de Lôme. In the **de Lôme letter,** as it came to be known, the ambassador denounced McKinley as, among other things, ''weak and a bidder for the admiration of the crowd.'' This was hardly strong language; Assistant Secretary of the Navy Theodore Roosevelt, for instance, described McKinley as having ''no more backbone than a chocolate eclair.'' Roosevelt, however, was an American citizen, whereas de Lôme was the representative of a foreign country, and the nation was outraged at the insult to its president. De Lôme resigned, but Spanish-American relations grew still worse.

A second incident was even more damaging. The battleship *Maine* had been sent to Havana Harbor in Cuba in January 1898 to protect American interests on the island. On February 15, the *Maine* exploded and sank in the harbor, causing the deaths of 260 Americans. An investigation at that time by the American government claimed that a mine had sunk the *Maine.* Actually, no one knows precisely what happened to the *Maine.* A careful study of the evidence by two American naval engineers in 1975, for example, concluded that the explosion resulted from an accident in the ship's coal bunkers. At any rate, the Spanish had no reason whatsoever for wanting to blow up the battleship. But Americans believed what they wanted to believe and what the yellow press told them–that the explosion was an act of Spanish treachery.

McKinley caved in to political pressure and sent a war message to Congress in April 1898. Congress demanded Spain's withdrawal from Cuba and authorized the president to use force, if necessary, to establish Cuba's independence. Spain refused, and the result was the **Spanish-American War.**

Manila Bay–The United States Navy was a powerful, modern fleet and was reasonably well prepared for war. Ironically, the war over the Caribbean island of Cuba started in the Pacific Ocean, where one of Spain's major fleets was located. America's Pacific fleet, under Commodore **George Dewey,** left Hong Kong and on May 1, 1898, engaged the Spanish fleet in Manila Bay, the main harbor of the Spanish-controlled Philippine Islands. The Americans wrecked the antiquated Spanish fleet, sending 381 sailors to the bottom. American

The U.S.S. Maine enters Havana Harbor, where its mysterious destruction would help spark a war between the United States and Spain.

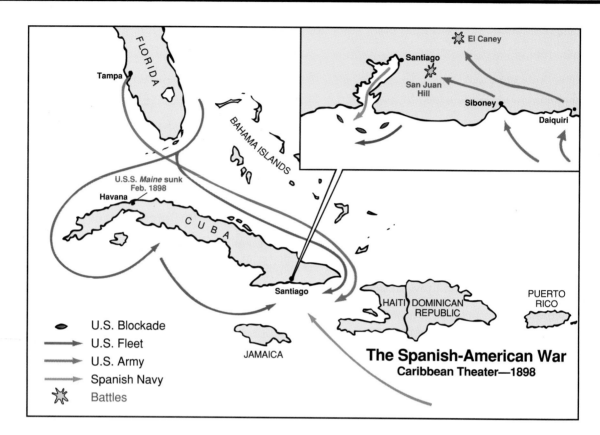

U.S. Blockade
U.S. Fleet
U.S. Army
Spanish Navy
Battles

The Spanish-American War
Caribbean Theater—1898

casualties were slight–only eight wounded. The **Battle of Manila Bay** destroyed Spanish sea power in the Pacific and left the Philippines in the hands of the United States.

Santiago–The American army was not nearly so well prepared as the navy. Little preparation had been made for transporting and supplying troops. Many soldiers had to fight in the steaming jungles of Cuba dressed in heavy blue woolen uniforms designed for winter campaigns against the Indians. The regular army in fact numbered only 26,000 men at the outbreak of the war, but Congress voted to raise several volunteer regiments. Probably the most famous of these volunteer units was the **"Rough Riders,"** a collection of cowboys and adventurers from the West, commanded by Colonel Leonard Wood and Lieutenant Colonel Theodore Roosevelt.

On May 19 Spain's Atlantic fleet entered Santiago Harbor in Cuba. The American fleet quickly blockaded the harbor, and the U.S. government decided to send the army into Cuba to capture Santiago and force the Spanish fleet out. In late June 17,000 American soldiers landed on the beaches of Cuba. In a series of sharp battles in late June and early July, the Americans pushed back the dispirited Spaniards and encircled the city. The most famous of these battles was probably the Battle of San Juan Hill in which Roosevelt and his Rough Riders helped storm the Spanish fortifications. (Ironically, the Rough Riders fought on foot because their horses were still in Florida.) The city of Santiago surrendered on July 17.

Even before that surrender, on July 3, the Spanish fleet tried to escape. The resulting **Battle of Santiago Bay** was a repetition of Manila Bay. The

American fleet decimated the Spanish. The Spanish suffered over three hundred fatalities; the Americans suffered one. Shortly thereafter American forces captured the island of Puerto Rico, and the Spanish sued for peace.

Aftermath—An American diplomat called the Spanish-American conflict "a splendid little war." Years later Theodore Roosevelt said, "It wasn't much of a war, but it was the best war we had." The Spanish-American War was indeed a "little war" in many ways. It lasted only four months, and only 379 Americans died in battle. (But over ten times that number died of disease either in Cuba or in unsanitary camps in the United States.) The results of the war, though, were anything but little.

At the beginning of the war, Congress had passed an amendment to a bill proclaiming that the United States wanted no territory in Cuba. That did not stop the U.S., however, from taking Puerto Rico, Guam, and the Philippines as a result of the war, although America paid the Spanish $20 million dollars for the latter. Furthermore, the United States virtually ruled Cuba as a protectorate for several years after the war, and the panic caused by the outbreak of the war had hastened American annexation of Hawaii. The United States was now widely recognized as a world power and had an empire of its own besides.

The nation soon found that empires can be extremely costly, however. For the first time in history, the United States had to maintain a large peacetime standing army and navy to protect the newly annexed areas. It also found that not all of the peoples liberated from Spain were eager to exchange Spanish control for American control. In the Philippines in 1899, **Emilio Aguinaldo** (ay-MEE-lee-oh AH-gee-NAHL-doh), a revolutionary who had aided the United States against the Spanish, led an insurrection to overthrow the Americans and establish Philippine independence. For two years the United States had to conduct a campaign in the islands that was far more difficult and costlier than the Spanish-American War before finally suppressing the insurrection.

The war and the resulting acquisition of distant islands that many Americans had scarcely heard of

"*Well, I hardly know which to take first,*" *says Uncle Sam to* "*waiter*" *William McKinley as he views the* "*expansionist menu*" *in this cartoon from the* Boston Globe.

before challenged the United States' traditional foreign policy of isolation. When the 1900 presidential election came around, the Democrats, once again headed by William Jennings Bryan, tried to make the election a referendum on American imperialism, which Bryan opposed. The Republicans embraced imperialism, renominating McKinley and adding "rough-riding" Theodore Roosevelt to the ticket as vice president. The resulting electoral landslide swept aside Bryan and his referendum. The forces driving America's growing role would not have been stemmed by a mere election, anyway. At the dawn of the twentieth century, America—burgeoning, energetic, and continental—was irresistibly moving toward leadership among the nations of the world.

Section Review

1. What three factors hastened the United States towards war with Spain?
2. Name the two editors and their papers who were the leading practitioners of yellow journalism.
3. What was the central issue of the presidential election of 1900? Who were the two leading candidates, and where did they stand on this issue?

Chapter Review

Terms

transcontinental railroad
Union Pacific
Central Pacific
Pikes Peak gold rush
Comstock Lode
cattle drive
cowboys
open ranges
Homestead Act
Oklahoma land rushes
Great Plains
dry farming
barbed wire
Plains Indians
Sioux
reservations
Sioux War (1876-1877)
George Armstrong Custer
Sitting Bull
Crazy Horse
Custer's Last Stand
Wounded Knee Massacre
A Century of Dishonor

Dawes Act
Maximilian I
commerce raiders
Treaty of Washington
Matthew Perry
Treaty of Kanagawa
Pan-Americanism
Open Door Policy
Boxer Rebellion
imperialism
purchase of Alaska
Hawaii
Student Volunteer Movement
Faith missions
yellow journalism
de Lôme letter
Maine
Spanish-American War (1898)
George Dewey
Battle of Manila Bay
Rough Riders
Battle of Santiago Bay
Emilio Aguinaldo

Content Questions

1. What method of transportation was most important in the development of the American West in the nineteenth century?
2. Name at least three factors that caused the end of the open-range cattle industry.
3. Why did Americans call the Great Plains "the Great American Desert" before the Civil War?
4. Name at least two actions that the United States government has taken in the twentieth century to alleviate the plight of the American Indians.
5. What were the three major goals of American foreign policy in the last half of the nineteenth century?
6. What American actions after the Boxer Rebellion promoted friendly relations between the United States and China?
7. What are the three methods by which an imperialist nation might acquire territory?
8. What event indirectly caused the United States to hasten to annex Hawaii?
9. Name at least one territory that the United States gained by each of the following methods: purchase, annexation, conquest.
10. What were the two major naval battles of the Spanish-American War?

Application Questions

1. Do you think that Helen Hunt Jackson's title for her book, *A Century of Dishonor,* was justified? Why or why not?
2. Do you think that the Spanish-American War was justified? Why or why not?
3. In what ways are the methods of yellow journalism a common tendency of media today?

PERSPECTIVES

THE OLD WEST

GUNFIGHTERS

This studio shot of western scouts includes two of the most famous: James Butler ("Wild Bill") Hickok (second from the left) and William Frederick ("Buffalo Bill") Cody (center).

Gunfighters of the American West were neither as noble nor as glamorous as their legends suggest. Many ''facts'' about James Butler ''Wild Bill'' Hickok, for example, were nothing more than embellished rumors and outright lies. For instance, Hickok once described to a reporter for *Harper's* magazine how he had handled the ''McCanles Gang'' in 1861 when they raided a wagon station. Hickok told the reporter that he had killed a gang of ten men with his rifle, Colt revolver, and bowie knife, ''striking savage blows, following the devils up from one side to the other of the room and into the corners, striking and slashing until everyone was dead.''

In reality, McCanles was the former owner of the station, a tough-fisted farmer who had nicknamed Hickok ''Duck Bill'' for his prominent upper lip. One day McCanles had come unarmed with his young son and two friends to collect payment on a debt from the station owner. In the argument that ensued, Hickok shot McCanles through the heart. He wounded the other two men and then watched while the wife of the station owner beat one to death with a hoe. Hickok then helped chase down the third man, who was shot in cold blood. Only McCanles's twelve-year-old son escaped.

Fierce reputations, however, were no guarantee of safety for the gunfighter. The famous James

Gang, led by the brothers Jesse and Frank James, terrorized Missouri and its neighbors for fifteen years after the Civil War, staging twenty-six raids. They were widely famous and even more widely feared. Yet Jesse was shot in the back of the head by one of his own men while at his home in St. Joseph, Missouri. Frank James later turned himself in, lamenting, ''I'm tired of running. Tired of waiting for a ball in the back. Tired of looking into the faces of friends and seeing a Judas.''

The fast draw on the street, one of the standard features of the gunfighter legend, was a myth. Hickok, for instance, was shot in the back of the head as he sat playing cards. The killer refused to risk facing Wild Bill, saying, ''I didn't want to commit suicide.'' No gunfighter would let the other man ''go for his gun first,'' because reaction time would be too slow to get off a shot against a quick-draw professional.

The author of a 1927 article in the *Nebraska History Magazine* described Wild Bill Hickok's gunfighting reputation, a description that is probably apt for most western gunfighters: ''From all accounts of killings in which Hickok subsequently

The mild features of Jesse James disguised the heart of a killer. A Confederate guerrilla in Missouri during the Civil War, he turned to robbery and murder after the war.

The Colt army service revolver became a favorite weapon of gunfighters and outlaws in the West.

took part, I have been unable to find one single authentic instance in which he fought a fair fight. . . . He was a cold-blooded killer without heart or conscience. The moment he scented a fight he pulled his gun and shot to kill.''

The "Peace Commissioners" of Dodge City, Kansas, pose for a photograph. Included are Wyatt Earp (front row, second from the left) and Bat Masterson (back row, on the far right).

There were several types of lawmen in the Old West. The lowest in prestige was the town marshal. Next up the ladder was the county sheriff, who, like the town marshal, appointed deputies to serve under him. In addition the U.S. government had an interest in establishing law and order in its territories. The president himself commissioned U.S. marshals and judges to enforce the law in the counties and towns. Finding qualified, honest men was difficult, however, and turnover was high. Further-

more, the lawmen were given unreasonably large territory to cover; one county marshal in Wyoming was responsible for 16,800 square miles of land.

Most of the U.S. Marshal's duties involved politics, tax collection, and paperwork; he usually left the field work to deputies. The town marshal's job was even less glamorous. His duties could include fire and health inspections and even shooting stray dogs. Town marshals, who rarely earned enough to live on, often supplemented their income by run-

ning gambling operations. The potential for graft was great.

In the absence of official justice, townspeople sometimes turned to their own brand of justice–lynching. The people of Laramie, Wyoming, once hanged their own town marshal when they found that he was drugging people and taking their money in the saloon that he managed. Vigilante groups (groups of private citizens who enforced the law without any authority) were another force for "order," even though they rarely had the sanction of the law. A few vigilante groups did manage to get tacit approval from the law, even winning legal status as stock growers' associations or homesteaders' associations.

Many businesses on the frontier also wanted to bring law and order to the West. For example, after suffering over two hundred stagecoach robberies in one month in 1877, the Wells Fargo shipping company hired a private detective agency, the Pinkerton National Detective Agency, to supplement the work of the government lawmen. The Pinkertons developed America's first extensive "most-wanted" file on criminals, an idea that was later adopted by the Federal Bureau of Investigation (FBI). The list of criminals included such men as Black Bart, a well-dressed "gentleman bandit" who robbed twenty-eight stagecoaches but never hurt any passengers. He was finally tracked down when he dropped a handkerchief at the scene of a crime. Pinkerton detectives traced the handkerchief to Black Bart after visiting ninety-one laundries across California all the way from Sonora to San Francisco.

Hanging was the most common form of execution in the Old West. In this photograph, "Black Jack" Ketchum is being prepared for "the final drop" in the New Mexico Territory, 1901.

The city prison in Larned, Kansas, was a typically ugly but reasonably secure jail in the frontier West.

Judges in the early years were often ill trained and not respected. At first they held court in improvised surroundings, such as a grocery store or a saloon. By their iron will, judges brought a grudging respect for the law. At the local level were the justices of the peace or the police court judges. The territories were divided among district judges, who often traveled great distances to hear a wide variety of cases.

Without a doubt the most famous judge of the West was Methodist Isaac Charles Parker, better known as ''the Hanging Judge.'' Parker's jurisdiction was over a rough slice of land in western Arkansas bordering on the Indian Territory (modern Oklahoma). Technically, only Indians were allowed in the vast Indian Territory, but the region had become a hideout for criminals. Although the tribes were self-governing, any case involving a white man was handed over to the single U.S. Court judge in West Arkansas, who had only one federal marshal to support him. As white settlers began to encroach upon the area, the situation became desperate. Legislators in Washington were wringing their hands when the position again became vacant in 1875, until–to

everyone's amazement–an honest, qualified man volunteered to serve for the $3,500 annual salary. The thirty-six-year-old Parker wanted to do what he could to bring justice to the territory.

Within eight days of bringing his family to the mudhole of Fort Smith, Arkansas, the imposing judge opened his court. He was given unique powers. The U.S. government granted him final say over any crime committed in Indian Territory, leaving outlaws with no recourse except a presidential pardon. He was also allowed to hire two hundred deputy marshals to scour the territory. Parker hired a fearsome collection of lawmen. Their instructions were plain: ''Bring them in, alive–or dead.'' During his first eight-week court session, he condemned to death six of the ninety-one people brought before him. A huge oak gallows was erected just for the occasion. Parker kept at his job, despite mounting criticism, for twenty-one years, working six days a week from sunup to sundown and sometimes holding court at night. He said of complaints, ''If criticism is due, it should be [for] the system, not the man whose duty lies under it.'' By the end of his career he had heard 13,940 cases, found 9,454 men guilty, and had sentenced 88 of them to the gallows. Through his tireless efforts, organizational skills, and firm grasp of the law, Judge Parker brought a measure of peace to a troubled land and won for himself a reputation as the West's greatest judge.

DRESS OF THE WEST

The clothing we associate with the American West was worn more for practicality than for style. Hats, for example, were designed to protect the cowboys from the elements–mainly sun and rain. The "Stetson," the hat commonly thought of as "a cowboy hat," was one of the most popular. (Because hats were sometimes used to carry water, the ample Stetson was jokingly called "the ten-gallon hat.") Many cowboys, however, preferred the Mexican sombrero with its wide brim. Likewise the bandana, or "neckerchief," was not simply a decoration. When the cowboy was trailing a herd or caught in a dust storm, the bandana provided him with a mask to protect his mouth and nose. (Villains, of course, found the bandana a convenient way to hide their identity.)

The cowboy's boots were tight at the top to help keep rocks and dirt out. Toes of the boots were often narrow and pointed so that a rider could get his feet in and out of stirrups easily. A cowboy's clothes were usually made of wool. Although wool was warm in hot weather, cowboys appreciated it during the cool nights and found that it wore much better than fabrics such as cotton. Some cowboys wore chaps, coverings for their trousers made of leather or other animal hides. The chaps were particularly helpful for protecting a cowboy riding through thorns and brush.

The most popular clothing to emerge from the Old West was the work of an immigrant Jew from Germany. Levi Strauss moved west to San Francisco in 1850, where he found a market for sturdy trousers that could endure the punishment that frontier life dished out. Using material out of which he had originally planned to make tents, Strauss built a booming trade as a tailor. He eventually began

to make the trousers out of a tough cloth from Nîmes, France, *serge de Nîmes,* from which the word *denim* comes. Other tailors named the material from the French name for Genoa, Italy–*Gênes*–where a similar cloth was manufactured. This name eventually became corrupted in English as "jeans." All that was left was for Strauss to decide to dye the material blue, and an American institution, "blue jeans," was born.

Buffalo Bill's Wild West Show set in the minds of most Americans the standard portrayal of the Old West. Buffalo Bill Cody's genuine experience as a western scout gave the program an aura of authenticity, but the Wild West Show was more romance than realism.

THE MYTH OF THE OLD WEST

The romantic image of the West–the world of "cowboys and Indians," gunfights, fearless lawmen, and lawless villains–often does not match the real history of the West. One of the creators of the modern image of the Old West was "Buffalo Bill's Wild West Show." As a rider for the Pony Express and a scout for both the army and the Kansas Pacific Railroad, William Frederick "Buffalo Bill"

Annie Oakley, nicknamed "Little Sure Shot" for her matchless skill with a rifle, was one of the most popular performers with Buffalo Bill's Wild West Show. Among her favorite tricks was shooting a dime tossed into the air. Her career abated after she was partially paralyzed in a railroad accident in 1901.

Cody was an authentic "knight" of the plains. A part in a hit Western play in New York, however, convinced Cody that greater opportunity for fame and fortune lay in the entertainment business than in the uncertain world of scouting. The result was "Buffalo Bill Cody's Wild West Show."

Buffalo Bill described his show as a kind of travel documentary, "a year's visit to the West in three hours." In reality, it was sheer entertainment. The climax, a "reenactment" of an Indian battle in which Cody had participated, promised "the grandest, most realistic and overwhelmingly thrilling war-spectacle ever seen." Cowboys rode bucking broncos and relived the pony express. Buffalo Bill tracked huge bison with guns loaded with blanks. Royalty and presidents in the audience gleefully volunteered to ride in the Deadwood Coach and be captured by whooping Indians. The show ran for thirty years (1883 to 1913) and included some of the leading figures in the lore of the American West, such as the famous Indian chief Sitting Bull and little Annie Oakley, whose sure shot could cut a playing card in two edgewise with a bullet.

Not only Buffalo Bill's show but also the many cheap "dime novels" written about him and others helped to glamorize "the Wild West." These sensational stories—written in a few days, garishly illustrated, and priced at 5¢ or 10¢ each— exaggerated the dramatic and ignored historical realities. Cody, for example, became famous through a magazine serial, *Buffalo Bill, The King of the Border Men.*

The modern western novel began in 1902 with the publication of Owen Wister's novel *The Virginian.* Wister presented what have become the standard stereotypes of western stories: the strong but silent "cowpoke" hero; the eastern "schoolmarm" who falls in love with the hero; the cowardly, bullying villain; and the showdown in the dusty street between hero and villain.

The Virginian

Such cowboy stars as Tom Mix, shown here, and the Lone Ranger thrilled American radio audiences with their weekly Wild West adventures during the 1930s and 1940s. Mix also made numerous successful motion pictures.

was Wister's only contribution to the western novel, but other writers quickly picked up where he left off. Ohio-born Zane Grey wrote some sixty westerns that, in his day, outsold all books except the Bible. In stories such as *Riders of the Purple Sage* (1912), Grey pioneered the standardized but popular formula for westerns that enabled him to sell over 17 million books. After Grey's death, Louis L'Amour assumed Grey's mantle as America's best-selling western novelist.

Movies and television, for better or—more often—for worse, have most shaped the modern perception of the Old West. The first movie with a plot was set in the Old West, *The Great Train Robbery* (1903), a nine-minute film containing many of the scenes that became stock favorites—the crime, the chase, the barroom brawl, and the showdown. A succession of western stars crossed the silver screen. Gene Autry, a "singing cowboy" popular in the 1930s and 1940s, typified the attempts to present the cowboy as a role model for children. Autry, for example, introduced the "Ten Commandments of the Cowboy" in the 1930s, which included such rules as "A cowboy always tells the truth" and "A cowboy is clean about his person and in thought, word, and deed." Radio and television likewise popularized the Lone Ranger, the "daring and resourceful masked rider of the

plains'' who neither drank nor swore and who never killed anyone with his silver bullets.

The most popular cowboy actor, John Wayne, and the long-running television series *Gunsmoke* successfully attempted to appeal to adults, but such efforts were often no more accurate historically. Indeed Hollywood often ignored history whenever it was convenient. Villains of the Old West, for example, such as Jesse James, became noble Robin Hood figures, and movies all too often caricatured Indians as mindless, bloodthirsty savages. Most Americans, however, were looking for entertainment, not history lessons, from the silver screen. As their cowboy heroes rode off into successive sunsets, what most Americans took away with them was the myth–not the reality–of the Old West.

Actor John Wayne (born Marion Michael Morrison) embodied for many Americans the swaggering cowboy of the mythic West. Real cowboys were far less glamorous and romantic.

Gun Fights!
Thundering herds!
Prairies ablaze!
Romance!

SAMUEL GOLDWYN presents

GARY COOPER

THE WESTERNER

directed by WILLIAM WYLER

with WALTER BRENNAN · DANA ANDREWS

With only a few exceptions, westerns on film and television tended to follow standardized patterns. The strong-but-silent hero, the true-hearted heroine, honest farmers, scheming ranchers, and notorious gunslingers were all part of the mixture.

The Progressive Era (1900-1920)

"The object of government is the welfare of the people."

Theodore Roosevelt, *The New Nationalism* (1910)

A milestone in history captured on film: Wilbur Wright watches as his brother Orville pilots their plane on its historic first flight.

On September 6, 1901, President William McKinley hosted a public reception at the Pan-American Exposition in Buffalo, New York. In the Exposition's Temple of Music, the president stood in a receiving line greeting the well-wishers who filed past him. McKinley smiled, shook hands, and murmured pleasantries. One tall, thin young man in the line wore what appeared to be a white bandage on his right hand. Kindheartedly, McKinley stretched out his left hand toward the other's unbandaged hand. The young man, however, pushed the president's outstretched hand aside, and from the "bandage" came the sharp *bang* of a pistol. Two shots struck the astonished president. As guards and bystanders swarmed over the assailant, the wounded president said pitifully, "Don't let them hurt him."

Eight days later President McKinley died, and Vice President Theodore Roosevelt took office as the nation's twenty-sixth president. The change was more than a simple switch in personnel. McKinley was quiet, reserved, and sedate; Roosevelt was energetic, active, and outgoing. More than that, McKinley was a political conservative, a cautious man who favored the tried-and-true Republican policy of supporting "big business" and advocating "little government." Roosevelt was a political progressive, an aggressive man who favored vigorous government action to curb abuses and to secure justice and fair treatment for all Americans. With the presidency of Theodore Roosevelt, Americans entered what historians call the "Progressive Era" of United States history.

Progressive Movement

Definition

Progressivism was an ideological movement of the early twentieth century that favored achieving political and social reform through education, wider political participation by all classes of society, and direct government action. The progressive movement had its roots in several movements of the nineteenth century. Some progressives, such as William Jennings Bryan, had been adherents of Populism. Many others were from the ranks of pro-reform Republican factions such as the Half-breeds and the Mugwumps. Many in the movement were members of the middle and upper classes who had been shocked by the abuses of industrialists, by corruption in government, and by the plight of the poor.

The motives of the progressives varied. Many were simply moral Americans whose sense of justice was outraged. They looked at the abuses and corruption around them and concluded that *something* had to be done. Some of the progressives, however, were evolutionary in their thinking. In their view, because man had been constantly evolving and improving from a lower form of life to a higher form, he should continue to improve and progress. To these Reform Darwinists (see p. 371), progress was a process of the natural order that could be aided by government intervention. Some Christians strongly opposed this un-Biblical evolutionary view of progress but still supported progressive reforms. For these believers, reform was an ''opportunity . . . [to] do good unto all men'' (Gal. 6:10).

Principles

The progressive movement was a broad coalition of diverse interests. In general, though, the progressives favored furthering reform through (1) promoting direct democracy, (2) increasing government efficiency, and (3) advocating government intervention.

Direct Democracy—For progressives, as historian George Brown Tindall has noted, ''The cure for the ills of democracy was more democracy.'' The progressives, because of their general faith in the basic goodness of man, believed that placing power in the hands of the people would naturally result in better government. For example, William Jennings Bryan said he favored ''anything that makes the government more democratic, more popular in form, anything that gives the people more control over government.''

Progressives furthered the growth of democracy through several specific reforms. They favored

America's burgeoning cities, typified by this scene from Mulberry Street on New York's lower East Side, presented numerous challenges to the nation at the turn of the century.

the **secret ballot** for elections. Before this time, Americans had to indicate publicly which candidate they preferred as they voted. For example, they would have to request a certain ballot for their candidate or sign their names on a list for the candidate. Such a system allowed unscrupulous political bosses to intimidate voters who favored the "wrong" candidate. The secret ballot reduced the possibility of influencing voters and also frustrated corrupt politicians who now could never be sure whether the votes they "bought" through bribery were actually cast.

Progressives also wanted to replace the nomination of candidates by party conventions and caucuses with **direct primaries,** the nomination of a party's candidates by popular vote. In theory, the direct primary took power over nominations away from party bosses and gave it directly to the people. Progressives also called for greater popular participation in legislation through the initiative and the referendum. **Initiative** is a process in which voters initiate legislation by presenting petitions to their legislature that require the legislators to consider some action. A **referendum** allows the people to vote yes or no in a regular election to determine whether a law should be enacted or rejected. Closely related to these two processes is **recall,** in which voters petition to hold a special election deciding whether to remove an elected official from office. Voters can also vote to "recall" specific legislation or even judicial decisions. Although the national government accepted none of these innovations except the secret ballot, many state and city governments embraced these reforms.

Government Efficiency–Progressives also sought to make government more efficient. They believed that problems in society and government could be remedied by elevating qualified technological experts to positions of responsibility in government. In the Progressive Era, city governments showed the greatest zeal for improving efficiency. Many cities abandoned the usual rule by an elected mayor and city council. Galveston, Texas, for instance, adopted the **city commission** form of municipal government. This system combined the duties of mayor and city council and invested them

in five city commissioners. Even more popular was the **city manager** form of government pioneered by Staunton, Virginia, in 1908. Under this system, the city council hired a qualified city manager who served as the administrator of the city government. In both systems, the goal was to fill positions of power with capable, qualified leaders.

Government Intervention–The progressives strongly believed that reform could best be accomplished by direct government action, although they did not always agree about which action to take. For instance, progressives were united in attacking the abuses and corruptions of trusts (large monopolies such as John D. Rockefeller's Standard Oil Company), but they differed on the method of dealing with the problem. Some progressives favored **"trust-busting,"** breaking up the monopolies and restoring competition to the marketplace. Others favored leaving the trusts intact but placing government regulations on their operations.

For many progressives, government ownership of businesses was the answer. The most extreme progressives–the socialists–wanted the government to take over nearly all business. The majority of reformers, however, preferred only limited government ownership. The most widely accepted form of control was **"gas and water socialism,"** control of utilities such as gas and water companies by city or state governments. The progressives argued that a monopoly was the most efficient way to operate a utility, and that the safest monopoly was one owned and operated by the government.

One plank of the progressive platform was government intervention in behalf of labor. Progressives favored legislation to allow labor unions to organize and to force businesses to negotiate fairly with the unions. In this way, unions could provide a check to the power of big business. Progressives also favored legislation directly helping the working man. Progressives on the city, state, and national levels sponsored laws establishing minimum wage levels, prohibiting child labor, limiting the number of hours in a work day, and mandating safety standards for factories.

It must be stressed that progressives conceived of government intervention as an extension of the idea of direct democracy. The people control the government, progressives argued; therefore, government control of business was really popular control of business. Only after time passed did people realize that popular control of government was more difficult to achieve in reality than in theory and that big government could be the ultimate monopoly.

Constitutional Progressivism

Sixteenth Amendment—Four progressive ideas eventually found their way into the United States Constitution. The first was federal income tax, established by the **Sixteenth Amendment** (ratified 1913). Progressives had two reasons for favoring the tax. First, income taxes would provide the government with funds it needed to initiate reforms and provide the expanded social services that the progressives demanded. Second, the tax rate was *graduated,* that is, the more money one makes, the higher percentage of his income he must pay in taxes. In this manner, the income tax took money from the very wealthy (usually the industrialists and monopolists whom the progressives opposed) and used it, theoretically, for the benefit of all Americans.

Seventeenth Amendment—The second of the "progressive amendments" was the **Seventeenth Amendment** (1913), calling for the direct election of U.S. senators. Under the constitutional procedure before that time (Article I, Section 3, Clause 1), state legislatures elected senators. Progressives charged that senatorial elections had become corrupt auctions in which the wealthy bribed legislators to elect them. Direct election ended this alleged abuse and gave the decision to the voters of each state. By replacing republicanism with increased democratization, however, the amendment also eliminated one of the safeguards which the Founding Fathers had so painstakingly built into our federal system of government.

Eighteenth Amendment—The third reform was **prohibition,** banning the manufacture, sale, or transportation of alcoholic beverages. Established by the **Eighteenth Amendment** (1919), prohibition proved to be the most controversial progressive amendment and was eventually repealed by the Twenty-first Amendment (1933). The progressives saw the amendment as a simple means of remedying major social problems. Social workers visiting the slums saw families in which drunken parents neglected or even abused their children and spent money on alcohol that would have been better spent on food and clothing. Prison reformers spoke to inmates who blamed alcohol for leading them into crime. Progressives naturally concluded that eliminating liquor would reduce crime and poverty.

The Eighteenth Amendment also demonstrates the widespread support that reform enjoyed in this period even beyond the progressive movement. Joining the progressives on behalf of prohibition was a large group of Christian leaders, who denounced alcohol as sinful. Perhaps the most famous of these Christian crusaders was Evangelist Billy Sunday. Although he did not show a consistent interest in progressivism, Sunday zealously championed the cause of prohibition. In his huge citywide evangelistic campaigns he vigorously attacked the "damnable, hellish, vile, corrupt, iniquitous liquor business." Also joining the progressives on this issue were businessmen. They saw prohibition as a means of increasing production by eliminating worker absences and accidents due to drunkenness. When America entered World War I, Americans had another reason to support prohibition; in the face of shortages of grains and other agricultural products caused by the war, it seemed wasteful to be using these products to manufacture alcoholic beverages.

Nineteenth Amendment—The fourth constitutional reform climaxed a movement much older than the progressive movement. The **Nineteenth Amendment** (1920) granted women *suffrage* (the right to vote). The drive for gaining the vote for women had begun before the Civil War. (See p. 227.) Throughout the nineteenth century "women suffragettes" had campaigned unceasingly for the right to vote. Led by women such as Elizabeth Cady Stanton and especially **Susan B. Anthony,** the crusade for women's suffrage was a part of an overall campaign for equal rights for women. Anthony, for example, also labored for the right of women to control their own property and to receive custody of children in divorce cases. Her campaign for the vote, however, garnered the most attention. Although she died fourteen years before it was ratified, the Nineteenth Amendment was often called the "Anthony Amendment" in her honor.

Personalities

Muckrakers—The literary leaders of progressivism were the **muckrakers,** writers who, through books and magazine articles, exposed abuse and corruption. Theodore Roosevelt gave the name "muckrakers" to this group, likening them to the man in John Bunyan's *Pilgrim's Progress* who

> could look no way but downwards with a muck-rake in his hand. There stood also one over his head with a celestial crown in his hand and proffered to give him that crown for his muck-rake; but the man did neither look up, nor regard, but raked to himself the straws, the small sticks, and dust of the floor (*Pilgrim's Progress,* Part II).

The muckrakers served an important purpose, however, in informing the public. The golden era of muckraking journalism began in 1902 when Lincoln Steffens published in *McClure's* magazine an exposé of municipal corruption in St. Louis. His work was soon followed by Ida Tarbell's *History of the Standard Oil Company* (1904), a scathing portrait of the unscrupulous, even dishonest, methods used by John D. Rockefeller to build his oil empire. Other muckraking articles and books followed—such as attacks on insurance fraud and on impure and worthless medicines. Unlike proponents of yellow journalism, who reported sensational stories simply to boost sales (see p. 398), muckrakers felt genuine concern for the causes they advanced. For the most part, muckrakers did not call for any specific action; they contented themselves with describing corruption in graphic detail and trusting in the revulsion of the American people to motivate reforms. In many cases, their faith proved justified as their attacks resulted in legislation addressing these abuses.

Political Progressives—Many politicians embraced the progressive movement. As mentioned earlier, William Jennings Bryan turned from Populism to progressivism and became the leader of the progressive wing of the Democratic party. One of the major Republican leaders was **Robert La Follette** (LUH FALL-ut) of Wisconsin. As a lawyer, governor, then senator, La Follette pressed for a series of reforms (such as the direct primary and railroad regulation) that made Wisconsin, as Theodore Roosevelt called it, "the laboratory of democracy."

There was also an extreme wing to the progressive movement—the socialists, those who advocated government ownership of the major means of production and distribution. The leading socialist of this era was **Eugene Debs,** former head of the American Railway Union (see p. 365). Debs ran for president on the Socialist ticket five times. His highest percentage of the vote came in 1912, when he won six per cent of the total. Debs's most interesting showing, however, was in 1920. In that year he won nearly a million votes while in prison for opposing American involvement in World War I. The vote totals of Debs, along with a few socialist victories in municipal elections, demonstrate that the call for radical reform was present, but only among a small segment of American society.

The boisterous Theodore Roosevelt in many ways personified the energetic, reformist tendencies of the Progressive Era.

DRAWING THE LINE IN MISSISSIPPI

Teddy Bears

Theodore Roosevelt's widespread popularity with the American public is illustrated by a fad from his presidency that has become an established part of American life for the young–and the young at heart. While Roosevelt was on a hunting trip in Mississippi in 1902, a guide captured a bear and brought it to camp for the president to shoot. Roosevelt indignantly refused to be so unsporting as to kill a captured animal. A reporter recounted the story, and an inspired cartoonist drew a caricature of the incident and labeled it "Drawing the line in Mississippi."

The incident caught the public fancy. Soon enterprising toy makers were selling stuffed bears labeled "teddy bears," and children all over the nation–and in fact all over the world–were sleeping with the soft, cuddly toys in their arms. Toy companies manufactured all sorts of teddy bears in all kinds of garb–including some dressed in Rough Rider uniforms. One toy maker, Morris Michtom, a Russian Jewish immigrant living in Brooklyn, actually wrote to Roosevelt, asking for his permission to market stuffed toy bears under the name "teddy bear." In a handwritten letter Roosevelt replied, "I doubt if my name will mean much in the bear business, but you may use it if you wish." Michtom successfully marketed the teddy bears, and his business eventually became the Ideal Toy Company, a multimillion-dollar corporation.

The president was by all accounts rather embarrassed by the teddy bear boom. He good-naturedly went along with the fad, however, and his political rallies were soon decorated with the toy. Roosevelt had one personal reason for disliking the toy, though; he had always hated the name "Teddy."

Progressive Presidents–Three presidents governed the United States during the Progressive Era: Theodore Roosevelt (1901-1909), William Howard Taft (1909-1913), and Woodrow Wilson (1913-1921). Each of these men reflected to some extent the progressive spirit, but **Theodore Roosevelt** was probably the most closely associated with progressivism. The son of a moderately wealthy New York family, a graduate of Harvard, and an accomplished historian, Roosevelt was in some ways the most "aristocratic" president since John Adams. Yet by living as a cowboy on his cattle ranch in the Dakotas and through his heroics with the Rough Riders in Cuba, Roosevelt shed much of his upper-class image and displayed a great appeal to the common man. Furthermore, as a New York state legislator, member of the U.S. Civil Service Commission, and a New York City police commissioner, Roosevelt had built a reputation as the friend of reform. The stage was set for a dramatic change in American government when Roosevelt took office in 1901.

Section Review

1. What were the three means proposed by the progressives to further reform?
2. What is the difference between an initiative and a referendum?
3. What were the two popular forms of city government developed during the Progressive Era?
4. What was the most controversial of the four "progressive amendments" to the Constitution?
5. Who was the leader of the progressive wing of the Democratic party?

Progressive Politics

Roosevelt and the Square Deal

Theodore Roosevelt approached the presidency as he approached life–zealously. He planned to govern actively, to lead instead of follow Congress in setting the political agenda for the nation. By persuasion, intimidation, and sheer force of personality, Roosevelt shaped the policies of the government. Central to his philosophy was his belief that every man and woman should receive fair treatment and equal opportunity, a **"Square Deal,"** as Roosevelt put it.

Trust-Busting—Early in his presidency, Roosevelt launched his attack on the abuses of the trusts by reviving the little-used Sherman Antitrust Act. In 1902 the federal government charged the Northern Securities Company with violating the act, and the government filed a lawsuit to break it up. The Northern Securities Company, which controlled the powerful Great Northern and Northern Pacific railroads, fought the suit, but the Supreme Court upheld the government. The **Northern Securities case** was a milestone in vindicating the government's authority to regulate trusts, and it encouraged Roosevelt to proceed against other monopolies. Although it is unclear how much this antitrust activity actually increased competition, it won Roosevelt widespread public acclaim as a "trust-buster."

Regulation—Roosevelt also sought to regulate the conduct of business and industry for what he viewed as the public good. He gave the most attention to railroads, the major means of transportation and shipping in the nation. Consumers often complained that the railroads, which operated as monopolies in some areas, charged excessively high rates and granted special concessions to businesses they favored. The **Hepburn Act** (1906) was Roosevelt's most important railroad-regulating legislation. This act strengthened the Interstate Commerce Commission's ability to set rates for railroads and also made provisions for a standard bookkeeping system that made it easier to compare and regulate these rates. Most important, the act shifted the burden of proof in rate-setting from the ICC to the railroads. Previously, the ICC had to take a rail

company to court to enforce its rate decisions. Under the Hepburn Act, the railroads had to take the ICC to court to overturn the commission's decisions. Increasingly, the railroads simply went along with the rates that the ICC set.

Roosevelt also pushed for regulation in the production of food and medicine. The **Pure Food and Drug Act** (1906) outlawed the interstate sale of impure food and drugs and also required honest labeling of such products. The **Meat Inspection Act** (1906) required the Department of Agriculture to oversee the preparation and packaging of meat and to inspect the health of animals before they were slaughtered. Passage of both of these acts was aided by the public outrage resulting from the publication of *The Jungle* (1906) by the muckraker Upton Sinclair. Although supposedly a work of fiction, Sinclair's book was a graphic portrayal of the filthy conditions in Chicago's meat-packing plants. (See the excerpt on the next page.) The supervisory agencies established by these two acts have unquestionably benefited the public, and their powers have not been so extensive that they have seriously hampered private production, as some regulatory agencies have done. In fact, increased public confidence in the quality of their food and drugs may actually have helped increase sales.

Coal Strike—Roosevelt's dedication to obtaining a "square deal" for labor and business was severely tested by a coal miners' strike in 1902. Coal was the major source of fuel for steam-operated machinery, including railroad locomotives, and the major source of heat for the entire nation. As winter drew near and the public grew concerned, Roosevelt tried to break the stalemate. He arranged a meeting between the owners and union leaders at the White House, but the owners refused even to speak to the union men assembled there. Losing his patience, Roosevelt threatened to use federal troops to operate the mines. For the first time, the threat of federal force was used against owners–whose arrogance had alienated public sentiment–rather than against workers. Reluctantly, the owners consented to a ten per cent pay raise and a nine-hour day. This was the first case of the federal government's acting as the mediator in a labor dispute, and the success of the effort increased Roosevelt's popularity even more.

Conservation—Nothing was more important to the rugged outdoorsman Roosevelt than the **conservation** of natural resources. The Reclamation Act, passed in 1902, set aside nearly 100 million acres of western land to be controlled by the federal government in addition to the millions of acres already set aside for national forests. Colorado's Mesa Verde National Park and Oregon's Crater Lake National Park are but two of the five national parks established during Roosevelt's presidency. During his last year in office, Roosevelt established the National Conservation Commission, headed by Gifford Pinchot (PIN shoh), chief of the U.S. Forest Service. The commission was assigned the task of reporting water, timber, soil, land, and mineral resources. A friend later told Roosevelt that his conservation efforts were "one of the greatest memorials to your farsightedness." Roosevelt replied,

"Bully, I had rather have it than a hundred stone monuments."

Race Relations—One of the great failures of progressivism was worsening race relations. In California, resentment of the growing Asian population resulted in discrimination and even violence. In 1906 the San Francisco school board touched off an international incident when it tried to segregate all Asian students into a separate public school. When the Japanese government strongly protested this treatment, Roosevelt pressured the school board to reverse this decision in return for voluntary Japanese restrictions on immigration.

The situation for blacks in the South (where the overwhelming majority of American blacks lived before World War I) actually worsened during the Progressive Era. Theodore Roosevelt stirred up controversy by inviting black educator Booker T. Washington to dine with him in the White House,

---

From *The Jungle*

They were regular alchemists at Durham's [a packing house]; they advertised a mushroom-catsup, and the men who made it did not know what a mushroom looked like. They advertised "potted chicken"—and it was like the boarding-house soup of the comic papers, through which a chicken had walked with rubbers on. Perhaps they had a secret process for making chickens chemically—who knows? . . . The things that went into the mixture were tripe, and the fat of pork, and beef suet, and hearts of beef, and finally the waste ends of veal, when they had any. They put these up in several grades, and sold them at several prices; but the contents of the cans all came out of the same hopper. And then there was "potted game" and "potted grouse," "potted ham," and "deviled ham"—de-vyled, as the men called it. "Devyled" ham was made out of the waste ends of smoked beef that were too small to be sliced by the machines; and also tripe, dyed with chemicals so that it would not show

white, and trimmings of hams and corned beef, and potatoes, skins and all, and finally the hard cartilaginous gullets of beef, after the tongues had been cut out. All this ingenious mixture was ground up and flavored with spices to make it taste like something. Anybody who could invent a new imitation had been sure of a fortune from old Durham, . . . but it was hard to think of anything new in a place where so many sharp wits had been at work for so long; where men welcomed tuberculosis in the cattle they were feeding, because it made them fatten more quickly; and where they bought up all the old rancid butter left over in the grocery stores of a continent, and "oxidized" it by a forced-air process, to take away the odor, rechurned it with skim milk, and sold it in bricks in the cities! Up to a year or two ago it had been the custom to kill horses in the yards—ostensibly for fertilizer; but after long agitation the newspapers had been able to make the public realize that the horses were being canned.

but progressives on the whole did little to alleviate growing racial discrimination. Until the 1890s there was some hope for improvement in racial relations in the South. The Redeemer governments that ruled the South after Reconstruction (see pp. 340-41) generally tried to keep their promises to protect black civil rights–if for no other reason than to lure black votes into the Democratic column. Blacks even held elective or appointive office under the Redemption governments. For example, in every session of Congress from 1869 to 1901 except one, there was at least one black member of the House of Representatives.

This situation began to change in the 1890s as southern states began passing **"Jim Crow laws,"** legislation that required the forced **segregation,** or separation, of the races in trains, restaurants, hotels, schools, and other social settings. ("Jim Crow" was a black character in a nineteenth-century minstrel song.) In fact, segregation was so extensive that whites and blacks even had separate restrooms and drinking fountains. In addition, southern governments began to deprive blacks of their right to vote by setting up literacy tests for voting (to which whites were often exempt) or requiring special "poll taxes" which one had to pay before voting. The number of registered black voters in Louisiana, for example, plummeted from over 130,000 in 1896 to slightly more than 1,300 in 1904.

There were several reasons for this change. First, the Redeemer politicians were gradually losing ground to overtly racist politicians who played on the fears and prejudices of white voters to rally support to their cause. Second, the alliance of blacks with some reform groups such as the Populists caused many conservative Democrats to disenfranchise blacks in order to dilute Populist political power. Third, the national government and the northern public in general lost interest in the cause of civil rights for blacks. Segregation in the South would not have been possible had not the Supreme Court issued a series of decisions that gutted the enforcement of the Reconstruction civil rights legislation. Perhaps the most famous of these cases was *Plessy* v. *Ferguson,* a case which decreed that "separate but equal" facilities for blacks and

Booker T. Washington

whites (in this case, on trains) were constitutional. These decisions gave state legislatures the legal justification they needed to pass whole "Jim Crow" law codes.

Blacks reacted to this increase in discrimination in differing ways. One approach was represented by the outstanding black leader of the era, **Booker T. Washington.** As described in his famous autobiography, *Up From Slavery,* Washington had risen from slavery to the presidency of Tuskegee Institute in Alabama, the nation's leading black industrial school. Washington was basically conservative; in a famous speech given in Atlanta in 1895, he urged blacks not to risk strife by agitating politically for their rights. Instead, they should concentrate on bettering themselves economically through vocational education and the establishment of black businesses and trades. As blacks became more powerful economically, Washington argued, whites would be forced to accept them and grant them political equality.

Opposing Washington was a group of black intellectuals led by **W.E.B. Du Bois.** They argued that blacks could not truly improve themselves economically until they enjoyed equal participation in the political process as American citizens. They opposed Washington's exclusive stress on technical and industrial education over liberal arts, fearing that it would force all blacks into an economically inferior laboring class and discourage higher education among blacks. Where Washington sought an economic solution to the problem, Du Bois pursued a political solution. In 1909 Du Bois and other like-minded leaders–black and white–formed the **National Association for the Advancement of Colored People (NAACP)** to fight legal battles on behalf of blacks. During Washington's lifetime, his views dominated American race relations; afterwards, however, the approach of the NAACP gained in strength and became the basis of the black civil rights movement of the 1950s and 1960s.

Roosevelt and the "Big Stick"

A favorite saying of Theodore Roosevelt's was "Speak softly and carry a big stick; you will go far." Just as the phrase "square deal" describes Roosevelt's domestic policy, so the "big stick" describes his foreign policy. The president pursued a vigor-ous, expansive foreign policy, one that involved the United States more actively in international affairs. His foreign policy was still in line with his reformist impulses; Roosevelt considered the expansion of a "civilized power" such as the United States into world affairs to be "a victory for law, order and righteousness."

Philippines–One major problem that Roosevelt inherited from McKinley was the situation in the Philippines after the Spanish-American War. Even after the surrender of Emilio Aguinaldo and the end of the insurrection (see p. 401), the people of the Philippines were not content with American rule; they wanted independence. Roosevelt approached the Philippine problem warily. The governor of the islands, his friend and adviser William Howard Taft, attempted to win the affection of the Philippine people through his genuine concern for them. American leaders feared that if the islands were granted independence too quickly, they might fall prey to another major power, such as Japan. Therefore, over a period of thirty years, the United States gradually gave the Filipinos increasing amounts of self-rule. After the liberation of the islands from Japanese occupation during World War II, the Philippines received their complete independence in 1946.

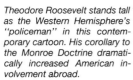

Theodore Roosevelt stands tall as the Western Hemisphere's "policeman" in this contemporary cartoon. His corollary to the Monroe Doctrine dramatically increased American involvement abroad.

Panama Canal—One of Roosevelt's favorite projects was the building of an American-controlled canal in Central America to link the Atlantic and the Pacific. Members of Congress, however, disagreed about the best route. Some favored a route through Nicaragua; others, a route through Panama (at the time a part of Colombia), where in the 1880s a French company had gone bankrupt trying to dig a canal. The French company, needing the money from the sale of their rights of construction, sent a representative, Philippe Bunau-Varilla (fuh-LEEP BOO-noh vuh-REE-yuh), to negotiate with the United States. In 1902 Congress passed an act authorizing purchase of the French rights for $40 million, and in 1903 the Senate passed a treaty with Colombia agreeing to purchase perpetual control of the canal zone for $10 million initially, with annual payments of $250,000 thereafter. However, the Colombian senate, hoping to get more money, rejected the treaty.

Infuriated by this action, Roosevelt denounced the Colombians as "foolish and homicidal corruptionists" who were attempting to blackmail the United States. Bunau-Varilla, who was still trying to promote the sale of his company's rights, quickly pointed out to the president that a revolution in Panama was imminent; many Panamanians resented the Colombian government and wanted to break away. Officers of the French company, led by Bunau-Varilla, helped finance and organize the revolt. Roosevelt, for his part, ordered the U.S. Navy to prevent Colombian troops from landing in Panama to crush the rebellion.

Mainly because of this American support, Panama's revolt succeeded on November 3, 1903. Three days later President Roosevelt recognized Panama's independence, and the Panamanians then appointed Bunau-Varilla as their minister to the United States. He and Secretary of State Hay signed an agreement on November 18 promising Panama the same payment for the canal that had been offered to Colombia.

The circumstances under which the United States acquired the canal zone were at least questionable, although the canal clearly benefited most of the nations of the Western Hemisphere. Colom-bia was understandably resentful, and other Latin American countries also expressed their fear of the United States—the "Colossus of the North," as they put it. Some congressmen raised ethical objections, but Roosevelt characteristically commented, "I took the Canal Zone and let Congress debate; and while the debate goes on the Canal does also."

Construction of the **Panama Canal** took approximately ten years. As many as forty thousand Americans were employed on the project at one time, despite the many hazards. The canal cost about $400 million, but its financial benefits to world shipping outweighed the cost. In August 1914–just days after World War I had broken out in Europe–the canal opened and linked ocean to ocean.

Roosevelt Corollary—Roosevelt's actions in Panama represented his general approach to affairs in Latin America. He envisioned the United States as the leader in the Western Hemisphere, protecting the region and regulating its behavior. Complicating Roosevelt's position was the sometimes irresponsible conduct of some Latin American nations. In 1902 Venezuela ran afoul of Great Britain and Germany when it proved unable to repay loans from those nations. Likewise a bloody revolution in the Dominican Republic in 1904 worried the European powers with sizable investments in that nation. Fearing European intervention in this hemisphere, Roosevelt devised an addition to the Monroe Doctrine that became known as the **Roosevelt Corollary.** As the president himself told Congress in 1904,

> Chronic wrongdoing . . . may in America, as elsewhere, ultimately require intervention by some civilized nation, and in the Western Hemisphere the adherence of the United States to the Monroe Doctrine may force the United States, however reluctantly, in flagrant cases of such wrongdoing or impotence, to the exercise of an international police power.

To the Monroe Doctrine's assertion that Europe could not intervene in the Americas, Roosevelt's corollary added that the United States would act as a "policeman" to keep Latin American nations in

A contemporary cartoon presents the Russo-Japanese War as a clash between the Russian bear and the Japanese samurai. Japan's crushing victory made the nation a major Pacific power and brought increased tension between it and the United States.

line. Roosevelt's new doctrine placed the United States in a position of constantly intervening in order to prevent European nations from intervening. During the next decade the United States intervened in Haiti, Honduras, Nicaragua, and the Dominican Republic in attempts to collect debts or maintain order. European and Latin American resentment toward the United States intensified as a result.

Relations with Japan–American trade with China and its possessions in the Pacific, such as the Philippines and Guam, brought the United States into closer contact with Japan. Throughout the Roosevelt years, relations with the proud and increasingly powerful Japanese were a sensitive issue. In February 1904 war broke out between Japan and Russia over conflicts of interest in Manchuria (a province of China). The Japanese won a series of quick naval and land victories that worried the other great powers, who feared growing Japanese might in the Pacific. The war, however, strained the finances of both nations, and they invited Roosevelt to mediate. In 1905 at a conference in Portsmouth, New Hampshire, Roosevelt negotiated a settlement which preserved most of Japan's gains but allowed Russia to escape with some of its honor intact. Roosevelt was later awarded the Nobel Peace Prize for his services. Unfortunately, both Russia and Japan were unhappy with the compromises embodied in the **Treaty of Portsmouth** (1905), and American relations with both nations soon cooled.

As mentioned earlier (p. 424), the Japanese were understandably offended at the discriminatory legislation directed at Asians on the west coast of the United States. Roosevelt finally negotiated what he called the "Gentleman's Agreement" with the Japanese government. Japan agreed to refuse passports to Japanese laborers leaving for the United States; Roosevelt forbade immigration of Japanese traveling by way of other nations. In return for these concessions, Roosevelt was able to win better treatment for Asians in California. The agreement all but stopped Japanese immigration, and tensions relaxed.

"Great White Fleet"–Japanese-American relations also sparked the climax of Roosevelt's foreign policy, a grand display of American naval power. In December 1907 sixteen battleships, referred to as the "Great White Fleet," steamed from Virginia heading around South America, into the Pacific, and on to Japan. Roosevelt's goal was to impress the Japanese with American strength. Instead of intimidating or provoking the Japanese, however, the navy was enthusiastically welcomed in Japan, and relations with Japan temporarily improved. In 1908, partly because of this "battleship diplomacy," the two countries signed the **Root-Takahira** (TAH kah HEE rah) **Agreement,** in which both powers pledged to respect each other's territorial claims in the Pacific and to maintain the "open door" for trade in China. The fleet itself imitated Magellan by sailing around the world, symbolizing American power wherever it went.

Section Review

1. What piece of muckraking literature spurred the passage of the Pure Food and Drug Act and the Meat Inspection Act? Who wrote the work?
2. How did Roosevelt manage to end the coal strike?
3. What decision by a school board in San Francisco angered the Japanese government?
4. Why did some Americans fear giving the Philippines their independence too quickly?
5. Why did Colombia reject the canal treaty with the United States in 1903? How did the United States acquire the canal anyway?

Taft and the Presidency

Roosevelt refused to run for a third term, but he hand-picked his successor, **William Howard Taft.** Taft was a huge man, weighing over three hundred pounds, whose pleasant nature made him almost instantly likable and whose physique gratified political cartoonists. The portly Taft had enjoyed a distinguished public career mostly in appointed positions such as governor of the Philippines and secretary of war. With Roosevelt's support, Taft easily captured the Republican nomination and then defeated William Jennings Bryan in the 1908 presidential election by a comfortable margin. Taft was sympathetic to reform, but he was far more reserved and cautious than Roosevelt. His subdued manner, orderly mind, and legal background actually suited him better for a judicial career than a political one. (He eventually did serve as Chief Justice of the Supreme Court.) Taft's instinctive caution led him into conflict with the progressives in his own party, despite his reformist intentions, and eventually resulted in a split between Taft and his former friend Roosevelt.

Tariff Fiasco—Taft's first effort at reform was a failure. Taft wanted to lower tariff rates–a controversial issue that Roosevelt had not dared to raise during his two terms. Taft's forces in Congress drafted a bill lowering the tariff moderately. However, by the time the probusiness Senate was finished with the bill, rates remained virtually unchanged. Progressives urged Taft to veto the bill, but the president accepted it as the best he could get. When Taft tried to defend the new tariff as "on the whole . . . the best [tariff] bill that the Republican party ever passed," progressives became even more dismayed.

Congressional Reform—Many members of the House of Representatives resented the dictatorial powers of the Speaker of the House, **Joseph ("Uncle Joe") Cannon.** As Speaker, Cannon assigned the members to and selected the chairman for each committee in the House. Furthermore, Cannon himself was chairman of the powerful Rules Committee, which controls when and how each bill will be debated. In 1910 a coalition of Democrats and Republican "insurgents" joined forces to reduce Cannon's power. They voted to increase the membership of the Rules Committee from five to fifteen members, to remove the Speaker as a member of the committee, and to elect members of the committee by the House. In addition, the insurgents stripped Cannon of his power to appoint members to other committees. Taft, however, did not share in the glory of this reform. Although he had originally supported trimming Cannon's power, Taft had relented when other Republican leaders warned him against antagonizing the powerful Speaker. As a result, the progressives thought that Taft had abandoned them, and another wedge was driven between the president and the progressives.

Split with Roosevelt—Theodore Roosevelt, after helping Taft reach the presidency, left in 1909 for a hunting trip in Africa followed by a tour of Europe. Even overseas Roosevelt began to hear complaints about Taft from progressives. One issue that divided the two men was especially dear to Roosevelt's heart: conservation. In reality, Taft was just as concerned with conservation as Roosevelt, and in his four years in office Taft actually withdrew more public lands to government control than Roosevelt had done in nearly eight years. Taft, however, disliked the way Roosevelt had stretched the law in reserving some lands; the new president preferred to withdraw lands only when the law was clearly and unquestionably on his side. As a result, Taft clashed with the head of the U.S. Forest Service, Gifford Pinchot, who was worried about the future of some of the public lands that Taft was returning to private use. Eventually Pinchot so publicized his conflicts with the president that Taft dismissed him. This act combined with Pinchot's denunciations cast public suspicion on Taft's devotion to conservation. Furthermore the fact that Pinchot was also a close friend of Roosevelt's placed a chill over the former president's relationship with Taft.

The final break between Roosevelt and Taft came over antitrust proceedings. Again, Taft built an impressive record in antitrust actions; he initiated more antitrust suits in one term than Roosevelt had done in two. One suit in particular, however, upset Roosevelt. In 1907, during Roosevelt's second term, U.S. Steel had wanted to purchase the Tennessee Coal and Iron Company, claiming that this action would help prop up a shaky brokerage house during a financial panic. The businessmen involved in the deal asked whether the government considered such a purchase too monopolistic. Roosevelt agreed that the move seemed necessary and gave his unofficial blessing to the purchase. The Taft administration, however, viewed the transaction as a step in building an illegal monopoly and filed suit against U.S. Steel. Since the charges included the suggestion that Roosevelt had allowed himself to be duped by the corporation, the former president was understandably angry and offended. A formal split was developing not only between Taft and Roosevelt but also between the conservatives and progressives within the Republican party.

Dollar Diplomacy—Taft also adopted a less confrontational foreign policy than the displays of military might that Roosevelt favored. Taft preferred to influence foreign affairs through the investment of American dollars in foreign countries, a policy that was soon nicknamed **"dollar diplomacy."** Concerned by Japan's efforts at expansion in China, he encouraged American companies to build railroads in China and establish themselves as competitors there. Taft also backed similar efforts in Latin America, particularly in Nicaragua. Most businesses, however, feared investing in areas of the world where trouble was brewing. Only as the U.S. government put pressure on American investors did they risk money on such projects. The results were mixed. Dollar diplomacy was mildly successful in increasing trade and industry in Latin America, where foreign governments realized that the United States might intervene militarily to protect American investments. It was less successful in regions such as China where interference was likely to bring little more than formal protests from the United States. Taft's dollar diplomacy was a well-intentioned plan to bring mutual economic benefit and to build better foreign relations between the United States and foreign nations. Its general failure disappointed both Taft and the public and contributed to the perception that Taft was an ineffective president.

Election of 1912

Roosevelt finally concluded that Taft was not wholly committed to the progressive cause. For that reason, among others, T.R. "threw his hat into the ring" and announced his candidacy for the Republican nomination in 1912. Roosevelt was still undeniably popular with the voters; he won nine of the twelve state primaries that chose delegates for the Republican convention. As the incumbent president, however, Taft held solid control of the nonprimary states, and he won the hard-fought campaign for the nomination.

Roosevelt declared that not only had Taft betrayed progressivism, he had also stolen the nomination. Therefore, Roosevelt and his followers formed a third party, the **Progressive party** (popularly known as the "Bull Moose" party because Roosevelt told a reporter that he felt "as strong as a bull moose.") Roosevelt ran on a platform that he called the **"New Nationalism."** The Progressive party called for strong federal regulation of business (instead of breaking up monopolies as Roosevelt had previously favored), a federal securities commission to supervise the sale of stocks and bonds, revision of the tariff, direct primary elections for nomination of candidates, easier amendment of the Constitution, and numerous social reforms, including women's suffrage and labor reforms.

The Democrats also nominated a progressive candidate, Governor **Woodrow Wilson** of New Jersey. As a historian, professor, and president of Princeton University, Wilson had both studied deeply and written intelligently about the American system of government. Elected governor of New Jersey in 1910, Wilson proved to be a zealous progressive. He initiated reforms such as the direct primary, state regulation of utilities, and legislation designed to drive monopolies out of the state. Wilson campaigned under the motto the **"New Freedom."** His platform sounded much like the progressive principles of Roosevelt's earlier years in the presidency. For example, Wilson called for increased competition through trust-busting rather than the greater regulation that Roosevelt was now campaigning for.

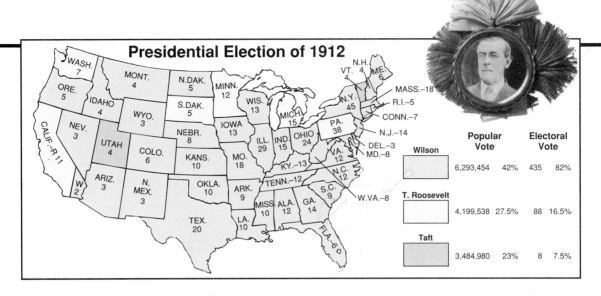

Presidential Election of 1912

	Popular Vote		Electoral Vote	
Wilson	6,293,454	42%	435	82%
T. Roosevelt	4,199,538	27.5%	88	16.5%
Taft	3,484,980	23%	8	7.5%

In the election, Roosevelt and the Progressives made the best third-party showing in presidential history. Roosevelt won 4.1 million votes to 3.5 million for Taft, and he won 88 electoral votes to Taft's 8. With the Republicans divided, however, Wilson won 6.3 million votes (43 per cent of the total) and 435 electoral votes. In addition, Wilson swept into office with Democratic majorities in both houses of Congress. For the first time in nearly twenty years, the Democrats controlled both Congress and the White House.

Wilson and the New Freedom

Most Americans today associate Woodrow Wilson with World War I and the complicated foreign affairs involved in that conflict (discussed in the next chapter). Wilson's first term, though, was really the climax of the progressive movement in America. For example, three of the four "progressive amendments" to the Constitution (17-19) were ratified during Wilson's time in office. His presidency represented the crowning achievements of the Progressive Era.

Revenue Revision—One of the first important reforms of the Wilson administration was the **Underwood Tariff Act** of 1913. Unlike Roosevelt and Taft, Wilson succeeded in achieving the first genuine tariff reform since the Civil War. The new tariff slashed overall rates by about a third from what they had been. Even more important, the act

made up for the loss of tariff revenue by adopting the first income tax under the recently ratified Sixteenth Amendment. The first income tax was one per cent of all annual incomes over $3,000 ($4,000 for married couples), gradually rising to six per cent of all incomes over $500,000. Since the average American income at the time was much less than $3,000, one writer joked, "It will be an exclusive circle, this income-tax class—one which the ordinary . . . man cannot hope to attain." The act nonetheless marked a significant change in American tax policies.

Federal Reserve Act—In 1907 the latest in a series of financial panics had left American businessmen desiring a better system of regulating currency and banking practices. These businessmen envisioned something similar to the Bank of the United States that Andrew Jackson had destroyed. Such a centralized, privately owned national bank could easily set standards for banks and regulate the flow of currency throughout the country. The nation's business interests, therefore, presented this request to the leaders in Washington.

Wilson and the progressives in Congress, however, developed a different system in the **Federal Reserve Act** (1913). This legislation divided the nation into twelve banking districts, each served by a private regional Federal Reserve Bank. Over these district banks was a central organization, the Federal Reserve Board, a government-run body.

This system represented a compromise between a totally private banking system (as businessmen wanted) and a totally state-controlled system (as many progressives wanted). The Federal Reserve Board, however, represented ultimate government control, if not actual government ownership. In addition to banking regulation, the act created a new currency, the Federal Reserve Note. These bills, issued by the various Federal Reserve Banks, eventually became the main currency of the United States. Today virtually all American currency consists of Federal Reserve Notes.

Business and Labor—Wilson's administration passed two important pieces of legislation in 1914 concerning the regulation of business and labor. The **Clayton Antitrust Act** strengthened the Sherman Antitrust Act by expanding the list of practices prohibited to corporations. It also exempted labor unions from antitrust legislation and legalized practices such as strikes, picketing, and boycotts. Samuel Gompers, head of the AFL, called the act labor's "Magna Carta."

Even more sweeping in its effects was the **Federal Trade Commission Act.** This act established the Federal Trade Commission (FTC), a board of five men authorized to help define and halt unfair business practices. The FTC Act marked a growing tendency in the nature of government regulation of business practices. Increasingly, the determining of unfair practices, the establishment of regulations, and the enforcement of policies were being left to regulatory agencies such as the FTC instead of to Congress or the courts. This legislation well represented the progressive tendency to view government as the solution to society's problems.

Section Review

1. Why did Taft's attempt to lower the tariff end up offending the progressives?
2. Why did Taft's antitrust suit against U.S. Steel result in a split between Taft and Roosevelt?
3. What method of raising revenue did the Underwood Tariff use in place of reduced tariff rates?
4. What two major pieces of legislation concerning business and labor were passed during Wilson's first term?

Progressive Society

The dramatic changes in American politics during the Progressive Era were paralleled by important changes in other aspects of American life. Just as politicians pushed for what they considered inevitable progress, so leaders in other areas called for progress and improvement in their fields—socially, economically, philosophically, and religiously. In some areas, particularly technological ones such as transportation and agriculture, there were genuine and remarkable advances. In education and religion, however, "progressive" proved to be *regressive* as far as the standards of God's Word are concerned.

Transportation Transformation

The development of two inventions in the Progressive Era—the automobile and the airplane—began the transformation of American transportation in the twentieth century. These innovations brought greater speed, power, flexibility, and dependability to transportation. The automobile in particular gave

Henry Ford

"Tin Lizzies" ready for the road. Ford's assembly-line process revolutionized American manufacturing and transportation.

the average American a mobility that he had never before experienced. Distances that would have daunted an early American pioneer became mere inconveniences in the increasingly hurried life of twentieth-century America.

Automobiles–In 1896 **Henry Ford,** an engineer for the Edison Illuminating Company in Detroit, unveiled in his garage an invention he had been tinkering with in his spare time–a motorized "horseless carriage." Ford did not invent the automobile; other inventors in America and Europe were experimenting with motorcars at the time, and there appeared to be nothing that would distinguish Ford from the rest. His vehicle, with its tiny two-cylinder engine, seemed little more than a novelty. However, Ford's grit, determination, and hard work–as well as generous financial support from several backers–enabled him to found the Ford Motor Company in 1903.

In 1908 Ford brought out the Model T automobile, a plain but remarkably sturdy car. Although the Model T was well designed, Ford's genius lay more in the manufacture of his vehicle.

Drawing on the ideas of several manufacturers, Ford perfected the **assembly line** method of production. "The way to make automobiles," said Ford, "is to make one automobile like another automobile, to make them all alike, to make them come through the factory just alike." Each car moved by stages along the assembly line, where at each stop a worker specializing in one task would attach his part or perform his process. By using standardized, interchangeable parts and the assembly line, Ford achieved a high degree of efficiency and speed in auto manufacturing. When he added the mass production of thousands of identical cars to this increased efficiency, Ford was able to lower costs and make the Model T affordable for nearly everyone. The price of a new Model T dropped steadily from over $800 when it first came out to $360 by 1916 to $260 by 1925. By the 1920s over half of the cars on America's roads were Fords.

Airplanes–Like the development of the automobile, the development of the airplane was the work of little-known, independent, midwestern inventors. The **Wright brothers**–Orville, born in

Wilbur and Orville Wright

Dayton, Ohio, and Wilbur, born near New Castle, Indiana–were not the only men of the era attempting to fly, but they were the first to succeed. The Wrights had first become interested in flight when as boys their father gave them a toy helicopter powered by rubber bands. Interest in flying, however, was only one aspect of the Wright brothers' mechanical and inventive interests. As young men in Dayton, they began a weekly newspaper printed on a press that they had built themselves. Later the popularity of bicycling led them to open a bicycle sales and repair shop which eventually became a successful bicycle-manufacturing firm.

The profits of their bicycle company enabled the Wrights to pursue their dream of flight. They read all the literature on flying that they could lay their hands on, and they experimented with home-built kites and gliders. Needing more room for their work, they set up an experimental testing grounds on the treeless, windswept dunes of Kitty Hawk, North Carolina. On December 17, 1903, after years of wearying work, Orville climbed into their flying machine, the Wright Flyer. In the damp chill of the morning, the Flyer rolled smoothly down its track and rose into the air. The 12-second, 120-foot trip was the first powered, sustained, and controlled flight in history. From this humble beginning at Kitty Hawk, the airplane rapidly developed into a faster means of shipping and transportation and a decisive military weapon.

George Washington Carver, *by Betsy Graves Reyneau, National Portrait Gallery, Smithsonian Institution*

George Washington Carver

One of the leaders in southern agriculture during and after the Progressive Era was George Washington Carver, a professor at Booker T. Washington's Tuskegee Institute. Born a slave in Missouri around 1861, he never knew his parents. Carver's father died when George was only two months old, and George, his mother, and his sister were kidnapped by guerrillas during the Civil War. George's master, Moses Carver, was able to locate George and purchase him back, but no trace was ever found of George's mother or sister.

Young Carver possessed an insatiable curiosity about nature. He was particularly interested in plants, and he taught himself so much about plants, soils, and growing that neighbors nicknamed him "the plant doctor." Carver also wanted more than anything else to get an education. Eventually he left the home of Moses Carver and traveled around Missouri, Kansas, and Iowa attending various schools and supporting himself by working as a cook, launderer, and common laborer. In each school, Carver stayed as long as he could learn anything from the often ill-educated teachers and then moved on.

When he was in his mid-twenties, Carver decided to go to college. He was accepted by one college, which then quickly rejected him when it discovered he was black. By persevering, Carver was able to get into college, and he graduated from Iowa's State Agricultural College in 1894 and received his master's degree there in 1896.

When Carver arrived at Tuskegee Institute in 1896, the school had little more than its land and a few ramshackle buildings. Carver stocked his laboratory by rifling through junk piles–milk bottles were cut down to form beakers, old coffee cups became mortars, and fruit jars held chemicals. To this odd assortment of mismatched equipment, Carver added his own natural genius for research and experimentation.

Carver was concerned that years of cotton growing had depleted southern soil. He found that certain plants–particularly peanuts–replenished the nitrogen that cotton removed from the soil. Farmers complained, however, that while peanuts might help the soil, they brought little profit to the growers. Carver, therefore, set to work to find uses for the peanut. After much experimentation, Carver developed over two hundred uses for the peanut, including dyes, a milk substitute, ice cream, livestock feed, fertilizer, and flour.

Carver's gentle spirit disarmed those who met him. Although he sometimes faced discrimination because of his race, Carver never lashed back at his tormentors. "No man can drag me down so low as to make me hate him," he said. He also refused to make any profit on his scientific discoveries. "God gave them to me," Carver said. "How can I sell them to someone else?" He refused all offers for more prestigious, better-paying jobs. In fact, he refused even to take any raises from Tuskegee. His salary always remained what it had been when he came in 1896–$29 a week. Carver cared only that he could use his knowledge to help others. As Theodore Roosevelt told him in 1915, "There is no more important work than what you are doing."

Agriculture

The era from 1898 to 1914 is often called the "golden age" of American agriculture because the profits of American farmers skyrocketed after years of depressed prices. At least two broad reasons for this growth stand out. First, America's population was shifting heavily from farms to the cities. This change left increasingly fewer farmers raising food for increasingly larger cities. Farmers were able to sell as much food as they could grow, and the demand naturally drove prices up, giving farmers heftier profits for their goods. Second, technology improved. Probably the most important technological advance was the development of the tractor, which provided more power and speed in sowing, cultivating, and harvesting crops. This greater speed in turn allowed farmers to sow and raise even more crops. In addition, improvements in veterinary science reduced the number of livestock dying from disease; improvements in transportation made it easier and cheaper to get produce to market. Farmers in this era saw little reason to question the progressive's claim that life for Americans was getting steadily better.

Medicine

Tremendous advances in medicine also occurred in the Progressive Era. Part of these changes involved improvements in medical organization and education. The Mayo Clinic, founded in Rochester, Minnesota, in 1901, developed the concept of private group medicine, that is, creating a center for medical research and practice which brought together several doctors. This plurality of doctors allowed each physician to contribute his strengths in medical knowledge and skill to the practice, thus providing better treatment for patients. Likewise, the founding of Johns Hopkins Medical School in Baltimore in 1893 created, as one educator described it, "a small but ideal medical school, embodying . . . the best features of medical education in England, France, and Germany." Johns Hopkins pioneered the modern medical school in which advanced medical research, laboratory experience, and actual hospital work were essential parts of a physician's education.

The medical advance that really captured public attention was the battle against **yellow fever.** The war in Cuba and failed French attempts to build a canal in Panama made Americans aware of how deadly this tropical disease was. Building on the research of Cuban Carlos Juan Finlay, a commission of army doctors led by Walter Reed proved that mosquitos transmitted the disease. On the recommendation of Reed's commission, William C. Gorgas, chief sanitary officer of Havana, launched a campaign aimed at destroying the nesting grounds of mosquitos, and yellow fever was virtually eliminated from the city. In 1904 Gorgas was appointed chief sanitary officer of the Panama Canal project. He improved sanitary conditions in Panama by draining swamps and pouring oil on standing water where mosquitos bred and by clearing away vermin-infested underbrush. By the time the canal was completed, Gorgas had reduced the deaths caused by malaria and yellow fever from about forty per one thousand workers to about seven per one thousand.

Education

What is commonly called **progressive education** actually had its greatest impact in America in the period from the 1920s to the early 1950s. The philosophy of the movement, however, is rooted firmly in the overall progressive movement. In general, progressive educators aimed at improving education by relating learning to the child's interests. As leading progressive **John Dewey** wrote, "The child becomes the sun about which the appliances of education revolve." Progressives emphasized that they were teaching *students,* not teaching *subjects.* Education should also be based on experience rather than simple memorization, according to progressives; therefore, activities such as laboratory experiments and field trips became part of the educational process. Progressives de-emphasized traditional academic subjects such as history and stressed vocational education, which seemed more relevant to the student's needs.

Progressives rightly stressed making education interesting and linking understanding to learning. There were shortcomings in the progressive methodology, though. Some necessary components of basic education, such as the multiplication table, can be learned only by rote memorization, regardless of whether they are relevant to student interest. Furthermore, progressive education was philosophically unsound. John Dewey, the leading representative of progressive education, typified the movement's philosophical problems. Dewey, an influential professor at the University of Chicago and Columbia University, was a major leader in the twentieth-century movement known as **secular humanism.** Secular humanism denies the existence of God and affirms the goodness and perfectibility of man. This philosophy replaces absolute standards of truth and morality with relative, pragmatic standards based on human experience (i.e., ''whatever works is right''). Obviously, the Christian must reject such a system. Ironically, public discontent over progressive education was based on the progressives' own results-oriented standard. Much of the criticism which arose in the 1950s resulted from the realization that progressive education had simply not done a good job of educating America's children.

John Dewey, *by Joseph Margulies, National Portrait Gallery, Smithsonian Institution*

Religion

"Progressive" Religion—Two closely allied religious movements make up what may be called the religious wing of progressivism. One was a theological movement known as **modernism.** Modernism applied Darwinian evolution to Christianity and ended up with a system of belief that was completely anti-Christian. For instance, modernists rejected the idea that Moses wrote the first five books of the Old Testament (Genesis through Deuteronomy). Instead, they contended, the Israelites preserved a series of stories, legends, and myths. Supposedly the priests and royal scribes gradually shaped these into the Biblical books that we know today, an evolutionary process which was completed after the Babylonian captivity of Israel (c. 450 B.C.). Likewise, modernists did not view Christian doctrine as an expression of God's revealed Word but as the result of an evolution of ideas within the Christian Church. Modernists, therefore, denied Biblical teachings such as the deity of Christ, His virgin birth, atonement for sin through His blood, and the inspiration of the Bible. Modernists gained a foothold first in American colleges and seminaries and soon began to spread their teachings to American pulpits.

The second progressive religious movement was the **social gospel** movement. Whereas modernism applied the evolutionary aspect of progressivism to religion, the social gospel applied its social reform ethic. The social gospel replaced the regeneration of the individual with the ''regeneration'' of society through social reform. Although some of these reforms were worthwhile, advocates of the social gospel joined with the modernists in rejecting the teachings of orthodox Christianity. Social salvation was the *only* salvation to proponents of the social gospel.

The leader of the movement was **Walter Rauschenbusch** (ROU shun b*oo*sh), Baptist minister in New York City and seminary professor in Rochester, New York. In 1907 he wrote *Christianity and the Social Crisis,* expounding the goals of the social gospel. Rauschenbusch denied that man has a depraved nature as the Bible teaches and believed instead that man's environment corrupted him. Im-

The widespread use of child labor, as in this Pennsylvania mine, spurred a call for reform from muckrakers, advocates of the social gospel, and other progressives.

Some Christians opposed anti-Christian teachings by thoroughly educating other believers in the truths of Scripture. One method was the **Bible institute,** a school similar to a college but whose curriculum usually consisted almost entirely of courses in Bible or church-related fields such as Sunday school work. Bible institutes normally granted "certificates" or "diplomas" instead of college degrees. One of the most important institutes was D. L. Moody's Chicago Bible Institute (renamed Moody Bible Institute after its founder's death). Not all Christians could attend Bible institutes, of course. Many spent their vacations at **Bible conferences,** sessions which featured noted preachers and Bible teachers and which were held in resort spots for a week or more during the summer months. The two pioneer American Bible conferences were the Niagara Conference, held in Ontario, and Moody's Northfield Conference in Massachusetts. Probably the most important twentieth-century conference in size and longevity was the Winona Lake Bible Conference in Indiana.

proving a man's environment, therefore, would allow his natural, inherent goodness to develop. Reformers such as Rauschenbusch were sometimes justified in accusing orthodox Protestants of lacking concern for the poor, and they were also correct in saying that Christ was always touched with compassion when He saw hunger, poverty, and suffering. They were wrong, however, when they made Jesus merely a social reformer and lost sight of His more important work in the souls of men. Social reform can never suffice when man's basic need of salvation from his sin is not met.

Orthodox Defense—Orthodox Christians did not ignore these attacks on their faith, and many believers responded vigorously. One of the centers for the defense of orthodox Christianity at this time was Princeton Theological Seminary. Theologians at Princeton responded pointedly and intelligently to modernist and evolutionist attacks on the Bible. Perhaps the greatest of these defenders of the faith in both the extent of his writing and the depth of his thought was **Benjamin B. Warfield,** professor at Princeton from 1887 until his death in 1921. Sadly, only a few years after Warfield's death, Princeton succumbed to the modernist influences that the earlier Princeton theologians had resisted.

Billy Sunday

One notable orthodox means of defending and furthering the Christian faith was the continuation of the urban revivals popularized by D. L. Moody. After Moody's death in 1899, the most important urban evangelist was William A. **"Billy" Sunday.** Born in Iowa in 1862, the athletic Sunday launched into a successful professional baseball career in 1883. In 1886, while on a drinking binge in Chicago with his teammates, Sunday heard a group of workers from the Pacific Garden Rescue Mission singing in the street. Reminded of the gospel songs his devout mother had sung, Sunday followed the singers back to the mission. After attending several services there, Sunday was converted. He married in 1888 and left baseball altogether in 1891 to work for the YMCA. He then spent two years as an assistant to Evangelist J. Wilbur Chapman. When Chapman temporarily left evangelism to return to the pastorate, Sunday was left without a job. Then three churches in Garner, Iowa, invited Sunday to conduct a campaign in their town, and he entered into a new career as an evangelist.

Sunday soon adopted an aggressive, popular style. In order to reach the masses, he added dramatic, almost athletic gestures to his sermons and spoke in a slangy vernacular. The following example is from his sermon "The Three Groups":

> I don't expect one of these ossified, petrified, mildewed, dyed-in-the-wool, stamped-on-the-cork, blown-in-the-bottle, horizontal, perpendicular Presbyterians or Episcopalians to shout "Amen!" but it would do you Methodists good to loosen up. . . . I believe half of the professing Christians amount to nothing as a spiritual force. They go to church, have a kindly regard for religion, but as for having a firm grip on God, . . . and [a] willingness to strike hard, staggering blows against the devil, they are almost failures.

When church and city auditoriums proved inadequate to hold the growing crowds at Sunday's meetings, the evangelist borrowed an idea that Moody had used in his early campaigns, the tabernacle. Tabernacles were wide but low wooden, barnlike structures built especially for the campaigns. To reduce noise, the floor of the tabernacle was covered with sawdust. When someone came down the aisle in response to one of Sunday's altar calls, he was said to be "hitting the sawdust trail."

Billy Sunday's reputation grew throughout the first decade of the twentieth century, and in the 1910s he was at the height of his fame. His most famous campaign was in New York City in 1917. In this ten-week campaign nearly one and a half *million* people attended Sunday's meetings and almost one hundred thousand responded to his altar calls. The New York campaign marked the height of Sunday's career and the climax of American urban evangelism.

Gradually, an orthodox alliance was forming in the United States. Orthodox theologians like Warfield, popular preachers such as Sunday, and other Christians were finding they had a common interest in defending the faith against modernism. In the 1920s there would come a major battle between orthodox Christianity and liberal religion for control of America's churches.

Progressivism Evaluated

The progressive movement was obviously a highly influential force in American history. One question remains: Were its effects generally beneficial or harmful to the nation? One must conclude, first, that many progressive reforms were worthwhile. Thanks to progressive efforts, Americans enjoyed, for example, purer food and drugs, better service from gas and water utilities, and greater participation in the political process. The value of these reforms is evident; the controversy is whether these advantages were worth the cost.

This controversy leads to a second observation: the cost of progressive reform was an increase in the powers of government. Only by increasing the government's authority could the progressives achieve the regulation of business and industry that they desired. The Founding Fathers had designed a limited government with limited powers; the progressives encouraged a shift in the role of government to an expanding government with expanding powers. The progressives did not fear the growth of government; after all, they argued, the people control the government, and so the government

CHICAGO White Stockings

Billy Sunday's Baseball Career

Billy Sunday spent eight seasons in the major leagues, compiling solid but not record-breaking statistics. Sunday was never an overpowering hitter; his highest batting average for one season was .291, perhaps a little better than average in that era. Sunday's first manager, "Cap" Anson of the Chicago White Stockings (now known as the Cubs), reported that Billy struck out his first thirteen times at bat.

Sunday was fast, however, and a good fielder. He won respect when he joined the Chicago team by racing their fastest man and beating him by fifteen feet in a hundred-yard race. The evangelist later said that he had set a record by rounding the bases in fourteen seconds from a standing start. While with Chicago, he had the honor of playing on pennant-winning teams in 1885 and 1886.

Throughout his evangelistic career, Sunday drew upon his baseball career for illus-

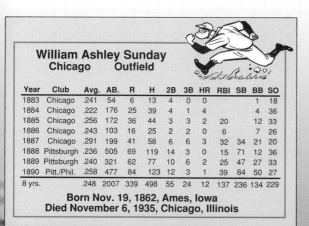

Year	Club	Avg.	AB.	R	H	2B	3B	HR	RBI	SB	BB	SO
1883	Chicago	.241	54	6	13	4	0	0			1	18
1884	Chicago	.222	176	25	39	4	1	4			4	36
1885	Chicago	.256	172	36	44	3	3	2	20		12	33
1886	Chicago	.243	103	16	25	2	2	0	6		7	26
1887	Chicago	.291	199	41	58	6	6	3	32	34	21	20
1888	Pittsburgh	.236	505	69	119	14	3	0	15	71	12	36
1889	Pittsburgh	.240	321	62	77	10	6	2	25	47	27	33
1890	Pitt./Phil.	.258	477	84	123	12	3	1	39	84	50	27
8 yrs.		.248	2007	339	498	55	24	12	137	236	134	229

William Ashley Sunday
Chicago   Outfield

Born Nov. 19, 1862, Ames, Iowa
Died November 6, 1935, Chicago, Illinois

trations. He was known, for example, to "slide into home" on the platform in order to clinch a point. He also sprinkled his sermons with baseball terminology. Sunday, for instance, recounted the deathbed experiences of a former teammate in a style more reminiscent of a sportscaster than a preacher: "It seemed like he was trying to stretch a three-base hit into a home run, and he rounded third with all his strength, and as he leaped as if to try and make it, the Umpire leaned over the battlements of the universe and said: 'You're out!' " When criticized for such informality in his preaching, Sunday replied, "I want to reach the people so I use the people's language."

could never get out of hand as private business had done. Experience has shown, however, that the government is not so easily controlled. Furthermore, some progressive reforms actually insulated the government from public control. The establishment of an independent government bureaucracy to oversee regulation and distribute government benefits created a class of bureaucrats who were immune to political changes and public pressure.

Third, most progressives had a faulty view of the nature of man. On the whole, they believed that man is basically good and that human nature might be improved. The stress on direct democracy (direct primaries, voter initiatives, etc.) assumed that while some institutions of society may be corrupt, the individual is not. Such a belief, of course, ignored the Biblical teaching that man is sinful by nature (Eph. 2:1-3). Progressives therefore also ignored the fact that the fallible men who built the corrupt institutions that they attacked were the same in nature as those who filled the political offices and staffed the regulatory agencies that were supposed to control the corruption.

Fourth, progressives mistakenly believed in the inevitability of progress, that things continually improve through some natural law. Many progressives based their belief in progress on evolution. The course of world history, evolutionary progressives argued, points to an ever upward progress toward perfection. Even some progressives who denied evolution still affirmed their faith in unchecked progress. Many Christians of the era, for example, believed that as the gospel spread throughout the world life on earth would continue to improve until the kingdom of God was established on earth and, at the climax, Christ would return. These sentiments were found in numerous sermons and hymns:

> Rise up, O men of God!
> His kingdom tarries long;
> Bring in the day of brotherhood
> And end the night of wrong.

The problem with this belief, whether evolutionary or Christian, is that progress is *not* inevitable. There may indeed be improvement in mankind's condition, but there is no guarantee that such improvements will occur as a matter of course.

Finally, progressives proposed false solutions to man's problems. They believed that through education, improving living conditions, and providing more equal political and economic opportunity, they could solve man's difficulties. Such a position ignores the Biblical teaching that man's basic problem is not his ignorance or his environment; it is his sin–a problem which can be remedied only through forgiveness and cleansing by God through the death and resurrection of Christ.

In conclusion, the results of the progressive movement were like the results of most movements in history–mixed. The progressive movement, however, did establish one major theme of twentieth-century American history, the gradual but almost continuous growth of the power of the federal government.

Section Review

1. What two inventions of the Progressive Era eventually transformed American transportation?
2. What was the most important technological advance in agriculture during the Progressive Era?
3. Who was the leading representative of progressive education? In what philosophical/religious movement was he a leader?
4. What two religious movements make up the religious wing of progressivism?
5. What major political and social theme of twentieth-century America did the progressives establish?

Chapter Review

Terms

progressivism
secret ballot
direct primaries
initiative
referendum
recall
city commission
city manager
"trust-busting"
"gas and water socialism"
Sixteenth Amendment
Seventeenth Amendment
prohibition
Eighteenth Amendment
Nineteenth Amendment
Susan B. Anthony
muckrakers
Robert La Follette
Eugene Debs
Theodore Roosevelt
"Square Deal"

Northern Securities case
Hepburn Act
Pure Food and Drug Act
Meat Inspection Act
The Jungle
conservation
Jim Crow laws
segregation
Plessy v. *Ferguson*
Booker T. Washington
W.E.B. Du Bois
National Association for the
    Advancement of Colored
    People (NAACP)
Panama Canal
Roosevelt Corollary
Treaty of Portsmouth
Root-Takahira Agreement
William Howard Taft
Joseph Cannon
"dollar diplomacy"
Progressive party

"New Nationalism"
Woodrow Wilson
"New Freedom"
Underwood Tariff Act
Federal Reserve Act
Clayton Antitrust Act
Federal Trade Commission Act
Henry Ford
assembly line
Wright brothers
yellow fever
progressive education
John Dewey
secular humanism
modernism
social gospel
Walter Rauschenbusch
Benjamin B. Warfield
Bible institute
Bible conferences
Billy Sunday

Content Questions

1. List at least three specific reforms that progressives proposed that expressed their faith in direct democracy.
2. Name which of the four "progressive amendments" to the Constitution is described by each phrase.
   a. "Anthony amendment"
   b. income tax
   c. repealed by Twenty-first Amendment
   d. popular election of senators
3. What is a graduated income tax rate?
4. Which of the three presidents of the Progressive Era is most closely identified with the progressive movement?
5. How did the Hepburn Act shift the burden of proof in rate-setting between the railroads and the Interstate Commerce Commission?
6. What phrase did Roosevelt use to describe his domestic policy? What phrase is commonly used to describe his foreign policy?
7. Name the three major presidential candidates and their parties in the 1912 election. Who won?
8. In what way was the progressive view of the nature of man faulty?
9. Who was America's most important urban evangelist after the era of D. L. Moody?
10. List at least three problems with the ideology of the progressive movement.

Application Questions

1. In what ways was America's Latin American policy good at the time? For what reasons could it be criticized?
2. One of the goals of progressivism was the expansion of democracy. Is the expansion of democracy always a benefit to a nation? Why or why not?
3. What should be the Christian's attitude toward social reform?

CHAPTER 19

The Great War (1913-1920)

"Sometimes people call me an idealist. Well, that is the way I know I am an American. America is the only idealistic nation in the world."

Woodrow Wilson *defending his record,* 1919

Actor Douglas Fairbanks rallies a crowd on Wall Street in support of the troops "over there," April 1918.

Macy's department store had men's summer suits on sale for $6.95, which shoppers could top off with cool straw hats for a low clearance price of $1.59. For readers of the Sunday edition of the *New York Times* on June 28, 1914, these ads were another reminder that vacation was just around the corner. Elsewhere in the paper, headlines told how the tough fists of boxing champ Jack Johnson had put yet another challenger on the canvas; the Brooklyn Dodgers made easy work of the Philadelphia Phillies in yesterday's double-header; Kay Laurell was appearing on Broadway with the Ziegfeld Follies. The newspaper's political cartoon that day, celebrating a number of successful diplomatic initiatives, depicted a rusty, scabbarded sword over the caption "Another Business Depression." It

was a comforting cartoon for that balmy summer morning in America. Halfway around the world, however, a distant disturbance on that sleepy Sunday was destined to shake an unwary America and the world off its nineteenth-century foundation. In many ways the twentieth century began on June 28, 1914, in an obscure little city in Central Europe called Sarajevo.

The day in the Austrian provincial capital promised to be gala, a day of parties and parades, for it was the Feast of St. Vitus. In addition, Austrian Archduke Franz Ferdinand, heir to the throne of the Austro-Hungarian Empire, and his wife, Sophie, were coming for a visit. The royal couple had cause for celebration as well, since that day was their fourteenth wedding anniversary.

Beneath the flags and bunting, however, a dark scene was quietly shaping. Seven Serbian youths, members of the terrorist group Black Hand plotting murder against the Austrians in the name of Serbian nationalism, positioned themselves along the parade route awaiting the archduke's motorcade. After narrowly escaping one assassin's bomb, the chauffeur took a wrong turn into a side street, stopping the car within five feet of another of the Serbian assassins, Gavrilo Princip. Being spared the necessity of even aiming, Princip raised his small Belgian pistol and fired two quick shots. The world would never be the same. Franz Ferdinand was shot in the neck, Sophie in the abdomen. As the blood ran from her husband's mouth, Sophie cried her last frantic words, ''For heaven's sake, what's happened to you?'' Then slumping over his wife's body, the dying archduke rasped his answer repeatedly: *''Es ist nichts, es ist nichts.''* (''It is nothing, it is nothing.'')

The sun that had risen over a festive city now sank blood-red over Europe. Ironically, what the archduke said was ''nothing'' sparked a blaze that engulfed the world. Four more summers would come and go before the bitter harvest of war was finally gathered. The body count to follow only coldly quantified the death of a generation–ten million killed, another six million crippled for life.

The ominous results that came from Princip's pistol were not readily apparent, however, either in Europe or in faraway America. The next day the killing was duly reported in the papers, and President Wilson wired the nation's condolences to the Austrians. In the weeks to follow, though, the European powers caught in a web of treaties and intrigues stumbled headlong into war. The **Central Powers** of Germany and Austria straddled the continent against the **Allies**–France, Britain, and Russia. Despite the broad Atlantic buffer and a long tradition of isolation, not even the United States could avoid the forces of war that pulled the world into Europe's trenches. Much of Woodrow Wilson's two terms would be occupied with avoiding the war, fighting the war, and concluding the war. By the end of the decade, America was shouldered with an ill-fitting mantle of world leadership.

Idealism

''It would be an irony of fate if my administration had to deal chiefly with foreign affairs,'' Woodrow Wilson privately remarked before his inauguration in 1913. Such irony would in fact be his ''fate.'' The bespectacled professor, along with his secretary of state, **William Jennings Bryan,** had little knowledge of international affairs and no experience in diplomacy; yet there was much in Wilson's background and character that would leave an enduring mark on America's foreign policy.

Woodrow Wilson grew up in a Presbyterian parsonage; his father, the Reverend Dr. Joseph Ruggles Wilson, instilled in his son sturdy moral convictions and a strong belief in God's sovereign direction in the universe. Wilson the president brought this moral vision to his foreign policy-making. He sought to make the United States the *moral leader* among nations, believing that America's role in the world was to promote democracy and peace by example and persuasion.

President Woodrow Wilson

Wilson saw America as having a *new* Manifest Destiny, not of territorial expansion but of political ideals. In a key foreign policy address delivered in Mobile, Alabama, in 1913, Wilson declared,

> We dare not turn from the principle that morality and not expediency is the thing that must guide us and that we will never condone iniquity because it is most convenient to do so. . . . It is a very perilous thing to determine the foreign policy of a nation in the terms of material interest. It not only is unfair to those with whom you are dealing, but it is degrading as regards your own actions.

> I want to take this occasion to say that the United States will never again seek one additional foot of territory by conquest. She will devote herself to showing that she knows how to make honorable and fruitful use of the territory she has.

Despite his noble goals, political realities soon challenged Wilson's ability to practice what he preached.

The Mexican Muddle

Wilson's idealism was first put to the test in Mexico. From 1876 to 1911 **Porfirio Díaz** (DEE ahz) ruled Mexico with an iron fist toward his opposition and an open palm toward foreign investors. Dictator Díaz and European and American businessmen all profited from the petroleum and mining resources of Mexico but left the Mexican people impoverished. In 1911 a popular revolt led by Francisco Madero drove Díaz into early retirement, but the rebellion also unleashed violent rivals for power, previously suppressed by Díaz's iron rule.

Just weeks before Wilson's inauguration, President Madero was murdered by his own military commander, the ruthless General **Victoriano Huerta** (WEHR tah). Though Huerta's regime has been described as "one of the most grotesque tyrannies in Mexican history," many countries quickly extended diplomatic recognition to the new Mexican government in hopes of re-establishing profitable business relations as in the days of Díaz. In addition, most countries, including the United States, traditionally extended recognition to a government if it simply *held* power, without concerning itself with *how* that power was obtained.

Woodrow Wilson, however, refused to recognize "government by murder." "My ideal is an orderly and righteous government in Mexico," he declared. He added, "My passion is for the submerged eighty-five per cent of the people of that Republic who are now struggling toward liberty." The former Presbyterian professor warned, "I am going to teach the South American republics to elect good men!"

Determined to drive, in Wilson's words, the "desperate brute" out of office, the president began to supply arms to Huerta's challengers, Venustiano Carranza (kah RAHN zah) and Pancho Villa (VEE yah) while at the same time cutting off arms shipments to Huerta. In April 1914 a group of American sailors enforcing this arms embargo at Tampico were arrested. Although they were immediately released and the local commander expressed regret to the American naval commander, the admiral of the American fleet demanded that the Mexicans hoist the U.S. flag and render a twenty-one-gun salute. Huerta, however, refused to grovel. Wilson, citing national honor, went to Congress and requested authority to use punitive force against the insubordinate Huerta. Congress granted the request on April 20, 1914.

Following a bloody clash between U.S. troops and Mexicans at Vera Cruz, the "ABC powers" (Argentina, Brazil, and Chile) mediated a truce between the United States and Mexico. The accumulated internal and international pressure encouraged by Wilson eventually toppled Huerta, bringing Carranza to power.

Peace, however, did not come with Huerta's exit. **Pancho Villa,** now vying for power against Carranza, sought to raise his popularity by becoming the chief enemy of the American "gringos"–an interesting indication of the success of Wilson's policies among the Mexican masses. Villa had eighteen American mining engineers murdered in cold blood then led a raid into New Mexico, where he killed seventeen more Americans and burned the border town of Columbus. In response, Presi-

The elusive Pancho Villa

dent Wilson sent General **John J.** (''Black Jack'') **Pershing** into Mexico with 11,000 troops to put the bandit out of business. After months of fruitless search for the elusive Villa, and as problems with the European war loomed ever larger, Wilson ordered Pershing to call off the hunt. To his credit Wilson resisted full-scale war with Mexico as many in Congress had urged; yet in the wake of the American withdrawal, Wilson's heavy-handed idealism had gained the president little more than ridicule at home and resentment abroad.

Caribbean Conflict

At the beginning of his administration, President Wilson denounced Taft's dollar diplomacy and Roosevelt's ''big stick'' policies as contrary to the United States' new moral leadership. However, the need to protect the strategic Panama Canal and Wilson's desire to see orderly democratic governments established among America's neighbors resulted in a number of military interventions in the Caribbean.

In Haiti virtual anarchy reigned from 1914 to 1915. Bloody power struggles left the countryside strewn with bodies and threatened to catch foreigners in the crossfire. Fearing the loss of American lives and property as well as European inter-

vention to quell the violence, Wilson ordered in the U.S. Marines. American forces occupied Haiti from July 1915 until 1934, bolstering the new civilian government, building schools and roads, and establishing order in the troubled country.

Next door to Haiti, in the Dominican Republic, civil war in 1916 brought a U.S. Marine police force that would occupy it until 1924. As in Haiti, the Dominican Republic benefited materially during the U.S. occupation, but resentment of the ''Colossus of the North'' in Latin America remained high.

It is ironic that Wilson, who set out to mend fences with America's southern neighbors, conducted more peacetime interventions than any of his predecessors. Wilson's idealism often ran afoul of strategic demands and uncontrollable events, sometimes creating sharp differences between rhetoric and reality. Despite Wilson's nagging foreign policy questions over Mexico, Central America, and the

John Joseph Pershing, by Douglas Volk, National Portrait Gallery, Smithsonian Institution

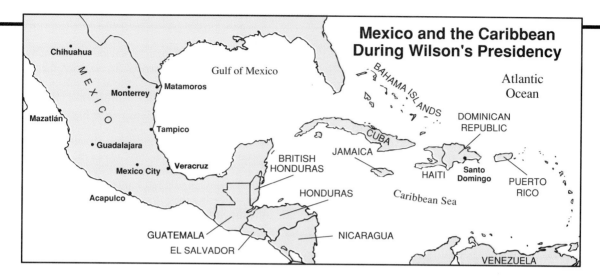

Mexico and the Caribbean During Wilson's Presidency

Caribbean, a far greater crisis loomed at the same time–the threat of American involvement in a European war that was bleeding that continent white.

The Web of War

After the murder of Austrian Archduke Franz Ferdinand by a pro-Serbian terrorist on June 28, 1914, fears and friendships among the nations of Europe caused them to fall like dominoes to the hand of war. The Austrian government, assuming that the Serbian government was at least passively responsible for the assassination, issued an incredible ultimatum on July 23. Austria demanded that Serbia submit to its rule until Serbia was purged of anti-Austrian sentiments. Surprisingly, Serbia replied that it was willing to accept most of Austria's demands. Austria was not satisfied, however, and declared war on Serbia on July 28.

Russia, fearing that Austria intended to establish control of the Balkans, mobilized its troops on July 30. Germany, Austria's ally, declared war on Russia two days later. Since the Russians had a mutual security pact with the French, Germany demanded to know France's intentions. The French, fearing the German buildup, mobilized their troops, an act the aggressive Germans interpreted as aggressive, and consequently declared war on France on August 3.

With France and Russia flanking Germany, the Germans turned to their long-standing plan for waging a two-front war, the Schlieffen Plan. According to its directives, the German army had to first crush France quickly by swinging through Belgium, occupying Paris within forty days after declaring war. The troops would then turn east to defeat the Russian hordes who were not expected to organize quickly.

Neutral Belgium naturally rejected Germany's demand to use its country as an invasion route. At the same time Britain, having treaty ties guaranteeing the neutrality of Belgium, warned Germany to call off the planned invasion by midnight of August 4 or the two countries would be at war. The German ruler, Kaiser **Wilhelm II,** sneered at Britain's commitment to a ''scrap of paper'' and ignored the ultimatum. Late that night, after a day of exhausting but vain negotiations, the British foreign minister, Sir Edward Grey, noticed the London street lamps being extinguished, and sadly–and prophetically–observed, ''The lamps are going out all over Europe; we shall not see them lit again in our lifetime.'' At the stroke of twelve, world war began.

As confident German troops marched into Belgium, the words of their Kaiser rang in their ears, ''You will be home before the leaves have fallen from the trees.'' Brave Belgian and British troops, however, offered tough resistance, buying precious time for the French. By the end of August, the Germans had pushed to the gates of Paris, where their war machine ground to a halt.

The French and British made valiant but costly attempts to push back the menace. In the first month of war, the French alone had 200,000 troops killed in action. By the end of 1914, a long bloody stalemate had settled over the front, as both sides dug into opposing trenches that stretched from Belgium to Switzerland. Between the trenches, in an ironic twist on the Kaiser's words, *millions* of men fell like leaves from the trees.

The Slippery Slope of Neutrality

When news of the war reached the United States, President Wilson issued the usual proclamations of neutrality; yet there was anything but neutral sentiment about the war. As the scope of the conflict became evident, the American people were deeply divided.

Melting Pot Problems—The New World could hardly ignore the Old World's war. Many Americans had been born in Germany or were descended from German immigrants. Many Irish immigrants and their descendants also favored Germany, mainly because they opposed Britain. Most Americans, however, had their roots in Great Britain, and American leaders admired British law, institutions, and culture. They also favored France because of her aid in America's War for Independence; as one poet glowingly declared:

> Forget us, God,
> If we forget
> The sacred sword of Lafayette!

Americans who favored the Allies tended to view Germany as an autocratic and militaristic aggressor—a view naturally encouraged by British and French propaganda. After the British seized control of the trans-Atlantic cables, they provided most of the war news available to Americans. After the war, many German "atrocities" reported in the news were exposed as exaggerated products of British propaganda writers. But the reality was bad enough. German troops burned Belgian homes and historic monuments, for example, and occasionally shot unarmed civilians whom they had chosen at random.

The Trade Trigger—American economic ties with the Allies, always strong, increased during the war. In addition, the British blockade of Germany and the British navy's control of the Atlantic meant that American trade with the Central Powers all but ceased. When the Allies used up their credit in buying American goods, Wilson allowed American loans to the Allies in order to avoid a collapse of American trade. In essence, the United States, while proclaiming its neutrality, was actually waging a *pro-Allies* neutrality. This policy would eventually pull the United States into the war as the Germans, suffering the effects of the British blockade, unleashed a deadly weapon on the high seas.

Submarine Warfare—Probably the most significant factor in America's entrance into the war was the violation of American rights on the sea by German submarines. Britain had blockaded Germany, prohibiting even the importation of food. A starving Germany countered by declaring the seas around Britain to be a war zone in which any ship would be liable to submarine attack. According to the rules of international law, warships were to warn and evacuate merchant ships before sinking them. Submarines, however, would not do this, since they were vulnerable to the merchant ship's deck guns and even well-directed prows.

Germany, fearing U.S. entanglement, had publicly warned American citizens not to travel into the war zone on British ships. But when the British passenger liner **Lusitania** left New York on May 1, 1915, a number of Americans were on board, despite a printed warning in the *New York Times* from the German government. When it entered the war zone near Ireland on May 7, no British patrol boat gave it the usual escort. The commander of a German submarine spotted the ship and fired a torpedo. Within eighteen minutes the large liner sank, and 1,198 passengers and crew, including 128 Americans, perished in the Atlantic.

President Wilson, though deeply moved by the tragedy, resisted the war hawks, with his moral idealism, declaring, "There is such a thing as a man being too proud to fight. There is such a thing as a nation being so right that it does not need to convince others by force that it is right."

Although political opponents would skewer Wilson with his own words, "too proud to fight,"

The sinking of the Lusitania *shocked many Americans out of their neutral attitude toward Germany.*

the president realized the country was too divided to fight. One cabinet official remarked after the *Lusitania* incident, for example, that Californians were more concerned with their citrus crop than with fighting. Even Wilson's cabinet was divided over how to respond to the German threat. After Wilson composed a sharply worded message to Berlin demanding a formal apology and reparation, or payment for losses, Secretary of State Bryan protested and resigned because he feared Wilson's message was *too* strong and might lead to war.

Germany replied to Wilson's demands with regret over the loss of life but asserted that the sinking was "just self-defense" since the passenger vessel was also carrying munitions. Whatever their justification, though, the *Lusitania* incident caused a change in American attitude toward the Germans. As one newspaper said, "The torpedo that sank the *Lusitania* also sank Germany in the opinion of mankind."

The battle over the *Lusitania,* however, remained a war of words, and the issue simmered on

the back burner until the spring of 1916. On March 24, 1916, an unarmed French passenger liner, the *Sussex,* was attacked by a German submarine in the English Channel, resulting in a number of deaths and injuries, including a number of Americans. The furor over the *Sussex* caused Wilson to instruct the Germans that another attack on passenger or merchant vessels would mean a break in diplomatic ties and likely war. This *"Sussex* **pledge"** of Wilson's quieted the seas for a time, but as one historian has pointed out, Wilson handed the Germans "a blank check which he could not honorably recall."

*Election of 1916—*The presidential campaign that geared up in the summer of 1916 naturally could not escape the shadow of the foreign crisis. In St. Louis, Democrats held a thunderous rally to renominate Wilson, cheering, "He kept us out of war." On the Republican side, Supreme Court justice Charles Evans Hughes left the bench to run for president.

In many ways the election mirrored the nation's mood. In the East, where war fever was highest, Hughes carried the states handily. However, the "hyphenates," the German-Americans and Irish-Americans of the Midwest, got behind Wilson, and on the Pacific coast, where Europe's war was a distant din, Wilson's neutrality was popular. Wilson's victory over Hughes on the winning slogan "He kept us out of war" seemed to indicate a mandate for his second term. Yet the slogan was in the *past tense*–it was not a pledge at all. The future remained as uncertain as it was threatening.

Section Review

1. Why did Wilson refuse to recognize the government of Huerta in Mexico?
2. Name the two countries in the Caribbean in which the United States intervened during Wilson's presidency.
3. The German invasion of what nation brought Great Britain into World War I?
4. The sinking of what ship caused Wilson to tell Germany that further attacks on passenger vessels would cause the United States to break diplomatic relations with Germany?

Intervention

The Great War was going badly for both sides. New technology born of industrialization gave the armies mass-produced weapons and mass-produced death. One tragic illustration of this change is the British offensive at the Somme. On the opening day, July 1, 1916, the British suffered 80,000 casualties–the bloodiest day in modern history. By the end of the Somme campaign, the British gained three or four miles of mud, but the price was steep, with half a million British soldiers killed or wounded. Winston Churchill wrote, "Before the war it had seemed incredible that such terrors and slaughters . . . could last more than a few months: After the first two years it was difficult to believe that they would ever end."

On the other side of the Atlantic, President Wilson feared the war would not end before America was dragged into it. Drawing on the idealism that characterized his foreign policy goals–if not his gains–Wilson appeared before the Senate and issued a historic declaration. He warned the deadlocked nations of Europe that only "peace without victory" could provide a lasting solution. Further, Wilson urged the formation of a League of Nations that would provide a forum for settling international disputes.

In Europe, where millions of men lay in untimely graves, Wilson's "peace without victory" was not even a consideration. A week after his speech the Germans, sorely pressed by the British blockade, replied by declaring **unrestricted submarine warfare.** *All* ships in the war zone, passenger or merchant, whether belligerent or neutral, would be sunk without warning.

Wilson, mindful of his *Sussex* pledge, yet knowing his actions would eventually lead to war, reluctantly severed diplomatic ties with Germany on February 3, 1917. Many Americans, including the president, held out a wishful hope that war could yet be avoided. Such thinking would quickly change, however.

Declaring War

On March 1 tensions were heightened by revelation of a secret, though clumsy, German diplomatic plot. The German foreign minister, Arthur Zimmermann, sought to gain Mexico's support in case the United States joined the Allies. He sent a telegram to Mexico offering Texas, New Mexico, and Arizona in return for Mexican support. He also asked Mexico to try to influence Japan to join the Central Powers. British intelligence intercepted and decoded the telegram and then enthusiastically forwarded it to the United States. When the details of the **"Zimmermann Telegram"** were first revealed, they seemed so fantastic that some believed the entire affair to be a British hoax. When the truth of Germany's hostility toward the United States finally dawned, however, Americans were outraged. Interestingly, Zimmermann's scheme succeeded in arousing the western United States, an area that had previously been indifferent to Europe's war. Now with their lands being "promised" to Mexico, even the West was on the warpath.

Two weeks later German submarines made good on their earlier threat by sinking four unarmed American merchant vessels. Wilson had run out of negotiating room. On April 2, 1917, the president appeared before a joint session of Congress requesting that the House and Senate formally recognize the state of war that had been "thrust" upon the United States by Germany. On April 6, Wilson signed the declaration–America had entered World War I.

Over Here

Raising an Army–"The world must be made safe for democracy," Wilson declared in his war message. "Its peace must be planted upon the tested foundations of political liberty." America, however, found itself ill prepared to answer Wilson's noble call.

At the time of the war declaration, the peacetime army and National Guard numbered only 379,000 men. Remarkably, that number increased tenfold to 3.7 million by the end of the war. This rapid recruitment to meet the tremendous manpower demands of modern war was the result of a national draft through the **Selective Service Act**. In 1917 all men ages 21 to 30 were required to register for the draft, and in 1918 the bracket was expanded to include those 18 to 45 years old. Altogether 2.8 million men were drafted into the army, with half that number eventually seeing action.

Wartime posters helped rally civilian support for bond drives and voluntary conservation measures.

When the raw recruits arrived at one of the hastily constructed boot camps, they quickly learned just how unprepared the United States was for the war to which they were being committed. Theodore Roosevelt, a long-time though often unheeded champion of military preparedness, wrote disappointedly that

> the enormous majority of our men in the encampments were drilling with broomsticks or else with rudely whittled guns. . . . In the camps I saw barrels mounted on sticks on which zealous captains were endeavoring to teach their men how to ride a horse.

The draft could provide the men but not the machinery of war. It took nearly a year for the nation's industry to convert to a full wartime footing. The importance of this industrial mobilization reflected the changing face of modern war; as President Wilson put it, "In the sense in which we have been wont to think of armies, there are no armies in this struggle; there are entire nations armed." All across the home front Americans enthusiastically met the challenge to war and to win.

"Hooverizing"—For Americans young and old the war was "fought" in backyard gardens and factory assembly lines. One of the key needs was providing an adequate food supply, not only for the American forces but for the beleaguered Allies as well.

In August 1917 the Lever Food and Fuel Control Act formed the **Food Administration** for the distribution of food and fuel to the war effort. Future president **Herbert Hoover** was made its administrator and gained national attention for organizing methods of saving and producing food. "Hooverizing" became the byword as citizens joined in "Meatless Mondays" and "Wheatless Wednesdays." Many, encouraged by the slogan "Food Will Win the War," raised their own food at home in "Liberty Gardens" so that more of the nation's commercial agricultural production could be sent to alleviate shortages in Europe.

Besides raising food, patriotic Americans raised money as well. The nationwide effort to invest in war bonds or "Liberty Loans" reaped $17 billion in revenue. Movie celebrities such as Doug-las Fairbanks and Mary Pickford appeared before huge rallies to boost bond sales. Even schoolchildren saved their pennies to fill Liberty Books with 25¢ stamps appropriately captioned "Lick a Stamp and Lick the Kaiser."

The war touched every area of life. Artists lent their pens and paints to the war effort to produce posters to recruit men and raise money. And in a day before radio and television, families often gathered around the piano in the evening to sing such sentimental ballads as "I'm Hitting the Trail for Normandy, So Kiss Me Goodbye" or the rollicking "Over There," the unofficial anthem of the American **"doughboy,"** or soldier.

Politics of Patriotism—The national fervor for the war effort understandably led to widespread anti-German sentiment. Courses in the German language were dropped from many high schools, and "liberty" replaced virtually everything connected with the hated Hun. As a result, German measles became "liberty measles," German shepherds were renamed "liberty dogs," and patriotic palates that had lost their taste for sauerkraut were doubtless relieved to discover "liberty cabbage."

The anti-German attitudes across America that changed everything from menus to street names changed laws as well. Under the **Espionage and Sedition Acts** it became a criminal offense to criticize the war effort in any way. These acts must be understood in their wartime context. A number of German spy plots, such as the successful sabotage of a New Jersey munitions plant, prompted lawmakers to enact stiff laws to safeguard national security. Undoubtedly, though, some of the enforcement of the Espionage and Sedition Acts, which resulted in over a thousand convictions, was the result of unfounded fears and hysteria. Despite examples of excessive enforcement, however, the Supreme Court ruled in the 1919 landmark decision *Schenk* v. *United States* that Congress could limit free speech, particularly during wartime, if such speech presented "a clear and present danger" to national interests. In the ruling, Justice Oliver Wendell Holmes noted, "Free speech would not protect a man in falsely shouting fire in a theater, and causing a panic."

Sergeant York

One of the greatest American heroes of World War I was a Christian. Alvin C. York, a shy man from the mountains of north central Tennessee, earned several medals and honors for his brave exploits in the Argonne Forest in France. Yet before the war, York had nearly registered as a conscientious objector (one who refuses to fight because of religious belief).

York had been converted in a revival meeting a few years before the war. When drafted into the army, he underwent a crisis; his church taught that killing was always wrong—even in time of war. York wanted to serve both God and his country. He later wrote, "I prayed and prayed. I prayed for two whole days and a night out on the mountainside. And I received my assurance that it was all right, that I should go."

York was a crack shot, one of the best marksmen in his county. In the army he quickly impressed his superiors with his accurate shooting and soon attained the rank of corporal. He was sent to France in May of 1918 as part of the 82nd Division, called the All-American division because it included soldiers from every state in the Union.

On October 8, 1918, York was part of a detachment exploring an enemy position in the Argonne Forest. The American soldiers went behind enemy lines and surprised a group of encamped Germans. The Germans surrendered, but a nearby machine gun nest opened fire on the Americans. Several of York's companions were killed, and the others dived for cover. York found himself facing the machine guns almost entirely alone.

York began to use his shooting skills to good effect. One by one the Germans peered over the embankment to take aim, and one by one York shot them dead. York fired quickly but efficiently, using only one bullet for each German. Finally a German major whom the Americans had captured told York that he would order his men to surrender if York would stop shooting.

As the Germans filed out of their positions, it became obvious that they far outnumbered the dozen or so Americans. When the group reached Allied lines, a lieutenant asked, "York, have you captured the whole Germany army?" York answered that he had "a tolerable few." The "tolerable few" turned out to be 132 prisoners. In addition, York had single-handedly killed twenty-five other Germans and silenced thirty-five machine guns.

York was promoted to sergeant and was given numerous awards for his heroism, including the Congressional Medal of Honor. On returning to his native Tennessee, York devoted his life to building schools for the mountain children of his home state. He even built a small nondenominational Bible college as a "school for God." When asked about his adventures in France, York would reply, "We know there were miracles, don't we? Well this was one. It's the only way I can figure it."

For most Americans support for the war came not as a result of coercion but as a matter of patriotism and idealism. None was better at defining and focusing that idealism than Woodrow Wilson. At the outset he declared,

> We desire no conquest, no dominion, we seek no indemnities for ourselves, no material compensation for the sacrifices we shall freely make. We are but one of the champions of the rights of mankind. . . . America is privileged to spend her blood and her might for the principles that gave her birth and happiness and the peace which she has treasured. God helping her she can do no other.

Wilson continued his theme of America's moral leadership in formulating a plan that he hoped would produce a lasting peace. His objectives, known as the **Fourteen Points,** proposed freedom of the seas, open diplomacy, and self-determination among the peoples of Central Europe and rejected reparation demands. Wilson's Fourteenth Point renewed his earlier ideas for a **League of Nations,** urging the formation of ''a general association of nations . . . for the purpose of affording mutual guarantees of political independence and territorial integrity to great and small states alike.'' In Wilson's idealistic, though unrealistic thinking, a League of Nations would prevent a recurrence of the events that ignited the 1914 conflagration. In addition, Wilson hoped to turn the war into a crusade for Americans and to use the olive branch of the Fourteen Points as a wedge between the battle-weary German people and their warlords. As such, Wilson's Fourteen Points were widely published in

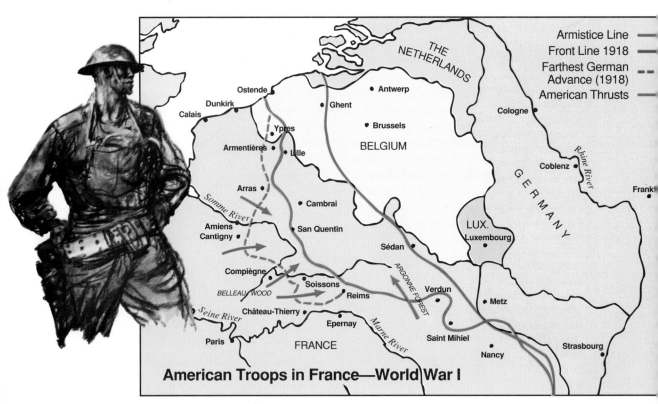

American Troops in France—World War I

Legend:
Armistice Line
Front Line 1918
Farthest German Advance (1918)
American Thrusts

THE NETHERLANDS
Ostende
Dunkirk
Calais
Antwerp
Ghent
Brussels
Cologne
Ypres
Armentières
Lille
BELGIUM
Coblenz
Rhine River
Arras
Cambrai
Somme River
Amiens
Cantigny
San Quentin
GERMANY
Frank
LUX.
Luxembourg
Sédan
Compiègne
BELLEAU WOOD
Soissons
Reims
ARGONNE FOREST
Verdun
Metz
Château-Thierry
Seine River
Epernay
Marne River
Saint Mihiel
Paris
FRANCE
Nancy
Strasbourg

Europe for everyone from kings to common laborers on both sides to consider.

While Wilson was waging war on the diplomatic front, American troops were making a timely entrance and crucial contribution on the *real* front.

Over There

"Lafayette, We are Here"—It was July 4, 1917, when the first contingent of U.S. troops of the American Expeditionary Force marched through the streets of Paris. The French were ecstatic. An American colonel, Charles E. Stanton, recalling an old debt and capturing the timeliness of their arrival, declared simply, "Lafayette, we are here."

For the Allies the American entry was pivotal. On the Eastern Front the bloody Bolshevik Revolution headed by Vladimir Lenin had swept the Communists to power in Russia in November 1917. In an effort to tighten his stranglehold over the country, Lenin negotiated a separate peace with Germany early in 1918. As a result hundreds of thousands of German troops were freed to join their comrades on the western front, hoping to deal a death blow to the Allies.

In addition morale among the beleaguered Allies was miserable. Seven million casualties had been suffered between the trenches in France and Belgium. Weary of the face of death, French troops in May and June of 1917 staged mass mutinies. In some trenches French soldiers even murdered their officers before running home. As the British and French teetered toward collapse, the arrival of the Americans, led by the tough, square-jawed "Black Jack" Pershing revived Allied spirit. Although the arriving Yanks were green, by the spring of 1918, the doughboys, a million strong, became the critical factor in the Allied recovery and ultimately in the Allied victory.

Holding the Line—The German commander Erich von Ludendorff, knowing that Germany could not prolong the war when the forces of the United States were added to those of the rest of the Allies, decided to wage a full offensive against the British and French, forcing them to surrender before the United States could give substantial support. Germany began the British phase of the offensive in northern France and Belgium on March 20, 1918, with the heaviest artillery fire ever used. Some 6,000 German guns, answered by 2,500 British guns, pounded the front with tons of steel and explosive shells for over four hours. Then the German infantry charged across no man's land. Flamethrowers, poison gas, hand grenades, and machine guns were used by both sides. The Germans, aided by a fog cover, succeeded in breaking through in some places, but the drive slowed and faltered. After several days of intense battle, the British, aided by the recently arrived American troops, succeeded in preventing a general collapse of the line.

Ludendorff's offensive having failed to break the British line, the Germans opened an attack on the French line to the south on May 27, 1918. The German assault broke the lines by May 30 and reached the Marne River only fifty miles from Paris. On June 2 and 3, though, jaunty Yanks eager for a fight poured into the gaps, halting the German drive at **Château-Thierry** (SHA-TOH TYEH-REE) **and Belleau** (BEL oh) **Wood.**

Push to Victory—On July 18 the Allies began a counterattack, slowly pushing the Germans back. The doughboys won an impressive victory at St. Mihiel (SAHN mee-YEL), but the largest effort was the American offensive in the Argonne beginning on September 26. The **Argonne offensive** was one of the costliest military campaigns in American history. One and a quarter million U.S. troops, concentrated on a twenty-five-mile front, fought for six weeks toward the central German rail center at Sedan. The Americans suffered 117,000 casualties including 26,000 killed in action, but the effort turned the tide. In October the German leadership began to negotiate for peace along the lines of Wilson's Fourteen Points. By early November the kaiser fled into exile, the German lines collapsed, and on November 11, 1918–at the eleventh hour of the eleventh day of the eleventh month–the **Armistice** was signed. The Great War was over.

The French commander Ferdinand Foch (FAHSH) recalled the unceremonious ceremony of the surrender signing: "I saw Erzberger [head of the German delegation] brandish his pen and grind his teeth. I was then glad that I had exerted my will . . .

Four Aces

Ever aware of the value of heroes in lifting spirits both on the home front and in the ranks, both sides in World War I glamorized the bravery of a new breed of warrior, the fighter pilots. These "flyboys," with their one-on-one aerial dogfights, seemed to embody the charm, chivalry, and daring of warfare that were lacking in the muddy carnage of trench warfare. For good reason, pilots were often called "knights of the air." Most famous were the "aces," those who scored at least five "kills" (enemy planes downed). The following are the top aces of the four major powers.

Manfred von Richthofen, better known as the "Red Baron" because of his scarlet red airplane, was the most successful ace in the war, scoring eighty kills in his career. Richthofen was a genuine baron, a member of the German nobility, and was probably the most popular war hero in Germany. On April 8, 1918, Richthofen scored his eightieth kill and

said afterwards as he climbed from his plane, "Eighty! That is really a decent number." The next day, the Red Baron was mortally wounded and forced down in combat near Allied lines. The British, respecting the valor of their fallen adversary, buried him with full military honors.

René Fonck was France's premier ace, with seventy-five kills. He embodied the jaunty, cocky, almost arrogant attitude that many people associated with the aces. Fonck, who called himself a "virtuoso," publicized his eccentricities (such as keeping a stork named Helen as mascot) and reveled in his reputation as an ace. At least his reputation was deserved. Fonck twice shot down six enemy planes in one day and once brought down three planes in ten seconds. Fonck survived the war and later, fittingly, became an exhibition pilot.

Edward "Mick" Mannock, the chief British ace (seventy-three kills), was an al-

America's top ace, Eddie Rickenbacker

together different kind of character–a moody, restless man. Mannock was blind in one eye, but he practiced his gunnery constantly to overcome his handicap. Mannock was not a carefree ''knight of the air.'' He took a grim delight in shooting down Germans, but he would go to his quarters and weep when one of his mates was shot down. Mannock suffered from a fear of fire and was tormented by dreams of being trapped in a burning plane. Ironically, he died in a fiery crash from antiaircraft fire in 1918.

Eddie Rickenbacker, America's ''ace of aces,'' scored twenty-six kills in the comparatively few months he saw action. Born in Columbus, Ohio, Rickenbacker was a race-car driver before the war who at one time had held the world land-speed record. During the war he combined his knowledge of engines with his personal bravery to become America's leading pilot. His most famous exploit, perhaps, was a solo attack on seven German planes. Rickenbacker downed two of the enemy craft and then escaped from the others unharmed. After the war Rickenbacker remained a leader in the field of aviation as president and later chairman of the board of Eastern Airlines.

Prominently displaying an American flag, an exuberant crowd in Paris celebrates the Armistice.

for the business was settled.'' Hardly. The next generation would add an enlarged second edition to the volume begun in 1914. In fact one of those who felt betrayed by the truce, willing to yet fight to the death for the fatherland, was a twenty-nine-year-old German corporal named Adolf Hitler. His dark mind burned with dreams of revenge. Of course none of this was apparent on Armistice Day, only jubilation that the fighting was over.

Section Review

1. What German decision caused Wilson to break diplomatic relations with Germany?
2. Name two methods that Americans on the home front used to raise food and money for the war effort.
3. What event on the Eastern Front in early 1918 made the entry of the United States crucial to the Allies?
4. What World War I offensive was the largest and costliest military campaign in American history up to that time?

The Big Four at Versailles: David Lloyd George of Great Britain, Vittorio Orlando of Italy, Georges Clemenceau of France, and Woodrow Wilson of the United States

Isolation

With their lines collapsing, their leadership fleeing, and their people starving, the Germans asked for an armistice, or truce, in hopes of getting the best peace terms possible–peace according to Wilson's Fourteen Points. After the Armistice, though, hopes for a favorable settlement proved empty. The German people, however, would not be the only ones disappointed in the results of what one writer referred to as "The Great War and The Petty Peace."

Treaty of Versailles

Wilson as Diplomat–Just one week after the Armistice was signed, Wilson announced that he would personally lead the peace delegation to meet at Versailles near Paris. Wilson's decision drew immediate fire from his critics, who charged that by personally negotiating the treaty the president would be more susceptible to public pressures and hasty decisions. For his part, Wilson believed that a personal appearance, given his tremendous prestige in Europe, would best help preserve his Fourteen Points (particularly the establishment of a

League of Nations that he believed would ensure lasting peace) among antagonistic Allied leaders. Wilson's critics charged that he had a "messiah complex."

Whatever Wilson's motivation, his peace mission was seriously flawed from the start, for the delegation included not a single prominent Republican from the Senate, where any treaty would have to be submitted for ratification. Just two weeks earlier, in the fall elections of 1918, the Democratic president had lost his majorities in both houses of Congress to the Republicans. Instead of cooperating with his opposition, Wilson and his partisan band headed for the cheering crowds of Europe while his enemies back home became entrenched.

Big Four, Big Differences–The Versailles conference, held from January to June 1919, was dominated by the **"Big Four"**–President Wilson, Frances's Premier Georges Clemenceau (KLEM MAHN SOH), Italy's Premier Vittorio Orlando, and Britain's Prime Minister David Lloyd George. Each nation had distinct aims. Wilson made it clear that the U.S. wanted no territory in return for its participation in the war. What Wilson wanted was acceptance of the Fourteen Points. Wilson was interested in peace; his Allied colleagues were interested in prey.

Clemenceau, though claiming to support the Fourteen Points, was more interested in revenge for France than in anything else. Conflicts between France and Germany over the mineral-rich coal- and iron-mining area west of the Rhine River, including the area known as Alsace-Lorraine, dated back to the days of the Franks and the Gauls. Germany had annexed Alsace-Lorraine in 1871, and France wanted it back. France also wanted a buffer zone east of the Rhine to ensure its future security.

Italy's Orlando represented a nation that had been Germany's ally at the beginning of the war and had then joined the Allies, in part because of British promises of territory in Austria. Orlando came expecting a large share of the spoils of victory to fall Italy's way at the peace table, although Italy had contributed little to the actual victory.

Lloyd George was a master politician, willing to do whatever was necessary to maintain British control of the seas. Though he had professed to support the terms of the armistice, he had campaigned for re-election in December 1918 promising that the Germans would be made to bear the entire cost of the war: "We will squeeze them till the pips squeak," Lloyd George crowed. And for good measure he promised to "Hang the Kaiser!" With a strong electoral victory, Lloyd George went to Versailles armed with his mandate of revenge.

Petty Peace—The **Treaty of Versailles** was signed on June 28, 1919–five long years after the Black Hand triggered a war that opened ten million untimely graves. The treaty drastically changed the map of Europe and had far-reaching consequences.

The Germans, who were permitted no part in the treaty negotiations, were in effect offered the treaty on a bayonet point and forced to sign a **"war-guilt"** clause stating that the German nation was responsible for the war. The German delegation in effect signed a blank check for the vengeful victors to fill in. If Germany was responsible, then Germany would pay the bill. As a result Britain and France demanded huge **reparation payments** to cover not just war damages, but the entire cost

of the war–over $30 billion. Such an unreasonable demand served only to deepen poverty and resentment in Germany.

After all the haggling among Allied leaders was over, only two major planks of Wilson's Fourteen Points were incorporated into the Treaty of Versailles: national self-determination for the peoples of Europe, and the formation of the League of Nations. Independence and national boundaries for Poland, Czechoslovakia, Yugoslavia, and the Baltic countries of Lithuania, Latvia, and Estonia were all drawn out of treaty provisions. While the new national identities satisfied the political aspirations of millions, they also created problems. Many of the new countries encompassed a number of ethnic groups whose own nationalist desires were further awakened by the changes. For example, Yugoslavia, composed of six major groups, was originally called the Kingdom of the Serbs, Croats, and Slovenes–hardly a name to inspire national unity. In addition, thousands of Germans found themselves living under foreign flags after the mapmakers in Versailles finished drawing the lines. Hitler would use this point of irritation to trigger a second world war twenty years later.

Wilson and others were not unaware of the problems of the Treaty of Versailles. They believed, though, that these flaws would be fixed by the League of Nations. First, however, if the U.S. were to take the lead in the newly formed League, Wilson would have to find enough senators to ratify the treaty. It would be the toughest fight of the president's life.

Rejection and Retreat

When Wilson returned from Europe, his most formidable opponent against the Treaty of Versailles and its most important component, the League of Nations, was Senate majority leader **Henry Cabot Lodge** of Massachusetts. Besides stubbornness, Wilson and Lodge had one other thing in common–they hated each other.

Most Democrats in the Senate naturally sided with their party leader, President Wilson; but the Democrats were in the minority. The focus was on the Republicans, who were divided into two groups:

the "irreconcilables," who opposed any entanglement in European politics, and the "reservationists," led by Lodge, who would ratify the treaty but only with reservations attached that would limit U.S. commitment. The reservationists feared that unqualified support of the League could drag Americans into future European wars by tying the country into unwanted alliances. Making a deliberate jab at Wilson's idealism, the hard-bargaining Lodge described the Versailles Treaty as "the beautiful scheme of making mankind virtuous by a statute or a written constitution." America's security, Lodge believed, was best protected by two oceans and a strong military force.

As the debate over treaty ratification dragged on, public opinion, which had initially favored the ideas behind the treaty, began to shift in Lodge's direction. Wilson, who opposed compromising on any of the treaty provisions, decided to take the issue to the people. In a marathon mission of eight thousand miles in twenty-two days, the president delivered forty speeches in favor of the treaty and membership in his brainchild, the League of Nations. The president declared,

> America does not want to feed upon the rest of the world. She wants to feed it and serve it. America . . . is the only national idealistic force in the world, and idealism is going to save the world.

Wilson's crusade, however, nearly killed him. On September 25, 1919, after an enthusiastic rally in Pueblo, Colorado, the president slumped over with exhaustion. The rest of the tour was cancelled and Wilson was taken back to Washington, where he suffered a serious stroke, paralyzing him on one side. Wilson's wife and a few close friends shielded his condition from the public, but his fighting days were over. For seven critical months Wilson did not meet with his cabinet, and a November vote on the treaty fell short of ratification. Wilson's attorney general, T. W. Gregory, perhaps best summed

up the nature of the president's lost cause: "The League was defeated in the United States, not because it was a League of Nations, but because it was a Woodrow Wilson league, and because the great leader had fallen and there was no one who could wield his mighty sword."

When public and administrative pressure brought a reconsideration of the treaty in March 1920, it seemed that the amended treaty would finally pass. Wilson, who had regained some of his strength, bitterly fought any changes, though. Ironically, Wilson sided with the irreconcilables to defeat his treaty in the interest of keeping it intact. The stricken president, having lost all contact with political and practical realities, became his own enemy.

The United States never joined the League of Nations nor ratified the Treaty of Versailles. It was not until July 2, 1921, after Wilson's term, that a joint resolution of Congress quietly ended the official state of war between the United States and Germany. By then Wilson–part president, part crusader–had been replaced by a Republican gladhander named Warren Gamaliel Harding, whose only qualification for the job was that he "looked like a president." Harding was no crusader, but he was an avid card player and he enjoyed cutting ribbons. Harding's striking contrast with Wilson illustrated the changing mood of the country. America, which had helped liberate the Old World, now shifted out of the uncomfortable harness of international leadership and retreated into the 1920s.

Section Review

1. Name the "Big Four" and the nation that each represented.
2. What two provisions of the Versailles treaty were most offensive to the Germans?
3. What was the difference between the Republican "irreconcilables" and "reservationists" concerning the Versailles treaty?

Chapter Review

Terms
Central Powers
Allies
William Jennings Bryan
Porfirio Díaz
Victoriano Huerta
Pancho Villa
John J. Pershing
Wilhelm II
Lusitania
Sussex pledge
unrestricted submarine warfare
Zimmermann Telegram
America enters the war (April 1917)
Selective Service Act
Food Administration
Herbert Hoover
doughboy
Espionage and Sedition Acts
Schenk v. *United States*
Fourteen Points
League of Nations
Château-Thierry and Belleau Wood
Argonne offensive
Armistice (November 11, 1918)
Big Four
Treaty of Versailles
"war-guilt" clause
reparation payments
Henry Cabot Lodge

Content Questions
1. What event sparked the First World War?
2. What Mexican rebel did General Pershing vainly pursue across Mexico?
3. How did the British blockade of Germany actually bring the neutral Americans closer to the Allies?

4. Why did William Jennings Bryan resign as secretary of state when Wilson sent a sharp message to Germany after the sinking of the *Lusitania?*
5. Place the following events in chronological order.
   a. Great Britain declares war on Germany.
   b. Germany declares war on France.
   c. Austria declares war on Serbia.
   d. Russia declares war on Austria.
6. The sinking of what two passenger ships helped push the United States into the war against Germany?
7. What German blunder roused prowar sentiment in the western United States?
8. Which two of Wilson's Fourteen Points were actually incorporated into the Treaty of Versailles?
9. Who was the main opponent of the Versailles Treaty in the Senate? Why was he opposed to the treaty?

Application Questions
1. Consider Woodrow Wilson's statement, "I am going to teach the South American republics to elect good men!" What characteristic of Wilson's foreign policy does this statement reflect? Is this characteristic necessarily a benefit in conducting foreign policy? Why or why not?
2. In the *Schenk* decision Justice Holmes said that government may limit free speech when such speech presents "a clear and present danger" to national interests. What are some potential problems with this position?
3. "Idealism will save the world," Wilson declared when trying to raise support for the League of Nations. What is the truth behind this statement? What are the fallacies?

UNIT VI

1919
"Red Scare"

1921
Washington
Naval
Conference

1924
National Origins
Act passed

1925
Scopes Trial

1928
Kellogg-Briand
Pact

1929
Stock Market
Crash

1931
Japan invades
Manchuria

1932
Franklin
Roosevelt
elected
president

1933
FDR's
"Hundred Days"

1936
*Gone with the
Wind* published;
Hitler militarizes
the Rhineland

1937
Japan attacks
China

1938
Hitler takes
Austria

1939
New York
World's Fair;
World War
II begins

1940
FDR elected
for third term

1941
Attack on Pearl
Harbor—U.S.
enters World
War II

1944
D-day

1945
End of
World War II

CHAPTER 20

The Twenties (1920-1929)

"The business of America is business."

President Calvin Coolidge *to the Society of American Newspaper Editors,* January 17, 1925

Flapper Suzette Dewey poses beside her roadster in 1927.

It was the age of flappers, foxtrots, Freud, and all that jazz. If the country was said to be growing up, then in the 1920s America reached adolescence. "Over There" was strangely out of date; America was singing "Ain't We Got Fun?" The generation coming of age in the 1920s enjoyed postwar prosperity and passive politicians. Moral crusades were out, replaced with a sometimes mindless pursuit of frolic and frivolity. The new heroes were on the silver screen, the sports field, and the radio waves. The roar of the twenties seemed to drown out problems at home and abroad, but by the decade's end the queues at America's movie palaces had turned into bread lines at soup kitchens. The party was over.

Normalcy and Naiveté

On the campaign trail in May 1920 Warren G. Harding pealed forth the political philosophy that carried the United States into the new decade. "America's present need is not heroics, but healing; not nostrums, but normalcy; not revolution, but restoration; . . . not surgery, but serenity." **"Normalcy"** was a new word, and whatever else it was, it became the goal of a people wishing to distance themselves from wartime pressures and problems.

Postwar Problems

In 1920 America was readjusting to the challenges of peacetime. The nation's industries and manpower were no longer demanded by the war effort. The people's emotions were no longer focused on defeating a foreign enemy. The drama of wartime had to be replaced with the more mundane activities of a work-a-day world, and the resulting changes in American life brought along some unpleasant side effects.

When the war ended and Johnny came marching home, he frequently discovered that once the parades down main street were over, America held few opportunities for him. War industries closed, but peacetime industries did not resume activities quickly. With over two million men returning from the American Expeditionary Force to a dismal job market, unemployment climbed to a staggering 11.9 per cent in 1921. Not until after this problematic peak would business activity boom and factory jobs begin to absorb the excess workers.

If a soldier returning from the Great War decided to return to the farm instead of seeking his fortune in the city, his prospects were no less bleak. Agriculture had been a profitable business during the war, for American farms were not only feeding the nation and its soldiers but also exporting farm products to war-torn regions. In response to this demand for their produce, American farmers had bought more land and equipment, planted more crops, and raised more livestock. With the war over, however, the agricultural market faced an upheaval. The bountiful harvest of 1920 brought farmers calamity instead of profit. Exports of farm products decreased as Europeans began to farm their own lands again, and the tremendous demand for foodstuffs created by the war vanished. All that remained to the farmer was the selling of his abundant produce for the ordinary peacetime needs of the nation. The huge surpluses caused food prices to plunge by the end of 1920, and farmers were devastated by the meager returns for their labors, especially since many were heavily in debt for their land and equipment purchases. Continued overproduction and low prices kept the agricultural market depressed, not just for a couple of years but for the entire decade. Thus, the farm problem would remain a major domestic issue throughout the decade of the 1920s.

Another change Americans had to face once the war ended was that of discarding the emotions raised by newspapers, war posters, rallies, and songs. The Kaiser was defeated, but some Americans feared that other enemies were still at large, particularly the Communists and anarchists (people who seek to destroy governmental authority) who had talked of overthrowing the government of the United States ever since the Bolshevik Revolution had engulfed Russia in 1917. The violent activities of a few leftists stirred this fear and created a temporary panic called the **Red Scare.**

The scare began in 1919 when a few anarchists sent small packages containing bombs through the mail to various government officials and businessmen who had opposed their actions by breaking strikes and prosecuting suspected leftists. One of the bombs blew up in the hands of a senator's maid, injuring her and the senator's wife. Although the other mail bombs were discovered before exploding, the violence set off a wave of leftist bombings resulting in death and great property destruction. Even the house of Wilson's attorney general, A. Mitchell Palmer, was bombed. The terrorism resulted in an intense government effort to track down foreigners with objectionable political views and either prosecute them for crimes or simply deport them. When a predicted "Red revolution" did not break out on May Day (a Communist holiday) in 1920, the scare quickly abated but left a widespread suspicion of foreign leftists that occasionally resurfaced in following years.

World Relations

The general theme of American foreign policy in the 1920s was one of **isolationism.** The taste of war had left many Americans disillusioned with idealistic efforts to change the world. Wilson's failure in persuading the United States to join the League of Nations punctuated the prevalent preference to take care of things at home rather than dabble in foreign matters. Nonetheless, America had proved itself to be a world leader, and in that role it could not avoid affecting the history of the 1920s.

The United States faced two basic foreign policy tasks in the twenties: to maintain world peace and to stabilize the world economy. Both of these tasks were undertaken with a focus on how any action would affect the peace and prosperity of the United States. Americans did not want foreign conflicts to draw their sons into battle, and they did not want foreign economic problems and policies to endanger American business.

Pursuit of Peace—Although America did send "unofficial observers" to meetings of the League of Nations, its major activities in pursuit of world peace were independent of that organization. The first of these was the **Washington Naval Conference** of 1921. The build-up of sea power sparked by the war did not come to an abrupt halt at the Armistice. Japan and Britain were continuing to strengthen their navies to acquire military advantages over potential enemies, and France and Italy were determined to enhance their naval strength as well. To keep these powers in check, the United States would have to continue the expansion of its navy, thereby participating in this dangerous (and expensive) armament. The Washington Naval Conference brought foreign diplomats to the nation's capital to negotiate an agreement to limit the growth of naval power. The result was a plan that called for Japan, Britain, and the United States to scrap some of their vessels, curtail battleship construction, and establish a $5:5:3:1.75:1.75$ ratio of naval power. For every 5 tons of naval vessels that the United States had, Britain would maintain 5 tons, Japan 3, and France and Italy 1.75 each.

The treaties devised at the Washington Naval Conference were idealistically heralded for their noble, ground-breaking effort. However, the agreements had some notable flaws that led to a future war in the Pacific. Although they limited the build-up of battleships, they did not restrict the build-up of cruisers, destroyers, and submarines–the kind of vessels that would prove more valuable in future naval warfare. Also, Japan left the conference unsatisfied. Because that nation resented having been given an inferior standing to Britain and the United States and because its militaristic goals encouraged a desire for naval expansion, Japan would later abandon any adherence to the treaties. Other conferences in 1927 and 1930 revived the principles established at Washington, but cooperation among the nations soon deteriorated.

While the supporters of arms control and peace efforts of the 1920s may have had laudable goals, their wrong thinking doomed them from the start. The Apostle James pinpointed the source of war when he wrote, "From whence come wars and fightings among you? come they not hence, even of your lusts that war in your members?" (4:1). International conflicts and hatred are simply compounded versions of personal conflicts and hatred. The source of war is sin in the heart of man, the only remedy for which is salvation through the Prince of Peace.

Another major peace initiative of the 1920s was one set forth by President Coolidge's secretary of state, Frank B. Kellogg, and the French Foreign Minister, Aristide Briand. These men proposed an international agreement that would make war illegal according to international law. Fourteen nations signed the **Kellogg-Briand Pact** in Paris on August 27, 1928, and most other nations gave assent later. This pact won great praise, but it had a severe flaw that in effect rendered it worthless. There was absolutely no means of enforcing the new law. This feature, however, allowed America to maintain its isolationist stance rather than entangle itself in the web of international politics.

In addition to making these efforts to maintain peace in Europe and the Pacific, the United States also modified its relationship with Latin American nations to promote peace with these near neighbors. President Wilson had maintained a forceful protection of American interests in the region. Presidents

Harding and Coolidge allowed this policy to continue so that in 1925 the United States had marines stationed in several of these lands and controlled the financial policies of half of the twenty countries in the region. Naturally, this interventionism created resentment toward the United States from its Latin neighbors. Eventually, many Americans began to question the wisdom of these dealings with fellow independent nations. Coolidge's secretary of state, Charles Evans Hughes, began softening the policies of the Roosevelt Corollary to the Monroe Doctrine, which had asserted the police power of the United States in the Western Hemisphere. Hughes also urged the withdrawal of troops from Latin American countries. There was a temporary lapse of this goodwill in 1927 when the United States sent troops into Nicaragua, but Herbert Hoover revived the effort to improve Latin American relations during his administration. This tack later came to be known as the Good Neighbor Policy under President Franklin Roosevelt.

Economic Entrapment—World War I had wreaked havoc on the economy of Europe. Not only were its farms and factories devastated by warfare, but also its surviving governments were saddled with an incredible burden of debt. The Treaty of Versailles had demanded that Germany pay $30 billion in reparations to the Allies, and also in the wake of the war the United States demanded that the Allies repay $22 billion in war loans, with interest. While the war had depleted the economic resources of Europe, the United States had escaped relatively unscathed with its finances in order and its factories intact. The Allies were appalled that America would insist on repayment, and the Germans were angered that reparations would be forcefully extracted from their nation. Nevertheless, these were the conditions that dictated the international economic activity of the 1920s.

The Allied debt had been received in the form of war materiel and foodstuffs; yet America required that it be repaid in cash (gold). The war had depleted the Allied coffers, and so the logical means of acquiring the needed sums was through the trade of European goods for the needed gold. However, the United States blocked this method entirely. Intent on

protecting America's own reviving industries, Congress passed the **Fordney-McCumber Tariff** in 1922. This high tariff, which would be supplanted by an even higher tariff in 1930, established a nearly insurmountable wall preventing European trade with the United States. Despite its many disagreeable consequences, protectionism remained entrenched in American policy.

With American trade blocked, the Allies had only one other source for the money to pay their debt–Germany. The German reparations payments, the Allies believed, would give them enough to cover their debts with extra left over for rebuilding their lands. There was a problem, however. Germany was in ruins and its economy was in shambles. The defeated foe had little with which to rebuild its industry, much less to make the colossal reparations payments. Germany had only one means of obtaining the needed cash, and that was through loans. Even so, what country in this postwar era could possibly have money to invest in loans to Germany? The answer was the United States. Thus a dangerous circular flow of money began: money lent by American financial institutions to Germany was passed on to the other Allies in reparations, which were in turn used to repay the United States for war debts. Money repaid to America provided investment capital to spare for more loans to Germany. In the process, Germany fell in heavy debt to the United States without having funds to improve its own economy. As the debts mounted, Germany could not meet its obligations. The Allies, deprived of reparations payments, could not make their loan payments, and American investors were alarmed by unpaid foreign loans.

In 1924 an American banker, Charles Dawes, led a panel of economic experts from the involved countries to resolve the impending crisis. The result was the **Dawes Plan,** which reduced German reparations payments significantly, while it encouraged private American institutions to continue lending money to help Germany rebuild. In addition, the American government reduced the interest charged on the Allied war debts and offered more generous terms for repayment. Despite this effort, the finan-

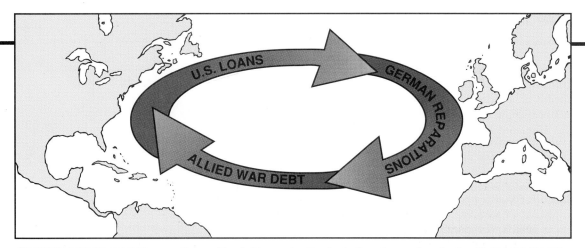

Attempts to settle the war debts–reparations problem led to an unhealthy circular flow of money from the New World to the Old and back again.

cial demands in the absence of free trade continued to sustain the ominous cycle of debt. The tensions of these arrangements plagued international relations throughout the decade, and eventually the Great Depression brought down the entire system of repayment.

Politicians

In an era when Americans generally wanted to mind their own business, have a good time, and make a fortune in the process, they chose political leaders who were in tune with their desires. After Versailles, Wilson's ill health and bitterness over the rejection of his peace plans left America and the Democratic party without leadership. Republicans easily won the White House, not only in 1920 but also in 1924 and 1928 as their party received the credit for the apparent peace and prosperity of the decade.

Harding—**Warren G. Harding,** the first of the Republican presidents of the 1920s, had been a newspaper editor in Marion, Ohio, until a state politician named Harry Daugherty took him under his wing. Daugherty thought Harding looked like a president, and as the leader of a group of state politicians called the Ohio Gang, he assisted the unassuming editor up the political ladder. Harding was elected to the Senate in 1914, but he was not particularly well known at the time of the 1920 Republican convention. However, his old friend Daugherty wished to change that. Several weeks before the convention, Daugherty predicted that a

deadlock would be overcome when in the middle of the night "fifteen men in a smoke-filled room" would agree to make Senator Harding the Republican candidate. The prediction came true, and Har-

President Harding on the stump

ding entered a race against the Democratic candidate, Governor James M. Cox of Ohio. Harding's theme of a **return to "normalcy"** pleased the nation, and he won decisively.

The American public generally liked Harding and approved of his policies, but some shenanigans in his administration brought his name into disrepute soon after his death in 1923. Most historians agree that Harding was generally honest, but he rewarded his friends in the Ohio Gang with high offices and imprudent favors. The improprieties of these friends soon put the president under extreme strain, possibly hastening his death. The most noted of the scandals was one involving his secretary of the interior, Albert B. Fall. Fall had won Harding's approval to take control of the navy's oil reserves at two locations, Teapot Dome in Wyoming and Elk Hills in California. In turn, Fall leased the oil rights on those properties to two friends, who were later found to have returned the favor to Fall in the form of sizable "loans." The **Teapot Dome scandal** also implicated various members of the administration, but it was not the only scandal of that era. Charles Forbes as head of the Veterans' Bureau, for example, defrauded that agency of over $200 million. And Harding's old pal, Attorney General Harry Daugherty, was brought to trial after being implicated in bribery schemes. Daugherty managed to have the case dismissed even though it was learned that he had burned the records of his account in his brother's bank. Daugherty refused to give his reason for destroying the records but cannily implied that the revelation would do further harm to the memory of the late President Harding.

Coolidge—When **Calvin Coolidge,** Harding's vice president, succeeded to the presidency after Harding's death from a heart attack in 1923, the Harding scandals were just beginning to unfold. Coolidge immediately made it clear that there would be thorough investigations into the underhanded dealings and that the guilty would be punished. As a result this man of few words from rural Vermont distanced himself from the corruption and won the praise of the American people as well as their votes in 1924. Coolidge had first gained national fame in 1919 as governor of Massachusetts

A cool Calvin Coolidge strikes a typical pose.

by quelling a Boston police strike. When Samuel Gompers of the American Federation of Labor asked Coolidge to acknowledge the right of the police to express their grievances, the governor replied, "There can be no right to strike against the public safety by anybody, anywhere, anytime." That strong statement had elicited the applause of the nation, then immersed in the Red Scare, and it soon brought him the vice presidency.

As president, Coolidge took a hands-off approach to administration. He was content to let big business have free reign, saying, "The business of America is business." Encouraged by his approval, investors watched the prices on the stock market climb and prosperity in the country boom. In light of his popularity, Coolidge therefore surprised the nation when he announced in 1927, "I do not choose to run for President in 1928."

Hoover—That proclamation opened the door for his secretary of commerce, **Herbert Hoover,** to seek the presidential nomination. After gaining a fortune as an engineer, Hoover had won acclaim for organizing American food relief efforts for Belgium during World War I and had served with distinction in both the Harding and Coolidge cab-

Herbert C. Hoover, *by Douglas Chandor, National Portrait Gallery, Smithsonian Institution*

inets. Having won the Republican nomination, Hoover faced governor **Al Smith** of New York in the 1928 election. Smith received the disapproval of many Americans for two reasons–he was Roman Catholic and he opposed prohibition. At the time Americans were not ready to accept a Catholic and a ''wet'' as their chief, and so Hoover won handily. However, Hoover reigned over American prosperity only briefly. Within a year of his inauguration the stock market crashed and America began to fall into the most severe economic depression in its history. Unfortunately for Hoover, he is associated more with the depression that he inherited than with the prosperous twenties.

Section Review

1. What temporary panic concerning fears of a leftist revolution beset America in 1919?
2. What two major efforts to maintain world peace did the United States endorse in the 1920s?
3. Describe the circular flow of money between the United States and Europe that developed following World War I.
4. What proposal for resolving the foreign debt crisis was introduced by an American banker?
5. Who were the three Republican presidents that took office in the 1920s?

The Mind of the Twenties

The twenties was the first decade of modern America and perhaps the most glamorous period in the nation's history. ''The greatest, gaudiest spree in history,'' novelist F. Scott Fitzgerald labeled it. Behind the glitter, however, new philosophies ravaged the moral character of a generation–a society which poet T. S. Eliot characterized as a ''waste land.''

New Ideas

Darwinism and Marxism – Modern ideas brought about the changes in American society that were evident in the 1920s. Although the writings of Charles Darwin and Karl Marx had appeared in the nineteenth century, their full impact did not become apparent until after World War I. Darwin's evolutionary theory undermined the Scriptural account of creation while Marx's economic philosophy denied the spiritual side of man as well as man's depravity. Although these ideas had been too radical for most nineteenth-century Americans to consider, evolution and socialism began to find widespread interest and acceptance in the 1920s. A growing disregard of Scriptural truth naturally accompanied the acceptance of these views.

Theory of Relativity – As the 1920s dawned, **Albert Einstein,** a German scientist, set forth a scientific theory that many writers and philosophers used to cast additional doubt upon the Scriptural and moral standards of Americans. Since the days of Sir Isaac Newton, scientists and philosophers had believed in an orderly world ruled by natural laws discovered by the scientific method. Through reason and common sense man could comprehend the universe, which was certain and machinelike. This comfortable view was shattered by Einstein's **theory of relativity**–that space, time, and matter are not absolute dimensions but are relative to the location and motion of the observer. By 1929 a Harvard mathematician confessed, ''The physicist thus finds himself in a world from which the bottom has dropped clean out.'' Seemingly, the absolutes of science were no longer absolute, and, unfortunately, many Americans erroneously transferred Einstein's ideas to the spiritual realm. (Einstein himself opposed this use of his theory.) According to

Albert Einstein

their faulty reasoning, Scripture could no longer be considered as absolute truth. Thus, they thought they were free of its moral restraints and responsibilities because these values were dependent upon the observer.

Freud—The ideas of **Sigmund Freud,** which became popular in the twenties, added further disdain to moral absolutes. For this Austrian psychologist, sexual disturbances in childhood explained the development of emotional problems later in life. Sex is pervasive in man's unconscious motivation, according to Freud, and he contributed to the popular sentiment that one has to get rid of inhibitions in order to have a healthy emotional life. Thereafter, many Americans argued that self-restraint, which they called "repression," led to emotional disorders, and that psychoanalysis was the cure. For some, having lost their moral bearings, the psychiatrist replaced the minister as counselor.

Literature and Art—Modern literature and art in the early twentieth century revealed the influence of the new ideas. In literature, as in art and music, traditional standards yielded to modern ones. Painting was abstract and depicted inner feelings rather than real images, and atonal music moved beyond normal harmony. Poetry written in free verse and novels in stream-of-consciousness form represented the modern break from the conventions of literature in the nineteenth century.

The themes as well as the techniques used in the literature of the twenties echoed the modern era. T. S. Eliot in his poetry spoke of despair and disillusionment and criticized the emptiness of modern society. William Faulkner, one of the great modern novelists, with his awkward syntax, his departure from traditional narrative, and his emphasis on man's evil, created a meaningless world with the old values removed.

The Roaring Twenties

The modern ideas that gained acceptance in the 1920s led to a social revolution in America. So obvious was the new disregard for moral standards that the decade has often been called the jazz age, the ballyhoo years, the age of excess, or more commonly, the "Roaring Twenties."

The young people caught up in this moral vacuum were known as "flaming youth," and they captured attention with their rebellious behavior. Before World War I police arrested women in towns and cities for smoking or for dressing immodestly, but during the twenties some young women in the cities flaunted their new-found freedom by drinking and smoking in public and by shortening their hemlines. Bobbed hair and the boyish look were fashionable for these "flappers." Immorality became glamorous and virtue was too old-fashioned for many of the pleasure-seeking young people of the era.

The breakdown in morality naturally weakened the family. From the 1870s to the 1920s the U.S. population increased three hundred per cent, but divorce increased two thousand per cent. Several factors contributed to this rapid rise in divorce. Women were freed from some of the chores around the house by the use of new inventions or the provision of new services from local businesses. In addition, families were generally smaller than in previous generations. The result was that wives often had time for work and social activities outside the home, and sometimes those interests interfered with family relationships. Also, the newspapers and the silent screen were ablaze with stories of immorality, and that emphasis naturally changed attitudes about purity and fidelity.

In addition to these evidences of moral and family breakdown, the 1920s witnessed an incredible popularity for the frivolous and the sensational. Young Americans rushed to follow the latest fads such as wearing raccoon coats, working crossword puzzles, playing a game called mah jong, marathon dancing, and flagpole sitting. Tabloids and radio informed a nation craving the details of scandalous love affairs, murders, and dramatic true-life stories. In a world where standards had been broken down, people tended to seek thrills and adventure to fill the void in their lives.

Heroes and Villains

The twenties was certainly a colorful time in American history. The spread of daily newspapers and the advent of radio and movies allowed people in every corner of the nation to keep tabs on rising stars in sports, entertainment, and politics as well as on notorious criminals.

American Idols–Organized sports became major entertainment in the twenties. In 1921, fans overflowed a 60,000-seat stadium near Jersey City to watch boxer Jack Dempsey knock out the Frenchman Georges Carpentier. It was the first "million-dollar gate" for sports in the United States and the first major sports event to be broadcast by radio. Babe Ruth, "the Sultan of Swat," thrilled huge crowds at baseball games in Yankee Stadium, and in the 1927 season he hit sixty home runs. Fans filled college football stadiums to thrill to the exploits of athletes such as Red Grange of Illinois

Sixth Avenue Elevated at Third Avenue, by John Sloan, 1928, Oil on canvas, 30 x 40 in. (76.2 x 101.6 cm.), Collection of Whitney Museum of American Art. (Purchase 36.154)

Babe Ruth, "the Sultan of Swat"

and the Four Horsemen of Notre Dame, coached by the legendary Knute Rockne.

Other sports heroes gained wealth, fame, and admiration during the 1920s while popularizing their sports for the enjoyment of millions of Americans. Bobby Jones became the king of the golf links, and William Tilden aspired to the heights of the tennis world. As ordinary people took note of the victories of these athlete idols, golf courses and tennis courts multiplied across the land.

By the end of the 1920s about a hundred million Americans, almost the entire population, went to the movies weekly to see famous comedians such as Charlie Chaplin and Laurel and Hardy or sensual stars such as Rudolph Valentino, Clara Bow, and Gloria Swanson. Popular "talkies" replaced silent films in 1927, and the more than twenty thousand movie palaces in the nation rivaled churches as the most important downtown buildings. Clearly by the twenties many middle-class Americans had become addicted to Hollywood, not just to the world of luxury and immorality portrayed on the screen but also to the promiscuity and glamor of the stars off the screen, as reported by the nation's tabloids.

America's Air Ambassador

At 7:52 on the morning of May 20, 1927, one man in a small silver airplane took off from Roosevelt Field on Long Island. The craft rose into the morning haze and carried its pilot into the headlines and history books. That man was **Charles A. Lindbergh, Jr.,** a twenty-five-year-old flyer from Minnesota. The *New York Times* used the first six pages of its paper the next morning to describe in detail the background of this pilot, the structure of his plane, the *Spirit of St. Louis,* and the nature of his daring attempt. He was trying to become the first person to fly solo nonstop across the Atlantic Ocean from New York to Paris.

The Lone Eagle, Charles Lindbergh, poses with his Spirit of St. Louis *at the time of his history-making flight.*

Lindbergh had received his flight training from the Army Air Service, graduating in 1925 with the rank of second lieutenant in the Air Service Reserve Corps. Soon he put his skills to work for the United States Mail Service, flying mail routes between St. Louis and Chicago. During this time he thought about the possibilities of aviation and considered the $25,000 prize that had been offered since 1919 for a nonstop flight from New York to Paris. Although two Englishmen had flown from Newfoundland to Ireland in 1919 and others had since flown to the continent by way of the Azores, none had yet won the prize. Lindbergh believed that with the right plane, he could make that flight, and several St. Louis investors were willing to help him try. He went to California to oversee the construction and outfitting of his specially built plane. After flying cross-country to New York, he learned that two Frenchmen had perished on their flight from Paris to New York. Undaunted, Lindbergh made the final preparations for his journey.

Though unknown before his historic flight, Lindbergh captured the attention of both the United States and Western Europe as they waited for news of his fate. Then, at last, word came that "the Lone Eagle" had reached his destination on the night of May 21. The next day the *New York Times* proclaimed in its headline, "LINDBERGH DOES IT! TO PARIS IN 33(1/2) HOURS; FLIES 1,000 MILES THROUGH SNOW AND SLEET; CHEERING FRENCH CARRY HIM OFF FIELD."

For the next two weeks Lindbergh faced throngs of admirers in parades and receptions in his honor, not only in France but also in Belgium and England. Kings and dignitaries greeted him with admiration for his courage and for the bridge of friendship he forged between their nations and America. After winning the hearts of the Europeans with grace and modesty, he boarded the U.S.S. *Memphis*, a cruiser sent by President Coolidge, and sailed back to the United States. On his arrival in Washington, crowds thronged to catch a glimpse of their daring hero, and Coolidge added the Distinguished Flying Cross to the many awards Lindbergh had already acquired. A ticker tape parade of grand proportion awaited Lindbergh in New York City, and St. Louis prepared a terrific welcome for the gallant hero whose plane bore its name. Although he modestly claimed to be only a stunt flyer, he riveted the world's attention on the potential of air power, and America showered him with acclaim and fondly remembered "Lucky Lindy's" heroic flight for years to come.

Concerned about the public image of Hollywood, movie makers hired Will Hays, Harding's postmaster general and a Presbyterian lay leader, to censor the films.

Pride and Prejudice—Around the turn of the century American culture became more diverse with the increased "new immigration" discussed in Chapter 16. From 1900 to 1910 almost nine million immigrants came to this country, the highest number for any one decade, and most were from Southern and Eastern Europe. These immigrants kept their language, religion, and culture and usually lived in crowded neighborhoods of the same nationality in the nation's major cities. Large numbers of Catholics and Jews in this immigration were perceived as a threat to the middle-class Protestant Americans that had long been predominant in the population. Many of the foreigners were poor and uneducated, and some had radical political ideas.

The Red Scare of 1919 had encouraged the public to associate crime with immigrants, and this association was evident in the famous **Sacco-Vanzetti case.** In 1920 Nicola Sacco and Bartolomeo Vanzetti allegedly murdered two men in connection with a robbery in South Braintree, Massachusetts. After their case received mounting publicity for several years, the two men were convicted and in 1927 were executed. Their defenders argued that they were condemned because they were Italian-born aliens and anarchists and not because of the evidence, which many viewed as doubtful.

The suspicion of foreigners combined with the surge in immigration after the war resulted in congressional restrictions. The **National Origins Act** (1924) set quotas to restrict immigration. It limited immigration of a nationality to two per cent of that nationality living in the U.S. as of the 1890 census. In addition it totally prohibited Japanese immigration. Clearly the government wanted to preserve America from a threat to its Anglo-Saxon heritage.

During World War I and the 1920s another trend altered American cities as blacks migrated from the South to the North. With the reduction in immigrants, northern industries needed workers, and the one million blacks who moved to northern cities between 1910 and 1930 helped fill that need. In this northern urban setting came political opportunities for blacks. Oscar DePriest from Chicago became the first black congressman from the North. Marcus Garvey of New York City, with his Universal Negro Improvement Association, organized urban blacks into a potent force. Touting racial pride, he enrolled six million members by 1923. Culturally blacks gained even greater visibility. With the Harlem Renaissance, black intellectuals and writers achieved prominence. Entertainers such as Louis Armstrong and Paul Robeson appealed increasingly to white Americans. Several fashionable night spots in the twenties featured black performers playing popular jazz music for all-white audiences.

The rapid social changes of the 1920s caused some Americans to react with violence. Fear of immigrants and blacks led in 1915 to the revival of the **Ku Klux Klan,** patterned after the organization founded during Reconstruction. Promoting "100% Americanism" and limited to native-born white Protestants, the Klan resembled a fraternal order complete with ritual and ceremony. Through skillful promotion the Klan expanded nationally from the South through the early 1920s, becoming a strong social and political force in many of the northern cities where immigrant and black popu-

Scarface

Journalist Lincoln Steffens once described Chicago as "first in violence, deepest in dirt, loud, lawless, unlovely, ill-smelling, irreverent, new, an overgrown gawk of a village, the 'tough' among cities, a spectacle for the nation." While the Windy City did not hold a monopoly on crime in the 1920s, it was the home and center of operations of a man who was probably the most infamous and notorious gangster of all time—**Al Capone.**

Prohibition achieved a measure of success in reducing alcohol consumption in the United States, but many Americans were not content to be "dry." They sought illegal alcohol in illicit taverns called "speakeasies," and they were willing to pay a handsome price to slake their thirst. Because of this demand, some people took advantage of the difficulties of enforcement to make tremen-

lations were rising. For example, in 1924 forty per cent of the Klan's total membership in the U.S. was located in the states of Ohio, Indiana, and Illinois, and a Klan-backed write-in candidate nearly won a three-way race for mayor of Detroit. Feeding on

dous profits on the illegal manufacture, transportation, or sale of alcoholic beverages. Organized crime leaders were quick to add this method of profit to their other corrupt practices, operating illegal breweries in private homes, providing the needed ingredients, and collecting the brew for delivery to customers. They also smuggled liquor into the country across the Canadian border or by boat along the nation's coasts and even stole legal alcohol from authorized warehouses. To ensure the sale of their liquor, they intimidated speakeasy operators to buy their drink only from the organization "or else," and they bribed politicians and police to look the other way as they conducted their business. With these bootlegging activities added to their other vice operations, gangsters of the 1920s were in a lucrative and dangerous business.

Several gangs entered the bootlegging business in Chicago during the 1920s. One of these gangs was led by Johnny Torrio with the help of a strong man, barely out of his teens, named Alphonse Capone. Son of Italian immigrants, Capone had grown up in Brooklyn and was well acquainted with the criminal elements of New York City. While there, he was slashed in a knife fight that left him with three prominent scars on the left side of his face (hence the nickname he detested, "Scarface").

Torrio brought Capone to Chicago in 1920 as a bodyguard, but Capone quickly proved to be clever and effective in operating the illegal businesses of the gang. After Torrio was wounded in a gangland attack in 1925, he decided to leave town and to give Capone command of his crime ring. Capone soon established himself as the king of Chicago's underworld, as people who stood in his way were likely to meet a sudden death. The most famous example of gang violence was probably the "Saint Valentine's Day Massacre" in 1929, when on that day members of Capone's gang, disguised as policemen, gunned down members of a rival gang in a garage. The violence between Capone and his rivals was termed *gangland war*, and for many of Chicago's citizens, it seemed that their city lay under the shadow of corruption and terror.

Despite Capone's opulent lifestyle, which was obviously the result of illegal gain, authorities struggled to find evidence that would put him behind bars. Capone richly rewarded subordinates who did his dirty work, and they were too loyal or too fearful to testify against him. Also Capone was careful not to allow any written evidence of his ill-gotten gain. Finally, at the prodding of President Hoover, federal investigators uncovered evidence of about $1 million in income (a small fraction of the total that Capone received in the late 1920s) on which he had not paid taxes. As a result, prosecutors brought Capone to trial for income-tax evasion in 1931. The court found the grand gangster guilty and sentenced him to eleven years in prison. Capone was sent to serve part of his sentence at Alcatraz, where he soon learned that his wealth and influence could no longer win him favor. While in prison venereal disease ravaged his brain. Although he lived until 1947, his days of power were over. At age forty-eight, the great kingpin of 1920s Chicago died without his fortune, yet with his well-earned notoriety intact.

bigotry and racism, the Klan's organizers resorted to intimidation and violence to keep blacks, Catholics, and Jews "in their place."

Paradoxically, the Klan in some areas of the country tried to be a means of reform, fighting the decline in morality and using the symbol of the cross. Klan targets were bootleggers, wife beaters, and immoral movies. In some communities it achieved a certain respectability as it worked with politicians. The 1924 Democratic National Convention refused, by a narrow margin, to condemn it by name. A secret organization, the Klan's membership reached several million according to some estimates, but that number declined after the mid-1920s. The 1924 immigration restriction law reduced the number of immigrants and the fears they generated. Also, the Klan's use of violence alienated mainstream America, and a sex scandal among the Indiana Klan leaders made a mockery of the Klan's moral crusade.

Fighting for the Faith

Rise of Fundamentalism—One religious movement reacted strongly to the modern trends of the 1920s. As mentioned in Chapter 18, several orthodox movements in the Progressive Era resisted the theological errors of modernism, the social gospel, and the inroads of evolution. Also arising to influence American Christianity at this time was premillennialism. Premillennialists rejected the unfounded liberal faith in progress, and they contended that the world was actually growing worse. Most important, premillennialists stressed that Christ could return at any time to establish His millennial kingdom. After World War I various conservative movements (such as premillennialism) from several denominations joined forces to form what became known as **fundamentalism.**

The origin of the term *fundamentalism* lies in the belief of some Bible-believing Christians that there are certain ''fundamental'' doctrines which no one can deny and be a Christian—doctrines such as the authority of Scripture and Christ's deity, vicarious atonement, resurrection, and Second Coming. In 1910 two Christian businessmen sponsored the publication of a series of essays to defend key doctrines. Called *The Fundamentals,* these essays by some of the leading Christian scholars of the day were sent at no cost to pastors, professors, and laymen all over the country. In 1920 a Christian editor wrote, ''We suggest that those who still cling to the great fundamentals and who mean to do battle royal for the fundamentals be called 'Fundamentalists.' ''

The Fundamentalist-Modernist Controversy— In the North the fundamentalist movement developed into a theological battle with modernists.

Called the **fundamentalist-modernist controversy,** this battle was waged over doctrine and the control of the schools, mission boards, and institutions of the major denominations. In the Northern Baptist Convention men such as William Bell Riley fought for the faith. J. Gresham Machen and others battled the liberals for the historic Christian faith in the northern Presbyterian church. Machen's book *Christianity and Liberalism,* written in 1923, forcefully pointed out that modernism was not Christianity but another religion.

Many conservatives were not willing to expel modernists from their denominations, however, if such action risked a major split. The more militant fundamentalists, therefore, began to leave the major denominations and form their own associations. Fundamentalists in the Northern Baptist Convention left to form the General Association of Regular Baptists (1932). Machen led a group of Presbyterian fundamentalists to form the Orthodox Presbyterian Church (1936).

Anti-Evolution Crusade—In the South where the major Baptist, Methodist, and Presbyterian denominations were generally sound in the twenties, one of the fundamentalist efforts there centered on removing the teaching of evolution from the public schools. As these Christians pointed out, evolution was not simply irreconcilable with the Biblical account of creation; it directly assaulted the authority of Scripture. With leaders such as William Jennings Bryan, they pushed for laws banning the teaching of evolution but succeeded in doing so in only a few southern states, one of them being Tennessee. Wanting to put their town on the map, some town leaders of Dayton, Tennessee, coaxed a high school teacher, **John T. Scopes,** to challenge the law.

The result was a media event as national attention focused on the town for the summer of 1925. Clarence Darrow, expert trial lawyer and agnostic, defended Scopes. Bryan, who helped the prosecution, also served as a witness, called by the defense as an expert on the Bible. Although Bryan showed commendable courage in his defense of the faith, he was no Bible scholar and did not make the best case for the cause. Scopes was convicted, but Bryan and the antievolutionists lost the publicity battle.

William Jennings Bryan: "He Kept the Faith"

William Jennings Bryan was one of the dominant figures of his era. From his first run for the presidency in 1896 until his death in 1925, Bryan made headlines as a three-time Democratic candidate for president, as secretary of state under Woodrow Wilson, and as a political crusader and reformer. Bryan also had one of the clearest Christian testimonies of any major political figure in American history. He recalled, "At the age of fourteen, I reached one of the turning points in my life. I attended a revival that was being conducted in a Presbyterian church and was converted." Bryan said that this event "has had more influence in my life for good than any other experience."

Bryan's reputation as a political progressive sometimes confuses those who associate conservative religious beliefs with conservative political beliefs. In the days before Franklin Roosevelt's New Deal—when the dangers of "big government" were not so obvious—some Christians supported progressive political reforms as a means of allowing the government to be "the minister of God . . . for good" (Rom. 13:4). For Bryan, supporting causes such as women's suffrage and the direct election of senators were matters of simple justice that would please God as well as help the common man. Opposing the abuses of "big business" was, to Bryan, fulfilling Christ's command to be "the salt of the earth" (Matt. 5:13).

Bryan always devoted himself to Christian causes, but he took a particular interest in them in the last ten years of his life, after his resignation as secretary of state. It was the defense of Christianity that took him to the antievolution Scopes trial in Dayton, Tennessee. When challenged by the agnostic defense attorney, Clarence Darrow, to testify as an "expert witness" on the Bible, the layman Bryan, according to his wife's later testimony, was not eager to do so. He feared that refusing, however, would make it seem that he thought the Bible could not stand up to scrutiny. He told the court, "I want the Christian world to know that any atheist, agnostic, unbeliever, can question me any time as to my belief in God, and I will answer him." Bryan therefore faced "foolish and unlearned questions" (II Tim. 2:23) from the cynical, scoffing Darrow, questions which Bryan frankly was sometimes neither scientist nor theologian enough to answer adequately. But there was no question about his courage. Following his death only days after the Scopes trial, Bryan was buried in Arlington National Cemetery. On his tomb was an epitaph simple and powerful, "He Kept the Faith."

Only a few days after the trial Bryan died. For many wishful critics, fundamentalism died with Bryan in Tennessee. The movement was still very much alive, however, as it demonstrated in 1928 when it assisted in defeating the antiprohibition, Roman Catholic Democratic candidate Al Smith in the presidential election.

Fundamentalist Successes—In a larger sense fundamentalists in the twenties were battling the modern culture that aggressively assaulted the old-time religion. Philosophers, writers, and even liberal ministers dogmatically trusted science as the source of true knowledge and extolled the virtues of Freud and Darwin. American society had become increasingly secular, as revealed in movies, magazines, radio, literature, jazz, and urban lifestyles. Fundamentalists fought this growing irreligious mood in America. The failure of World War I to bring peace and the corruption in government and society gave credibility to their message.

Despite the Scopes Trial debacle, fundamentalism flourished in the twenties. By 1930 more than fifty Bible colleges and seminaries offered training for those who could no longer trust their denominational colleges and seminaries. Fundamentalists also took to the airwaves. In 1932 *Sunday School Times* listed over four hundred evangelical programs on eighty different radio stations in the country. Ironically, while the mainline denominations that had resisted fundamentalism suffered a decline, fundamentalist institutions prospered.

Section Review

1. Name four men whose philosophical and scientific theories helped to reshape the moral attitudes of the 1920s in ways detrimental to Christianity.
2. What term describes the young people of the 1920s who lacked moral values?
3. In what two occupational groups did Americans of the 1920s find many of their heroes?
4. What were two major evidences of American resentment toward immigrants and blacks in the 1920s?
5. What two groups were involved in a major religious controversy during the 1920s?

From Roar to Ruin

As the 1920s passed, Americans grew accustomed to the prosperity of the era. Business thrived and living standards improved to make life more comfortable, in a material sense, for most Americans. When Herbert Hoover accepted the Republican nomination in 1928, he even predicted a total eradication of poverty in the land.

> One of the oldest and perhaps the noblest of human aspirations has been the abolition of poverty. . . . We in America today are nearer to the final triumph over poverty than ever before in the history of any land. The poorhouse is vanishing from among us. We have not yet reached the goal, but, given a chance to go forward with the policies of the last eight years, we shall soon, with the help of God, be in sight of the day when poverty will be banished from this nation.

Hoover's rosy prediction must have seemed legitimate at the time, but events would soon prove that prosperity was fleeting.

We've Got the Goods

If America was on the road to ruin, it was certainly driving there in style. In 1920 there had been only about nine million automobiles in the United States. During the decade that number nearly tripled. Henry Ford had made his black Model Ts affordable and commonplace, but they were also dull and drab compared to the sleek styles and colors introduced by other automakers in the twenties. Chevrolet and other competitors attracted buyers who wanted something different, forcing Ford to introduce the Model A in 1927. With installment loans available to finance the price, Americans eagerly stepped into the driver's seat and sped away in debt.

The automobile had social as well as economic influence. Good roads improved transportation and gave rise to the suburbs, as workers no longer had to live within walking distance of their jobs. Rural families could visit the cities frequently rather than just a few times a year, and tourism boomed as the average family could travel for vacations. Also with the car young people had opportunities for unchaperoned dates.

In the 1920s radio became the major medium of news and entertainment for the nation, a dominance that radio did not lose until the advent of television after World War II.

Radio was another influential item of the 1920s. From the time the first commercial station **KDKA** went on the air in Pittsburgh, Americans began to tune in to the news, music, sports, and other entertainment that it offered. At first the enthralled listeners built crude crystal sets to receive their broadcasts, but during the decade those archaic radios gave way to bigger and better receivers, many of them in the form of fine pieces of furniture. Rural and urban Americans alike gathered around these prized possessions to listen to the songs of their favorite crooners, to thrill to stories of adventure, and to laugh at the jokes of popular comedians.

In addition to cars and radios, Americans acquired many more new material possessions in the 1920s. With electricity available in smaller towns as well as large cities, electric appliances multiplied. Phonographs, refrigerators, irons, and other devices brought pleasure and comfort into many homes. Telephone wires spread to many more homes as well, allowing people to communicate more easily with one another. There seemed to be an unlimited array of desirable possessions to catch the eye of the American consumer and make modern life more enjoyable.

On a Spending Spree

The materialism of the twenties was widely evident, but there were other elements corrupting American society in more subtle ways. Advertising

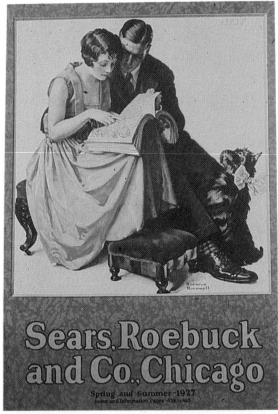

America's "wish book," the Sears, Roebuck and Co. catalog, was one of several in the 1920s which encouraged consumer spending.

practice self-denial. Materialistic values undercut Biblical values as advertisers increasingly persuaded Americans to be better consumers of goods than producers of them. Buying on credit through **installment plans** (making small monthly payments until the item is paid for) made that possible.

Ever in debt for their purchases, Americans searched for ways to acquire the money they needed to maintain their comfortable lifestyles. Some resorted to fraud, bootlegging, and other illegal means, while others turned to **speculation,** buying something at a low price and selling it at a higher price for profit. One hot item for speculation in the 1920s was land in Florida. Billed as a tropical paradise, acreage there began to sell for high prices. Speculators bought large tracts of land and subdivided them for sale. As the land boom progressed, the properties were sold and resold for higher and higher amounts. Much of the land was marshland or otherwise undesirable, but promises of future golf courses, shopping areas, and other developments tempted many to buy a lot nearby for $20,000 or more. Then in 1926 a severe hurricane hit the Miami area, killing four hundred people and destroying thousands of houses. The disaster brought a sudden end to the land boom as people awoke to the hazards of their speculation. The credit which had sustained the boom collapsed as land prices plummeted. Many fortunes made in the frenzy were lost overnight, and thousands of unwary Americans were left with a heavy debt and a worthless land deed.

As a great **bull market** (a stock market characterized by rising prices and optimism) began in 1927, stock became the prime target for American speculation. Wall Street had prospered throughout the decade as public infatuation with business grew and as ordinary people who had gained experience buying bonds to support the war effort now became aware of the promising securities market. Easy credit also fueled an interest in owning shares of corporations as investors were allowed to buy stock **"on the margin."** In this process investors would purchase stock through a broker but pay only a percentage (thirty per cent to fifty per cent on the average) of the purchase price. The broker would finance the remaining amount for the investor with

began to coax the public to buy even if they did not need the product or have the money. Mass production was providing greater and greater numbers of products that needed to be sold. Therefore, mass consumption was also necessary. Through increased newspaper and magazine advertisements along with ads on the newly popularized radio, businessmen promoted goods ranging from cigarettes to soap, and automobiles to mouthwash. Advertising appeals emphasized youth, sex, happiness, luxury, and keeping up with one's neighbors. Celebrity endorsements began to add glamour to a product. Ads bombarded consumers with temptations to spend, not save; to enjoy the present, not worry about the future; to pamper themselves, not

money he had borrowed from a bank or other sources. As long as the stock's value remained constant or increased, the broker was assured of collateral to cover the loan. However, if the stock price dropped, he would call in the investor's loan and force him to increase his margin or pay for the stock immediately. During the late 1920s Americans watched stock prices climb dramatically and almost steadily. Many began to buy stock on the margin, hoping to sell it at a huge profit, pay off their stock broker, and pocket a tidy sum without ever risking a large amount of their own money.

From March of 1928 to September of 1929 prices of many favored stocks doubled, and nearly every stock rose. The possibilities of profits from stock speculation fueled tremendous activity on Wall Street and created even greater admiration and expectations of American business. President Coolidge disapproved of speculation, but he had certainly encouraged American faith in business, and Hoover's election helped to prompt the amazing stock market flourish that followed for several months. Republicans reveled in the prosperity that seemed to abound.

Boom Goes Bust

While Wall Street was booming, Americans naturally focused their attention on the excitement and affluence that it afforded. However, the nation's economic condition was dependent on far more than the price of corporate stock. Several fundamental problems had been developing

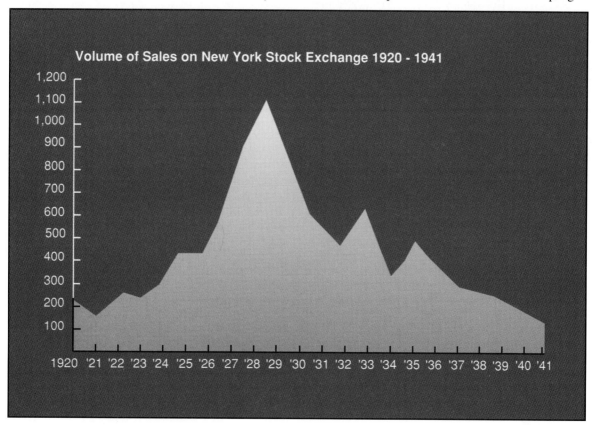

through the decade, but the possible dangers they entailed were brushed aside by optimistic Americans until October of 1929.

In the middle of that month stock prices began to sag, and investors began to grow wary. On October 24 (''Black Thursday'') fear began to encourage panic selling. Millions of shares were offered for sale, but there were virtually no buyers. Prices dropped dramatically until New York's leading financiers pooled their resources to buy stock and halt the devastating decline. The attempt to prop up the market worked for that day, but not before stock prices had taken a significant fall. As a result, banks began to pressure brokers, and brokers began to pressure investors who had bought stock on the margin to pay up. Because most of these speculators did not have the extra cash, they opted to sell the stock. This action resulted in a new wave of selling at the stock exchange and an accompanying drop in prices. On **Black Tuesday,** October 29, the bottom fell out of the market. More than sixteen million shares were dumped on the market and investors lost $30 billion in the process. Americans hoped that this **stock market crash** was only a temporary ''readjustment'' of the inordinately high stock prices caused by speculation. Those hopes eroded, however, as prices on the market continued to decline gradually for three years.

What were the problems that contributed to the demise of prosperity? A few were at hand in the stock market itself. Buying stock on credit had resulted in over $8 billion in loans from banks to brokers by October 1929. All of that credit was based on the presumed value of stocks in a speculative market, and that value was shaky indeed. The inherent worth of many of the stocks had not increased during the bull market because many American industries became no more prosperous during that era. Neither their profits nor the dividends they paid shareholders had increased significantly. The crash ended the speculative inflation of stock prices and consumed the money that banks, brokers, and investors had tied up in them. The resulting collapse of credit was devastating to America's financial market.

Another problem was that American industries faced a shrinking market for their products. By the late 1920s most American families had bought a car if they needed one, and many were still making payments on the purchase. Under these conditions the demand for new cars decreased. Similar effects were felt in other industries as Americans had bought houses, appliances, and the other things they wanted on credit, and now they did not need or could not afford additional purchases. Not only did the domestic market for goods decline, but the high tariffs closed the possibility of selling American products abroad. These conditions caused many industries to decline and resulted in significant unemployment even before the crash.

Problems were evident in other areas of the nation's economy as well. America's farm population, about half of all Americans in the 1920s, continued to struggle with the adverse conditions of the agricultural market noted earlier. Also the nation's banks were beginning to suffer not only from defaults on loans made for stock purchases, but also from losses on the huge loans made to European countries and losses on many loans made to Americans for land, equipment, and other major purchases.

Americans, now mired in debt and pessimistic about their future, tightened their belts in an attempt to regain their own economic security. Unfortunately, reduced consumer spending only augmented the growing economic depression, and the cycle of despair grew. The fearful emotions combined with these and other inherent economic problems helped to push America into the Great Depression and ushered the nation into a new and difficult decade.

Section Review

1. What two inventions in particular had a tremendous effect on American life in the 1920s?
2. Name two practices that encouraged Americans to spend money extravagantly during the 1920s.
3. In what year did the stock market crash?

Chapter Review

Terms

"normalcy"
Red Scare
isolationism
Washington Naval Conference
Kellogg-Briand Pact
Fordney-McCumber Tariff
Dawes Plan
Warren G. Harding
return to "normalcy"
Teapot Dome scandal
Calvin Coolidge
Herbert Hoover
Al Smith
Albert Einstein
theory of relativity
Sigmund Freud
Charles A. Lindbergh
Sacco-Vanzetti case
National Origins Act
Ku Klux Klan
Al Capone
fundamentalism
fundamentalist-modernist controversy
John T. Scopes
radio
KDKA
installment plans
speculation
bull market
"on the margin"
Black Tuesday
stock market crash (1929)

Content Questions

1. Why was there a "farm problem" in the years following World War I?
2. What were the two basic foreign policy tasks faced by the United States in the 1920s?
3. How did U.S. foreign policy toward Latin America change during the 1920s?
4. Why did President Harding's reputation become tarnished after his death?
5. What trends in the ethnic and racial make-up of America's population disturbed many people in the 1920s?
6. What was one of the main focuses of fundamentalist efforts in the North? in the South?
7. List at least three social effects of the automobile upon American society in the 1920s.
8. How did Americans' spending habits change during the 1920s?
9. List at least four problems that contributed to the demise of prosperity in the 1920s.

Application Questions

1. What are some potential dangers of hero worship, such as that practiced in the 1920s toward sports and film stars?
2. What are arguments for and against placing strict limits on the immigration of certain nationalities and ethnic groups as the United States did in the 1920s?
3. Consider the statement of the Christian editor who described fundamentalists as those "who mean to do battle royal for the fundamentals" of the faith. Is "doing battle royal" a proper attitude for the Christian to take in defending the faith?

CHAPTER 21

The Thirties (1929-1939)

"I can't. This is my sister's day to eat."

*A little girl's response to a teacher's suggestion that she go home
and eat something* (c. 1932)

I. Hoover Gets the Blame
  A. Call It a Depression
  B. Too Little, Too Late
  C. A Demand for Change
II. FDR and the New Deal
  A. Fighting Fear
  B. Roadblocks and Pitfalls
  C. Elusive Recovery
III. Worst of Times, Best of Times
  A. Depths of Depression
  B. The Good Times

Out of work and out of luck, Americans line up for relief assistance during the Great Depression. Photographed by Dorothea Lange.

The jobless stood on city street corners, hoping to sell apples for 5¢ each. The homeless rode the rails from freight yard to freight yard, often camping in "hobo jungles." Down-and-out "Okies" left their dust-choked farms on the Great Plains looking for work in the bean fields of California. Poor teachers in Chicago prepared little meals from their meager resources to feed their hungry students.

The nation that had come to be the wealthiest and most powerful in the world was somehow thrown into a confusing economic quagmire, entrapping millions of its people in poverty and despair. Although the majority of Americans escaped severe deprivations, few passed through the 1930s without some hardship and anxiety. All around were unwanted reminders that the prosperity of the 1920s was gone and that the future was full of doubt. Franklin Roosevelt, during his 1932 campaign, described the prevalent despondency when he commented, "I have looked into the faces of thousands of Americans. . . . They have the frightened look of lost children." Hard times and great challenges gripped the nation in the decade of the **"Great Depression."**

Hoover Gets the Blame

During the 1928 election Republicans had promised the nation "A Chicken in Every Pot, Two Cars in Every Garage." The party gladly accepted credit for the prosperity of the 1920s and promised more, a promise that the American people wanted to believe. Americans gave their support to Herbert Hoover, expecting him to extend their carefree existence for another four years. But when the stock market crash of 1929 knocked them out of their bed of roses, blame for the end of prosperity began to fall on the shoulders of one man: Herbert Hoover.

Call It a Depression

Actually, America's economic prosperity did not evaporate overnight in October 1929. The conditions that had led to the stock market crash had been developing during the twenties, and their impact was compounded in the months of uncertainty that followed the crash. The problems of unemployment, poverty, and despair began to surface but did not become widespread until about a year after the collapse on Wall Street. Even so, the economic decline could not be ignored very long. Because President Hoover was intent on keeping the morale of Americans intact, he avoided the standard historical terms for an economic decline–"panic" or "crisis"–and instead chose to call the downturn by a title evoking less emotion. He called it a "depression." Although the economic term *depression* seemed less alarming at the time, the word would come to strike fear in the hearts of Americans in the decade that followed and would bring to mind painful memories for the remainder of the century.

Historians, economists, and politicians endlessly analyze the causes of the 1930s depression, and while certain factors clearly contributed to the economic demise of the decade, there are no easy answers. It is evident that the growing debts of consumers in the 1920s eventually resulted in a loss of purchasing power by the end of that decade. This loss decreased demand for industrial production, which in turn caused businesses to slow production and to lay off workers. The increase in unemployment led to further decline in the purchasing power of consumers, and this in turn led to further cutbacks in industry. The regressive cycle continued and was made worse by the harsh realities of the stock market crash, until the nation was seized with bewilderment and fear over its economic future.

But what caused the dreadful stagnation of the economy? Some have found fault with America's greedy businessmen who reaped large profits during the 1920s while they paid meager wages to their workers. Some have condemned the federal government for its blatant support of laissez-faire capitalism and its failure to intervene boldly in the nation's economic affairs when problems began to arise. Others, including President Hoover, have blamed the international economic situation involving the unpaid debts of the Allies and Germany to the United States. The decline of international trade in response to high tariffs should also be added. And, of course the eagerness of the Ameri-

can people to incur heavy debts for autos, land, homes, stock, and other purchases before the downturn certainly could be cited as a contributing factor. One more point that should not be overlooked is the growth of pessimism in response to foreboding conditions. A gloomy outlook prompted people to make the situation worse. But whatever led the nation to experience a decade of economic decline (and it was undoubtedly a combination of many conditions), the easiest thing for the people of the 1930s to do was to blame Herbert Hoover.

In response to his being blamed for the depression, Hoover once commented sarcastically that the ascription was a "great compliment to the energies and capacities of one man." Obviously, Hoover was not the cause of the "Great Depression," but his name was forever linked with the hardships of that era. Since Hoover was the president on watch when the crisis struck, a disappointed public laid the responsibility for their plight squarely on his doorstep. As conditions grew bleaker in 1931 and 1932, the president's name was attached to practically everything that symbolized the adversities of the depression. Cardboard shacks sheltering homeless people in the parks and vacant lots of American cities were called "Hoovervilles." Newspapers used for a covering on cold nights were "Hoover blankets," and empty pockets turned inside out became "Hoover flags." As unemployment, business failures, and apprehension spread, the pressure mounted on the president to do something to bring the nation out of its trouble and hasten the return of prosperity.

Too Little, Too Late

On October 25, 1929, the day after Black Thursday, Hoover had declared that "the fundamental business of the country, that is production and distribution of commodities, is on a sound and prosperous basis." His intent was to restore American confidence in order to avoid a financial panic, but his words of encouragement were not enough. Black Thursday was soon followed by Black Tuesday (see p. 486), and the nation went into a downward economic spiral. Nonetheless, the president continued to try to convince Americans, telling a group that asked for more government works projects in June 1930, "Gentlemen, you have come sixty days too late. The Depression is over." It was not so easy, Hoover found, to inspire the same optimism in the nation.

It has often been implied that Hoover made little effort to combat the depression other than to try to assure the nation that everything was going to be all right. This reputation for inaction, however, was not well earned. Hoover was a progressive Republican who was willing to make prudent changes, and he began to take steps to deal with the situation almost immediately. He quickly got Congress to cut taxes by $140 million, and he encouraged an increase of $420 million on spending for federal **public works** (government-financed construction of public facilities) to create jobs. These were not small steps, but they gained little notice and, unfortunately, provided few immediate substantial results.

Voluntary Uncooperation—President Hoover also launched a major campaign for voluntary cooperation in the fight against depression. In December of 1929 the president called a meeting of four hundred of the nation's leading business executives. He urged these leaders to voluntarily keep their workers and maintain satisfactory wage levels. He also asked that they continue to invest in new construction and equipment rather than cut back industrial growth. Although the businessmen attempted to cooperate, by the end of 1930 economic realities made support impossible. To abide by the agreement would have sent many firms into bankruptcy; so unemployment grew, wages were cut, and industrial expansion virtually ceased.

Even before the stock market crash, Hoover had directed Congress to create the Federal Farm Board. This agency, intended to relieve the prolonged hardships of American farmers, instituted public stabilization corporations chartered by the states rather than the federal government. These were supposed to bolster the prices of farm products by buying surpluses while also trying to persuade farmers to cut back their production volun-

tarily. When the depression began and needs increased, Hoover hoped that these efforts would ease the farm problems, but the plan quickly fell apart as overproduction continued and funds for propping up farm prices ran out. The price for wheat fell from $1.05 a bushel in 1929 to 68¢ in 1930 and 39¢ in 1931. Other farm prices dropped in similar fashion, throwing farmers deeper into debt and despair.

Other voluntary efforts initiated by the Hoover administration included the President's Emergency Committee for Employment (PECE), formed in October 1930. This committee attempted to coordinate the efforts of public and private charities as they provided needed assistance to the poor and funneled information about relief conditions back to the government. About a year later the President's Organization for Unemployment Relief (POUR) superseded PECE, but no matter what name it held, it never had the resources to deal effectively with the growing crisis. Another program was the National Credit Corporation (NCC). In the face of growing numbers of bank failures (from 651 in 1929 to almost 2,300 in 1931), Hoover wanted banks to cooperate in an effort to maintain their own stability. He expected the nation's prosperous banks to help establish a credit reserve fund that would be used to provide assistance to banks in danger of failing. By helping each other in this

The impact of the Great Depression forced many former wage-earners to seek their meals in free "soup kitchens."

way, they could avoid further panic in the banking industry. This idea also met a humiliating end. Years later Hoover commented on the effort saying that it quickly "became ultraconservative, then fearful, and finally died."

Hoover sincerely believed that it was the duty of private individuals, not the government, to reach out and help the needy with voluntary assistance. Unfortunately, in the face of an uncertain future and an apparently steady economic decline, Americans were reluctant to risk their own capital and positions in cooperative efforts. Therefore, by the fall of 1931, the public outcry for government action was mounting rapidly.

Government Involvement–President Hoover was not opposed to government action in the face of the financial emergency. After all, some of his first efforts involved tax cuts and public works programs. And when voluntary cooperation did not provide the needed results, he turned to possible government measures intended to hasten recovery. However, he was adamantly opposed to the use of any form of dole (an unearned government handout) to meet the needs of impoverished Americans. He believed that **work relief** was far better. Employment in a government relief job would at least discourage idleness and preserve the self-respect of the needy. Hoover also wanted to keep most of the relief efforts under the control of state and local government rather than to create large federal relief agencies. In this way the measures taken could be adapted more easily to the needs in each local area. Finally, Hoover was determined to keep the federal budget in balance. He declared that "the course of unbalanced budgets is the road to ruin." Because this view was shared by most Americans, the president believed that deficit spending would jeopardize confidence in the nation's financial stability and further discourage industrial recovery.

These reservations, though commendable, led Hoover to reject many of the relief proposals that Congress scrambled to enact. Finally, in 1932 he approved the Emergency Relief and Construction Act, which established the **Reconstruction Finance Corporation (RFC)**. This agency, patterned after the War Finance Corporation of World War

I, was given $500 million to loan to businesses (primarily banks). While this bold move did help to stabilize the banking industry and a few other economic concerns for a time, it did not inspire the expansion of credit and return of confidence that Hoover wanted. Furthermore, the RFC was roundly criticized for helping the wealthy–bankers and businessmen–rather than the truly needy.

Probably one of the worst actions Hoover did take was to sign the **Hawley-Smoot tariff** in June 1930. This action pushed tariffs on foreign industrial and agricultural prices to their highest level in history, up from thirty-three per cent to forty per cent. The high protectionist tariff, though intended to help American producers and stabilize prices, served primarily to shut off foreign trade and thereby reduced the market for American goods. The American Farm Bureau Federation concluded that the Hawley-Smoot tariff provided farmers with a $30 million benefit from the agricultural tariffs while it also imposed a $330 million loss. It is impossible to measure the total effect of the tariff revision on the economy, but this action certainly did not help to bring recovery to the depressed nation.

The increase in the tariff undoubtedly helped to precipitate an economic collapse in Europe in 1931. Hoover was especially concerned about this international crisis because he believed America's foreign economic ties contributed to the depression the nation now experienced. He soon declared an unpopular but unavoidable moratorium on European debt payments to the United States. He also called for an international economic conference to solve international economic problems. Even so, no action was taken to lower the tariff until 1934.

Even though Hoover's efforts to overcome the depression did not turn the nation's economy back to prosperity, his actions set the stage for a significant increase in federal government involvement in America's economic affairs. In 1930 he asked for a $25 million loan to the Department of Agriculture for the provision of seed and feed to impoverished farmers, an action that established a precedent for future agricultural subsidies. He began the expansion of public works, provided the first (though meager) federal funds for relief, established some pioneer programs in home financing and public housing, and established the Reconstruction Finance Corporation, a major lending agency that would become an integral part of his successor's relief efforts. Such federal activity would be embraced and greatly expanded in the administrations to come.

A Demand for Change

Although Hoover did not neglect the mounting economic crisis, the spread of poverty and despair was beginning to take a toll on the American people, and they began to cry for action to stop their suffering. In 1932 the situation was obviously bleak. The nation's measure of productivity, its GNP (Gross National Product, the annual sum of all goods and services that a nation produces) fell to $41 billion, down from $104 billion in 1929. More than 5,000 American banks had failed, 86,000 businesses had closed, and a quarter of a million families had been evicted from their homes. In September of that year *Fortune* magazine estimated that twenty-eight per cent of the population or about thirty-four million men, women, and children were without any income whatsoever. As the hardships of the depression spread, many Americans began to clamor for help and for change.

A striking characteristic of depression America, however, was that the hardships and uncertainties of those times did not spark a true revival of Biblical Christianity. Many Americans looked to government rather than God to meet their temporal needs.

The Bonus Army—A major episode in the Hoover administration's struggle with the depression took place in the summer of 1932. A large group of World War I veterans, now unemployed, made their way to Washington, D.C., to ask for an early payment of the bonus promised to them by the Adjusted Compensation Act of 1924. These former members of the American Expeditionary Force now called themselves the Bonus Expeditionary Force (BEF), but this "army" did not win support from Congress. They turned to Hoover for help, but he would not deal with them. Dismayed but unwilling to concede defeat, a large number of the more than twenty thousand BEF marchers, some with their wives and children, settled into a hastily built shantytown on the edge of the city and into some vacant buildings near the Capitol. As weeks of the BEF occupation of Washington passed, Hoover became more and more frustrated by their embarrassing presence in the capital city.

On July 28 the situation came to a head. Government agents were sent to inform the **Bonus Army** that they must move out of the downtown buildings, but they refused. Police were sent with nightsticks in hand to force the illegal occupants out of the buildings, but the BEF, reinforced with men from the main camp, met the officers with a volley of bricks. In the melee, some of the policemen began to fire on the veterans, killing two and wounding two others. Hoover learned of the trouble and sent General Douglas MacArthur with troops to quell the disorder and complete the eviction of the buildings. MacArthur, contrary to Hoover's orders, determined to use all necessary force to drive the BEF not only out of the condemned buildings but also completely out of the capital. After an hour's warning the general's forces marched in with tear gas, tanks, and brandished bayonets. Once the downtown buildings were cleared, MacArthur moved on the main camp, driving out the BEF that remained and burning their shacks.

Though the action had been much harsher than he intended, Hoover took full responsibility for the affair. In doing so the president seemed to be even more callous to the needs of struggling Americans than ever. A desire for change was leading many people to look elsewhere for relief. Some began to espouse various socialistic plans, even praising the Communist Soviet Union. Mussolini's fascist regime in Italy also won admiration for dealing with economic difficulties. Such extreme political views were not the norm, but people without food and other necessary provisions and without jobs to provide money for those needs were becoming desperate.

Election of 1932—As the fall election approached in 1932, Republican prospects for reelection were certainly bleak. Hoover had lost his appeal to the impatient public, but there were no other bright stars on the Republican horizon that year. Republican Congressmen and governors had generally fallen out of favor along with Hoover as voters held the whole party responsible for the continuing depression. As a result, Hoover won renomination easily, but the Republicans entered the fall campaign with little confidence.

The Democrats, however, did have a rising star to offer to the 1932 campaign. For some time **Franklin Delano Roosevelt** had desired the office once held by his Republican cousin Theodore, but that ambition had seemed to be shattered in August 1921 when polio struck the young politician, paralyzing him from the waist down for life. Nonetheless, Roosevelt's courageous struggle to overcome his disability added appeal to his public image. In 1928 Roosevelt won the governorship of New York, despite the overwhelming support for Republicans in that year. With the rising disapproval of the Republicans in 1930, the governor won re-election easily. Although the measures Roosevelt took to combat the depression in New York were not particularly daring or successful, he managed to maintain his popularity, placing himself in an advantageous position as the presidential election approached.

Roosevelt entered the Democratic convention in 1932 as the front-runner for the nomination. Although the governor met some stiff opposition from certain factions of the party, Roosevelt managed to appease the conservatives with his vice-presidential pick, John Nance Garner of Texas. Roosevelt won on the fourth ballot, and on notification of that fact he flew from Albany to Chicago to make his acceptance speech in person at the convention. This unprecedented action helped to picture the candidate as a daring man who was willing to change tradition.

That perceived defiance of traditional actions proved to be the central issue of the campaign between Hoover and Roosevelt. Hoover pointed out this theme when he said, ''My countrymen! The fundamental issue that will fix the national direction for one hundred years to come is whether we shall go in fidelity to American traditions or whether we shall turn to innovations.'' Because many Americans were critical of Hoover's insistence on tradition in the face of their great needs, they were ready to turn to innovations. Roosevelt promised them action and they believed him. Even his campaign song renewed hope in a change for the better:

> Happy days are here again!
> The skies above are clear again!
> Let's all sing a song of cheer again–
> Happy days-are-here-a-gain!

Republicans, caught in the crossfire of events, were not in a singing mood.

Roosevelt was in an enviable position throughout the race against Hoover. Because so many Americans wanted something different in their new president, Roosevelt would be an easy winner unless he foolishly antagonized the public. Therefore he was careful to avoid explaining the details of his economic plans. He pledged to increase direct federal relief to the poor, while he promised to cut government expenditures and balance the budget. No one seemed to question how he could possibly accomplish both of these popular moves at the same time. Roosevelt spread hope and his assurance of action to meet the crisis. In his acceptance speech he had stated, ''I pledge you, I pledge myself, to a New Deal for the American people.'' That promise of a **''New Deal''** (a name that would soon be permanently attached to his efforts to conquer the depression) was what the people wanted to hear, regardless of his ambiguity on the particulars. The people were willing to look to a man who had overcome a serious handicap and to trust that he would be able to help the nation overcome its serious difficulties. Surprisingly, even the poor identified with the wealthy and aristocratic Roosevelt because of his physical adversity. Such popularity could only result in a decisive win for the New York governor. Roosevelt won over 57 per cent of the popular vote in November and 472 electoral votes to Hoover's 59.

Final Desperate Days–During the months between the November election and the March 4 inauguration of Roosevelt, the defeated president was left to struggle with the continuing problems of the depression. Hoover was not only somewhat bitter about his fate but also deeply concerned that Roosevelt would take the nation in a dangerous direction. A brief and temporary upturn in the economy during the latter months of 1932 convinced the outgoing president that his policies were working. He blamed Roosevelt, with some legitimacy, for scaring business with vague references to economic planning and deliberate inflation. Hoover feared that these hints of future socialism would destroy his efforts to encourage a business recovery.

Nonetheless Hoover tried to enlist Roosevelt's help in a cooperative effort to deal with the difficulties that were arising in the early weeks of 1933. For any new effort to gain acceptance, it must have the approval of the popular president-elect. Roosevelt, however, avoided placing his favor on any of Hoover's programs for fear that the people would transfer the blame for failures to him. Roosevelt wanted to start his job without any ties to the unpopular moves of the outgoing administration. This position was wise, politically, for Roosevelt, but it was disastrous for the nation during those intervening weeks. Despite the efforts of the Reconstruction Finance Corporation and other Hoover initiatives, a terrible **banking crisis** began to sweep the country. The nation's banking system was on the brink of total collapse. Depositors across the land were rushing to their banks to withdraw their money before it was too late, but that panic only hastened the failure of many of these institutions and jeopardized the savings of other depositors. Roosevelt continued to refuse cooperation, leaving Hoover unable to act. As the hours passed before Roosevelt's inauguration, the nation seemed to be slipping into economic chaos.

Section Review

1. Why did Hoover call the economic decline a "depression"?
2. What two steps did Hoover take almost immediately to combat the oncoming depression with federal action?
3. What kind of assistance to the poor did Hoover favor in place of a dole?
4. What episode involving World War I veterans in Washington, D.C., became a problem to the Hoover administration?
5. Who were the two major party candidates for the presidency in 1932?

FDR gleams and Hoover glowers in this New Yorker *caricature celebrating Roosevelt's inauguration.*

FDR and the New Deal

The drama of the banking crisis provided an emotional backdrop to the inauguration of the new president. The sense of imminent danger made Roosevelt appear as a knight in shining armor rushing in to save a nation in distress. Radiating confidence, he quickly calmed apprehensions with a terse statement in his inaugural address: "First of all, let me assert my firm belief that the only thing we have to fear is fear itself."

Fighting Fear

Immediately after assuming office, Roosevelt began to set government in motion once again. His first two actions were to call Congress into a special session and to declare a **"bank holiday."** Because Congress, according to the Constitution, was not due to convene until December, the new president needed to call an immediate meeting to deal with the emergency and begin the implementation of his proposals. The banking crisis had brought the financial markets of the nation to a virtual standstill. By March 4, the day of his inauguration, thirty-eight states had closed their banks, and elsewhere the institutions were operating on a restricted basis. The collapse would be devastating if order and confidence were not restored. Therefore, Roosevelt called for a four-day closing of all banks in order to calm the fears of a jittery public. The banks that proved that they were basically sound were allowed to reopen (and all but five per cent did eventually). This action renewed the people's confidence in banks and greatly reduced panic withdrawals.

The First Hundred Days—Congress convened on March 9 and remained in their emergency session until June 16. In those crucial one hundred days Roosevelt's New Deal programs began to pass, one after another. The support that the president had won in the election, along with the many newly elected Democratic congressmen, guaranteed a smooth passage for most New Deal legislation. Rarely has a president enjoyed such cooperation in accomplishing his agenda. And all the while the nation watched in approval of the quick action. "The whole country is with him," commented the popular humorist Will Rogers. "Just so he does something. If he burned down the Capitol, we would cheer and say, 'Well, we at least got a fire started anyhow.' "

Besides his cabinet members (which included the first woman, Secretary of Labor Frances Perkins), Roosevelt had collected a group of advisers to help him formulate his plans for combating the depression. This group, called the **"Brain Trust,"** was composed mostly of professors from Columbia and other universities who could offer ideas, many of them shaped by socialistic thinking, on economic policies and legislation. Roosevelt used some of these ideas to frame his legislative agenda.

On the first day of the emergency session, Congress approved the Emergency Banking Act, a measure that endorsed Roosevelt's bank holiday and authorized measures to deal with an impending currency shortage due to the bank closures and hoarding. That action was followed by a dozen more significant pieces of New Deal legislation in the days that followed. Among other things, these laws took the nation off the gold standard, established a Civilian Conservation Corps, provided nearly $4 billion in federal relief, created the Agricultural Adjustment Administration to deal with farm problems, legalized beer (a measure followed shortly by the national repeal of prohibition), provided insurance for bank deposits, established regulations for the financial activities of Wall Street, provided for the refinancing of home mortgages, attempted to provide some regulation for the nation's industries, and approved the Tennessee Valley Authority.

To keep the nation informed and inspired, Roosevelt used the radio. His frequent **"fireside chats,"** beginning on March 7, became a useful means of inspiring confidence and keeping public approval for the New Deal. About half of all American families owned radios in 1933, and many of those that did not made their way to the homes of neighbors or local businesses to hear the president's messages. His personal charm and fatherly manner carried over the airwaves to persuade Americans that they could trust him to make the government work for their benefit.

ABCs of the New Deal—New Deal legislation created a vast array of programs and agencies that often came to be known by their initials. The nation's conversations were soon filled with talk of the CCC, the AAA, the NRA, and the TVA. Former Democratic presidential candidate Al Smith said of these labels, "It looks as if one of the absent-minded professors had played anagrams with the alphabet soup." The goal of Roosevelt's New Deal involved "three Rs"–not "reading, writing, and 'rithmetic" but *relief, recovery,* and *reform.* Because these New Deal efforts played a major role in broadening the activities and authority of the federal government during the Roosevelt administration, a brief survey of some of the most important programs is warranted.

Providing work relief to furnish income to the millions of needy unemployed was a responsibility that several new agencies assumed. One was the

Franklin Roosevelt holds a fireside chat over radio with America in 1934.

Civilian Conservation Corps (CCC). The CCC put young, unmarried men to work in reforestation and soil conservation projects under the supervision of the army, and it proved to be one of the most popular New Deal agencies, lasting until after American entry into World War II. Another provider of work relief was the **Public Works Administration (PWA),** which during its six years of existence built school buildings, courthouses, hospitals, bridges, and other public facilities all over the country. The PWA also built ships and planes for the nation's military. In a similar vein the short-lived Civil Works Administration (CWA) put the jobless to work building roads, playgrounds, and airports. It also supported teachers, artists, and writers in public enrichment activities. The Federal Emergency Relief Administration (FERA) carried on some CWA projects and created others. All of these programs, however, were not able to provide enough jobs to eliminate the dole. Therefore, one other major program, the **Works Progress Administration (WPA),** was created in 1935 in an attempt to finally eliminate the despised relief doles. The WPA employed almost anyone in almost any kind of job. It constructed public buildings and recreational areas; supported actors, directors, writers, and artists in programs for the arts; and manufactured a wide variety of other jobs. Yet, even this vast effort, it alone costing almost $5 billion, was not enough to eradicate widespread unemployment.

The New Deal launched two major measures to attack the widespread problems in American agriculture and industry. The **Agricultural Adjustment Act (AAA)** and its supplements established a new method of subsidizing farm products and aided debt-ridden farmers in danger of losing their farms to foreclosure. To reduce the huge surpluses expected in the 1933 harvest, the AAA offered benefit payments to farmers who plowed up cotton and slaughtered pigs. That policy, however, was contemptible to a nation in which thousands of children wore rags and remained undernourished, and it brought rampant criticism of the entire program. The **National Industrial Recovery Act (NIRA)** attempted to organize voluntary guidelines for industries to increase employment, maintain wages, and reduce unwanted competition. Businesses that complied with the devised codes were allowed to display the blue eagle symbol of the **National Recovery Administration (NRA),** the agency designed to carry out the activities prescribed by the NIRA. This unsuccessful government attempt at industrial planning also met opposition and ultimate elimination along with the AAA.

One more large group of New Deal programs was intended to provide security, improved conditions, or other benefits for large groups of Americans. A banking act led to the formation of the **Federal Deposit Insurance Corporation (FDIC),** an agency devised to insure the bank deposits of millions of Americans against loss. The **Tennessee Valley Authority (TVA)** undertook an extensive project to build dams along the Tennessee River that would provide flood control and cheap electricity for the valley residents. Congress passed the **Social Security Act** in 1935, instituting old-age pensions and unemployment insurance for American

workers. Another program was the Rural Electrification Administration (REA), which offered funds to farmer cooperatives for extending electricity to the many rural areas still lacking that utility.

Roadblocks and Pitfalls

Roosevelt's extensive New Deal activities sought to meet the nation's demand for change. He had stated during his 1932 campaign that

> the country needs and, unless I mistake its temper, the country demands bold, persistent experimentation. It is common sense to take a method and try it: If it fails, admit it frankly and try another. But above all, try something.

Because he was taking action, he received widespread praise from many Americans, especially the poor, regardless of whether their lives were improved. One woman wrote Roosevelt in 1935 to tell him of the undernourishment of her children, but she did not neglect to add, ''you are the best president we ever had.'' Such praise for FDR was not uncommon, but then neither was criticism.

Opposition from the Right—People on the political right of Roosevelt, including most Republicans and a few Democrats, found much in the New Deal to criticize. First of all was its great expense. The government was spending billions of dollars to support the various programs, sending the nation into heavy debt in the process. Also, many of the programs were taking the nation into greater and greater government regulation of American businesses, a tendency that looked suspiciously socialistic. For instance, the NRA was a significant step toward the nationalization of industry, and the TVA was simply government ownership and control of a large electricity-producing industry. And finally, the New Deal was not bringing recovery. American businesses were still in the doldrums, and millions of people were still unemployed.

Roosevelt's opponents found cause for rejoicing in 1935 when the Supreme Court, still dominated by conservative Republican appointees, began to reject some New Deal legislation. Until that time the Court had not found occasion to strike down popular measures, especially in light of the ''national emergency.'' But after two years of compliance,

The Struggles of the Sharecropper

"We seem to move around in circles like the mule that pulls that syrup mill. We are never still, but we never get anywhere. For twenty-three long years we have begun each year with nothing and when we settled in November we had the same," a sharecropper's wife told an interviewer in the 1930s. That system she described began after the devastation of the Civil War when large land owners needed laborers but did not have money for wages. Poor whites and blacks with no money to buy land, tools, or supplies needed work. Sharecropping provided a solution. The farmer paid the landowner with a share of the income from the crop as rent; most sharecroppers did well if they just broke even. Annual income at best would be a few hundred dollars. If the farmer provided his own tools and supplies, he could keep as much as two-thirds of the income. Since sharecroppers had little cash, they had to borrow, often at high interest rates, to pay for mules, fertilizer, and seed. Typically at the end of the year after "settling up" with the merchant and landlord, the sharecropper continued in debt. "It was like slavery," the son of a sharecropper recalled. "You could leave. That was the only difference." In fact many sharecroppers did just that, moving from farm to farm in search of a better life for their families.

Three Virginia sharecroppers gather for a Sunday afternoon photograph in 1938.

By the 1930s sharecropping was pervasive: one out of two southern farmers did not own the land he farmed. Already poor, the farmer suffered more during the Great Depression. The New Deal brought some assistance through relief programs. The farmer might get a WPA construction job and perhaps the wife a WPA sewing job, while the sons might enroll in the CCC. The Rural Electrification Administration brought electricity for lights, radios, and appliances that improved the quality of life in the backcountry. New Deal farm policy with the AAA, while it improved prices for their crops, drove thousands of sharecroppers off the land. Government policy that called for less production meant fewer farmers were needed. That along with mechanization forced many sharecroppers to move yet again in search of work.

it began to question certain New Deal actions and even to strike down some minor pieces of legislation. Then, on May 27, 1935, the court declared the National Industrial Recovery Act unconstitutional in a unanimous decision. Roosevelt denounced the decision, but his NRA was doomed. Early in 1936 the Supreme Court, in a 6-3 decision, struck down the Agricultural Adjustment Act. Clearly this phase of the New Deal was losing its momentum.

Opposition from the Left—Besides those who thought the president was doing too much, there were others who complained that he was not taking enough decisive action. Three different men gained wide followings for advocating bolder governmental moves to combat the depression. One was Senator **Huey Long,** a former governor of Louisiana. His "Share Our Wealth" scheme proposed that the government impose heavy taxes on the rich and then redistribute that wealth to the poor. The idea was alarming, not to mention impractical, but it became popular among the uneducated poor who thought that they could get rich quick. Long appeared to be stealing some support from Roosevelt in advance of the 1936 election, but the rise of the Louisiana "Kingfish" ended suddenly with his assassination in September 1935.

Another popular plan, especially among older Americans, was that espoused by Dr. **Francis Townsend.** He proposed that the government pay a pension of $200 every month to each citizen over sixty, provided that they agree to hold no job and to spend every penny they received. This pension would be financed, supposedly, by a two per cent national sales tax. Thousands joined Townsend clubs, and many began to buy merchandise on credit in expectation of receiving the monthly checks. The plan's supporters, however, failed to recognize that it would simply rob younger Americans of their purchasing power to give that power to the elderly.

One other challenger who promoted his own brand of government action during the 1930s was Reverend **Charles Coughlin,** a Roman Catholic priest from Royal Oak, Michigan. Coughlin turned his weekly radio program of religious sermons into a national political broadcast. By 1934 the eloquent Father Coughlin was telling his huge radio audience that the nation needed to abandon the ''pagan god of gold'' and coin large amounts of silver (thereby inflating the money supply). He also began to propose that capitalism be replaced with his own system of ''social justice.'' Coughlin allied with Townsend briefly in 1936 to help support a third-party candidate for the presidency. The effort died, however, as the radio priest became increasingly violent in his verbal attacks against President Roosevelt and began to praise fascism.

Although this radical opposition to the New Deal was ultimately unsuccessful, the wide popularity evoked by these socialistic schemes certainly posed a threat to America's economic foundations. The New Deal, in comparison, was definitely the lesser of the evils.

Elusive Recovery

Despite the criticisms Roosevelt met during his first term in office, his popularity remained widespread. Millions of Americans had received some aid through the CCC, the PWA, and other programs, making these people as grateful to Roosevelt as they had been bitter toward Hoover. On the surface, economic conditions seemed to be improving, insuring the New Deal of some credit in the upcoming election.

1936 Election—In 1936 the Republicans had only one viable candidate to offer in the race against Roosevelt, **Alf Landon.** As one of only seven current Republican governors and the only one to have won re-election in 1934, Landon was the ''most available'' man. Also, being from Kansas, he was free of the image of Wall Street and big business, an image that had plagued the Republican party since the depression began. Although Landon had a progressive record and supported much of the New Deal, Republicans hoped that he would be ''the Kansas Coolidge,'' bringing a return of business prosperity to the nation. Unfortunately for Landon, the big business interests launched a major effort to elect the Kansas governor, thereby linking him with this unpopular segment of society after all. Roosevelt jumped at the chance to lash out at the forces of ''organized money,'' thereby solidifying his support from the poorer classes.

Nevertheless, Landon maintained hopes of winning the election when a poll conducted by the *Literary Digest* predicted a decisive Republican victory. This straw vote, however, was based on replies from people with telephone listings and automobile registrations, thereby overlooking the preferences of the poor entirely because they lacked those luxuries. On election day the votes of the poor were not overlooked, and Roosevelt won by a landslide. Landon won only two states, Maine and Vermont, and only 8 electoral votes to Roosevelt's 523. Republicans were able to salvage only a few seats in the Senate and House of Representatives, and the future of their party was in doubt, while the Democrats and their leader, Franklin D. Roosevelt, were clearly in control of the nation's political machine.

''A Switch in Time Saves Nine''—Roosevelt believed that his overwhelming victory had given him a clear mandate to carry on with his New Deal. The decisions of the Supreme Court in 1935 and 1936 declaring various New Deal measures unconstitutional, however, disturbed the president greatly. At first he thought about a constitutional amendment to protect New Deal legislation but dismissed the strategy because it could be defeated easily and

would take too long. On February 5, 1937, he announced instead a plan to enlarge the court. For every justice over seventy who did not retire, he wanted the right to appoint an additional justice up to a maximum of six. Roosevelt argued that the new members would make the court more efficient.

The president's proposal generated a storm of opposition from many quarters and for many reasons. Many attacked the plan because it threatened the American tradition of an independent judiciary. Conservatives argued that efficiency was not the issue, since more justices would actually delay Court proceedings. Rather Roosevelt, they pointed out, wanted to "pack the court" with liberal New Dealers. Politicians who before had not dared oppose Roosevelt publicly because of his popularity spoke out against the **court-packing plan** because they sensed the public was on their side.

Because of the extensive opposition to the plan, court reform failed to win approval even in the Democratic-controlled Congress, but Roosevelt won the "war." One of the justices announced his retirement from the court, and this gave the president the opportunity to replace him with a liberal appointee. Meanwhile another justice left the conservative bloc on the court and voted with a new majority that approved New Deal programs in several decisions. Newspapers characterized it as a "switch in time saves nine." Roosevelt eventually had the opportunity to nominate several members

of the Supreme Court. By 1940 five out of the nine justices were his appointees. In the end, however, Roosevelt did pay a price. The fight over the court divided his party and strengthened the enemies of the New Deal.

No Way Out—Despite his impressive victory in the 1936 election, Roosevelt still faced major problems. Four years after he took office and initiated his myriad of New Deal programs, the nation was still beleaguered by a severe economic depression. When Roosevelt took his oath of office again in 1937 he saw "one-third of a nation ill-housed, ill-clad, ill-nourished." What is more, in that year the nation experienced a sharper economic decline than the one that had occurred following the stock market crash. Any gains that had been credited to the New Deal were washed away. The government was pumping billions of dollars into the economy and plunging the nation into debt only to find that recovery was as illusive as ever and millions of Americans were still in need. In addition, Roosevelt's aura of invincibility would soon be badly wounded during the court-packing episode.

To add to the other problems of the time, labor unions were gaining strength and using strikes to cripple big industries. **John L. Lewis,** president of the United Mine Workers, recognized that recent legislation had provided the opportunity to organize the workers in large industries. The American Federation of Labor (AFL) had limited its unions to skilled craftsmen, but millions of unskilled industrial workers suffering hardships wanted more from their jobs. As a result, Lewis organized the **Congress of Industrial Organizations (CIO)** to accommodate these workers, and the CIO broke off from the AFL in 1936. The CIO quickly made the headlines when its rubber industry workers at Firestone, Goodyear, and Goodrich plants in Akron, Ohio, staged a simultaneous sit-down strike. The workers simply sat down on the job, refusing both to work and to leave the factories until their point was made with the management. Two of the companies gave in to the worker demands, but Goodyear refused until a month-long strike forced it to concede.

The success of the CIO in Akron gave new hope to thousands of disgruntled workers and sent

ALL I SAID WAS GIMME SIX MORE JUSTICES!"

FDR's court-packing plan raised a storm of criticism, even from Democrats in Congress.

a shudder through the nation's employers. Later in 1936 the automobile industry began to feel the pressure of increased CIO membership among its workers. The CIO's ranks soon swelled to 400,000, and, with the increase, sit-down strikes multiplied as well. Violence was inevitable, and it came on Memorial Day 1937 when, in response to a barrage of rocks and sticks, police killed ten striking workers at the Republic Steel mill in South Chicago. Besides their dismay at the violence, middle-class Americans were alarmed by the sit-down tactic which endangered private property rights. (The strikers frequently abused, destroyed, or pilfered company property while they occupied their work places.) Finally, the Supreme Court outlawed the sit-down strike in 1939. This decision eliminated the CIO's most effective weapon, but the union remained powerful, eventually reuniting with the AFL to become the AFL-CIO.

Many domestic problems plagued the United States during the later years of the depression. However, the focus would soon shift to foreign concerns. The unemployment, poverty, and despair of the depression would ultimately give way to the excitement and activities of World War II. Only in the build-up of a new war machine were American industries finally rejuvenated and the economy sent on an upward course. The New Deal did not rescue the nation from the depression, but it did install the framework for a burgeoning federal bureaucracy.

Section Review

1. What were the first two actions that Roosevelt took after his inauguration to deal with the depression?
2. What was the name for Roosevelt's radio talks used to inspire confidence and approval for his New Deal measures?
3. What was the common purpose of the CCC, the PWA, and the WPA?
4. What New Deal program involved the government in the ownership and control of a large electricity-producing industry?
5. How did Roosevelt attempt to make the Supreme Court support the New Deal?

Worst of Times, Best of Times

The 1930s was a bewildering decade for Americans. They often did not understand the reasons for their plight, and they found it difficult to believe that there was a hope of something better tomorrow. Too many dreams had been shattered when the crash and depression hurled financiers, factory workers, and farmers alike into unemployment, bankruptcy, and desperation. Yet in the midst of the depression, life went on in the nation and the people found ways to cope and even to laugh in the face of difficulty.

Depths of Depression

The Hunger—Once the depression struck, almost anything that President Hoover said was used to mock him, especially when he told reporters, "Nobody is starving. The hoboes, for example, are better fed than they have ever been. One hobo in New York got ten meals in one day." Soon a flood of newspaper headlines appeared to refute the President on this point. Ninety-five cases of starvation were reported in New York City during 1931. This is probably an inflated figure because substantiated reports were few, but some starvation did occur. And malnutrition was commonplace among the poor. In 1932 the New York City Health Department declared that over twenty per cent of the city's public school children were suffering from malnutrition. Jobless men who happened to find work were sometimes too weak from hunger to handle their new responsibilities.

Private charities had maintained rescue missions and soup kitchens for the down and out in the past, but they were not prepared to give aid to the vast numbers now swelling the ranks of the unemployed. The federal funds given to states for relief were in part used to provide the needed extra provisions for the hungry. Soon **"bread lines"** formed along city streets as the desperate sought food in the soup kitchens. Local agencies were set up to provide some cash for relief to those who applied and met all of the strict guidelines of destitution. Even then, the sums given were hardly enough to feed a family, much less clothe and house them. A FERA representative in North Carolina reported that a good relief payment to help support a family of five totaled $5.25 per week. The amount was $2.39 in New York City. When New Jersey's relief funds ran out, that state decided to issue licenses for begging.

The Humiliation—Often it was the parents' concern for their children that finally brought the family to apply for relief, but that concern could not cover the sense of humiliation felt by the adults. Husbands and fathers who had trudged from business to business trying to find work blamed themselves for their inability to gain and hold a job. Wives struggled with their own cares, trying to keep the ragged clothes that their families wore from falling apart, and even searching for housecleaning jobs or other employment that might bring in some money.

Thousands of people wrote letters to President Roosevelt and his wife, telling them their trials and needs and asking for some help. A disabled man from Tennessee wrote, "My family is barfooted and naked and an suferns and we all are a goin to purish if I cannot get some help some way." Some women pleaded with Mrs. Roosevelt to send them clothing for their children or old clothes discarded by the first lady for themselves. Many of these petitioners added a final request, asking that their letters be kept private so that no one else would know of their disgrace.

Homelessness—About two million people were totally uprooted from their homes in the 1930s. A few of these had deliberately fled from the torment of watching their families suffer, but many were simply young, unmarried men and teen-age boys who had given up all hope of finding a job and settling down. They rode in or under boxcars on freight trains from place to place, eating in soup kitchens, sleeping in city parks or camping in hobo jungles, and perhaps dreaming that the next stop might hold promise for a job.

Besides the hoboes there were countless thousands of families facing the threat of homelessness. Some had mortgages on modest homes, but now without income they could not keep up their payments. Banks were seldom quick to foreclose, but many institutions eventually had to repossess the

An Okie mother and her children on a desperate road to California

houses. Others rented houses or apartments for which they now had no money to pay. Rent in those days was typically low (often around $10 to $12 per month), but even that was beyond the means of a family on relief. As renters were evicted and homes and farms foreclosed, thousands of families were left to scramble for a place to live. Some moved in with relatives; some built their own shack in a Hooverville; and some found other landlords with more patience.

Blacks—The hardships of the depression fell heavily on American blacks, even though hardships were not new to them. In 1932 about half of all black workers were unemployed, a rate of joblessness double that of the general population. Farm problems and government policies drove sharecroppers in the South off the land, continuing the migration of blacks from the South to the cities of the North and West that had begun with World War I. With unemployment wracking America's

The Dust Bowl

On April 15, 1935, Washington, D.C.'s *Evening Star* reported a story on the spreading drought that was devastating the southern Great Plains. "Three little words–achingly familiar on a Western farmer's tongue–rule life in the dust bowl of the continent–'If it rains.'" From that line in the newspaper came the name that denoted not only drought, but the anguish of a whole region's farm families: the **"Dust Bowl."**

In the opening decades of the twentieth century, farmers had poured into the Great Plains region. They had ploughed the tough prairie sod, sowed wheat, and met enough success to build a respectable life for themselves and their families. In the process they converted millions of acres from prairie grassland to fields of fertile, powdery soil. In the late 1920s abundant rains brought bountiful crops and temporary prosperity to the farmers. But soon came the depression with its fall of farm prices joined by a ruinous drought that began in 1932. For four years rainfall was rare, and the region's produce all but vanished. To add to the woes that the farmers were experiencing, the prairie winds began to pick up the powdery dust from the plains and carry it across the land. Billowing black clouds of dust sometimes engulfed the region, the dirt sifting through every crack in a farmer's house, piling in huge drifts against buildings and fences, obscuring sunlight, and nearly suffocating anyone who ventured outdoors. Even indoors the people often slept with wet cloths over their faces to keep from breathing the dust.

The Dust Bowl reached into Colorado and Kansas in the north and Texas and New Mexico in the south, but its most brutal effects were felt in Oklahoma. Some of the stricken farmers resorted to relief through WPA jobs and various agencies while they tried to reclaim their farms. Others gave up and moved away. Thousands of these "Okies" loaded their cars or trucks with all their possessions and headed west to California. There they sought jobs as migrant farm workers, harvesting various crops as they came in season. The uprooted farm families generally remained in poverty until the end of the depression, but the fields of the Far West offered more opportunity than the dust-choked lands of the Great Plains.

The hardships of the Dust Bowl drove many farmers off the land, and those that remained soon learned to adjust their farming methods to the needs of their arid land. Much acreage was returned to grassland and used as pasture for livestock, and soil conservation techniques prevailed on the remaining fields. These ongoing efforts continue to keep the dust of the plains settled in an attempt to avert any dreadful reappearance of the Dust Bowl.

idled cities, the North was hardly a promised land for jobless blacks.

Government relief efforts were slow to reach needy blacks. At first Roosevelt was reluctant to press for needed steps for fear of angering southern Democrats, and some aspects of his AAA and NRA were actually harmful to the interests of blacks. However, Roosevelt's wife, Eleanor, helped to turn attention to problems of discrimination by openly befriending black leaders. FDR then began to try to prohibit racial discrimination in some federal programs, beginning in 1935 with the WPA. The PWA also constructed a large share of its public housing projects for blacks. Although the immediate benefits of the New Deal were meager for blacks, subtle changes in governmental attitudes were opening a path for a more potent black civil rights movement in the future.

The most noticeable effect of Roosevelt's policies was the winning of black votes for the Democratic party. Blacks had voted strongly Republican ever since the Civil War, even for Herbert Hoover in 1932. But while Republicans offered no hope for efforts to relieve the problems of blacks, the actions of FDR and the Democrats at least seemed encouraging. In 1936 Roosevelt collected 76 per cent of the black vote, initiating a long-term political trend.

The Good Times

Although the 1930s witnessed a quarter or more of the population in want, there were eighty million Americans who did not experience great deprivations. While they may have experienced some hardships since the departure of the prosperous roaring twenties, they still had food on their tables, clothes on their backs, and a roof over their heads. For these Americans there were at least some good times in the midst of the depression.

Amusements—Americans often seemed to be intent on forgetting their troubles during the rough times. Many found escape from their cares in reading books such as Margaret Mitchell's epic Civil War novel, *Gone with the Wind,* which appeared in 1936 (and was turned into a popular movie in 1939). Hollywood produced over five thousand feature films of fantasy and drama, providing escape and entertainment for millions of Americans. Walt Disney's first full-length animated presentation, *Snow White*, debuted in 1938, and many new movie stars began to draw wide admiration–among them a little girl named Shirley Temple who became the darling of the nation.

Radio became the most popular means of home entertainment in America. Old and young alike laughed at the comedy of "Amos and Andy," swooned to the songs of crooner Bing Crosby, and thrilled to the adventures of the Lone Ranger. Children listened devotedly to the tales of Little Orphan Annie and cowboy hero Tom Mix. Clarinetist and band leader Benny Goodman introduced "swing music" in 1935, and soon a host of big bands were broadcasting jazzy orchestra numbers on popular radio programs. The radio created one of the most

dramatic and comic episodes of the 1930s when Orson Welles presented his version of H. G. Wells's *War of the Worlds,* a tale of a terrifying invasion from Mars, on a major network in 1938. Thousands of listeners tuned in to the program as it was in progress, unaware that the frightening account of a spaceship landing in New Jersey was only fiction. Radio stations and public officials hastened to quell the growing panic, but several days passed before emotions were entirely calmed.

Other Diversions–Real-life drama captured the nation's attention during the 1930s. One of the biggest headlines was the kidnapping of aviator hero Charles Lindbergh's infant son in 1932. All across the nation people were anxious to hear of any developments in the case, and they grieved when word finally came that the child had been found dead. The search for the murderer required

On May 6, 1937, the hydrogen-filled Hindenburg exploded mysteriously as it approached its mooring mast in Lakehurst, New Jersey, after a trans-Atlantic flight.

Comic Relief

During the depression, Americans wanted some escape, no matter how brief, from their pressing problems. Some sought relief through destructive means, such as alcohol. Most, however, found harmless diversion through popular entertainment. One source of drama, adventure, and comedy was as near as the daily newspaper–the comic strip.

Comic strips had been appearing in newspapers since the 1890s. The 1930s, however, proved to be a golden age of comics. Whether in the black-and-white strips found in the daily papers or in the four-color "funny papers" found in Sunday editions, comics provided millions of readers (children *and* adults) with an avenue into adventure.

One of the most popular strips was *Little Orphan Annie.* Annie, an orphan waif with open, pupilless eyes, and her dog Sandy overcame the challenges of the depression with pluck and courage. Adopted by a wealthy weapons manufacturer (aptly named Daddy Warbucks), Annie was a reflection of her creator's philosophy. Harold Gray, who began the strip in 1924, was a conservative Republican and dedicated opponent of FDR's New Deal. Through Annie and her friends, Gray espoused his views in favor of self-help through hard work. As Daddy Warbucks says in one early strip, "Annie doesn't need charity–Just give her an even break and she'll do the rest–Charity!!–BAH!"

The lawlessness of the 1920s and 1930s also gave birth to one of the toughest detectives comics have ever seen–Dick Tracy. Created by Chester Gould in 1931, *Dick Tracy* brought a realism to police comics never before seen. In the best "crime does not pay" tradition, villains in *Dick Tracy* often died realistically (and sometimes gruesomely). The police used the most advanced scientific methods of crime detection, such as "two-way wrist radios" (miniature walkie-talkies). Tracy's grotesque rogues' gallery of villains–such as Flattop, Pruneface, the Mole, and Mumbles–was an important part of the comic strip's appeal.

Those who wanted to escape the problems of the 1930s could travel by comic strip to exotic, faraway locales. *Tarzan* took the reader to "deepest, darkest Africa" with the adventures of Edgar Rice Burroughs's "Lord of the Jungle," or readers could follow the Stone Age exploits of *Alley Oop.* Those who really wanted to escape could try other planets with the science fiction strip *Flash Gordon* or the twenty-fifth-century adventures of *Buck Rogers.* The diversion might have been for only a few minutes a day, but comics became one small means of facing the depression with a smile.

over two years of intense detective work and ended in the conviction and execution of Bruno Hauptmann, a German immigrant.

Other crimes gained wide attention during the depression, particularly those of bank-robbing gangs. Although sometimes lauded as modern-day Robin Hoods, these desperate criminals were brutal. John Dillinger topped the ''most wanted list,'' but he was joined by desperados such as Pretty Boy Floyd, Machine Gun Kelly, and Baby Face Nelson, along with the couple-in-crime, Bonnie Parker and Clyde Barrow.

Amelia Earhart gave Americans a new flying hero as she became the first woman to cross the Atlantic in 1932. But in 1937, after nearly completing an adventurous round-the-world flight, the aviatrix disappeared somewhere in the Pacific. Hers was not the only air tragedy of the 1930s, however. Popular humorist Will Rogers perished in a crash while on a tour of Alaska. And the most dramatic of the 1930s air tragedies was the explosion and crash of the zeppelin *Hindenburg*. As the giant, blimplike craft approached its moorings in Lakehurst, New Jersey, in 1937, it suddenly burst into flames. A radio announcer watching the landing described the catastrophe for the nation with uncontrollable emotion:

> Oh, flames four or five hundred feet into the sky, it's a terrific crash, ladies and gentlemen, the smoke and the flames now and the crashing to the ground, not quite to the mooring, oh the humanity, and I told you, I can't even talk, mass of smoking wreckage, I can, I can hardly breathe!

Thirty-six of the airship's ninety-seven passengers perished.

Sports continued to attract many fans, and fads such as miniature golf and Chinese checkers gained momentary popularity. World's fairs also became a big attraction in the decade. Chicago hosted one on its lake shore in 1933, but it was surpassed by the spectacular **New York World's Fair.** From its opening in 1939 to its closing two years later, the New York fair attracted 45 million visitors to its 1,500 exhibits. People marveled at the technological innovations on display at this event christened ''The World of Tomorrow,'' and they delighted in the breathtaking carnival rides. One of the most popular attractions, General Motors' ''Futurama,'' carried fairgoers on a 15-minute tour of America in 1960. The 1939 prophets provided breathless audiences with a fast-lane future of 100 m.p.h. highways traveled by Americans in radio-controlled, rain drop–shaped cars, enjoying their two months of vacation each year. And in retrospect, the seers provided a good example of man's inability to predict the future.

New Decade Dawning—For America emerging out of the depression, the ''world of tomorrow'' would be as fast-paced as the fair prophets predicted, but it would be no carnival. Even as the 1939 audiences marveled at future prospects of peace and prosperity, undercurrents of war were roiling the world's already troubled waters. Soon the tides of war would reach America's shore.

War would shake the nation's lethargic economy in ways that FDR had only dreamed of, turning bread lines into assembly lines and forging a new role of world leadership in the decade to come.

Section Review
1. In what way did American blacks change their voting patterns during the depression?
2. What famous kidnapping case captured national attention in the 1930s?
3. What was the most popular means of home entertainment during the depression?

Chapter Review

Terms

Great Depression
public works
work relief
Reconstruction Finance Corporation (RFC)
Hawley-Smoot tariff
Bonus Army
Franklin Delano Roosevelt
New Deal
banking crisis
bank holiday
Brain Trust
fireside chats
Civilian Conservation Corps (CCC)
Public Works Administration (PWA)
Works Progress Administration (WPA)
Agricultural Adjustment Act (AAA)
National Industrial Recovery Act (NIRA)
National Recovery Administration (NRA)
Federal Deposit Insurance Corporation (FDIC)
Tennessee Valley Authority (TVA)
Social Security Act
Huey Long
Francis Townsend
Charles Coughlin
Alf Landon
court-packing plan
John L. Lewis
Congress of Industrial Organizations (CIO)
bread lines
Dust Bowl
New York World's Fair

Content Questions

1. Why was Hoover blamed for the depression?
2. What was the result of Hoover's attempt to use voluntary cooperation in efforts to deal with the depression?
3. What American governmental action in 1930 probably precipitated a European economic collapse in 1931 by dealing a harmful blow to world trade?
4. Why was Hoover unable to take action against the crises of the depression in the final months of his administration?
5. What problematic situation arose to heighten economic tensions in the final days before Roosevelt's inauguration?
6. How did Roosevelt calm the banking crisis?
7. What two major pieces of New Deal legislation were struck down by the Supreme Court?
8. Name three demagogic leaders who denounced Roosevelt's New Deal for not doing enough to combat the depression's problems.
9. What proposal made by President Roosevelt following the 1936 election alarmed many Democrats as well as Republicans?
10. What tactic did the CIO introduce to gain concessions for workers from industries?

Application Questions

1. Why could it be said that Hoover instigated a wider governmental role in the nation's economy and that Roosevelt merely expanded on what Hoover had begun?
2. How did the defeat of the court-packing plan serve to preserve the integrity and power of the Supreme Court?
3. In what ways was the increased role of government in American life that resulted from the New Deal beneficial to the nation? In what ways was it harmful?

U.S. torpedo bombers (Grumman TBF-1 Avengers) on a mission over the Pacific during the Second World War

It's a long one down to around the three-yard line. . . .

The radio announcer's voice crackled across the airwaves. The New York Giants, the champs of the National Football League's eastern division, were getting a surprise beating from the Brooklyn Dodgers at the Polo Grounds in New York. . . .

Ward Cuff takes it . . .
Coming up to his left . . . he's over the 10 . . .
Nice block by Leemans! Cuff still going . . .

Listeners across the country edged up in their seats.

He's up to the 25 . . .
And now he's hit and hit hard about the 27-yard line!

Bruiser Kinard made the tack—

We interrupt this broadcast to bring you this important bulletin from the United Press:
FLASH Washington:
The White House announces Japanese attack on Pearl Harbor. . . .

The announcement on that Sunday afternoon of December 7, 1941, did more than interrupt a football game; it shattered America's uneasy peace. The nation now plunged into the largest, costliest war in history. Isolation was over; the heroic effort to liberate the Pacific from the Japanese warlords and Europe from the Nazi war machine was underway. The global conflict changed the face of the world for the rest of the century and gave America a superpower role in that new world.

A Time of Tyrants

Clouds on the Horizon

Germany: Adolf Hitler—In 1923 a German war veteran, who sought to satisfy his hunger for revenge with radical politics, attempted to overthrow the Bavarian government in Munich. The failed coup landed **Adolf Hitler** in jail, which gave him time to seethe and write his personal memoir of hate, *Mein Kampf* ("My Struggle"). In a ranting, rambling style, Hitler set forth his ideas for a new German order. He advocated scrapping the League of Nations, ridding Germany of the "weakening" influence of democracy, uniting all Germans, and eliminating all Communists and Jews. After his release he began to preach his doctrines to growing audiences of all classes. Hitler and his National Socialist German Workers' Party, or *Nazi* party, came to power in Germany in 1933. Just ten years after his failed coup, Hitler was elected chancellor of Germany. Yet for him it was no democratic office. Hitler used his new power to crush all opposition and establish himself as the *Führer* (FYOOR ur). He described the Nazi regime as the "Third Reich," a German empire that would last a thousand years.

In foreign affairs Hitler moved cautiously while he consolidated his power. Gradually he forged a police state of blind nationalism, anti-Semitism, and totalitarianism unique in history. For years, in violation of the Versailles agreements, the German navy, army, and air force were secretly rebuilt. This war machine employed all of the latest technological improvements and would prove to be a fearful instrument in Hitler's grasping hands.

Italy: Benito Mussolini—Nazism was the German version of a growing force during the 1920s and 1930s known as **fascism.** Fascism, first established as a governing force in Italy in 1922 under **Benito Mussolini,** was a nationalistic, militaristic, totalitarian mass movement that often profited from the discontent spawned by hard times. The jut-jawed Mussolini promised the Roman masses gathered at his feet that he would restore the glory of Caesar's empire. His black-shirted followers pronounced him *Il Duce* (DOO chay), the leader; and

The face of tyranny, Adolf Hitler with his storm trooper chief, Ernst Röhm. Shortly after this photograph was taken, Hitler had Röhm executed in order to further consolidate his power within Nazi Germany.

together they crushed all visible opposition.

If Italy were to have power and prestige in the world, Mussolini reasoned, the country would have to acquire foreign territories and markets. In search of easy prey, Mussolini moved against the backward but resource-rich African nation of Ethiopia in 1935. Ethiopian tribesmen bravely but vainly fought machine guns and tanks with swords and stones. Mussolini quickly conquered and annexed Ethiopia. When the League of Nations in Geneva tried to condemn Italy by voting sanctions and shutting off military supplies, the Italian representatives simply walked out. Soon Italy initiated an alliance with its Fascist friends to the north, the Nazis.

Japan: Hideki Tojo—A new threat also arose to the east. The Japanese, who had come late to the scene of industrialism and world trade, found that many trade barriers had already been established by European nations that had carved out their "spheres of influence" in the East during the late nineteenth century. With growing militarism the Japanese sought to carve out their own spheres through direct conquest, making their first show of force by subjugating Manchuria, a province of China, in 1931. In 1937 the expanding Japanese empire launched a full-scale war against the nation of China, a war that would not end until 1945. Later, under the guidance of the cruel **Hideki Tojo,** the "warlords" were able to take complete control of the Japanese government.

With the distraction of the Great Depression at home, the United States took little action to check Japanese aggression. In 1934 Japan cancelled the Washington Naval Treaty, and relations with Japan continued to deteriorate during Roosevelt's first term. Encountering no real opposition from America or the other world powers, Japan continued to lay plans for greater gain, ever nursing its hatred for its chief rival in the Pacific—the United States. In 1940 Japan joined Italy and Germany to form the Rome-Berlin-Tokyo **Axis,** an alliance of dictator states.

Soviet Union: Joseph Stalin—The Bolshevik Revolution and the subsequent consolidation of Communist power in Russia are among the bloodiest chapters in human history. Directing this systematic terror and bloodshed throughout much of the 1920s and 1930s was one of the greatest tyrants of the times—**Joseph Stalin.**

By 1924, after taking the reins of power from the ailing Vladimir Lenin, leader of the Communist revolution, Stalin moved to crush all opposition, both within and without the Communist party. Beginning in 1928, for example, Stalin ordered the destruction of all resistance to his agricultural "reforms," or collectivization (basically the government's seizure of all private land and crops). The result was the killing of at least ten million men, women, and children, with another ten million dying in Siberian slave-labor camps. Throughout the 1930s Stalin continued to push Russia into the industrial age and fortify his own power with a chilling callousness perhaps best summed up by Stalin himself: "A single death is a tragedy; a million deaths is a statistic." By the late 1930s Stalin would find a kindred spirit in the leader of the growing, aggressive German reich.

The Coming of War

Hitler was not a skilled diplomat nor, as later blunders would underscore, was he a military genius. He was, however, a master politician who could size up other leaders, predict their responses, and outmaneuver them. Despite Hitler's open violations of the Treaty of Versailles and the growing threat he represented to European security, the rest of Europe allowed Hitler to make numerous territorial gains without going to war. He assured other nations that he was interested only in consolidating German territory that had been fragmented by the Treaty of Versailles—simply re-establishing German control over German areas "stolen" by the victors in World War I.

Easy Acquisitions—Meanwhile the western alliance stood by with folded arms, practicing a policy of **appeasement** toward Hitler, trying to satisfy the dictator by giving in to his stated demands. Appeasement, however, was a weak and wishful response to Nazi aggression and succeeded only in whetting Hitler's appetite for more territory.

In March 1936 German troops moved into the **Rhineland,** an industrial region of Germany near Alsace-Lorraine that under the terms of the Versailles Treaty was to remain demilitarized. The League of Nations of course filed all the necessary paperwork of protest against Hitler's government, but favorable world opinion was hardly a priority with the Nazis. The Germans then began building the Siegfried Line, a series of fortifications built along the German bank of the Rhine River from the Swiss border to the North Sea. This construction, claimed Hitler, was in response to the Maginot (mah zhee NOH) Line, a similar French fortification on the west side of the river. Except for Winston Churchill's, a lone voice in the British Parliament, few protests were raised.

Hitler's next aggression was against Austria. The German dictator had long dreamed of union, or *Anschluss* (AHN schl*oo*s), with Austria, a German-speaking land and Hitler's birthplace. Despite explicit opposition to such unification in the World War I peace treaties, in 1938 Hitler incited Austrian Nazis to stage a coup, and then the Austrians "invited" German Nazis to join them. Hitler naturally accepted the invitation, since the British and French lacked the will to stop him.

Munich—Czechoslovakia was next on Hitler's menu. The Führer declared that Germany had a right to annex the **Sudetenland** (soo DATE un LAND), a predominantly German area in western Czechoslovakia. Actually, at least a quarter million Sudeten Germans had fled there from Hitler's tyranny. The Czech leadership appealed to the British and French to protect them from this act of naked aggression. Unfortunately, for the Czechs, the appeasers were in power.

England's Prime Minister Neville Chamberlain and France's Premier Edouard Daladier agreed to meet with Hitler in Munich, Germany, in September 1938. Hitler was determined to get his way at the conference, even if it meant going to war. To "preservé the peace," Chamberlain and Daladier agreed to "give" Hitler the Sudetenland–and nothing more. Hitler, managing to keep a straight face, promised, "This is the last territorial claim I have to make in Europe." Believing him to be a man of his word, Chamberlain returned to England proclaiming "peace for our time."

"Munich" became an adjective for appeasement and defeatism. Churchill observed bitterly, "The German dictator, instead of snatching his victuals from the table, has been content to have them served to him course by course." In March 1939 Hitler took another bite–the rest of Czechoslovakia. Public outrage over Hitler's betrayal of his promise forced the British and French leadership to sign security agreements with Romania and Poland in hopes of ringing in Hitler.

Tyrants Prey—If Hitler were to continue his expansion eastward, he would have to calm Soviet fears. Throughout the spring and summer of 1939 Hitler sought a nonaggression treaty with Stalin. Politically Hitler and Stalin were on different ends of the spectrum or perhaps more accurately different sides of the same coin, for both tyrants understood power. Hitler secretly offered Stalin a free hand to take the Baltic countries of Lithuania, Latvia, and Estonia as well as Finland and a slice of eastern Poland. In exchange Hitler wanted a free hand for the Germans to invade Poland from the west. Stalin agreed to the deal. The pact was based on no mutual trust, but like vultures feeding on a carcass, the tyrants' mouths were too full of flesh to be concerned with devouring each other.

On August 23, 1939, the surprising announcement of the **Nazi-Soviet nonaggression pact** was published. Hitler lost little time taking advantage of its secret clauses. Munich had emboldened the Führer to ignore British and French threats to intervene. On **September 1, 1939,** fifty-six German divisions rolled across the Polish border, while sixteen hundred *Luftwaffe* aircraft bombed and strafed military and civilian targets. The swift assault coined a new word: *blitzkrieg,* "lightning war." Forty-eight hours after the assault began, the brave Polish defenders had suffered 100,000 casualties. By the end of September, Hitler's conquest was complete. By war's end, between the Germans and Russians, six million Poles would be killed, half of them Jews.

On September 3 Chamberlain reluctantly acknowledged his commitment to Poland and declared war on Nazi Germany. With equal dread and even more foot-dragging, France followed Britain. While these hesitant Allies tried to do as little as they could, the initiative was left with Hitler.

German Victories

Denmark and Norway—In the spring of 1940, Hitler began his biggest push to date. The true meaning of the word *blitzkreig* became apparent in April, when powerful German armored divisions, or panzers, superbly assisted by fighters, bombers, and paratroopers, occupied neutral Denmark in a matter of hours. That same day Germany attacked neutral Norway to gain naval bases and access to iron-rich Sweden. Norway became the scene of fierce resistance, however. The fighting lasted sixty-two days before the Norwegians were betrayed. German destroyers sailed under land-based guns that could have sent them to the bottom. The guns, though, had been rendered useless by sabotage, because of a prominent Norwegian political official named Vidkun Quisling. Quisling had assisted German agents for months prior to the invasion and then became a puppet governor during the occupation of his land as the reward for his treason. Quisling's name added a new loathsome synonym for *traitor* to the vocabulary. Through the acquisition of Denmark and Norway, the Third Reich had secured its northern border in preparation for future conquests. The securing of the southern was next.

Fall of France—On May 10 Germany launched a coordinated attack on the countries on her western border from southern France to the North Sea. Against the overwhelming German force, resistance in the Low Countries was short-lived. Luxembourg fell after two days; Holland lasted five; Belgium was forced to surrender in eighteen.

In June 1940 the French army, reinforced by the British, found itself outflanked and penetrated by swift armored units. The *Luftwaffe* destroyed French fortifications far ahead of German armored divisions and infantry; millions of refugees scattered, trying to escape their doomed cities. German *Stuka* dive-bombers dominated the air. These new weapons and tactics were a total departure from the trench warfare of World War I. For the French, who relied on the old methods of the last war, *blitzkrieg* was disastrous.

The German forces surrounded the British and French forces, driving them northward to the French port of **Dunkirk** on the English Channel. Before the Germans could move to annihilate the Allied army, a dense fog rolled in over the Channel for several days, grounding the *Luftwaffe*. Shortly before, Hitler had ordered his land armies to hold back so that the *Luftwaffe* could receive the glory for destroying the enemy. Communication failed, and the army continued to hold back even though the air force was grounded by bad weather. The usually efficient Nazi forces ground to a halt. The Allies, encouraged by what was apparently divine intervention on their behalf, moved to rescue their men. Using fishing boats, yachts, and almost anything else that would float, British citizens crossed the English Channel to deliver some 330,000 men. The twenty-two-mile-wide Channel was soon filled with craft bringing out France's defeated defenders.

With the British gone, the French reserves gone, and Paris abandoned by the government, France accepted the inevitable. In the same railroad car in which the Germans had signed the humiliating armistice terms in 1918, France accepted the German terms of surrender on June 22, 1940, before an audience of grinning Nazis, crowing over their long-awaited revenge.

The fall of France stunned the world and left Britain on the brink of destruction. At that dark hour one of England's greatest leaders came to power—**Winston Churchill.** The new prime minister inspired the beleaguered Britons with his grand defiance and fighting spirit.

> I have nothing to offer but blood, toil, tears, and sweat. . . . You ask, what is our policy? I will say: It is to wage war, by sea, land, and air, with all our might and with all the strength God can give us. . . . You ask, what is our aim? I can answer in one word: It is Victory.

Britain Alone—Britain now faced the Nazi menace alone. Hitler decided to bomb the island into submission, hoping to "soften" it up before landing troops. Throughout the late summer and fall of 1940, the great **Battle of Britain** took place in the skies above southern England and the Channel. Bombing during the daylight hours became too expensive for the *Luftwaffe*. The Germans lost three

London in the blitz. St. Paul's Cathedral stands in majestic defiance in this famous wartime photograph.

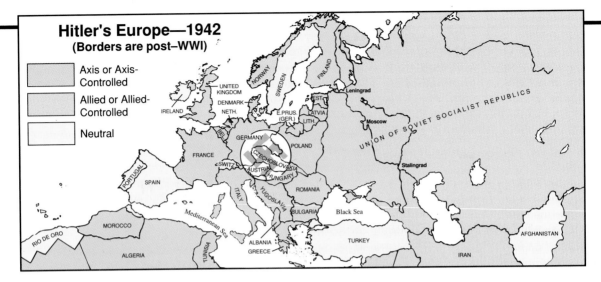

Hitler's Europe—1942
(Borders are post–WWI)

- Axis or Axis-Controlled
- Allied or Allied-Controlled
- Neutral

times as many planes as the British, and many more pilots; the British pilots who were shot down were usually rescued to fight again. The *Luftwaffe*, forced to change its tactics, began night bombing with incendiaries, or fire bombs.

London, Plymouth, Manchester, Birmingham, Dover, Portsmouth, and Coventry were heavily damaged, and tens of thousands of Britons were killed or injured. Yet the British resolve in the face of the enemy was firm. During those fearful days when the fate of the nation hung in the skies above them, the British were steeled and inspired by Churchill, who declared,

> Hitler knows that he will have to break us on this island or lose the war. If we can stand up to him all Europe may be free and the life of the world may move forward into broad, sun-lit uplands. But if we fail, then the whole world, including the United States, including all we have known and cared for, will sink into the abyss of a new Dark Age. . . . Let us therefore brace ourselves to our duties, and so bear ourselves that if the British Empire and its Commonwealth last for a thousand years, men will still say: "*This* was their finest hour."

Barbarossa—In the wake of the fall of France, continued bombing of Britain and conquests in the Mediterranean, Hitler again seized the initiative, this time by launching a massive surprise attack on his eastern ally, the Soviet Union. On June 22, 1941, the ***Wehrmacht*** (VAIR MAHKT; the German armed forces), three million strong, rolled deep into Russia, covering five hundred miles of territory within two months on a front that stretched from the Black Sea to the Arctic. In an operation code-named "Barbarossa," the Germans aimed their attacks at three strategic cities–Leningrad to the north, Moscow in the center, and Stalingrad to the south–engulfing the Soviet heartland with some of the fiercest, costliest fighting of the war.

By September 1941 the Russians were reeling and England was badly battered. Just two years after launching his *blitzkrieg* against Poland, Hitler was virtually master of Europe.

Section Review

1. Name the dictators who rose to power in Italy and the Soviet Union in the 1920s and in Germany in the 1930s.
2. What African nation did Italy conquer in the 1930s?
3. What was *Anschluss?*
4. What nation was forced to surrender one region of its land to Germany at the Munich Conference? What was the name of that region?
5. Place the following nations in the proper chronological order in which they fell to Germany: Belgium, Denmark, France, Norway, Poland.

Isolation and Infamy

While Europe was being crisscrossed with panzer tracks, America was safe behind its ocean walls. Three major forces kept the United States on the sidelines as war clouds gathered over Europe and Asia. First, the force of tradition returned America to an isolationist foreign policy. Rejection of membership in the League of Nations was symptomatic of the return to the old attitudes prior to the Great War. Franklin Roosevelt, who had begun his political career under the good graces of Woodrow Wilson, was in 1920 an outspoken supporter of his mentor's League. Yet by 1932 Roosevelt campaigned on his *opposition* to the League. The Great War had not kept the world "safe for democracy," and many Americans preferred to ignore what seemed to be only the latest European brawl.

Second, isolationism was spurred by the war debt problem (see pp. 470-71), which created resentment on both sides of the Atlantic. Americans viewed the huge war loans to the Allies during World War I, which totaled $22 billion, as just that, a loan. Payment from the debtor nations, however, was difficult not only because of the slowness of their postwar recovery but also because trade with the U.S., which would have helped pay their bill, was effectively cut off by America's high protective tariffs. In addition Europeans took a different view of their debts. The old Allies observed that much of the American credit was used to purchase American goods which fueled the American economy. Europeans viewed settling their American debt with all the enthusiasm of making a funeral payment. After bitter losses of millions killed and maimed, the British and French pointed to miles of graves as payment enough. By 1933 most of America's former allies had repudiated their war debts.

Third, the Great Depression kept most Americans focused on domestic rather than international concerns. Leaders in Washington were too occupied with economic recovery to take more than a sideline role in the turbulent world of European and Asian politics.

Despite the drift to isolationism, the sympathies of most Americans were with the beleaguered Allies. As in the days preceding U.S. entry into the First World War, Americans felt their strong cultural ties to Britain. They also felt a natural sympathy for the nations devastated by the vicious *Wehrmacht*. Yet Americans wanted no part of the war itself, if it were possible to avoid it. They hoped that the Allies would succeed in quashing the German aggressions without direct U.S. military support. These hopes were based on a number of illusory beliefs. Many Americans, like the French, believed that France's Maginot Line would stop Hitler's tanks. They believed that the German war effort could not be long sustained without oil, rubber, and food–supplies that Germany could not easily acquire in adequate amounts. And many hoped that the German people themselves would not long support their mad dictator's bloody ambition.

Nervous Neutrality

Changing with the Times–In September 1939, while the Germans were mopping up the last remnants of Polish resistance and the Russians were devouring the Baltic states, President Roosevelt called

This contemporary cartoon ridiculed Roosevelt's announced policy of isolation in the face of Nazi aggression.

Congress into special session to consider changes in the Neutrality Act of 1937. This law had cut off American military supplies to belligerents–nations engaged in war. Ironically, the Neutrality Act had not greatly affected Germany, because Hitler had been rearming for years and had little need for U.S. arms; it had, however, seriously hurt the democratic nations because they could not purchase military supplies from the United States when they had their greatest need.

After stiff debate, Congress passed the **Neutrality Act of 1939,** which provided that belligerents could purchase weaponry from the United States, but only on a cash basis. It further stipulated that the buyers must transport the weapons in their own ships. This ''cash-and-carry'' policy was a help to England, which had a large navy. In addition the act forbade U.S. ships and passengers to enter the ports of belligerent nations. This unwittingly helped Germany by ensuring that U.S. ships would not be traveling into the ports of Germany's enemies; thus Hitler could initiate unrestricted submarine warfare with less fear of becoming involved with the United States.

The more vocal isolationists and militant pacifists organized into **America First committees** with Charles Lindbergh as one of their leading spokesmen. These organizations, many of which were centered in the Midwest, acted as watchdog groups to keep Allied sympathy and American involvement in check.

Despite the isolationist tendencies of most Americans, including President Roosevelt, there was an increasing sense of the need for preparedness as the *Wehrmacht* rumbled through Scandinavia and France. In addition to changes in the neutrality laws, a peacetime draft–the first in American history–was instituted in September 1940. The following month, Congress approved a huge $17 billion defense budget.

1940 Election–Despite these measures, the American public and their leaders vacillated between preparedness and pacifism. During the election of 1940, Franklin Roosevelt, running for an unprecedented third term, promised from the stump, ''I have said this before, but I shall say it again and again and again: Your boys are not going to be sent into any foreign wars.''

Such empty, crowd-pleasing statements were also being proclaimed by FDR's opponent, Republican **Wendell Willkie,** a former New Deal Democrat. Willkie had early recognized the Hitler menace and urged preparedness and support of the Allies but was careful not to seem to support U.S. intervention. Willkie, a former Indiana farm boy turned wealthy businessman, drew enthusiastic followings across the country with his down-home charm. As one respectful Democrat keenly but wryly observed, Willkie was ''a simple, barefoot, Wall Street lawyer.'' Willkie received twenty-two million votes in the November election, but with Nazis having their way in Europe, most Americans agreed with the Democratic slogan that year: ''Don't switch horses in the middle of the stream.'' The next four years for Franklin Roosevelt and the nation would be among the most demanding in American history.

The Arsenal of Democracy

Roosevelt's election in 1940 ensured further aid to England and the other Allies. In January 1941 Roosevelt outlined what he called the ''Four Freedoms'': freedom of speech and of worship and freedom from want and from fear. Backed by a growing popular attitude that the United States would have to fight the enemies of free people alone if England were destroyed, he asked for and received from Congress ''all-out aid'' to the Allies. ''They do not need manpower,'' the president stated. ''They do need billions of dollars' worth of weapons of defense.'' On March 11 the **Lend-Lease Act** was signed, and $7 billion was appropriated to provide supplies for the embattled nations. Under the provisions of the act, President Roosevelt was empowered to supply any Allied nation with war materiel, on almost any terms the president desired. America was now, as Roosevelt had earlier urged, ''the great arsenal of democracy.'' Eventually nearly $50 billion worth of military supplies was distributed to thirty-eight countries. In addition U.S. forces were stationed in Iceland and Greenland to protect the vital shipping lanes of the North Atlantic as American supplies were ferried to Britain.

The indomitable Winston Churchill on board a ship anchored off Newfoundland at the time of his Atlantic Charter meeting with Franklin Roosevelt

The Atlantic Charter–The growing alliance between the United States and Britain was galvanized in August 1941, when Churchill and Roosevelt secretly met at Placentia Bay, Newfoundland. In an exchange of meetings aboard the American cruiser *Augusta* and the British warship *Prince of Wales,* the two leaders drew up the **Atlantic Charter**, a list of "common principles" such as self-determination, freedom of the seas, and economic cooperation, which would provide "a better future for the world." The Atlantic Charter was essentially a list of the goals of the anti-Axis nations, and it expressed America's moral commitment to the Allied cause. Increasingly President Roosevelt's rhetoric against Germany and massive supplies to the Allies were making America, as one newspaper editor observed, "as unneutral as possible without getting into war."

Hitler was not unaware of America's "unneutral" neutrality. In May 1941 a German submarine attacked and sank an American merchant vessel in the waters off Brazil. In September the U.S. destroyer *Greer* was fired on by a German submarine, after which Roosevelt ordered the fleet to "shoot on sight" German or Italian attack vessels. In October another U.S. destroyer, the *Kearny,* was torpedoed, and eleven sailors were killed in the attack. That same month the destroyer *Reuben James* was sunk west of Iceland with the loss of over a hundred Americans. In the waning days of 1941, escalating tensions in the Atlantic brought America to the verge of war. Yet surprisingly when the blow finally came, it fell not in the Atlantic, but in the Pacific.

"Remember Pearl Harbor!"

Japan's insatiable appetite for territory had placed increasing strain on U.S. relations. The decade-long rape of China culminated in the summer of 1941 with the Japanese seizure of the strategic oil fields and rubber plantations of French Indochina in Southeast Asia. President Roosevelt responded by placing an oil embargo on the Japanese, freezing Japanese assets, and placing all American forces in the Far East under the command of General **Douglas MacArthur.**

The Japanese, though, had bigger plans than simply taking French Indochina. With England being pounded by Hitler and the Netherlands under Nazi occupation, the Japanese eyed the resource-rich British and Dutch colonies of the Pacific rim. First, however, the Japanese warlords would have to deal with the chief naval threat in the Pacific, the United States.

Pearl Harbor—At 7:53 A.M. on Sunday, **December 7, 1941,** Japanese warplanes swept across the blue Hawaiian sky over Pearl Harbor. With the cry of *Tora! Tora! Tora!* ("Tiger! Tiger! Tiger!"), the surprise strike commenced. In a series of bomber attacks, the Japanese sank three battleships and seriously damaged sixteen other warships. They also destroyed about 150 aircraft at nearby Hickam Field. The two-hour raid took a heavy toll in American lives as well, with 2,400 killed and 1,200 wounded. In a whirlwind follow-up, Japanese forces conquered many other U.S. and British bases throughout the South Pacific during the rest of December, including Guam, Hong Kong, Wake Island, and the Gilbert Islands.

Despite the heavy American losses, Pearl Harbor was not a complete success for the Japanese. First, they had missed the American aircraft carriers, which were out on maneuvers at the time; and in the coming fight, the carrier, not the battle cruiser, would be the decisive factor. Second, with one stroke the Japanese had done what Hitler's accumulated atrocities and aggressions had not—united the American nation to war and to win.

A day of infamy—the U.S.S. Shaw *explodes during the Japanese attack on Pearl Harbor.*

"Fear Itself"—The Nisei Internment

In the wake of the sneak attack on Pearl Harbor, many Americans feared anyone of Japanese ancestry, including other *Americans*. The fear of potential spies and saboteurs was especially great on the West Coast, where most Nisei (nee SAY), or second-generation Japanese-Americans, lived. Early in 1942 the former attorney general of California asked Congress to restrict the freedom of Japanese-Americans because "they are not of an assimilable race and they are strangers to our customs, our way of life. . . . If they are permitted to live at large among us, the possibility of disaster cannot be reckoned."

Reflecting this wartime hysteria, President Roosevelt on February 19, 1942, authorized the War Department to restrict Japanese-Americans. Some 120,000 were forced from their homes in California, Oregon, and Washington and placed in detention camps further inland. None was ever charged with or convicted of treason or espionage. Despite such violations of their civil liberties, 30,000 Nisei demonstrated their patriotism by serving in combat units in Europe.

In 1976 President Gerald Ford marked the thirty-fourth anniversary of Roosevelt's action by issuing a proclamation, which ended with these words: "We have learned from the tragedy of that long-ago experience forever

Nisei family awaits transfer to an internment camp.

to treasure liberty and justice for each individual American, and resolve that this kind of action shall never again be repeated." In 1988 a formal apology and financial redress were offered to the Japanese-Americans who had been interned as a result of what a congressional commission called "race prejudice, war hysteria, and a failure of political leadership."

The day following the Pearl Harbor attack, President Roosevelt addressed a joint session of Congress, declaring December 7, 1941, a date that would "live in infamy." Congress quickly declared war on Japan, as did Britain that same day. In a flurry of war declarations, China declared war on the Axis on December 9, and on the 11th Germany and Italy declared war on the United States, which responded by declaring war on them. Pearl Harbor had triggered war on a global scale.

Fall of the Philippines—In the Philippines the Japanese forced the American and Philippine forces to withdraw to the Bataan Peninsula early in January 1942. Slowly the huge Japanese force advanced in the face of stiff American resistance. In March, to prevent the capture of General Douglas MacArthur, Roosevelt ordered him to leave. Vowing "I shall return," MacArthur left for Australia, where he laid plans for thwarting and reversing Japanese gains in the Pacific. In April the surviving American defenders on Bataan surrendered to the Japanese and were forced to make a brutal eighty-mile "death march" to prison camps. On May 6 the last American troops, holding out on the island fortress of Corregidor, surrendered—the conquest of the Philippines was complete.

Battle of Midway—With the fall of Corregidor in May 1942, the Japanese controlled a huge Pacific empire stretching from Burma to the Bering Sea. Yet May 1942 was the high-water mark of the Japanese advance. A naval and air battle in the Coral Sea in May checked the Japanese advance toward Australia. Japanese expansion was again halted at Midway Island in the northern Pacific in June. The **Battle of Midway** was a critical battle—perhaps the turning point of the war in the Pacific. By breaking the Japanese radio codes, the U.S. intercepted war messages and anticipated Japanese moves. U.S. Admiral **Chester W. Nimitz** skillfully directed carrier forces against the Japanese, destroying four Japanese carriers. The outstanding victory at Midway, combined with the Battle of the Coral Sea, turned the tide of Japanese conquest. Despite these victories, Tokyo was far away; the road ahead to victory would be long and bloody.

Home Front

The idea that "each citizen should be a soldier" was born in the French Revolution, but it had its greatest demonstration during the Second World War. The war would not be won, as in olden days, by one army defeating another on the field of battle. Rather the war would be won in both the field and the factory.

Through Roosevelt's generous lend-lease program, the economic output of the United States had already been critical to sustaining not only Britain but also the Soviet Union, which was teetering on the brink of Nazi conquest. Now America's tremendous production capability would be a crucial factor in bringing victory over the Axis.

Mobilizing the Economy—Under the new War Powers Act of 1941, Congress authorized President Roosevelt, as commander in chief, to get the nation's economy on a war footing. The **War Production Board** (WPB), which began operation in January 1942, immediately halted nearly all building construction in order to conserve materials for war production. Production of many consumer goods was discontinued through much of the war. In addition, the WPB ordered massive industrial conversion from civilian to military production.

Automakers in Detroit switched from making Cadillacs to making tanks; clothing manufacturers turned out uniforms, blankets, and parachutes; even small manufacturers such as the maker of Hoover vacuum cleaners switched to producing helmets and bomb fuses.

Conserving vital goods such as foodstuffs, rubber, and gasoline for diversion to the war effort required a system of nationwide **rationing** under the direction of the Office of Price Administration. Every man, woman, and child was issued ration books containing stamps needed to purchase various goods such as meat, sugar, and shortening. Even the purchase of shoes was limited to three pair a year. A new generation of "Victory Gardens" also sprang up in backyards across America, to offset the shortages created by the war. By 1943 these gardens produced one-third of the nation's vegetables. Gasoline was rationed as motorists received a monthly portion in relation to the importance of their vehicle to the war effort. In addition, several states established a "Victory Speed" of 35 m.p.h. in order to conserve necessary fuel.

Besides conservation measures, recycling was an important part of the national war effort. Boy Scouts fanned out through their neighborhoods collecting cooking grease and discarded metal and rubber goods. Farm boys scoured the fields for old

Women made a major contribution to America's war industries. Here women put the finishing touches on B-25 bomber nose cones, 1942.

plow tips and even junk cars, doing their part to help "scrap" the Axis.

Manpower and Womanpower—The war also created massive changes in the labor force and as a result dramatic changes in American society. The call to arms was answered by 15 million men and women throughout the course of the war. The war increased the production needs of industry but at the same time subjected every able-bodied man between the ages of eighteen and forty-five to the draft. Consequently, a huge demand for workers was created.

The war brought dramatic numbers of women into the job market, from twenty-five per cent in 1941 to thirty-six per cent by 1944. In addition female workers filled many traditionally male-oriented jobs, particularly in the defense industry. "Rosie the Riveter" symbolized the American woman on the assembly line and in the shipyard, filling a vital role in the war on the home front. The contribution that women made in the work force was not without its cost, however. During the war, for the first time, married women outnumbered single women, and working mothers placed new strains on the home and created new concerns over child care.

Axis Taxes—Paying for the war would not only be a political football for the duration of the conflict; it would also have long-term effects on the taxed and the taxer alike. America's war bill totaled over $300 billion, a figure which President Roosevelt believed should be paid with increased taxes rather than allowing the nation to lapse into debt. Congress, however, was less enthusiastic about raising taxes. With elections looming in 1942, Congress supported only half the tax increase recommended by Roosevelt. Altogether, about forty-five per cent of the war's cost was paid through taxation, while the national debt increased sixfold. Not only were new taxes imposed but new means of collecting them as well. Payroll deductions for income tax were introduced on a national scale in 1943 to help improve the government's tax flow.

But for most Americans the war was about far more than taxes and ration books. With the mobi-

These pilots of the Women's Auxiliary Corps (WACs) did their part for the war effort by ferrying bombers for America's air force. Behind them is one of their planes, a B-17 christened Pistol Packin' Mama.

lization of millions of men, nearly every family had a very personal interest in the news from the war front. Blue star banners proudly hung in windows across America representing a son gone to war. "Gold star mothers" replaced the blue banner with the gold in memory of a fallen son who would not be coming home. The war required of millions of Americans their courage, patriotism, sacrifice, and sometimes their grief.

Section Review

1. What three forces kept the United States out of the war until late 1941?
2. Who was the leading spokesman for the isolationist America First committees?
3. What three actions did FDR take in response to Japan's seizure of French Indochina?
4. What was the turning point of the Pacific war?
5. What action did several states take during World War II in order to conserve gasoline?

Fight for Fortress Europe

Hitler's occupied Europe was imposing and seemingly invincible. Yet by 1942 faint cracks in his empire could be detected. The eastern "wall" of this "Fortress Europe," deep within Russia, was locked in bitter cold and bitter fighting, with German casualties mounting to a million since the invasion was launched. Westward, Hitler's defenses, which ringed from the Aegean Sea to the Arctic Ocean, did not invite attack. Yet the Führer underestimated his enemy–a fatal mistake. The British, led by Churchill, had much fight left in them and Hitler's latest enemy, the United States, loomed beyond the Atlantic. Hitler's air chief, Goering, dismissed the now awakened industrial giant, "All the Americans can make are razor blades and refrigerators," he said. But Americans turned their plowshares into swords and soon showed their eagerness to fight for Fortress Europe.

Desert War

Mussolini, seeking to expand his African empire by building on his Ethiopian conquest, moved to conquer more territory in North Africa. To protect their interests in the Middle East, the British sent troops to halt the Italian advance. In February 1941 the British cornered the Italians in Libya and forced them to surrender.

The British triumph was short-lived, however, due to their exhausted resources and the arrival of German panzers led by the famed **Erwin Rommel.** Rommel arrived at Tripoli to take command of the Axis forces in North Africa. With the superb military strategy that earned him the nickname "Desert Fox," Rommel began to move his *Afrika Korps* eastward toward the Suez Canal, hoping to force Britain into a desert showdown. For months the tank war in the desert moved back and forth from Egypt to Libya. At times the fall of Egypt seemed imminent. After a string of stinging British defeats at the hands of Rommel, Churchill ordered Field Marshall **Bernard** ("Monty") **Montgomery** to take command.

This desert war was the first in which U.S. forces took part. On November 8, 1942, **Operation Torch,** commanded by General **Dwight D. Eisenhower,** landed 850 ships on the west coast of Africa at Casablanca, at Oran, and at Algiers. In a three-day advance the American tanks raced eastward to Tunisia. With the feisty Montgomery coming from the east, the German and Italian tank corps were caught in the middle. After suffering repeated defeats and numerous shortages, the last German outpost at Tunis fell on May 13, 1943.

Italian Campaign

Casablanca Conference–In January 1943, while the desert war was raging far to the east in Tunisia, Franklin Roosevelt and Winston Churchill met in **Casablanca** to forge an Allied strategy for the assault on Hitler's Europe. Stalin, who was not present, was urging a Second Front in France to relieve the German pressure on the Russian front. Both Roosevelt and Churchill refused to commit themselves to such an invasion, citing a lack of troop strength and preparedness for such a grand assault. They did agree, however, to open up a front against Mussolini's Italy, what Churchill described as Europe's "soft underbelly." A successful invasion would not only thrust into the heart of Europe but would also reopen crucial Mediterranean sea lanes.

Up the Boot–The invasion of Italy began with the capture of Sicily, an island at the foot of the Italian boot. In **Operation Husky,** three thousand ships and landing craft carried troops and equipment to Sicily. Although suffering heavy casualties, the Allied forces defeated the Italian army and forced the German army off the island. By the end of the summer, Sicily was an Allied base. From there the Allies, led by General Mark Clark, moved to Italy, landing at Salerno and Anzio, and, after fighting bitter battles with the German forces there, finally marched into Rome on June 4, 1944. The cheering Romans viewed the conquest of their city as a deliverance. One of their "deliverers," an American GI, viewing the ancient ruins of the Forum for the first time, whistled and said with amazement, "I didn't know our bombers had done *that* much damage in Rome."

Top: *General Dwight Eisenhower, the Supreme Allied Commander, exhorts the troops involved in the D-day landings.*
Bottom: *Allied troops wade ashore under heavy enemy fire during the Normandy landings.*

Despite the successful occupation of Rome, the Italian campaign was far from over. The push into northern Italy continued to be costly as the "soft underbelly" turned out to be rock-ribbed with tough Nazi resistance. It was not until the closing days of the war that the Allies finally crossed the Po River at the foot of the Alps.

D-day

On June 4, 1944, far from the cheering crowds in Rome, the German legend Rommel looked at his impressive coastal defenses on the French side of the English Channel and glanced at the threatening skies. There would be no Allied invasion for now, he thought. Why not surprise his wife back in Berlin with a visit on her birthday in two days? As it turned out, Mrs. Rommel was not the only one who was surprised on June 6.

In January 1944 General Eisenhower had been appointed Supreme Allied Commander with the immediate task of coordinating a cross-channel invasion into occupied France. Eisenhower, or "Ike" as his men called him, was not only a strategist but also an organizer who had demonstrated in Africa and Italy his ability to work with the motley multinational Allied army. The fifty-three-year-old midwesterner now faced his greatest challenge ever–an amphibious assault on the "Atlantic Wall of Fortress Europe." Three million Allied soldiers, sailors, and airmen–half of them Americans–were readied in southern England for the grand invasion.

The invasion code-named Operation Overlord began on the morning of "D-day," June 6, 1944. In spite of bad weather and deadly opposition, the Allied Expeditionary Force (AEF) established a beachhead along a sixty-mile stretch of the Normandy coast of France. Beaches with code names immortalized by their courageous conquerors–Gold, Utah, Sword, and Omaha–were taken in fierce fighting. The invaders encountered mines and pilings along the beaches and under the water level, and on the shore the Germans had set up miles of barbed wire, machine guns, and heavy artillery. The initial assault was made by 175,000 troops under intense enemy fire while gliders carried more troops behind the German lines. Airborne troops cut vital transportation and communication lines for miles around the invasion site.

The Nazis resisted fiercely but could not stop the surprise invasion. They were out-planned, out-equipped, and outnumbered. The Allies, who controlled the skies, bombed roads, bridges, and supply depots to prevent reinforcements from reaching the front. This greatest invasion in history, despite its complicated nature and enormous losses of men and supplies, was a crucial success.

After intense street fighting at St. Lô the Allied forces broke out into the French countryside for the push to Paris. The hard-fighting American General George Patton led the rapid advance to Paris, which Allied soldiers liberated on August 25, 1944. Another invading army landed in southern France, opening new ports and supply bases. The troops pushed quickly up the Rhone Valley to join the forces in northern France. By the end of 1944, France, Holland, and much of Luxembourg and Belgium were freed of German armies. The three million-man Allied force was at Germany's borders, ready to break the famous Siegfried Line and move on to Berlin.

Battle of the Bulge

As snow fell in early December, mounting victories and thoughts of home had many Allied soldiers believing the war would be over by Christmas. Hitler had other plans, however. At 5:00 A.M. on December 16, 1944, Hitler unleashed a terrific counter offensive out of Belgium's Ardennes Forest in a bold drive to cut the Allied forces in two.

The massive Nazi spearhead against the weakest point in the Allied line sent green American troops reeling. The thrust created a "bulge" fifty miles deep into the Allied lines giving the battle its name, the **Battle of the Bulge**. By Christmas Day

Maxwell Taylor's "Crickets"

General Maxwell Taylor, commander of America's 101st Airborne Division, was the kind of officer that inspired *esprit de corps* in his fighting men. He combined integrity, courage, duty, and creativity with a practical concern for his men. Taylor was not the sort of general to view a battle as a series of pins on a wall map at a safe distance from the shooting; he was on the front line. As he and his command prepared to parachute into Normandy on D-day, the general grew concerned about scattered paratroopers distinguishing friend from foe at night behind enemy lines. Taylor's solution was as simple as it was original; he ordered thousands of toy "crickets." Each man received one of the clicking noise-makers as a signaling device, and during that tough Normandy night many lives were spared and the operation was expedited by General Taylor's "crickets."

the Germans had captured thousands of troops and had completely surrounded American forces in Bastogne. When the German commander ordered the American commander, Anthony McAuliffe, to surrender his outnumbered army, the defiant general sent a one-word reply–"Nuts!"

Elsewhere along the Allied lines the same fighting spirit prevailed. Eisenhower ordered Montgomery to go against the northern face of the Bulge while he sent the irrepressible Patton against the

The Holocaust

As Allied forces freed Europe from Nazi tyranny, they came across unexpected horrors in the liberated areas. In Nazi prison camps Allied soldiers found gruesome evidence of mass murder, the widespread slaughter of certain racial and ethnic groups. This astounding massacre of millions of people became known as the **Holocaust.**

Hitler and his ruthless Gestapo (secret police) had carried out secret programs to exterminate "lesser peoples" such as Poles, Czechs, and especially Jews. The Nazis referred to their mass-murder program in official communiqués as the "final solution." The depths of human depravity evidenced in Hitler's Holocaust nearly defy belief. In a routine day of exterminations at one camp, 6,700 people got out of the freight cars in which they had arrived. A loudspeaker blared instructions, telling the prisoners to take off all their clothes and valuables—including artifical limbs. Guards dragged the women and girls to a barber who quickly cut off all of

Nazi troops round up Polish Jews in the Warsaw Ghetto.

their hair. The pitiful masses were told to relax, that they were simply going to take a shower. As they neared the chambers, though, the stench of death confirmed the dread that most already felt–that they were witnessing their own murder.

A witness to these events described the scene afterwards: "The wooden doors are opened. . . . Inside the chambers, the dead stand closely pressed together, like pillars of stone. . . . Even in death one recognizes the families. They still hold hands, so they have to be torn apart to get the chambers ready for their next occupants."

southern face to free Bastogne. Together, they had squeezed the Bulge back by the middle of January 1945. Hitler's last mad gamble had cost him 100,000 casualties, 1,000 aircraft, and 800 tanks. American troops who had borne the brunt of the attack suffered heavy losses also, but they had stood the test, ready now to cross the Rhine for the final push into the German heartland.

Section Review

1. What was the first military operation of World War II in which the United States took part?
2. At their conference at Casablanca, where did FDR and Churchill agree to open another front against the Axis?
3. In what region of France did the landings in Operation Overlord take place?
4. What battle resulted from Hitler's last gamble to win the war in the West?

War in the Pacific

While war raged in Europe against Hitler's *Wehrmacht,* the United States also took on the task of defeating the Japanese in the Pacific. Japan's expansion had been halted with its defeat at Midway in June 1942, but victory for America came only after several costly battles at sea over tiny islands known only because they were the scene of some of the most desperate fighting of the entire war.

In broad terms the Pacific war consisted of a two-prong drive, with General Douglas MacArthur of the U.S. Army heading the southern force from New Guinea and Admiral Chester Nimitz of the U.S. Navy commanding the Central Pacific force. These two separate campaigns would converge to reclaim the Philippines and then make the final assault on the Japanese islands.

World War II in the Pacific

Japanese Occupied Territory

Extent of Japanese Control (1942)

"Island Hopping"

In August 1942 the drive to defeat Japan began when U.S. Marines landed on **Guadalcanal** (GWAD ul kuh NAL), a ninety-mile stretch of jungle island in the Solomon Islands, three thousand miles from Tokyo. After several desperate sea battles and months of bloody jungle fighting, Japanese troops abandoned the island in February 1943. American forces then began **"island hopping"** toward Tokyo, bypassing the heavily fortified islands and securing advance air bases on those less fortified. From these runways, bombers such as the B-17 Flying Fortress and the B-29 Superfortress bombed Japanese fortifications and cut supply lines.

For the next year U.S. forces slowly reduced the area of Japanese control in the South and Central Pacific. In March 1943 U.S. and Australian air forces caused severe damage to Japanese transports in the Bismarck Sea. Then from May to June, the U.S. retook the western Aleutian Islands occupied by Japan. Early in 1944 U.S. troops captured the Marshall Islands and in April attacked New Guinea, cutting off fifty thousand Japanese troops there.

The Marianas—The war for the Pacific became even more bitter during the summer of 1944 as Japanese resistance became desperate. The most significant fight of the summer was the taking of the Mariana Islands, including Saipan and Guam. While the amphibious assault on Saipan was underway, a massive air battle took place between carrier-based fighters. The Hellcats, new U.S. warplanes, devastated the force of Japanese Zeroes, knocking 346 enemy aircraft out of the sky, a victory which the Americans quickly dubbed "the Great Marianas Turkey Shoot." The capture of the Marianas enabled Allied bombers to fly to the Japanese home islands and the occupied Philippines to deliver their destructive cargoes.

Fight for the Philippines—By the fall of 1944 the two-pronged Pacific strategy converged on the Philippines. The first major assault on the heavily fortified Philippines began around the central island of Leyte (LAY tee). The **Battle of Leyte Gulf** was the largest sea battle in history and a critical blow to Japanese naval and air forces. The Japanese lost 3 battleships, 9 cruisers, 10 destroyers, and 180

Marines raise the flag over Mount Suribachi during the desperate fight for Iwo Jima.

aircraft to American firepower, opening the gate to Manila and the liberation of the Philippines. The Battle of Leyte Gulf was also a turning point in another way. The Japanese, in desperation over their losses, organized squadrons of suicide pilots, or **kamikazes** (KAH mih KAH zeez). Their mission was as simple as it was deadly—crash their bomb-laden planes into American ships. Although many of the fanatical missions were stopped by concentrated antiaircraft fire, too many got through. The emperor's kamikazes sank or crippled 300 U.S. warships in the final ten months of the war and inflicted 15,000 casualties.

Iwo Jima—While MacArthur's forces were pushing on to Manila, American strategists were looking ahead. The key target for 1945, from which the final assault on Japan would be launched, was Okinawa. In addition the planners determined that a secondary foothold would need to be secured. Scanning the map dotted with tiny island fortresses, they settled on a little speck of volcanic ash called **Iwo Jima** (EE-woh JEE-muh).

U.S. Marines landed on the island of Iwo Jima on February 19, 1945, beginning what would become the toughest, costliest battle of their illustrious history. On the cave-riddled volcanic island, the marines fought for every foot of black sand against 21,000 Japanese defenders. Over 6,800 American soldiers were killed and 20,000 more were wounded before the Japanese resistance was crushed. Admiral Nimitz pronounced a fitting elegy over the heroes of Iwo Jima: "Uncommon valor was a common virtue."

Okinawa–The grim victory at Iwo Jima opened the way to **Okinawa** (OH kih NOW wuh), the bloodiest single campaign in the Pacific. Both sides knew the importance of Okinawa to the final stages of the war and fought accordingly. For the Americans, Okinawa was the dagger that could pierce the Japanese defense perimeter by providing a base for intensive bombing raids and a launch site for an amphibious assault on the Japanese home islands. For the Japanese, the loss of Okinawa would mean the beginning of their death struggle.

The American invasion was launched on Easter Sunday, April 1, 1945, beginning a fierce two-and-a-half-month fight for Okinawa. While the infantry fought for the island, the U.S. Navy found itself locked in combat with an equally determined foe from the air and sea. Nearly two thousand kamikazes flew their mad missions against the American fleet, leaving 5,000 sailors dead and sinking 38 ships. By mid-June Okinawa was conquered at a cost of 12,000 American servicemen killed and 50,000 wounded. The Japanese casualty figures underscored their suicidal resistance. Of the 117,000 casualties, 110,000 were killed. Committed to fighting to the death, most of the Japanese captives were those so seriously wounded as to be unable to kill themselves.

The grim tale of Okinawa cast a pall over plans for the invasion of the Japanese home islands. As the war neared an end in Europe, fear of "an Okinawa from one end of Japan to the other," which would leave a million Americans dead, raised thorny questions about how to conclude the conflict. These problems weighed heavily on the mind of President Roosevelt as he met with fellow Allied chiefs Churchill and Stalin to discuss the future of war and peace.

A Thief in the Camp

A week prior to the marine assault on Iwo Jima in February 1945, a meeting of the Big Three–Roosevelt, Churchill, and Stalin–took place at the Soviet Union's Black Sea resort of **Yalta.** Much had happened since their first meeting at Teheran in November 1943, when plans were discussed for the opening of a second front. Now, with Allied forces pushing Hitler's crumbling army from the east and the west, the Big Three laid plans for postwar Europe.

Roosevelt came to Yalta enjoying the wide support of the American people. The previous November he had won a fourth term at the polls over New York governor Thomas Dewey. In fact, one of the biggest fights for FDR during the 1944 election was not with the Republicans but with his own party over his vice president, Henry Wallace. Southern conservatives did not like Wallace's ties to the left, and political bosses in the North did not like his ties to labor. As a result Roosevelt tapped a little-known senator from Missouri named **Harry Truman** for the second spot. Just as he had handled

The Big Three at Yalta

a split in his own party, Roosevelt came to Yalta expecting to handle the growing rift between the Western nations and their at-arms-length ally, the Soviet Union.

Roosevelt came to Yalta with two misconceptions, however. First was the idea that if the United States simply corrected the mistake, as FDR saw it, that it had made after World War I of not joining the League of Nations, then the postwar world would be secure. As a result, formation of an international organization for peace was at the top of the Yalta agenda. Getting the Soviet Union to join the United Nations, however, would not prove to be a panacea for peace.

Roosevelt's second misconception was over his ability to deal with Stalin. FDR thought he could deal with Stalin as one party boss to another. But Stalin was no politician; he was a tyrant. The Big Three agreed to support democratic elections and government in all of the liberated nations of Europe. Stalin gave the appropriate nods and smiles that FDR wanted on the issue, and all the while the Soviet army was destroying democratic forces in Eastern Europe and setting up puppet governments. Wherever the Red Army advanced, Nazi control was simply replaced with Communist control. Roosevelt was not unaware of the gulf between Soviet promises and practices, but, because of Stalin's agreement to join the war against Japan after Germany was defeated, FDR did not press the issue.

At the time, this concession was paramount in Roosevelt's thinking. With Americans bogged down in costly fights in the South Pacific and the atomic bomb still on the drawing board, Roosevelt wanted Russia's help in defeating the Japanese. Stalin agreed to join the fight, but he wanted additional Asian territory for his trouble. Roosevelt agreed.

Franklin Roosevelt's disappointing performance at Yalta reflected political realities, wishful thinking, and the president's declining health. Just eight weeks after Yalta, on April 12, Roosevelt died of a cerebral hemorrhage at Warm Springs, Georgia. After less than three months on the job as vice president, Harry Truman became the new commander in chief.

Victory!

Victory in Europe–On April 20, 1945, Hitler celebrated his fifty-sixth birthday in his command bunker deep in the heart of Berlin. The only fireworks for the occasion were the sound of the opening round of Soviet artillery shells falling on the streets of his beloved city. Allied forces to the west under Eisenhower had pushed as far as the Elbe River in central Germany, where he halted his armies while the Soviets devoured eastern Germany.

By April 30 the Battle of Berlin raged less than a quarter mile from Hitler's underground headquarters. That morning the Führer fed cyanide to his favorite dog, Blondi, and her pups in order to test the effectiveness of the poison. That afternoon he used it on himself. The ruinous Reich was ended. On May 7 and 8 the Nazis surrendered on both fronts. News of victory in Europe triggered joyous celebrations from Times Square to Red Square.

In his victory address to the nation, President Truman pointed to the unfinished task.

> We must work to bind up the wounds of a suffering world–to build an abiding peace, a peace rooted in justice and law. We can build such a peace only by hard, toilsome, painstaking work–by understanding and working with our Allies in peace as we have in war.

Truman would soon learn that "working with our Allies," particularly the Soviet Union, would be the hardest work of all.

Potsdam–Truman traveled to Berlin in July 1945 to meet with Churchill and Stalin to plan the conclusion of the war in the Pacific. Truman was not the only new face among the Big Three at Potsdam. Elections in Britain during the conference swept Churchill's party out of power, replacing the great war leader with a new prime minister, Clement Attlee.

In other ways the Potsdam conference underscored changes in the alliance. Stalin had installed puppet governments throughout much of the area his armies occupied. Truman could do little more than remind Stalin of his promises to support free

American infantry march through the rubbled streets of Bensheim, Germany, in March 1945 as a resident gazes in anguish at the destruction.

elections in eastern Europe, but Stalin's problem was not memory loss. The previous spring, shortly after Yalta, the dictator had boasted, "This war is unlike all past wars. Whoever occupies a territory imposes his own social system . . . as far as his army can advance."

One item on which the Big Three at Potsdam could agree was the demand for Japan's unconditional surrender. Behind this declaration was perhaps the biggest event to occur during the conference. Shortly after arriving at Potsdam, President Truman received the following message:

TOP SECRET
PRIORITY
WAR 33556
TO SECRETARY OF WAR FROM HARRISON. DOCTOR HAS JUST RETURNED MOST ENTHUSIASTIC AND CONFIDENT THAT THE LITTLE BOY IS AS HUSKY AS HIS BIG BROTHER. THE LIGHT IN HIS EYES DISCERNIBLE FROM HERE TO HIGHHOLD AND I COULD HAVE HEARD HIS SCREAMS FROM HERE TO MY FARM.

The code words meant that the test of the **atomic bomb** had been successful; the noise of the blast could be heard for forty miles. The secret weapon awaited the president's orders for use against Japan.

"These Proceedings Are Closed" – The Allied ultimatum to Japan, surrender or face destruction, was pronounced "absurd" by the Japanese premier. Truman's warning, however, was not an idle one. On the morning of August 6, a B-29 christened *Enola Gay,* piloted by Colonel Paul Tibbets, flew over the sun-drenched city of **Hiroshima** (HIR uh SHEE muh) and delivered the first atomic bomb. The extraordinary weapon destroyed half the city with a single blast. Three days later the second bomb was dropped on **Nagasaki** (NAH guh SAH kee), and the Japanese emperor Hirohito accepted the inevitable. On September 2, 1945, the Japanese surrendered aboard the U.S.S. *Missouri* anchored

in Tokyo Bay. General MacArthur stood on deck and addressed victor and vanquished alike:

> We are gathered here, representatives of the major warring powers, to conclude a solemn agreement whereby peace may be restored. The issues, involving divergent ideals and ideologies, have been determined on the battlefields of the world and hence are not for our discussion or debate. Nor is it for us here to meet, representing as we do a majority of the people of the earth, in a spirit of distrust, malice, or hatred. But rather it is for us, both victors and vanquished, to serve, committing all our people unreservedly to faithful compliance with the understanding they are here for-

mally to assume. It is my earnest hope . . . that from this solemn occasion a better world shall emerge . . . a world dedicated to the dignity of man. . . . Let us pray that peace be now restored to the world, and that God will preserve it always. These proceedings are closed.

The aftermath of the atomic bomb–Nagasaki is reduced to a wasteland and the Japanese sue for peace. Inset: *Surrender ceremony aboard the U.S.S.* Missouri *anchored in Tokyo Bay.*

Operation Downfall, The Invasion That Never Occurred

Before the development of the atomic bomb was completed, the U.S. military assumed that the Pacific war would climax in what would be the bloodiest, most difficult campaign in history—the invasion of Japan. Given the code name "Operation Downfall," the projected invasion of Japan would have required the entire U.S. Pacific Fleet and a force of four and a half million men. Plans for the invasion actually involved two separate amphibious assaults, either of which would have made the Normandy invasion pale by comparison. One attack would seize Japan's southernmost island, Kyushu, as a base for further operations. The second landing would be on Honshu, Japan's main island and the site of its capital, Tokyo.

American commanders did not look at Operation Downfall with any eagerness. In the hard fighting on the Pacific islands, not a single Japanese unit had ever surrendered. Instead, the Japanese soldiers showed an almost fanatical tendency to fight to the last man. In the fierce battle for the tiny island of Guadalcanal in 1942, for example, 1,500 Americans lost their lives in six months of fighting while 25,000 Japanese died there rather than surrender. An attack on Japan itself could only be worse. It would, in fact, be even harder than the pessimistic Americans expected. Unknown to the American high command, the Japanese military had two million troops stationed in Japan for the nation's defense. Furthermore, ten million Japanese civilians were being prepared to conduct guerrilla warfare if the islands were invaded.

When President Truman took office and reviewed the plans for Operation Downfall, he was appalled. The armed forces expected at least a million American casualties. Truman was also dismayed to learn that even if everything went according to plan, the military commanders did not expect Japan to fall until the end of 1946. These facts weighed heavily with Truman when he made the decision to drop the atomic bombs on Hiroshima and Nagasaki. As devastating as those actions were, they were far less deadly for both sides than Operation Downfall would have been.

Silent Guns—While victory celebrations erupted around the world, in those lands where the victory took place, survivors in search of food picked through the rubble of what had once been their homes. For the millions of destitute refugees in Europe, peace did not follow victory. Beside their struggle for survival, perhaps a million civilians died in 1945 from exposure or from the vengeful guns of Russian soldiers. Throughout the world the wounds of war ran deep. The grim tally was simply overwhelming: fifty million men, women, and children killed, with millions more maimed for life.

The United States, insulated by oceans, suffered no direct civilian loss, but 292,000 American soldiers, sailors, and airmen gave their lives for the cause of freedom. Victory placed the heavy mantle of world leadership on the shoulders of the United States. As the spectre of communism hung over the rubbled cities of Europe and the wasted fields of Asia, America found that vigilance in peace would be as important as vigilance in war.

Section Review

1. Who was the military commander of each of the two prongs of the Allied attack in the Pacific War?
2. What was the largest sea battle in history?
3. What island did American forces capture as a launching point for the final assault on Japan?
4. What two cities were the sites of the first use of the atomic bomb in warfare?

Chapter Review

Terms

Adolf Hitler
fascism
Benito Mussolini
Hideki Tojo
Axis
Joseph Stalin
appeasement
Rhineland
Sudetenland
Nazi-Soviet nonaggression pact
beginning of World War II
(September 1, 1939)
blitzkrieg
Dunkirk
Winston Churchill
Battle of Britain
Wehrmacht

Neutrality Act of 1939
America First committees
Wendell Willkie
Lend-Lease Act
Atlantic Charter
Douglas MacArthur
Japanese attack on Pearl Harbor
(December 7, 1941)
Battle of Midway
Chester W. Nimitz
War Production Board
rationing
Erwin Rommel
Bernard Montgomery
Operation Torch
Dwight D. Eisenhower
Casablanca

Operation Husky
D-day
St. Lô
Battle of the Bulge
Holocaust
Guadalcanal
island hopping
Battle of Leyte Gulf
kamikazes
Iwo Jima
Okinawa
Yalta
Harry Truman
Potsdam
atomic bomb
Hiroshima
Nagasaki

Content Questions

1. The invasion of what nation sparked World War II?
2. Place the following events in their correct chronological order.
   a. Battle of Britain
   b. Invasion of the Low Countries
   c. Operation Barbarossa
   d. Invasion of Denmark and Norway
   e. Invasion of Poland
   f. Evacuation of Dunkirk
3. Why was the United States called "the arsenal of democracy"
4. What event sparked American involvement in World War II? When did it occur?
5. Why did the war force many women to take traditionally male jobs in the factories?
6. Who was the supreme commander of the Allied forces from 1944 on?

7. What is the term for the Allied strategy in the Pacific of bypassing heavily fortified Japanese islands in favor of less fortified ones?
8. What nations made up the Big Three? Who represented each nation at Yalta? at Potsdam?

Application Questions

1. How did the American government justify its internment of Japanese-Americans during World War II? Were these arguments valid? Why or why not?
2. Realistically, could President Roosevelt have made the outcome of the Yalta Conference more beneficial to the United States? Why or why not?
3. Was President Truman right to use the atomic bomb against Japan? Defend your answer.

UNIT VII

1945
United Nations founded; atomic bombs dropped on Japan

1948
European Recovery Program (Marshall Plan); World Council of Churches formed

1949
NATO formed; China falls to Communists

1950
National Council of Churches formed

1950-1953
Korean War

1954
Brown v. *Board of Education*

1959
Castro sets up Communist government in Cuba

1961
First American space flight

1963
Civil rights march on Washington

1964
Civil Rights Act of 1964

1964-1973
American involvement in Vietnam War

1965-1967
Urban riots

1969
First landing on moon

1972
President Nixon visits Communist China

1974
President Nixon resigns

1975
South Vietnam falls to communism

1980
Ronald Reagan elected president

1989
Communist governments in most Eastern European nations collapse

1991
Gulf War

1998
Impeachment of President Clinton

2000
George W. Bush elected president

CHAPTER 23

The Postwar Era (1945-1963)

"Let every nation know, whether it wishes us well or ill, that we shall pay any price, bear any burden, meet any hardship, support any friend, oppose any foe, in order to assure the survival and success of liberty."

President John F. Kennedy, *Inaugural Address,* January 20, 1961

I. **Cold War**
   A. United Nations
   B. Containing Communism
   C. Accommodating Communism
II. **Domestic Reform**
   A. Truman and the Fair Deal
   B. Eisenhower and "Dynamic Conservatism"
   C. Kennedy and the New Frontier
III. **Life in Postwar America**
   A. The Affluent Society
   B. Family
   C. Emergence of Minority Rights
   D. Religion

America enters the ominous atomic age: a test explosion of the atomic bomb in the South Pacific, 1946.

On April 12, 1945, the day Franklin Roosevelt died, **Harry Truman** took the presidential oath of office. "Boys, if you ever pray, pray for me now," the overwhelmed Truman confided to reporters the next day. "I don't know whether you fellows ever had a load of hay fall on you, but when they told me yesterday what had happened, I felt like the moon, the stars and all the planets had fallen on me." Truman indeed seemed unprepared for the White House. Taking office after serving less than three months as vice president, Truman had little experience in foreign policy. Left out of briefings by FDR, he did not even know about the project to develop the atomic bomb until he became president. Little in his background foreshadowed greatness. Only a high school graduate, Truman failed in the clothing business; then, working with a local political machine in Missouri, he was elected county judge. In 1934 he won a U.S. Senate seat and there gained praise for his work as chairman of a committee to investigate war mobilization. In 1944 President Roosevelt–seeking a moderate vice-presidential candidate to replace the radically liberal Henry Wallace–turned to Truman as an alternative.

Prepared or not, Truman proceeded to make his mark on American policy at home and in the world. Aided by his own toughness and common sense, along with the best advice he could get, the president charted a course unknown to America for peacetime. After involvement in wars, presidents typically had resumed an isolationist position. Truman, however, led the United States into membership in, and even sponsorship of, international organizations such as the United Nations and the North Atlantic Treaty Organization (NATO). Furthermore, in a departure from tradition, he pushed for a peacetime buildup of America's armed forces, a buildup anchored by atomic weapons.

Truman was followed as president by Dwight Eisenhower and John Kennedy, two men who exhibited a different style from the peppery Truman. Eisenhower was a former commanding general and grandfatherlike figure; Kennedy was a handsome young senator and war hero. Both Eisenhower and Kennedy, however, pursued Truman's goal of

American leadership in international affairs. They even followed Truman to a lesser extent in domestic affairs, particularly in the gradual increase in the size and power of government. These three presidents reflected the burgeoning military, political, and economic growth of postwar America.

Cold War

United Nations

An idealistic effort to maintain peace was the **United Nations** (UN). Born out of wartime cooperation among the Allies, the UN began on April 25, 1945, in San Francisco with delegates from fifty nations writing a charter for the organization. The UN includes three major agencies. The first, the General Assembly, includes delegates from all member nations and meets annually. It provides a forum in which all member nations may express their views. The second, the Security Council, currently includes five permanent members and ten elected by the General Assembly for two-year terms. Permanent members of the Security Council–the United States, Russia, Britain, France, and China–have veto power over UN proposals. The third agency, the Secretariat, is the bureaucracy and center of administration. The United States Senate ratified the UN charter in 1945 by an overwhelming margin, and eventually the UN made its permanent home in New York City.

Proponents of the United Nations hoped that the body would provide a forum for rational discussion and a means of furthering world peace. Instead, it has often become a sounding board for propaganda, particularly for Communist and anti-American views. The ability of any permanent member of the Security Council to veto an action limits the UN's ability to act. Likewise the inability of the organization to force members to recognize its authority has hampered its efforts to preserve peace. Good intentions lay behind the founding of the United Nations, but its record as a mediator and preserver of the peace has been uneven.

Containing Communism

***Declaring the Cold War**–The failures of the United Nations in the postwar era are highlighted by the struggle of the Free World against the aggressive policies of the Soviet Union. Presidential adviser Bernard Baruch dubbed this hostility between the two superpowers–the United States and the Soviet Union–and their allies the **"cold war."** By this term, Baruch meant that the U.S. and USSR entered a period of tension and intense competition which only occasionally flared up into actual military conflict (i.e., a "hot war"). Although the two countries had been allies in World War II and Soviets had received Lend-Lease aid, the relationship had never been a cordial one. After the Bolshevik Revolution in 1917, American troops had briefly intervened with the Allies in the Russian Civil War on the side of the anti-Communists. The United States government did not grant diplomatic recognition to the Soviet Union until 1933. Even when fighting their common enemy, Hitler, during World War II, Roosevelt and Stalin disagreed about the location and timing of the Second Front, the invasion of Western Europe to ease pressure on the Russian, or eastern, front. What really launched the cold war, however, was the realization that the USSR intended to spread its dominion throughout the world. The Soviet Union, the Free World discovered, was perhaps a greater threat to peace and liberty than Nazi Germany. The cold war was fought around the world as the forces of democracy and communism squared off in nation after nation.

***Eastern Europe**–The first campaign of the cold war took place in Eastern Europe. The Soviets, invaded twice in the twentieth century by Germany, sought security by imposing pro-Soviet governments in neighboring Eastern Europe, contrary to their guarantees at Yalta of free democratic elections in those nations. In the spring of 1945, before the war ended, the Soviet Union had installed "puppet" governments in Poland and Rumania. After 1945 East Germany, Hungary, Bulgaria, Albania, and Yugoslavia fell under Communist control. In 1948 Czechoslovakia was the last Eastern European country to succumb to Soviet conquest. Winston Churchill described the unfolding events in Europe as the descent of an **"iron curtain"** separating the Communist East from the free West. Ironically, the Allies fought World War II over the fate of Eastern Europe only to see it pass into totalitarian Communist control.

President Truman responded to the Soviet presence in Eastern Europe with the policy of **containment.** Unwilling to dislodge the Red Army through military action, the West conceded the area to the Soviets. Truman declared, however, that further Communist aggression would be resisted. In 1945, for example, the combative Truman confronted Soviet Foreign Minister Molotov about Poland. ''I have never been talked to like that in my life,'' Molotov said. ''Carry out your agreements and you won't get talked to like that,'' Truman shot back. Faced with the growing Communist menace, Truman was intent on pursuing the policy of containment by providing military and economic support to halt Soviet expansion.

Middle East and Mediterranean—The policy of containment enjoyed some success. In 1946 the Soviets withdrew their forces from Iran, a strategically important country in the Middle East. More critically, that same year civil war erupted in Greece, where Communists tried to take over the country. The Soviet Union also pressured Turkey for territory and the right to establish naval bases on the Bosporus, the strategic waterway providing access between the Black Sea and the Aegean Sea. To prevent Soviet influence from spreading to the Mediterranean, Truman asked Congress for $400 million in economic aid for Greece and Turkey. This policy of aiding countries fighting Communist takeovers became known as the **Truman Doctrine.** With American help, both Greece and Turkey successfully warded off Communist threats. The United States was backing words with actions.

Western Europe—After 1945 American attention focused on Western Europe, where economic ruin from the war created an opportunity for Communist advances. France and Italy, for example, already had strong left-wing parties that could pave the way for Communist takeover. To blunt the appeal of the Soviets, Secretary of State George C. Marshall in 1947 offered a plan for massive economic aid to all European countries. The Soviet Union and its puppet governments in Eastern Europe refused the aid, but Western Europe welcomed

it. In 1948 Congress passed this European Recovery Program, better known as the **Marshall Plan.** By 1951 the United States had spent $13 billion on restoring the economy of Western Europe. The Marshall Plan not only further immunized that region against communism but also restored these European countries as trading partners with the United States.

Reacting to the Soviet military threat in Europe, the Middle East, and the Mediterranean, the Western nations forged a military alliance to defend themselves in the event of Soviet attack. In April 1949 representatives from ten Western European countries and the United States and Canada formed the **North Atlantic Treaty Organization (NATO),** a mutual defense pact. The United States Senate overwhelmingly ratified the North Atlantic Treaty, and in 1950 NATO named General Dwight Eisenhower as the head of its combined defense force in Western Europe. Participation in NATO showed again how far America had ventured from isolationism. It also hardened divisions between East and West in Europe. In 1955 the Communist countries of Eastern Europe created the **Warsaw Pact,** their military alliance to counter NATO.

The division of Germany after the war into Communist East Germany and Allied-controlled West Germany created special tensions between the United States and the USSR. In 1948 the Americans, the British, and the French consolidated their occupied zones in western Germany and began the process of forming its government. Threatened by the prospect of a unified West Germany, the Soviets in 1948 blockaded West Berlin. That city, located deep in East Germany, had also been divided into Communist East Berlin and free West Berlin after the war. Surrounded by the Communist East, West Berlin was especially vulnerable. By cutting off all access to West Berlin, Stalin hoped to take over all of Berlin or force the West to stop the unification of West Germany. Truman responded quickly with a massive airlift of food and supplies to West Berlin, and by May 1949 the **Berlin airlift** had forced the Soviet Union to end the blockade. Afterwards, the Soviets reacted to the formation of the Federal Republic of Germany

(West Germany) by fashioning East Germany into a Communist state, the German Democratic Republic. Germany remained divided for over forty years, until 1990.

"Year of Shocks"—Despite progress in the cold war with the Marshall Plan, the formation of NATO, and the resolution of the Berlin crisis, 1949 proved to be a "year of shocks" for the Free World. Since the 1920s China had endured a civil war between the Nationalists of **Chiang Kai-shek** (CHANG KYE-SHEK) and the Communists of **Mao Zedong** (MOU DZUH-DONG). World War II interrupted their fighting as they battled the Japanese, but after 1945 civil war resumed. The United States supported the Nationalists with $2 billion in aid from 1945 to 1949, but it was not enough. Mao had captured strong support among the peasants, undermining Chiang's leadership and economic strength. In 1949 Communist forces gained control of mainland China and the Nationalist forces set up a government on the island of Taiwan, off the coast of China. The United States continued to recognize the Nationalists in Taiwan as the "real" China in the UN and until the 1970s did not recognize the government of Mao on the mainland.

The same year that China fell to communism, the United States lost its monopoly on nuclear weapons. The existence of nuclear weapons heightened the cold war tensions (although from 1945 to 1949 the Communists seemed little intimidated by this exclusive American power, and the United States resisted temptations to use it as blackmail). In 1949 the Soviet Union detonated its first atomic bomb and forced Truman to evaluate America's defense policy. He called first for building up conventional military forces, since the Soviets possessed "the bomb" and America's nuclear threat now carried less punch. Truman also escalated the arms race by ordering development of a more powerful weapon, the hydrogen bomb. When the hydrogen bomb, or "H-bomb" as it was popularly known, was finally developed in 1952, it had an explosive power hundreds of times greater than the bomb dropped on Hiroshima. Within a year the Soviet Union revealed that it too had developed a hydrogen bomb.

The Korean War—The most serious military conflict of the cold war occurred on the Asian peninsula of Korea. Freed from Japanese control after World War II, Korea had been divided along the **38th parallel** of latitude into Communist North Korea and non-Communist South Korea. On June 25, 1950, the Communist North invaded the South in an attempt to unite the peninsula under Communist rule. President Truman reacted boldly to this aggression. Rather than ask Congress for a declaration of war, the president worked through the Security Council of the United Nations. The USSR, which could have vetoed the action, was temporarily absent in protest of America's refusal to recognize the government of Communist China. Although fourteen other nations sent troops, the United States contributed the most men, and General **Douglas MacArthur,** America's hero of the Pacific in World War II, was in charge of the UN military forces.

General Douglas MacArthur

American troops advance on Communist forces in the Korean conflict, June 1951.

Initially, the North Koreans penetrated deeply into the South, easily brushing aside both disorganized South Korean resistance and the first American units sent to Korea. MacArthur, however, reversed the situation by a brilliant maneuver. Taking advantage of his superior air and naval power, MacArthur launched an amphibious invasion behind North Korean lines at **Inchon,** a seaport halfway up the western coast of Korea. In one magnificent stroke, MacArthur cut the North Korean supply lines and began destroying the North Korean forces. Soon the UN forces had pushed the Communists back across the 38th parallel and pressed into the North to unify the peninsula under a non-Communist government. MacArthur boasted in October 1950 that the troops would be home by Christmas.

His success had an unexpected effect, however. Communist China intervened in the conflict, sending thousands of troops into North Korea to rescue the North's Communist government. The Chinese sent the overextended UN forces reeling back down the peninsula. MacArthur, who had downplayed the possibility of Chinese intervention, now admitted, "We face an entirely new war." Communist forces pushed the UN troops once again back to the 38th parallel. Soon a replay of the trench warfare of World War I was in effect, with the two well-entrenched sides fighting each other desperately for a few square miles of worthless land. The Korean conflict had become a stalemate.

MacArthur, declaring "There is no substitute for victory," argued for breaking the stalemate by expanding the war into China. Truman, however, held to the principle of **limited war,** a war with a limited objective short of total victory over the enemy. Calling war with China a "gigantic booby trap," Truman refused to expand the conflict and risk, as he thought, a third world war. MacArthur disagreed publicly with the president's decision, and Truman relieved him of his command. Neither side in the war could gain a decisive advantage, and they began truce talks in July 1951. Fighting continued for two years until a truce was reached on July 27, 1953. More than 33,000 Americans had died in a war that left the boundary between North and South Korea about where it was before the war began. The United States had succeeded in saving South Korea from communism, however, and in maintaining a beachhead for freedom on the perimeter of the Communist empire.

Accommodating Communism

In part because of the unpopularity of the Korean War, Truman did not seek re-election in 1952. Instead **Dwight Eisenhower** became chief executive, and after two terms he was followed by **John Kennedy.** Containment of communism remained the goal of U.S. foreign policy under Eisenhower and Kennedy, but with a twist. Containment was mixed with more of a willingness to accommodate

---

Frozen Chosin

The entrance of the Red Chinese forces into the Korean War caught MacArthur's army dangerously off guard. One force engulfed in the Chinese offensive was the 1st Division, U.S. Marines. Holding a position by the Chosin Reservoir not far from the Yalu River, the marines were nearly surrounded by the oncoming Chinese. Their escape was one of the great episodes of daring during the Korean War.

The division's only hope of escape was to break out to the south toward the seaport of Hungnam. One colonel told his men, "The enemy is in front of us, behind us, to the left of us, and the right of us. They won't escape *this* time." The commanding general of the division, Oliver P. Smith, denied that this action was a retreat. "We are simply attacking in another direction," he said. His words were not just bravado; escape would involve combat just as fierce as any offensive operation.

Complicating the situation was the bitterly cold weather. Soldiers joked about how *Chosin* rhymed with *frozen,* but the subzero temperatures were no laughing matter. An action as simple as tossing a grenade involved removing a glove and risking frostbite. Weapons froze up. (One ingenious soldier found that lubricating his gun with Wild Root hair cream oil kept it in operation.) One of the few advantages of the severe cold was that wounds did not bleed long; they froze.

The marine breakout involved countless individual acts of bravery. One sergeant, his legs paralyzed from a bullet wound, died holding off the enemy on a hilltop for ten minutes while his comrades escaped. Others used shovels like baseball bats to bat back grenades that the enemy tossed at them. A private was being treated for severely frostbitten feet when he found out his unit was in danger. Without hesitation he took off toward his buddies, his feet leaving bloody footprints in the snow. A sergeant holding off the Chinese in one gap was hit twice but refused medical attention. "There isn't time," he said. "They're only small holes anyway." The sergeant died of blood loss, but his unit held the line.

One unit, Fox Company, stood out for special commendation. The company had to hold the heights of Toktong Pass south of Chosin Reservoir against overwhelming odds or the enemy would cut off the withdrawal. The 240 men would have to fight to the last man if necessary; there could be no retreat. For five days, Fox Company stayed and hung on grimly in the face of waves of attacking Chinese soldiers. A total of 115 of Fox Company's men were killed or wounded, including all but one of its officers. Even when relief arrived, the remains of the unit stayed until the last truck was safely through Toktong Pass. The peak they defended was thereafter known as Fox Hill.

The withdrawal took fourteen days, and the Chinese contested almost every foot of the more than fifty miles from the reservoir to Hungnam. However, by Christmas Day 1950 the UN forces had been evacuated. The marines suffered nearly 13,000 casualties from both battle and the bitter cold; the Chinese took even heavier losses—37,500 casualties. In the face of the worst that winter and enemy could deliver, the marines added "Frozen Chosin" to their roll call of valor.

---

communism. **"Peaceful coexistence"** was the phrase coined to describe the goal of U.S.-USSR relations. The United States, at least, was beginning to change its goal in the cold war from pursuit of total victory over communism to achieving some sort of agreeable accommodation.

Indochina—One cold war trouble spot was the Asian territory known as Indochina. France had controlled Indochina from the middle of the nineteenth century until Japan captured it during World

War II. After the war France attempted to reclaim its former colony. Communists in Vietnam, the largest part of Indochina, played on the anti-French sentiment of the people to foment a revolution. The Communist leader, **Ho Chi Minh** (HOE CHEE MIN), successfully conducted a guerrilla war against the French which climaxed in 1954 with the Battle of Dien Bien Phu, a decisive defeat for the French. The United States had sent limited economic aid to the French but had rejected sending military aid.

In 1954 an international conference at Geneva followed the postwar pattern of Germany and Korea by dividing Vietnam between the Communist North and French-controlled South. The United States did not sign the Geneva agreement, but the U.S. continued to aid South Vietnam under its anti-Communist president **Ngo Dinh Diem** (dee EM) after the French withdrew. In short, the United States was willing to tolerate the existence of the Communist North while helping to check the threat of Communist influence in South Vietnam. Eisenhower sent 2,000 military advisers to aid Diem in training and organizing his forces. Eisenhower's rationale for helping anticommunism in Vietnam was what became known as the **domino theory,** that if one non-Communist nation in Southeast Asia fell to communism, then other nations would fall like a row of dominoes. As Eisenhower himself described it: "You have a row of dominoes set up. You knock over the first one, and what will happen to the last one is a certainty that it will go over very quickly."

President John F. Kennedy boosted the American commitment to 16,000 advisers, but the situation in Vietnam did not improve. A coup in 1963 resulted in Diem's overthrow and murder, and the Communists' guerrilla war intensified, with increasing help from North Vietnam. The stage was set for massive American military intervention in South Vietnam under Kennedy's successor, Lyndon Johnson. Vietnam was soon to replace Korea as the cold war's hottest conflict. (See pp. 567-71, 581-83.)

Cuba—In Cuba, as in Vietnam, America accommodated the further spread of communism, in violation of the spirit of containment. In 1959 **Fidel Castro** overthrew the Cuban dictator Fulgenico Batista y Zaldivar. But instead of installing a de-

mocracy, he created a Communist state only ninety miles from Florida. He nationalized foreign-owned property and signed a trade agreement with the Soviet Union. President Eisenhower responded with trade sanctions, broke diplomatic relations, and authorized the CIA to plan a counterattack to topple Castro. That CIA project culminated during the Kennedy administration when Cuban exiles with the assistance of the CIA invaded their homeland on April 19, 1961. The **Bay of Pigs** operation ended in total failure after only three days of struggle. An embarrassed John Kennedy was philosophical: "Victory has a thousand fathers, but defeat is an orphan."

Cuban dictator Fidel Castro brought communism to the Western Hemisphere.

The most dramatic confrontation over Cuba did not come until October 1962, a time when the cold war teetered on the brink of nuclear war. Soviets apparently interpreted Kennedy's refusal to use enough military force to overthrow Castro as a sign of weakness, and they challenged the president by attempting to install in Cuba missiles capable of carrying nuclear warheads. American intelligence confirmed the existence of missile sites under con-

struction, and Kennedy demanded their removal. In what became known as the **Cuban missile crisis,** he ordered a blockade of Cuba, and fortunately the Soviets honored it. Shortly thereafter, Soviet premier Khrushchev agreed to remove the missiles

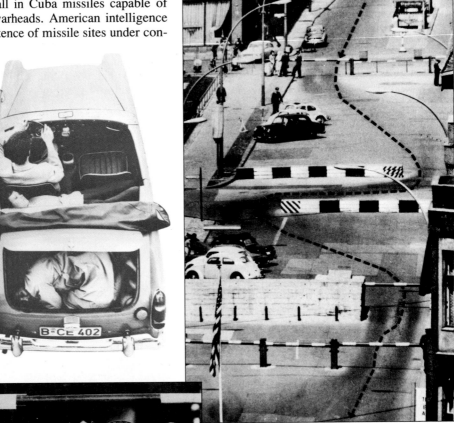

The Berlin Wall slowed but could not stop the flow of refugees to the free West. In May 1963 one ingenious young Austrian rented a sports car low enough to pass under the barriers between East and West Berlin. Placing an East German girl in the back seat and his mother in the trunk, the driver negotiated the sharp turns of his escape route and dashed by the astonished guards before they could fire.

The Postwar Era (1945-1963)

in return for a pledge by the United States not to invade Cuba. Kennedy accepted the proposal, and a very tense week ended.

When he learned that the Soviets had chosen to honor the blockade of Cuba, Secretary of State Dean Rusk said, "We're eyeball to eyeball and I think the other fellow just blinked." Indeed, most Americans viewed the crisis as a clear-cut American triumph. What the public did not know was that Kennedy had secretly agreed to remove a number of missiles in Turkey in exchange for the Soviet concession. That secret deal and Kennedy's pledge not to invade Castro's Cuba showed the president's willingness to accommodate the Communists and to tolerate a Communist foothold in the Western Hemisphere.

Berlin Wall—Just as Cuba was an insult to American pride, West Berlin remained an embarrassment to the Communist East because it was a "showcase of democracy" and a haven for refugees fleeing from East Germany. In 1961 Khrushchev met with Kennedy in Vienna and threatened to restrict western access to Berlin. In response Kennedy asked Congress for increased defense spending, but he did not respond with force when the East German government began construction of the **Berlin Wall** in August 1961. The wall solved the East German refugee problem but demonstrated the failure of communism as the second Berlin crisis of the cold war ended.

Section Review

1. What was the last Eastern European nation to fall to Soviet domination after World War II?
2. Name the two countries whose resistance to communism caused Truman to announce the Truman Doctrine.
3. What act by the Allies caused Stalin to blockade West Berlin?
4. In addition to calling for stronger conventional forces, what did Truman do in reaction to the Soviet development of the atomic bomb?
5. Why were the Soviets unable to veto the UN's decision to intervene in Korea?
6. What country became a Communist foothold in the Western Hemisphere in the late 1950s?

Domestic Reform

While the United States was waging the cold war in foreign affairs from 1945 to 1963, events on the domestic front were also moving rapidly. Each U.S. president during this period pursued a policy of domestic reform. The "Fair Deal" (Truman), "Dynamic Conservatism" (Eisenhower), and the "New Frontier" (Kennedy) became the slogans that America's postwar presidents used to describe their policies.

Truman and the Fair Deal

Shortly after the war President Truman sent Congress a list of proposals which signaled that his domestic program would be an expansion of the New Deal. By 1949 he was calling his legislative goals the **Fair Deal.** The president sought a government commitment to full employment (federal spending designed to insure jobs for the unemployed), but conservative opposition killed it. Truman settled instead for the Employment Act of 1946, which created the Council of Economic Advisers to advise the president on the economy. Congress in 1946 also created the Atomic Energy Commission, which gave control over atomic energy to civilian rather than military authorities.

With economic problems, foreign policy setbacks, and charges of Communists in government, Truman's approval ratings sank and Democrats suffered. The wife of a leading Republican senator captured the mood best when she quipped, "To err is Truman." "Had enough?" was an effective Republican slogan. In the 1946 elections Republicans captured both Houses of Congress for the first time since 1928. With control of Congress, Republicans pushed through the **Taft-Hartley Act** of 1947. This antiunion measure, passed over Truman's veto, permitted states to pass "right-to-work" laws banning the union shop, which required union membership as a condition for hiring. The act also required an eighty-day cooling-off period for strikes in businesses involving national interests, and union officials had to swear they were not Communists. In another matter of national security Congress in 1947 changed the American military establishment with the **National Security Act.** World War II, especially the Pearl Harbor disaster, revealed the need for greater coordination among the armed forces. This act created the post of secretary of defense, a civilian cabinet position set over the army, navy, and air force. The National Security Council and Central Intelligence Agency (CIA) were also created to assist the president in foreign policy matters.

Election of 1948—Truman faced the voters in the 1948 election, and his prospects for victory looked dim. The left wing of the Democratic party was enraged over the president's firing of Secretary of Commerce **Henry A. Wallace** for his pro-Soviet positions. These extreme liberals bolted the party and supported Wallace on the Progressive ticket. (This was a far different Progressive party from the one Theodore Roosevelt had run under in 1912.) Conservative southern Democrats, upset over Truman's civil rights record, walked out of the Democratic National Convention and eventually nominated Governor **Strom Thurmond** of South Carolina on a States' Rights party ticket, more commonly known as **"Dixiecrats."** Confident because of the disarray among Democrats, Republicans chose **Thomas Dewey,** the popular governor of New York, as their candidate.

Undaunted, Truman campaigned vigorously against the odds. He called the Republican-controlled Congress back into a special session. When it refused to act on several of his proposals, he dubbed it the "do-nothing" Eightieth Congress and used it as a campaign issue. Truman targeted his appeals to labor and blacks in the cities as well as to farmers in the Midwest and West in hopes of keeping the old New Deal coalition alive. On a 31,000-mile "whistle-stop" train tour, Truman continued his attacks on the Republicans. On election day he made good on his promise that "I will

Displaying the Chicago Daily Tribune's premature headline, an elated Harry Truman celebrates his upset victory over Thomas Dewey.

Harry S.? or Harry S?

Harry S. Truman holds the distinction of being the president with the shortest middle name. When he was born, his parents wanted to avoid offending his grandfathers, Anderson Shippe Truman and Solomon Young; trouble would almost certainly arise if the child were named for one but not the other. The Trumans compromised by giving young Harry the middle initial *S*—but no middle name. Thus each grandfather could claim that Harry was named for him. Truman personally preferred the name *Shippe* and occasionally used it.

The odd middle name naturally caused some confusion. When Truman was sworn in as president after the death of Roosevelt, Chief Justice Harlan Fiske Stone administered the oath of office. He began, "I, Harry Shippe Truman...." Truman responded, "I, Harry S. Truman...." Journalists were also troubled by the name. Since the president's middle name was really simply *S,* shouldn't the period be omitted? Many newspapers, deciding that it should, referred to him as "Harry S Truman." Although the omission was sensible, it looked too much like a mistake. Stimulated by this controversy, one style manual devised a special rule: "For convenience and consistency, . . . it is recommended that all initials given with a name be followed by a period." The president, incidentally, agreed.

Harry Truman

extended social security coverage, and gave more aid to farmers. Congress, however, rejected civil rights bills, federal aid to education, and national health insurance. Like most presidents, Truman got only part of what he wanted from Congress.

Anticommunism in America—One important domestic issue throughout the postwar era was a growing anti-Communist crusade in the United States. Just as a "Red Scare" (widespread fear of communism) followed World War I in the United States, so a second **Red Scare** followed World War II. Many Americans blamed subversives in their own government for Soviet advances, and several events in the postwar era gave credibility to the charge. The most sensational case involved **Alger Hiss,** a former State Department official. In 1948 Whittaker Chambers, a former Communist, went before Congress and accused Hiss of passing secret documents to him ten years before when Chambers was a Soviet agent. Hiss could not be tried for espionage, since the statute of limitations had expired, but he was convicted of perjury when he denied the accusations under oath. The Hiss case also launched the political career of Congressman **Richard Nixon,** whose aggressive work eventually sent Hiss to jail. In addition to the charges against

Richard Nixon rose to national attention in the late 1940s and 1950s through his unflinching attacks on communism. He is pictured here in 1958 confronting an Uruguayan Communist.

win this election and make the Republicans like it." Although many Americans went to bed on election night thinking that Dewey had won, the ballot count the next morning revealed that Truman had beaten Dewey easily in one of the biggest upsets in the history of presidential elections. After his election, Congress passed many of the president's Fair Deal proposals, which basically updated the New Deal. Congress raised the minimum wage,

COMMUNIST PARTY OR

Senator Joseph McCarthy points to a map during televised hearings on alleged Communist subversion in the United States Army. On the left sits an emotionally drained Boston attorney Joseph Welch. Only shortly before, Welch–in response to McCarthy's reckless charge that a member of Welch's staff was a Communist–had demanded in anger, "Have you no sense of decency, sir, at long last?"

Hiss, the government in 1950 revealed the existence of a British-American spy ring. Two members of this ring, Julius and Ethel Rosenberg, were convicted of passing atomic secrets to the Soviets during World War II. They were executed in 1953 for their treason.

The government quickly reacted to these threats. In 1947 President Truman instituted a loyalty program to check federal employees. The House Un-American Activities Committee (HUAC) in Congress conducted extensive investigations, such as that for the Hiss case and an in-depth study of Communist activity in the entertainment industry. With fears heightened by revelations of subversion, Congress in 1950 passed, over Truman's veto, the McCarran Internal Security Act, which made it easier for the government to combat espionage. One provision of this act required Communists and their organizations to register with the Justice Department.

The man most closely associated with the Red Scare in the 1950s was Senator **Joseph McCarthy** of Wisconsin. In 1951 in a speech at Wheeling, West Virginia, McCarthy declared boldly that the State Department harbored Communists; in fact, he said, he had a list of their names. A Senate committee investigated the charges and concluded that the charges were "a fraud and a hoax." McCarthy continued his attacks, however, and he even headed a Senate subcommittee which probed into the presence of Communists in government. His political power was greatest during the Korean War, when no one dared attack him for fear of being suspected of Communist sympathies. Republicans encouraged McCarthy, some because they believed him but others simply because fighting Communists was a winning political issue. Despite his well-publicized investigations, the senator never found a single Communist in the government. (This failure was in part due to Truman's previous success

A Couple of Spies

No incident better illustrates the reality of the Communist threat to America during and after World War II than the theft of the secret of the atomic bomb. At the heart of this act of espionage were traitors who rival Benedict Arnold in infamy. The main leader, Julius Rosenberg, had been reared in a Jewish home and had even considered becoming a rabbi. In college, however, Rosenberg became a Communist, and he later married another Communist, Ethel Greenglass. A talented engineer, Rosenberg won a civilian job with the U.S. Army during World War II.

While keeping his Communist ties secret, Rosenberg became the center of a Soviet spy ring. Among those he recruited was David Greenglass, his brother-in-law, who worked at the top-secret atomic bomb research center in Los Alamos, New Mexico. In 1944 and 1945 Rosenberg, with his wife's knowledge and complicity, helped funnel classified information concerning the atomic bomb to the Soviets, thus helping speed the USSR's development of atomic weapons.

In 1950 British investigators uncovered a major figure in the spy ring, scientist Klaus Fuchs, who had been one of the most important developers of the atomic bomb. Fuchs confessed in full, and using information gained from him, the FBI began to track down other Soviet agents. The trail eventually led to David Greenglass. To save himself, Greenglass became a witness for the government and led government investigators to his sister and brother-in-law, Ethel and Julius Rosenberg.

The Rosenbergs were arrested and tried, claiming all the while that they were innocent. The jury looked at the evidence, however, and thought otherwise. Convicted of espionage, the Rosenbergs were sentenced to death in the electric chair. Despite pleas for mercy from various leftist groups to the president and the Supreme Court, the Rosenbergs were executed in 1953. Many left-wing writers have tried to make the Rosenbergs "martyrs" of the Red Scare, victims of paranoid hysteria. The facts, though, reveal that the Rosenbergs were guilty of one of the greatest acts of treason in American history–they had given a totalitarian nation the most destructive weapon in history.

in rooting security risks out of the government.) By the end of 1954 McCarthy's charges had become increasingly irresponsible, and his Senate colleagues censured him for his conduct. His opponents coined a new word, **"McCarthyism,"** to describe his alleged use of lies, distortion, and innuendo. What was often ignored in the outrage over McCarthy's methods was the reality of the Communist threat in America. By his exploitation of the Communist issue, McCarthy probably brought genuine anticommunism into disrepute.

As a part of the fight against communism, several new conservative leaders and organizations emerged in the 1950s. Most prominent perhaps was **William F. Buckley, Jr.** Soon after his graduation from Yale he wrote a bestseller, *God and Man at Yale,* a critique of the University's liberal political philosophy. In 1955 he founded *National Review,* a magazine that promoted conservative views. Buckley and other conservatives such as senators Robert Taft and Barry Goldwater opposed the growth of the welfare state, rejected government regulation of the economy, and decried weakness in the face of Communist aggression. Some conservatives went further. In 1958 Robert Welch founded the **John Birch Society,** named for a Baptist missionary killed by Chinese Communists at the end of World War II. The Birch Society held that Communist subversion affected high public officials in the country, and it questioned the patriotism of those who pursued the policy of peaceful coexistence with the Soviet Union.

The ticket of Eisenhower and Nixon brought the Republicans two lopsided presidential election victories in the 1950s.

Eisenhower and "Dynamic Conservatism"

His popularity at a low ebb, due mainly to the Korean War, Truman declined to run for re-election in 1952. Republicans, frustrated with defeat in 1948, looked for victory with Dwight Eisenhower, former Allied commander in World War II and commander of NATO, as their standard bearer. The popular war hero balanced the Republican ticket by choosing thirty-nine-year-old Senator Richard Nixon, a conservative, as his vice-presidential running mate. The Democrats nominated the governor of Illinois, **Adlai Stevenson,** for president. Pompously intellectual, Stevenson could not match the popularity and charm of Eisenhower, captured in the slogan "I like Ike." Eisenhower promised to end corruption in Washington and the war in Korea. Elected in a landslide, Eisenhower was the first Republican president since Herbert Hoover. The new president described his philosophy as **"Dynamic Conservatism,"** calling himself "conservative when it comes to money and liberal when it comes to human beings." In 1954 his new budget cut expenditures by nearly ten per cent. Eisenhower abolished the Reconstruction Finance Corporation, a holdover from the depression, and reduced farm price subsidies. Furthermore, the presence of millionaire businessmen in the cabinet gave the administration a strong conservative image. Because several cabinet members were from the auto industry, Adlai Stevenson quipped that the New Dealers had been replaced by the "car dealers."

Like the Truman administration, however, Eisenhower expanded the New Deal in many ways, much to the frustration of conservatives. Congress broadened social security to cover professionals, domestics, farm workers, armed services personnel, and other groups that had previously been excluded. In 1955 Congress increased the minimum wage from 75¢ to $1 an hour. The federal bureaucracy grew as the government created a new cabinet department in 1953–Health, Education, and Welfare (now Health and Human Services)–to coordinate federal social programs. Eisenhower supported the National Defense Education Act, which poured federal funds into education in unprecedented amounts. One of his most enduring projects was a new federal highway act. This legislation committed the national government to pay for ninety per cent of an extensive **interstate highway system.** These limited-access "interstates," as they are commonly known, have become the main arteries of highway transportation in the United States.

Kennedy and the New Frontier

In the election of 1960, two World War II veterans competed for the leadership of a new generation of Americans. John F. Kennedy–youthful, handsome, and witty–skillfully promoted himself as an author and war hero. As a result of eight years of service in the Senate (and lots of money from his millionaire father), Kennedy won a close election over Vice President Richard Nixon, the Republican nominee. Despite a lackluster record in the Senate, where he had avoided controversies such as McCarthyism and civil rights, Kennedy had impressed the voters with a vigorous campaign. His apparent grasp of the issues overcame doubts about his age. (At forty-three Kennedy was the youngest elected president.) He also eased doubts about his religion as he became the first Catholic to serve as president. Kennedy deftly used television as a new political weapon. Poised and charismatic, Kennedy bested Nixon–at least in image–in four televised presidential debates.

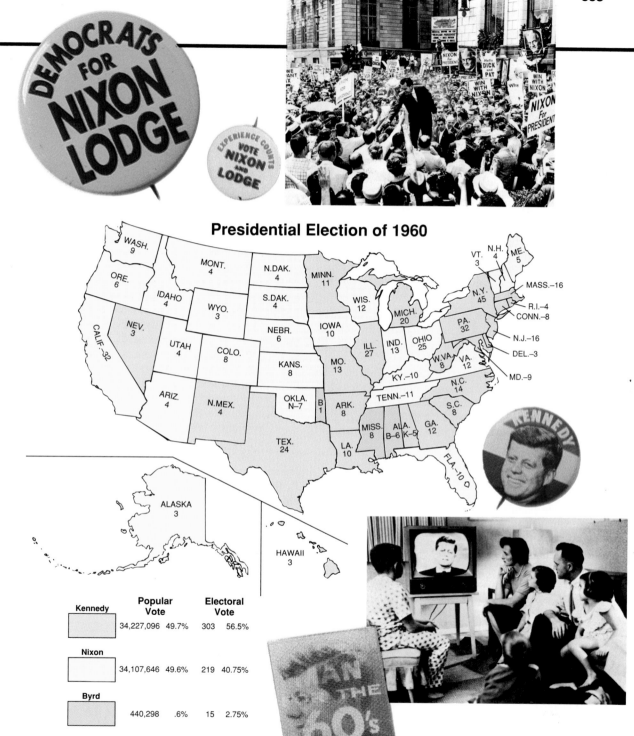

Presidential Election of 1960

Map electoral votes by state:

WASH. 9
ORE. 6
CALIF.–32
NEV. 3
IDAHO 4
MONT. 4
WYO. 3
UTAH 4
ARIZ. 4
N.MEX. 4
COLO. 8
N.DAK. 4
S.DAK. 4
NEBR. 6
KANS. 8
OKLA. N–7
TEX. 24
MINN. 11
IOWA 10
MO. 13
ARK. 8
LA. 10
WIS. 12
ILL. 27
IND. 13
MICH. 20
OHIO 25
KY.–10
TENN.–11
MISS. 8
ALA. B–6 K–5
GA. 12
N.C. 14
S.C. 8
FLA.–10
VA. 12
W.VA. 8
MD.–9
DEL.–3
N.J.–16
PA. 32
N.Y. 45
CONN.–8
R.I.–4
MASS.–16
VT. 3
N.H. 4
ME. 5
B 1

ALASKA 3
HAWAII 3

		Popular Vote		Electoral Vote	
Kennedy		34,227,096	49.7%	303	56.5%
Nixon		34,107,646	49.6%	219	40.75%
Byrd		440,298	.6%	15	2.75%

An exuberant John F. Kennedy, pictured with his daughter Caroline, on the day after his election victory in 1960

Because of his youth and vigor, Kennedy seemed to embody a dramatic change in government. People admired the handsome, glib Kennedy; and his lovely young wife, Jacqueline, became a model and trendsetter for women's fashion. The sight of the young president romping with his children in the White House presented a pleasing picture to most Americans. Kennedy himself proclaimed a change in emphasis. In his inaugural speech the president said,

> Let the word go forth from this time and place, to friend and foe alike, that the torch has been passed to a new generation of Americans–born in this century, tempered by war, disciplined by a hard and bitter peace, proud of our ancient heritage–and unwilling to witness or permit the slow undoing of those human rights to which this Nation has always been committed, and to which we are committed today at home and around the world.

Kennedy appealed to American idealism, as demonstrated by the famous line from his inaugural address: "And so, my fellow Americans, ask not what your country can do for you: Ask what you can do for your country." He gave his legislative program the inspiring name the **New Frontier.** An example of this idealism was one of Kennedy's most popular programs, the **Peace Corps,** a government project designed to send skilled volunteers overseas to help underdeveloped nations. The "Kennedy mys-

tique," heightened by the youthful president's tragic assassination in 1963, gave the impression of great changes in America under Kennedy.

In reality Kennedy's administration differed from previous ones more in style than in substance. Entering office in 1961, Kennedy faced one of the worst recessions in the postwar period. The government sharply increased its spending to stimulate the economy; Congress expanded public works, appropriated almost $5 billion for housing, gave financial aid to distressed areas, increased social security benefits, and raised the minimum wage. Kennedy's record in office was sometimes marked by a conservative bent, however. Business endorsed his 1962 Trade Expansion Act, which stimulated trade with the European Common Market. The Telstar satellite system aided the communications industry, and Kennedy's challenge to put a man on the moon by the end of the decade expanded the space program, a boon to aerospace companies. In 1962 the Revenue Act gave $1 billion in tax credits to business. Later that year he proposed a drastic tax cut in an address that a liberal economist called "the most Republican speech since William McKinley." Congress enacted it, however, a few months after Kennedy's death.

Liberals criticized Kennedy not only for pro-business policies but also for a lack of leadership in federal aid to education, medical care for the elderly, and civil rights. "We get awfully sick of this 'moderation,'" a columnist wrote in the *New Republic,* a liberal magazine. Kennedy's defenders argued that the foreign affairs of the cold war demanded more attention; moreover, his narrow victory over Nixon dictated caution in the White House. His death in Dallas, Texas, in November 1963 brought an end to an administration that was more symbol than substance.

Section Review

1. What is a "right-to-work" law?
2. Name the four major candidates and their parties in the 1948 presidential election.
3. Give at least one example each of how Truman and Eisenhower expanded the New Deal.
4. What new political weapon was important in helping Kennedy defeat Nixon in 1960?

Life in Postwar America

The Affluent Society

After World War II many Americans feared another economic decline since the war demand had been the cure for the economic woes of the 1930s. They need not have worried, for the postwar era brought unprecedented economic prosperity. Between 1945 and 1960 the Gross National Product (GNP; see p. 493) almost doubled. The biggest reason for the economic improvement was defense spending, a necessary expense given the challenges of the cold war, especially in Korea. With Europe and Japan devastated from the war, America had little competition as a major supplier of industrial goods to the world. With new industries such as aerospace, electronics, and chemicals, along with technological improvement in automation, productivity jumped dramatically. Also American consumers went on an unrestrained buying spree after sacrificing and saving during the war. They bought automobiles as well as washing machines, televisions, refrigerators, and numerous other items for their new homes. The number of home owners in the United States increased by fifty per cent between 1945 and 1960. By 1955 about twice as many people belonged to the middle class as did in 1929, before the Great Depression. In the title of his book *The Affluent Society* (1958), economist John Kenneth Galbraith gave the prosperous era a label that stuck.

The economic growth altered American culture as well. Less attuned to "producing," that is, working hard, Americans turned their attention to consuming, buying the latest goods in the marketplace. Business carefully orchestrated this "consumer culture." Borrowing from the 1920s, advertisers taught the public to forget the frugality of the depression and war years and to spend. Manufacturers offered different models and styles so that eventually certain possessions would become out of date. This "planned obsolescence" fueled the urge to buy. Marketing specialists appealed to self-gratification, social status, and materialism. With televisions in ninety per cent of American homes by 1960, almost no one was immune to these appeals.

Consumers, less thrifty and less concerned about debt, could use the credit card when they did not have the money. In 1950 Diner's Club inaugurated the credit card, and by 1965 more than a million people had one. Other cards, such as American Express, soon equaled the success of Diner's Club. Retail activity in the postwar period shifted from the downtown to the suburban malls, and the number of malls mushroomed from eight in 1945 to almost four thousand by 1960. Shopping–drudgery for previous generations of housewives–became a significant leisure activity for millions. Young people also became avid consumers. When rock music exploded on the scene in the 1950s, businessmen capitalized on the craze by marketing transistor radios, phonographs, and "forty-fives" (small records played at forty-five revolutions per minute). The pop culture also included magazines and movies that featured all the teen idols. Many, such as actor James Dean and rock singer Elvis Presley, symbolized rebellion against traditional values.

Family

Baby Boom—Postwar America witnessed enormous changes in the family. Young adults had postponed marriage and children during the war, and after 1945 they married and started families. Americans had one of the highest marriage rates in the world for the period 1944 to 1948. Some fifteen million returning soldiers who became new fathers contributed also to the **"baby boom,"** a massive rise in the birth rate lasting until 1964. Between 1945 and 1960 America's population increased by almost thirty per cent. With the prosperity of the 1940s and 1950s, more couples were having more children. Television, which replaced movies as the chief source of entertainment, celebrated the American middle-class family. The Andersons of *Father Knows Best* and the Cleavers of *Leave it to Beaver* were models of the perfect family, presided over by a patient and dutiful father who had all the answers. Jackie Gleason's *The Honeymooners* carried the theme with working-class families, and Lucille Ball's *I Love Lucy* program gave a comic dimension to the ideal family.

The ideal family faced some daunting threats in the real world, however. Divorce rates climbed

Television had a tremendous social impact after World War II, making numerous actors familiar faces in American homes.

in 1946, leveled off for several years, then increased again after 1958. The 1950s also experienced a national concern over juvenile delinquency. Some people blamed television, movies, and crime comic books, while others cited the breakdown of discipline in the home and the school. Dr. Benjamin Spock's *Baby and Child Care* book may have contributed to underlying permissiveness, according to his conservative critics, by advocating less structured methods of child-rearing. Spock, popularizing theories of psychologist Sigmund Freud and philosopher John Dewey, wanted children eventually to become well-adjusted, guilt-free adults. His child-care book sold 23 million copies between 1946 and 1976. Only the Bible, a much better answer to the problem of human guilt, outsold it during that same period.

Women at Work–The role of women changed after World War II. According to the popular ideal, women married, had children, and reigned over the middle-class suburban household as "queens of domesticity." Mother, wife, and family manager, they juggled numerous tasks—ranging from cooking, gardening, and club meetings to Little League for the sons and piano lessons for the girls—all with a self-sacrificing spirit. The family was still important to society in the 1950s, and being a housewife was considered a rewarding career for a woman.

Much in the postwar society contradicted this picture of the ideal housewife image, however.

More women than ever before worked outside the home. Government policy encouraged it during the war because of the shortage of workers in the defense industries. When "Rosie the Riveter" came marching home, she was accustomed to the income and independence and often continued to work, not just in traditional female jobs but in male ones as well. By 1970 forty-one per cent of married women were in the work force. The increase in divorce posed another problem for women; the number of single-parent heads of household rose dramatically. Such trends did not bode well for the family.

Emergence of Minority Rights

The push for equality of the races gained momentum after the war with the rise of the **civil rights movement.** Technically, a *civil right* is a specific privilege or entitlement that is granted by law and that the government is responsible for actively protecting from both government and individual encroachment. In modern American history, however, the phrase "civil rights movement" refers primarily to attempts by blacks to secure the exercise and protection of their civil rights. Truman was the first president to accept civil rights for blacks as an issue, as shown by his appointment of black judges and territorial governors and his order ending discrimination in the armed forces.

The first great victory of the modern civil rights movement was the Supreme Court decision ***Brown***

v. *Board of Education* (1954), the climax of years of legal action by the NAACP. Citing sociological evidence, the Court concluded that segregated public schools stamped blacks as inferior and that such institutions no longer had a place in American society. The Court then ordered an end to segregated schools. Compliance came slowly because some states resisted. The most dramatic stand-off occurred in 1957 in Little Rock, Arkansas, when Governor Orval Faubus used the National Guard to block nine black students from entering a high school. He later withdrew the force under court order, and Eisenhower used troops to protect the black students, to keep order in the school, and to enforce obedience to the *Brown* decision.

In 1955 the civil rights struggle shifted from legal to mass action with a **bus boycott** in Montgomery, Alabama. At that time, blacks sat in the back of all city buses in Montgomery and had to give up their seats to whites and stand if the buses became crowded. On December 1, 1955, a tired black seamstress named Rosa Parks refused to give up her seat to a white male. She was arrested and fined for refusing the bus driver's order to stand. Her small act of defiance energized the black community of Montgomery. Over ninety per cent of the city's blacks joined a boycott of the city's bus system. The boycott financially devastated the Montgomery city bus system, but the fight did not end until a Supreme Court decision forbade discrimination in public transportation.

The boycott also launched a popular and charismatic figure in the civil rights movement, Baptist pastor **Martin Luther King, Jr.,** leader of the fight against Montgomery's bus system. Brought up in a pastor's home, King turned from his religiously conservative upbringing and received his theological training at the liberal Crozer Seminary, followed by a Ph.D. in systematic theology from the equally liberal Boston University. While in graduate school, King was profoundly influenced by reading American transcendentalist Henry David Thoreau and Hindu political philosopher Mohandas Gandhi. From them, King borrowed the idea of

The Reverend Martin Luther King, Jr., the major leader of the civil rights movement in the 1950s and 1960s

Jackie Robinson

Professional sports, like most areas of American life before the 1950s, were segregated along racial lines. America's national pastime, baseball, was no exception. The best white players joined the major league teams of the National and American leagues. Blacks played in the "negro leagues," loose organizations of all-black teams. There was an unofficial, unspoken rule in the major leagues—no blacks allowed. That color barrier was finally broken, however, by a brave and talented ballplayer named Jackie Robinson.

Robinson was born in Georgia but moved with his family to California while still a child. A gifted athlete, Robinson won a scholarship to UCLA, where he starred in football, basketball, track, and baseball. After serving in the army during World War II, Robinson joined the Kansas City Monarchs, a team in one of the negro leagues. It was there he came to the attention of Branch Rickey, president of the Brooklyn Dodgers.

Rickey was determined to break the color barrier in the major leagues. He knew that the player who would break it, however, would have to be special. Rickey needed a man who was unquestionably a talented player, but the man also had to have the strength of character to withstand intense public scrutiny and even open bigotry. As Rickey observed Jackie Robinson, he became convinced that Robinson had the necessary talent and character to become baseball's black pioneer.

After a season in the minor leagues, Robinson joined the Dodgers in 1947 as their sec-

using nonviolent resistance and civil disobedience (refusing to obey laws that one thinks are unjust) in order to achieve social and political change. King became convinced that black churches could serve as the vehicles of such reform in the United States, and the Montgomery effort seemed to vindicate his ideas. In 1957 King and his associates organized the Southern Christian Leadership Conference to further the cause of black rights.

The early 1960s brought greater exposure to the civil rights movement. Black young people staged "sit-ins" at restaurants and lunch counters in 1960 in six southern states to focus more attention on social equality for minorities. Testing the effect of Supreme Court decisions prohibiting discrimination in interstate transportation, black and white "freedom riders" traveled in buses across the deep South in 1961 to challenge segregated buses and terminals. In 1962 James Meredith enrolled as the first black student at the University of Mississippi after federal marshals and troops overcame a defiant governor and mob. Television also became an ally of the civil rights movement. As news cameras showed police dogs, tear gas, and fire hoses being used against demonstrators in their protests, middle-class Americans increasingly sympathized with the victims.

In August 1963 over two hundred thousand people—both black and white—gathered in the nation's capital for the **march on Washington,** the largest civil rights protest in United States history. The highlight for the protestors was Martin Luther

ond baseman. Rickey had not overestimated the challenge Robinson faced. He heard racial slurs and insults from hecklers in the crowd from his first time at bat. Once in Philadelphia the entire Dodger team was turned away from a hotel because of the presence of a black player on the roster. In many cities Robinson had to stay in a separate hotel from his white teammates. Aware that the national eye was on him, Robinson curbed both his natural competitiveness and his resentment of the treatment he received. He knew that—fairly or not—many Americans would judge his whole race by his behavior. For Robinson, Branch Rickey later wrote, "There could be but one direction of dedication—the doctrine of turning the other cheek. *There* came in the greatness of Jackie Robinson."

In his first season, Robinson won honors as baseball's Rookie of the Year. In 1949 his .342 batting average and 37 stolen bases helped him win the league's coveted Most Valuable Player Award. In Robinson's ten seasons with Brooklyn, the Dodgers won six pennants and one World Series, and after his retirement, he was elected to baseball's Hall of Fame.

King's speech in front of the Lincoln Memorial. King said,

> I have a dream that one day this nation will rise up and live out the true meaning of its creed: "We hold these truths to be self-evident: that all men are created equal." I have a dream that one day on the red hills of Georgia sons of former slaves and the sons of former slave-owners will be able to sit down together at the table of brotherhood. . . . I have a dream that my four children will one day live in a nation where they will not be judged by the color of their skin but by the content of their character.

The events of 1963 pushed the previously cautious John Kennedy to publicly support a major civil rights bill. The legislation was not passed, however, until after his assassination. (See p. 565.)

Religion

Americans displayed a renewed interest in religion in the postwar era as memberships in religious groups rose from fifty to over sixty per cent in the decade after the war. Unfortunately, this was more a bland public piety than a genuine spiritual revival. In 1953 President Eisenhower joined a church for the first time in his public life and began to promote religion in general with comments such as "Our government makes no sense, unless it is founded in a deeply felt religious faith—and I don't care what it is." Congress in 1954 added "one nation under God" to the Pledge of Allegiance and the next year required that "In God We Trust" be placed on U.S. currency. *The Power of Positive Thinking* (1952) by Norman Vincent Peale, a leading liberal Protestant minister, was a bestseller in the 1950s. His emphasis on how to be happy was more psychological therapy than Biblical faith, but he touched a chord in a generation anxious about life and seeking material success. The message from the liberal religious establishment was soothing but ultimately unsatisfying.

Paralleling the "uniting" of the world in the UN was a movement for unity among nominal Christians, the **ecumenical movement,** whose advocates often quoted Christ's words from John 17:20-21:

> Neither pray I for these alone, but for them also which shall believe on me through their word; that they all may be one; as thou, Father, art in me, and I in thee, that they also may be one in us: that the world may believe that thou hast sent me.

The goal of the movement was to promote greater unity among professing Christians, ultimately resulting in one great church to which all Christians would belong. One aspect of this movement was the uniting of different bodies with similar denominational backgrounds. American Methodists, for example, healed their 1844 North-South split in 1939, and in 1968 merged with the Evangelical United Brethren to form the United Methodist Church. Another aspect was in uniting dissimilar bodies in cooperative organizations, sort of religious versions of the UN. The World Council of Churches, founded in 1948, was the main international ecumenical body, and the National Council of Churches, founded in 1950, was the primary body in the United States. The great shortcoming of the ecumenical movement, however, was that it compromised the truths of Scripture in order to achieve outward unity. Significant differences in doctrine and even modernistic unbelief were all tolerated in the interests of unity. Proponents of the movement did not seem to realize that true Christian unity involves spiritual unity built on God's truth.

Conservative Christian groups grew in the 1940s and 1950s. Generally ignored by the media and the religious establishment, fundamentalist Protestants expanded through large local churches and evangelistic ministries. Charles E. Fuller on his very popular "Old Fashioned Revival Hour" radio program preached to millions the simple gospel message of saving faith in Christ. His audience was huge, despite the fact that the major networks would not carry his broadcasts. Youth rallies during the war led to the creation in 1945 of a large evangelistic outreach called Youth for Christ. Many Christians who had served in the military felt a burden for missions in the foreign nations they visited and returned to those lands as soldiers for the Lord.

The first full-time evangelist for Youth for Christ was **Billy Graham,** who, after being promoted by the press in a 1949 Los Angeles tent revival, gained worldwide fame. Graham, however, became the center of the major postwar dispute in fundamentalist Christianity. In 1957 Graham accepted the sponsorship of liberal Protestants in a New York City crusade. To Graham and his supporters, such a move would help bring fundamentalism into the mainstream of public life and allow it to build bridges to liberal Christianity. However, many fundamentalists broke with Graham over the issue. Having come through the fierce struggles with modernism in the 1920s, these militant fundamentalist Christians would not compromise their faith by joining with unbelieving liberals. Conservative Protestants who accepted Graham's cooperation with liberal churches adopted the label

The ecumenically oriented evangelistic campaigns of Billy Graham became a major point of division among conservative Christians in the 1950s.

"new evangelicals" or simply "evangelicals." The militants kept the name "fundamentalist."

There were other divisions in American society that would deepen into wounds in the coming decade. Divisions during the turbulent decade that followed Kennedy's assassination–divisions over war and peace, over poverty and plenty, over rights and rioting–would tear at America's social fabric and produce fundamental changes in the nation's politics and moral direction.

Section Review

1. During the postwar era, what replaced the downtown area in most cities as the center of retail business activity?
2. What became the nation's chief source of entertainment in the 1950s?
3. Technically, what is a "civil right"?
4. What act sparked the Montgomery bus boycott? Who emerged as the leader of the boycott?
5. What is the major international ecumenical body? What is the major national ecumenical body in the United States?

Chapter Review

Terms

Harry Truman
United Nations
cold war
iron curtain
containment
Truman Doctrine
Marshall Plan
North Atlantic
   Treaty Organization (NATO)
Warsaw Pact
Berlin airlift
Chiang Kai-shek
Mao Zedong
38th parallel
Douglas MacArthur
Inchon
limited war
Dwight Eisenhower

John Kennedy
"peaceful coexistence"
Ho Chi Minh
Ngo Dinh Diem
domino theory
Fidel Castro
Bay of Pigs
Cuban missile crisis
Berlin Wall
Fair Deal
Taft-Hartley Act
National Security Act
Henry A. Wallace
Strom Thurmond
"Dixiecrats"
Thomas Dewey
Red Scare
Alger Hiss
Richard Nixon

Joseph McCarthy
"McCarthyism"
William F. Buckley, Jr.
John Birch Society
Adlai Stevenson
"Dynamic Conservatism"
interstate highway system
New Frontier
Peace Corps
The Affluent Society
"baby boom"
civil rights movement
Brown v. *Board of Education*
Montgomery bus boycott
Martin Luther King, Jr.
march on Washington
ecumenical movement
Billy Graham

Content Questions

1. What are the three major agencies of the United Nations? Which agency has veto power over the UN's actions?
2. Name three nations that were split into Communist and non-Communist divisions after World War II.
3. Who was the first commander of the NATO forces? What organization did the Soviets form in response to NATO?
4. Which of the two Chinese governments did the United States recognize as the "real" China after 1949?
5. What event caused MacArthur to say that the Korean conflict had become "an entirely new war"?
6. How did the Communists respond to the flight of refugees to West Berlin?
7. What American politician first rose to fame by conducting the congressional investigation of Alger Hiss?
8. What senator most exploited anticommunism as a political issue in the 1950s?
9. Under which president was the interstate highway system begun?
10. What city was the scene of a confrontation over the desegregation of public schools in 1957?

Application Questions

1. Was the Korean War a success or failure for the United States? Why?
2. How does the career of Joseph McCarthy illustrate the danger of pursuing a worthy cause in an unworthy manner?
3. What are the dangers of the ecumenical movement?

CHAPTER 24

The Shattered Society (1963-1973)

"The 'Great Society' has become the sick society."

Senator William Fulbright, 1968

This Pulitzer Prize-winning photograph of Dallas nightclub-owner Jack Ruby shooting Lee Harvey Oswald, alleged assassin of President Kennedy, epitomizes the violence of the 1960s.

On the afternoon of November 22, 1963, millions of Americans were watching the soap opera "As the World Turns" on the CBS television network. Suddenly an announcer interrupted with a shocking news bulletin: "In Dallas, Texas, three shots were fired at President Kennedy's motorcade in downtown Dallas. The first reports say that President Kennedy has been seriously wounded by the shooting." Soon the horrifying news came–President Kennedy was dead. Only two days later, Kennedy's alleged assassin, Lee Harvey Oswald, was gunned down by a Dallas nightclub owner in front of seventy policemen as well as a national television audience.

Over the next ten years, Americans endured a series of similar news bulletins flashing across their television screens–civil rights leader Martin Luther King, Jr., slain on the balcony of a motel in Memphis; Senator Robert Kennedy assassinated in a California hotel during his presidential campaign; Democratic presidential candidate Governor George Wallace cut down in the parking lot of a shopping mall in Maryland. (Wallace, at least, survived but was paralyzed for life.) These acts of violence were but the individual highlights of a decade of unrest. Viewers saw urban riots punctuated by looting and killing, student protests often climaxing in bloody clashes between protesters and police, and, above all, scenes of the frustratingly endless carnage of the war in Vietnam. This war in Southeast Asia might have been far away in miles, but television brought it into the living rooms of America. As he reviewed the dramatically widespread unrest in the United States, one California newspaper editor lamented, "We just seem to be headed toward a collapse of everything."

In the midst of apparent chaos, many Americans looked to their political leaders for guidance–and deliverance. The presidents during this era were two of the shrewdest, most experienced politicians in America, Democrat Lyndon B. Johnson and Republican Richard M. Nixon. Yet both found that America's problems defied their efforts to solve them. Johnson's presidency was wrecked by his inability to deal with violence at home and the growing American involvement in Vietnam. Nixon finally ended the war, and domestic violence at least subsided, but serious divisions remained. For the ten years from 1963 to 1973, the United States was a society shattered by hatred and conflict. More than a few wondered whether the social fabric could stand the strain.

Johnson and the Great Society

Although lacking Kennedy's charisma, President **Lyndon Johnson** was well prepared for politi-

A somber Lyndon Johnson takes the oath of office on the presidential plane shortly after John F. Kennedy's assassination.

An assembly of politicians and civil rights leaders, including Martin Luther King, Jr., watch as Lyndon Johnson signs the Voting Rights Act of 1965.

cal leadership. He was one of the country's most experienced, energetic, and crafty politicians. Johnson had spent twelve years in the Senate, including five years in the powerful position of majority leader. Few other presidents have known how to work with Congress as well as Johnson did. He also came to the presidency with a clear vision of what he thought the United States must accomplish. Johnson believed that the government had the power and resources to eliminate poverty and inequality, to create a **"Great Society"** in which government would help all citizens have the opportunity to better themselves politically, socially, and economically.

Building the Great Society

Civil Rights—By dedicating legislation to the slain Kennedy and using his considerable political skill, Johnson won from Congress the legislation he needed to build his Great Society. A major part of his agenda was civil rights legislation. The first and most important of Johnson's civil rights bills was the **Civil Rights Act of 1964.** This comprehensive law called for an end to a number of racial injustices. It established fairer procedures for voter registration, forbade racial discrimination in public buildings such as restaurants and stores, promoted

the desegregation of public schools, authorized withholding federal funds from projects or institutions which discriminated against minorities, and created the Equal Opportunity Commission to ensure that job seekers did not encounter discrimination.

The following year Johnson encouraged Congress to pass the **Voting Rights Act of 1965,** which sent federal officials into states to help register blacks to vote and which outlawed literacy tests for voters. Such tests were often administered only to blacks in order to prevent them from voting. This measure augmented the provisions of the **Twenty-fourth Amendment,** ratified in January 1964, which outlawed the use of poll taxes, similarly used to prevent black suffrage. The intent of both the amendment and the Voting Rights Act was to help blacks acquire more nearly equal treatment by giving them a greater political voice.

War on Poverty—In his first State of the Union message, Johnson also declared a **"War on Poverty."** Through the newly formed Office of Economic Opportunity (OEO), the government attacked poverty through job-training and job-placement programs; Head Start (a preschool program for children in poor families); and Volunteers in Service to

America (VISTA), a sort of domestic Peace Corps in which thousands of enthusiastic young people volunteered to work in government programs helping the poor. The programs of the War on Poverty did succeed in helping raise thousands of people above the poverty level (although the general economic prosperity of the Johnson years may have had much to do with that success). The "war," however, did not come close to eliminating poverty in the United States.

1964 Election—A factor that helped Johnson push his program through Congress was his landslide victory in the 1964 presidential election. Even before Kennedy's assassination, most political observers had predicted a Democratic victory in 1964; afterwards, the shock of the president's death made Americans even less likely to want to change leaders again in less than a year. Johnson was further helped by the Republican nomination of Senator **Barry Goldwater** of Arizona. Goldwater was an honest, unbending conservative. He rejected the usual political practice of tailoring his message to

Senator Barry Goldwater, Republican candidate in the 1964 presidential election

please his audience. He denounced the social security system in front of senior citizens in Florida, for example, and suggested in a speech in Knoxville that the government sell the Tennessee Valley Authority (see p. 498). Goldwater advocated a philosophy of government almost diametrically opposed to Johnson's; the Arizona senator believed that *less* government activity and regulation would benefit the nation. Goldwater, for instance, voted against the Civil Rights Act of 1964, not because he opposed equal rights for blacks but because he thought that the bill gave the federal government too much power to interfere in the private lives of citizens.

Goldwater fought a losing battle from the beginning. Blacks resented Goldwater's vote on the Civil Rights Act, and liberal Republicans refused to support him. Besides representing a minority party, Goldwater frightened many voters by his indiscreet statements about how he would conduct the war in Vietnam, such as how he would "defoliate" the jungle with nuclear weapons. Johnson, on the other hand, soberly committed himself to "no wider war" in Vietnam. Johnson scored an overwhelming victory with 61 per cent of the vote, gaining 486 electoral votes to only 52 for Goldwater, who won only his home state and five states of the Deep South. Johnson now believed he had an unquestioned mandate for the Great Society.

A Flood of Legislation—The 1964 elections had also given the Democrats huge majorities in Congress, 68-32 in the Senate and 295-140 in the House. In the first session of Congress, Johnson used his tremendous victory and lopsided majorities to push no fewer than eighty-nine bills through the legislature, such as a bill increasing federal aid to education ($1.5 billion worth). The program having the widest impact, perhaps, was **Medicare,** a government health insurance program established in 1965 to help elderly people pay for medical care. Medicare was designed to ensure that the nation's elderly would be able to afford proper medical treatment, but it did so by taxing other Americans in order to pay for the program. In that respect, Medicare typified the Great Society as a whole.

The Warren Court—Even before the Johnson years, the Supreme Court had followed the same liberal reformist approach that Johnson advocated. Led by Chief Justice **Earl Warren,** the Warren Court (1953-1969) pursued a policy of **judicial activism,** interpreting the law and the Constitution broadly in order to address what judges perceive as major social problems. Activist judges do not wait for legislation to attack a problem; they more or less make the laws themselves by handing down sweeping decisions and ordering their enforcement.

The Warren Court is probably best known for its civil rights decisions, beginning with *Brown* v. *Board of Education* (1954; see pp. 556-57). The Court did not limit itself to civil rights, however; it handed down decisions touching all areas of American life. The Court placed tighter restrictions on law enforcement officials and gave greater protection to accused criminals in cases such as *Gideon* v. *Wainwright* (1963), which required the state to provide an attorney for defendants who could not afford one, and *Miranda* v. *Arizona* (1966), which required that criminal suspects be informed of their constitutional rights before they could be questioned. In *Engel* v. *Vitale* (1962) the Court banned state-sponsored prayers in public schools as a so-called violation of the First Amendment's guarantee of the separation of church and state. In *Roth* v. *United States* (1957) the Supreme Court ruled that obscenity was not protected by the First Amendment's guarantee of freedom of speech, but it defined "obscenity" so narrowly that the decision actually struck down many obscenity laws. As a result, a flourishing pornography industry began to grow in the United States in the 1960s.

In a typical example of judicial activism, the Court ordered the redrawing of legislative districts, such as those in the House of Representatives, in a series of **"one man, one vote" decisions.** In these cases the justices ruled that districts that were unequal in population violated the guarantees for "equal protection of the law" in the Fourteenth Amendment. The Court eventually extended the "one man, one vote" principle all the way to city councils and local school boards.

Not all of the justices agreed with the Court's policy of activism. In a dissenting opinion in 1964, Justice John Harlan warned,

The Constitution is not a panacea for every blot upon the public welfare, nor should this Court, ordained as a judicial body, be thought of as a general haven for reform movements. . . . This Court . . . does not serve its high purpose, when it exceeds its authority even to satisfy justified impatience with the slow workings of the political process.

Unfortunately, the majority of Harlan's associates did not listen to him.

Evaluating the Great Society—The Great Society was, on the whole, a failure. Individual programs alleviated some effects of poverty and inequality, and part of the legislation aimed at eliminating discrimination (such as civil rights legislation) did, in Johnson's words, "replace . . . despair with opportunity." However, Johnson's utopian goal ("to use [our] wealth to enrich and elevate our national life—and to advance the quality of American civilization . . . upward to the Great Society") remained an unrealized dream. Poverty, inequality, and unrest remained; in fact, the nation seemed to be even more riven with dissent at the end of Johnson's presidency than at the beginning.

Liberal critics claimed that the president did not do enough; they said that he should have spent much more on his antipoverty programs. Yet the cost of the War on Poverty, combined with the cost of the war in Vietnam, was already creating a huge deficit in the federal budget. Conservative critics said that the failure proved what they had maintained all along: government legislation and regulation are not sufficient to solve society's problems. Ultimately the individual is responsible for helping himself, conservatives argued, and only such self-help will produce lasting results. Christians, of course, recognize that the root of society's problems is sin; only when this root problem is dealt with can society's problems as a whole be approached.

Johnson and Vietnam

America's commitment to maintaining the non-Communist government in South Vietnam had begun under Eisenhower (see pp. 543-44). From the 2,000 military advisers that Eisenhower had sent, to the 16,000 that Kennedy had sent, this commit-

U.S. Marines disembark at Khe Sanh, a major military base near the border of North and South Vietnam. American forces tenaciously and successfully defended Khe Sanh against a Communist siege in 1968.

ment had slowly grown. Ostensibly the troops were there to train the South Vietnamese army and to protect American personnel. However, the situation in Asia, as one historian has noted, was proving to be like a "tar baby": the more the United States tried to free itself, the more entangled it became. Under Lyndon Johnson, the "advisers" became combatants, and the United States became engaged in a full-fledged war.

Escalation—During his campaign against Goldwater, Johnson had said, "We are not about to send American boys nine or ten thousand miles away from home to do what Asian boys ought to be doing for themselves." Yet an incident occurred off the coast of Vietnam during the campaign that would change the complexion of the war. In the midsummer of 1964 the American destroyer *Maddox* repulsed an attack by North Vietnamese patrol boats in the Gulf of Tonkin. Although the affair was relatively minor, Johnson denounced this attack on an American vessel and asked Congress to pass a joint resolution giving him authority to respond to Communist aggression in Vietnam. Congress overwhelmingly approved the **Gulf of Tonkin resolution,** approving "the determination of

the President . . . to take all necessary measures to repel any armed attack against the forces of the United States and to prevent further aggression."

Armed with this resolution, Johnson began to *escalate* the war in Vietnam, increasing the number and expanding the role of American troops. Americans began to take over a large part of the fighting from the South Vietnamese army, and by 1968 U.S. forces there numbered over 500,000. In addition, Johnson ordered American bombers to extend the war to North Vietnam by bombing supply lines and military sites in that nation.

Several factors made the war far more difficult to win than American politicians and generals had imagined. First, the war was not a clear-cut conflict between two separate nations, as the Korean War had been. Americans were fighting both the North Vietnamese and pro-Communist South Vietnamese (called the **Viet Cong**). It was a guerrilla war fought mainly within South Vietnam between the cities (held by the government of South Vietnam) and the countryside (controlled by the Viet Cong). Second, supplies for the Communist forces from North Vietnam flowed not only across the North-South border but also through the neighboring and supposedly neutral countries of Laos and Cambodia. Such supply lines would be impossible to cut without attacking those nations, and American political leaders were hesitant to do so. Third, the government of South Vietnam—although non-Communist—was corrupt, undemocratic, and unstable. The only advantage it offered to Americans was that it was "better than the Communists." Fourth, and most important, Johnson was committed to the idea of a limited, defensive war. He did not want to risk an outright war against North Vietnam—a war which might draw in the Soviet Union or Communist China, divert dollars from the Great Society at home, and prove politically damaging.

For many soldiers, the war took on an unreal, nightmarish hue. The enemy Viet Cong looked, dressed, and acted just like the friendly South Vietnamese—until they opened fire. There were no clear fronts or lines of battle; enemy forces would suddenly emerge from the jungle, attack, and then fade back into the thick forests. Americans tried to cope by using their superior technology. Huge helicopters armed with machine guns and carrying troops swooped like warbirds over the jungles; napalm and other chemical defoliants burned away the jungle cover; American fighters and bombers pounded enemy positions. Yet the enemy kept coming back. Almost out of frustration the American army at times seemed to be trying to win the war by sheer firepower. In an extreme case, one major said after a fierce battle for one town, "It became necessary to destroy the town to save it."

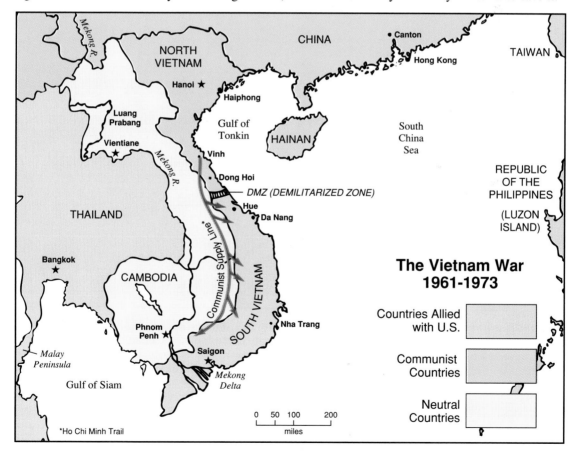

The Vietnam War 1961-1973

Countries Allied with U.S.

Communist Countries

Neutral Countries

0 50 100 200 miles

*Ho Chi Minh Trail

Air War in Vietnam

Portrayals of the Vietnam War on television and in motion pictures tend to emphasize the worst aspects of the war–the confused guerrilla fighting, the spread of drug addiction among American troops, and the ultimate failure of the effort. What is often ignored in these negative accounts is the bravery and courage that many American servicemen displayed, as they have done in every war in American history. Just as typical of the war as the darker portrayals is the following account by Colonel Robert Scott of a bombing raid into North Vietnam in 1969. After making their deadly delivery on a target in North Vietnam, Scott and his fellow airmen faced a tough fight with swift Soviet MiG jets and surface-to-air missiles (SAMs) as the pilots attempted to reach their base in Thailand. Colonel Scott recalled:

We know there are at least a hundred guns in the immediate vicinity and right now I think they are all firing at me–37 and 57mm plus radar-controlled 85mm.

My number three yells, *"MiGs!"* At almost the same instant I see two missiles go overhead. Then I see two *MiG*-21s flash up and away. They missed us–too eager.

We had been briefed about a new *MiG* field (Hoa Lac) just south of our target. Al-

Tet Offensive — There were some grumblings about the war among the American people, and a student protest movement was growing. One girl joked bitterly, "I was told if I voted for Goldwater we would be at war in six months. I did–and we were." The large majority of Americans, however, tended to support the war. Unfortunately, that support was partially the result of misrepresentation and outright deception by the government. President Johnson feared that if Americans knew how deeply committed the United States was to the war and how it was actually going, they would stop supporting the programs of the Great Society. Therefore, he attempted to disguise the number of U.S. troops involved in the conflict and to cover setbacks. All that the American people generally heard were cheery, optimistic reports of how well the war was going.

most automatically after the near fatal encounter I lower a wing and pull hard, bending my bird in the direction of the field. Zing! I meet a *MiG* head-on, right after takeoff. He whistles under me to make like an air-show thriller. I latch onto a *MiG*-17 in the traffic pattern but he turns too tight. With my excess speed I am unable to line up for a missile shot. I yo-yo up and down, reducing my speed to 475 knots. The *MiG* reverses–I pull up. As I go down, he reverses again and we both go across the runway at five hundred feet. He pulls up to the clouds, . . . then down to the treetops. I'm pulling 7 Gs in afterburner, determined to nail him! Now the *MiG* relaxes his turn and heads west–his mistake. I open up with my 20mm Gatling gun and a steady stream of metal closes the gap. For a fraction of a second, his left wing lights up, then–pow! Half of the wing snaps off and he crashes inverted in a split second.

Two heartbeats later, a scream in my earphones, "SAM at three o'clock!"

Instinctively, I whip the controls right and forward. My bird responds violently to the right and down. The SAM arches over me at about two hundred feet. I'm impressed but there isn't time for fear–everything's at high speed. The SAM left a telltale smoke trail right back to the site. Too bad! My wingmen bore down the smoke trail preceded by their deadly 20mm emissaries. Scratch one SAM mobile unit!

This situation changed with the **Tet Offensive** by the Communists in January 1968. During the South Vietnamese celebration of Tet, the lunar new year (January 30), the Viet Cong infiltrated the major cities in the South. They smuggled in arms, for example, by carrying them into the cities in coffins during funeral processions. On the first day of the new year, 60,000 Viet Cong troops launched attacks on nearly every major strategic point in South Vietnam. One force even captured part of the U.S. Embassy for a time. In the weeks that followed the attacks, American and South Vietnamese forces drove back the enemy, recapturing what had been lost and inflicting massive casualties. Militarily, the Tet Offensive was a failure for the Communists, but it had a dramatic effect on the American public. Television newscasts emphasized the negative aspects–the suddenness of the attack and the heavy losses–thus leading many Americans to believe that Tet was a Communist victory. The U.S. government, to some extent, reaped what it had sown. Having misled the American people and media about the course of the war, the government now faced the wrath of a public who wanted to know how things could come so close to disaster so suddenly. After Tet, many Americans were seemingly no longer looking to win the war; they only wanted a way out.

Paris Peace Talks–In May 1968 the North Vietnamese offered to hold peace negotiations, and the United States accepted. The **Paris Peace Talks** began with a heated discussion over a critical topic: what shape of table to use. After this unpromising start, the peace talks dragged on for nearly five years while the fighting continued. The United States wanted out but also wanted to preserve South Vietnam as a non-Communist nation. North Vietnam wanted the reunion of the two nations under Communist rule. The talks droned on while casualties continued to mount on the battlefields of Vietnam.

Section Review

1. What method of keeping blacks from voting was outlawed by the Twenty-fourth Amendment? by the Voting Rights Act of 1965?
2. Why did *Roth* v. *United States* spur a pornography industry in the U.S. even though the decision said that obscenity is not protected by the First Amendment?
3. List at least three of the factors that made the Vietnam War harder to win than American politicians and military leaders had thought.
4. What event caused the American people to begin to doubt government reports of progress in the Vietnam War?

Upheaval

Violence at home paralleled the fighting in Vietnam as the United States endured some of its worst civil disturbances since the Civil War. Even those Americans who lived nowhere near the unrest often saw it in graphic detail on their television sets. As the violence and bloodshed increased, many citizens felt a sense of despair and helplessness. One Democratic senator moaned, "The 'Great Society' has become the sick society."

Racial Conflict

Fighting in the Streets—The civil rights movement had never been free from violence. Early protest marches and demonstrations sometimes ended with assaults on the demonstrators by mobs of angry whites or even by policemen using tear gas and police dogs. These incidents, however, paled in comparison to what happened during the Johnson years. In 1964 in Mississippi, members of the Ku Klux Klan brutally murdered three civil rights workers who were trying to help blacks register to vote. Likewise, during a voting rights protest in Selma, Alabama, three white civil rights advocates died in separate incidents at the hands of Klansmen and other extremists. (Johnson used the Selma incident to spur Congress to approve the Voting Rights Act.) Violence only increased as the civil rights movement moved north. Northerners who had approved of the negro cause when it centered in the South suddenly found it a far different matter when northern blacks began to call for desegregated schools and neighborhoods.

Racial hostility blazed the hottest in the cities during the summers of 1965, 1966, and 1967. Black resentment of discrimination and apparent slowness in meeting black grievances led to uncontrolled riots. The first of this series of **urban riots** began in a predominantly black section of Los Angeles known as Watts. Only days after Congress passed the Voting Rights Act, a white policeman in Watts tried to arrest a young black for drunk driving. Angry crowds began to gather in the summer heat, and wild tales of police brutality began to circulate. Finally, the tension exploded into an orgy of destruction. Mobs roamed Watts, burning and looting. Police and eventually the National Guard tried to restore order. In six days of violence, thirty-four people died, nearly nine hundred were wounded, and $45 million in property was destroyed. The Watts riot was followed by over thirty others. A few were in southern cities, such as Atlanta and Nashville, but most were in the North. The worst riot was in Detroit in 1967. Forty-three people died there while looters ransacked shops and arsonists set hundreds of fires. Detroit took on the appearance of Vietnam as tanks rolled down smoldering streets trying to restore order and troops exchanged fire with snipers on the buildings.

The effect of this violence was traumatic. Blacks felt the brunt of the destruction; black homes and businesses suffered most of the damage, and most of the casualties were black. One reporter, watching black rioters destroying Watts, wrote, "The rioters were burning their city now, as the insane sometimes mutilate themselves." There was also a backlash of fear and revulsion among whites. In 1964 only thirty-four per cent of Americans thought blacks "were seeking too much, too fast"; by 1966 that figure had risen to eighty-five per cent.

Radicalization—Accompanying these riots was an increased radicalization of the civil rights movement. Even Martin Luther King, usually an advocate of nonviolence, became more strident in his language. He urged his followers "to get out and demonstrate and protest" until they shook "the very foundations of this nation." King came out in opposition to the Vietnam War and called the United States government "the greatest purveyor of violence in the world today."

King's language was mild compared to the radical wing of the civil rights movement represented by the misnamed Student Nonviolent Coordinating Committee (SNCC). Rejecting King's call for peaceful protests, the black radicals proclaimed that they would meet violence with violence. One SNCC leader announced, "Violence is as American as cherry pie." The radicals advocated the idea of **"Black Power,"** a call for the securing of black rights, even black supremacy over whites, by any means including violence. At one rally in Mississippi, Black Power advocates chanted, "Hey! Hey!

Protests against the Vietnam War were one of the major expressions of the rebelliousness of the counterculture in the late 1960s and early 1970s.

Whattya know! White folks must go–must go!'' Some extremists formed paramilitary organizations such as the Black Panthers, the black version of the Ku Klux Klan. Racial divisions seemed to be deepening in America. Some began to fear a race war which blacks could not win but in which all races would suffer.

Radical Youth

The radicalization of young blacks was but one aspect of a general radicalization of youth. By the late 1960s fully half of the population of the United States was under the age of twenty-five. These young people had grown up in the midst of prosperity and affluence. Some began to question and then rebel against the materialistic values of the day–the virtual worship of material possessions and the constant striving after luxuries. Finding that materialism did not satisfy them spiritually, young people became dissatisfied and disillusioned. Unfortunately, the means that the young used to satisfy themselves often turned out to be worse than their parents' materialism.

Antiwar Movement–The rallying point for disaffected youth was opposition to the Vietnam War. Antiwar demonstrations grew in proportion to the number of troops Johnson was sending overseas. Demonstrators held rallies to protest the war; antiwar radicals seized control of college buildings, barricaded themselves inside, and dared police to come after them; a number of young men fled to Canada rather than be drafted into the army.

One force behind the antiwar movement was the **"New Left,"** radical groups which hoped to use resentment of the war as a means of overthrowing established American institutions. The Students for a Democratic Society (SDS) was the largest New Left group, with a total of over five thousand members on more than two hundred campuses. An even more radical group, the Weathermen, actually engaged in terrorist bombings of buildings in order to "bring the war home."

Left-wing sympathies were not sufficiently powerful to motivate the whole antiwar movement, however. Much of the energy for the movement came from the resistance to authority that is always present in unregenerate man. The New Left merely harnessed this discontent. The antiwar movement directed its rage at the president, the ultimate symbol of authority. Johnson suffered cruel and vicious attacks, such as thousands of demonstrators in Washington chanting, "Hey! Hey! LBJ! How many kids did you kill today?" Antiwar sentiment began to spread to older age groups, and the number of protesters multiplied. By the end of Johnson's term, military bases were the only places the president could speak without being heckled.

Counterculture–The antiwar movement was itself only a part of an overall youth movement known as the **counterculture.** More an attitude

The Day the Music Died

Rock music, which became a powerful cultural force in the 1960s, originated in the mid-1950s. A blend of several styles—jazz, blues, swing, and country and western being the more obvious—rock music emerged as a popular form of music among teens. Popularized by songs such as "Rock Around the Clock" (from the

Crowds throng the Woodstock rock concert; by John Dominis, The Image Works.

movie *The Blackboard Jungle,* in which it symbolized juvenile delinquency), rock music found its first major star in Elvis Presley, a former truck driver from Memphis who became a national sensation.

Presley illustrated the dual nature of rock songs prior to the 1960s. Lyrically, the songs were similar to earlier love songs from sheet music, motion pictures, and stage plays: basic pledges of "undying love," laments for broken hearts, and so on. (One historian of rock music satirically typified the lyrics of early rock songs as "I love you baybee, oop wee ooh, ooh I do.") The music was another matter. By the use of a driving beat, emphasized by drums and bass guitars in particular, rock music contained an

undertone of sexual aggressiveness. Presley stressed this sexual aspect in his stage performances through his hip-shaking movements—considered shocking at the time—and vocal intensity.

This dichotomy between "innocent" words and provocative music disappeared with the counterculture's embrace of rock in the 1960s. The leaders in this change were a British rock group, the Beatles, who took America by storm in 1964. Their early songs bore such innocent-sounding titles as "I Want to Hold Your Hand." Within a few years, however, the Beatles began to write more poetically accomplished songs that reflected their experimentation with drugs and sex. In 1967 the group released *Sgt. Pepper's Lonely Hearts Club Band,* a milestone in the open glorification of the drug culture. It contained songs such as "Lucy in the Sky with Diamonds" (a play on the letters *LSD*) and lyrics such as "I get high with a little help from my friends."

The combination of drugs and rock gave birth to new forms of rock music. "Head music" was designed to enhance the effects of marijuana. "Acid rock" attempted to reproduce the effects of LSD (nicknamed "acid") and was often composed by writers under the influence of the drug. San Francisco became a center of drug-related rock and the hippie culture, and thousands of runaway teens swarmed to the West Coast to be part of the rock and drug "scene."

The rock culture of the 1960s reached its height with the Woodstock Rock Festival in upstate New York in August 1969. A crowd of 400,000 young people—eight times what the promoters expected—gathered for three days to hear popular rock groups perform. With hopelessly inadequate sanitary facilities and insufficient supplies of food and water, the festival succeeded only because the huge crowds were able to work together to overcome their problems. Even with this cooperation, the festival

The Beatles hit the American scene in 1964 with an appearance on the television show of Ed Sullivan (pictured here with the group). © Bettmann/ CORBIS

was hardly an unqualified success. Two people died (one of a drug overdose and one who was crushed by a tractor as he slept), and hundreds were arrested or suffered adverse effects from the rampant drug abuse. Counterculture proponents, however, chose to view the festival as a vindication of their philosophy of love and sharing. The "Woodstock Nation," they claimed, symbolized what the young could do for civilization if they had the chance.

A few months later in December, another popular British rock group, the Rolling Stones, held a free concert near Altamont Speedway in California in imitation of Woodstock. Again there was widespread drug use and immorality, but this time there was no sugar-coating of "love" and cooperation. To serve as security guards, the concert's promoters hired a motorcycle gang known as "Hell's Angels." In "policing" the concert, the "Angels" indulged in acts of violence, climaxing during one of the performances when they beat and killed a young black who had pulled out a gun.

The Altamont experience so shattered the rock culture that within two years a folk rock singer referred to it simply as "the day the music died." Above all, the Altamont concert revealed a truth that undercut the main premise of the whole youth movement: when left to themselves, the young were just as prone to violence, corruption, and disorder as their parents were. It was a sobering lesson.

than an ideology, the counterculture of the 1960s and early 1970s had its roots in rebellion, specifically a rejection of the materialism as well as the morals and values of the previous generation. Proponents of the counterculture believed that the solution to society's problems included self-expression and espousing a philosophy of love and sharing. "Do your own thing" and "All you need is love" (the title of a popular rock song) were simplistic expressions of the counterculture creed. Counterculture also praised youth as having the answers to society's problems, as illustrated by the popular saying "Don't trust anyone over thirty."

The popular expression of counterculture was the "hippie" movement (derived from the slang term *hip,* being aware of current tastes and attitudes). Hippies made a virtue of nonconformity. In place of the neat clothing and appearance of their

Robert Indiana's "pop art" painting Love, *commemorated here on an 8¢ U.S. postage stamp, aptly captures the emphases of the counterculture. Its bright primary colors typify the art of the period: eye-catching, almost garish color. Even more its theme of "love" represents the counterculture's professed faith in "love" to solve society's problems–a faith that ultimately proved vain as it left the nature of that love undefined.*

parents, they wore jeans and t-shirts that were dirty, patched, and garishly colored. Young men grew their hair and beards long as a sign of protest. Rejecting traditional standards, hippies repudiated marriage and advocated unrestricted sexual activity. They embraced rock music, which, with its provocative lyrics and heavy beat, symbolized their rebellion. Hippies were also leaders in the drug culture. They experimented with numerous illegal hallucinogenic drugs, notably LSD. The most popular drug was marijuana, a product of the hemp plant that is smoked like tobacco. The American Medical Association estimated that eight million people had experimented with marijuana by the late 1960s.

The Christian quickly recognizes that much within the counterculture was completely ungodly–the illicit sex, drug use, and other immoral behavior. Indeed, many hippies embraced the counterculture lifestyle simply so that they could live a carefree life without assuming any responsibility for their actions; it was a philosophy which provided a license to sin. Even when they were sincere, however, the hippies were wrong. Their belief that expressing "love" was the answer to man's problems was naive and simplistic; they did not realize that genuine love requires sacrifice and discipline. Furthermore they believed that material possessions and moral restrictions corrupted man. The Bible teaches that man is born corrupt (Ps. 58:3; Rom. 5:12), and forsaking possessions or breaking restrictions does nothing to free man from the power of sin. "Curing man's ills" requires changing his sinful nature through the power of God in salvation.

Radicalism in Perspective

One can make too much of the radicalism of the 1960s. Even among young people and blacks, the radicals were a decided minority. Domestic violence can likewise be overstated; the United States came nowhere near equaling the death and destruction through civil disorder that occurred in other nations in the era. (In Nigeria in the late 1960s, for example, a full-blown civil war resulted in the deaths of tens of thousands of people.) The violence shocked Americans, however, especially after the relative calm of the Eisenhower and Kennedy years. They wondered how a nation so advanced and so wealthy could suddenly be convulsed with such disorder. As 1968 neared–a presidential election year– Americans began looking for a leader who could cure the country's ills.

Section Review

1. What incident did Johnson use to motivate Congress to pass the Voting Rights Act of 1965?
2. What city was the site of the worst urban riot in the United States in the 1960s?
3. What was the rallying point for disaffected young people in the 1960s and early 1970s?
4. What was the popular expression of the counterculture?
5. What was the most widely used illegal drug of the 1960s?

1968

Certain years bear a singular importance in United States history. Nearly all Americans, for example, immediately identify 1776 as the year of American independence. The violence and conflicting ideologies of the era from 1963 to 1973 are encapsulated to a great extent in one year: 1968. Against the background of presidential politics, American leaders offered their respective answers to the nation's problems. In a campaign marred by bloodshed, Americans had to choose the man they thought could resolve the crisis they faced.

Johnson Bows Out

Lyndon Johnson bemoaned the failure of his Great Society to solve America's problems. He said on one occasion,

> I tried to make it possible for every child of every color to grow up in a nice house, eat a solid breakfast, to attend a decent school, and to get a good and lasting job. I asked so little in return. Just a little thanks. Just a little appreciation. That's all. But look at what I got instead. Riots. . . . Looting. Burning. Shooting. . . . Young people by the thousands leaving the university, marching in the streets, chanting that horrible song about how many kids I had killed that day. . . . It ruined everything.

President Johnson scans the headlines announcing his decision not to seek re-election.

Despite his unpopularity, Johnson was favored to win renomination by the Democrats. His only challenger was an antiwar Democrat, Senator **Eugene McCarthy** of Minnesota. Johnson's staff did not take McCarthy's threat seriously. Then the Tet Offensive in January stirred up the Vietnam issue with fresh vigor. In the New Hampshire primary in March, the underdog McCarthy nearly upset the president. Senator **Robert Kennedy** of New York, a younger brother of the slain president who possessed much of the Kennedy charm, suddenly announced that he too would challenge Johnson. When Johnson's advisers warned him that he could lose badly to McCarthy in the upcoming Wisconsin primary, Johnson stunned the nation by withdrawing from the race.

Johnson's withdrawal created a scramble among the Democrats. Kennedy and McCarthy competed for the antiwar vote. Vice President **Hubert H. Humphrey** also joined, more or less representing the Johnson approach to Vietnam and the nation's problems. The result was a wide-open race for the nomination. Humphrey ignored the primaries, depending instead on President Johnson's still formidable power and prestige within the Democratic party organization to win delegates in nonprimary states. McCarthy and Kennedy battled it out in the primaries to win the right to challenge Humphrey at the convention in Chicago.

Death Times Two

In early April 1968, while the presidential candidates fought over the nomination, Martin Luther King went to Memphis to support a strike by garbage workers. On the balcony of his hotel, King was shot and killed by a white sniper, his death sparking a new wave of urban violence. Ironically, the death of a man who had won the Nobel Peace Prize for his advocacy of nonviolence became the cause of fighting, looting, and bloodshed. The riots served as a fresh reminder to voters of the troubles that America was experiencing.

The campaign went on. Robert Kennedy pulled ahead of McCarthy and threatened to wrest the nomination from the well-entrenched Humphrey. After a major victory in the California primary,

Kennedy was greeting scores of supporters in a Los Angeles hotel corridor as he made his way to speak to the press. Suddenly a young Arab nationalist–who opposed Kennedy's support of Israel–thrust forward a revolver and fired. Kennedy fell, mortally wounded. Within a period of two months, two major American leaders had died violently.

Nixon Takes the Center

While the Democratic candidates jockeyed for position, the Republican race narrowed to one question: Could anyone stop **Richard Nixon?** After his narrow loss to John Kennedy in 1960 and a defeat in the California governor's race in 1962, the former vice president practiced law in New York City but remained heavily involved in politics. Unlike most moderate Republicans, Nixon campaigned for Goldwater in 1964 and won the respect of Republican conservatives. In 1968, after thorough preparation and hard work, he won a series of primaries that made him the front-runner for the Republican nomination.

Nixon attempted to take the "middle of the road" on political issues. Only then, he thought, could he appeal to the general public and win the fall election. Unwittingly helping Nixon present this moderate image were his main opponents: Governor Nelson Rockefeller of New York, a staunch liberal, and Governor Ronald Reagan of California, the man who had replaced Goldwater

Richard Nixon and his running mate Spiro Agnew celebrate their nomination at the Republican convention in Miami in 1968.

as the hero of Republican conservatives. Nixon was able to place himself solidly in the political center between these two men. At the Republican convention in Miami, Nixon beat back the challenges by Rockefeller and Reagan to win the nomination.

Nixon sensed the dismay of the American electorate with the violence that racked their country. He realized that they felt helpless in the face of apparently uncontrollable unrest. Therefore, Nixon struck a nerve with the public when he called for "law and order," a firm response to the anarchy that seemed ready to engulf the nation. Ironically, one of the biggest boosts to Nixon's "law and order" campaign was the Democratic convention.

Democratic Disarray

With the death of Robert Kennedy, Hubert Humphrey easily captured the nomination at the party's convention in Chicago. Some Democrats, though, wondered whether the nomination would be worth anything. As Americans watched on television, police and radical demonstrators battled outside the convention hall. Inside the hall they saw the Democratic mayor of Chicago shouting obscenities at a Democratic senator who was denouncing what he called the "Gestapo tactics" of Chicago's police. In addition to these nationally televised clashes, Humphrey's candidacy was weighed down with Johnson's unpopular policy in Vietnam, which Humphrey, as vice president, was virtually bound to defend.

The Wallace Factor

Another element in the confused campaign was the third-party candidacy of Alabama's **George Wallace,** who ran as the candidate of the newly formed American Independent party. The fiery Wallace had risen to fame as a prosegregation governor during the civil rights struggles of the early 1960s. He sought to draw on popular discontent with the civil rights movement, urban violence, rampant immorality, rising crime rates, and the seemingly endless war in Vietnam. Wallace's political pronouncements were generally conservative but couched in tough, pugnacious language. He attacked the "pointy-headed intellectuals" who ran the government bureaucracy. "When I get to

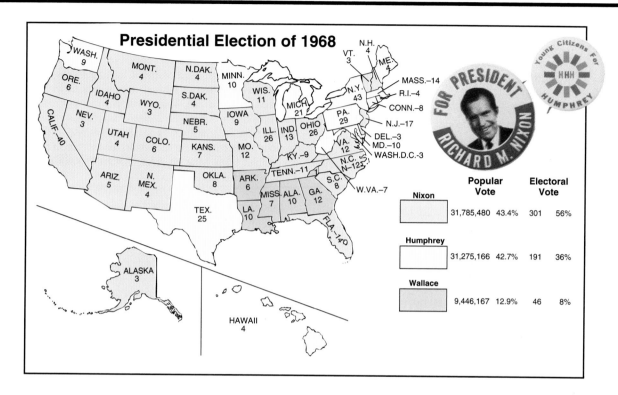

Presidential Election of 1968

	Popular Vote		Electoral Vote	
Nixon	31,785,480	43.4%	301	56%
Humphrey	31,275,166	42.7%	191	36%
Wallace	9,446,167	12.9%	46	8%

Washington," he said, "I'll throw all these phonies and their briefcases into the Potomac." As for demonstrators, Wallace told delighted audiences, "If any demonstrator ever lays down in front of my car, it'll be the last car he'll ever lay down in front of." Wallace did not really believe that he could win the election, but he believed that a strong showing would "send a message" to Washington that there was a bloc of conservative Americans that the politicians could not afford to ignore.

Election: Nixon's the One

The election results reflected the fragmented state of American society in 1968. After losing by the thinnest of margins in 1960, Nixon won by only a slightly larger margin in 1968. He won 31,785,480 votes (43.4 per cent) to Humphrey's 31,275,166 (42.7 per cent); Nixon's lead in the electoral college was more substantial, 301-191. Wallace won nearly ten million votes (13.5 per cent) and 46 electoral votes. The results represented

a repudiation of Johnson's policies but not an overwhelming mandate for Nixon. Furthermore, Nixon was the first president since Zachary Taylor to begin his first term with both houses of Congress in the hands of the opposing party. The voters clearly did not want what they had had under Johnson, but it was unclear what they *did* want in its place.

Section Review

1. Who was the first antiwar Democrat to challenge the renomination of Lyndon Johnson?
2. After the withdrawal of Johnson in the 1968 campaign, which Democratic candidate best represented the incumbent president's policies?
3. What two major American leaders died violently in 1968?
4. Name the Republican nominee, the Democratic nominee, and the major third-party candidate in the presidential election of 1968.

Nixon and the Silent Majority

In a speech during his first year in office, Richard Nixon appealed to "the great silent majority of . . . Americans" to support him. With the term **silent majority,** the president affirmed his belief that the majority of Americans were not violent radicals wholly discontent with the status quo. The bulk of the population, he believed, were quiet, respectable, hard-working, decent citizens who wanted only peace and order. Nixon claimed that he represented the interests of this silent majority and that his administration would give voice to their values. Many writers called Nixon's statement an appeal to "Middle America," the views of the dominant middle class.

Domestic Problems

Busing—Nixon confronted a highly emotional issue early in his presidency, one that outraged many of his middle-class supporters. Despite Supreme Court orders for the desegregation of schools since the 1950s, the integration of schools had proceeded slowly. One of the main obstacles to integration was that nearly all schools drew their students from surrounding neighborhoods. Most neighborhoods, however, tended to be segregated by race because of years of legal restrictions and social pressure. As a result, blacks went to predominantly black schools in their neighborhoods, and whites went to predominantly white schools in theirs. To overcome this fact, the courts ordered the **busing** of students by school buses out of their neighborhoods into other schools until all schools reflected the overall racial make-up of the city or community as a whole.

Busing was controversial. Some parents opposed busing simply because they opposed racial integration. Other parents feared the destruction of the neighborhood school as a center of community life and values. Angry protesters–mostly blue-collar and middle-class whites this time–demonstrated against court busing orders. Sometimes violence resulted, as in Pontiac, Michigan, where protesters fire-bombed empty school buses. Nixon attempted to placate antibusing forces by slowing the process of integration. The courts, however, pressed the issue, and busing continued.

Economic Problems—Nixon inherited a deteriorating economic situation. President Johnson had attempted to pay for both the Great Society and the Vietnam War without raising taxes. The result was a growing budget deficit which in turn resulted in inflation. When Nixon tried to control inflation by trimming the federal budget and raising interest rates, inflation remained unchanged but unemployment rose and a recession set in. Nixon then responded with what he called his **New Economic Policy.** First, he imposed a ninety-day freeze in 1971 on all wages and prices. This was followed, second, by the establishment of a board to regulate all wage and price increases. Finally, the third phase in 1973 replaced the mandatory guidelines with voluntary ones. The freeze and mandatory regulations did slow inflation, but they did not reduce unemployment. Also, once the guidelines became voluntary, prices began to rise again.

Diplomatic Successes

China—Nixon scored his most notable triumphs in the realm of foreign affairs. Probably his biggest breakthrough was establishing relations with the Communist People's Republic of China. Since the flight of Chiang Kai-shek's Nationalist government to the island of Taiwan in 1949 (p. 542), the United States had recognized Chiang's government on Taiwan as the legitimate government of China rather than that of the Communists on the mainland. Nixon hoped to exploit dissension between Communist China and the Soviet Union to America's advantage by currying favor with the Chinese. In 1971 the president announced that he would visit the People's Republic the following year, and he endorsed the admission of Communist China to the United Nations as an equal of Taiwan. (Contrary to Nixon's wishes, the United Nations expelled Taiwan when it admitted Communist China in 1971.)

Nixon's visit was an enormous public relations success. Television cameras followed the president as he toured the Great Wall and other scenic sites closed to foreigners for years; the president banqueted with Communist leaders and exchanged messages of good will with them. The effect of the visit was to portray Nixon as an astute diplomat

President and Mrs. Nixon visit the Great Wall during their historic trip to Communist China in 1972.

and able statesman. Nixon laid the groundwork for resuming trade with mainland China and also for the possible reunification of the mainland with Taiwan. The president did not actually abandon Nationalist China by granting full diplomatic recognition to the Communist government, however. That act remained for President Carter to perform in 1978 when he recognized the People's Republic and severed official ties with Nationalist China.

Soviet Union—At least in part because of his overtures to China, Nixon was able to win some concessions from the Soviet Union. Through the influence of Nixon and his secretary of state, **Henry Kissinger,** the United States entered a period of **détente** (day TAHNT), a relaxation of the tension that had existed between the two nations since World War II. As a result of Strategic Arms Limitations Talks (SALT), the U.S. and the USSR reached an agreement limiting the number of missiles and warheads each nation would have. Nixon also arranged the sale of large amounts of grain to the Soviets. Americans watched in surprise as Richard Nixon, the former anti-Communist "cold

warrior," did more to build relations between the United States and Communist nations than any other president in history. What was often ignored in Nixon's dealings with China and the Soviet Union was that for the first time the United States was actively seeking the support of repressive Communist regimes.

Nixon and Vietnam

De-escalation and Expansion—In a reversal of Johnson's Vietnam policy, President Nixon began to *de-escalate* the war by bringing American troops home and leaving the bulk of the fighting to the South Vietnamese. Nixon gradually reduced American forces in Vietnam from more than 500,000 when he took office to fewer than 140,000 by the beginning of 1972. Nixon called this policy of reducing American forces and increasing the role of the South Vietnamese the **Vietnamization** (VYET nah muh ZAY shun) of the war.

At the same time he was reducing the number of American soldiers, however, Nixon took other steps that expanded the war. In an effort to force the North Vietnamese to make peace, the president authorized raids into neutral Cambodia in 1970 and Laos in 1971 to destroy enemy bases. In 1972 he approved a massive bombing and naval blockade of North Vietnam. Although these efforts destroyed some enemy bases and strained the resources of North Vietnam, they did not end the war. In fact, with Cambodia and Laos drawn directly into the conflict, the fighting was even more widespread.

Dissent at Home—The antiwar movement entered a lull when Nixon took office as protesters waited to see what the new president would do. The bombing of North Vietnam and the expansion of the war into Cambodia and Laos, however, revitalized the movement. At least three traumatic events at home further divided the country over the war.

The first was the court-martial of Lieutenant **William Calley.** In 1968 Calley led his platoon into the South Vietnamese village of My Lai (MEE LYE), where they killed over three hundred unarmed civilians who were suspected of supporting the Viet Cong. When word of the massacre leaked out, the army launched an investigation and a series of courts-martial lasting from 1969 to 1971. Only Calley was convicted. Americans were appalled at such a slaughter by American troops, but a large segment of the nation sympathized with Calley. They believed either that he was being made a scapegoat by the army to cover up for other officers or that he was being persecuted by the antiwar movement in anger over the whole war effort. President Nixon reduced Calley's life sentence to twenty years and then placed him under a mild form of house arrest.

A second event took place in May 1970 at **Kent State** University near Cleveland. Demonstrators protesting the invasion of Cambodia rioted on and near the campus and even burned an ROTC building at the university. The governor of Ohio called out the National Guard. On May 4 a group of protesters taunted the Guardsmen and hurled rocks at them. A few of the soldiers panicked and fired. Four students died, two of whom were simply walking to class and had nothing to do with the protest. The event revealed the deep divisions in the nation over the war. One faction considered the

A girl screams in horror as she kneels by the body of a student killed by a stray bullet fired by National Guardsmen at Kent State University.

slain students martyrs for peace. Another faction, angered at what they considered a lack of patriotism by the antiwar movement, claimed that the students "had it coming to them." Peace seemed no closer at home than it did in Vietnam.

The third event was the publication of the **Pentagon Papers** in 1971. Pentagon staff analyst Daniel Ellsberg stole a number of confidential documents concerning the progress of American involvement in Vietnam and released them to the *New York Times.* The Nixon administration tried vainly to block publication in the interests of "national security." The documents were more embarrassing to the government than they were dangerous to the nation, however. They revealed the blunders and deceptions of primarily the Kennedy and Johnson administrations in the conduct of the war. Readers learned, for example, that Johnson had drafted what became the Gulf of Tonkin resolution months before the actual incident in the Gulf of Tonkin took place. These revelations of government deceit prompted even more antiwar sentiment.

"Peace"—Although Nixon's Vietnam policy was unpopular at home, it was wearing down North Vietnam. The North Vietnamese were not near defeat, but the constant casualties and bombing were draining the Communists' resources. After an extremely heavy "Christmas bombing" late in 1972, the war-weary Americans and North Vietnamese reached an agreement at the Paris Peace Talks early in 1973. The United States recalled its troops and received back its prisoners of war. South Vietnam

received huge amounts of American arms to protect itself, but North Vietnam still maintained troops and guerrillas in the South. Nixon hoped that the supply of arms and the threat of future American intervention would protect South Vietnam. Secretary of State Kissinger hinted, however, that all the United States wanted was a "decent interval" between the removal of American forces and the fall of South Vietnam.

Aftermath—In the spring of 1975 North Vietnam launched a massive offensive, and South Vietnamese resistance collapsed with astonishing speed. Nixon was no longer in office, and President Ford was unable to persuade Congress to help South Vietnam. With no outside help and torn by internal dissension and corruption, the South fell to the North. Vietnam was finally united and at "peace"—under Communist rule.

The results of the war at least partially justified Eisenhower's "domino theory" (see p. 544). South Vietnam, Laos, and Cambodia all fell to Communist domination. Fears of Communist atrocities in the fallen nations proved justified as well. The worst example was the cruel Communist regime in Cambodia which slaughtered 1.2 million Cambodians—a fifth of the nation's population. "Relief" came to the Cambodians in 1979 when Vietnam invaded the nation, toppled the murderous Cambodian Communist government, and installed its own "milder" totalitarian rule. In America the result was a wave of isolationism. Citizens wanted "no more Vietnams," which usually meant almost no commitment of U.S. troops to fight anywhere. Upset at how American presidents—particularly Johnson and Nixon—had run the war on their own authority, Congress passed a series of acts to limit the president's power to use American troops abroad. The War Powers Act (1973), for example, required the president to withdraw American troops from combat abroad after sixty days unless Congress specifically approved such use of these forces.

Why did America lose in Vietnam? Liberal critics argued that, given the unpopularity and corruption of the South Vietnamese government, the war was unwinnable; Communist domination was inevitable. Conservative critics charged that an ear-

lier commitment of larger forces or even an invasion of North Vietnam would have won the war; only the halfhearted concept of "limited war" prevented victory. Conservatives also stressed the role that the American media played in sapping American support for the war by unsympathetic and even distorted reporting. Such questions are, of course, ultimately unanswerable. What was certain was that the American people had been deeply wounded by the trauma of the Vietnam experience and that they would not soon recover.

1972 Election

In the presidential election of 1972, President Nixon's chances of re-election looked good. His trip to China and de-escalation of the Vietnam War strengthened his position. His opposition for the Republican nomination was minor: a liberal congressman who accused the president of being too conservative and a conservative congressman who accused him of being too liberal. The Democrats, furthermore, were divided. George Wallace campaigned for the Democratic nomination and by crusading against busing was able to win not only in the South but also in primaries in northern industrial states such as Massachusetts and Michigan. Wallace's campaign was cut short, however, when a would-be assassin shot him in Maryland, leaving him paralyzed for life.

The Democratic nomination eventually went to a candidate who was almost the exact opposite of Wallace, the zealously liberal Senator **George McGovern** of South Dakota. McGovern's campaign, though, was almost hopeless. He was far to the left of most American voters, and he managed to botch his best issue—discontent with the war in Vietnam—by saying that he would "crawl" to North Vietnam if necessary for peace. When it was revealed that his running mate, Thomas Eagleton, had twice undergone electroshock treatments for a nervous disorder, McGovern first announced that he was "1000 per cent" behind Eagleton and then a week later forced him off the ticket. Five leading Democrats turned McGovern down before he could find someone else to run with him.

The election was much like that of 1964: the incumbent president crushed an unpopular challenger. Nixon won 61 per cent of the popular vote and captured every state except Massachusetts and the District of Columbia for a 520-17 edge in the electoral college. Yet the election would prove to be like 1964 in another respect: the president who won a landslide victory would be discredited and even hated before the next presidential election. Within two years of his overwhelming triumph, Richard Nixon would be disgraced and out of office.

Section Review

1. What method did the courts order to speed the integration of public schools?
2. What were the three components of Nixon's New Economic Policy?
3. What three actions did Nixon take in 1970, 1971, and 1972 to force the North Vietnamese to make peace?
4. What two other Southeast Asian nations fell to communism after the fall of South Vietnam?

Chapter Review

Terms

Lyndon Johnson
Great Society
Civil Rights Act of 1964
Voting Rights Act of 1965
Twenty-fourth Amendment
"War on Poverty"
Barry Goldwater
Medicare
Earl Warren
judicial activism
"one man, one vote" decisions

Gulf of Tonkin resolution
Viet Cong
Tet Offensive
Paris Peace Talks
urban riots
"Black Power"
New Left
counterculture
Eugene McCarthy
Robert Kennedy
Hubert H. Humphrey
Richard Nixon

George Wallace
silent majority
busing
New Economic Policy
Henry Kissinger
détente
Vietnamization
William Calley
Kent State killings
Pentagon Papers
George McGovern

Content Questions

1. Give at least three reasons for Barry Goldwater's unpopularity with most American voters in 1964.
2. What does it mean that Johnson *escalated* the Vietnam War?
3. Match each of the following slogans with the tenet of counterculture philosophy that it describes.
    a. "Do your own thing."
    b. "All you need is love."
    c. "Don't trust anyone over thirty."
    (1) the ability of man to work out his problems in a spirit of cooperation
    (2) the belief that youth alone has the answer to society's problems
    (3) the importance of nonconformity
4. Why were the results of the 1968 election a repudiation of Johnson but not a mandate for Nixon?

5. What was Nixon's greatest triumph in foreign affairs?
6. What three traumatic events in the United States during Nixon's term of office deepened the division in the nation over the Vietnam War?

Application Questions

1. Why is a policy of judicial activism such as that pursued by the Warren Court dangerous?
2. Why is a philosophy inadequate that simply espouses "love" as the solutions to man's problems?
3. What is the danger of the isolationist philosophy illustrated by the postwar phrase "no more Vietnams"?

PERSPECTIVES
Space Race

The race to the moon between the United States and the Soviet Union began as a cold war competition and ended for Americans as a demonstration of technological achievement, an expression of national pride and a witness to the Creator's handiwork.

THE CHALLENGE

Above: *May 5, 1961, a Mercury Redstone rocket carries Astronaut Alan Shepard in his* Freedom 7 *spacecraft on America's first manned space flight.*
Left: *Astronaut Shepard after his maiden suborbital flight*

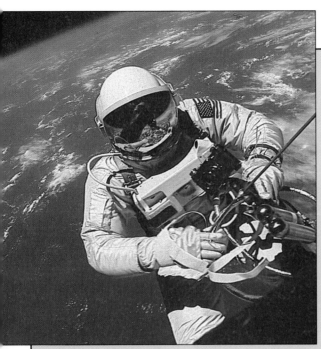

Astronaut Edward H. White becomes the first American to walk in space.

The United States, the world's technological leader in the cold war, was shocked when the Soviets announced the successful launch of *Sputnik 1*– the world's first satellite–on October 4, 1957. A month later the Soviets launched the dog Laika in a 1,121-pound space capsule. America's feeble attempt to launch a two-pound satellite in December failed when the rocket exploded five feet off the launch pad. In an effort to get out of the starting block, Congress approved the formation of the National Aeronautics and Space Administration (NASA) to direct America's space program. But the Soviet Union continued to set records and embarrass the U.S. scientific community. It soon became obvious that the Soviets were planning to send a man to the moon; and unless something changed, they were likely to succeed in getting there first.

In April 1961, the world was again stunned when the Soviets announced that a cosmonaut, Yuri Gagarin, had orbited the earth. America responded on May 5 with a fifteen-minute sub-orbital flight by astronaut Alan Shepard. Yet the nation was energized by a challenge. Twenty days later President John F. Kennedy announced to Congress and the nation, ''I believe that this nation should commit itself to achieving the goal, before this decade is out, of landing a man on the moon and returning him safely to earth.''

With these words Kennedy committed the resources of the nation to achieve in less than ten short years what man for centuries had only dreamed of; the ''space race'' for the moon was on. It was the greatest technological challenge this nation had ever taken, dwarfing even the development of the nuclear bomb. A quarter million miles of cold, empty space lay between Earth and its moon. The rocket boosters, spacecraft, and sophisticated equipment did not even exist for such a mission. The obstacles ahead seemed insurmountable. Yet by the end of the decade, Americans had planted their flag on lunar soil.

Perspectives

Race Through a Decade

1957	
1958	**Jan. 31** U.S. launches *Explorer 1*, an eighteen-pound satellite that discovers the Van Allen radiation belt. **Dec. 6** U.S. probe fails to escape the atmosphere.
1959	
1960	**April 1** U.S. launches the world's first weather satellite. **Aug. 10** U.S. makes the first recovery of a capsule from space.
1961	**Jan. 31** A chimpanzee named Ham is sent into outer space and is recovered. **May 5** Astronaut Alan Shepard, Jr., reaches suborbital flight *(Mercury)*. **May 25** Kennedy announces goal to land a man on the moon "before this decade is out."
1962	**Feb. 20** Astronaut John Glenn, Jr., orbits the earth.
1963	**May 15** U.S. Astronaut Gordon Cooper makes an extended space flight (34 hours 20 minutes).
1964	**July 28** Lunar probe, *Ranger 7*, sends back close-up photographs of possible landing sites on moon.
1965	**March 23** A two-man crew reaches space; first pilots to maneuver a craft in space *(Gemini 3)*. **June 3** Edward White walks in space *(Gemini 4)*. **Aug. 21** Astronauts spend a record eight days in space, the time needed for a moon flight *(Gemini 5)*. **Dec. 4-15** Two U.S. spacecraft rendezvous *(Gemini 6-7)*.
1966	**March 16** Two orbiting U.S. spaceships dock *(Gemini 8)*. **May 30** U.S. lands *Surveyor 1*, an unmanned probe, on the moon. **Aug. 10** Lunar orbiter maps the moon's surface for possible manned landing sites.
1967	**Jan. 27** Tragic fire kills astronauts Grissom, White, and Chaffee during a count-down rehearsal, delaying the manned Apollo program eighteen months. **Sept. 7** Capsule studies effects of weightlessness in space.
1968	**Oct.11** A three-man U.S. crew orbits the earth *(Apollo 7)*. **Dec. 21** Three U.S. astronauts orbit moon *(Apollo 8)*.
1969	**March 3** Astronauts practice lunar maneuvers in earth orbit *(Apollo 9)*. **May 18** Astronauts descend close to the moon in the Lunar Module *(Apollo 10)*. **July 20** Astronauts Neil Armstrong and Edwin Aldrin walk on the moon *(Apollo 11)*.

Oct. 4 U.S.S.R. launches *Sputnik 1*. *Nov. 3* U.S.S.R. launches *Sputnik 2*, a 1,121-pound spacecraft carrying a dog.	1957
	1958
Jan. 2 A Soviet space probe flies past the moon. *Sept. 12* A Soviet spaceship hits the moon. *Oct. 4* A Soviet space probe circles the moon.	1959
	1960
April 12 Cosmonaut Yuri Gagarin makes the first manned space flight *(Vostok 1)*. *Aug. 6* Cosmonaut Gherman Titov makes the first extended space flight (25 hours 18 minutes).	1961
Aug. 11/12 Two Soviet vessels perform the first dual mission.	1962
June 16 U.S.S.R. sends the first woman into space (Valentina Tereshkova).	1963
Oct.12 A three-man Soviet crew reaches space. *(Voshkod 1)*.	1964
March 18 Alexei Leonov becomes the first man to walk in space *(Voshkod 2)*.	1965
Jan. 31 U.S.S.R. makes the first soft landing on the moon with an unmanned probe. *March 31* Soviet satellite placed in lunar orbit.	1966
April 23 Cosmonaut Vladimir Komarov dies during re-entry *(Soyuz 1)*.	1967
Sept. 14 U.S.S.R. recovers a capsule from lunar orbit.	1968
	1969

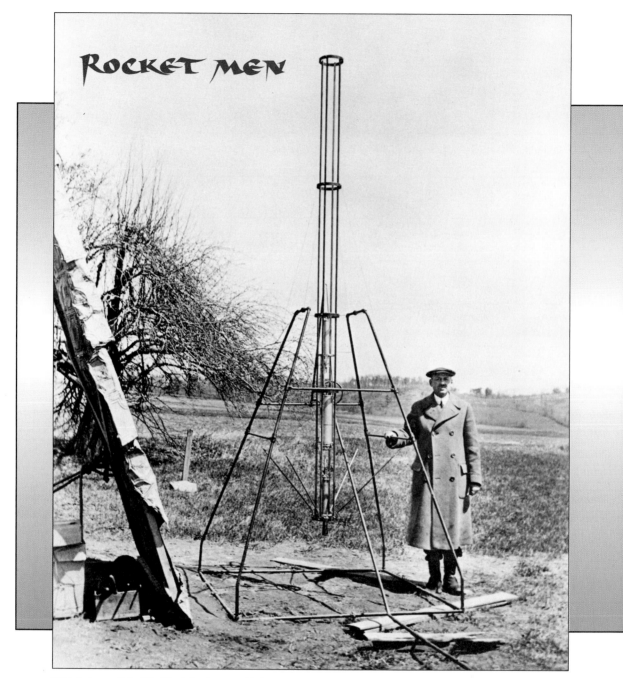

Rocket pioneer Robert Goddard stands next to his liquid propulsion rocket in Auburn, Massachusetts, 1926.

Landing on the moon could not have taken place without the decades of scientific advances that preceded it. Yet the scientists who dared to dream about reaching the stars faced not only technological barriers but also the scoffing of those who dismissed them as dreamers.

One of the greatest of these early pioneers was American Robert H. Goddard, the father of modern rocketry. As a teen-ager Goddard began experimenting with rockets, beginning a lifelong pursuit of reaching beyond the sky. Goddard was the first to prove that propulsion could take place in a vacuum, and he won over two hundred patents from his various experiments. After experimenting with various fuels, he switched to liquid propellants (oxygen and gasoline). In 1926 on his aunt's farm in Massachusetts, he launched the world's first liquid-propelled rocket; it flew an amazing 184 feet.

"Moony" Goddard was laughed at for his fanciful dreams, but his experiments won the respect of the scientific world. With help from Charles A. Lindbergh, he won enough financial assistance to open a shop in New Mexico and hire a crew. By 1935 one of his rockets flew faster than the speed of sound. He developed a steering mechanism, a rocket fuel pump, and multiple-stage rockets. The aging Goddard abandoned his rocket experiments during World War II to assist the military in the then experimental field of jet propulsion. His contribution to science and to his country was not fully recognized until after his death, when jets and rockets came of age.

Another rocket pioneer was Germany's Wernher Von Braun. While most countries cancelled their rocket experiments during World War II, the Germans accelerated theirs. "Until 1936," Von Braun admitted, "Goddard was ahead of us all." But with the support of the Nazi military, Von Braun was given huge facilities and oversaw the technical development of the dreaded V-2 bombs that were used to blitz London.

In 1945, as the invading Soviet armies drew closer, Von Braun and his entire rocket team fled to the American side and surrendered, many of them later becoming U.S. citizens. The V-2 was adapted and updated to continue scientific experiments in America. Von Braun eventually became the technical director of the U.S. Army ballistic-weapons program. While most rocket engineers kept to their duties and balked at the fanciful idea of space travel, Von Braun led a popular crusade for it. He proposed three stages: a guided satellite, manned flights in orbit, and then flights to the moon and Mars. Von Braun found little support for his far-fetched ideas.

Sputnik 1, however, forced scientists, politicians, and the public to see things Von Braun's way. When NASA was formed, Von Braun directed the development of the huge Saturn launch vehicle, the thirty-six-story rocket used to launch Americans to the moon. A brilliant engineer and organizer, Von Braun oversaw the greatest engineering feat of mankind to that date, assembling millions of parts on schedule and meeting unprecedented reliability standards. Each booster was launched without failure. He was a prolific writer and promoter of the space program until his death in 1977.

Mercury & Gemini Projects

America's seven original astronauts: (Front row, left to right) Walter M. Schirra, Jr., Donald K. Slayton, John H. Glenn, Jr., and Scott Carpenter; (back row) Alan B. Shepard, Jr., Virgil I. "Gus" Grissom, and L. Gordon Cooper

Now that man has walked on the moon, it is easy to forget the drama during the years before this achievement. Without the pioneering Mercury and Gemini projects, the Apollo moon landing would not have been possible.

The Mercury project, named after the mythological messenger of the gods, was designed to lift a man into orbit. The maiden project did not have a promising start in 1958, however. Mercury's complex wiring and parts were placed deep within the craft, requiring dismantling for repairing even the smallest problems. The cramped compartment (about seven feet long) had small control jets that merely adjusted the direction in which it tilted. The "flying rock," as some called it, was designed to fall almost helplessly back to the earth. Yet NASA troubleshooters overcame the problems one by one.

The Mercury pilots were true pioneers of the last frontier. These original seven astronauts, se-

lected after rigorous psychological and physical tests, underwent grueling training to prepare them for every conceivable problem of space flight, including coming out of a three-dimensional spinning tumble, learning to navigate by the stars, and jungle survival in case of a crash. John Glenn, Jr., flew the first American orbit, returning to a hero's welcome; Walter Schirra's "textbook flight" performed so well that it landed less than four miles off its target; and Gordon Cooper spent over thirty-four hours in orbit, traveling 600,000 miles.

Begun in 1961, the Gemini program was supposed to bridge the Mercury project and the complex Apollo project. Named after famous twins in Greek mythology, Gemini was designed to lift a two-man spacecraft into orbit and test the technology necessary to maneuver two spacecraft so that they could meet and then dock in outer space. At first scientists planned simply to change the scale

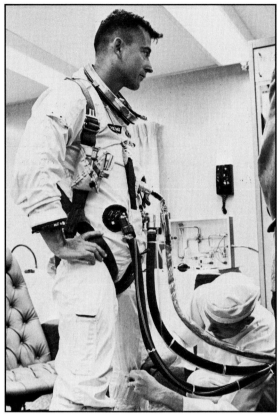

Astronaut John Young suits up for a Gemini flight.

of the Mercury project—adding a seat and the necessary power to put it into orbit (from the Titan 2 ballistic missile, which had twice the thrust of Mercury's Atlas missile). But technicians made some fundamental improvements in the Gemini craft. For instance, they placed the wiring and serviceable parts near the outside of the craft for easy repair. They also added thrusters to give the ships maneuverability and designed two complex hatches to allow the astronauts to leave the ship and walk in space.

The Gemini project marked a turning point in the space race. The first manned Gemini flight (March 1965) performed hand-operated maneuvers in space (a necessary prerequisite in the complex operation of finding another spacecraft in space and docking with it). Although a Soviet cosmonaut became the first to walk in space, the United States responded quickly. In less than two months, astronaut Edward H. White also became a human satellite as he maneuvered outside the ship for twenty-one minutes—twice as long as his Soviet rival. Four flights and less than a year later, a Gemini craft accomplished the difficult task of finding another craft that had already been launched into orbit and then docking with it. With the Gemini program complete, the stage was set for Apollo and the reach for the moon.

Down to Earth

The huge cost of the space program was questioned from the very start. Critics called the program an expensive boondoggle for dreamy scientists and extravagant politicians, when the money could be better spent on human needs on earth. Yet the discoveries and inventions of the space program have improved life on earth in thousands of ways, from the medical laboratory to the supermarket shelf.

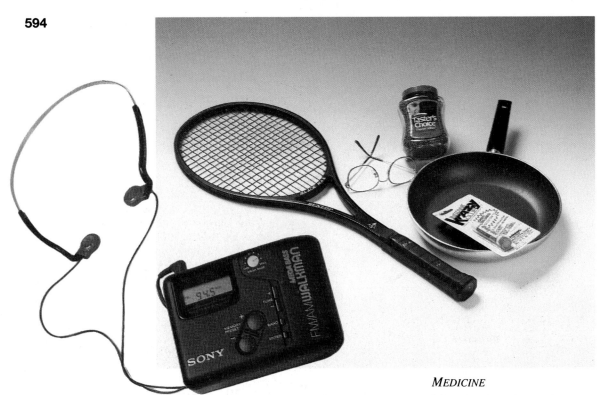

HOME

synthetics and materials from parachutes for clothes, furniture upholstery, and drapes

miniature electronics and bearings have changed television and radio

epoxy resin used as a powerful glue

new silicons and lubricants for cars and appliances

fluxless aluminum soldering for home repairs

mercury cell batteries provide power for cordless drills, razors, flashlights, radios, etc.

freeze-dried food

precise electronic thermometers

self-cleaning ovens

Teflon® filters for brewing coffee

light-sensitive sunglasses

pots and pans made from Pyroceram, developed for covers over radar equipment

manufacturing technology for compact discs

lightweight tennis rackets

MEDICINE

improvement and miniaturization of dental instruments

improved electrodes for electrocardiograms

automatic blood pressure cuff

a chemical derivative of the rocket propellant hydrazine relieves tuberculosis and certain forms of mental illness

improved dental braces

heart pacemakers

laser surgery technology

INDUSTRY

the plasma arc torch (temperatures of 30,000° F, or three times as hot as the sun), a new tool in industry

an electron beam gun used to weld precision parts and new materials

improved thermostat controls

scratch-resistant plastic for eyeglasses and instruments

microprocessors (computer chips)

low-radiation x-ray equipment for airport security

Apollo 11

The powerful Saturn V rocket was America's launch vehicle for manned Apollo flights to the moon.

Perspectives

"Houston, Tranquility Base here. The *Eagle* has landed." A voice crackled across the vast night of space. Americans were on the moon! Flight controllers in Houston, Texas, along with a worldwide audience of six hundred million, either cheered or sat in speechless amazement when they learned that the *Eagle* lunar module had landed Americans on the moon.

Three men made that historic venture: Neil Armstrong, the mission commander; Edwin Aldrin, Jr., pilot of the lunar module, *Eagle;* and Michael Collins, pilot of *Columbia,* the command module. Armstrong and Aldrin made the descent to the moon while Collins circled overhead. A few hours after landing on July 20, 1969, Armstrong climbed down the spindly spacecraft and stepped onto the gray dust of the moon, pausing to say, "That's one small step for a man, one giant leap for mankind." Aldrin soon followed, awestruck. "Beautiful, beautiful, beautiful," he said. "A magnificent desolation."

After Armstrong and Aldrin raised the Stars and Stripes over the barren moonscape, a call from President Nixon was transmitted to them. "Because of what you have done," the president said, "the heavens have become a part of man's world." The astronauts spent about two and a half hours walking on the moon, gathering samples and setting up experiments with a laser reflector, a seismic detector, and a solar wind composition detector. When later asked, "Was there ever a moment on the moon when either one of you were just a little bit spellbound by what was going on?" Armstrong responded, "About two and a half hours."

Astronaut Edwin Aldrin's visor reflects the history-making images of Apollo 11–the Eagle resting on lunar soil and the first man on the moon, Astronaut Neil Armstrong.

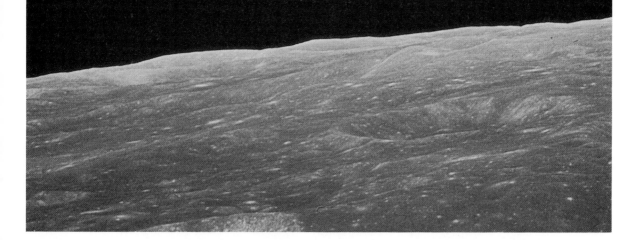

They left behind a plaque on *Eagle's* descent stage, signed by the three astronauts and President Nixon:

HERE MEN FROM THE PLANET EARTH
FIRST SET FOOT UPON THE MOON
JULY 1969, A.D.
WE CAME IN PEACE FOR ALL MANKIND

Man's first infant steps outside his planet—a drop of blue on the corner of an incomprehensible universe—were steps shrouded in mystery. But it was a mystery not of science but of creation. Aldrin, scanning the celestial expanse from Tranquility Base, began to quote from Psalm 8: "When I consider thy heavens, the work of thy fingers, the moon and the stars, which thou hast ordained; What is man that thou art mindful of him?"

CHAPTER 25

A Nation Adrift (1973-1980)

"I did not take the sacred oath of office to preside over the decline and fall of the United States of America."

President Gerald Ford, September 1975

Hounded by charges of corruption, President Richard Nixon resigns from office on August 9, 1974.

An average American watching the evening news on December 1, 1979, would have noticed a difference from broadcasts from only a few weeks before. Each night Walter Cronkite, anchorman of the "CBS Evening News," always closed his program with his trademark line "And that's the way it is. . . ." On this night–shortly after Muslim extremists had seized fifty-three American hostages in the American embassy in Teheran, Iran–viewers heard Cronkite add a final phrase ". . . on the twenty-seventh day of captivity for the American hostages in Iran." Each night Cronkite added another day to the total; it became thirty days, forty, fifty, one hundred, two hundred, and still more with no end in sight. The nightly broadcasts were like a drumbeat to Americans, each beat echoing the helplessness of the United States, its decline as a world power, and above all the inability of its president to deal with the world situation. Cronkite continued the demoralizing count until the 444th day, the day on which the hostages were freed and the day on which Americans inaugurated the new president that their frustration had in part led them to elect.

The president repudiated in 1980 was Jimmy Carter, but he was only the last in a series of presidents rejected by the American public. For much of the 1970s the United States suffered a "leadership crisis." It began when one president, hounded by scandal, resigned from office. It continued as his successor, a man who had never won an election outside of his congressional district in Grand Rapids, Michigan, tried vainly to unite the nation. It ended with Carter, a man elected in part because of the failures of his predecessors, being driven from office by a disillusioned American electorate. The United States, for much of the 1970s, was a nation adrift.

The Embattled Presidency

The Fall of Richard Nixon

Watergate Affair–In the summer of 1972, during the heat of the presidential campaign, police arrested five burglars, carrying electronic listening devices, who were trying to break into the headquarters of the Democratic National Committee at the Watergate Office Complex in Washington. The

Republican Senator Howard Baker of Tennessee (left) *and Democratic Senator Sam Ervin of North Carolina* (center) *directed the Senate's nationally televised hearings concerning the Watergate Affair.*

event caused little stir at the time. The White House vigorously denied any connection with this "third-rate burglary," and George McGovern's campaign was already in such deep trouble that few listened to his charges against Nixon of criminality and corruption.

After the election, however, more of the story began to leak out. One of the convicted burglars alleged to the judge trying the case that authorities "higher up" were behind the break-in and were trying to cover up the affair. Further investigation revealed a pattern of questionable and illegal activities that had been organized by Nixon's Committee to Re-elect the President. Some Nixon aides, for example, had sent libelous letters to newspapers accusing Democratic candidates of racism and sexual immorality. Others had burglarized the office of the psychiatrist of Daniel Ellsberg, the man who had stolen the Pentagon Papers, in an attempt to find material with which to discredit Ellsberg. In 1973 investigations by Congress and by a federal court resulted in the firing or resignation of several members of Nixon's staff and cabinet. The contro-

versy did not go away with these dismissals, however; people wondered how deeply the president himself was involved.

Resignation of Agnew—Nixon's administration was also plagued by startling revelations that Vice President **Spiro Agnew** had taken bribes from building contractors while governor of Maryland and even while vice president. By striking a bargain with prosecutors, Agnew was allowed to plead guilty to a lesser charge, and he received only a fine and probation. He had to resign as vice president, though, in October 1973, the first vice president to resign from office since John C. Calhoun had resigned for political (not criminal) reasons in 1832. Although Agnew's crimes were unrelated to Watergate, they increased the perception that the Nixon administration was thoroughly corrupt. Using the procedure outlined by the Twenty-fifth Amendment (ratified 1967), President Nixon nominated House minority leader **Gerald Ford** of Michigan to succeed Agnew; both houses of Congress confirmed the nomination by overwhelming margins. Nixon hoped that Ford's popularity in Congress and reputation for honesty would help deflect criticism from his administration.

Resignation of Nixon—Despite all of the charges and investigations, no evidence had come to light that implicated President Nixon himself in the Watergate scandal. That situation changed in the middle of 1973, when a White House aide revealed that Nixon had installed a secret recording system in the Oval Office that taped every conversation there. Immediately, both the courts and Congress began to press Nixon to release the tapes. The president refused, claiming that national security and the separation of powers were at stake. This refusal began a long struggle over control of the tapes. Nixon tried to placate investigators by first releasing edited transcripts of the tapes and then releasing just a portion of the tapes. All the while, he maintained his complete innocence of wrongdoing. The president's approval rating with the public plummeted. Wrenching judicial and congressional inquiries exposed the seamy side of the Nixon administration—the political "dirty tricks," subtle lies, and outright deceit that Nixon's followers had practiced.

The Watergate affair became a national trauma. For months the government seemed paralyzed by the accusations and rumors that flew about. Televised congressional hearings kept the scandal constantly before the public eye. Finally, in July 1974, the Supreme Court ruled unanimously that Nixon must release all of the tapes. The previously unreleased tapes showed that although the president had not known about the Watergate break-in beforehand, he had participated in attempts to cover up involvement of his White House subordinates. With impeachment by the House and conviction by the Senate now a virtual certainty in the Democratic-controlled Congress, Richard Nixon resigned on August 9. Gerald Ford, in his first speech as president, said, "My fellow Americans, our long national nightmare is over."

The Unelected President

Gerald Ford enjoyed a flood of good will when he took office. The American people indeed wanted to put the "long national nightmare" behind them.

President Gerald Ford

Furthermore, Ford's reputation as a decent, honest man was a welcome contrast after the bitter struggle between the White House and Capitol Hill. Then after only a month in office, Ford dashed his popularity with one stroke: he granted a full **pardon** to Richard Nixon for any crimes he might have committed while in office. The president maintained that his action would put the Watergate affair behind the nation and that it would save the United States the agony of enduring the trial of a former president. President Ford's act was brave but politically damaging. Many critics thought it unfair that Nixon should escape punishment while his subordinates suffered. Some cynics even hinted that there had been a "deal," that Nixon had agreed to resign only if Ford promised to pardon him later. Ford's popularity fell dramatically after the pardon.

President Ford faced several obstacles, in addition to the pardon, which hampered his effectiveness. One was the fact that he was the nation's first unelected president. He owed his elevation to the nation's highest office not to a national election but to an appointment and resignation. As Ford himself said, "I am acutely aware that I have received the votes of none of you." A second obstacle was the public's increasingly critical perception of Ford. Despite Ford's athletic ability (which included a stint as a star center for the University of Michigan's football team), a series of public accidents gave the impression that he was clumsy. Ford stumbled as he descended the ramp of the presidential jet, for example, and accidentally hit spectators with balls when he played golf. Malicious critics quoted Lyndon Johnson's old insult that Ford had "played too much football with his helmet off."

Ford's greatest obstacle, however, was a hostile Congress. The Democrats held comfortable majorities in both houses, and they were determined to control the government after the excesses of the Nixon administration. Ford's main weapon against Congress was the veto, and he vetoed sixty-one bills in less than three years in office in an attempt to hold down government spending and protect the powers of the presidency. Congress, however, overrode twelve of his vetoes, one of the highest number of overrides since the beleaguered presidency of Andrew Johnson. The standoff between Ford and Congress created a legislative deadlock.

In addition to the pardon and the clashes with Congress, factors beyond the president's control damaged his reputation. In 1975 America tasted final defeat in Southeast Asia as South Vietnam, Cambodia, and Laos fell to the Communists. A sluggish national economy also worried voters. Under Nixon and Ford, the paralyzed presidency had sunk to its lowest level of prestige since the era of Warren G. Harding.

Section Review

1. Why did the release of the presidential tapes cause President Nixon to resign?
2. What event early in Ford's administration drastically lowered his popularity with the American people?
3. What was Ford's greatest obstacle to effectiveness in his presidency?

Domestic Difficulties

The problems of the 1960s–urban violence, student unrest, and racial conflict–gave way to problems in the 1970s that were less overtly dramatic but perhaps just as important. In spite of all its problems, the 1960s had been economically prosperous; in the 1970s, however, economic conditions became the nation's primary concern. Also the success of the civil rights movement in the 1960s spurred other groups to agitate for their "rights"–some legitimate and some not–in the 1970s.

Economic Woes

Energy Crisis–In October 1973 the Arab nations of Egypt and Syria attacked the neighboring Jewish state of Israel. The United States, as it had done since Israel became a nation in 1948, supported the Israelis against the Arabs. In retaliation, the oil-producing Arab nations–all members of the Organization of Petroleum Exporting Countries (OPEC)–announced an **oil embargo** against the United States, prohibiting the sale of any oil to America. When the embargo came, the United States was still under President Nixon's wage and price controls. With a shrinking supply of gasoline (which is made from petroleum) held at an artificially low price, supplies became scarce. Service stations were open fewer hours and limited the amount of gas each customer could buy. Motorists often had to wait in long lines to buy the gas that was available. When price controls were finally lifted, the price of gasoline shot up, from about 35¢ a gallon at the beginning of 1973 to well over a dollar a gallon by 1980.

The gasoline shortages were only part of an overall **energy crisis,** a combination of higher prices for and shortages of American energy resources. Until the 1970s, Americans had always assumed that there would be enough cheap fuel resources to power any project that American industry undertook. Now the realization began to set in that America's energy sources were not inexhaustible and would no longer be inexpensive. Petroleum production had already begun to drop before the embargo, and the embargo itself simply heightened the shortages and drove up prices more quickly. Even when the Arabs lifted the oil embargo, they increased their prices for crude oil fourfold, nudging prices even higher. All petroleum products–everything from heating oil and fuels for power plants to phonograph records and asphalt–went up in price.

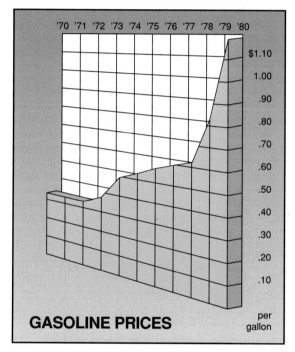

GASOLINE PRICES per gallon

'70 '71 '72 '73 '74 '75 '76 '77 '78 '79 '80

$1.10
1.00
.90
.80
.70
.60
.50
.40
.30
.20
.10

Contributing to the energy crisis was the **environmental movement,** a growing concern with the effects of industrial development on the earth's environment. Beginning in the 1960s, environmentalists began to sound warnings about the pollution of the water and air by industry in general and automobiles in particular. Under pressure from environmental groups, Congress passed a number of laws regulating pollution. Chief among Congress's acts were the establishing of the Environmental Protection Agency in 1970 to oversee and coordinate environmental regulations and the passage of the Clean Air Act (1970; amended 1977) and the Clean Water Act (1977), both of which empowered the government to control air and water pollution.

These actions helped reduce pollution of the environment, but they also increased the demands on the nation's energy resources. Many industries, for example, began to switch from highly pollutant coal to oil as a power source, straining American oil resources even further. Likewise regulations aimed at reducing air pollution by cars required adding emission-control devices which reduced fuel efficiency along with the pollution. For environmentalists, of course, their goal was worth the higher energy costs. Many industries, on the other hand, began to plead for delays in implementing the environmental regulations to give them time to make the costly adjustments.

Stagflation—In general, the economic problems of inflation and high unemployment are mutually exclusive. Normally, when inflation is high, unemployment is low; and when unemployment is high, inflation is low. In the 1970s, however, the United States experienced high inflation and high unemployment at the same time, a condition economists called **stagflation.** Three factors caused the stagflation. First, the energy crisis had created a scarcity of many products and pushed prices up. Second, President Johnson created a large budget deficit by attempting to pay for both the Vietnam War and the Great Society without raising taxes. As a result the government had to print more money to cover the deficit and thus fueled inflation further.

The third and most complicated cause was the United States' decision to abandon the gold standard for currency. From World War II to 1971, the United States had promised foreign nations that anyone outside the United States could redeem any American currency he held for American gold at a price of $30 an ounce. (The U.S. had not allowed American citizens to redeem currency for gold, however, since 1933.) While the United States was exporting more goods than it imported, this policy was not a problem, because few foreign investors held sizable amounts of American currency. In 1971, however, the United States suffered its first **trade deficit** since the 1890s; it imported more goods than it exported. Foreign investors, primarily in Europe, now had abundant amounts of American currency and began to exchange them for gold.

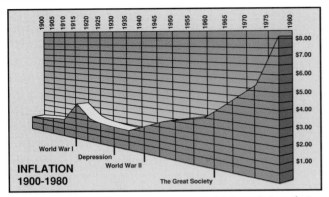

INFLATION
1900-1980

World War I
Depression
World War II
The Great Society

$8.00
$7.00
$6.00
$5.00
$4.00
$3.00
$2.00
$1.00

Prices have risen continuously since 1900. Items that cost $1 in 1900 cost over $8 (an increase of 800%) by 1980.

Faced with the possible depletion of America's gold reserves, President Nixon stopped the redeeming of gold for currency. As a result of Nixon's action, nothing backed U.S. currency except the government's promise. Without any fixed value, the dollar began to drop in value in relation to foreign currencies, and the costs of buying foreign goods rose.

The energy crisis, the budget deficit, and abandoning the gold standard all fueled inflation without providing a means of reducing unemployment. Stagflation left Congress in a dilemma. Attacking inflation by cutting government spending added to the already high unemployment, because many jobs depended on federal funds. On the other hand, attacking unemployment through government spending added to the already alarming inflation rate. By 1980 the majority of Americans listed economic issues—primarily inflation—as their main concern.

Rights Movements

Since blacks had made dramatic gains in securing their civil rights, many other minorities attempted to broaden their legal rights, with varying degrees of success. American Indians, for example, held protests to dramatize their plight: a high rate of unemployment and lower life expectancy. One of the most publicized protests was at Wounded Knee, South Dakota, in 1973, on the hundredth anniversary of the Wounded Knee Massacre (see p. 391). Some Indian groups sued the government for violating its numerous treaties with the Indians, and the courts often granted the Indians generous

financial compensation. Some "rights movements" of the era were less legitimate. One of the worst was the "gay rights" movement, in which homosexuals tried to remove legal prohibitions to their immoral lifestyle and to gain legal recognition of homosexual "marriages" for purposes of adoption and the like.

Without doubt the largest and most influential movement in the 1970s was the **women's rights movement.** Although not a numerical minority, women as a group suffered from various forms of discrimination. It was not at all uncommon, for instance, for a woman to receive less pay than a man working at the same job simply because she was a woman. In some states, a married woman could not own property in her own name, whereas a married man could. A widow would discover after the death of a spouse that the excellent credit rating they had built as a couple no longer existed, but a widower's credit rating continued unimpaired. With such injustices as illustrations, **feminists** (advocates of women's rights) successfully appealed to the public's sense of fairness to address these problems.

The women's rights movement was complicated, though, by a radical element which generally preferred the name **women's liberation movement.** These extreme feminists portrayed modern American marriage as a form of slavery in which wives labored in the "demeaning" roles of mother and homemaker. They wanted to "liberate" women from this "slavery" and looked down on women who preferred the traditional role of wife and mother in the home. To achieve their vision of equality, women's liberationists advocated a platform of bold immorality: "free love" (premarital and extramarital sex), easier divorce laws, recognition of lesbian "marriages," and above all a woman's unquestioned right to abortion on demand. State laws had long restricted or even prohibited the practice of abortion. In the landmark case ***Roe v. Wade*** (1973), however, the Supreme Court struck down most state abortion laws. As a result of the Court's decision, the slaughter of unborn children by abortion rose to over one million a year by 1978. Women's liberationists were elated with the decision.

The Woman Who Stopped the ERA

The leader of the fight against the Equal Rights Amendment was one determined woman named Phyllis Schlafly. But then, she was a woman used to competing against long odds. She worked her way through college during World War II by test-firing bullets in an ammunition plant. She compiled a brilliant college record, winning recognition from the Phi Beta Kappa scholastic honor society and receiving her master's degree from Radcliffe College, one of the nation's most prestigious women's schools. After her marriage to a prominent attorney, Schlafly worked as a homemaker and brought up six children—and ran for Congress twice, served as a delegate to the Republican National Convention four times, and wrote nine books. She said, "I'm a housewife, but not *just* a housewife."

Phyllis Schlafly first made headlines in 1964 when she published *A Choice Not an Echo,* an examination of Republican national politics that is often credited with helping Barry Goldwater win the Republican presidential nomination. After Congress sent the ERA to the states for ratification in 1972, however, she really made her mark as the nation's chief opponent of the amendment. Tirelessly and relentlessly she visited the states that had not ratified the ERA in order to stress the dangers of the amendment to the traditional rights of women. She warned that it would strike down laws requiring husbands to support their wives financially, for example, and eliminate protections preventing women from fighting in combat in the armed services.

She took abuse for her stand. Female reporters virtually hissed when questioning her. A radical feminist, after being bested in a debate with Schlafly, shrieked, "I'd like to burn you at the stake!" She was often insulted, sometimes spat upon, and on one occasion was hit in the face with an apple pie. Through it all, Schlafly kept a calm, even, and always courteous composure. She stated her arguments in crisp tones supported by a wealth of careful research. When opponents scorned her for speaking out on legal and constitutional issues without being a lawyer, she entered law school and earned her law degree in her "spare time."

Schlafly warred against not only the ERA but also the whole radical feminist idea that the history of the United States was a history of the oppression of women. "The claim that American women are downtrodden and unfairly treated is the fraud of the century," Schlafly said. She pointed to her own success: "I've achieved my goals in life and I did it without sex-neutral laws." To Phyllis Schlafly, the wise woman "spends her time, ingenuity, and efforts seizing her opportunities—not whining about past injustices."

Although radical feminists seized much of the public's attention, the real strength of the women's movement lay in the basic justice of its demands in the marketplace. Many women who were uninterested in or even opposed to the demands of the liberationists were very much interested in economic equality. Both higher inflation and rising divorce rates were forcing more women out of the home and into the work place simply to survive. These women desired only the chance to make a living and support their families. Therefore, Congress and the states passed legislation giving women equal access to employment and equal pay for performing the same jobs as men.

The most controversial and divisive piece of profeminist legislation was the **Equal Rights Amendment** (ERA) passed by Congress in 1972. Section 1 of this amendment said briefly, ''Equality of rights under the law shall not be denied or abridged by the United States or by any state on account of sex.'' Proponents of the amendment claimed that it would reinforce the basic rights as citizens that women held under the Constitution. Opponents claimed that sufficient laws were already in effect to guarantee these rights. Furthermore, opponents warned that the amendment's overlooked Section 2–''The Congress shall have the power to enforce, by appropriate legislation, the provisions of this article'' (language similar to that contained in eight other amendments)–would open the door to an enormous growth of abusive government power. Opponents feared that the amendment would break down the traditional protections that women enjoyed, such as laws against rape, and would increase government intrusions into individual privacy, such as matters of adoption and child custody. A bitter fight over ratification of the ERA ended in 1982 when the amendment failed to garner the necessary approval of three-fourths of the state legislatures before its deadline for ratification had passed. Its failure was a blow to the radicals but did not diminish the genuine gains that women had made.

Section Review

1. Why did Arab nations place an oil embargo on the United States in 1973?
2. Name the agency and the two major acts which were Congress's main attempts to protect the environment from pollution.
3. What were the three causes of stagflation in the 1970s?
4. What is the name for the radical wing of the women's rights movement?

The Ineffectual Presidency

Rise of Jimmy Carter

1976 Election–Gerald Ford entered the 1976 presidential race encumbered by numerous weights. Although he was the incumbent, he was an unelected incumbent, having never won a national election. The nation's high unemployment rate, the pardon of Nixon, and the public perception of Ford as a good-natured bumbler all hampered the president's re-election efforts. Furthermore, Ford was not even the preferred choice of many in his own party. Former California governor **Ronald Reagan,** the hero of the Republican conservatives who dominated the party, mounted a strong challenge to Ford in the primaries. The president won renomination but only by a narrow margin after a bruising fight. One Democrat, noting Ford's plight, said gleefully, ''We could run an aardvark this year and win.''

The Democrats did not run an aardvark, but their candidate proved to be an unusual one. **Jimmy Carter,** a well-to-do peanut farmer whose political experience consisted of one term in the Georgia state senate and one term as governor of Georgia, surprised the experts by winning the Democratic nomination. Carter's strategy was clever. He placed himself in the political center where he could attract the most voters, to the right of a host of liberal Democratic candidates but to the left of Democratic firebrand George Wallace. He also ran as an ''outsider,'' a candidate untainted by the corruption in Washington and therefore supposedly better able to clean it up. As a further contrast to the dishonesty of the Nixon years, Carter claimed to be a ''born-again'' Christian who wanted a government ''as filled with love as the American people.'' After the trauma of Watergate, Americans were attracted to a candidate who said plainly, ''I'll never tell a lie.''

The 1976 election looked at first as though it would be a landslide for Carter. Ford, however, fought back. The incumbent hammered away at Carter's vagueness on the issues. ''Jimmy Carter will say anything anywhere to be president of the United States,'' Ford said. ''He wavers, he wanders, he wiggles, and he waffles.'' Ford hurt himself, though, by proclaiming in a televised debate

By using his nickname "Jimmy" and dressing in casual clothing such as sweaters, President Carter attempted to portray himself as a "common man," a chief executive who was unpretentious and accessible to the public.

that he did not believe Eastern Europe was under Soviet domination, despite the presence of Soviet-imposed governments and thousands of Soviet troops in those nations. This gaffe merely reinforced the perception of some that Ford was a bungler. In the end, Carter won narrowly, 50.1 per cent to 48 per cent in the popular vote; the vote in the electoral college, 297 to 240, was the closest since Woodrow Wilson defeated Charles Evans Hughes in 1916.

The Carter Style—Carter entered office professing his desire to be a "people's president" with an open, honest, and compassionate administration. He surprised and delighted the American people by walking down Pennsylvania Avenue after his inauguration instead of riding in the usual armored limousine. He made televised addresses wearing a sweater instead of a suit; photographs often showed him relaxing in blue jeans. The new president appointed record numbers of women and minorities to government positions. Not all of Carter's healing gestures were appreciated, though. When he granted amnesty (a general pardon) to all those who had evaded the draft in order to avoid fighting in Vietnam, Carter felt the wrath of those veterans who had loyally fulfilled their obligation and fought in the war.

Carter had his negative characteristics as well. Like James Polk, he was a compulsive worker who tried to control every aspect of running the government; as a result, the president often found himself bogged down by details that could have been delegated to subordinates. Carter's "outsider" status in Washington, and his aloof, humorless personality gave him trouble in dealing with Congress, despite large Democratic majorities in both houses. The president's subdued, low-key speaking style displayed, said former senator Eugene McCarthy, the "eloquence of a mortician." These flaws did not prove damaging to Carter at first, but as Americans became disenchanted with his policies, these characteristics added to the public perception of him as a colorless and ineffective leader.

Foreign Affairs

Jimmy Carter attempted to pursue a foreign policy based on fairness and morality, much as Woodrow Wilson had attempted to do in the 1910s. The cornerstone of Carter's foreign policy was the defense of **human rights,** protecting people from oppression by their governments. However, President Carter learned—just as Wilson had—that morality is more easily preached than imparted. Communist nations, some of the worst violators of human rights, were impervious to Carter's pressures; they continued their oppressive policies without interference. The United States could influence only friendly nations concerning human rights. An example of the shortcomings of Carter's foreign policy was Nicaragua. The Carter administration began to pressure a friendly but dictatorial regime in that Central American nation to improve its human rights record. Eventually revolutionaries, with the American government's quiet approval, overthrew the Nicaraguan dictator. Afterwards, a Marxist government which was just as repressive as the previous government but far more hostile to the United States took power. The human rights doctrine seemed to typify Carter's foreign policy: high ideals, low performance.

Panama Canal Treaty—Carter's first great challenge in foreign affairs concerned the Panama Canal. Panamanians had resented American control of the canal for many years, despite the fact that the United States had helped Panama win its independence and had paid that nation for control of the Canal Zone, according to the original treaty, "in perpetuity." The Nixon and Ford administrations had begun negotiations to return the canal to Panama; Carter merely completed the process. President Carter signed a treaty with Panama in 1977, and the Senate narrowly ratified it the following year. The new treaty allowed Panama and the United States to operate the canal jointly until the year 2000, when Panama would take over the operation completely.

The treaty created controversy in the United States. Administration officials, numerous leading Democrats, and even some Republicans such as Gerald Ford defended the treaty. They claimed that the canal's narrow width and the growth of air power made the canal neither militarily nor economically important to the United States. (They pointed out, for example, that aircraft carriers and oil tankers were too wide to use the canal.) Supporters also hoped that the United States' action would build better relations with Latin America. Opponents of the treaty claimed that the waterway was still vital to American interests and that it should not be handed over to the authoritarian and sometimes unstable government of Panama. Despite passage of the treaty, U.S.-Latin American relations did not perceptibly improve. Furthermore, surrender of the canal increased the perception at home and abroad that the United States was declining in power and influence.

Camp David Accords—President Carter's greatest triumph came in diplomacy in the Middle East. Since the nation of Israel had come into existence in 1948, it had been in constant conflict with its Arab neighbors. They had fought four brief wars, and the region suffered from constant unrest. Egypt, one of Israel's most powerful opponents, was tired of the fighting, which brought no gain to the Egyptians. In 1978 Carter invited the president of Egypt and the prime minister of Israel to meet with him at Camp David, the private presidential retreat in Maryland. After thirteen days of arduous negotiations, the three hammered out an agreement known as the **Camp David Accords.** In return for Egypt's recognition of Israel's sovereignty (which no other Arab nation had recognized) and a guarantee of peace, Israel returned to Egypt the Sinai Peninsula that it had taken in the Six-Day War (1967). Although some parts of the accords eventually broke down, the agreement marked one of the greatest advances for peace in the Middle East since World War II.

Soviet Union—Carter's success with the Camp David Accords was overshadowed by several setbacks in foreign policy. His dealings with the Soviet Union were one example. Like Nixon and Ford before him, Carter pursued a policy of *détente,* relaxing of tensions, with the Soviet Union. The key to good relations, Carter decided, would be passage of the **SALT II Treaty.** This treaty was the result of Strategic Arms Limitation Talks (SALT) between the Soviets and the Americans to limit the number and kinds of nuclear weaponry each superpower would have. The president signed the treaty in June 1979, but he faced a stiff challenge in getting it ratified by the Senate. Conservatives charged that the treaty would put the Soviet Union ahead of the United States in nuclear weaponry and that, given the Communists' consistent treaty violations, the U.S. could not be sure that the Soviets would maintain the agreement in any case.

Two days after Christmas in 1979, all chance of passing the treaty vanished when the Soviet Union invaded the neighboring nation of Afghanistan. The Soviets claimed that they were going to "help" the pro-Communist ruler of Afghanistan,

President Jimmy Carter (center) *enjoyed his greatest foreign affairs triumph in negotiating the Camp David Accords between Egypt's President Anwar Sadat* (left) *and Israel's Prime Minister Menachem Begin* (right).

but he was quickly assassinated and replaced by a more pliable Soviet puppet. Furious, President Carter announced an embargo on all sales of grain to the Soviets and an American boycott of the 1980 summer Olympic Games to be held in Moscow. He also withdrew the SALT II Treaty from the Senate's consideration and called for a new registration of young men for the discontinued draft (although he did not revive the draft itself). In his State of the Union Address for 1980, he enunciated what became known as the "Carter Doctrine," that the United States would resist by military force if necessary any Soviet attempt to push further south to the Persian Gulf.

Yet even this relatively mild reaction brought down a storm of criticism on Carter. Liberals described the Carter Doctrine, draft registration, and withdrawal of the SALT II Treaty as harsh, provocative overreactions which threatened world peace. Farmers complained about their financial losses due to the grain embargo. Conservatives claimed that Carter was all talk, that his few concrete actions–such as the Olympic boycott–were pitifully weak. Whether he tried firmness or conciliation, Carter seemed unable to please anyone.

Iran–The Middle East gave Carter his greatest triumph with the Camp David Accords, but it also gave him his most damaging defeat when revolution convulsed the nation of Iran. The "shah" (king) of that nation, **Mohammed Reza Pahlavi** (known as the Shah of Iran), was long known to be pro-West in his outlook but repressive in his rule. In January 1979, after months of violent disorder, the Shah fled the country, and a fanatical Islamic extremist, the **Ayatollah Ruhollah Khomeini** (koh MAY nee) took power. Khomeini denounced everyone who was not as zealous as he and his followers were–the Shah, other Arab nations, the Soviet Union, and especially "the great Satan" who had supported the Shah, the United

States. When the exiled Shah went to the United States to receive medical treatment for terminal cancer, enraged Muslims stormed the American embassy in Teheran, Iran, in November and took fifty-three Americans hostage.

The **Iranian hostage crisis** became President Carter's greatest foreign policy nightmare. American citizens raged helplessly as television networks almost daily broadcast footage of Iranians burning American flags and chanting anti-American slogans. The Iranians toyed with the United States for months, raising hopes that they would release the hostages, then dashing those hopes with an almost sadistic glee. Carter, with few options open to him short of military invasion, vainly tried using economic sanctions, negotiations, and world opinion to move the Iranians to release the hostages. In April 1980 an attempted military rescue of the hostages turned into a fiasco. Two American helicopters collided in the desert of Iran, and eight American soldiers died without ever getting near the hostages. As the weeks dragged on, part of the American public's frustration and anger turned from Iran to the president himself. The whole nation seemed to be asking, ''Why doesn't the president *do* something?'' Carter's inaction–which was perhaps not entirely his fault considering his limited choices–made him seem weak, indecisive,

even spineless. Significantly, the hostages were finally released after 444 days of captivity on January 20, 1981–the day Americans inaugurated a new president who promised to bring the United States back to world leadership.

Domestic Disaster

Carter's foreign problems were matched by his domestic difficulties. The economy was the primary problem. President Ford had managed to get the rate of inflation down to 5 per cent, but the cost had been a recession and an unemployment rate of 8 per cent by the time he left office. In four years in office, President Carter was able to bring down unemployment only slightly, to 7.5 per cent. Inflation, however, soared. By 1980 the inflation rate rose to 12-13 per cent annually. Depositors and investors worried about how inflation was ravaging their hard-earned savings. Consumers complained loudly about rising prices for food, clothing, fuel, and other necessities of life. The American economy was careening out of control, and President Carter appeared helpless to do anything about it.

Aggravating domestic problems was Carter's difficulty in getting along with Congress. The president's reserved personality and Congress's determination to show its independence after the excesses of Watergate combined to paralyze legislation. Americans were frustrated that a president and a

The rise of Islamic extremist groups and Arab terrorism in the late 1970s and the 1980s presented President Carter and later President Reagan and President Bush with some of their thorniest problems in foreign affairs. Pictured here is an Islamic military unit in Beirut, Lebanon. That city in particular suffered from the conflict between Muslims, nominal Christians, and Jews.

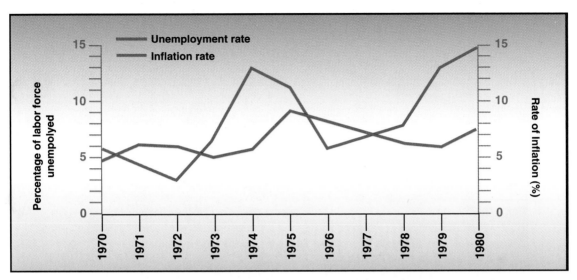

majority of Congress from the same party could not agree on a course of action to help the nation. Furthermore, the Iranian revolution in 1979 diminished oil supplies in the United States again, reviving the long lines and rising prices at gas stations that had characterized the early 1970s. As American anger rose, Carter's popularity dropped. By December 1979 only nineteen per cent of the American people approved of President Carter's performance as president–a rating lower than that of Richard Nixon during the depths of the Watergate affair. The American people–fed up with the failures of Nixon, Ford, and Carter–were looking for bold, new leadership.

Section Review

1. Name at least two difficulties President Ford faced in his campaign for re-election.
2. What act did Carter perform at his inauguration to symbolize his desire to be a "people's president"?
3. Why was the narrow width of the Panama Canal an argument against its value to the United States?
4. What was President Carter's greatest diplomatic triumph?
5. What event virtually eliminated all chance of the Senate's ratifying the SALT II Treaty?

The Rising Conservative Tide

Thunder on the Right

Among those dissatisfied with the course America was taking in the 1960s and 1970s were political conservatives, typified by Republicans Barry Goldwater and Ronald Reagan. These traditional conservatives held to a firm ideology of limited powers for the national government and staunch opposition to the growth of communism. They opposed increased government spending, especially since the nation's budget deficit was growing at an alarming rate. These conservatives feared particularly that the United States was falling behind the Soviet Union in military power and therefore opposed initiatives such as President Carter's SALT II Treaty. They also denounced Carter's decision to break relations with Nationalist China on Taiwan in order to establish relations with Communist China. Such an action was to them a cowardly betrayal of a long-time friend and anti-Communist force in order to accommodate a totalitarian Communist regime. Likewise most political conservatives opposed the Panama Canal Treaty as a symbol of America's declining power and prestige. These events served to energize conservatives as a political force.

New Right–Joining these old-line conservatives was a faction called the **New Right.** These

The Supreme Court decision legalizing abortion sparked a groundswell of opposition and launched a "right-to-life" movement dedicated to finding legal means to overturn the decision.

conservatives shared many of the beliefs of the traditionalists, notably opposition to communism and belief in limited government. The New Right, however, was also motivated by numerous social and moral issues, and many New Right groups focused on a single overriding issue. The *Roe v. Wade* decision legalizing abortion, for example, spurred a Right-to-Life movement which opposed abortion and sought to use some means, such as a constitutional amendment, to overturn the *Roe* decision. Other New Right activists called for reduction of the heavy burden of taxation that national, state, and local governments were increasingly laying on taxpayers. The most publicized event in this "taxpayers' revolt" was the passage of **Proposition 13** in California in 1978. This initiative, overwhelmingly approved by California voters, forced the state to drastically roll back property taxes.

Religious Right–One important component of the New Right was the **religious right,** various conservative Christian leaders and organizations concerned primarily with moral issues. The religious right grew in reaction to immoral trends in the United States, such as widespread drug abuse, the legalization of abortion, and increased toleration and even advocacy of homosexuality. The religious right hoped to stem this tide of immorality through political action that would re-establish America's traditional standards of morality, standards that reflected the unique contribution of the Christian faith to American history.

Many of the most prominent leaders of the religious right were adherents of the **Charismatic movement.** (See the special feature on pp. 614-15.) By using television extensively to advance their views, the Charismatics managed to motivate many Christians to become active politically. The most influential of these Charismatic television evangelists was **Pat Robertson.** He had begun his career by founding the first Christian television station in the United States in 1961. From this start he built the Christian Broadcasting Network (CBN) and became host of a prominent Christian talk show, the "700 Club."

Not all of the leaders of the religious right were Charismatics. Catholics, Mormons, and numerous non-Charismatic Protestants joined this vaguely religious crusade for morality. One of the most controversial was Baptist pastor **Jerry Falwell** of Virginia, who, like Robertson, utilized television to promote his cause. Falwell founded a religious political action group called Moral Majority to help elect conservative candidates and further conservative political causes. Falwell drew heated criticism, however. Liberals attacked him for supposedly breaking down the separation of church and state by attempting to force his religious views on the general public and by using a religious organization to achieve political ends. (Many of these liberals were silent, however, when many civil rights leaders were using black churches to register voters and advance liberal causes.) Even other religious conservatives criticized Falwell. A number of fundamentalists charged that Falwell's political activities distracted Christians from their primary purpose of preaching the gospel. Others pointed out that he was using politics to bring together religious groups which differed strongly on important points of Scriptural teaching, linking Bible-believers with Mormons and Catholics, for example.

The religious right also benefited from the fact that more Americans were turning from theologically liberal churches to more doctrinally conservative ones. In a 1977 survey, seventy million Americans described themselves as "born-again" Christians. Although their varied definitions of "born again" did not always agree with the Scriptural doctrine of regeneration, these numbers meant that a large portion of the American population was at least sympathetic to conservative religious views.

A major fear of the religious right was that the government was undercutting the nation's traditional religious freedoms. The Supreme Court decisions against prayer and Bible reading in public schools were major examples. Another fear was government control of Christian schools. Since the 1960s, many Christians had placed their children in private Christian day schools or had even begun to educate them at home in order to protect them from the secular influence and declining educational standards of the public schools. Some state and federal authorities began to call for regulating or even closing Christian schools. Religious conservatives, realizing that growing governmental power could threaten all constitutional religious freedoms, began to fight back with their dollars and their ballots.

Baptist pastor Jerry Falwell, pictured here in a 1984 rally with Vice President George Bush, maintained a highly visible presence on the American political scene in the late 1970s.

The Charismatic Movement

One of the most influential religious forces in modern America is the Charismatic movement. Charismatics are distinguished by their belief in the revival of certain New Testament "gifts": the power to heal illnesses, speaking in "tongues" (ecstatic speech) as a sign of the baptism of the Holy Spirit, and the gift of prophecy (giving out special revelations from the Spirit). The name *charismatic* comes from the Greek word *charisma,* meaning "gift." Most Bible scholars have traditionally held that these particular gifts ended after the age of the apostles when the New Testament was completed.

The roots of Charismatic teaching lie in Pentecostalism, a religious movement arising in America around 1900. Pentecostals were the first modern American denomination to advocate healing and speaking in tongues. (A few minor sects, such as the Shakers, had earlier practiced tongues.) For the first half of the twentieth century, Pentecostalism remained a small force, limited to only Pentecostal denominations and scorned by older, established Protestant denominations.

Pentecostalism began to change in the 1950s. Several prominent Pentecostal preachers sought wider approval from the general public and the established denominations. Pentecostal evangelist Oral Roberts led this movement by beginning a television ministry, founding a college (Oral Roberts University), and joining the United Methodist Church in 1968. While Pentecostals were reaching out to non-Pentecostals, many non-Pentecostals were embracing Pentecostal teaching. In the 1960s ministers and laymen in the mainline denominations adopted Pentecostal practices–healing, tongues, and prophesying–without becoming Pentecostals themselves. These non-Pentecostals most often referred to themselves as Charismatics.

The Charismatic movement spread like wildfire among other denominations. Episcopal, Lutheran, Baptist, and even Roman Catholic Charismatics appeared on the scene. Some preachers founded large interdenominational Charismatic churches. Old-line Pentecostal denominations tended to join forces with the Charismatics, thus blending most advocates of these "gifts" into one great Charismatic movement. By the 1970s even the liberal dean of Harvard Divinity School was claiming to be a Charismatic. Public awareness of the Charismatic movement grew primarily through the extensive television ministries of Oral Roberts, Pat Robertson, and numerous others.

American Evangelist Oral Roberts (b. 1918), seated on a chair, prays for a man's healing while laying on his hands (early 1960s). Archive Photos

Election of 1980

Nomination of Reagan–Riding this surge of conservatism to the Republican nomination was Ronald Reagan. A polished speaker whose tone conveyed a sense of absolute sincerity, Reagan had been a leading and persuasive advocate of conservative causes since the 1950s. Reagan used his

Charismatics have received their share of criticism from other Christians. Most often critics simply reject the existence of the gifts of tongues, healing, and prophecy in the modern church. Some point out that the Charismatic movement un-Scripturally unites groups who have little in common spiritually save a belief in Charismatic gifts; the large number of Roman Catholic Charismatics is the primary example. Critics also cite un-Biblical tendencies among Charismatics: the emphasis on the work of the Holy Spirit over the saving work of Jesus Christ, the accepting of "special revelations" over the revealed Word of God, and the separation of the baptism of the Spirit from the time of conversion. Several Bible scholars have also accused Charismatics of violating the standards for speaking in tongues that Paul set down for the Corinthian church (I Cor. 14:26-32), such as limiting such speaking to no more than two or three persons in one service.

As part of the religious right, the Charismatics exerted enormous political as well as religious power beginning in the 1970s. The movement received several setbacks in the 1980s, however. Oral Roberts raised both alarm and ridicule by claiming that God would "take him home" (i.e., to heaven) unless Roberts's supporters raised $8 million for his ministry. Pat Robertson lost a well-publicized effort to capture the Republican presidential nomination in 1988. Two other prominent Charismatic television evangelists were enmeshed in sex scandals. These defeats left the Charismatic movement still powerful but uncertain of its popular appeal.

Ronald Reagan's confident leadership combined with Carter's foreign and domestic ills helped Reagan pull an upset victory in 1980.

governor of California by a huge margin and re-elected in 1970. Reagan had made two previous runs at the Republican presidential nomination, a brief attempt to halt Richard Nixon in 1968 and a nearly successful try at wresting the nomination from Gerald Ford in 1976. By 1980 Reagan was certainly the best-known and most popular Republican in the nation.

Reagan brushed aside his competition in the 1980 primaries and won the nomination easily. To unify the party, he chose one of his politically moderate opponents, George Bush, to run as his vice-presidential candidate. With Reagan at the head of the ticket and the nation in a conservative mood, Republicans believed that they could win back the presidency that they had lost four years earlier.

Carter's Problems–Jimmy Carter had more than Reagan to worry about. Despite his moderately liberal social policies, Carter found that his more conservative economic policies did not please the liberal wing of the Democratic party. Liberals rallied behind Massachusetts senator **Edward Kennedy,** the younger brother of John and Robert. Kennedy soon realized that he had almost no chance to beat Carter, but he stubbornly remained in the campaign to force the president to pursue more liberal policies. This divisive candi-

vocal skills honed as a radio broadcaster and actor to rouse conservatives by his defense of free enterprise, his call for shrinking the size of the federal government, and his steadfast opposition to Communist expansion. He rose to fame politically by giving a persuasive television address on behalf of Barry Goldwater in 1964. In 1966 he was elected

Presidential Election of 1980

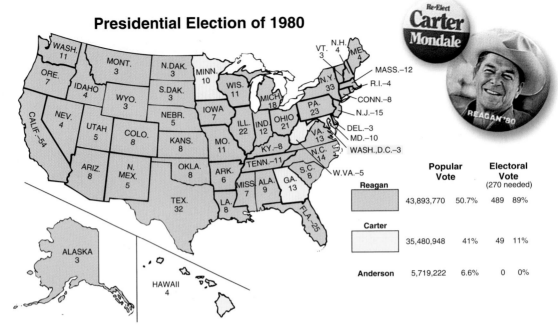

	Popular Vote		Electoral Vote (270 needed)	
Reagan	43,893,770	50.7%	489	89%
Carter	35,480,948	41%	49	11%
Anderson	5,719,222	6.6%	0	0%

dacy hampered Carter's attempts to unify the party behind him.

Even after Carter had defeated Kennedy, he faced another liberal opponent. Liberal Republican **John Anderson** of Illinois, proclaiming that he thought both Reagan and Carter too conservative, announced that he would run as an independent third-party candidate. Anderson had no chance to win, of course, but he was more likely to draw votes from the moderately liberal Carter than from the staunchly conservative Reagan.

Campaign–Conservative fervor alone was not enough to win a national election. The Republicans were banking on popular discontent with Carter and the Democrats to help them. The hostages in Iran were like a cancer eating away at the Carter candidacy, ever reminding voters of his foreign policy failures. Even more immediate was the state of the economy, mainly the dangerously high rate of inflation. Reagan shrewdly perceived the public sentiment. At the close of a televised debate with Carter only a week before the election, Reagan turned to the camera and asked the American people,

> Are you better off than you were four years ago? Is it easier for you to go and buy things in the stores than it was four years ago? . . . Is America as respected throughout the world as it was? . . . I would like to lead

that crusade to take government off the backs of the great people of this country and turn you loose again to do those things that I know you can do so well, because you did them and made this country great.

Up until the last days of the campaign, the polls predicted a close race. It was not. On election day, Reagan won 50.7 per cent of the popular vote to Carter's 41 per cent and John Anderson's 6.6 per cent. In the electoral college, Reagan carried forty-four states for a massive 489-49 landslide victory. In addition, the Republicans picked up twelve seats in the Senate and captured control of that body for the first time since Eisenhower's first term. The nation had decisively rejected not only Jimmy Carter but also his party. It was now up to Ronald Reagan and the Republicans to demonstrate their ability to do a better job.

Section Review

1. What was the goal of the Right-to-Life movement?
2. Name the most important Charismatic and non-Charismatic political leaders of the religious right.
3. Who was the major third-party candidate of the 1980 presidential election? Why did he run?
4. What foreign policy issue hurt Carter the most in the 1980 election? what domestic issue?

Chapter Review

Terms

Watergate affair
Spiro Agnew
Gerald Ford
Nixon pardon
oil embargo
energy crisis
environmental movement
stagflation
trade deficit
women's rights movement
feminists
women's liberation movement
Roe v. Wade
Equal Rights Amendment
Ronald Reagan
Jimmy Carter
human rights
Panama Canal Treaty
Camp David Accords
SALT II Treaty
Mohammed Reza Pahlavi (Shah of Iran)
Ayatollah Ruhollah Khomeini
Iranian hostage crisis
New Right
Proposition 13
religious right
Charismatic movement
Pat Robertson
Jerry Falwell
Edward Kennedy
John Anderson

Content Questions

1. Under the provisions of what amendment did Gerald Ford become vice president? Whom did he replace?
2. Why did attempts to make automobiles produce less pollution actually heighten the energy crisis?
3. What was the most controversial piece of pro-feminist legislation? What happened to this legislation?
4. Why did conservatives oppose the SALT II Treaty?
5. Who challenged President Carter for the 1980 Democratic nomination?
6. Who won the presidential election of 1976? of 1980?

Application Questions

1. Some political observers in the late 1970s claimed that the presidency had grown too large for one man to handle. Why would they think so? Do you agree or disagree with their claim? Why?
2. How can some of the extreme "rights movements," such as the homosexuals' gay rights movement, undermine genuine civil liberties?
3. Is political activity by Christians, such as that of the religious right, legitimate in light of the separation of church and state? Why or why not?

CHAPTER 26

Resurgence (1981-1992)

"It's morning again in America."

Ronald Reagan on the campaign trail in 1984

President Ronald Reagan and Soviet Premier Mikhail Gorbachev stand in front of St. Basil's Cathedral on Red Square during one of Reagan's visits to the Soviet Union.

The bullet had stopped an inch from his heart. For the man and the times one critical, providential *inch*. The victim, looking up from the gurney into the worry-lined faces of the crowding physicians, smiled weakly and said, "Please tell me you're Republicans." Their faces brightened. "Mr. President, today we're all Republicans," they answered with a chuckle.

The March 1981 wounding of **Ronald Reagan** in a spray of gunfire from a crazed assailant brought an outpouring of national concern and prayer for the life of the president. Reagan's coolness, pluck, and recovery during his administration's first spring symbolized much of the national spirit that reawakened during the succeeding decade.

The Reagan Revolution

The Reagan years marked a clear shift in the nation's leadership, policies, and attitudes. After a quartet of failed presidencies, Ronald Reagan projected an image of confident leadership, restoring public faith in the White House. Many Americans, tired of the cardigan sweater days of Jimmy Carter, welcomed the new president's strong presence and inspiring rhetoric.

Yet Reagan brought more than polished images to the White House; he also brought new policy directions. As Reagan himself observed near the end of his tenure, "A revolution of ideas became a revolution of governance on January 20, 1981." The **"Reagan Revolution"** had two simple points: America must be strong, and Americans must be free. Reagan believed that with Communist threats from Central America to Central Asia, the United States had no choice but to maintain a vigilant grip on the reins of Free World leadership. In addition, America's economic strength must be unleashed by breaking the shackles of big government and heavy taxes that hindered growth and opportunity. Also according to his ideal, Reagan wanted to strengthen and restore America's moral fiber by curbing government intrusion into the home, the church, and the school.

The Reagan Magic

After a decade of Vietnam, Watergate, Iran, and national "malaise," Ronald Reagan revived hope, restored pride, and put new polish on patriotism. During his years in office Reagan was a kind of commander in chief of the American spirit, marshalling national emotion with a skill that few leaders have been able to muster. When Reagan came to Washington, many critics dismissed him as a has-been B-grade actor clearly out of his element in the rough-and-tumble national scene. But the critics underestimated both Reagan and the American people. It was said that Reagan was "simply saturated in the American identity." His talents were not those of an administrator nor of an economist; they were that unquantifiable quality called leadership. In the following excerpt, written for Independence Day 1986, Lance Morrow, a senior writer for Time, *describes something of the magic of Reagan's leadership, perhaps the most important and most successful presidency of the postwar era.*

Ronald Reagan has found the American sweet spot. The white ball sails into the sparkling air in a high parabola and vanishes over the fence, again. The 75-year-old man is hitting home runs. Winning a lopsided vote on a tax-reform plan that others had airily dismissed. Turning Congress around on the Contras. Preparing to stand with a revitalized Miss Liberty on the Fourth of July. He grins his boyish grin and bobs his head in the way he has and trots around the bases. . . .

The business of magic is sleight of hand: now you see it, now you don't. Ronald Reagan is a sort of masterpiece of American magic–apparently one of the simplest, most uncomplicated creatures alive, and yet a character of rich meanings, of complexities that connect him with the myths and powers of his country in an unprecedented way.

Sleight of hand: during a meeting of the Economic Policy Council last year, the Secretary of State and the Secretary of Agriculture started lobbing grenades at each other over a proposal to sell grain to the Soviet Union. Others entered the argument. Voices rose, arms waved. Through it all, Ronald Reagan sat silently, apparently concentrating on picking the black licorice jelly beans from the crystal jar on the table in front of him. Occasionally, he would look up. Once, as he did so, he caught the eye of an aide sitting opposite him at the back of the room. The President winked. The tumult gradually subsided. When it was peaceful again, Reagan looked up, turned to Treasury Secretary James Baker, and said, "What's the next item, Jim?"

It had been a very private wink, but it seemed to its one witness to go beyond the walls of the White House, out over the Rose Garden and well outside the Beltway that surrounds the nation's capital. It was as if Ronald Reagan had winked at America, sharing the people's amused disdain for the sort of thing that goes on in Big Government.

These simple yet ambitious goals of strength and freedom answered a need that many Americans keenly felt in the wake of humiliations abroad and hardships at home. That these goals were never quite achieved and that Reagan's rhetoric often fell short of reality did not diminish the revolution of spirit that America experienced at the dawn of its third century.

Reaganomics

Tackling the nation's economic woes was at the top of the Reagan agenda. Frustration over the economic recession, with its double-digit inflation and high unemployment, had helped elect the new president, and Reagan determined to address the problem quickly. In his inaugural speech he declared an end to a "tax system which penalizes successful achievement and keeps us from maintaining full productivity." The days of big government spending sprees were also numbered, according to Reagan, because deficits were

> mortgaging our future and our children's future for the temporary convenience of the present. To continue this long trend is to guarantee tremendous social, cultural, political, and economic upheavals. . . . We must act today in order to preserve tomorrow. And let there be no misunderstanding—we are going to begin to act beginning today.

Reagan's prescription for America's inflation ills was **supply-side economics** (or **Reaganomics,** as it was popularly called). The supply-side approach seeks to lower inflated prices by enhancing productivity and increasing the supply of goods. Higher productivity and a larger supply of goods satisfy the demand for goods, which helps lower prices and energizes the economy by providing fuller employment. The supply-side way of increasing productivity fit nicely into Reagan's conservative, limited-government agenda: cut taxes so that citizens will have incentive to earn, save, and invest; encourage economic expansion by reducing government regulations on business and by providing corporate tax breaks.

The Tax Axe—The centerpiece of Reagan's economic policies was tax cuts. With his skills of persuasion, Reagan took his cause not only to Congress but also to the taxpayers. Congress, fearful of a popular backlash, mustered majorities in both houses to pass the **Economic Recovery Tax Act of 1981.** The new law cut income taxes by twenty-five per cent over a two-and-a-half-year period. The act reduced maximum tax rates for upper incomes from seventy to fifty per cent and also lowered business taxes.

Budget Battles—Another important part of Reagan's economic plans was budget cuts. In 1981 Congress approved budget cuts of $35 billion, reducing funding for some highway programs as well as educational, welfare, and arts assistance. Critics who feared that the conservative Reagan would have a "take no prisoners" approach to the huge federal budget had little to fear, however. Fully 90¢ of every federal budget dollar went for programs that Congress considered untouchable, since cutting them would be politically damaging. It soon became clear that much of the budget was simply a collection of special interest entitlements. As a result there were no big budget bites, only some gnawing on the edges.

Despite promises of a "safety net" for the needy, the budget cuts were neither without effect on the poor nor without drawbacks for the economy as a whole. Budget restraints, for example, forced cutbacks in Aid to Families with Dependent Children (AFDC), stopping payment to those who had worked for only a four-month period. With over a quarter of all children in America living in single-parent homes, the effect was extensive. AFDC payments ended for four hundred thousand homes. Many welfare mothers, without jobs programs to bridge the gap from the welfare rolls to the work force, found it necessary—lacking a ladder of opportunity—to simply "stay in the safety net" and remain on welfare. The growing problems and inadequacies of the welfare system, however, often had more to do with the mounting social problems of drug addiction and illegitimacy than with the budget.

One budget area that did receive a boost by the Reagan administration was defense spending. The administration added $12 billion to defense programs in 1982, and the buildup continued through the end of the decade. Critics of the defense buildup, altering a famous remark of humorist Will Rogers, charged that President Reagan had never met a weapons system he did not like. In the post-Vietnam era of the 1970s, however, America's military had lost ground in both morale and materiel. Given Communist expansion in Asia, Africa, and Central America and the need to protect vital oil interests in the Middle East, Reagan continued throughout his term to push for a superior military force and fleet.

Deficit Debacle–Tax cuts, defense hikes, and particularly the unwillingness of Congress and the White House to make serious budget cuts added up to a huge deficit problem. This gap between what the government spent and what it took in contributed to a growing national debt. At the end of the 1970s the debt amounted to a huge bill of $834 billion. By 1990, though, the figure had soared to the stratospheric sum of $2.3 trillion. By then interest payments alone on the debt reached over $150 billion, effectively wiping out any ground gained by budget cuts. The huge debt placed a continuing threat to America's present and future economic strength.

By late 1985, with public outcries over dozen-digit deficits, Congress made an effort at self-discipline with the **Gramm-Rudman Act.** The law, largely the work of Senator Phil Gramm of Texas, imposed automatic deficit reduction through across-the-board spending cuts if Congress would not curb the budget on its own. In addition it mandated a balanced budget by 1991. As sweeping as the measure appeared, Congress exempted many programs from being subject to Gramm-Rudman. The president and Congress were not the only ones lacking the will to deal with the debt, however. Many Americans representing many interests supported the *idea* of budget cuts so long as someone *else's* budget was being cut. The idea of government services on an easy credit plan, though, soon sank in a sea of red ink.

Recession and Recovery–During the 1980 campaign, while the country was experiencing a deep recession, President Carter quibbled with candidate Reagan over the challenger's assertion that

Strom Thurmond: "Rebel" Politician

Born in the South Carolina upcountry that had produced John C. Calhoun, James Strom Thurmond followed a path that likewise led to prominence in the United States Senate. Although he has worn a number of party labels throughout his career, Thurmond was at heart a populist and an individualist ready to fight the political establishment. This characteristic of Thurmond's often landed him at the forefront of political trends mirroring momentous changes in American politics. A 1923 graduate of Clemson University, Thurmond was soon bitten by the political bug. In 1928, at the age of twenty-five, he was elected county superintendent of education. After being taught law by his father, he was admitted to the state bar in 1930. Election to the state senate followed and then service as a circuit judge, interrupted by a stint with the army in World War II .

Returning from Europe as a decorated war hero, Thurmond soon found himself in a

Senator Strom Thurmond (far left) takes questions from reporters on the floor of the 1968 national Republican convention.

fierce political fight in South Carolina. In a campaign that pitted him against the party bosses, Thurmond won election to the governorship in 1946. Most politicians run for the presidency as the culmination of their careers, but Thurmond mounted a White House campaign in 1948, early in his career. Southern delegates, including Thurmond, walked out of the 1948 Democratic National Convention because of opposition to its civil rights position. Conservative southern Democrats met in Birmingham, organized the States' Rights Democratic Party, and nominated Thurmond as president and Gov. Fielding Wright of Mississippi as vice president. The "Dixiecrats," as they were called, hoped to throw the election to the House, where a southern bloc could reach a compromise with liberal Democrats. The South Carolina governor carried four states and received the largest third-party vote for president since Theodore Roosevelt and the Progressive party in 1912.

Thurmond's career entered a new phase in 1954 with his election to the United States Senate after a write-in campaign. The state Democratic executive committee, after the death of the incumbent, selected a replacement with the general election about two months away. Attacking "back-room" nominations by party bosses, Thurmond again bolted the party establishment by organizing a grass-roots write-in campaign for the Senate seat, and with strong newspaper support he won handily. He became the first candidate for Congress or state-wide office ever to win with a write-in vote. While serving in the Senate, he achieved another distinction: delivering the longest speech in the United States Senate history. He defended jury trials in a filibuster lasting twenty-four hours and eighteen minutes.

Thurmond had defied Democratic party regulars by running against Truman in 1948, endorsing Republican nominee Eisenhower in 1952, and beating their Senate choice in 1954. Ten years later he rebelled again by endorsing conservative Republican presidential candidate Barry Goldwater. Moreover, he switched to the Republican party. Thurmond's action symbolized the end of the solidly Democratic South and the emergence of a two-party system in the region. The Democratic party had become too liberal for Thurmond and other Southerners. His most important service for his newly adopted party came in 1968, when he campaigned hard for Richard Nixon in a "southern strategy" that would keep third-party candidate George Wallace from sweeping the South. In Nixon's close win that followed, Thurmond's support proved crucial and perhaps even decisive.

After years of fighting the government's civil rights agenda, Thurmond in the 1970s softened his position on the issue. Blacks registered in increasing numbers after the Voting Rights Act of 1965, and Thurmond's willingness to change with the time helped him survive politically. He courted blacks by appointing them to his staff, voting for congressional representation for the District of Columbia, and supporting the appointment of a black federal judge in South Carolina. Thurmond perhaps reached the pinnacle of his career when Republicans captured the Senate with the election of Ronald Reagan. From 1980 to 1986 South Carolina's "rebel" served as president pro tempore of the United States Senate and chairman of its Judiciary Committee. Strom Thurmond's re-election to an eighth term in 1996 at the age of ninety-three made him the oldest and longest-serving senator of all time.

the country was in an actual depression. Reagan responded, "I'm talking in human terms and he is hiding behind a dictionary. If he wants a definition, I'll give him one. A recession is when your neighbor loses his job. A depression is when you lose yours. A recovery is when Jimmy Carter loses his."

Candidate Reagan's punch line drew a good round of guffaws in 1980, but by 1982 President Reagan found that a recession was no laughing matter. That year the economy slumped along with the president's approval rating, and unemployment grew to over ten per cent. The president's response was mixed. Abandoning his anti-tax policies, Reagan pushed through a huge tax-increase package aimed mainly at business, hoping to calm jitters over the deficit. At the same time, Reagan urged Americans to "stay the course" while the Reaganomic tax cuts and probusiness policies turned the employment problem around.

By 1983 America's economy experienced an upturn. The prosperity to follow (for which Reagan could take only partial credit, but credit nonetheless) began, as one economist observed, "the longest and strongest noninflationary expansion in our history." The result was a boom time of lower unemployment, lower interest rates, and lower oil prices. Nineteen million new jobs were created during the 1980s, and unemployment dropped to below five per cent. With some regional unemployment figures down to two per cent, some areas of the country actually had a *labor* shortage rather than a job shortage. The housing market, an important indication of American economic strength, mushroomed. Twenty per cent of all homes standing in 1990 were built during the 1980s. In addition, per capita income during Reagan's term grew by an unprecedented seventeen per cent. Reminiscent of the prosperity of an earlier decade, the Reagan years could well be called the "Roaring 80s."

Section Review

1. In addition to cutting taxes for all citizens, what two actions did supply-side economics propose for business in order to promote economic expansion?
2. What was the "centerpiece" of Reagan's economic policies?
3. Which of the two parts of Reagan's program for economic recovery (tax cuts or budget cuts) was he less successful in carrying out?
4. What three factors helped to dramatically increase the budget deficit in the 1980s?

Reagan Doctrine

America faced challenges abroad as well as at home. After years of post-Vietnam paralysis in American foreign policy, Soviet troops in Afghanistan and the exporting of Communist revolutions around the world renewed the debate over containment. From the beginning, President Reagan demonstrated his determination to confront the aggression. During his first month in office Reagan characterized the Communist leadership as those who "reserved unto themselves the right to commit any crime, to lie, to cheat," and who were still bent on "world domination." Critics groaned that Reagan's harsh words were putting the cold war into a deep freeze. However, the ongoing genocide in Afghanistan; the Soviets' shooting down of a Korean airliner in September 1983, killing all 269 passengers; and the 1985 murder of an American army major, Arthur Nicholson, in Communist East Germany clearly gave substance to Reagan's characterization of the Soviet Union as an "evil empire."

One of the key aspects of Reagan's foreign policy, in keeping with America's tough stance toward the Soviets, was known as the **Reagan Doctrine.** This policy theme pledged America's support to insurgent groups battling Communist governments in the Third World. As a result, military and economic aid flowed to anti-Communist fighters on three continents, putting pressure on both regional Communists and their backers in Moscow. The Reagan Doctrine also sparked battles on the home front as Congress struggled with the White House over the new directions in foreign policymaking.

Central America—Early in 1981 fighting between Communist rebels and the democratic government of El Salvador flared in the tiny Central American republic. Reagan responded to the aggression of the Soviet and Cuban-backed guerrillas by supplying arms, military advisors, and economic aid to the beleaguered Salvadoran government under President José Napoleon Duarte.

American assistance in propping up democracy in El Salvador led to further involvement in Central America when it was revealed that the Salvadoran insurgents were being supplied with arms by the Communist Sandinista government of neighboring

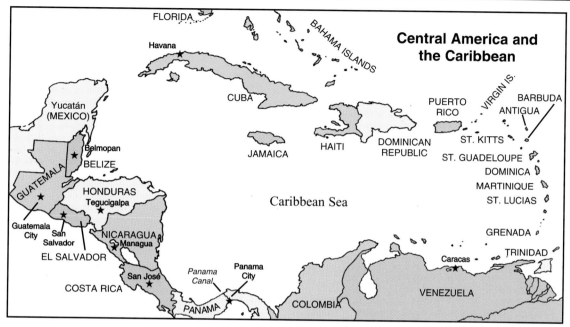

Central America and the Caribbean

Nicaragua. Under the direction of the Central Intelligence Agency, groups of anti-Sandinista guerillas known as **Contras** were organized. Many of these fighters had been ousted from power when the Communists seized control of the government in 1979. Other Contras came from groups actively repressed by the Sandinistas such as the fiercely independent Miskito Indians of northeastern Nicaragua.

Reagan's support for anti-Communist forces in Nicaragua ignited fierce debates in Congress. Critics charged that reviving "big-stick" policies would renew anti-Americanism throughout the region. They urged compromise with the Sandinistas and increased economic aid to the region. Reagan, however, believed that the Sandinistas posed a threat not only to the democratic elements within Nicaragua but also to the security of all of Central America. With the Soviets supporting Nicaragua's Communist government, particularly through its satellite state of Cuba, support of the Contras also represented a vital test of American commitment to the Monroe Doctrine. Reagan, however, would soon have an opportunity to deal the Cuban dictator, Castro, a telling blow.

Grenada, a tiny island in the Caribbean, was being transformed into a fueling station for Cuban troops sailing for Africa and Soviet advisors heading for Nicaragua. In October 1983 the Communist government of Grenada under Maurice Bishop was overthrown by a more radically Communist faction, led by General Hudson Austin. Bishop was murdered, and calls to the United States for help came quickly from neighboring islands. Armed with this appeal, concerned over the safety of a number of American medical students living on Grenada, and fearful of a second Cuba in the Caribbean, President Reagan ordered nearly 2,000 U.S. Marines and airborne troops to liberate the island. Although a relatively small military operation, Grenada had huge symbolic importance. It sent a clear signal of American resolve to Communist leaders and ended much of the post-Vietnam fears and frettings over the use of American military force.

Angola–In Angola 35,000 Cuban troops, backed by Soviet advisors and sophisticated weaponry, propped up the Communist regime against anti-Communist forces led by Jonas Savimbi. At the urging of Congressman Jack Kemp, President Reagan began funneling supplies to Savimbi in 1986. The aid to Savimbi was critical and proved decisive. By 1988 the Cubans and Soviets began withdrawing their tentacles of control from central Africa.

Afghanistan–The front line of the Reagan Doctrine was in Soviet-occupied Afghanistan. Since the 1979 invasion the Red Army had waged a brutal war not only against the guerrilla *Mujahideen* (moo JAH hih DEEN) but also against Afghan civilians of all ages. Besides mass bombings, executions, and the use of a chemical weapon known as Yellow Rain, the ruthless Red Army left toy trucks strewn in villages. The toys, however, were actually booby traps left not for the purpose of killing children–only of blowing their hands off so that they might be a continuing burden on a society already writhing beneath the Soviet boot.

Reagan supplied the *Mujahideen* insurgents with military advisors and state-of-the-art weapons such as surface-to-air Stinger missiles. American support combined with determined rebel resistance dealt a stunning blow to Moscow's troops. After ten years the Soviet army withdrew in the spring of 1989, leaving Afghanistan bloodied and battered. Yet the humiliating Soviet defeat was the first in a generation, and it marked a great triumph for the Reagan Doctrine.

Terrorism–In contrast to Reagan's successes in Afghanistan, the problem of terrorism dogged his administration and produced many setbacks, mainly in Lebanon. The land of Lebanon, renowned since Bible times for its beauty, became a battlefield in the 1970s, subdivided in a complex war among Druse, Sunni Muslims, Shiite Muslims, Arab Christians, Syrians, and Yasser Arafat's Palestine Liberation Organization (PLO). With the threat of PLO terrorists on its northern border, Israel sent troops into Lebanon to destroy them in June 1982. The Israelis sent the PLO reeling back into Beirut, where Arafat's forces hunkered down under heavy shelling. Israel's presence, though, complicated an already complex situation.

Eventually Reagan ordered American troops into Lebanon to join a multinational "peace-keeping" force to oversee the withdrawal of the PLO from Lebanon. There was, however, little

peace to keep as fighting continued to boil over into the rubbled streets of Beirut. In addition, U.S. soldiers were viewed by the Arab factions not as peace-keepers but as allies of Israel and thus a target. After repeated attacks on American positions, the U.S. Navy began shelling terrorist bases. On October 23, 1983, a terrorist driving a bomb-laden truck crashed through barricades and into the U.S. Marines barracks at Beirut airport, killing 241 Americans. The ill-defined U.S. peace-keeping mission soon ended with troops returning to off-shore warships and leaving battered Beirut to its own bloody fate.

Unfortunately not all Americans escaped the terror of Lebanon. A number of U.S. citizens, some working in Beirut as teachers and journalists, were taken hostage during the 1980s. Efforts by the Reagan administration to gain the release of the hostages from their shadowy captors were largely futile as the American public watched in helpless anger.

Reagan had somewhat more success against terrorism outside the muddled Middle East. In 1985 Arab terrorists hijacked the Italian cruise ship *Achille Lauro* and brutally murdered a wheelchair-bound American, Leon Klinghoffer. The terrorists returned to safety in Egypt in high spirits over their cowardly crimes, but when they flew to Tunis the happy hijackers were hijacked. In a skillful operation engineered by Lt. Col. Oliver North, the Egyptian airliner was forced by U.S. fighter planes to land at the American air base in Sicily. The jailed terrorists soon had a visitor; Klinghoffer's widow stopped by to identify her husband's murderers and to spit in their faces. Elsewhere in the Mediterranean, the 1986 terrorist acts against Americans ordered by Libya's ruler Muammar Qaddafi were answered with a successful surprise air strike on the shores of Tripoli.

Four More Years

Forty-Nine-State Landslide–In 1984 Democrats renewed some of their old themes against Ronald Reagan: the president's trigger-happy foreign policy, as the Democrats characterized it, was an embarrassment in the international community, and his social policies isolated the poor, ignored the working classes, and insulted women. Despite the fact that Reagan had appointed the first woman Supreme Court justice, Sandra Day O'Connor, in 1981 and had named a number of women to important government posts, feminists in the Democratic party charged that the president had ignored the female half of the electorate, and thus a gender gap in his support had developed.

Walter Mondale, former vice president under Jimmy Carter, outlasted all others in the Democratic field to win the nomination. Mondale quickly came under criticism that he was controlled by liberal special-interest groups such as labor unions and feminists. The charges seemed confirmed when Mondale chose New York Congresswoman **Geraldine Ferraro** as his running mate. Although Ferraro was the first female vice-presidential candidate for a major party, her narrow, liberal record provided no counterbalance to Mondale's position. On election day Reagan won one of the greatest state landslides in history, losing only Mondale's home state of Minnesota (by two-tenths of one per cent of the vote) and

Walter Mondale

the District of Columbia. Ironically the only gender gap in 1984 was against Mondale, with women voting 57 to 42 per cent in favor of the president.

Reagan's second term was plagued with few of the domestic economic issues that had confronted his administration's first years. Despite mounting deficits, the continuing slide in oil prices helped keep the economy strong. Much of the focus of Reagan's second term was on foreign policy: improving relations with the Soviet Union and, after 1986, dealing with the political fallout over the Iran-Contra affair.

Cold War Thaw–The Soviet Union went through a procession of dictators during the Reagan years, but it was more like a *funeral* procession as death took its toll on the old-guard rulers. Leonid Brezhnev died in 1982; his successor Yuri Andropov died in 1984; and his successor Konstantin Chernenko died in 1985. **Mikhail Gorbachev** (mik-HEL GOR-bah-chof) took the Kremlin reins in 1985, presenting a new, polished style in contrast with his stodgy predecessors.

When the new Soviet chief came to power, the Russian economy was on the verge of collapse and the Red Army was sunk in the costly quagmire of Afghanistan. In confronting these problems, throughout the late 1980s Gorbachev called for *perestroika* (PEHR uh STROY kah), or "restructuring" of the stagnant Communist economy, shifting to more free-market policies and private ownership. In order to make the transition to the Western economic mainstream, Gorbachev urged *glasnost* (GLASS nost), or "openness," in Soviet society. The Soviet leader believed that loosening some of the shackles of Communist control, allowing greater self-expression, would help motivate the masses to move from a passive to a more active economic role.

Gorbachev spoke of new ideas, however, while mostly clinging to the old ones. The practice of *perestroika* turned out to be a series of half-measures that raised Soviet expectations rather than the standard of living. Yet in contrast to the slow progress of *perestroika, glasnost* was perhaps *too* successful from Gorbachev's point of view. The taste of freedom only awakened a thirst for more, as

Vice President Bush, President Reagan, and Premier Gorbachev meet in New York City. Reagan's presidency saw a thaw in the cold war between the U.S. and the USSR.

nationalism replaced Marxism. The diverse ethnic groups of the Soviet Empire, bound together by a Marxist philosophy that in both theory and practice was now an official failure, called for greater freedom from Kremlin control. Gorbachev and the Red Army responded to these stirrings of independence and nationalism with tear gas and bullets. *Glasnost* was even more successful on the fringes of the Iron Curtain as, one by one, Communist governments were ousted in Central Europe in 1989, and a Germany divided since World War II was united in 1990.

During his second term, Ronald Reagan made a dramatic shift in Soviet relations. The president improved ties on the diplomatic front, meeting with Gorbachev on five occasions during Reagan's last three years in office. The summit meetings between the two leaders were aimed primarily at reaching a **Strategic Arms Reduction Talks (START)** agreement actually cutting the size of long-range nuclear arsenals in half, rather than simply slowing their growth as earlier agreements had aimed for. Despite the fact that the Soviets had consistently cheated on previous arms agreements, Reagan placed a newfound faith in the power of treaties to correct Soviet behavior. At the Washington Summit in 1987, Reagan and Gorbachev signed the **Intermediate Nuclear Forces (INF) Treaty,** which eliminated most medium-range missiles from Europe. Events in Eastern Europe, though, soon lessened the importance of the INF Treaty. Nonetheless, with leaders

eager to show progress, the superpowers' agreement was heralded as a symbol of friendlier relations.

While Reagan worked the summit circuit, he also kept pressure on the Soviets in two other areas: supplying weapons to anti-Communist forces in Asia and Africa, and developing the **Strategic Defense Initiative (SDI).** First announced by Reagan in 1983, SDI–or "Star Wars," as it came to be known–was a proposed space-based defense shield of satellites, missiles, and lasers which would safeguard the country from nuclear attack. Although SDI was many years, many billions of dollars, and not a few technological hurdles away from reality, the program seriously affected the nuclear arms equation. Gorbachev knew that SDI would force the Soviet Union to develop its own defense shield–a long and costly endeavor. With the Soviet economy on the verge of collapse, SDI development strengthened Reagan's bargaining position, and by the early 1990s more down-to-earth problems such as empty store shelves would further weaken Gorbachev's position.

Iran-Contra–On election day 1986 President Reagan received two strikes against his second-term successes. First, Reagan lost his Republican majority in the Senate. The Republican Senate had been a key factor in getting Reagan's programs through Congress during his first term. With Democrats in firm control of both houses of Congress, they could now take more control from the popular

When the Walls Came Tumbling Down

No Joshua gave a signal for the walls of communism that imprisoned Eastern Europe to come tumbling down, but they did fall in a few remarkable months in 1989. Forty years of Soviet domination came to an end as one by one the Iron Curtain countries cast off communism and threw open their borders to Western influence. Sadly, in China after a brief springtime of freedom, authorities ruthlessly crushed democratic forces in the bloody Tiananmen Square massacre. In Europe, however, the amazing developments that year not only captured the attention of sympathetic Americans but also presented the United States with a whole new slate of foreign policy questions to be answered in the decade to come. The following simplified chronicle recounts some of the more startling events of those memorable days.

April 18, 1989 Poland legalizes the Solidarity union and opens the way for the first free elections in forty years.

May 2, 1989 Hungarians begin to tear down the fences along their Austrian border.

June 4, 1989 Solidarity candidates win stunning victories over Communists in Poland's parliamentary elections.

August 25, 1989 Poland's new non-Communist government takes power.

September 10, 1989 Hungary opens its western borders. Many East Germans and Rumanians begin to use Hungary as an escape route to the West.

October 11, 1989 Hungary's Communist party abandons communism and changes its name in order to compete better in free elections.

October 18, 1989 East German Communist leader Erich Honecker resigns under pressure, later to be placed under house arrest and charged with criminal acts.

October 23, 1989 Hungary declares itself an independent republic.

October 25, 1989 Soviet leader Mikhail Gorbachev tells the West that his nation will no longer use force to keep the governments of Eastern Europe under Communist control, thereby opening the way for greater change in the region.

November 9, 1989 East Germany opens its borders. The Berlin Wall is no longer a barrier for East Germans as the gates swing open. The Wall, the symbol of cold war division, will begin to come down in three more days, and East Germany and West Germany will be on the road to reunification.

November 24, 1989 Czechoslovakia's Communist politburo resigns, leaving the nation to hold free elections. Bulgaria's Communist leader has been ousted, and thousands of demonstrators in Sofia chant for democracy and free elections.

December 22, 1989 A popular uprising leads to the capture, trial, and execution of Rumania's oppressive Communist dictator, Nicolae Ceausescu. The once-solid walls of Communist control have fallen in the last of the Soviet bloc nations of Eastern Europe.

East and West Germans alike celebrate atop the Berlin Wall before the Brandenburg Gate.

president over domestic and foreign policymaking. The Democrats were shortly given the opportunity to do just that, for the second strike came from an underground newspaper in faraway Beirut which reported that the administration had traded arms to Iran in exchange for the release of American hostages in Lebanon.

As the stunning story unfolded, it was revealed that members of the White House National Security Council (NSC)–principally the NSC chief John Poindexter, his aide U.S. Marine Lt. Col. Oliver North, and Central Intelligence Agency director William Casey–had set up secret arms sales to Iran. At the time Iran was locked in a costly war with neighboring Iraq and in need of missiles and military spare parts. Because of strategic interests in Iran, the covert operation was aimed at cultivating a moderate successor to the aging Ayatollah Khomeini. In addition, it was hoped that the arms deal would encourage Iran to help gain the release of American hostages in Lebanon held by terrorists loyal to Khomeini.

Investigations as to what happened to the money from the arms sales thickened the plot even more. The money, funneled through Swiss banks, was used to supply the Nicaraguan Contras battling the Communist Sandinistas, giving the whole matter the name **Iran-Contra affair.** The support came at a time when Congress had cut off military aid to the Contras, under the provisions of a law known as the Boland Amendment. The Reagan White House was already embarrassed over the disclosures of the Iranian arms sales, essentially an attempt to pay ransom to kidnappers, contrary to long-stated policy. Now the administration faced a Democratic-controlled Congress eager to pin criminal charges on the president's men for supplying funds to the Contras. Reagan distanced himself from his subordinates, but the whole matter raised questions about Reagan's management of the White House.

Throughout 1987 investigations and congressional hearings dragged out details of the Iran-Contra affair. The White House insisted that the Boland Amendment did not apply to the president's National Security Council. Congressional investigators disagreed. Eventually North and Poindexter were brought to trial and convicted on some lesser criminal charges. When the dust of dispute had settled, however, North's indictments were overturned on appeal in 1990. The court ruling signaled that the Iran-Contra affair was essentially another chapter in the long-running political dispute between the president and Congress over control of foreign policy, rather than a criminal conspiracy.

One More for the Gipper–Despite the shadow of Iran-Contra over Reagan's last two years in office, the president remained strong, popular, and the only chief executive in a generation to complete two terms. With a constitutional cap on two terms, Democrats and Republicans alike were jockeying for a chance at Reagan's job as the election year 1988 approached.

A number of Republicans claimed the right to Reagan's mantle, from **Jack Kemp,** one of the architects of Reaganomics, to newcomer Pat Robertson of the religious right. The nominee to emerge, however, was Reagan's vice president, **George Bush.** Having been in the shadow of a strong president for nearly eight years, however, Bush struggled to establish his own identity beyond his Republican ranks. Also surviving a crowded field of contenders, Governor **Michael Dukakis** of Massachusetts emerged to win the Democratic nomination.

Bush and Quayle celebrate their nomination at the 1988 Republican National Convention.

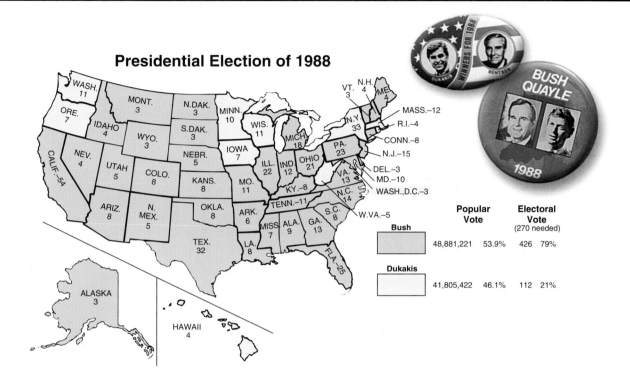

Presidential Election of 1988

	Popular Vote		Electoral Vote (270 needed)	
Bush	48,881,221	53.9%	426	79%
Dukakis	41,805,422	46.1%	112	21%

The Democrats held a euphoric convention in Atlanta buoyed by polls that showed Dukakis with a substantial lead over candidate Bush.

Republicans gathered in New Orleans for their national convention, where they gave a last hail to their chief. President Reagan, in an emotional farewell to his party faithful, urged them again to "go out there and win one for the Gipper." "The Gipper" recalled a familiar line from Reagan's old movie days in which he played George Gipp of Notre Dame, a dying football hero whose name became a rallying cry when his team was down–and in the opinion polls the Republican team was down. After a shaky start, Bush rallied support largely under the mantle of the Gipper's popularity and positions: American strength at home and abroad and no new taxes. The result for Bush and his running mate **Dan Quayle** was a decisive win on election day. George Bush's victory was in many ways a final vote of approval for Ronald Reagan. His hand-picked understudy won forty states, becoming the first vice president since Martin Van Buren in 1836 to be elected from the second spot to the presidency.

Section Review

1. What Caribbean nation was liberated by American forces in 1983, symbolizing America's willingness to use military force in the post-Vietnam era?

2. What Asian country's resistance to a ten-year Soviet occupation marked a great triumph for the Reagan Doctrine?

3. Terrorism in what Middle Eastern nation gave the Reagan administration its greatest setbacks in foreign policy?

4. Who was the first female Supreme Court justice?

5. What was the proper name for the "Star Wars" project?

The Bush Presidency

Unfortunately for George Bush, he followed in the footsteps of Van Buren in other ways as well. After eight years under a popular boss, Bush inherited problems of economic decline and foreign challenge that demanded immediate attention. He proved astonishingly successful in his greatest foreign policy challenge, but his domestic difficulties doomed his presidency.

Problems at Home

One of the signs of economic trouble was the failure of a number of the nation's savings and loan banks. Unsound investments and a drop in oil prices drove several of the "S&Ls" into bankruptcy. Because government guarantees underwrote the deposits in the banks, some $300 billion of government money ($3,000 per adult taxpayer) was required to cover the debts of the defaulting banks. Voters and federal prosecutors wanted to know why so many troubled S&Ls were allowed to stay afloat for so long. Some suspected that political favors, more than financial soundness, kept the S&Ls open. Investigators in several states delved into the murky, even shady transactions behind the S&Ls. Among those investigated in the scandals was the then little-known governor of Arkansas, Bill Clinton.

President Bush lost some public support by first opposing and then finally signing the **Americans with Disabilities Act.** This legislation prohibited job discrimination based on disabilities. It also required local governments and businesses to improve and alter their accommodations (e.g., provide special parking places for the disabled, install ramps for wheelchairs) to benefit the disabled. When he opposed the legislation as an intrusion by the federal government on local governments and private citizens, Bush was labeled as uncompassionate by the bill's supporters. When he finally did give in and sign the act, Bush angered those who opposed the new costs and the flood of lawsuits that resulted from the act's adoption.

Probably the most damaging mistake George Bush made was breaking a promise. During the 1988 presidential election campaign, he had undercut the Democrats by declaring, "Read my lips, no new taxes." Americans took him at his word and sent him into office. But budget deficits and pressure from Democrats in Congress made him

---

The Twenty-seventh Amendment

The Bush administration saw the adoption of a new amendment to the Constitution—one drafted by James Madison over two hundred years before! When he originally proposed the Bill of Rights, Madison offered twelve amendments, not just the ten that we are familiar with today. One of the two that were not adopted by the states read, "No law, varying the compensation for the services of the Senators and Representatives, shall take effect, until an election of Representatives shall have intervened." Since it was not adopted along with the other ten, the amendment remained in legal limbo. Only six states had ratified it by 1792. Ohio joined them by ratifying it in 1873.

This old amendment took new life in the 1980s. Taxpayers were outraged when Congress attempted to vote itself pay raises, even when the national economy was in a downturn. In 1989 Congress voted itself not only a hefty pay raise but also automatic adjustments for inflation. This furor gave a fresh push to the old Madison amendment. On May 7, 1992, Michigan became the thirty-eighth state to ratify the amendment. Now when Congress passes pay raises, they do not take effect until after the next election—giving the voters a chance to register their opinion with their ballots.

"Communist Dominoes Are Falling"

In an interesting reversal of the "domino theory," the idea of free states in a region sequentially falling to Communist aggression (see p. 544), Ronald Reagan in a speech on May 18, 1990, described the collapse of communism in post–cold war Europe and the moral high ground that America occupies in the struggle between free and totalitarian states.

Let me tell you the basis of my optimism for our future. What has made the United States great is that ours has been an empire of ideals. The ideals of freedom, democracy, and a belief in the remarkable potential of the individual. Power isn't simply wealth or troops. Power is also spirit and ideas. And these we have in abundance.

The attitude of wanting to be the biggest and to go the farthest and to get there first and to do the most good when we arrived is part of our national character. Americans have always been larger than life. We wanted to establish the best government on Earth. We wanted to put a man on the moon. This is the spirit we set loose. This is the passion that invented revolutionary technologies and a culture young people everywhere envy.

And this is the attitude that has defeated communism. At some dark, lonely moment during the last decade, a terrible realization set in upon the leaders of the Soviet Union. They realized that their system could not take them where the United States and the rest of the free world was going.

The West's economics and technologies were a powerful booster blasting us into orbits the Communist world could not hope to reach. Our communications technology sailed over the barbed wire and concrete walls, letting their citizens know what democracy could offer, what free markets could provide. Our computer technology left them bewildered and behind, paper societies in an electronic age. . . .

Children rest on a fallen statue of Stalin in Monument Park, Moscow. AP Photo/Dieter Endlicher

Communist dominoes are falling all over the world. We must continue to give Communist dominoes a good push whenever and wherever we can. There are still those that must fall–China, North Korea, North Vietnam, North Yemen, and of course, Cuba. Cuba is next in democracy's sweep. And let me say directly to Fidel Castro–like Honecker in East Germany, like Ceausescu in Romania, like Noriega in Panama, like all the other has-been dictators of despair, you cannot fight democracy's destiny. Fidel, you're finished! . . .

We should not be timid in our embrace of democracy. We should be as bold and brash in our democratic ideals as ever in our history. The Golden Age of Freedom is near because America has remained true to her ideals. This is not the time to let our support for democracy wane.

Allied fire rains down on Baghdad during the air phase of the Gulf War. Associated Press AP

rethink his vow. Persuaded by Democrats in Congress, the president agreed to a budget deal that sought to tame the federal deficit by increasing taxes. Although both president and Congress worked on the legislation, Bush took most of the blame for the tax hike and disappointed voters by breaking his "no new taxes" vow.

Triumph Abroad

The Bush administration saw the final collapse of the iron curtain and the end of the Cold War. By the time George Bush left office, there was no longer a Soviet Union, and Eastern Europe was free of Communist domination. Despite the decline of communism, however, tyranny did not vanish from the face of the earth. The United States soon faced a new challenge in a different hot spot, the Middle East. The **Gulf War** was to be Bush's finest hour as president.

Confrontation–On August 2, 1991, the Middle Eastern nation of Iraq, led by dictator Saddam Hussein (sah-DAHM hoo-SANE), launched a military blitzkrieg that overwhelmed the tiny neighboring nation of Kuwait. With Kuwait crushed beneath its war machine, Iraq stood poised with the threat of further conquest as Saddam massed his forces on the border of Saudi Arabia. Opposing this naked aggression and fearing that much of the world's oil supply was about to fall under the control of the dictator Saddam, President Bush vowed, "This shall not stand." Working through the Security Council of the United Nations, the United States coordinated, first, a defensive operation. Code-named Operation Desert Shield, the plan deployed allied forces (chiefly American) in Saudi Arabia to forestall further Iraqi aggression.

Storm in the Desert–The United Nations voted overwhelmingly to authorize the use of military force to push the Iraqis out of Kuwait if they did not voluntarily withdraw by January 15, 1991. The allies (the United States, Kuwait, Saudi Arabia, Egypt, Great Britain, France, and several other nations) gathered a force 700,000 strong in Saudi

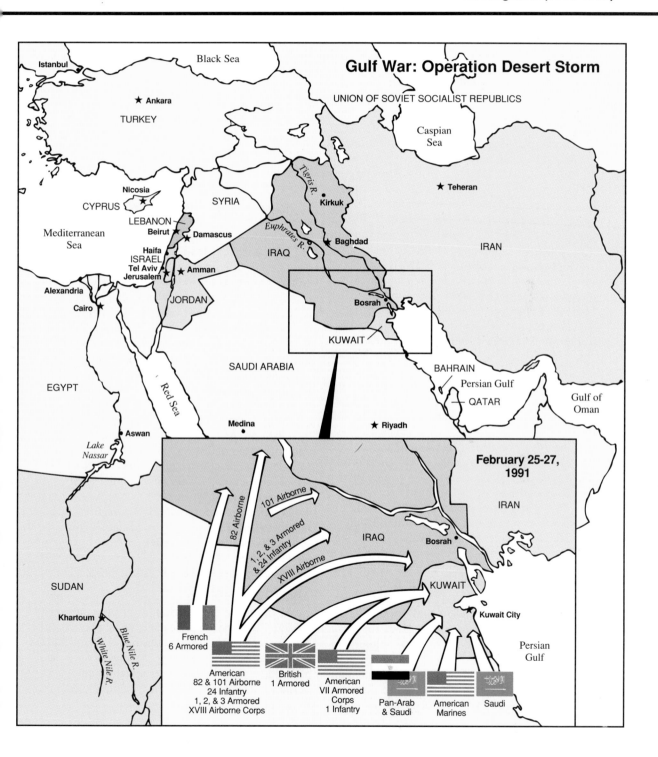

Gulf War: Operation Desert Storm

February 25-27, 1991

Arabia. Before launching this force, the allies tried every sort of diplomatic effort to get the Iraqis to withdraw. All failed. Finally, on January 12, 1991, the U.S. Congress voted to authorize President Bush to use force if necessary to get Iraq out of Kuwait. America had declared war for the first time since World War II.

The January deadline became a battle line as the Iraqi forces defiantly dug in deeper. On January 16 President Bush ordered a massive military assault on Iraqi military targets. Code-named **Operation Desert Storm,** the liberation of Kuwait began. The allied commander, American general Norman Schwarzkopf, told his forces, "Now you must be the thunder and lightning of Desert Storm."

The war began with more than five weeks of massive, around-the-clock bombing and air strikes on military targets in Iraq and Kuwait. Allied bombers, fighters, and missiles pounded enemy installations. Enjoying almost complete air superiority over the outgunned Iraqi air force, the U.S.-led forces destroyed much of Iraq's military capability–communications networks, airfields, bridges, roads, chemical-weapons plants, and missile-launching sites. Then the attacks targeted Iraq's ground forces, demolishing tanks and artillery and relentlessly pounding Saddam's entrenched legions.

The 100-Hour War–The second stage of the war was a ground attack on the Iraqis. On February 24, a coalition of American, Arab, and British troops assaulted enemy positions in southern Kuwait, pinning down the Iraqis, who thought this attack was the main thrust. But while this attack was going on, American and British forces, supported by French units, moved into southern Iraq to the west of Kuwait. With amazing speed, this force of armor and infantry swept around the lines of Saddam's soldiers, encircling and entrapping the main Iraqi force in Kuwait and southern Iraq. Dispirited by the weeks of bombing and now virtually surrounded, thousands of Iraqi soldiers deserted and surrendered to the coalition army. Some Iraqi units fought fiercely, but with the communication between units cut off, they were destroyed piecemeal by the allies. On February 27–just a hundred hours after the ground war began–President Bush addressed a television audience.

> Kuwait is liberated. Iraq's army is defeated. Our military objectives are met. . . . No one country can claim this victory as its own. It was not only a victory for Kuwait, but a victory for all the coalition partners. This is a victory for the United Nations, for all mankind, for the rule of law, and for what is right.

Aftermath–The Gulf War was the most intensive American military effort since World War II. Allied planes flew over 100,000 missions during the six-week war, losing fewer than 50 aircraft. With losses of fewer than 200 men and women, the American-led coalition wrecked nearly 4,000 enemy tanks and captured over 50,000 prisoners as it destroyed the effectiveness of an enemy force numbering more than 500,000 soldiers. General Schwarzkopf said, "The loss of one human life is intolerable to any of us who are in the military. But . . . casualties of that order of magnitude, considering the job that's been done and the number of forces that are involved, is almost miraculous."

Long-term, the results were not so positive for the coalition. Although defeated, Saddam Hussein still ruled Iraq and threatened the stability of the Middle East. He resisted all efforts by UN inspectors to inspect his military sites and defied an embargo placed on him by the victors. Among the allies, differences forgotten in war were soon remembered in peace. Trouble continued to simmer in the Middle East long after Desert Storm had blown over. For George Bush personally, great victory was a prelude to bitter political defeat.

The 1992 Election

In the glow of the triumph in the Gulf War, George Bush looked unbeatable as he prepared to run for reelection. As a result, major Democratic candidates hesitated to enter the presidential race and endure what looked to be certain failure. This hesitance opened the door for a political unknown to capture the nomination.

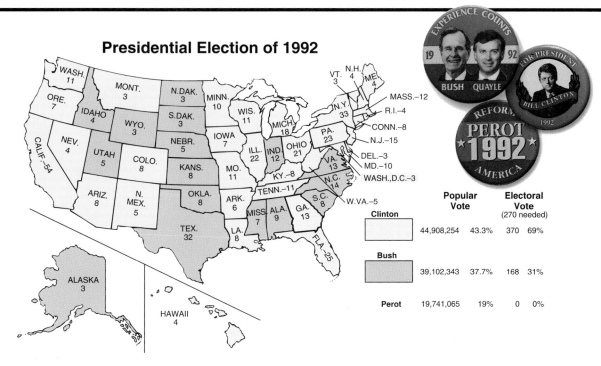

Presidential Election of 1992

	Popular Vote		Electoral Vote (270 needed)	
Clinton	44,908,254	43.3%	370	69%
Bush	39,102,343	37.7%	168	31%
Perot	19,741,065	19%	0	0%

Bill Clinton, the governor of Arkansas, surprised the experts by winning the Democratic nomination. A shrewd politician with a strong popular appeal, Clinton sidestepped and deflected charges concerning his past behavior. First his Democratic opponents and then the Republicans leveled charges concerning Clinton's alleged sexual immorality, marijuana use, draft dodging during the Vietnam War, and shady financial transactions as governor of Arkansas. Clinton shrugged off these attacks. Instead, he put forth himself as a **"New Democrat."** He claimed that he would not follow the pattern of promoting big government and would end the policies of high taxes and free spending that the Democrats had followed in the past.

Complicating the campaign was an unusual third-party candidate. Billionaire **Ross Perot** financed his own campaign for the presidency. A small, folksy man with the spirit of a Texas maverick, Perot promised to put an end to "politics as usual" and to trim the budget deficit. He made a virtue of the fact that he was no politician. Many Americans–put off by the candidates of the major parties and what they saw as the dirty politics of Washington–warmed to a candidate who was a true outsider. Even his wealth, which might have offended some voters, made Perot appear independent and self-sufficient. No special interests could "buy" him in return for their financial support.

The campaign was a confused one. Perot first dropped out of the race and then returned. Bush focused on Clinton's moral failings and tried, unsuccessfully, to label him another "tax-and-spend" liberal like those Ronald Reagan had vanquished. Clinton wisely made the economy his central issue as a recession had followed the Gulf War. With the Cold War won and no immediate foreign threats, Americans worried about domestic issues such as education, health care, and especially the economy.

On Election Day 1992, Americans gave a decided rejection of Bush and a faint endorsement of Clinton. Democrats lost ground in Congress but still controlled both the Senate and the House. In the presidential race Perot won 19% of the popular vote, the largest total for a third-party candidate since Theodore Roosevelt in 1912. Clinton defeated

Bush by only a plurality, 43% to 37%. But in the electoral college, he won a landslide of 370 to 168. Although he did not have a majority of the voters behind him, Bill Clinton had become the new president and brought an end to the Reagan era.

Section Review

1. How did George Bush offend many voters by breaking a pledge?
2. What amendment was added to the Constitution during the Bush administration? What issue did it address?
3. The invasion of what country sparked a Middle Eastern war in the early 1990s? What country invaded it?
4. Through what organization did the United States coordinate its efforts in the Gulf War?
5. Who was the significant third-party candidate in the election of 1992?

Bill Clinton

Third Parties

After the 1992 election, many observers suggested that it was Ross Perot's candidacy which enabled Bill Clinton to defeat George Bush. If this claim is true, then Perot was one of a line of third-party candidates who shaped the history of America's presidential elections. Listed below are some of the most significant third-party candidacies in American history.

Year	Candidate	Party	% of Popular Vote	Electoral Votes
1844	James Birney	Liberty	2.3%	—
1848	Martin Van Buren	Free Soil	10.1%	—
1856	Millard Fillmore	American ("Know Nothing")	21.5%	8
1892	James B. Weaver	Populist	8.5%	22
1912	Theodore Roosevelt	Progressive	27.5%	88
	Eugene V. Debs	Socialist	6.0%	—
1924	Robert LaFollette	Progressive	16.6%	13
1948	Strom Thurmond	States' Rights ("Dixiecrat")	2.4%	39
	Henry Wallace	Progressive	2.4%	—
1968	George Wallace	American Independent	13.5%	46
1980	John Anderson	Independent	6.6%	—
1992	Ross Perot	Independent	19.0%	—
1996	Ross Perot	Reform	8.4%	—
2000	Ralph Nader	Green	2.7%	—

Chapter Review

Terms
Ronald Reagan
"Reagan Revolution"
supply-side economics (Reaganomics)
Economic Recovery Tax Act of 1981
Gramm-Rudman Act
Reagan Doctrine
Contras
Grenada
Mujahideen
Walter Mondale
Geraldine Ferraro
Mikhail Gorbachev
perestroika
glasnost
Strategic Arms Reduction Talks (START)
Intermediate Nuclear Forces (INF) Treaty
Strategic Defense Initiative (SDI)
Iran-Contra affair
Jack Kemp
George Bush
Michael Dukakis
Dan Quayle
Americans with Disabilities Act
Gulf War
Operation Desert Storm
Bill Clinton
"New Democrat"
Ross Perot

Content Questions
1. What part of government spending did the Reagan administration actively increase during the time of the budget cuts?
2. Name at least two countries in which anti-Communist forces benefited from American aid under the Reagan Doctrine.
3. What was the only state carried by Walter Mondale in the 1984 presidential election?
4. Which of Soviet leader Gorbachev's reform policies–*perestroika* or *glasnost*–was more successful?
5. How did the results of the congressional elections of 1986 hamper President Reagan in the final two years of his second term?
6. What financial crisis during the Bush administration required $300 billion in "bail-out" funds from the federal government?
7. What is the difference between Operation Desert Shield and Operation Desert Storm?

Application Questions
1. How does the unwillingness of the federal government to control spending reflect on the American public?
2. The Reagan Doctrine, as well as the defense buildup of the 1980s, was said to exhibit "peace through strength." What does this slogan mean?
3. Review the feature on the Twenty-seventh Amendment on p. 632. Why would such an idea be popular with voters?
4. Do you agree or disagree with the Americans with Disabilities Act? Why?
5. Is the United States right to involve itself in military efforts such as the Gulf War in which its own territory is not threatened? Why or why not?

CHAPTER 27

New Challenges (1993-2000)

"There is a religious war going on in our country for the soul of America. It is a cultural war, as critical to the kind of nation we will one day be as was the Cold War itself."

Pat Buchanan at the Republican National Convention, August 17, 1992

William Jefferson Clinton takes the oath of office as the forty-second president of the United States.

In honor of Presidents' Day (February 21, 2000), a cable television network invited a team of historians to rank America's presidents from best to worst. They rated the presidents on several criteria, such as public persuasion, crisis leadership, moral authority, and economic management. The results, for the most part, were not too surprising. Abraham Lincoln ranked first, just ahead of Franklin Roosevelt and George Washington. Lincoln's predecessor, James Buchanan, came in last, just behind Lincoln's successor, Andrew Johnson.

The president in office at that time, Bill Clinton, finished in the middle of the pack. He was twenty-first, behind George Bush (the man he had defeated for the presidency) and just ahead of Jimmy Carter. How President Clinton rated on the various criteria revealed the strengths and weaknesses of his administration. He ranked near the top in economic management–fifth overall. But in moral authority, he came in dead last, trailing even Richard Nixon, the president forced to resign from

office because of the Watergate scandal. Economic strength and moral poverty–this was the Clinton administration.

Early Stumbles

Bill Clinton had been overcoming obstacles even before he was born. Three months before his birth, his father had died in a car accident. He was raised by an alcoholic and sometimes abusive stepfather. Yet he graduated from Yale Law School, went on to become attorney general of Arkansas, and in 1978, at age 32, became governor of that state. After a single two-year term as governor, however, Clinton lost a reelection bid when the people began to view him as arrogant and too liberal. This event caused him to revamp his political philosophy. Clinton pursued more moderate policies and kept a close ear tuned to public opinion. He recaptured the governor's office in 1982 and won successive reelection until he assumed the presidency. He became known as a major leader in

The Brady Bill, passed early in the Clinton administration, required a five-day waiting period before a purchaser could buy a gun. © Peter Johnson/CORBIS

the moderate faction of the Democratic Party opposed to the liberal extremes that had led to so many Republican victories.

Defeats and Victories

On assuming the presidency, Clinton seemed to forget the lessons he had learned in Arkansas. He proposed, for example, to permit open homosexuals to serve in the armed forces. The plan roused an uproar of opposition from the military, from Congress, and from the public at large. Quickly, Clinton backed down and adopted a policy of "don't ask, don't tell" for homosexuals in the military: They were not to declare their homosexuality, and no one was to ask them about it. It was an uneasy compromise.

Past controversies also dogged Clinton. A series of women from the president's past accused him of sexual immorality. The most significant scandal, however, was the **"Whitewater" scandal.** It took its name from the president's past investment in the failed Whitewater Development Corporation, a re-

sort in northeastern Arkansas. Rumors surfaced that Governor Clinton had unethically used his influence to promote the Whitewater scheme for his private benefit. Eventually the federal justice department hired an independent counsel (an attorney not under the control of the executive branch) to investigate the Whitewater affair. This investigation went on throughout the Clinton administration and eventually led to the president's greatest humiliation late in his second term.

President Clinton by no means suffered constant defeat. With a Democratic majority in Congress, he was able to push through some significant legislation. The new **Family and Medical Leave Act** required businesses to give employees up to twelve weeks of unpaid leave to care for newborn children or seriously ill family members. The **Brady Bill** (named for a member of the Reagan administration who was seriously wounded in the assassination attempt on President Reagan) was one of Congress's most significant pieces of gun control legislation. Before a gun shop could sell an individual a gun, the law required a five-day waiting period and a background check on the purchaser. The **National Voter Registration Act** was commonly called the "motor voter act" because it required states to allow voters to register when they applied for or renewed a driver's license. Also, with the help of Republicans and over objections of his own party, the president herded through legislation opening free trade with Mexico (North American Free Trade Act, or **NAFTA**).

All of this legislation represented an extension of the federal government's power over state and local governments, businesses, and individuals. But it was one of the most sweeping attempts at reform that led to Clinton's first major defeat.

Health Care Fiasco

When he undertook to reform American health care, Clinton found that even a Democratic Congress was no guarantee of legislative victory. Joining the president in this effort (and in the blame for its defeat) was the First Lady, **Hillary Rodham Clinton.** Like her husband, she was an attorney, but she was more openly liberal than the president. During the presidential election, she had quickly taken a back seat when the Clinton staff realized her views made her unpopular with moderate voters. With the health care plan, she again stepped forward to take an open role in administration policy.

Mrs. Clinton took charge of a task force to plan the best way to implement health care reform. In late 1993 she presented a massive 1,342-page plan addressing what candidate Bill Clinton had called a health care "crisis" during his presidential campaign. The plan would allegedly take care of those who had insufficient medical insurance (or no insurance) and would hold down rising costs.

At first, the promises of universal insurance coverage and low costs for medical care attracted many Americans. Then, as details of the plan emerged, the public realized that someone would have to pay for those lower costs. The First Lady suggested raising taxes to pay for the plan. She added further controversy by insisting that the plan provide tax support for abortion. The sheer size of the plan gave many pause. The Clinton health care plan would create a new government bureaucracy, with some experts estimating that one-seventh of American business would come under government regulation. Soon, an outcry arose from those who saw the plan as too expensive and too intrusive into American life.

Conservative Backlash

The Clinton health care plan fell before an alliance of Republicans, the medical profession, and even some Democrats who were lukewarm to the plan. The battle over health care also revealed the power of a new and surprising force in America: **"talk radio."** Radio had not been a great political force since the 1950s, when television displaced it as America's favorite source of entertainment and information. Radio became mostly a medium for music and brief news reports. In talk radio, speech replaced music. Aggressive and impassioned radio hosts expressed their usually conservative views and took phone calls on the air in which listeners earnestly and heatedly voiced their protests about conditions in America. The most important of these talk radio hosts was Rush Limbaugh. He built a nationwide network of listeners energized to speak out on political issues.

Also displaying new political muscle was the religious right. The Moral Majority (see p. 613) had gradually weakened and dissolved in the late 1980s. New conservative religious organizations took its place. Probably the most important was the **Christian Coalition.** Religious broadcaster Pat Robertson had begun this organization after his failed attempt to win the Republican presidential nomination in 1988. Although he lost, Robertson revitalized the religious right by putting together a grassroots network of Roman Catholics, Charismatics, and evangelicals who were united on moral issues such as abortion and homosexuality. The Coalition issued "voter guides" through the mail and through churches to show how candidates had voted on moral issues. The organization also focused on electing conservative candidates on the local level, as in races for school boards.

Another conservative force, combining the appeal of radio and religion, was the broadcast *Focus*

A Christian Coalition rally in Washington, D.C. (1996). The Christian Coalition was a leading voice of religious political conservatives during the Clinton administration. Archive Photos

on the Family hosted by James Dobson. Although less directly involved than the Christian Coalition in specific election campaigns, the program took a conservative stand on issues such as abortion and homosexuality. The program encouraged Christians to get involved politically. A nationwide audience listened as Dobson and his guests promoted various pieces of legislation and advised ways for Christians to "take their nation back" from those who had allegedly moved the country from its Christian foundations.

As the 1994 congressional elections approached, Republicans in the House of Representatives issued what they called a **"Contract with America."** House Republicans laid out ten popular bills they promised to bring up for a vote–if they were elected–within their first hundred days in office. This legislation dealt with issues such as balancing the federal budget and limiting the number of terms a congressman could be elected. Displeasure with the Clinton health care plan, the opposition to Democratic policies stirred up by talk radio, the efforts of the Religious Right, and the Contract

with America all contributed to a stunning repudiation for the president. In the fall elections, the Republicans captured control of both houses of Congress for the first time since Dwight Eisenhower's first term. Politically, President Clinton was like a fighter on the ropes under the hammering of his opponent. Some Republicans confidently predicted that he would be a one-term president like George Bush. But as those opponents would soon learn, the president was only down, not out.

Section Review

1. Why was the National Voter Registration Act commonly called the "motor voter act"?
2. What ambitious legislative effort by the Clinton administration sparked a backlash in public opinion?
3. Name the two organizations that represented the resurgence of the religious right in the 1990s and their founders.
4. What was the result of the congressional elections of 1994?

"The Comeback Kid"

Throughout his career, Bill Clinton had often been called "the comeback kid." After his defeat in the 1980 Arkansas governor's race, he came back to recapture that office two years later. After allegations of sexual immorality led to his defeat in the 1992 New Hampshire presidential primary, he rebounded to capture the Democratic nomination. Now faced with embarrassing defeats over his health care plan and in the congressional elections, Clinton began another comeback.

Battling with Congress

The Republican Congress began with a rush. Under the aggressive leadership of House Speaker Newt Gingrich, House Republicans kept their "Contract with America" by pushing through votes on the promised legislation. But only two of these bills actually made it past the House and through the Senate to be signed into law by the president. And one of these two bills, giving the president the **line-item veto** (allowing the president to eliminate spending items in the federal budget), was later struck down by the Supreme Court. The "Contract" had attracted voters, but Republicans had trouble getting its agenda through, particularly with the president ready to veto their efforts.

Meanwhile, President Clinton picked his battles with Congress shrewdly. Despite the defeat of his party in the 1994 Congressional elections, the president still retained his popularity with the public. He also proved to have more skills than the Republicans in shaping public opinion. He showed these strengths in a battle over the federal budget. The new Republican Congress insisted on real spending cuts that addressed the government's budget deficit. Clinton and the Democrats opposed cuts in which they alleged the poor and needy would suffer. A core of determined Republicans refused to pass *any* budget if it did not deal with the deficit. As a result, twice (in November 1995 and again in December and January of 1995-96) the government technically ran out of money and shut down "nonessential" federal agencies, such as national parks. Unfortunately for Republicans, these events caused the public to think of Republicans as irresponsible and cold-hearted. Under public pressure, Congress passed a budget more to the president's liking.

Move to the Middle

In addition to outmaneuvering Republicans by swaying public opinion, the president also carried out a sharp shift to the middle of the political spectrum. Aware that many voters had begun to view him as liberal, Clinton went back to the centrist, middle-of-the-road stance he had used to get elected. In his 1996 State of the Union Address, Clinton presented himself again as a New Democrat–tough on crime, supportive of family values, and ready to reform welfare. He declared, "The era of big government is over."

The president soon took steps to the political center. Despite his endorsement of the drive for homosexual rights, he signed the **Defense of Marriage Act,** which secured federal benefits, such as health insurance, for spouses in traditional marriages only, denying any status to homosexual "unions." Then he signed the Republicans' welfare reform bill. The **Welfare Reform Act of 1996** rolled back federal guarantees for the poor for the first time since FDR's New Deal. The new law required welfare recipients to go back to work within two years and put a lifetime cap of five years for assistance. It also gave blocks of federal funds to the states to address welfare reform as they saw fit, without federal strings attached. It was an attempt, as Clinton said, to "end welfare as we know it." These shifts bothered members of the president's own party. One Democratic Congressman said, "I think most of us learned some time ago that if you don't like the president's position on a particular issue, you simply need to wait a few weeks."

Election of 1996

The success of Clinton's comeback became evident in the 1996 presidential election. The Republicans nominated Senate Majority Leader **Bob Dole** of Kansas. Dole was a decorated World War II veteran with a conservative voting record. He was an experienced legislator with a thorough knowledge of the operation of Washington politics. Dole was a lackluster campaigner, however. He avoided social issues, such as abortion, leaving Republican activists apathetic about his campaign. Even his considerable political experience turned off voters who blamed "politics in Washington" for many of the nation's problems. Dole tried to rouse Americans

The "Gay Rights" Movement

When President Clinton suggested allowing open homosexuals to serve in the U.S. military and later when he signed the Defense of Marriage Act, he was reacting to a rising political force in America, the **"gay rights" movement.** Openly practicing homosexuals sought ways to secure legal recognition of their lifestyle and, by doing so, hoped to make themselves more accepted by the American public.

The term *gay* has been used in reference to homosexuality since the early 1900s, although that use was not widespread until the 1970s. Sometimes it is used just of male homosexuals and sometimes of homosexuals in general. The birth of the "gay rights" movement was the Stonewall riots of June 1969. When police in New York City raided a homosexual bar called Stonewall, the patrons resisted and violence broke out. For homosexuals, this event marked the beginning of a war for public acceptance.

The effort saw some success. In 1973 the American Psychiatric Association voted to stop considering homosexuality a disorder. In cities with large homosexual populations, such as San Francisco, pro-homosexual forces put through local ordinances banning discrimination against homosexuals. But the majority of the American people opposed these trends. Christians realized that the Bible expressly condemns homosexuality (e.g., Rom. 1:26-27). Even non-Christians could see that the behavior was unnatural and immoral.

Nonetheless, homosexual activists made strides. They enlisted the entertainment industry and news media to portray homosexuality as normal and to demonize those who opposed it as "hate-mongers" and "homophobes" (people who irrationally fear homosexuality). Homosexual politicians began to win election to city councils, state legislatures, and even Congress. They labeled any criticism of the homosexual lifestyle as "gay-bashing," putting sermons against the sin in the same class as brutal acts of violence against homosexuals.

By the 1990s homosexuals had succeeded in normalizing their behavior to a large segment of the American people. Doing so allowed them to present legislative favors as simply their "rights." Attempts to redefine marriage to recognize homosexual "unions" was such an effort, which activists likened to the African American civil rights movement. When critics pointed out that homosexuality is a behavior, not an inherited characteristic like race, the pro-homosexual lobby contended that everyone is born with a "sexual orientation" about which the individual has no choice.

The "gay rights" movement challenges Christians to think biblically. They must not allow public opinion, no matter how strong, to reshape their view of sin. It is true that because of their sinful nature, humans are born bent to sin, and for some that bent is toward the sin of homosexuality. But Jesus Christ died to redeem people from sin–from its penalty and from its power. At the same time, Christians cannot condone violence against homosexuals or any other group and must not allow their abhorrence of the sin of homosexuality to quench compassion for the sinner. Paul's admonition to be "speaking the truth in love" (Eph. 4:15) means that believers must hold to both truth *and* love in their dealings with others.

America's intervention in Somalia was an early disaster in Clinton's foreign policy. © Peter Turnley/CORBIS

with a call for tax cuts and by accusing Clinton of double-dealing, but these attacks had little effect. In addition, Ross Perot was on the ballot again with his Reform Party, splitting the votes of those opposed to the Clinton administration.

President Clinton cruised to reelection. Although he failed again to get a majority of the popular vote, he had 49 percent to Dole's 41 percent and Perot's 8 percent. In the electoral college, the president swamped Dole 379-159. But the Republicans retained control of Congress and maintained their hold on the majority of governors' chairs. Bill Clinton "came back," but his party remained in the minority in Congress.

Section Review

1. During Congress's showdown with President Clinton over the federal budget, what events caused the public to view the Republicans as irresponsible?
2. What were the provisions of the welfare reform act passed during the Clinton administration?
3. What is the significance of the Stonewall riots?
4. Who was the Republican candidate in the 1996 presidential election? Who was the significant third-party candidate? What was his political party?

The Second Term

Economic Prosperity

One of the reasons for Clinton's sweeping reelection was the nation's booming economy. During the 1992 presidential election, the Clinton campaign staff had posted a slogan in campaign headquarters: "It's the economy, stupid." In 1992 that motto reminded candidate Clinton to hammer President Bush on economic issues, which were the greatest concern of American voters. By the dawn of Clinton's second term, the slogan took on a new twist. The United States was enjoying unparalleled economic growth, and citizens generally credited the president for their prosperity. A strong economy bolstered the president's popularity as most Americans remained generally satisfied, even optimistic, about the nation's economy.

There was good reason for the American people to be satisfied. Inflation stayed low and unemployment fell steadily to its lowest levels in thirty years. Businesses had to offer higher salaries and benefits not only to attract but also just to keep skilled employees. The stock market roared to record levels, fueled especially by growth in "e-technology," computer-related businesses. The Internet, an international computer network, opened new markets as people began to make purchases on-line. By Clinton's second term, the government was actually showing a budget surplus instead of the deficits that had characterized the federal budget since the days of the Vietnam War. The president's popularity surged with the economy.

Foreign Affairs

As the governor of a small state, Bill Clinton came to the presidency with little experience in foreign affairs. Early in his first term, he displayed that lack of experience when he encountered disaster in the famine-stricken country of Somalia. President Bush had sent American soldiers to that country in 1992 to aid United Nations peacekeeping forces. But the military factions in Somalia resisted all attempts to control or disarm them. Clinton eventually sent in army specialists, called Rangers, to track down the most brutal of the Somali warlords. Instead, the Somalis shot down an army military helicopter, and Americans watched their televisions in horror as the victorious Somalis dragged the body of an American soldier through the streets. Baffled by his inability to deal with the warlords, Clinton withdrew all American forces from the country.

He was somewhat more successful in Haiti. A brutal military junta in that country had overthrown a democratically elected president in 1991. When he took office, Clinton began to pressure the Haitian regime to allow the ousted president to take office once more. When he gathered a military force off the island and threatened armed intervention, the Haitian military backed down. The United States succeeded in putting the president back in office but could provide little help for Haiti's serious long-term problems of poverty and political corruption.

Probably the most significant American involvement overseas in the Clinton years was in the Balkans. The fierce ethnic and religious divisions of that corner of Europe had long been an explosion waiting to happen. Religiously, Catholics, Muslims, and Orthodox Christians compete fiercely with each other. Ethnically, the Serbs and Croats are the dominant groups, with several smaller groups added to the mix. Some fifty years of cruel Communist oppression after World War II

The Information Revolution

Just after World War II, electronic computers began to attract widespread public notice for the first time. In the 1950s, computers were huge machines, taking up whole rooms and consisting of a maze of wires and vacuum tubes. Advances in miniaturization rapidly shrank the size of computer components. In the late 1970s America saw the release of the first "personal computers," machines small enough to sit on a person's desk or be used at home. The 1980s saw an incredible boom as computer technology invaded offices and homes. Typewriters, long considered a traditional part of office equipment, became almost extinct.

The 1990s marked another advance in the computer revolution with the explosion in popularity of the **Internet.** Stand-alone computers need connection to a network of computers so that users can communicate information to one another. The Internet is an international network that joins thousands of smaller networks into one united network. The roots of the system lie with the U.S. Defense Department. Concerned that an enemy attack could cripple a nation's computer system if it had only one or just a few centralized points, American engineers in 1969 proposed a completely decentralized system. The idea was that if an attack destroyed part of the network the rest could still function.

Thus the Internet began, but it was still just a tool for government experts and scientists who had access through a computer hookup. The birth of the personal computer, however, made it possible for millions of Americans to get access to a network. Tapping into the Internet could become as simple as hitting a few keys on a keyboard or clicking a mouse. Commercial possibilities emerged. One of the most popular computer advances was electronic mail, or "e-mail."

Without pen, paper, or stamps, people could send electronic messages around the world through the Internet. E-mail reduced not only normal correspondence (now called "snail mail" by computer users) but also telephone calls.

The economic possibilities of the Internet became evident with the development of the **World Wide Web.** Often confused with the Internet in the public mind, "the Web" is itself a network of local servers connected electronically with each other around the world. The Web uses the Internet to allow users to communicate with each other. By typing in a web address (usually beginning with the prefix "www.") when logged into an Internet server, those connected to the Web can find access to diverse resources. Those with the technical knowledge can even construct their own websites, as users as young as elementary school have proved.

"Dot coms" (sites ending with the suffix ".com" for "commercial") became the heart of Internet/Web commerce. Entrepreneurs began to offer more items for sale through the Internet than one could find in the Mall of America. Customers began to buy books, airline tickets, clothes, groceries, and whatever else they wanted by credit card through the Web. Some found other creative ways to use the system; a few states allowed citizens to vote via the Internet.

There is a dark side to the Web as well. Since virtually any kind of information is available, users can find sites on how to make homemade bombs or how to manufacture illegal drugs or sites filled with pornographic content. Pornography became one of the Web's biggest sources of profit.

Any technology can be used for good or ill, according to who is using it. Despite the problems of the Internet, Christians have found it a helpful tool. Missionaries with computer access are able to contact family and supporters around the world without incurring high long-distance telephone charges or waiting for mail to be delivered. Churches can distribute information about their ministries and present the gospel to all who visit their sites. Used wisely, the Internet can be a means of education and even Christian edification.

had, at least, kept relative peace in the region. When communism fell in most of the region in the 1980s and 1990s, however, conflict broke out again. The nation of Yugoslavia became the focus of the trouble as it splintered into several different nations.

The United States became involved in Bosnia first. Located in the center of the former Yugoslavia, Bosnia embodied all the conflicts in the region. While other countries were predominantly Croat or Serb, Bosnia's population has both Croats and Serbs. In addition, Bosnia had one of the largest Muslim populations in the Balkans. In 1992 civil war broke out–a war furthered by Croatia in the west and what was left of Yugoslavia in the east.

President Clinton did not, at first, send soldiers to Bosnia, but he did provide air support for the United Nations' efforts to keep the peace. Furthermore, American diplomats took a leading role in trying to negotiate a peaceful settlement in the area. Finally, all the parties met together at Wright-Patterson Air Force Base and hammered out the **Dayton Accords.** This fragile agreement fashioned Bosnia into a confederation in which the Serbs, Croats, and Muslims shared power. To enact the

agreement, the United Nations worked with NATO (the North Atlantic Treaty Organization formed in 1949 to protect Western Europe from Soviet communism; see p. 541). The UN was responsible for the civil duties, while NATO took the burden of the military duties. As part of the peacekeeping efforts, President Clinton sent American troops to Bosnia. An uneasy peace settled over the bitterly divided nation.

The creation of new nations in the Balkans reduced Yugoslavia to a federal union of two small states, Serbia and Montenegro. Even in the shrunken Yugoslavia the province of **Kosovo,** became the scene of ethnic clashes. The majority of the people in the province were Albanian Muslims while a large minority were Serbs who were nominally Christian. In the mid-1990s an Albanian Muslim group, the Kosovo Liberation Army, began armed resistance to the Serb government. In response, Yugoslavia cracked down on any sign of Kosovar independence. Violence flared, with both sides committing massacres and atrocities. Eventually, the conflict forced thousands of Albanians caught between the revolutionaries and the government to flee the province. The Yugoslav government encouraged the flight, as their armed forces sought ruthlessly to bring order to the province.

The plight of the Kosovar refugees and the brutal policies of the Serb government caught the world's attention. President Clinton committed American forces to join the United Nations and NATO in stopping the oppression. When negotiations with the Yugoslav government failed, the military stepped in. In March 1999 NATO forces, including Americans, launched massive air strikes against Yugoslavia. The strikes hit military and government targets, along with accidental attacks on civilians. Casualties mounted, and finally, in July, the Yugoslavs gave in. NATO and Russian forces moved in and restored peace in Kosovo.

On the whole, the foreign policy of the Clinton administration showed a surprising willingness to use military force. In most cases (Somalia was an exception), these efforts achieved the government's immediate goals. But tactical military victories were not long-term solutions for regions. The intervention in Kosovo in particular raised questions about how the United States or any other country should intervene in another country's internal affairs. The United States possesses great power; the challenge is using that power for good.

Impeachment

No event in America or elsewhere in the world dominated the second term of Bill Clinton–or indeed his entire presidency–as the **Lewinsky scandal** and the history-making impeachment trial that followed. The investigation of the Whitewater affair (see p. 642) had continued into the president's second term. The investigation of wrongdoing in Arkansas had led to the trial and convictions of several friends of the president, including the governor of Arkansas who succeeded Clinton. Yet the evidence never touched the president himself. Then in January 1998 a new story hit the headlines. While digging into Whitewater, the independent counsel Kenneth Starr found evidence that the president had been having an adulterous relationship with a young White House intern named Monica Lewinsky and that he and his staff were trying to cover it up.

When the story broke, the president declared, "I did not have sexual relations with that woman. . . . I never told anybody to lie." He had in fact said the same thing about Lewinsky under oath in an earlier investigation. Evidence soon confirmed, however, that he had been involved sexually with her. Moreover, there was strong indication that the White House staff had tried to hinder the investigation of the matter.

There was little question that the president committed perjury, lying under oath about the relationship. He was likely guilty of obstruction of justice in not only the Lewinsky matter but also in a separate investigation in which a woman had accused him of sexual impropriety. As a result, the House of Representatives conducted an investigation marked by bitter conflict between Republicans and Democrats. Finally, in December 1998, the House voted to impeach the president–to put him on full trial before the Senate. For only the second time in American history, the president would be tried and, if convicted, removed from office.

Headlines from newspapers in the Miami area proclaim President Clinton's impeachment in English and Spanish. Associated Press AP

Andrew Johnson barely survived his Senate trial in 1868; he was acquitted by a single vote. By comparison, President Clinton was in little danger. Two-thirds of the senators would have to vote against him before he could be removed from office. The support of the Democratic minority for the president almost guaranteed that Clinton would be acquitted. Furthermore, polls indicated the American public did not want him removed from office. Many Americans apparently did not consider his behavior anything more than a private matter. Other Americans were disgusted with what the president had done, but they did not feel that "lying about sex" was sufficient grounds for removing him from office.

The trial before the Senate took place in January and February of 1999. Members of the House of Representatives conducted the prosecution while Chief Justice William Rehnquist presided. The Senate weighed two charges: whether the president was guilty of perjury and of obstruction of justice. By a vote of 45-55 the Senate declared him not guilty of perjury, and the vote tied 50-50 on the charge of obstruction of justice. Not a single Democrat voted against him. In neither case was there anything close to the 67 votes needed to remove him from office. Bill Clinton, "the comeback kid," had survived again, and he claimed complete vindication. This time, however, his reputation was seriously damaged, even among his supporters and members of his own party.

Section Review

1. What African country was the scene of a disastrous military effort early in the Clinton administration?
2. What are the two major ethnic groups in the Balkans?
3. The splintering of what nation in the Balkans led to deep unrest in the region? In what nation did the United States first become involved?
4. What were the two charges against President Clinton in his trial before the Senate?
5. How many Democrats voted to convict the president?

Election of 2000

Against a backdrop of financial prosperity and sexual scandal, the presidential election of 2000 took place. The race developed into a referendum on the Clinton presidency. On the one hand, the Democrats nominated Clinton's vice president, former Tennessee senator **Al Gore.** As a leading member of the Clinton administration, Gore represented the policies and approach of President Clinton. The vice president was not involved in the Lewinsky scandal, but he had loyally stood by the president during the impeachment. More than any other candidate, he represented the Clinton heritage. The Republicans turned to the son of the man whom Clinton had defeated in 1992. Texas governor **George W. Bush** ran on a theme of "compassionate conservatism." He promised educational reforms and swore that he would restore honor and dignity to the White House.

The two sides ran a closely contested campaign, the closest in a generation. Each man chose a running mate who buttressed his apparent weaknesses. Since Bush had little experience in Washington politics, he selected **Richard Cheney,** a former congressman from Wyoming who had served as secretary of defense under the elder Bush during the Gulf War. Gore, needing to distance himself from the scandals of the Clinton presidency, chose Connecticut senator **Joseph Lieberman.** The first practicing Jew ever to run on a major ticket, Lieberman had criticized President Clinton's behavior in the Lewinsky scandal (although he did not vote to impeach the president). In addition Lieberman had severely criticized the entertainment world for the deplorable morals portrayed in film and television. He added a moral tone to the Democratic ticket.

The two candidates differed significantly on some issues. Governor Bush was pro-life, for example, and Vice President Gore was pro-abortion. But both tried to appeal to the undecided middle-of-the-road voters as each advanced moderate agendas. Both wanted tax cuts, for example, but of a different nature. Gore wanted tax cuts for selected groups while Bush favored cuts for all taxpayers. Many of the dominant issues turned more on personalities. The Gore team tried to portray Bush as an "intellectual lightweight" who was incapable of

Presidential Election of 2000

	Popular Vote		Electoral Vote (270 needed)	
Bush	49,820,518	48.0%	271	50%
Gore	50,158,094	48.4%	266	49%
Nader	2,703,722	2.7%	0	0%

*One Gore elector cast a blank ballot in protest of D.C.'s lack of representation in Congress.

handling the job of president. The Bush forces responded by highlighting the vice president's numerous exaggerations, including his remarks suggesting he invented the Internet.

The election turned out to be the most bizarre since Rutherford B. Hayes's disputed election over Samuel Tilden in 1876. (See pp. 345-47.) It was, in fact, about as close to being a tie as a national election could be. Gore narrowly won the popular vote by a little more than 500,000 votes out of over 100,000,000 cast, a margin of about one-half of one percent of the vote. In the twentieth century, only John F. Kennedy's margin over Richard Nixon in 1960 was smaller.

The Electoral College, however, not the popular vote, decides the presidency. The candidate who could win enough states to garner 270 electoral votes would be president. After the dust from Election Day settled, the count stood at 267 electoral votes for Gore and 246 for Bush. The crucial state of Florida (with 25 electoral votes) was too close to call. Bush led after the initial count in that state by only about 1,800 votes out of some 6,000,000 cast. A recount of the votes in Florida (required by

Florida law because the result was so close) cut Bush's lead in half to just under 1,000 votes.

At this point, with the presidency at stake, both sides began to plead their case before the American people and especially before the courts. The Democrats claimed that many of the computer-read ballots should be recounted by hand, but they asked for these recounts only in heavily Democratic counties where the results would favor Vice Presi-

The Florida Recount

The tight outcome in the race for Florida's presidential electors led to confusion, anger, and even some laughter.

George W. Bush takes the oath of office as the forty-third president of the United States.

dent Gore. Republicans replied that such hand-counting was done by arbitrary standards and therefore unfair.

Some recounting took place, and Bush's lead shrank again to about 500 votes. A flood of some-times contradictory court decisions from Florida state courts, federal courts, and the U.S. Supreme Court interrupted the recount. Weeks dragged by as some court decisions favored Bush and some fa-vored Gore. Finally, on December 12–exactly five weeks after election day–the Supreme Court ruled for Bush, halting all recounts and, by default, mak-ing him the winner of Florida's votes and thus giv-ing him the presidency. Gore became the first candidate since Grover Cleveland in 1888 to win the popular vote but lose in the Electoral College.

This dramatic contest illustrated divisions within the government. The two candidates had al-most equal support in the nation. Republicans con-trolled both houses of Congress, but only by narrow margins. In fact, the Senate was tied 50-50, and only Vice President Cheney's vote as president of the Senate gave Republicans control. George W. Bush during his campaign had promised to bring a spirit of cooperation to Washington, saying, "I'm a uniter, not a divider." A divided Congress and a slender electoral mandate would give Bush the op-portunity to prove this claim.

Section Review

1. Who were the presidential candidates of the Democratic and Republican parties in the presidential election of 2000? How did they differ on the issues of abortion and tax cuts?
2. Which candidate won the most popular votes? Which won the majority of votes in the Elec-toral College?
3. The electoral votes of which state ultimately decided the presidential election?

Chapter Review

Terms

"Whitewater" scandal
Family and Medical Leave Act
Brady Bill
National Voter Registration Act
NAFTA
Hillary Rodham Clinton
"talk radio"
Christian Coalition
"Contract with America"
line-item veto
Defense of Marriage Act
Welfare Reform Act of 1996
"gay rights" movement
Bob Dole
Internet
World Wide Web
Dayton Accords
Kosovo
Lewinsky scandal
Al Gore
George W. Bush
Richard Cheney
Joseph Lieberman

Content Questions

1. What was President Clinton's "don't ask, don't tell" policy for homosexuals in the military?
2. What is an independent counsel?
3. Name two indications of the strength of the economy during the Clinton administration.
4. What are "dot coms"?
5. How did the popularity of personal computers enhance the growth of the Internet?
6. What province of Yugoslavia was the scene of a civil war in the late 1990s? To what ethnic and religious group did the majority of the people in this province belong?
7. What factor had dampened ethnic and religious conflict in the Balkans after World War II?
8. How did the Whitewater investigation lead to the impeachment of President Clinton?

Application Questions

1. What themes characterized the Clinton administration? Name at least two and explain your answers using specific examples.
2. Is it right for the United States to intervene militarily in another nation's internal affairs, as it did in Kosovo? Why or why not?
3. Do you think the Senate was right to acquit President Clinton? Explain your answer.
4. Do you think the United States should keep or abolish the Electoral College as a means of electing its president? Defend your answer.
5. List at least three events that have occurred since the beginning of the school year that you think will be included in future history books.

"Now We See Through a Glass Darkly"

Five hundred years have passed since the blue Atlantic horizon first beckoned explorers. The curious, the restless, and the persecuted soon sailed in their wake to brave the New World. But it was not an easy land. For many it meant only an early grave; for others it meant a struggle simply to survive. Still they came. There was no Statue of Liberty to light their way, no Bureau of Immigration and Naturalization to see that their paperwork was in order, no welcome wagon waiting–only the land before them and the sea behind them. They were pioneers on a new shore, strong men and women with sturdy backs and sturdy faith to match.

These Americans were remarkable. They wrestled their farms and villages out of the wilderness, raised churches, built schools, established governments, and when the time came, defended their right to do all of those things for themselves. "Life, liberty, and the pursuit of happiness," as their Declaration put it, were not only inalienable rights; they were the elements of the American mettle.

For pioneers and patriots alike, individualism was ingrained. Across the gallery of our nation's past it has been the individual of noble character, ready sacrifice, and tireless labor whose portrait is framed with true greatness. One such portrait of greatness can be seen in the scarlet snows of Valley Forge, bloodied by the bare feet of soldiers who did not know how to quit. Another can be seen by the flickering camp light as Stonewall Jackson, who bowed to none but God, kneels in prayer. Framed nearby is a twin portrait of two brothers, who over the sands of Kitty Hawk give wings to mankind's dream of flight. Still another portrait may be seen astride a weary horse as Francis Asbury blazes trails for God in the trackless Appalachians. After forty-five years of ceaseless labor, Asbury died penniless according to the world's accounting. But Asbury could count other things: thousands of men called to preach and growing churches with believers two hundred thousand strong.

Asbury–like Bradford, Bradstreet, and Brainerd, like Whitefield, Moody, Judson, Warfield, and countless other believers who have been a blessing to America–understood the definition of greatness given in Matthew 20:26-27: "Whosoever will be great among you, let him be your minister; And whosoever will be chief among you, let him be your servant." Christ gave this definition to His disciples at a time when some among them were jockeying for position and prestige. They thought, as much of the world thinks, that the way to stand out in the crowd is to step on other people's feet. The Lord pointed out, however, that true greatness is not the result of prestigious titles or fistfuls of money. It is not measured by headlines and handshakes. It comes from hearts and hands of service.

The wonderful thing about such greatness is its accessibility. As surely as the Lord said "whosoever will" may find salvation, He also taught "whosoever will" may be great. These great ones may be spiritual giants, Christian heroes, crowned not with the laurels the world crafts for its own, but with the character of the One who was crowned with thorns.

At no time in America's history has there been a greater need for such spiritual leaders driven by the compelling demands of Calvary. In a humanistic and often hostile society that has drifted far from its spiritual moorings, perhaps the opposition to such Christian leadership has never been greater, but then neither has the opportunity for Christian service been greater.

Each day we journey past the pages of this history book down an uncertain path to a certain future. Paul wrote, "Now we see through a glass darkly"; likewise our understanding of the past and our vision for the future is often clouded. We cannot even predict tomorrow's headlines. Yet as believers we have a sure destiny as we walk with the Author and Finisher of time to "a new heaven and new earth." Our New World discovery, however, unlike Columbus's voyage, will not be an accidental landing on a hostile shore. As America was to weary pilgrims long ago, this New World will be a refuge, a welcome shore, a city upon a hill.

Appendixes

The States of the Union

Order of Admission into Union	State	Year of Admission	Postal Abbrev.	Capital City	Nickname	Area in Sq. Miles
1	Delaware	1787	DE	Dover	Diamond State, First State	2,044
2	Pennsylvania	1787	PA	Harrisburg	Keystone State	45,308
3	New Jersey	1787	NJ	Trenton	Garden State	7,787
4	Georgia	1788	GA	Atlanta	Empire State of the South, Peach State	58,910
5	Connecticut	1788	CT	Hartford	Constitution State, Nutmeg State	5,018
6	Massachusetts	1788	MA	Boston	Bay State, Old Colony	8,284
7	Maryland	1788	MD	Annapolis	Old Line State, Free State	10,460
8	South Carolina	1788	SC	Columbia	Palmetto State	31,113
9	New Hampshire	1788	NH	Concord	Granite State	9,279
10	Virginia	1788	VA	Richmond	Old Dominion State	40,767
11	New York	1788	NY	Albany	Empire State	49,108
12	North Carolina	1789	NC	Raleigh	Tar Heel State, Old North State	52,669
13	Rhode Island	1790	RI	Providence	Little Rhody, Ocean State	1,212
14	Vermont	1791	VT	Montpelier	Green Mountain State	9,614
15	Kentucky	1792	KY	Frankfort	Bluegrass State	40,409
16	Tennessee	1796	TN	Nashville	Volunteer State	42,144
17	Ohio	1803	OH	Columbus	Buckeye State	41,330
18	Louisiana	1812	LA	Baton Rouge	Pelican State	47,752
19	Indiana	1816	IN	Indianapolis	Hoosier State	36,185
20	Mississippi	1817	MS	Jackson	Magnolia State	47,689
21	Illinois	1818	IL	Springfield	Land of Lincoln, Prairie State	56,345
22	Alabama	1819	AL	Montgomery	Heart of Dixie, Camellia State	51,705
23	Maine	1820	ME	Augusta	Pine Tree State	33,265
24	Missouri	1821	MO	Jefferson City	"Show Me" State	69,697
25	Arkansas	1836	AR	Little Rock	Natural State, Razorback State	53,187
26	Michigan	1837	MI	Lansing	Wolverine State, Great Lakes State	58,527
27	Florida	1845	FL	Tallahassee	Sunshine State	58,664
28	Texas	1845	TX	Austin	Lone Star State	266,807
29	Iowa	1846	IA	Des Moines	Hawkeye State	56,275
30	Wisconsin	1848	WI	Madison	Badger State	56,153
31	California	1850	CA	Sacramento	Golden State	158,706
32	Minnesota	1858	MN	St. Paul	North Star State, Gopher State	84,402
33	Oregon	1859	OR	Salem	Beaver State	97,073
34	Kansas	1861	KS	Topeka	Sunflower State	82,277
35	West Virginia	1863	WV	Charleston	Mountain State	24,231
36	Nevada	1864	NV	Carson City	Sagebrush State, Silver State, Battle Born State	110,561
37	Nebraska	1867	NE	Lincoln	Cornhusker State	77,355
38	Colorado	1876	CO	Denver	Centennial State	104,091
39	North Dakota	1889	ND	Bismarck	Peace Garden State	70,702
40	South Dakota	1889	SD	Pierre	Coyote State, Mt. Rushmore State	77,116
41	Montana	1889	MT	Helena	Treasure State	147,046
42	Washington	1889	WA	Olympia	Evergreen State	68,139
43	Idaho	1890	ID	Boise	Gem State	83,564
44	Wyoming	1890	WY	Cheyenne	Equality State, Cowboy State	97,809
45	Utah	1896	UT	Salt Lake City	Beehive State	84,899
46	Oklahoma	1907	OK	Oklahoma City	Sooner State	69,956
47	New Mexico	1912	NM	Santa Fe	Land of Enchantment	121,593
48	Arizona	1912	AZ	Phoenix	Grand Canyon State	114,000
49	Alaska	1959	AK	Juneau	The Last Frontier	591,004
50	Hawaii	1959	HI	Honolulu	Aloha State	6,471
	District of Columbia	1791	DC	Washington		70

The Presidents of the United States

President	Term	Political Party	Home State	Vice President
George Washington	1789-1797	None	Virginia	John Adams
John Adams	1797-1801	Federalist	Massachusetts	Thomas Jefferson
Thomas Jefferson	1801-1809	Republican	Virginia	Aaron Burr
				George Clinton
James Madison	1809-1817	Republican	Virginia	George Clinton
				Elbridge Gerry
James Monroe	1817-1825	Republican	Virginia	Daniel D. Tompkins
John Quincy Adams	1825-1829	Republican	Massachusetts	John C. Calhoun
Andrew Jackson	1829-1837	Democrat	Tennessee	John C. Calhoun
				Martin Van Buren
Martin Van Buren	1837-1841	Democrat	New York	Richard M. Johnson
William H. Harrison	1841	Whig	Ohio	John Tyler
John Tyler	1841-1845	Whig	Virginia	
James K. Polk	1845-1849	Democrat	Tennessee	George M. Dallas
Zachary Taylor	1849-1850	Whig	Louisiana	Millard Fillmore
Millard Fillmore	1850-1853	Whig	New York	
Franklin Pierce	1853-1857	Democrat	New Hampshire	William R. King
James Buchanan	1857-1861	Democrat	Pennsylvania	John C. Breckinridge
Abraham Lincoln	1861-1865	Republican	Illinois	Hannibal Hamlin
				Andrew Johnson
Andrew Johnson	1865-1869	Republican	Tennessee	
Ulysses S. Grant	1869-1877	Republican	Illinois	Schuyler Colfax
				Henry Wilson
Rutherford B. Hayes	1877-1881	Republican	Ohio	William A. Wheeler
James A. Garfield	1881	Republican	Ohio	Chester A. Arthur
Chester A. Arthur	1881-1885	Republican	New York	
Grover Cleveland	1885-1889	Democrat	New York	Thomas A. Hendricks
Benjamin Harrison	1889-1893	Republican	Indiana	Levi P. Morton
Grover Cleveland	1893-1897	Democrat	New York	Adlai E. Stevenson
William McKinley	1897-1901	Republican	Ohio	Garret A. Hobart
				Theodore Roosevelt
Theodore Roosevelt	1901-1909	Republican	New York	Charles W. Fairbanks
William H. Taft	1909-1913	Republican	Ohio	James S. Sherman
Woodrow Wilson	1913-1921	Democrat	New Jersey	Thomas R. Marshall
Warren G. Harding	1921-1923	Republican	Ohio	Calvin Coolidge
Calvin Coolidge	1923-1929	Republican	Massachusetts	Charles G. Dawes
Herbert Hoover	1929-1933	Republican	California	Charles Curtis
Franklin D. Roosevelt	1933-1945	Democrat	New York	John Garner
				John Garner
				Henry A. Wallace
				Harry S. Truman
Harry S. Truman	1945-1953	Democrat	Missouri	Alben W. Barkley
Dwight D. Eisenhower	1953-1961	Republican	Pennsylvania	Richard M. Nixon
John F. Kennedy	1961-1963	Democrat	Massachusetts	Lyndon B. Johnson
Lyndon B. Johnson	1963-1969	Democrat	Texas	Hubert H. Humphrey
Richard M. Nixon	1969-1974	Republican	California	Spiro T. Agnew
				Gerald R. Ford
Gerald R. Ford	1974-1977	Republican	Michigan	Nelson A. Rockefeller
Jimmy Carter	1977-1981	Democrat	Georgia	Walter F. Mondale
Ronald Reagan	1981-1989	Republican	California	George Bush
George Bush	1989-1993	Republican	Texas	Dan Quayle
Bill Clinton	1993-2001	Democrat	Arkansas	Al Gore
George W. Bush	2001-	Republican	Texas	Richard Cheney

In CONGRESS, July 4, 1776.

The unanimous Declaration of the thirteen united States of America

When in the course of human events, it becomes necessary for one people to dissolve the political bands which have connected them with another, and to assume among the powers of the earth, the separate and equal station to which the laws of Nature and of Nature's God entitle them, a decent respect to the opinions of mankind requires that they should declare the causes which impel them to the separation.

We hold these truths to be self-evident, that all men are created equal, that they are endowed by their Creator with certain unalienable rights, that among these are life, liberty and the pursuit of happiness. That to secure these rights, governments are instituted among men, deriving their just powers from the consent of the governed. That whenever any form of government becomes destructive of these ends, it is the right of the people to alter or to abolish it, and to institute new government, laying its foundation on such principles and organizing its powers in such form, as to them shall seem most likely to effect their safety and happiness. Prudence, indeed, will dictate that governments long established should not be changed for light and transient causes, and accordingly, all experience hath shewn, that mankind are more disposed to suffer, while evils are sufferable, than to right themselves by abolishing the forms to which they are accustomed. But when a long train of abuses and usurpations, pursuing invariably the same object, evinces a design to reduce them under absolute despotism, it is their right, it is their duty, to throw off such government, and to provide new guards for their future security. Such has been the patient sufferance of the colonies; and such is now the necessity which constrains them to expunge their former systems of government. The history of the present king of Great Britain is a history of the unremitting injuries and usurpations, all having in direct object the establishment of an absolute tyranny over these states. To prove this let facts be submitted to a candid world.

He has refused to pass other laws for the accommodation of large districts of people, unless those people would relinquish the right of representation in the legislature, a right inestimable to them, and formidable to tyrants only.

He has called together legislative bodies at places unusual, uncomfortable, and distant from the depository of the public records, for the sole purpose of fatiguing them into compliance with his measures.

He has dissolved representative houses repeatedly and continually for opposing with manly firmness his invasions on the right of the people.

He has refused for a long time after such dissolutions to cause others to be elected whereby the legislative powers incapable of annihilation have returned to the people at large for their exercise, the state remaining in the meantime exposed to all the dangers of invasion from without and convulsions within.

He has endeavored to prevent the population of these states, for that purpose obstructing the laws for naturalization of foreigners, refusing to pass others to encourage their migrations hither, and raising the conditions of new appropriations of lands.

He has suffered the administration of justice totally to cease in some of these states, refusing his assent to laws for establishing judiciary powers.

He has made judges dependent on his will alone, for the tenure of their offices and the amount and payment of their salaries.

He has erected a multitude of new offices, and sent hither swarms of officers to harass our people and eat out their substance.

He has kept among us, in times of peace, standing armies without the consent of our legislatures.

He has affected to render the military independent of and superior to the civil power.

He has combined with others to subject us to a jurisdiction foreign to our constitutions and unacknowledged by our laws, giving his assent to their acts of pretended legislation, for quartering large bodies of armed troops among us; for protecting them, by a mock trial, from punishment for any murders which they should commit on the inhabitants of these states; for cutting off our trade with all parts of the world; for imposing taxes on us without our consent; for depriving us in many cases of the benefits of trial by jury; for transporting us beyond seas to be tried for pretended offenses; for abolishing the free system of English laws in a neighboring province, establishing therein an arbitrary government, and enlarging its boundaries so as to render it at once an example and fit instrument for introducing the same absolute rule into these colonies; for taking away our charters, abolishing our most valuable laws, and altering fundamentally the forms of our governments; for suspending our own legislatures and declaring themselves invested with power to legislate for us in cases whatsoever.

He has abdicated government here by declaring us out of his protection, and waging war against us.

He has plundered our seas, ravaged our coasts, burnt our towns, and destroyed the lives of our people.

He is at this time transporting large armies of foreign mercenaries to complete the works of death, desolation, and tyranny, already begun with circumstances of cruelty and perfidy scarcely parallel in the most barbarous ages, and totally unworthy the head of a civilized nation.

He has excited domestic insurrection amongst us, and has endeavoured to bring on the inhabitants of our frontiers, the merciless Indian savages, whose known rules of warfare is an undistinguished destruction of all ages, sexes and conditions.

He has constrained our fellow citizens, taken captive on the high seas, to bear arms against their country, to become the executioners of their friends and brethren, or to fall themselves by their hands.

In every stage of these oppressions we have petitioned for redress in the most humble terms; our repeated petitions have been answered only by repeated injuries. A prince whose character is thus marked by every act which may define a tyrant is unfit to be the ruler of a people.

Nor have we been wanting in attentions to our British brethren. We have warned them from time to time of attempts by their legislature to extend an unwarrantable jurisdiction over us. We have reminded them of the circumstances of our emigration and settlement here. We have appealed to their native justice and magnanimity and have conjured them by the ties of our common kindred to disavow these usurpations which would inevitably interrupt our connection and correspondence. They too have been deaf to the voice of justice and of consanguinity. We must therefore acquiesce in the necessity which denounces our separation and hold them, as we hold the rest of mankind, enemies in war, in peace, friends.

We, therefore, the Representatives of the United States of America, in General Congress assembled, appealing to the Supreme Judge of the world for the rectitude of our intentions, do, in the name, and by authority of the good people of these colonies, solemnly publish and declare, that these united colonies are, and of right ought to be, free and independent states; that they are absolved from all allegiance to the British Crown, and that all political connection between them and the state of Great Britain is, and ought to be, totally dissolved; and that as free and independent states, they have full power to levy war, conclude peace, contract alliances, establish commerce, and to do all other acts and things which independent states may of right do.

And for the support of this Declaration, with a firm reliance on the protection of divine Providence, we mutually pledge to each other our lives, our fortunes, and our sacred honor.

Appendixes

The Constitution of the United States

We the People of the United States, in order to form a more perfect union, establish justice, insure domestic tranquility, provide for the common defense, promote the general welfare, and secure the blessings of liberty to ourselves and our posterity, do ordain and establish this Constitution for the United States of America.

Article I: The Legislative Branch

Section 1

All legislative powers herein granted shall be vested in a Congress of the United States, which shall consist of a Senate and House of Representatives.

Section 2

1. The House of Representatives shall be composed of members chosen every second year by the people of the several states, and the electors in each state shall have the qualifications requisite for electors of the most numerous branch of the state legislature.

2. No person shall be a representative who shall not have attained to the age of twenty-five years, and been seven years a citizen of the United States, and who shall not, when elected, be an inhabitant of that state in which he shall be chosen.

3. Representatives and direct taxes shall be apportioned among the several states which may be included within this Union, according to their respective numbers, *which shall be determined by adding to the whole number of free persons, including those bound to service for a term of years, and excluding Indians not taxed, three-fifths of all other persons.* The actual enumeration shall be made within three years after the first meeting of the Congress of the United States, and within every subsequent term of ten years, in such manners as they shall by law direct. The number of representatives shall not exceed one for every thirty thousand, but each state shall have at least one representative; *and until such enumeration shall be made, the state of New Hampshire shall be entitled to choose three, Massachusetts eight, Rhode Island and Providence Plantations one, Connecticut five, New York six,* *New Jersey four, Pennsylvania eight, Delaware one, Maryland six, Virginia ten, North Carolina five, South Carolina five, and Georgia three.*

4. When vacancies happen in the representation from any state, the executive authority thereof shall issue writs of election to fill such vacancies.

5. The House of Representatives shall choose their speaker and other officers; and shall have the sole power of impeachment.

Section 3

1. The Senate of the United States shall be composed of two senators from each state, *chosen by the legislature thereof,* for six years; and each senator shall have one vote.

2. Immediately after they shall be assembled in consequence of the first election, they shall be divided as equally as may be into three classes. *The seats of the senators of the first class shall be vacated at the expiration of the second year, of the second class at the expiration of the fourth year, and of the third class at the expiration of the sixth year,* so that one-third may be chosen every second year; *and if vacancies happen by resignation, or otherwise, during the recess of the legislature of any state, the executive thereof may make temporary appointments until the next meeting of the legislature, which shall then fill such vacancies.*

3. No person shall be a senator who shall not have attained to the age of thirty years, and been nine years a citizen of the United States, and who shall not, when elected, be an inhabitant of that state for which he shall be chosen.

4. The vice president of the United States shall be president of the Senate, but shall have no vote, unless they be equally divided.

5. The Senate shall choose their other officers, and also a president pro tempore, in the absence of

[Note: Sections in *italics* are sections of the Constitution which are no longer in force.]

the vice president, or when he shall exercise the office of president of the United States.

6. The Senate shall have the sole power to try all impeachments. When sitting for that purpose, they shall be on oath or affirmation. When the president of the United States is tried, the chief justice shall preside: And no person shall be convicted without the concurrence of two-thirds of the members present.

7. Judgment in cases of impeachment shall not extend further than to removal from office, and disqualification to hold and enjoy any office of honor, trust or profit under the United States; but the party convicted shall nevertheless be liable and subject to indictment, trial, judgment and punishment, according to law.

Section 4

1. The times, places and manner of holding elections, for senators and representatives, shall be prescribed in each state by the legislature thereof; but the Congress may at any time by law make or alter such regulations, except as to the places of choosing senators.

2. The Congress shall assemble at least once in every year, *and such meeting shall be on the first Monday in December, unless they shall by law appoint a different day.*

Section 5

1. Each house shall be the judge of the elections, returns and qualifications of its own members, and a majority of each shall constitute a quorum to do business; but a smaller number may adjourn from day to day, and may be authorized to compel the attendance of absent members, in such manner, and under such penalties as each house may provide.

2. Each house may determine the rules of its proceedings, punish its members for disorderly behavior, and, with the concurrence of two-thirds, expel a member.

3. Each house shall keep a journal of its proceedings, and from time to time publish the same, excepting such parts as may, in their judgment, require secrecy; and the yeas and nays of the members of either house on any question, shall, at the desire of one-fifth of those present, be entered on the journal.

4. Neither house, during the session of Congress, shall, without the consent of the other, adjourn for more than three days, nor to any other place than that in which the two houses shall be sitting.

Section 6

1. The senators and representatives shall receive a compensation for their services, to be ascertained by law, and paid out of the treasury of the United States. They shall in all cases, except treason, felony, and breach of the peace, be privileged from arrest during their attendance at the session of their respective houses, and in going to and returning from the same; and for any speech or debate in either house, they shall not be questioned in any other place.

2. No senator or representative shall, during the time for which he was elected, be appointed to any civil office under the authority of the United States, which shall have been created, or the emoluments whereof shall have been increased during such time; and no person holding any office under the United States, shall be a member of either house during his continuance in office.

Section 7

1. All bills for raising revenue shall originate in the House of Representatives; but the Senate may propose or concur with amendments as on other bills.

2. Every bill which shall have passed the House of Representatives and the Senate, shall, before it becomes a law, be presented to the president of the United States; if he approves, he shall sign it, but if not, he shall return it, with his objections, to that house in which it shall have originated, who shall enter the objections at large on their journal, and proceed to reconsider it. If after such reconsideration, two-thirds of that house shall agree to pass the bill, it shall be sent, together with the objections, to the other house, by which it shall likewise be reconsidered, and if approved by two-thirds of that house, it shall become a law. But in all such cases the votes of both houses shall be determined by yeas and nays, and the names of the per-

Appendixes

sons voting for and against the bill shall be entered on the journal of each house respectively. If any bill shall not be returned by the president within ten days (Sundays excepted) after it shall have been presented to him, the same shall be a law, in like manner as if he had signed it, unless the Congress by their adjournment prevent its return, in which case it shall not be a law.

3. Every order, resolution, or vote to which the concurrence of the Senate and House of Representatives may be necessary (except on a question of adjournment) shall be presented to the president of the United States; and before the same shall take effect, shall be approved by him, or, being disapproved by him, shall be passed by two-thirds of the Senate and House of Representatives, according to the rules and limitations prescribed in the case of a bill.

Section 8

The Congress shall have power

1. To lay and collect taxes, duties, imposts and excises, to pay the debts and provide for the common defense and general welfare of the United States; but all duties, imposts, and excises shall be uniform throughout the United States.

2. To borrow money on the credit of the United States;

3. To regulate commerce with foreign nations, and among the several states, and with the Indian tribes;

4. To establish a uniform rule of naturalization, and uniform laws on the subject of bankruptcies throughout the United States;

5. To coin money, regulate the value thereof, and of foreign coin, and fix the standard of weights and measures;

6. To provide for the punishment of counterfeiting the securities and current coin of the United States;

7. To establish post-offices and post-roads;

8. To promote the progress of science and useful arts, by securing for limited times to authors and inventors the exclusive right to their respective writings and discoveries;

9. To constitute tribunals inferior to the Supreme Court;

10. To define and punish piracies and felonies committed on the high seas, and offenses against the law of nations;

11. To declare war, grant letters of marque and reprisal, and make rules concerning captures on land and water;

12. To raise and support armies, but no appropriation of money to that use shall be for a longer term than two years;

13. To provide and maintain a navy;

14. To make rules for the government and regulation of the land and naval forces;

15. To provide for calling forth the militia to execute the laws of the Union, suppress insurrections and repel invasions;

16. To provide for organizing, arming and disciplining the militia, and for governing such part of them as may be employed in the service of the United States, reserving to the states respectively, the appointment of the officers, and the authority of training the militia according to the discipline prescribed by Congress;

17. To exercise exclusive legislation in all cases whatsoever, over such district (not exceeding ten miles square) as may, by cession of particular states, and the acceptance of Congress, become the seat of the government of the United States, and to exercise like authority over all places purchased by the consent of the legislature of the state in which the same shall be, for the erection of forts, magazines, arsenals, dock-yards, and other needful buildings; and

18. To make all laws which shall be necessary and proper for carrying into execution the foregoing powers, and all other powers vested by this Constitution in the government of the United States, or in any department or officer thereof.

Section 9

1. *The migration or importation of such persons as any of the states now existing shall think proper to admit, shall not be prohibited by the Congress prior to the year 1808, but a tax or duty may be imposed on such importations, not exceeding ten dollars for each person.*

2. The privilege of the writ of habeas corpus shall not be suspended, unless when in cases of rebellion or invasion the public safety may require it.

3. No bill of attainder or ex post facto law shall be passed.

4. No capitation, or other direct tax shall be laid unless in proportion to the census or enumeration herein before directed to be taken.

5. No tax or duty shall be laid on articles exported from any state.

6. No preference shall be given by any regulation of commerce or revenue to the ports of one state over those of another: nor shall vessels bound to, or from one state, be obliged to enter, clear, or pay duties in another.

7. No money shall be drawn from the treasury but in consequence of appropriations made by law; and a regular statement and account of the receipts and expenditures of all public money shall be published from time to time.

8. No title of nobility shall be granted by the United States: and no person holding any office of profit or trust under them, shall, without the consent of the Congress, accept of any present, emolument, office, or title, of any kind whatever, from any king, prince or foreign state.

Section 10

1. No state shall enter into any treaty, alliance, or confederation; grant letters of marque and reprisal; coin money; emit bills of credit; make any thing but gold and silver coin a tender in payment of debts; pass any bill of attainder, ex post facto law, or law impairing the obligation of contracts, or grant any title of nobility.

2. No state shall, without the consent of the Congress, lay any imposts or duties on imports or exports, except what may be absolutely necessary for executing its inspection laws; and the net produce of all duties and imposts, laid by any state on imports or exports, shall be for the use of the treasury of the United States; and all such laws shall be subject to the revision and control of the Congress.

3. No state shall, without the consent of Congress, lay any duty of tonnage, keep troops, or ships of war in time of peace, enter into any agreement or compact with another state, or with a foreign power, or engage in war, unless actually invaded, or in such imminent danger as will not admit of delay.

Article II: The Executive Branch

Section I

1. The executive power shall be vested in a president of the United States of America. He shall hold his office during the term of four years, and, together with the vice president, chosen for the same term, be elected as follows.

2. Each state shall appoint, in such manner as the legislature thereof may direct, a number of electors, equal to the whole number of senators and representatives to which the state may be entitled in the Congress; but no senator or representative, or person holding an office of trust or profit under the United States, shall be appointed an elector.

The electors shall meet in their respective states, and vote by ballot for two persons, of whom one at least shall not be an inhabitant of the same state with themselves. And they shall make a list of all the persons voted for, and of the number of votes for each; which list they shall sign and certify, and transmit sealed to the seat of the government of the United States, directed to the president of the Senate. The president of the Senate shall, in the presence of the Senate and House of Representatives, open all the certificates and the votes shall then be counted. The person having the greatest number of votes shall be the president, if such number be a majority of the whole number of electors appointed; and if there be more than one who have such majority, and have an equal number of votes, then the House of Representatives shall immediately choose by ballot one of them for president; and if no person have a majority, then from the five highest on the list, the said House shall, in like manner, choose the president. But in choosing the president, the votes shall be taken by states, the representation from each state having one vote; a quorum for this purpose shall consist of a member or members from two-thirds of the states, and a majority of all the states shall be necessary to a choice. In every case, after the choice of the president, the person having the greatest number of votes of the electors shall be the vice president. But if there should remain two or more who have equal votes, the Senate shall choose from them by ballot the vice president.

Appendixes

3. The Congress may determine the time of choosing the electors, and the day on which they shall give their votes; which day shall be the same throughout the United States.

4. No person except a natural born citizen, *or a citizen of the United States, at the time of the adoption of this Constitution,* shall be eligible to the office, who shall not have attained to the age of thirty-five years, and been fourteen years a resident within the United States.

5. In case of the removal of the president from office, or of his death, resignation, or inability to discharge the powers and duties of the said office, the same shall devolve on the vice president, and the Congress may by law provide for the case of removal, death, resignation, or inability, both of the president and vice president, declaring what officer shall then act as president, and such officer shall act accordingly, until the disability be removed, or a president shall be elected.

6. The president shall, at stated times, receive for his services, a compensation, which shall neither be increased nor diminished during the period for which he shall have been elected, and he shall not receive within that period any other emolument from the United States, or any of them.

7. Before he enter on the execution of his office, he shall take the following oath or affirmation:–"I do solemnly swear (or affirm) that I will faithfully execute the office of president of the United States, and will to the best of my ability, preserve, protect and defend the Constitution of the United States."

Section 2

1. The president shall be commander in chief of the army and navy of the United States, and of the militia of the several states, when called into the actual service of the United States; he may require the opinion, in writing, of the principal officer in each of the executive departments, upon any subject relating to the duties of their respective offices, and he shall have power to grant reprieves and pardons for offenses against the United States, except in cases of impeachment.

2. He shall have power, by and with the advice and consent of the Senate, to make treaties, provided two-thirds of the senators present concur; and

he shall nominate, and by and with the advice and consent of the Senate, shall appoint ambassadors, other public ministers and consuls, judges of the Supreme Court, and all other officers of the United States, whose appointments are not herein otherwise provided for, and which shall be established by law. But the Congress may by law vest the appointment of such inferior officers, as they think proper in the president alone, in the courts of law, or in the heads of departments.

3. The president shall have power to fill up all vacancies that may happen during the recess of the Senate, by granting commissions, which shall expire at the end of their next session.

Section 3

He shall, from time to time, give to the Congress information of the state of the Union, and recommend to their consideration, such measures as he shall judge necessary and expedient; he may, on extraordinary occasions, convene both houses, or either of them, and in case of disagreement between them, with respect to the time of adjournment, he may adjourn them to such time as he shall think proper; he shall receive ambassadors and other public ministers; he shall take care that the laws be faithfully executed, and shall commission all the officers of the United States.

Section 4

The president, vice president, and all civil officers of the United States shall be removed from office on impeachment for, and conviction of, treason, bribery, or other high crimes and misdemeanors.

Article III: The Judicial Branch

Section I

The judicial power of the United States shall be vested in one Supreme Court, and in such court and in such inferior courts as the Congress may from time to time, ordain and establish. The judges, both of the Supreme and inferior courts, shall hold their offices during good behavior, and shall, at stated times, receive for their services a compensation, which shall not be diminished during their continuance in office.

Section 2

1. The judicial powers shall extend to all cases, in law and equity, arising under this Constitution, the laws of the United States, and treaties made, or which shall be made under their authority; to all cases affecting ambassadors, other public ministers and consuls; to all cases of admiralty and maritime jurisdiction; to controversies to which the United States shall be a party; to controversies between two or more states; *between a state and citizens of another state;* between citizens of different states, between citizens of the same state claiming lands under grants of different states, and between a state, or the citizens thereof, and foreign states, citizens or subjects.

2. In all cases affecting ambassadors, other public ministers and consuls, and those in which a state shall be party, the Supreme Court shall have original jurisdiction. In all the other cases before mentioned, the Supreme Court shall have appellate jurisdiction, both as to law and fact, with such exceptions, and under such regulations as the Congress shall make.

3. The trial of all crimes, except in cases of impeachment, shall be by jury; and such trial shall be held in the state where the said crimes shall have been committed; but when not committed within any state, the trial shall be at such place or places as the Congress may by law have directed.

Section 3

1. Treason against the United States shall consist only in levying war against them, or in adhering to their enemies, giving them aid and comfort. No person shall be convicted of treason unless on the testimony of two witnesses to the same overt act, or on confession in open court.

2. The Congress shall have power to declare the punishment of treason, but no attainder of treason shall work corruption of blood, or forfeiture, except during the life of the person attained.

Article IV: Interstate Relations

Section I

Full faith and credit shall be given each state to the public acts, records and judicial proceedings of every other state. And the Congress may by general laws prescribe the manner in which such acts, records and proceedings shall be proved, and the effect thereof.

Section 2

1. The citizens of each state shall be entitled to all privileges and immunities of citizens in the several states.

2. A person charged in any state with treason, felony, or other crime, who, shall flee from justice, and be found in another state, shall, on demand of the executive authority of the state from which he fled, be delivered up, to be removed to the state having jurisdiction of the crime.

3. *No person held to service or labor in one state, under the laws thereof, escaping into another, shall, in consequence of any law or regulation therein, be discharged from such service or labor, but shall be delivered up on claim of the party to whom such service or labor may be due.*

Section 3

1. New states may be admitted by the Congress into this Union; but no new state shall be formed or erected within the jurisdiction of any other state, nor any state be formed by the junction of two or more states, or parts of states, without the consent of the legislatures of the states concerned as well as of the Congress.

2. The Congress shall have power to dispose of and make all needful rules and regulations respecting the territory or other property belonging to the United States; and nothing in this Constitution shall be so construed as to prejudice any claims of the United States, or any particular state.

Section 4

The United States shall guarantee to every state in this Union a republican form of government, and shall protect each of them against invasion; and on application of the legislature, or of the executive (when the legislature cannot be convened), against domestic violence.

Article V: Amending the Constitution

The Congress, whenever two-thirds of both houses shall deem it necessary, shall propose amendments to this Constitution, or on the application of the legislatures of two-thirds of the several states, shall call a convention for proposing amendments, which, in either case, shall be valid to all intents and purposes, as part of this Constitution, which ratified by the legislatures of three-fourths of the several states, or by conventions in three-fourths thereof, as the one or the other mode of ratification may be proposed by the Congress; Provided that *no amendment which may be made prior to the year 1808 shall in any manner affect the first and fourth clauses in the ninth section of the first article; and that* no state, without its consent, shall be deprived of its equal suffrage in the Senate.

Article VI: Constitutional and National Supremacy

1. All debts contracted and engagements entered into, before the adoption of this Constitution, shall be as valid against the United States under this Constitution, as under the confederation.

2. This Constitution, and the laws of the United States which shall be made in pursuance thereof; and all treaties made, or which shall be made, under the authority of the United States, shall be the supreme law of the land; and the judges in every state shall be bound thereby, anything in the constitution or laws of any state to the contrary notwithstanding.

3. The senators and representatives before mentioned, and the members of the several state legislatures, and all executive and judicial officers, both of the United States and of the several states, shall be bound by oath or affirmation, to support this Constitution; but no religious test shall ever be required as a qualification to any office or public trust under the United States.

Article VII: Ratifying the Constitution

The ratification of the conventions of nine states shall be sufficient for the establishment of this Constitution between the states so ratifying the same. Done in convention by the unanimous consent by the states present, the seventeenth day of September, in the year of our Lord 1787, and of the independence of the United States of America the twelfth. In witness whereof we have hereunto subscribed our names.

George Washington, President and Deputy from Virginia

New Hampshire
John Langdon
Nicholas Gilman

Massachusetts
Nathaniel Gorham
Rufus King

Connecticut
William Samuel Johnson
Roger Sherman

New York
Alexander Hamilton

New Jersey
William Livingston
David Brearley
William Paterson
Jonathan Dayton

Pennsylvania
Benjamin Franklin
Thomas Mifflin
Robert Morris
George Clymer
Thomas Fitzsimons
Jared Ingersoll
James Wilson
Gouverneur Morris

Delaware
George Read
Gunning Bedford, Jr.
John Dickinson
Richard Bassett
Jacob Broom

Maryland
James McHenry
Daniel of St. Thomas Jenifer
Daniel Carroll

Virginia
John Blair
James Madison, Jr.

North Carolina
William Blount
Richard Dobbs Spaight
Hugh Williamson

South Carolina
John Rutledge
Charles Cotesworth Pinckney
Charles Pinckney
Pierce Butler

Georgia
William Few
Abraham Baldwin

Amendments to the Constitution
Amendment I: Foundational Freedoms
Congress shall make no law respecting an establishment of religion, or prohibiting the free exercise thereof, or abridging the freedom of speech or of the press; or the right of the people peaceably to assemble, and to petition the government for a redress of grievances.

Amendment II: The Right to Bear Arms
A well-regulated militia being necessary to the security of a free state, the right of the people to keep and bear arms shall not be infringed.

Amendment III: No Quartering of Troops
No soldier shall, in time of peace, be quartered in any house without the consent of the owner, nor in time of war but in a manner to be prescribed by law.

Amendment IV: No Unreasonable Searches
The right of the people to be secure in their persons, houses, papers, and effects, against unreasonable searches and seizures, shall not be violated, and no warrants shall issue but upon probable cause, supported by oath or affirmation, and particularly describing the place to be searched, and the persons or things to be seized.

Amendment V: Rights of the Accused
No person shall be held to answer for a capital or other infamous crime unless on a presentment or indictment of a grand jury, except in cases arising in the land or naval forces, or in the militia, when in actual service, in time of war or public danger; nor shall any person be subject for the same offense to be twice put in jeopardy of life or limb; nor shall be compelled in any criminal case to be a witness against himself, nor be deprived of life, liberty, or property, without due process of law; nor shall private property be taken for public use without just compensation.

Amendment VI: Rights of the Accused in Criminal Trials
In all criminal prosecutions, the accused shall enjoy the right to a speedy and public trial, by an impartial jury of the state and district wherein the crime shall have been committed, which district shall have been previously ascertained by law, and to be informed of the nature and cause of the accusation; to be confronted with the witnesses against him; to have compulsory process for obtaining witnesses in his favor, and to have the assistance of counsel for his defense.

Amendment VII: Rights of Citizens in Civil Trials
In suits at common law, where the value in controversy shall exceed twenty dollars, the right of trial by jury shall be preserved, and no fact tried by a jury shall be otherwise re-examined in any court of the United States than according to the rules of the common law.

Amendment VIII: Cruel, Unusual, and Unjust Punishments
Excessive bail shall not be required, nor excessive fines imposed, nor cruel and unusual punishments inflicted.

Amendment IX: Unspecified Rights
The enumeration in the Constitution of certain rights shall not be construed to deny or disparage others retained by the people.

Amendment X: Unlisted Rights Go to States or to the People
The powers not delegated to the United States by the Constitution, nor prohibited by it to the states, are reserved to the states respectively, or to the people.

Amendment XI: Suing States
(Proposed March 4, 1794; ratified January 8, 1798)
The judicial power of the United States shall not be construed to extend to any suit in law or equity, commenced or prosecuted against one of the

Appendixes

United States, by citizens of another state, or by citizens or subjects of any foreign state.

Amendment XII: Separate Ballots for President and Vice President

(Proposed December 9, 1803; ratified September 25, 1804)

The electors shall meet in their respective states, and vote by ballot for president and vice president, one of whom, at least, shall not be an inhabitant of the same state with themselves; they shall name in their ballots the person voted for as president, and in distinct ballots, the person voted for as vice president, and they shall make distinct lists of all persons voted for as president and of all persons voted for as vice president, and of the number of votes for each, which lists they shall sign and certify, and transmit sealed to the seat of the government of the United States, directed to the president of the Senate; the president of the Senate shall, in the presence of the Senate and House of Representatives, open all the certificates and the votes shall then be counted; the person having the greatest number of votes for president, shall be the president, if such number be a majority of the whole number of electors appointed; and if no person have such majority, then from the persons having the highest numbers not exceeding three on the list of those voted for as president, the House of Representatives shall choose immediately, by ballot, the president. But in choosing the president, the votes shall be taken by states, the representation from each state having one vote; a quorum for this purpose shall consist of a member or members from two-thirds of the states, and a majority of all the states shall be necessary to a choice. And if the House of Representatives shall not choose a president whenever the right of choice shall devolve upon them, *before the fourth day of March next following,* then the vice president shall act as president, as in the case of the death or other constitutional disability of the president. The person having the greatest number of votes as vice president shall be the vice president, if such number be a majority of the whole number of electors appointed, and if no person have a majority, then from the two highest numbers on the list, the Senate shall choose the vice president; a quorum for the purpose shall consist of two-thirds of the whole number of senators, and a majority of the whole number shall be necessary to a choice. But no person constitutionally ineligible to the office of president shall be eligible to that of vice president of the United States.

Amendment XIII: Slavery

(Proposed January 31, 1865; ratified December 18, 1865)

Section 1. Neither slavery nor involuntary servitude, except as a punishment for crime whereof the party shall have been duly convicted, shall exist within the United States, or any place subject to their jurisdiction.

Section 2. Congress shall have power to enforce this article by appropriate legislation.

Amendment XIV: Citizenship

(Proposed June 13, 1866; ratified July 28, 1868)

Section 1. All persons born or naturalized in the United States, and subject to the jurisdiction thereof, are citizens of the United States and of the state wherein they reside. No state shall make or enforce any law which shall abridge the privileges or immunities of citizens of the United States; nor shall any state deprive any person of life, liberty, or property without due process of law; nor deny to any person within its jurisdiction the equal protection of the law.

Section 2. Representatives shall be apportioned among the several states according to their respective numbers, counting the whole number of persons in each state, *excluding Indians not taxed.* But when the right to vote at any election for the choice of electors for president and vice president of the United States, representatives in Congress, the executive and judicial officers of a state, or the members of the legislature thereof, is denied to any of the male inhabitants of such state being of twenty-one years of age, and citizens of the United States, or in any way abridged, except for participation in rebellion or other crime, the basis of representation therein shall be reduced in the proportion which the number of such male citizens shall bear to the whole number of male citizens twenty-one years of age in such state.

Section 3. No person shall be a senator or representative in Congress, or elector of president and vice president, or hold any office, civil or military, under the United States, or under any state, who having previously taken an oath, as a member of Congress, or as an officer of the United States, or as a member of any state legislature, or as an executive or judicial officer of any state, to support the Constitution of the United States, shall have engaged in insurrection or rebellion against the same, or given aid and comfort to the enemies thereof. But Congress may, by a vote of two-thirds of each house, remove such disability.

Section 4. The validity of the public debt of the United States, authorized by law, including debts incurred for payment of pensions and bounties for services in suppressing insurrection or rebellion, shall not be questioned. But neither the United States nor any state shall assume or pay any debt or obligation incurred in aid of insurrection or rebellion against the United States, or any claim for the loss or emancipation of any slave; but all such debts, obligations, and claims shall be held illegal and void.

Section 5. The Congress shall have power to enforce, by appropriate legislation, the provisions of this article.

Amendment XV: Black Voting Rights
(Proposed February 26, 1869; ratified March 30, 1870)

Section 1. The right of the citizens of the United States to vote shall not be denied or abridged by the United States or by any state, on account of race, color, or previous condition of servitude.

Section 2. The Congress shall have power to enforce this article by appropriate legislation.

Amendment XVI: Income Tax
(Proposed July 12, 1909; ratified February 25, 1913)

The Congress shall have power to lay and collect taxes on incomes, from whatever source derived, without apportionment among the several states, and without regard to any census or enumeration.

Amendment XVII: Direct Election of Senators
(Proposed May 13, 1912; ratified May 31, 1913)

The Senate of the United States shall be composed of two senators from each state, elected by the people thereof for six years; and each senator

shall have one vote. The electors in each state shall have the qualifications requisite for electors of the most numerous branch of the state legislatures.

When vacancies happen in the representation of any state in the Senate, the executive authority of such state shall issue writs of election to fill such vacancies; provided, that the legislature of any state may empower the executive thereof to make temporary appointments until the people fill the vacancies by election as the legislature may direct.

This amendment shall not be so construed as to affect the election or term of any senator chosen before it becomes valid as part of the Constitution.

Amendment XVIII: Prohibition
(Proposed December 18, 1917; ratified January 29, 1919)

Section 1. *After one year from the ratification of this article the manufacture, sale, or transportation of intoxicating liquors within, the importation thereof into, or exportation thereof from the United States and all territory subject to the jurisdiction thereof, for beverage purposes is hereby prohibited.*

Section 2. *The Congress and the several states shall have concurrent power to enforce this article by appropriate legislation.*

Section 3. *This article shall be inoperative unless it shall have been ratified as an amendment to the Constitution by the legislatures of the several states, as provided in the Constitution, within seven years from the date of submission hereof to the states by the Congress.*

Amendment XIX: Women's Suffrage
(Proposed June 4, 1919; ratified August 26, 1920)

Section 1. The right of the citizens of the United States to vote shall not be denied or abridged by the United States or by any state on account of sex.

Section 2. The Congress shall have power to enforce this article by appropriate legislation.

Amendment XX: Lame Duck Amendment
(Proposed March 2, 1932; ratified February 6, 1933)

Section 1. The terms of the president and the vice president shall end at noon on the 20th day of January, and the terms of senators and representatives at noon on the 3rd day of January, of the years in which such terms would have ended if this arti-

Appendixes

cle had not been ratified; and the terms of their successors shall then begin.

Section 2. The Congress shall assemble at least once in every year, and such meeting shall begin at noon on the 3rd day of January, unless they shall by law appoint a different day.

Section 3. If, at the time fixed for the beginning of the term of president, the president-elect shall have died, the vice president–elect shall become president. If a president shall not have been chosen before the time fixed for the beginning of his term, or if the president-elect shall have failed to qualify, then the vice president–elect shall act as president until a president shall have qualified; and the Congress may by law provide for the case wherein neither a president-elect nor a vice president–elect shall have qualified, declaring who shall then act as president, or the manner in which one who is to act shall be selected, and such person shall act accordingly until a president or vice president shall have qualified.

Section 4. The Congress may by law provide for the case of the death of any of the persons from whom the House of Representatives may choose a president, whenever the right of choice shall have devolved upon them, and for the case of the death of any of the persons from whom the Senate may choose a vice president, whenever the right of choice shall have devolved upon them.

Section 5. Sections 1 and 2 shall take effect on the 15th day of October following the ratification of this article.

Section 6. *This article shall be inoperative unless it shall have been ratified as an amendment to the Constitution by the legislatures of three-fourths of the several states within seven years from the date of its submission.*

Amendment XXI: Repeal of Prohibition
(Proposed February 20, 1933; ratified December 5, 1933)

Section 1. The eighteenth article of amendment to the Constitution of the United States is hereby repealed.

Section 2. The transportation or importation into any state, territory, or possession of the United States, for delivery or use therein of intoxicating liquors, in violation of the laws thereof, is hereby prohibited.

Section 3. *This article shall be inoperative unless it shall have been ratified as an amendment to the Constitution by conventions in the several states, as provided in the Constitution, within seven years from the date of the submission thereof to the states by the Congress.*

Amendment XXII: Presidential Terms
(Proposed March 24, 1947; ratified February 27, 1951)

Section 1. No person shall be elected to the office of the president more than twice, and no person who has held the office of president, or acted as president, for more than two years of a term to which some other person who was elected president shall be elected to the office of the president more than once. *But this article shall not apply to any person holding the office of president when this article was proposed by the Congress, and shall not prevent any person who may be holding the office of president, or acting as president, during the term within which this article becomes operative from holding the office of president, or acting as president during the remainder of such term.*

Section 2. *This article shall be inoperative unless it shall have been ratified as an amendment to the Constitution by the legislatures of three-fourths of the several states within seven years from the date of its submission to the states by the Congress.*

Amendment XXIII: Voting for Washington, D.C.
(Proposed June 16, 1960; ratified April 3, 1961)

Section 1. The District constituting the seat of government of the United States shall appoint in such manner as Congress may direct:

A number of electors of president and vice president equal to the whole number of senators and representatives in Congress to which the District would be entitled if it were a state, but in no event more than the least populous state; they shall be in addition to those appointed by the states, but they shall be considered, for the purposes of the election of president and vice president, to be electors appointed by a state; and they shall meet in the District and perform such duties as provided by the twelfth article of amendment.

Section 2. The Congress shall have power to enforce this article by appropriate legislation.

Amendment XXIV: No Poll Tax
(Proposed August 27, 1962; ratified February 4, 1964)

Section 1. The right of citizens of the United States to vote in any primary or other election for president or vice president, for electors for president or vice president, or for senator or representative in Congress, shall not be denied or abridged by the United States or any state by reason of failure to pay any poll tax or other tax.

Section 2. The Congress shall have the power to enforce this article by appropriate legislation.

Amendment XXV: Presidential Succession
(Proposed July 6, 1965; ratified February 23, 1967)

Section 1. In case of the removal of the president from office or of his death or resignation, the vice president shall become president.

Section 2. Whenever there is a vacancy in the office of the vice president, the president shall nominate a vice president who shall take office upon confirmation by a majority vote of both houses of Congress.

Section 3. Whenever the president transmits to the president pro tempore of the Senate and the Speaker of the House of Representatives his written declaration that he is unable to discharge the powers and duties of his office, and until he transmits to them written declaration to the contrary, such powers and duties shall be discharged by the vice president as acting president.

Section 4. Whenever the vice president and a majority of either the principal officers of the executive departments or of such other body as Congress may by law provide, transmit to the president pro tempore of the Senate and the Speaker of the House of Representatives their written declaration that the president is unable to discharge the powers and duties of his office, the vice president shall immediately assume the powers and duties of the office as acting president.

Thereafter, when the president transmits to the president pro tempore of the Senate and the Speaker of the House of Representatives his written declaration that no inability exists, he shall resume the powers and duties of his office unless the vice president and a majority of either the principal officers of the executive department or of such other body as Congress may by law provide, transmit within four days to the president pro tempore of the Senate and the Speaker of the House of Representatives their written declaration that the president is unable to discharge the powers and duties of his office. Thereupon Congress shall decide the issue, assembling within forty-eight hours for that purpose if not in session. If the Congress, within twenty-one days after receipt of the latter written declaration, or, if Congress is not in session, within twenty-one days after Congress is required to assemble, determines by two-thirds vote of both houses that the president is unable to discharge the powers and duties of his office, the vice president shall continue to discharge the same as acting president; otherwise, the president shall resume the powers and duties of his office.

Amendment XXVI: Eighteen-Year-Old Vote
(Proposed March 23, 1971; ratified July 5, 1971)

Section 1. The right of citizens of the United States, who are eighteen years of age or older, to vote shall not be denied or abridged by the United States or by any state on account of age.

Section 2. The Congress shall have power to enforce this article by appropriate legislation.

Amendment XXVII: Congressional Pay Raises
(Proposed June 8, 1789; ratified May 7, 1992)

No law, varying the compensation for the services of the senators and representatives, shall take effect until an election of representatives shall have intervened.

Federalist No. 10

Securing the Public Good and Private Rights Against the Dangers of Faction

by James Madison

10.1   Among the numerous advantages promised by a well-constructed Union, none deserves to be more accurately developed than its tendency to break and control the violence of faction. The friend of popular governments never finds himself so much alarmed for their character and fate, as when he contemplates their propensity to the dangerous vice. He will not fail, therefore, to set a due value on any plan which, without violating the principles to which he is attached, provides a proper cure for it.

The Public Good Is Disregarded in the Conflicts of Rival Parties

10.2   The instability, injustice, and confusion introduced into the public councils, have, in truth, been the mortal diseases under which popular governments have everywhere perished; as they continue to be the favorite and fruitful topics from which the adversaries to liberty derive their most specious declamations. The valuable improvements made by the American constitutions on the popular models, both ancient and modern, cannot certainly be too much admired; but it would be an unwarrantable partiality, to contend that they have as effectually obviated the danger on this side, as was wished and expected. Complaints are everywhere heard from our most considerate and virtuous citizens, equally the friends of public and private faith, and of public and personal liberty, that our governments are too unstable, that the public good is disregarded in the conflicts of rival parties, and that measures are too often decided, not according to the rules of justice and the rights of the minor party, but by the superior force of an interested and overbearing majority.

10.3   However anxiously we may wish that these complaints had no foundation, the evidence of known facts will not permit us to deny that they are in some degree true. It will be found, indeed, on a candid review of our situation, that some of the distresses under which we labor have been erroneously charged on the operations of our governments; but it will be found, at the same time, that other causes will not alone account for many of our heaviest misfortunes; and, particularly, for that prevailing and increasing distrust of public engagement, and alarm for private rights, which are echoed from one end of the continent to the other. These must be chiefly, if not wholly, effects of the unsteadiness and injustice with which a factious spirit has tainted our public administrations.

A Faction Is Defined as a Group of People Adverse to the Rights of Other Citizens

10.4   By a faction, I understand a number of citizens, whether amounting to a majority or minority of the whole, who are united and actuated by some common impulse of passion, or of interest, adverse to the rights of other citizens, or to the permanent and aggregate interest of the community.

There Are Two Methods of Curing the Mischiefs of Faction

10.5   There are two methods of curing the mischiefs of faction: the one, by removing its causes; the other, by controlling its effects.

There are Two Methods of Removing the Causes of Faction

10.6   There are again two methods of removing the causes of faction: the one, by destroying the liberty which is essential to its existence; the other, by giving to every citizen the same opinions, the same passions, and the same interests.

The First Remedy Is Worse Than the Disease

10.7   It could never be more truly said than of

the first remedy, that it was worse than the disease. Liberty is to faction what air is to fire, an aliment without which it instantly expires. But it could not be less folly to abolish liberty, which is essential to political life, because it nourishes faction, than it would be to wish the annihilation of air, which is essential to animal life, because it imparts to fire its destructive agency.

The Second Remedy Is Impracticable

10.8   The second expedient is as impracticable as the first would be unwise. As long as the reason of man continues fallible, and he is at liberty to exercise it, different opinions will be formed. As long as the connection subsists between his reason and his self-love, his opinions and his passions will have a reciprocal influence on each other; and the former will be objects to which the latter will attach themselves.

Protection of the Rights of Property Is the First Object of Government

10.9   The diversity in the faculties of men, from which the rights of property originate, is not less an insuperable obstacle to a uniformity of interests. The protection of these faculties is the first object of government. From the protection of different and unequal faculties of acquiring property, the possession of different degrees and kinds of property immediately results; and from the influence of these on the sentiments and views of the respective proprietors, ensues a division of the society into different interests and parties.

The Latent Causes of Faction Are Sown into the Nature of Man

10.10   The latent causes of faction are thus sown in the nature of man; and we see them everywhere brought into different degrees of activity, according to the different circumstances of civil society. A zeal for different opinions concerning religion, concerning government, and many other points, as well of speculation as of practice; an attachment to different leaders ambitiously contending for pre-eminence and power; or to persons of other descriptions whose fortunes have been interesting to the human passions, have, in turn, divided mankind into parties, inflamed them with mutual animosity, and rendered them much more disposed to vex and oppress each other than to cooperate for their common good. So strong is this propensity of mankind to fall into mutual animosities, that where no substantial occasion presents itself, the most frivolous distinctions have been sufficient to kindle their unfriendly passions and excite their most violent conflicts.

The Most Common Source of Factions Has Been over the Unequal Distribution of Property

10.11   But the most common and durable source of factions has been the various and unequal distribution of property. Those who hold and those who are without property have ever formed distinct interests in society. Those who are creditors, and those who are debtors, fall under a like discrimination. A landed interest, a manufacturing interest, a mercantile interest, a moneyed interest, with many lesser interests, grow up of necessity in civilized nations, and divide them into different classes, actuated by different sentiments and views.

The Principal Task of Modern Legislation Is to Regulate Various Interfering Interests

10.12   The regulation of these various and interfering interests forms the principal task of modern legislation, and involves the spirit of party and faction in the necessary and ordinary operations of government.

10.13   No man is allowed to be a judge in his own cause, because his interest would certainly bias his judgment, and, not improbably, corrupt his integrity. With equal, nay with greater reason, a body of men are unfit to be both judges and parties at the same time; yet what are many of the most important acts of legislation, but so many judicial determinations, not indeed concerning the rights of single persons, but concerning the rights of large bodies of citizens? And what are the different classes of legislators but advocates and parties to the causes which they determine? Is a law proposed concerning private debts? It is a question to which the creditors are parties on one side and the debtors on the other. Justice ought to hold the balance between them. Yet the parties are, and must be, themselves the judges; and the most numerous party, or, in other words, the most powerful faction must be expected to prevail. Shall domestic manufactures be encouraged, and in what degree, by restrictions

Appendixes

on foreign manufactures? are questions which would be differently decided by the landed and the manufacturing classes, and probably by neither with a sole regard to justice and the public good.

Property Taxes Provide a Great Opportunity and Temptation to Trample the Rules of Justice

10.14   The apportionment of taxes on the various descriptions of property is an act which seems to require the most exact impartiality; yet there is, perhaps, no legislative act in which greater opportunity and temptation are given to a predominant party to trample on the rules of justice. Every shilling with which they overburden the inferior number, is a shilling saved to their own pockets.

Enlightened Statesmen Will Not Always Be at the Helm

10.15   It is vain to say that enlightened statesmen will be able to adjust these clashing interests, and render them all subservient to the public good. Enlightened statesmen will not always be at the helm. Nor, in many cases, can such an adjustment be made at all without taking into view indirect and remote considerations, which will rarely prevail over the immediate interest which one party may find in disregarding the rights of another or the good of the whole.

It Is Necessary to Control the Effects of Faction

10.16   The inference to which we are brought is, that the causes of faction cannot be removed, and that relief is only to be sought in the means of controlling its effects.

The Constitution Protects the Majority of the People from a Faction of the Minority

10.17   If a faction consists of less than a majority, relief is supplied by the republican principle, which enables the majority to defeat its sinister views by regular vote. It may clog the administration, it may convulse the society; but it will be unable to execute and mask its violence under the forms of the Constitution.

10.18   When a majority is included in a faction, the form of popular government, on the other hand, enables it to sacrifice to its ruling passion or interest both the public good and the rights of other citizens.

Securing the Public Good and Private Rights Against the Dangers of Faction Is the Great Object

10.19   To secure the public good and private rights against the danger of such a faction, and at the same time to preserve the spirit and the form of popular government, is then the great object to which our inquiries are directed. Let me add that it is the great desideratum by which this form of government can be rescued from the opprobrium under which it has so long labored, and be recommended to the esteem and adoption of mankind.

10.20   By what means is this object attainable? Evidently by one of two only. Either the existence of the same passion or interest in a majority at the same time must be prevented, or the majority, having such coexistent passion or interest, must be rendered, by the number and local situation, unable to concert and carry into effect schemes of oppression. If the impulse and the opportunity be suffered to coincide, we well know that neither moral nor religious motives can be relied on as an adequate control. They are not found to be such on the injustice and violence of individuals, and lose their efficacy in proportion to the number combined together, that is, in proportion as their efficacy becomes needful.

A Pure Democracy Can Admit of No Cure for the Mischiefs of Faction

10.21   From this view of the subject it may be concluded that a pure democracy, by which I mean a society of a small number of citizens, who assemble and administer the government in person, can admit of no cure for the mischiefs of faction. A common passion or interest will, in almost every case, be felt by a majority of the whole; a communication and concert result from the form of government itself; and there is nothing to check the inducements to sacrifice the weaker party or an obnoxious individual.

Democracies Have Ever Been Found Incompatible with Personal Security and the Rights of Property

10.22   Hence it is that such democracies have ever been spectacles of turbulence and contention; have ever been found incompatible with personal security or the rights of property; and have in general been as short in their lives as they have been violent in their deaths.

Politicians Have Made Erroneous Assumptions Regarding Political Rights

10.23   Theoretic politicians who have patronized this species of government, have erroneously supposed that by reducing mankind to a perfect equality in their political rights, they would, at the same time, be perfectly equalized and assimilated in their possessions, their opinions, and their passions.

Republican Government Promises to Secure the Public Good and Private Rights against the Danger of Faction

10.24   A republic, by which I mean a government in which the scheme of representation takes place, opens a different prospect, and promises the cure for which we are seeking. Let us examine the points in which it varies from pure democracy and we shall comprehend both the nature of the cure and the efficacy which it must derive from the Union.

There Are Two Main Differences between a Democracy and a Republic

10.25   The two great points of difference between a democracy and a republic are: first, the delegation of the government, in the latter, to a small number of citizens elected by the rest; secondly, the greater number of citizens, and greater sphere of country, over which the latter may be extended.

The Virtues of Patriotic and Just Representatives Are Founded in Their Desire for Public Good

10.26   The effect of the first difference is, on the one hand, to refine and enlarge the public views, by passing them through the medium of a chosen body of citizens, whose wisdom may best discern the true interest of their country, and whose patriotism and love of justice will be least likely to sacrifice it to temporary or partial considerations. Under such a regulation, it may well happen that the public voice, pronounced by the representatives of the people, will be more consonant to the public good than if pronounced by the people themselves, convened for the purpose.

Sinister Representatives May Betray the Interests of the People

10.27   On the other hand, the effect may be inverted. Men of factious tempers, of local prejudices, or of sinister designs, may, by intrigue, by corruption, or by other means, first obtain the suffrages, and then betray the interests, of the people.

Large Republics Are More Favorable to the Election of Proper Representatives

10.28   The question resulting is, whether small or extensive republics are more favorable to the election of proper guardians of the public weal; and it is clearly decided in favor of the latter by two obvious considerations:

10.29   In the first place, it is to be remarked that, however small the republic may be, the representatives must be raised to a certain number, in order to guard against the cabals of a few; and that, however large it may be, they must be limited to a certain number, in order to guard against the confusion of a multitude. Hence, the number of representatives in the two cases not being in proportion to that of the two constituents, and being proportionally greater in the small republic, it follows that, if the proportion of fit characters be not less in the large than in the small republic, the former will present a greater option, and consequently a greater probability of a fit choice.

The Constitution Provides for the Public to Be Protected from Unworthy Candidates

10.30   In the next place, as each representative will be chosen by a greater number of citizens in the large than in the small republic, it will be more difficult for unworthy candidates to practice with success the vicious arts by which elections are too often carried; and the suffrages of the people being more free, will be more likely to center in men who possess the most attractive merit and the most diffusive and established characters.

The Federal Constitution Provides a Proper Combination for Best Representation

10.31   It must be confessed that in this, as in most other cases, there is a mean, on both sides of which inconveniences will be found to lie. By enlarging too much the number of electors, you render the representatives too little acquainted with all their local circumstances and lesser interests; as by reducing it too much, you render him unduly attached to these, and too little fit to comprehend and pursue great and national objects. The federal Constitution forms a happy combination in this respect; the great and aggregate interest being referred to the national, the local and particularly the State legislatures.

A Republican Government Can Encompass a Large Territory

10.32   The other point of difference is, the greater number of citizens and extent of territory which may be brought within the compass of republican than of democratic government; and it is this circumstance principally which renders factious combinations less to be dreaded in the former than in the latter. The smaller the society, the fewer probably will be the distinct parties and interests composing it; the fewer the distinct parties and interests, the more frequently will a majority be found of the same party; and the smaller the number of individuals composing a majority, and the smaller the compass within which they are placed, the more easily will they concert and execute their plans of oppression. Extend the sphere and you take in a greater variety of parties and interests; you make it less probable that a majority of the whole will have a common motive to invade the rights of other citizens; or if such a common motive exists, it will be more difficult for all who feel it to discover their own strength, and to act in unison with each other. Besides the other impediments, it may be remarked that, where there is a consciousness of unjust or dishonorable purposes, communication is always checked by distrust in proportion to the number whose concurrence is necessary.

A Large Republic Has the Advantage over a Small Republic in Controlling the Effects of Faction

10.33   Hence, it clearly appears, that the same advantage which a republic has over a democracy, in controlling the effects of faction, is enjoyed by a large over a small republic–is enjoyed by the Union over the States composing it. Does the advantage consist in the substitution of the representatives whose enlightened views and virtuous sentiments render them superior to local prejudices and to schemes of injustice? It will not be denied that the representation of the Union will be most likely to possess these requisite endowments. Does it consist in the greater security afforded by a greater variety of parties, against the event of any one party being able to outnumber and oppress the rest? In an equal degree does the increased variety of parties comprised within the Union, increase this security. Does it, in fine, consist in the greater obstacles opposed to the concert and accomplishment of the secret wishes of an unjust and interested majority? Here, again, the extent of the Union gives it the most palpable advantage.

Numerous States Provide a Bulwark Against Factious Leaders

10.34   The influence of factious leaders may kindle a flame within their particular States, but will be unable to spread a general conflagration through the other States. A religious sect may degenerate into a political faction in a part of the Confederacy; but the variety of sects dispersed over the entire face of it must secure the national councils against any danger from that source.

Equal Division of Property Is Considered Wicked

10.35   A rage for paper money, for an abolition of debts, for an equal division of property, or for any other improper or wicked project, will be less apt to pervade the whole body of the Union than a particular member of it; in the same proportion as such a malady is more likely to taint a particular county or district, than an entire State.

10.36   In the extent and proper structure of the Union, therefore, we behold a republican remedy for the disease most incident to republican government. And according to the degree of pleasure and pride we feel in being republicans, ought to be our zeal in cherishing the spirit and supporting the character of Federalists.

Federalist No. 51

The Federal Republic of America

by James Madison

51.1   To WHAT expedient, then, shall we finally resort, for maintaining in practice the necessary partition of power among the several departments, as laid down in the Constitution? The only answer that can be given is, that as all these exterior provisions are found to be inadequate, the defect must be supplied, by so contriving the interior structure of the government as that its several constituent parts may, by their mutual relations, be the means of keeping each other in their proper places. Without presuming to undertake a full development of this important idea, I will hazard a few general observations, which may perhaps place it in a clearer light, and enable us to form a more correct judgment of the principles and structure of government planned by the convention.

Separation of Power Is Essential to the Preservation of Liberty

51.2   In order to lay a foundation for that separate and distinct exercise of the different powers of government, which to a certain extent is admitted on all hands to be essential to the preservation of liberty, it is evident that each department should have a will of its own; and consequently should be so constituted that the members of each should have as little agency as possible in the appointment of the members of the others.

The Fountain of All Authority Is the People

51.3   Were this principle rigorously adhered to, it would require that all the appointments for the supreme executive, legislative, and judiciary magistracies should be drawn from the same fountain of authority, the people, through channels having no communication whatever with one another. Perhaps such a plan of constructing the several departments would be less difficult in practice than it may in contemplation appear. Some difficulties, however, and some additional expense would attend the execution of it. Some deviations, therefore, from the principle must be admitted. In the constitution of the judiciary department in particular, it might be inexpedient to insist rigorously on the principle: first, because peculiar qualifications being essential in the members, the primary consideration ought to be to select that mode of choice which best secures these qualifications; secondly, because the permanent tenure by which the appointments are held in that department must soon destroy all sense of dependence on the authority conferring them.

The Three Branches of Government Should Be as Independent as Possible

51.4   It is equally evident, that the members of each department should be as little dependent as possible on those of the others, for the emoluments annexed to their offices. Were the executive magistrate, or the judges, not independent of the legislature in this particular, their independence in every other would be merely nominal.

We Need to Guard Against a Gradual Concentration of Power in One Department of Government

51.5   But the great security against a gradual concentration of the several powers in the same department consists in giving to those who administer each department the necessary constitutional means and personal motives to resist encroachment of the others. The provision for defense must in this, as in all other cases, be made commensurate to the danger of attack.

Man's Human Nature Must Be Controlled Whenever It Leads to Unrighteous Dominion Over Others

51.6   Ambition must be made to counteract ambition. The interest of the man must be connected with the constitutional rights of the place. It may be a reflection on human nature, that such devices should be necessary to control the abuses of government. But what is government itself, but the greatest of all reflections on human nature? If men were angels, no government would be necessary. If angels were to govern men, neither external nor internal controls on government would be necessary. In framing a government which is to be administered by men over men, the great difficulty lies in this: you must first enable the government to control the governed; and in the next place oblige it to control itself.

The Primary Control on the Government Is Its Total Dependence on the People

51.7   A dependence on the people is, no doubt the primary control on the government; but experience has taught mankind the necessity of auxiliary precautions.

The Constant Aim Is to Divide and Arrange the Different Government Offices so that They Check Each Other

51.8   This policy of supplying, by opposite and rival interests, the defect of better motives, might be traced through the whole system of human affairs, private as well as public. We see it particularly displayed in all the subordinate distribution of powers, where the constant aim is to divide and arrange the several offices in such a manner as that each may be a check on the other–that the private interest of every individual may be a sentinel over the public rights. These inventions of every prudence cannot be less requisite in the distribution of the supreme powers of the State.

In Republican Government the Legislative Authority Is Predominant

51.9   But it is not possible to give each department an equal power of self-defence. In republican government, the legislative authority necessarily predominates. The remedy for this inconveniency is to divide the legislature into different branches; and to render them, by different modes of election and different principles of action, as little connected with each other as the nature of their common functions and their common dependence on the society will admit.

It May Be Necessary to Guard Against Encroachments of Power by the Legislative Branch

51.10   It may even be necessary to guard against dangerous encroachments by still further precautions. As the weight of the legislative authority requires that it should be thus divided, the weakness of the executive may require on the other hand, that it should be fortified. An absolute negative on the legislative appears, at first view, to be the natural defence with which the executive magistrate should be armed. But perhaps it would be neither altogether safe nor alone sufficient. On ordinary occasions it might not be exerted with the requisite firmness, and on extraordinary occasions it might be perfidiously abused. May not this defect of an absolute negative be supplied by some qualified connection between this weaker department and the weaker branch of the stronger department, by which the latter may be led to support the constitutional rights of the former, without being too much detached from the rights of its own department?

Two Considerations Are Applicable to the Federal System of America

51.11   If the principles on which these observations are founded be just, as I persuade myself they are, and they be applied as a criterion to the several State constitutions, and to the federal Constitution, it will be found that if the latter does not perfectly correspond with them, the former are infinitely less able to bear such a test.

51.12   There are, moreover, two considerations particularly applicable to the federal system of America, which place that system in a very interesting point of view.

In the Compound Republic of America the Power Surrendered by the People Is Divided Between Two Distinct Governments

51.13   First. In a single republic, all the power surrendered by the people is submitted to the administration of a single government; and the usurpations are guarded against by a division of the government into distinct and separate departments. In the compound republic of America, the power surrendered by the people is first divided between two distinct governments, and then the portion allotted to each subdivided among distinct and separate departments. Hence a double security arises to the rights of the people. The different governments will control each other, at the same time that each will be controlled by itself.

It Is Very Important that a Republic Guard the Rights of the Minority

51.14   Second. It is of great importance in a republic not only to guard the society against the oppression of its rulers, but to guard one part of the society against the injustice of the other part. Different interests necessarily exist in different classes of citizens. If a majority be united by a common interest, the rights of the minority will be insecure.

There are but two methods of providing against this evil: the one by creating a will in the community independent of the majority–that is, of the society itself; the other, by comprehending in the society so many separate descriptions of citizens as will render an unjust combination of a majority of the whole very improbable, if not impracticable. The first method prevails in all governments possessing an hereditary or self-appointed authority. This, at best, is but a precarious security; because a power independent of the society may as well espouse the unjust views of the major, as the rightful interests of the minor party, and may possibly be turned against both parties. The second method will be exemplified in the federal republic of the United States. Whilst all authority in it will be derived from and dependent on the society, the society itself will be broken into so many parts, interests and classes of citizens, that the rights of individuals, or of the minority, will be in little danger from interested combinations of the majority.

The Security of Civil and Religious Rights Must Be the Same

51.15   In a free government the security for civil rights must be the same as that for religious rights. It consists in the one case in the multiplicity of interests, and in the other in the multiplicity of sects. The degree of security in both cases will depend on the number of interests and sects; and this may be presumed to depend on the extent of country and number of people comprehended under the same government.

Justice Is the End of Government

51.16   This view of the subject must particularly recommend a proper federal system to all the sincere and considerate friends of republican government, since it shows that in exact proportion as the territory of the Union may be formed into more circumscribed Confederacies, or States, oppressive combinations of a majority will be facilitated: the best security, under the republican forms, for the rights of every class of citizens, will be diminished; and consequently the stability and independence of some member of the government, the only other security, must be proportionally increased. Justice is the end of government. It is the end of civil society. It ever has been and ever will be pursued until it is obtained, or until liberty be lost in the pursuit.

In a Society Where the Weaker Faction Is Not Protected from the Stronger Faction, Anarchy Reigns

51.17   In a society under the forms of which the stronger faction can readily unite and oppress the weaker, anarchy may as truly be said to reign as in a state of nature, where the weaker individual is not secured against the violence of the stronger; and as, in the latter state, even the stronger individuals are prompted, by the uncertainty of their condition, to submit to a government which may protect the weak as well as themselves; so, in the former state, will the more powerful factions or parties be gradually induced, by a like motive, to wish for a government which will protect all parties, the weaker as well as the more powerful. It can be little doubted that if the State of Rhode Island was separated from the Confederacy and left to itself, the insecurity of rights under the popular form of government within such narrow limits would be displayed by such reiterated oppressions of factious majorities that some power altogether independent of the people would soon be called for by the voice of the very factions whose misrule had proved the necessity of it.

The Principles of Justice and Common Good Are to Reign in America

51.18   In the extended republic of the United States, and among the great variety of interests, parties, and sects which it embraces, a coalition of a majority of the whole society could seldom take place on any other principles than those of justice and the general good; whilst there being thus less danger to a minor from the will of a major party, there must be less pretext, also, to provide for the security of the former, by introducing into the government a will not dependent on the latter, or, in other words, a will independent of the society itself.

The Larger the Society the More Capable It Will Be of Self-Government

51.19   It is no less certain than it is important, notwithstanding the contrary opinions which have been entertained, that the larger the society, provided it lie within a practical sphere, the more duly capable it will be of self-government. And happily for the *republican cause,* the practicable sphere may be carried to a very great extent, by a judicious modification and mixture of the *federal principle.*

Index

Italic type indicates that an illustration of the entry appears on that page.

Index

Index

Index

Index

Acknowledgements

A careful effort has been made to trace the ownership of selections included in this textbook in order to secure permission to reprint copyrighted material and to make full acknowledgment of their use. If any error or omission has occurred, it is unintentional and will be corrected in subsequent editions, provided written notification is made to the publisher.

Chapter 18, page 424
Excerpt from THE JUNGLE by Upton Sinclair, copyright 1905, 1906 by Upton Sinclair. Used by permission of Viking Penguin, a division of Penguin Putnam Inc.

Chapter 20, page 482
Hoover acceptance speech for Republican nomination in 1928, courtesy of the Herbert Hoover Presidential Library.

Chapter 21, page 494
"Happy Days Are Here Again," by Jack Yellen and Milton Ager, 1929 (Renewed) Warner Bros. Inc. All Rights Reserved. Used by Permission. WARNER BROS. PUBLICATIONS U.S. INC., Miami, FL. 33014

Chapter 22, pages 515 and 516
Excerpts from Churchill's speeches, reproduced with permission of Curtis Brown Ltd, London, on behalf of the Estate of Sir Winston Churchill. Copyright Winston S Churchill 1948.

Chapter 22, page 533
Excerpt from MacArthur's speech, courtesy of the General Douglas MacArthur Foundation, Norfolk, Virginia.

Chapter 22, page 531
Excerpt from Truman's speech, courtesy of Harry S. Truman Library.

Chapter 23, page 559
Excerpt from "I Have a Dream," reprinted by arrangement with The Heirs to the Estate of Martin Luther King, Jr., c/o Writers House Inc, as agent for the proprietor. Copyright 1963 by Martin Luther King Jr., copyright renewed 1991 by Coretta Scott King

Chapter 26, page 634
Quotation from IT DOESN'T TAKE A HERO by Norman Schwarzkopf, published by Random House, Inc.

Chapter 26, page 636
Excerpt from Bush's speech, courtesy of George Bush Presidential Library and Museum

Photograph Credits

The following agencies and individuals have furnished materials to meet the photographic needs of this textbook. We wish to express our gratitude to them for their important contribution.

Suzanne R. Altizer
AP/Wide World Photos
Architect of the Capitol
Archive Photos
Arizona Historical Foundation
The Art Institute of Chicago
Beinecke Rare Book and Manuscript Library, Yale University
Bettmann/CORBIS
BJU Press files
Bob Jones University Collection
Bob Jones University Museum & Gallery
Boston Athenaeum
James Brooks
Buffalo Bill Historical Center
Jimmy Carter Library
Chessie System Railroads
Chicago Historical Society
George R. Collins
Colt Industries, Firearms Division
CORBIS
CORBIS/Digital Stock
Jeff Danziger
Denver Public Library
Department of Defense
Eastman Kodak
Dwight D. Eisenhower Library
John Ficaro/The White House
John Filo
Gene Fisher
Gerald R. Ford Library
Harper's Encyclopedia of United States History (1902)
The Image Works/John Dominis
Independence National Historical Park
Bob Jackson
LBJ Library, Photo by Yoichi Okamoto
Lyndon B. Johnson Library
Peter Johnson/CORBIS
Kansas State Historical Society
Gillie Gibson Keesee
Tim Keesee
King Feature Syndicate
Library of Congress
Lick Observatory
Marblehead, MA
The Mariner's Museum
The Maryland Historical Society
The Metropolitan Museum of Art
Museum of the City of New York
NASA

National Archives
National Baseball Library, Cooperstown
National Gallery of Art, Washington
The National Gallery, London
National Gallery of Canada, Ottawa
National Museum of American History, Smithsonian Institution
National Park Service
National Park Service/Richard Frear
National Portrait Gallery, London
National Portrait Gallery, Smithsonian Institution
Nebraska State Historical Society
The New-York Historical Society
The New York Public Library
Ohio Historical Society
Peabody Essex Museum
Philadelphia Museum of Art
PhotoDisc. Inc.
Ronald Reagan Library
Reuters/Ron Thomas/Archive Photos
Franklin D. Roosevelt Library
Royal Ontario Museum
Terry Rude
The San Jacinto Museum of History
Phyllis Schlafly
The Schlesinger Library, Radcliffe Institute, Harvard University
Sears, Roebuck and Co.
Senate Historical Office
Pete Souza/The White House
Smithsonian Institution
Tennessee State Library and Archives
Strom Thurmond Library, Clemson University
Peter Turnley/CORBIS
Union Pacific Railroad Museum Collection
United States Air Force
United States Energy Department and Resources Administration
United States Naval Academy Museum
The University of Texas at Arlington Libraries
University of Virginia Library
Unusual Films
U.S. Senate Collection
Utah State Historical Society
Valentine Museum
Washington and Lee University

Westinghouse Broadcasting and Cable, Inc.
West Point Museum Collection, United States Military Academy
The White House
Robert Whitmore
Whitney Museum of American Art
Winterthur Museum
Woolaroc Museum
Perry Wright
Yale University Art Gallery
Young America's Foundation

Cover
CORBIS (Jefferson Memorial); Unusual Films (flag)

Title Pages
CORBIS (Jefferson Memorial); Unusual Films (flag)

Front Matter
Unusual Films v, vi, viii;

Unit I
Unusual Films xiv-1

Chapter 1
Unusual Films 2; Library of Congress 3, 11; Architect of the Capitol 4; Bob Jones University Museum & Gallery, Photo by Unusual Films 6; By courtesy of the National Portrait Gallery, London 12; National Portrait Gallery, Smithsonian Institution 15

Chapter 2
Unusual Films 18, 26; Architect of the Capitol 19, 22, 23; Library of Congress 25; Detail from Pocahontas, National Portrait Gallery, Smithsonian Institution; transfer from the National Gallery of Art, Gift of the A. W. Mellon Educational and Charitable Trust, 1942. 31; University of Virginia Library 33; From the Collections of The Mariners' Museum, Newport News, Va. 34

Perspectives Eastern Indians Photograph courtesy of the Royal Ontario Museum, © ROM 37; Library of Congress 39, 42; Ohio Historical Society 40; National Gallery of Art, Washington, Photograph © 2000 Board of Trustees (Andrew W. Mellon Collection) 44

Chapter 3
Unusual Films 46; National Gallery of Art, Washington, Photograph © 2000 Board of Trustees (Andrew W. Mellon Fund) 47, Gift of Edgar William and Bernice Chrysler Garbisch. 57, 59; Philadelphia Museum of Art, Gift of the Barra Foundation, Inc. 50 (right); Library of Congress 52

Chapter 4
Unusual Films 62; Collection of The New-York Historical Society (accession number S-117, negative no. 27117) 63; Courtesy Peabody Essex Museum, Salem, Mass. (Neg.# 15,539) 66; BJU Press Files (James Brooks, artist) 70; Rare Books Division, The New York Public Library, Astor, Lenox and Tilden Foundations 74; Library of Congress 76 (left), 78; Courtesy of Gene Fisher 76 (right)

Unit II
Unusual Films 84-85

Chapter 5
Unusual Films 86; National Gallery of Canada, Ottawa 87; Library of Congress 92, 96, 102; National Portrait Gallery, Smithsonian Institution 101

Chapter 6
Unusual Films 104; Yale University Art Gallery 105; Library of Congress 107; Washington and Lee University, Lexington, VA 113; Architect of the Capitol 115, 128; The Metropolitan Museum of Art, NY 117; Courtesy of Marblehead, MA 120; National Portrait Gallery, Smithsonian Institution 122; National Park Service 123; © The National Gallery, London 125; Independence National Historical Park 126

Chapter 7
Unusual Films 132; Architect of the Capitol 133, 149; Courtesy, Winterthur Museum 135; Courtesy of Tim Keesee 139; National Portrait Gallery, Smithsonian Institution 140; Library of Congress 142, 147

Chapter 8
Unusual Films 152; United States Naval Academy Museum 153; National Portrait Gallery, Smithsonian Institution 154 (lower right), 163; Library of Congress 157; Tennessee State Library and Archives 160; National Archives 161; Print Collection,

Miriam and Ira D. Wallach Division of, Art, Prints and Photographs, The New York Public Library, Astor, Lenox & Tilden Foundations 164

Unit III
Unusual Films 168-169

Chapter 9
Unusual Films 170; United States Naval Academy Museum 171; Library of Congress 172 (both); National Portrait Gallery, Smithsonian Institution 174, Gift of Mrs. Herbert Lee Pratt, Jr. 182 (right); Chicago Historical Society (sepia tone added) 180; Harper's Encyclopedia of United States History (1902) 182 (left); United States Naval Academy Museum 186; The Maryland Historical Society, Baltimore, Maryland 188

Chapter 10
Unusual Films 192, 204; Library of Congress 193, 197, 207, 208; National Gallery of Art, Washington, Photograph © 2000 Board of Trustees (Andrew W. Mellon Collection) 199; National Portrait Gallery, Smithsonian Institution; transfer from the National Gallery of Art, Gift of the A. W. Mellon Educational and Charitable Trust, 1942. 202, National Portrait Gallery, Smithsonian Institution 205; Woolaroc Museum, Bartlesville, OK 206

Chapter 11
Unusual Films 212, 217; National Gallery of Art, Washington, Photograph © 2000 Board of Trustees, Gift of Edgar William and Bernice Chrysler Garbisch. 213; Colt Industries, Firearms Division 215; Library of Congress 219, 223, 224, 229, 231, 234; Chessie System Railroads 222; National Portrait Gallery, Smithsonian Institution 225, 233; The Schlesinger Library, Radcliffe Institute, Harvard University 227; Bob Jones University Collection, Photo by Unusual Films 228; The Metropolitan Museum of Art, NY 230; Used by permission, Utah State Historical Society, all rights reserved 237

Chapter 12
Unusual Films 240; Courtesy, Fort Worth Star-Telegram Photograph Collection, The University of Texas at Arlington Libraries, Arlington,

Texas 241; Harper's Encyclopedia of United States History (1902) 245 (left); The San Jacinto Museum of History, Houston 245 (right); Library of Congress 247, 249, 253, 254, 255 (both), 256; Yale Collection of Western Americana, Beinecke Rare Book and Manuscript Library, Yale University 250

Unit IV
Unusual Films 258-259

Chapter 13
Unusual Films 260; Kansas State Historical Society 261; Library of Congress 262, 269, 271 (both), 277 (left), 281; Photographic History Collection, National Museum of American History, Smithsonian Institution (negative number: 38416C) 264; National Portrait Gallery, Smithsonian Institution 265, 267 (left); Print Collection, Miriam and Ira D. Wallach Division of, Art, Prints and Photographs, The New York Public Library, Astor, Lenox & Tilden Foundations 273; National Archives 275, 277 (right); Boston Athenaeum (sepia tone added) 278

Chapter 14
Unusual Films 284, 305; Valentine Museum/Richmond History Center, Richmond, Virginia, Cook Collection 285; Library of Congress 293, 294, 299, 310, 315; National Archives 297, 304, 308, 309, 311; United States Naval Academy Museum 300; National Portrait Gallery, Smithsonian Institution 303; West Point Museum Collection, United States Military Academy 314

Perspectives Photography Courtesy of Tim Keesee 317, 318 (all), 319 (all but round), 322 (top left), 329 (5 photos at bottom); Eastman Kodak 319 (round); Unusual Films 320; National Archives 321, 323, 326, 327, 329 (top); Library of Congress 322 (top right, bottom left, bottom right), 324, 325; "Five Cents a Spot"; Lodgers in a Bayard Street Tenement, c. 1889 The Jacob A. Riis Collection, #155 Museum of the City of New York 328

Chapter 15
Unusual Films 330; Library of Congress 331, 332, 335 (left), 338, 341, 342, 346; National Portrait Gallery,

Photograph Credits

Smithsonian Institution 333; National Archives 335 (left); Valentine Museum/Richmond History Center, Richmond, Virginia, Cook Collection 337; U.S. Senate Collection 348

Unit V
Unusual Films 350-351

Chapter 16
Unusual Films 352; The Metropolitan Museum of Art, NY 353; Library of Congress 354,355, 357, 359, 361, 362, 366, 367, 369, 373; Courtesy of Tim Keesee 368, 374; The Art Institute of Chicago 372; National Portrait Gallery, Smithsonian Institution 376

Chapter 17
Unusual Films 380; Union Pacific Railroad Museum Collection 381, 382, 383; National Archives 384, 392, 393, 399; Nebraska State Historical Society, Solomon D. Butcher Collection 386; Architect of the Capitol 389; Buffalo Bill Historical Center, Cody, WY 391 (top); Library of Congress 391 (bottom), 397, 401; National Portrait Gallery, Smithsonian Institution 394; General Research Division: The New York Public Library, Astor, Lenox & Tilden Foundations 395

Perspectives, The Old West Denver Public Library, Western History Collection (sepia tone added) 404; Unusual Films / Courtesy of Terry Rude 405 (bottom), 413; National Archives 406, 407; Kansas State Historical Society 408; Library of Congress 410, 411, 415; Courtesy of Tim Keesee 412

Chapter 18
Unusual Films 416, 438 (bottom); Library of Congress 417, 418, 421, 425, 426, 433, 434; Courtesy of Tim Keesee 431; Detail from George Washington Carver, by Betsy Graves Reyneau, National Portrait Gallery, Smithsonian Institution; transfer from the Smithsonian American Art Museum, Gift of the George Washington Carver Memorial Committee to the Smithsonian Institution, 1944. 435, Smithsonian Institution 437; National Archives 438 (top); National Baseball Library, Cooperstown, NY 440

Chapter 19
Unusual Films 444; National Archives 445, 448 (top), 455, 458, 459; Library of Congress 446, 460; National Portrait Gallery, Smithsonian Institution 448 (bottom); BJU Press Files 451; Courtesy of Tim Keesee 453 (all); Smithsonian Institution 456

Unit VI
Unusual Films 464-465

Chapter 20
Unusual Films 466, 483 (right); Library of Congress 467, 471, 472, 474, 481; Detail from Herbert C. Hoover, by Douglas Chandor, National Portrait Gallery, Smithsonian Institution 473; Whitney Museum of American Art, New York 475, National Baseball Library, Cooperstown, NY 476 (left); National Archives 476 (right); Chicago Historical Society (image cropped) 478; Westinghouse Broadcasting and Cable, Inc. 483 (left); Sears, Roebuck and Co. 484

Chapter 21
Unusual Films 488; Franklin D. Roosevelt Library 489, 495, 497, 498; National Archives 491, 506; Courtesy of Gillie Gibson Keesee 499; Library of Congress 501, 503, 504, 505; Reprinted with special permission of King Feature Syndicate 507 (both)

Chapter 22
Unusual Films 510; Library of Congress 511, 512, 515, 517, 519, 522, 525 (top); National Archives 520, 521, 523, 525 (bottom), 527, 529, 530, 532, 533 (top); LBJ Library, Photo by Yoichi Okamoto 526; United States Energy Department and Resources Administration 533 (bottom)

Unit VII
Unusual Films 536-537

Chapter 23
Unusual Films 538, 560; National Archives 539, 542, 545, 546 (all), 548, 549, 553 (both), 554; Library of Congress 543, 557; Senate Historical Office 550; Dwight D. Eisenhower Library 552; Courtesy of Tim Keesee 553 (buttons); National Baseball Library, Cooperstown, NY 558

Chapter 24
Unusual Films 562; Bob Jackson 563; Lyndon B. Johnson Library 564, 565, 577; Arizona Historical Foundation 566; Department of Defense 568; United States Air Force 570-71; George R. Collins 573; John Dominis/The Image Works 574; © Bettmann/CORBIS 575; National Archives 578, 581; Courtesy of Tim Keesee 579; John Filo 582

Perspectives Space Race Lick Observatory 585 (large); NASA 585 (inset), 586 (both), 587, 590, 592, 593, 595, 596, 597; Unusual Films 594

Chapter 25
Unusual Films 598; National Archives 599, 609; Senate Historical Office 600; Gerald R. Ford Library 601; Courtesy of Phyllis Schlafly 605; Courtesy of Tim Keesee 607 (buttons), 616; Jimmy Carter Library 607; Perry Wright 610; Suzanne R. Altizer 612; Robert Whitmore 613; Archive Photos 614; The White House 615

Chapter 26
Unusual Films 618; National Archives 619; The White House 620, 638; Strom Thurmond Library, Clemson University, 622; Courtesy of Tim Keesee 627, 631, 637 (buttons); Courtesy Ronald Reagan Presidential Library 628; Young America's Foundation 629; Pete Souza/The White House 630; AP/Wide World Photos 633, 634

Chapter 27
Unusual Films 640; The White House 641, 654; Peter Johnson/CORBIS 642; Reuters/Ron Thomas/Archive Photos 644; PhotoDisc. Inc. (image manipulated) 646; © Peter Turnley/CORBIS 647; AP/Wide World Photos 651; John Ficaro/The White House; Courtesy of Tim Keesee 653 (buttons); Courtesy of Jeff Danziger (artist) 653 (bottom)

Back Matter
National Park Service/Richard Frear 657; PhotoDisc. Inc. (Mount Rushmore) 658-659; CORBIS/Digital Stock (flag) 658-659